WITNESS TO THE GOSPEL

Witness to the Gospel

The Theology of Acts

Edited by
I. Howard Marshall
and
David Peterson

WILLIAM B. EERDMANS PUBLISHING COMPANY
GRAND RAPIDS, MICHIGAN / CAMBRIDGE, U.K.

© 1998 Wm. B. Eerdmans Publishing Co.
255 Jefferson Ave. S.E., Grand Rapids, Michigan 49503 /
P.O. Box 163, Cambridge CB3 9PU U.K.

Printed in the United States of America

02 01 00 99 98   5 4 3 2 1

Library of Congress Cataloging-in-Publication Data

Witness to the Gospel : the theology of Acts /
edited by I. Howard Marshall and David Peterson.
p.   cm.
Includes bibliographical references and indexes.
ISBN 0-8028-4435-9 (pbk. : alk. paper)
1. Bible. N.T. Acts — Theology. I. Marshall, I. Howard.
II. Peterson, David, 1944- .
BS2625.2.W 1998
226.6′06 — dc21   98-14685
                                                      CIP

TABLE OF CONTENTS

LIST OF CONTRIBUTORS   xi

PREFACE   xv

INTRODUCTION   1

1   HOW DOES ONE WRITE ON THE THEOLOGY OF ACTS?
Howard Marshall

I. Was Luke a 'theologian'?   3
II. What do we mean by 'the theology of the book of Acts'?   5
III. What can we learn from previous investigators?   8
IV. Why are we attempting this book?   15

PART I: THE SALVATION OF GOD   17

2   THE PLAN OF GOD   19
John T. Squires

I. Introduction   20
II. The plan of God in Acts   23
III. Conclusion   37

3   SCRIPTURE AND THE REALISATION OF GOD'S PROMISES   41
Darrell Bock

I. Introduction   42
II. Hermeneutical axioms   43
III. Five scriptural themes in Acts   49
IV. Conclusion   62

4   SALVATION-HISTORY AND ESCHATOLOGY   63
     John Nolland

     I. Introduction   64
     II. Parousia hope   65
     III. Kingdom as present and future   68
     IV. Repetition and escalation in salvation-history   70
     V. Jewish unbelief not the basis for good news to Gentiles   76

5   SALVATION TO THE END OF THE EARTH: GOD AS
     THE SAVIOUR IN THE ACTS OF THE APOSTLES   83
     Joel B. Green

     I. Introduction   84
     II. 'The message of this salvation'   87
     III. 'God has brought a saviour'   95
     IV. 'What must I do to be saved?'   101
     V. 'You and your entire household will be saved.'   105

6   THE DIVINE SAVIOUR   107
     H. Douglas Buckwalter

     I. Introduction   108
     II. A survey of Luke's christology   108
     III. A deity who reigns supreme   112
     IV. A deity who waits on tables   120
     V. Conclusion: the christological pulse of Acts   122

7   THE NEED FOR SALVATION   125
     Christoph Stenschke

     I. Introduction   126
     II. How and why people need to be saved   129
     III. Forgiveness of sin   132
     IV. Luke's 'generation' and humanity in general   135
     V. Repentance   140
     VI. Some clues from Acts 2 (prior to Acts 2:37)   142
     VII. Conclusion   144

8   SALVATION AND HEALTH IN CHRISTIAN ANTIQUITY: THE SOTERI-
     OLOGY OF LUKE–ACTS IN ITS FIRST CENTURY SETTING   145
     Ben Witherington III

     I. Introduction   146
     II. Salvation in a Graeco-Roman mode—spared, healed, blessed 147
     III. Helped, cured, delivered in Luke–Acts   150
     IV. The means of salvation in Luke–Acts   155
     V. The meaning and the benefits of salvation in Luke–Acts   159
     VI. Conclusions and corollaries   163

PART II: THE CALL OF GOD   167

9   THE ROLE OF THE APOSTLES   169
     Andrew Clark

     I. Introduction   170
     II. The twelve Apostles   170
     III. Peter as representative of the Twelve   172
     IV. The roles of the twelve Apostles   173
     V. Paul and Barnabas   181
     VI. Peter and Paul parallels   185
     VII. Conclusion   190

10   MISSION AND WITNESS   191
     Peter Bolt

     I. Introduction   192
     II. Vocabulary   192
     III. The witnesses and their witness   196
     IV. Mission, witness and the readers of Acts   210

11   THE PROGRESS OF THE WORD   215
     Brian Rosner

     I. Introduction   216
     II. Progress anticipated   217
     III. Progress confirmed   221
     IV. The author of progress   223
     V. Patterns of progress   225
     VI. Unending progress   229
     VII. Conclusion   233

12   OPPOSITION TO THE PLAN OF GOD AND PERSECUTION   235
     Brian Rapske

     I. Introduction   236
     II. Jewish opposition   236
     III. Christian opposition   239
     IV. How the persecuted fulfil the plan of God   245
     V. Conclusion   254

13   THE PREACHING OF PETER IN ACTS   257
     Hans F. Bayer

     I. Introduction   258
     II. The context of the Petrine speeches and the emerging
     portrait of Peter   258
     III. Peter as a preacher of repentance and salvation   262
     IV. Peter as a preacher of Christ: the christology of the
     collective apostolic witness with some Petrine emphases   269
     V. Conclusion   273

14   THE SPEECH OF STEPHEN   275
Heinz-Werner Neudorfer

I. Introduction   276
II. Context and meaning of Stephen's speech   277
III. Stephen's speech as an 'historical review' in the context
of Jewish literature   281
IV. Theological motives and building-blocks in Stephen's speech   283
V. Concerning the theological roots of Stephen's speech   290
VI. Conclusion   294

15   THE PREACHING AND DEFENCE OF PAUL   295
G. Walter Hansen

I. Introduction   296
II. Mission speech to Jews   297
III. Mission speeches to Gentiles   307
IV. Defence speeches   317
V. Conclusion   324

PART III: THE RENEWING WORK OF GOD   325

**16   THE 'SPIRIT OF PROPHECY' AS THE POWER OF ISRAEL'S
RESORATION AND WITNESS**   327
Max Turner

I. Introduction   328
II. The Spirit as the 'Spirit of Prophecy' in Acts   333
III. The gift of the Spirit and conversion–initiation   337
IV. A Donum Superadditum or a soteriological necessity   339
V. Conclusion: Luke's pneumatology and the theology of Acts   347

17   THE NEW PEOPLE OF GOD   349
David Seccombe

I. A revolutionary transformation   350
II. Israel's restoration begins   351
III. The remnant of Israel   352
IV. A messianic people   353
V. Leadership of the new people   354
VI. God in their midst   355
VII. Condemnation of Israel's rulers   356
VIII. A creed for the people of God   357
IX. Assembling the outcasts   359
X. Gentile breakthrough   360
XI. Severance of church and synagogue   363
XII. The culture of the new people of God   365
XIII. An appeal to the Jews   366
XIV. A partial hardening of Israel   370
XV. The new people of God   371

18   THE WORSHIP OF THE NEW COMMUNITY   373
David Peterson

I. Introduction   374
II. The earliest disciples in the temple   374
III. The challenge to the Gentile world   382
IV. Homage and service under the new covenant   384
V. The character and function of early Christian gatherings   389
VI. Conclusion   394

19   THE CHRISTIAN AND THE LAW OF MOSES   397
Craig Blomberg

I. Introduction   398
II. Analysis   400
III. Conclusion   415

**20   MISSION PRACTICE AND THEOLOGY UNDER CONSTRUCTION
       (ACTS 18–20)**   417
Philip H. Towner

I. Introduction   418
II. Formative events and patterns   419
III. Modification of the pattern and developments in Corinth
and Ephesus: Acts 18–19 (20)   424
IV. Conclusion   435

**21   ISRAEL AND THE GENTILE MISSION IN ACTS AND PAUL:
       A CANONICAL APPROACH**   437
Robert Wall

I. Introduction   438
II. Israel and the Gentile mission in Acts   441
III. Israel and the Gentile mission in Romans 9–11   452

22   SOCIOLOGY AND THEOLOGY   459
Stephen C. Barton

I. Prologomena   460
II. Sociology and theology in Acts: two case studies   467
III. A theological postscript   472

**23   THE INFLUENCE OF JEWISH WORSHIP ON LUKE'S
       PRESENTATION OF THE EARLY CHURCH**   473
Brad Blue

I. Introduction   474
II. Jewish antecedents   475
III. Apostles, Christian benefactors and early gatherings   479
IV. Conclusion   496

24 RECIPROCITY AND THE ETHIC OF ACTS   499
Brian Capper

I. Introduction   500
II. Literary resonances and the narrative tension of Acts   504
III. Friendship, reciprocity and meal-fellowship   512

CONCLUSION   519

25 LUKE'S THEOLOGICAL ENTERPRISE: INTEGRATION AND INTENT
David Peterson   521

I. Introduction   522
II. Some brief preliminaries   522
III. Integrating the themes of Acts   523
IV. Luke's intention   532

BIBLIOGRAPHY   545

INDEXES   577

Index of Authors   577
Subject Index   585
Index of Biblical References   595

LIST OF CONTRIBUTORS

Stephen C. Barton lectures in New Testament at the University of Durham, and is a non-stipendiary minister of the Church of England. He studied at Macquarie University in Sydney and also at Lancaster University. He obtained his doctorate at King's College London. His publications include *The Spirituality of the Gospels* (1992), and *Discipleship and Family Ties in Mark and Matthew* (1994).

Hans F. Bayer is Associate Professor of New Testament at Covenant Theological Seminary, St. Louis, Missouri, following ten years as *Dozent* of New Testament Exegesis at the Freie Theologische Akademie in Giessen, Germany. He is the author of *Jesus' Predictions of Vindication and Resurrection* (Tübingen, 1986). He read divinity at the University of Tübingen, Germany and at Ashland Theological Seminary, Ohio, and obtained his PhD at the University of Aberdeen, Scotland.

Craig L. Blomberg is Professor of New Testament at Denver Seminary, Colorado. His doctorate is from the University of Aberdeen. He has published *The Historical Reliability of the Gospels* (1987), *Interpreting the Parables* (1990), *Matthew: New American Commentary* (1992), and *1 Corinthians: NIV Application Commentary* (1994), as well as numerous articles.

Brad Blue who is a faculty member of Ramsay International Fine Arts Center, Minneapolis obtained a PhD from King's College, University of Aberdeen on 'In Public and in Private: The Role of the House Church in Early Christianity' in 1989 and contributed 'Acts and the House Church' to the second volume of A1CS.

Darrell Bock is Research Professor of New Testament Studies at Dallas Theological Seminary and Professor of Spiritual Development and Culture for its Center for Christian Leadership. He earned his doctorate in New Testament at the University of Aberdeen. His publications include *Proclamation from Prophecy and Pattern: Lucan Old Testament Christology*, a two volume technical commentary on Luke (*Luke 1:1–9:50; Luke 9:51–24:53)* and a more popular study for InterVarsity Press on *Luke*.

xi

Peter Bolt who is a Lecturer in Biblical Studies at Moore Theological College in Sydney completed his MA (Hons) from Macquarie University and a PhD in New Testament, Kings College, London on the theme of Jesus' defeat of death and Mark's early readers' and has published articles on Mark's Gospel.

Douglas Buckwalter is Assistant Professor of New Testament at Evangelical School of Theology, Myerstown, Pennsylvania. He did his doctoral studies at the University of Aberdeen; his dissertation on *The Character and Purpose of Luke's Christology* was published as a Cambridge University Press monograph in 1996.

Brian Capper is presently Senior Lecturer in Religious Studies, Christ Church College, University of Kent at Canterbury. He has previously taught at the Universities of Edinburgh and St. Andrews, and at Ripon College Cuddesdon, University of Oxford. He holds his doctorate from Cambridge University and also pursued research at the University of Tübingen.

Andrew C. Clark has served with the Overseas Missionary Fellowship in Hong Kong since 1978, and has taught at several theological colleges there, most recently at the Chinese Mission Seminary, where he was Librarian and New Testament Lecturer. He completed his PhD thesis on the theme of Paul among the Apostles in Acts at London Bible College in association with Brunel University and presently works for Scripture Union.

Joel Green is New Testament Professor, Asbury Theological Seminary, Wilmore, Kentucky. Among his books is the recently published examination of *The Theology of the Gospel of Luke* (1995). He is currently completing a commentary on Luke for the New International Commentary on the New Testament and is also preparing the Word Biblical Commentary on the Acts of the Apostles. He received his PhD from the University of Aberdeen.

G. Walter Hansen is Associate Professor of New Testament and Director of the Global Research Institute, Fuller Theological Seminary and has taught at Trinity Theological College, Singapore. His PhD is from Wycliffe College and the Toronto School of Theology, University of Toronto. He has published *Abraham in Galatians: Epistolary and Rhetorical Contexts* (1989) and a commentary on *Galatians* (1994).

I. Howard Marshall holds the chair of New Testament Exegesis, King's College, Aberdeen University where he read classics and divinity as an undergraduate. He has written extensively on Luke and Acts with a commentary on the Greek text of *Luke* (1978) and on the English text of *Acts* (1980) *Luke: Theologian and Historian* (ed. 3, 1988) and *The Acts of the Apostles: New Testament Guides* (1992).

Heinz-Werner Neudorfer is Studienleiter of Albrecht-Bengel-Haus, Tübingen (Germany). Having researched in North African Judaism at Tübingen Institutum Judaicum, he completed his doctoral dissertation on Der Stephanuskreis in der Geschichte der Forschungseit F.C. Baur and published a two-volume German commentary on Acts (1986/1990), and articles on the new Tübingen research in Paul's theology in the *Jahrbuch für Evangelikale Theologie* of which he is the General Editor. He was Columbia guest professor at the Freie Hochschule für Mission (Korntal).

John Nolland is Vice-Principal and Lecturer in New Testament Studies at Trinity College, Bristol. He has published a three volume commentary on Luke in the Word Biblical Commentary Series (1989, 1993). His doctorate is from the University of Cambridge on Luke's readers in Luke/Acts.

David Peterson who was formerly Head of the Department of Ministry at Moore Theological College, Sydney is now the Principal of Oak Hill College, London. He has published *Hebrews and Perfection* (1982), *Engaging with God: a Biblical Theology of Worship* (1992) and *Possessed by God: a New Testament Theology of Sanctification and Holiness* (1995). He is a graduate of Sydney and London Universities and obtained his doctorate from Manchester University.

Brian M. Rapske received his PhD from the University of Aberdeen and is Senior Pastor of Trinity Baptist Church, Vancouver and sessional lecturer in New Testament at Regent College. He has published in the area of New Testament background and is the author of *The Book of Acts and Paul in Roman Custody* and a contributor to *The Book of Acts in Its Graeco-Roman Setting*, Volume 2 in A1CS series.

Brian S Rosner obtained his PhD from the University of Cambridge and is Lecturer in New Testament at the University of Aberdeen. He contributed to volume one of A1CS, is the author of *Paul, Scripture and Ethics* (1994) and edited *Understanding Paul's Ethics: Twentieth Century Approaches* (1995).

David Seccombe took his PhD from the University of Cambridge with a dissertation entitled *Possessions and the Poor in Luke Acts* (Linz: SNTU, 1982). He was minister of an Anglican student church in Perth, Western Australia from 1979-92, a co-founder of the Perth Centre for Applied Christianity, and since 1993 has been the Principal of George Whitefield College in Cape Town.

John Squires is a graduate of the Universities of Sydney and Yale. His Yale PhD dissertation, a comparative exploration of divine providence in Luke–Acts, Josephus, and Hellenistic historians, has been published as *The plan of God in Luke-Acts* (1993). He is currently Lecturer in New Testament Studies at the United Theological College, Sydney.

Christoph Stenschke holds degrees from the Freie Theologische Akademie, Giessen, Germany, and has completed his doctoral research at the University of Aberdeen on anthropology in Acts. He lectured in New Testament at the International Baptist Seminary in Prague in 1996 and is now undertaking further study in Berlin.

Philip H. Towner received his PhD from the University of Aberdeen, and subsequently taught at China Evangelical Seminary in Taipei, Taiwan, and held the post of Research Fellow in New Testament in the University of Aberdeen. He is the author of *The Goal of Our Instruction: The Structure of Theology and Ethics in the Pastoral Epistles* (1989), and is Translation Consultant, United Bible Societies.

Max Turner is Director of Research and Senior Lecturer in New Testament at London Bible College, and has previously taught at the University of Aberdeen. He earned his PhD from Cambridge University which was published as *Power from on*

High: the Charismatic Spirit of Israel's Restoration in Luke–Acts (1996) and *The Holy Spirit and Spiritual Gifts: Then and Now* (1996).

Robert Wall is Professor of Biblical Studies, Seattle Pacific University, Seattle, Washington. He undertook his doctorate at Dallas Theological Seminary and has published commentaries on Revelation (1991) and Colossians and Philemon (1993). His book *The Community of the Wise: A Commentary on James* is forthcoming. He has written extensively on the canonical approach to biblical interpretation, including *The New Testament as Canon* (1992), which he co-authored.

Ben Witherington III received his PhD from the University of Durham, and subsequently taught at Ashland Theological Seminary before coming Professor of New Testament Studies at Asbury Theological Seminary. His numerous books include *Women in the Earliest Churches, The Christology of Jesus, Paul's Narrative Thought World,* and *Jesus the Sage.* He has also edited a collection of essays on *History, Literature and Society in the Book of Acts* and has just completed a commentary on Acts in the Socio–Rhetorical Commentary Series.

PREFACE

During the past few years a project aimed at a better understanding of the Book of Acts in its First Century Setting has been carried on under the auspices of Tyndale House, Cambridge. Five of a planned six volumes have already appeared. Alongside this work there seemed to be scope for a book which would offer a comprehensive survey of the theology of Acts. Various recent works have covered aspects of the theology of Acts or discussed it with a commendable succinctness, but at present there is no one volume that attempts to cover the topic as a whole by bringing together the insights of a broad group of scholars. A panel of contributors was enrolled and draft papers were produced for mutual discussion at a conference held at Tyndale House in 1995. These essays have subsequently been carefully revised for publication. They are offered now, not only as a contribution to the ongoing study of the theology of Acts by specialists in the field, but also as a collection of essays which will form a useful textbook for students for whom Acts may be a set text. The approaches of the contributors vary considerably from thematic to narrative approaches. Some topics are treated more than once in different ways, and there are inevitably differences in interpretation and emphasis among the contributors. Even within a volume of this length it has not been possible to cover every topic that might have been discussed. Readers will note, for example, that the important subject of women in the early church has not been given separate treatment, although it might be pleaded in extenuation, that this is a subject related to Luke's social concerns rather than to purely theological ones.

We as editors of the volume would like to thank all who have shared in its production including the contributors, Dr. Knut Heim (the translator of chapter 14), and those who worked very hard to bring a set of essays by different authors into a more uniform format and produce the camera-ready copy.

September, 1997   I. Howard Marshall
                                                  David Peterson

INTRODUCTION

CHAPTER 1

HOW DOES ONE WRITE ON THE THEOLOGY OF ACTS?

Howard Marshall

Summary

The introduction sets the scene for the rest of the volume by offering some reflections on what is implied by characterising Luke as a theologian and Acts as a theological work. Insights into how to approach Acts as a theological document are drawn from the work of previous investigators including especially J.C. O'Neill. The theological centre of Acts lies in God's gift of salvation through Jesus Christ, the task of proclaiming it, and the nature of the new people of God empowered by the Holy Spirit.

I. Was Luke a 'theologian'?

The question of the author of Acts (hereinafter referred to as 'Luke') as a theologian can be raised from various angles. What do we mean by a theologian? It is sometimes said that all Christians are theologians inasmuch as all Christians must hold some theological opinions and think about them. But we normally use the term more narrowly. The word 'theologian' may be applied to a person who is knowledgeable in theology as opposed to a person who has little knowledge or understanding. Bernard Ramm once wrote a comparison of Karl Barth and Lewis Sperry Chafer as theologians, and the question was seriously raised whether they were on the same intellectual level, whereas I imagine that most people might want to assess their relative abilities rather differently.

Or people may be regarded as theologians in that they are writing a specifically theological work as opposed to a work with a different aim. Barth is certainly writing as a theologian in the *Church Dogmatics*, but he is perhaps doing something different when he writes a commentary on a biblical book or a book of sermons preached in Basle Prison; no doubt, these latter two examples are also 'theological', but the 'genre' is not specifically theological.

Again, we may use the term perhaps in respect of somebody who has a particular theological emphasis or understanding to impart, a person with an axe to grind. We might think of R. Bultmann's *New Testament Theology*, which is not simply a descriptive account of the thought of the NT but is at the same time the presentation of a particular 'theological' angle on the NT. Or again we might use Barth as an example with his commentary on *The Epistle to the Romans*.

Applying these three possible understandings to Acts or, rather, to its author, we may note, first, that Luke is often compared with Paul who is said to be a more profound theologian; Paul has thought things through more deeply and comes up with discussions on a different level of understanding. But this comparison does not deny that Luke was indeed a theologian, and indeed it may be in danger of drawing false conclusions if it ignores the important differences in genre between the letters of Paul and Luke–Acts. Second, then, we should want to ask whether the writing of a 'history' (if that is what Acts is) produces a less obviously theological result than the writing of a pastoral letter to a congregation (which is what Romans is). Certainly the prologue to the Gospel (Luke 1:1-4), which in my view serves as an introduction to the Gospel and Acts, does not promise a theological treatise to follow. However, especially when the history contains a good deal of theological material, I doubt if we can deny that it is by a theologian. It is true that H. Schürmann disputed whether Luke was a theologian, and preferred to think of him as more concerned with pastoral issues.[1] But this is a dubious antithesis. Third, we are back to the question whether Luke was deliberately pushing a particular 'line' or acts (unconsciously) as the representative of a specific kind of theology over against others (such as third-generation Christianity over against first-generation or second-generation). This leads us directly into our next section.

II. What do we mean by 'the theology of the book of Acts'?

A major concern of writers on Acts has been to discover to what extent the theology of the author differs from that of the actors, or, to reverse the point, to determine whether the actual theology of the first Christians can be recovered from an account which belongs to, and is said to reflect the theology of, a later period.

1. As it stands, Acts purports to give an account of certain aspects of the history of the early church. It is presented as a story in more or less chronological order of what happened between the resurrection of Jesus and the end of Paul's two-year stay in Rome. It contains a substantial amount of material in direct speech representing what leading early Christians said, mainly in public, before various audiences. It describes what they did. It is a familiar story that in an earlier day Acts was taken at what seemed to many readers to be its face value, namely as a historical record of aspects of the mission of the early church, from which information could be gleaned as to the theology of the principal actors, Peter, Stephen, James and Paul. If this position can still be maintained, it would be possible, at least in theory, to draw up a systematic presentation of what is offered piecemeal as the beliefs of the early church, to draw out the theological significance of what its leaders and members did (or give the theological reasons why they did it) and to reconstruct the underlying set of theological assumptions which may be necessary to fill the gaps and to give coherence to what is actually said. That would be a theology of the early church according to Acts.

Questions would arise, of course, as to whether the theological views changed and developed with the passage of time, and whether

---

[1]H. Schürmann, *Das Lukasevangelium*, I, 16f.

there were differences between the various principal actors. In fact, Luke tells us that there were differing points of view not only on practical matters but also on theological points (or points with theological implications) between the leaders and others. He shows how possible conflict among the leaders was overcome through dialogue and seeking the mind of God. It is clear that he was conscious of tensions, differences and developments, and that he presented them incidentally in his narrative. It is much less likely that he set himself as one of his deliberate goals the task of presenting an account of the development of the theology of the church.

At the same time, Luke as narrator permits himself explanatory remarks on what was happening, and on the strength of these it may well be possible to identify some of the strands and expressions of the theology of the early Christians with his own mind. It could, of course, also be assumed that he agreed broadly with the consensus expressed in his account of the early Christians. Indeed, one might perhaps expect this to be so, given the high regard which he evidently has for the early Christians. Thus, it might be argued that Luke's own outlook, with any characteristic variations and developments from the early church, might emerge alongside the presentation of the early church's view. In fine, it is a possibility that the theology (or theologies) of the early church as presented by Luke is faithfully recorded, and Luke himself is in substantial agreement with it.

2. But it could also be argued that Luke's account of the early church does not accurately mirror reality. This could happen in at least two ways which are not mutually exclusive.

On one hand, the sources from which Luke gained his material may have been inaccurate in that they may have been misinformed, or they may have attributed their own views to the early Christians in an anachronistic manner. It would be easy, for example, for later Christians to attribute their own rather developed view of the person of Jesus to the earliest Christians without recognising that development had taken place. Luke, therefore, could have been aiming to produce the sort of account already suggested (option 1.) and yet been the prisoner of the information available to him. He himself could have been like his contemporaries in lack of historical discernment.

On the other hand, and more radically, it could be suggested that Luke (or his sources) was presenting a picture of the early church which reinforced the validity of his own theology by attributing to the early Christians views which they may not have held. This could have been a more deliberate procedure.

To be sure, the lines are not easy to draw here. If we consider the well-known view that Luke was an exponent of what has been called 'third generation Christianity', then it might be hard to say whether the anachronistic picture of the first Christians which he is alleged to present was due to (a) a deliberate attempt to present the first Christians in this kind of way, although the author knew that this was unhistorical; or (b) an unconscious pressure from the author's own situation and experience which led him to present the first Christians in this way without realising that he was being unhistorical (he simply thought that it must always have been so. *Cf.*, how people on church councils today justify practices by saying 'we have always done it this way', where 'always'='for the last ten years'). On this second view we have two factors at work: (i) the assumption of the author that (at least in some respects) things have been unchanged over the period in question; (ii) the effects of a pressure of which he may or may not have been unaware which had resulted in the theology of his time having a different character from that of the previous period. Since there is no indication that Luke thought that he was expressing a different point of view in his own remarks from that which emerges in the direct speech of the main actors, we are probably to assume that he thought that his own view did not seriously differ from theirs. But if there are cases where it is arguable that he knew that the historical facts were of a particular character and yet chose to present them differently, then this would indicate that he knew that there had been changes but wished to hide them.

The question is manifestly a necessary one and it cannot be avoided. The tendency in recent scholarship is to argue that the theology is at every point the theology of Luke, that earlier sources cannot be recovered, and that the speeches represent what Luke thought that people should have said. In terms of the well-known passage from Thucydides, Luke was not able to give 'the general purport of what was actually said' (because he had no, or a negligible amount of information) and had to 'put into the mouth of each speaker the sentiments proper to the occasion, expressed as I thought he would be likely to express them', but again Luke had little idea as to how 'he would be likely to express them' and had to rely on a well-developed historical imagination. G. Lüdemann, who is otherwise well disposed to the possibility of detecting traditions Luke uses and testing their historical value, brackets off the speeches at the outset of his investigation.[2]

---

[2]G. Lüdemann, *Das frühe Christentum nach den Traditionen der Apostelgeschichte*, 53.

However, we cannot proceed in such an abrupt manner without considering the point more fully. It is arguable that there is sufficient evidence of historical verisimilitude in the narrative and in the character of the speeches to make it worthwhile to ask whether the latter do not rest to some extent on 'the general purport of what was actually said' if not on a specific occasion at least in the general period of the earliest Christians.[3] How are we to go about settling these issues and formulating an approach? A glance at previous practitioners of the art is the obvious next step.

III. What can we learn from previous investigators?

Books on the theology of Acts are not all that common, although studies of theological themes in Acts are plentiful.[4] Conzelmann's *Die Mitte der Zeit* has been so often summarised and discussed by writers on Luke–Acts that it is not necessary to do so here. It is often regarded as the first attempt to trace a theology of Luke, the author of Luke–Acts, but this is disputable. H. von Baer's work on the Holy Spirit, *Der heilige Geist in den Lukas-schriften*, is recognised as a notable predecessor. It is significant because it was asking what Luke's view of the Spirit was, and it rightly picked out a topic on which Luke makes a distinctive contribution.

Both of these writers considered Luke–Acts as a whole,[5] and Conzelmann certainly did not think that it was a viable enterprise to write a book on the theology of Acts.[6] His opinion has not been shared by others who claimed that it was possible to write on *The Theology of Acts* (J.C. O'Neill) and consider Acts separately from the Gospel. The fact that O'Neill wrote two editions of his book which differ very considerably from each another is probably a testimony to his fertility of mind and capacity for fresh ideas rather than to any inherent difficulty in the enterprise. But what exactly did he do? A summary of

---

[3]See the nuanced position of C.L. Gempf, 'Public Speaking and Published Accounts', *A1CS* 1, 259-303.

[4]See the bibliography at the end of this book.

[5]We shall not consider further other notable works on the theology of Luke–Acts as a whole such as H. Flender, *St Luke: Theologian of Redemptive History*; E. Franklin, *Christ the Lord: A Study in the Purpose and Theology of Luke–Acts*; idem., *Luke: Interpreter of Paul, Critic of Matthew*; A. Hastings, *Prophet and Witness in Jerusalem*.

[6]In his review of O'Neill's book Conzelmann commented on the impossibility of the proceeding (H. Conzelmann, Reviews of the two editions of O'Neill, J.C., *The Theology of Acts*).

his work may be helpful.

1. He began by placing Acts in its historical setting, in this case an unusual one, in that he argued for a very late date for Acts, namely between AD 115 and 130.

2. He discussed the structure of Acts and its theology. He argued for a fivefold division of Acts, based on geography with Jerusalem controlling the history. The church comes of age when it leaves Jerusalem and enters Rome.

3. He focused on the attitude to the Jews who rejected the gospel despite every effort to persuade them through Scripture and preaching. Here come two crucial statements:

> The theology of Acts consists not so much in the doctrines which are put into the mouths of the chief historical characters as in the movement of the history.[7]

> Luke was a theologian who believed that God had revealed his solution to the theological decisions facing the contemporary church in the history of the primitive church. He believed that God had used the rebelliousness of the Jews to drive the church out into the Gentile world, and that it should boldly accept its destiny and try to capture the Roman Empire for the faith, as he was himself by writing Luke–Acts; he also believed that the practice of the early church provided a model for the relationship which should exist between Jewish and Gentile Christians in his day.[8]

Therefore it is more important to discuss the relations between groups of people than between doctrines like gospel and law.

4. Luke tries to show that a workable relationship between Jews and Gentiles in the church was a possibility (Acts 15).

5. A lengthy discussion of the titles given to Jesus follows. The chapter is not summarised, but on the whole the result seems to be that the usage represents that of the date assigned to the composition of Acts, while preserving some primitive echoes.[9]

6. In the next section the argument for Luke being indebted to the Judaism of the Dispersion is developed. The use of a history for apologetic reasons is traced to the Greek-speaking Jewish apologists.

---

[7]O'Neill, *Theology*, 94 (1st ed.).
[8]O'Neill, *Theology*, 117 (1st ed.).
[9]O'Neill, *Theology*, 119 (1st ed.).

The methods employed come from the same source. Some important topics are in this chapter.

7. Finally, it is held that Luke's theological presuppositions are those of early catholicism in the second century:

> This is indicated by: the way he regarded the Apostolic Age as normative and as part of salvation-history; his attitude to the Jews; the way he used the OT; and the comprehensive collection of christo-logical titles which he had inherited. An eschatology which puts the 'end' into the indefinite future, a pneumatology which confines the work of the Spirit to open and tangible effects, and a clear conception that heresy began when the apostles died (20.29), all point to the same conclusions. Luke took it for granted that the churches were objective historical bodies with an established ministry and sacraments, and that salvation was ratified by entering their fellowship and sub-mitting to their discipline....in Paul there is a dimension of hiddenness which is lacking in Luke. To Luke nothing of God's saving work in history is hidden; at Pentecost it was completely revealed to any who would listen.[10]

The central purpose, however, is to persuade educated Romans to become Christians. Acts is not just a history of Christian missions but aims to show how the church found its true nature in the move from Jerusalem to Rome.

In the second edition, some omissions seem to be due to lack of space rather than to change of mind. There are a number of additions which do not essentially alter the argument. Of greatest interest is a fresh chapter in which O'Neill develops his new opinion that Luke used written sources and claims that it is necessary to discern three 'layers of ideas'. These are: (a) the ideas found in Luke's sources which he passed on more or less unchanged; (b) the ideas 'presupposed by Luke because he was a man of his own particular time and situation'; and (c) 'the result of the conscious intentions of Luke as he composed Luke–Acts'.[11]

My concern is not to comment on the specific theology (or theol-ogies) that O'Neill finds in Acts, but rather the pointers to method and approach that emerge from his work. He draws the following con-clusions regarding the character and content of the theology of Acts.

1. Luke's background is the second century church. It is important to

---

[10]O'Neill, *Theology*, 166f. (1st ed.).
[11]O'Neill, *Theology*, 160f. (2nd ed.).

'fix' him and see him against the correct background.

2. Luke derives important influences from Hellenistic Judaism.

3. His deliberate purpose is evangelistic.

4. He uses a story to make his points, because that is what is effective.

5. He uses the primitive church as a model.

6. He does a take-over of the OT.

7. Thus Luke is early catholic.

8. It is possible to consider the theology of Acts as a topic on its own while recognising that it is part of Luke–Acts.

What is important for us is to note the kind of questions which were being asked in order to come up with these conclusions. Already at this point I will express the view that, however we may judge the specific conclusions reached by O'Neill, he is basically asking the right questions and going through the right agenda, but unfortunately he stands almost alone in making the attempt.

A more recent, more popular and less ambitious volume is that of H.C. Kee, *Good News to the Ends of the Earth*. Kee announces that he sees the relation of the Church to Israel as a key feature in Acts, and he thinks the way forward is by an examination of the social, political, literary and cultural features of the contemporary situation. He sums up his aim as: 'to discern the distinctive features of defining participation in the covenant and the messianic role in this book, and to see how these factors shape the attitudes towards politics, culture, ethics and other religious traditions expressed therein'.[12] After his introduction he tackles five themes. First, there is christology. He considers 'Jesus as God's agent for the renewal of his people', and does so by a discussion of his titles. His aim seems to be to bring out the connection between God and Jesus. Second, comes a survey of the 'Spirit as God's instrument in the present age'. This is a useful summary of the varied modes of action of the Spirit. Third, Kee examines the church 'reaching out across religious and cultural boundaries'; this is essentially a re-telling of the story of Acts. Fourth, he discusses 'structure and strategy in the new community'. Finally, the theme of 'witness' is isolated as a key to what God still wants the church to do.

Between them, these five themes cover a good deal of material, and in particular the emphasis on witness picks up an issue which is surely of central significance in the theology of the book. An important feature is the recognition of a kind of social dimension to the theology, but otherwise there is not a lot of reflection on method in this book.[13]

---

[12]Kee, *Good News*, 5.

Perhaps surprisingly, that is all that we have, so far as comprehensive treatments of the theology of Acts are concerned, with the
exception of J. Jervell's outstanding treatment.[14] An article by B.R.
Gaventa may take us a little further.[15] She argues that no one understanding of Luke's theology has won the day because there is no
agreement on the method to be pursued. Conzelmann's work fails
because he sought Luke's theology only in his redactional changes to
his sources, and this is a methodological blooper of the first rank.[16] She
then outlines four approaches that might be followed.

The first is redaction criticism which builds on the way Luke
uses his sources. This method is rejected because in Gaventa's view it
is doubtful whether Luke had sources for Acts in the same way as for
the Gospel, and also because material that appears to be traditional
may in fact be Luke's own creation.

The second approach is to concentrate on the speeches on the
assumption that Luke had greater freedom in their composition than
in the narrative. It is also assumed, says Gaventa, that narrative cannot
convey theology. But no real criticism of this approach is offered.

Third is the identification of what Gaventa calls 'key' texts, passages which stand out for their programmatic or strategic significance.
Gaventa wonders whether reader-response criticism will help explain
how the identification of these passages and their significance is affected by the situation of the readers who make these identifications.

Fourth, there is the identification of specific theological themes

---

[13]I regret that the work of E. Rasco, *La teologia de Lucas: origen, desarrollo, orientaciones* is inaccessible to me. (There is a summary in Bovon, *Luc le théologien: Vingt-
cinq ans de recherches. [1950-1975]*, 79-81, from which it appears that it is a corrective to Conzelmann.) F. Bovon has written a survey, *Luke the Theologian: Thirty-three
years of research (1950-1983)*, which summarises the various contributions to an
understanding of different areas of theology in Luke–Acts. It is not an attempt to
write a theology of Acts or Luke–Acts. But its list of contents may be significant: 1.
The plan of God. Salvation history and eschatology; 2. The Interpretation of the
OT; 3. Christology; 4. The Holy Spirit; 5. Salvation; 6. The Reception of Salvation;
7. The Church. These are topics which have been discussed in recent study,
although they have not all commanded the same attention.
[14]This chapter was completed before the publication of J. Jervell, *The Theology of the
Acts of the Apostles* in the CUP series on *New Testament Theology* (1996). Jervell's
book is an outstandingly clear exposition of his approach to Acts, developed in his
earlier books of essays, and is largely concerned to demonstrate his understanding
of Luke's view of the people of God. Although it does not contain any discussion
of how to write a theology of Acts, it is a first-class example of how it can be done.
[15]B.R. Gaventa, 'Towards a Theology of Acts. Reading and Rereading'.
[16]*Cf.*, I.H. Marshall, *Luke: Historian*, 19f.

and threads. Here the criticism is that those who take this approach tend to single out a particular theme without relating it to the others in this complex book.

Having found all these approaches wanting, Gaventa then develops a case for the study of narrative as an approach to theology. Acts does not provide a theological thesis which has been wrapped up in a narrative from which it can be separated. The theology is inextricably bound up with the narrative, and be it noted that it is a 'narrative' rather than a historical account which may or may not be true to the facts. She then suggests various questions to ask which may help us to analyse the narrative as theology. Her test case or example is a refutation of Conzelmann's thesis that Acts contains a theology of triumph and growth; she has little difficulty in showing that the development of the story supports rather C.K. Barrett's case that Acts contains a *theologia crucis*: the triumph of God, or rather of his Word, and the suffering of the messengers of the Word go hand in hand in the pattern of the book.[17]

As is often the case with scholars, Gaventa appears to be right in what she affirms but on shakier ground in what she denies. None of her arguments against the four approaches which she dismisses is sufficient to disqualify them. It is easiest to dismiss the redaction-critical method, since the discrimination between tradition and redaction is so speculative, and since there is no indication that Luke disagreed theologically with his sources. No real argument is offered against looking to the speeches for theological light, and the discussion of 'key passages' contains warnings against subjectivity rather than reasons for rejection in principle. The study of themes is manifestly legitimate, provided that we pay attention to the intricate interplay of numerous themes and do not hitch our wagon to a single star.

As for her own stress on narrative, we had already found this exemplified by O'Neill who wrote (happily?) before the development of the modern approaches to the method.

It is surely the case that an approach to the theology of Acts, as of any NT book, must be eclectic and use all the legitimate methods that there are. Part of the responsibility for the variety of views may lie in the fact that different scholars have different goals. It is one thing to attempt a survey of Luke's teaching on theological topics in Acts; it is another thing to attempt a characterisation of either the influences that affected him or the general shape and flavour of his theology. These

---

[17]Barrett, *'Theologia crucis*–in Acts?'

goals suggest a couple of other approaches that must be brought into the matter. The one is the search for the influences that went into the theology: where did Luke get his theology from? The other is a comparison of the theology of Acts with that of other early Christians so as to give it its proper place on the map of the early church and perhaps even on a time-chart of evolution and development.

When we put all these insights together, we find that the agenda that should be in the minds of people who write on the theology of Acts should include such questions as the following:

1. What is Luke's ecclesiastical background? And what was the life-situation of those whom he addressed and for whom he framed his account? Luke's own setting in the church establishes his context for what he was doing. This may be deduced from his writing and/or from other evidence. The setting and the theology may well form a hermeneutical circle.

2. What kind of influences affected him? Luke's broader setting in the Jewish and Graeco–Roman world indicates the kind of thinking that may be expected from him. Attention must also be paid to any sociological factors which may have influenced the formation of the theology.

3. What was he trying to do? Insight into Luke's purpose in writing will help to set the parameters for what he may be expected to provide and for what he may be expected to omit (*e.g.*, the fact that he is more concerned with mission than with the development of local church leadership). We need to identify his theological interests and themes, in particular those which may be considered to be of central significance.

4. What sort of writing did he produce? What does the character and shape of the book say about its theology? The 'genre' of Acts is clearly relevant in determining the nature of what Luke writes. Here the question of his use of 'narrative' is especially important.

5. What relationship has the theology of Acts to that of earlier Christians? How far is Luke recording what the early church believed and how far is he reading back or imposing the theology of his own day upon the early Christians? And what light is thrown on his work by a comparison with what other figures in the church, especially Paul and any so-called Deutero–Paulinists, were doing?

6. What relationship has the theology of Acts to the OT?

7. How is what is going on in Acts related to what is going on in the Gospel? We must consider the place of Acts within the total programme of Luke in his two-volume work. For example, what

parallelism exists between the two works, and what is its theological, as distinct from its literary, significance?

8. What general character has the resulting theology? Do any such phrases as 'delay of the Parousia; salvation-history; subordinationist christology; faded Paulinism; interpretation of Paul; early catholicism' help us to characterise the theology in terms of its motivation or matrix or method?

9. What are the particular themes of Luke's theology in detail, and how are they to be understood?

10. Finally, since we inevitably approach Acts as modern readers and cannot avoid doing so, we need to ask both how our situation affects our understanding of the text, and how the text should affect us who are not the original readers.

IV. What are we attempting in this book?

This is a book of essays on aspects of the study of the theology of Acts rather than a unified and complete account of its theology. The editors have attempted to cover many of the topics that would properly find their way into an account of the theology of Acts, although in the nature of things it is difficult to cover every aspect in a symposium and to avoid a certain amount of overlap between the contributions. Further, it needs to be emphasised that the contributors worked on a tight time-schedule and within rigorous word-limits on topics, each of which could have merited a monograph. Nevertheless, the attempt was made to unify the volume by holding a conference at which a significant number of the contributors were present and all of the papers were discussed before their final drafting. We have attempted to lay a solid exegetical foundation rather than to ask questions about the significance of our studies for contemporary theology and the life of the contemporary church.

It should perhaps be added at this point that in general the contributors share the view that Acts is to be understood as the second volume of the two-part work Luke–Acts. According to H.J. Cadbury 'Acts is neither an appendix nor an afterthought. It is probably an integral part of the author's original plan and purpose'.[18] While recognising the force of the points made especially by M.C. Parsons

---

[18]H.J. Cadbury, *The Making of Luke–Acts*, 8f.; *cf.*, R. J. Maddox, *The Purpose of Luke–Acts*, 3–6.

and R.I. Pervo to the effect that the Gospel and Acts are independent
works and that they have significant differences in theology,[19] we
would claim that Acts is the intended sequel to the Gospel and that,
while it is proper to consider its theology separately from that of the
Gospel, it should not be considered in isolation from it.[20]

The structure which has been followed, as is inevitable in a
symposium, is a thematic one with different writers exploring different aspects of the theology of Acts. The aim has been to give some
account of the state of research in each of the areas discussed and to
provide a creative interpretation of the topic. The general structure
and method of the theology of Acts and the different themes that
appear to be important to the author are handled in turn.

The shape of the volume reflects our broadly-shared understanding of the nature of the book of Acts. We believe that Acts is
primarily about God's action in offering salvation through Jesus Christ
to both Jews and Gentiles and thereby creating a new people. Therefore the book has three main sections. In the first section on 'The
Salvation of God' we consider the divine provision of salvation with
essays on the plan of God and its adumbration in Scripture, and the
role of Jesus as the Saviour. The second section on 'The Call of God' in
effect tells the story of how the message of salvation is made known to
Jews and Gentiles. Section three on 'The Renewing Work of God'
considers the experience and character of the saved people. These
three sections, which form the core of the book, are followed by some
final, methodological considerations. We have attempted to look at
how Luke 'did' his theology, what comes to expression on various
topics, how the 'narrative' develops, and what may be said about the
resulting composition as a whole. We hope that the result will be
sufficiently comprehensive and detailed to do justice to one of the most
fascinating books in the New Testament.

---

[19]M.C. Parsons and R.I. Pervo, *Rethinking the Unity of Luke and Acts*.
[20]See I.H. Marshall, 'Acts and the "Former Treatise"', *A1CS* I, 163-82. On the
alleged differences between the anthropologies of Luke and Acts see the chapter
by C. Stenschke in this volume.

Part I

THE SALVATION OF GOD

CHAPTER 2

THE PLAN OF GOD IN THE ACTS OF THE APOSTLES

John Squires

Summary

Luke sets his story of the early church into the broadest possible theological context: that of the plan of God. As he narrates the events that take place in Acts, Luke explicitly interprets them as being in accord with the divine plan, which has an inherent necessity about it. This plan is implemented by various means, including the action of the Holy Spirit, the intervention of divine agents such as angels, the occurrence of miracles, and the fulfilment of scriptural prophecies. The chapter ends with comments on the scope of the divine plan, and the purpose of such 'divine plan' language in Acts.

I. Introduction

Lines of interpretation

Throughout his two-volume work, Luke tells the story of the life of
Jesus and the growth of the early church. He sets this into the broadest
possible theological context: that of the plan of God.[1] The surface level
of the events which he narrates has its focus on concerns which appear,
at first glance, to be of a different nature. In volume one (the Gospel),
the narrative recounts the life of Jesus from his conception and birth,
through his public ministry as an adult and his journey to Jerusalem,
the centre of the Jewish world, to his crucifixion, burial, resurrection
and ascension. In volume two (Acts), the narrative is of the establishment of the earliest Christian community in Jerusalem, the expansion
of the church through Samaria and around the Mediterranean basin,
and the arrest of Paul in Jerusalem and his transportation to Rome,
where he testifies to the gospel in the centre of the Roman Empire.
These events form the most immediate foreground to Luke's narrative.

One line of interpretation is concerned with investigating the
historical verisimilitude of the narrative at this level. At stake is the
value of Luke's work as a source for the critical reconstruction of the
life of Jesus and the development of the early church.[2] Another line has
been concerned with the kind of community for which this two-
volumed work was written. Much recent work has been devoted to
this fertile area of investigation, with impressive results.[3] Some writers
within this approach, drawing on the notion that the figure of

---

[1]I assume the literary and theological unity of Luke–Acts; see Maddox, *Purpose*, 3-
6, 24 n. 14; and Marshall, ' Former Treatise'. On the plan of God, see Squires, *Plan
of God*, especially the survey of literature, 3-10; and Kee, *Good News*, 6-27. Throughout this chapter, the terms 'plan', 'providence' and 'guidance' are used inter-
changeably to refer to the same concept.

[2]This has largely been argued by citing the number of details in Acts which, when
read alongside other ancient sources, can be considered to be historically accurate;
see Cadbury, *Acts in History*, Hemer, *Acts*, and see chs. 8–11 of A1CS 1, as well as
many parts of A1CS 2. The claim seems to be that these details render the narrative, as a whole, as historically reliable. Therefore, Luke's theological interests do
not render his work null and void as a historical witness. The discussion by
Marshall, *Luke: Historian*, permits a more nuanced attitude towards the historical
value of Luke's work, without devaluing his theological tendencies.

[3]Karris, 'Poor and Rich', 112-25; Esler, *Community and Gospel*; Neyrey (ed.), *Social
World*; and, with a more limited question in view, Alexander, *Preface*,168-212.

Theophilus represents a broadly Gentile audience, have understood Luke–Acts within the context of hellenistic historiography.[4]

Our interest in this chapter, however, is directed more to what lies 'beneath' the text, in terms of the ideas and influences which appear to have shaped Luke's presentation of the events he narrates. This kind of interpretation of the theological interests of Luke has marked numerous recent studies.[5] This article is a contribution to this line of interpretation and will focus on 'the plan of God' as a singularly important motif running throughout Acts. In investigating this theme, we will proceed section by section throughout Acts. Before doing so, however, a preliminary word needs to be said about the layering of ideas which can be perceived 'beneath' the narrative.

Levels 'beneath' the narrative

The surface level of the narrative of Acts begins with a recapitulatory preface[6] and an extended opening scene in Jerusalem (1:1-26).[7] The body of the work contains a description of the earliest Christian community in Jerusalem (2:1-8:3); a pivotal section validating the 'turn to the Gentiles', featuring especially Saul of Tarsus, and the apostle Peter (8:4–12:25); an account of missionary activity with a focus on Saul, now renamed Paul (13:1-21:14); and a detailed description of the arrest and trials of Paul in Jerusalem, Caesarea, and en route to Rome (21:15–28:15). Acts ends with an extended final scene in Rome (28:16-31).[8]

Embedded within this surface level narrative are numerous references to all that Jesus did and taught (1:1)—that is, the events already narrated in the Gospel. These events are recounted in the apostolic preaching reported throughout chapters 2–26. In addition, within the narrative of these speeches there are references to events before the time of Jesus, concerning 'this people Israel' (13:17). Thus, Acts already

---

[4]Aune, *Literary Environment*, 77-157; Johnson, *Acts*, 11-12, 20-23; Sterling, *Historiography*, 363-69; compare the critical discussion of Palmer, 'Acts and the Ancient Historical Monograph', 1-29.

[5]Marshall, *Luke: Historian*; O'Toole, *Unity*; Kee, *Good News*; Schweizer, *Luke*; many more recent monographs on specific theological topics could also be mentioned.

[6]Palmer, 'Acts and the Ancient Historical Monograph', 21-26.

[7]Henceforth, references to Acts are made by numerals only.

[8]A slightly different structuring of Acts is provided by Satterthwaite, 'Classical Rhetoric', 337-79, here 348-49. My reasons for the structuring used here are noted in the argument below; they relate to the geographical and theological 'markers' which appear to delineate the sections.

contains a surface level narrative, as well as other levels of the
narrative which rehearse matters from Luke's Gospel and from the
Hebrew Scriptures.[9] These other narrative levels are presented within
an explicit interpretive framework. The story of Jesus is to be
understood within the parameters of the things that 'God did through
him' (2:22); likewise, the history of Israel is consistently interpreted in
by the claim that 'the God of this people Israel chose our ancestors and
made the people great' (13:17).

Similarly, events within the surface level narrative of both
volumes are presented within an understanding that everything takes
place under the guidance of God. Frequently, this guidance is mediated through the Spirit sent by God. This is signalled at key places in
each volume: when Jesus announces 'the Spirit of the Lord is upon me'
(Luke 4:18) and Peter states 'God declares, I will pour out my Spirit
upon all flesh' (2:17).[10] With similar frequency, the characters in the
story interpret key events in the narration as being 'nothing but what
the prophets and Moses said would take place' (26:22)—that is, that
these events (in both volumes) are the fulfilment of prophecies found
in Scripture.[11] These two second-level themes are supplemented
throughout the narrative by periodical interjections of divine agents,
such 'as an angel of the Lord coming and speaking' (10:3), and occasional references to miracles, to the effect that 'the Lord granted
signs and wonders to be done through them' (14:3).[12]

In turn, these second-level themes (guidance by the Spirit, fulfilment of scriptural prophecy, appearances of divine agents, and occurrences of miracles) assume a more fundamental, or third-level, assertion, namely, that the events of both volumes can be understood as' all
that God had done' (14:27, 15:4). Our contention is that this theme—

9Henceforth, whenever 'scripture' is used it will refer to the Hebrew Scriptures
(the Christian OT).
10There have been a number of recent explorations of the Spirit in Luke–Acts; see
Dunn, 'Baptism', 3-27; Menzies, *Development*; Shelton, *Mighty*; Stronstad,
Charismatic Theology. The direction of these studies has largely been influenced by
questions of the Spirit's soteriological role and the modern charismatic understanding of the Spirit. However, for a good survey of 'The Spirit as God's
Instrument' in Acts, see Kee, *Good News*, 28-41.
11Squires, *Plan of God*, 121-55; Talbert, 'Promise and Fulfillment', 91-103; Peterson,
'The Motif of Fulfilment', 83 -104. See ch. 3 in this volume, D. Bock, 'Scripture and
the Realisation of God's Promises', for other dimensions in Luke's use of Scripture.
12On these two themes, see Squires, *Plan of God*, 78-102 (miracles), 103-120
(epiphanies); for the way that these themes cluster together throughout Luke–
Acts, see *op. cit.*, 3-5, 186-89.

the plan of God–functions as the foundational theological motif for the complete work.[13] Some direct statements of this divine guidance can be found at the surface level of the narrative. Additional comments can be noted, stating the necessity that events must take place as they do.[14] However, the complete infusion of this theme throughout Luke's work can be seen once the cluster of second-level themes is explored. The broad theological context of Luke–Acts is that God has been at work in the events narrated. This is the interpretive framework within which Luke is writing; and this is the framework which will help us to discern something of the scope and the purpose of Luke's writing.

II. The plan of God in Acts

Preface and opening scene in Jerusalem (1:1-26)

Luke's second volume begins with a narrative recapitulation of the conclusion of his first volume. In Acts 1, the account of the ascension (already reported at Luke 24:50-53) is expanded through the explicit noting of some significant features of that occasion. The last words of Jesus to the disciples, 'you will receive power when the Holy Spirit has come upon you' (1:8), reinforce the programmatic role of the Spirit throughout this volume. The description of 'two men in white robes' (1:10) and the prominence they have at this point identifies the role that such epiphanies will play throughout the second volume. The following scene, which completes the gap in the twelve which has been created by the death of Judas, includes the doubly significant note that 'the Scripture had to be fulfilled, which the Holy Spirit through David foretold' (1:16; also 1:20=Ps. 69:25).[15] Thus, the opening chapter has indicated that the Spirit will guide, angelic figures will lead, a certain necessity will drive events as they occur, and these events can be understood as fulfilling scriptural prophecy.[16] The narrative moment is ripe to turn immediately to the day of Pentecost.[17] According to

---

[13]This is worked out in detail throughout Squires, *Plan of God*, with reference to the hellenistic understanding of providence. On the resonances with Jewish understandings of 'God's control of history', see Sterling, *Historiography*, 359-63; Rosner, 'Acts and Biblical History', 78-80.

[14]The key word is δεῖ, which appears throughout Luke–Acts; see Squires, *Plan of God*, 2 n. 6, 166-85; Cosgrove, 'The Divine ΔΕΙ in Luke–Acts', 168-90.

[15]See Peterson, 'The Motif of Fulfilment', 95-96.

Luke, what happens at Pentecost, is that apparently supernatural phenomena occur (2:1-4), and are interpreted by Peter (with reference to Scripture) as being an irruption of God into human history (2:14-21). In the ensuing speech (2:22-36), the first of many such speeches, Peter expands on other aspects of divine guidance.

The apostolic preaching (chapters 2–28)

When the speeches are viewed together as a cohesive unit, each of the themes identified forms a part of the consistent apostolic message.[18]

(1) Spirit: Peter's first speech is introduced by a quotation from the Scriptures which refers to God's action, through the Spirit, in fulfilment of a scriptural prophecy: 'God declares, I will pour out my Spirit upon all flesh' (2:17=Joel 2:28). The role of the Spirit receives acknowledgement in subsequent speeches by Peter (5:32; 10:38), Stephen (7:51), and Paul (20:23; 28:25). Direct narrative comments also note the role of the Spirit immediately following speeches after the death of Stephen (7:55) and the preaching of Peter (10:44). In his speech at Caesarea, Peter declares that 'God anointed Jesus of Nazareth with the Holy Spirit' (10:38). This theme thus relates the present activity of God, from Pentecost onwards, to the past actions of God through the Spirit in the life of Jesus.

(2) Fulfilment: Also in focus throughout the speeches is the affirmation that scriptural prophecies are fulfilled in the events of Jesus' life.[19] Paul's climactic defence speech concludes with the claim that he has been 'saying nothing but what the prophets and Moses said would take place' (26:22). This claim has a twofold orientation, as explained immediately in 26:23. First, Paul notes the fulfilment of prophecies relating to events recorded in Luke's first volume, namely, 'the suffering of the Messiah'. The claim that events relating to Jesus (namely, his life, death, resurrection and exaltation) fulfil scriptural prophecies had

---

16The same cluster of themes can be found in the extended prologue of Luke 12; see Squires, *Plan of God*, 27-32.
17The ten days elapsing between 1:1-14 and 2:1-42 are represented by the single incident–1:15-26. The concern seems to be to get to Pentecost as rapidly as possible.
18Soards, *Speeches*, argues persuasively that the speeches form a cohesive whole. For a treatment of the cluster of themes relating to providence in one speech (Paul to Agrippa and Festus, 26:1-29), see Squires, *Plan of God*, 32-35.
19Peterson, 'The Motif of Fulfilment', 96-100.

been stated in earlier speeches, by Peter (at 2:25-28,31,34; 4:11), the believers in Jerusalem (4:25-26), and Paul himself (13:33-35; and see the summary comment at 17:2-3). Furthermore, Peter relates the anticipated return of Jesus to the fulfilment of prophecy; Jesus' return is expected at 'the time of universal restoration that God announced long ago through his holy prophets' (3:21); indeed, this event, he claims, is predicted by 'all the prophets, as many as have spoken, from Samuel and those after him' (3:24).

Second, Paul interprets the key events of the narrative of Acts—those acts of 'proclaim[ing] light both to our people and to the Gentiles'—as also being in fulfilment of scriptural prophecies. This claim had already been made by Paul himself (13:41; 13:47), as well as by Peter at 15:16-17.[20] It is noteworthy that, when Paul addresses a completely Gentile audience in Athens, the argument he presents is consistent with a scripturally-based viewpoint; but the 'ancient authorities' he quotes are drawn, not from Hebrew Scriptures, but from Gentile writers (17:28). The argument can equally well be understood in Greek philosophical terms.[21] The function of the Gentile quotations is the same as scriptural quotations elsewhere, namely, to interpret current events through ancient writings which are authoritative for the particular audience.

(3) Divine agents: The two manifestations of such agents in the speeches are in Stephen's recital of Israel's history (7:30-38) and Paul's recounting of his conversion and commissioning (22:7-11; 26:13-18). In the case of Israel, the angel calls Moses to his leadership role in the Exodus; 'God sent [him] as both ruler and liberator through the angel who appeared to him in the bush' (7:35). In the case of Paul, his commission is conveyed both through the dramatic effect of the light (22:6,9; 22:11; 26:13) and by the heavenly voice (22:8-9; 26:14-18). In Paul's Jerusalem defence speech, the voice clearly identifies that the purpose of the epiphany is to inform Paul that 'the God of the ancestors has chosen [you] to know his will' (22:14), that is to serve as a witness (22:15). In Paul's Caesarean defence speech, the voice declares that God has appeared 'to appoint you to serve and testify' (26:16) to epiphanies both already seen (9:3) and yet to occur (16:6-9; 18:9-10; 23:11; 27:23-24).

---

[20]Stephen also refers to the fulfilment of scriptural prophecies, in relation to Israel's exile (7:42-43) and to the nature of the temple (7:49-50).
[21] See Squires, *Plan of God*, 71-75, esp. nn. 182, 184.

(4) Necessity: Statements indicating the divine necessity are made in a number of speeches. Peter notes that Jesus 'must remain in heaven until the time of universal restoration' (3:21) and emphasises the necessity, in the meantime, of responding in obedience (3:22; 4:12). Peter and all the apostles reiterate this before the council ('we must obey God rather than any human authority', 5:29), but the result is that they suffer a flogging (5:40-41). A similar conjunction is found in the words of the Lord which tell Saul both of the imperative of obedience ('you will be told what you must do', 9:6) and the necessity of suffering ('how much he must suffer for the sake of my name', 9:16). Luke has Paul himself recall the motif of necessary suffering, in relation to the obedience required of believers ('through many persecutions we must enter the kingdom of God', 14:22) as well as in relation to Jesus ('the Messiah must suffer', 26:23).

(5) Miracles: Occurrences of divine portents are noted in the life of Jesus (Peter, at 2:22) and in the history of Israel (Stephen, at 7:36). In both instances, it is clear that God is the one who has performed these signs and wonders.

(6) God: Most prominent of all in these speeches is the acknowledgement of the direct, unmediated action of God in the events narrated.[22] Thus, the body of Peter's speech at Pentecost begins with a full explanation of God's activity in Jesus (2:22-24) and concludes with the affirmation that 'God has made him both Lord and Messiah' (2:36). Subsequent speeches expand the activity of God in Jesus: God 'has glorified his servant Jesus' (3:13), 'sent a message to the people of Israel' (10:36), 'raised Jesus from the dead' (13:30; see also 2:24, 32; 3:15; 5:30; 10:40; 17:31), and 'will have the world judged in righteousness by a man whom he has appointed' (17:31). Yet the sphere of God's activity stretches beyond Jesus; other speeches note that before Jesus, God had guided Israel (7:2-50; 13:17-22), especially Abraham (7:2-8), Joseph (7:9-16), Moses (7:20-38) and David (13:22,36). Beyond the time of Jesus, God is at work in the early church (2:16-18) and in choosing Paul to bear witness (22:14-15; 26:16-18). Finally, God's actions can be seen in the creation of the world (4:24; 14:15; 17:24-25).

Throughout the speeches in Acts, each theme reinforces the overall interpretation that the events reported take place within the providence of God. Luke's consistent intention in the apostolic

---

[22]See my detailed consideration of six speeches in *op. cit.*, 63-76; Soards, *Speeches*, 184-89, provides a synthesis of this theme in the speeches.

preaching he reports in Acts, is to interpret both the story of Jesus and the history of Israel within the framework of divine providence. This same theme forms the framework for Luke's account of the earliest Christian community.

The earliest Christian community in Jerusalem (2:1-8:3)

All the events narrated in this section concerning the earliest Christian community take place in Jerusalem ('in one place', 2:1, refers back to 1:12-13). Each of the second-level themes already noted find a place in the narrative; together, these themes reinforce the idea that these events are guided by God.

(1) Spirit: The theme of guidance by the Spirit is clearly signalled in the first four verses of this section. With the coming of the day of Pentecost 'all of them were filled with the Holy Spirit' (2:4). This is a divinely-motivated act which is explained at the start of Peter's speech (2:14-18). This same concept is repeated in later descriptions of the community at prayer ('filled with the Holy Spirit', 4:31) and the seven ('full of the Holy Spirit', 6:3, and particularly Stephen at 6:5,10). Even at his moment of death, Stephen is 'full of the Holy Spirit' (7:55). The on-going role of the Spirit is also indicated in Peter's interpretation of the disobedience of two members of the community: Ananias has 'lied to the Holy Spirit' (5:3) and his wife Sapphira has 'put the Spirit of the Lord to the test' (5:10).

(2) Miracles: Of similar prominence in this section is the constant stream of wonders and signs being performed by the apostles (2:43; 5:12). One particular instance is the healing of the lame man (3:1-10), which Peter interprets as an indication that such portents have a divine origin; he declares it is not by our own power or piety that the man is healed, but rather, it is by faith in the name of Jesus (3:16), who is none other than the servant of the God of Abraham, the God of Isaac, and the God of Jacob (3:13). The same understanding, that divine power enables healings, is expressed by the believers in their prayer to God: you stretch out your hand to heal, and signs and wonders are performed (4:30).

(3) Other themes: Peter has previously offered the interpretation of the coming of the Spirit as a fulfilment of prophecy—'this is what was spoken through the prophet Joel' (2:16). Alongside of the Spirit,

another divine agent indicates how God's purposes are at work. During their second imprisonment, Peter and John are released by an angel of the Lord (5:19), who explicitly commands them to resume their preaching in the temple (5:21). In the same context, when Peter and the apostles stand before the Jerusalem council, they declare that their preaching and healings happen out of divine necessity—'we must obey God rather than any human authority' (5:29). The response of Gamaliel, a member of the council, is a clear Lukan formulation indicating God's role in these events (5:38-39).[23]

(4) God: The primary theme for interpreting the events of this section is clearly 'all that God had done'. The close of the all-important initial scene, at Pentecost, comes with the comment that 'day by day the Lord added to their number' (2:47). This then provides the interpretive key for the subsequent statements about the growth of the community (4:4; 5:14; 6:1a, 7): this growth is due to divine action. The comment that 'great grace was upon them all' (4:33) reinforces this perception. Thus, throughout this section, divine guidance is evident in a variety of ways. The explicit interpretation offered by characters in the narrative is reinforced by events in the narrative itself.

The section closes with a geographical reference to the scattering of the believers outside of Jerusalem (8:1) and a proleptic glance of Saul (8:3), who will play a key role in each subsequent section. At this point in the narrative—Stephen has been martyred, persecution begins, believers are scattered, Saul ravages the church—divine providence appears to be temporarily obscured. However, the narrative will return immediately to this theme in the next section.

Pivotal section: the 'turn to the Gentiles' (8:4-12:25)

This section begins by recapitulating the geographical reference (8:4) and summarising the successful missionary activity of Philip (8:5-8). The narrative then outlines a series of steps beyond Jerusalem and Judaea, each of which includes events which validate the movement out of Jerusalem into the wider Hellenistic world. This section is marked by the prominence of miracles, divine agents, and the Spirit. The combination of these themes, along with explicit statements of God's plan, reinforces the validity of the move to the Gentiles at each step.

---

[23]H. Conzelmann, *Acts*, 43.

(1) Miracles: This section of Acts is permeated by miraculous events: the casting out of many demons (8:7a), the healing of many people (8:7b), and the performing of great signs and miracles (8:13); the complete turnaround of a persecutor, including his blinding and then restoration to sight (9:1-31); the resurrection of a dead woman (9:36-42); a complementary set of visions to a Jew and a godfearer, leading to an epoch-making visit and a renewed outpouring of the Holy Spirit (10:1-11:18); and the death of a tyrannical, persecuting ruler (12:1-23). Usually there is no explicit claim that God is performing these miracles; such an interpretation, however, is not alien to the intention of this section. It can readily be drawn in various ways. Often throughout Luke–Acts, portentous events are interpreted as occurring due to divine power. Such an understanding is made clear early in this section, when Philip's ability to heal and exorcise is explained as being due to the power of God (8:10). The related indications of divine providence that recur throughout this section make it clear that Luke sees God's hand resting on all that takes place as the storyline turns towards the Gentiles.

(2) Spirit: Guidance by the Spirit is central in each step taken towards the Gentiles.[24] The initial step, focused on Philip (8:4-40), is set immediately outside of Judaea. The Samaritans who have accepted the message of Philip received the Holy Spirit at the hands of Peter and John (8:15-17). The conversation on the wilderness road to Gaza between Philip and the Ethiopian eunuch is both initiated by the Spirit (8:29) and ended by the Spirit, when Philip is snatched away immediately after baptising the Ethiopian (8:39). The second step in this section, focused on Saul (9:1-31), begins on the road to Damascus, and foreshadows the ultimate move into the Gentile world (9:15). After being blinded, Saul is brought back to wholeness by the command of Ananias, be filled with the Holy Spirit (9:17). After this action of the Spirit, Saul is not only able to see, but also to begin his calling of preaching, with success, in the synagogues (9:20-22) and among the believers (9:27-29).

The third step towards the Gentiles, focused on Peter (9:32-11:18), moves to Caesarea, and brings the Gentiles firmly into view (10:28, 45; 11:1,18). It is the Spirit who instructs Peter to accompany the messengers from Cornelius (10:19-20); as a result, Peter enters the house of Cornelius (11:12). Thus, the Spirit initiates the contact which results in Peter's powerful preaching to the Gentiles in Caesarea, at

---

24Kee, *Good News*, 34-35.

which time 'the Holy Spirit fell upon all who heard the word' (10:44). For Luke, the significance of this moment is that 'the gift of the Holy Spirit had been poured out even on the Gentiles' (10:46). He subsequently reports Peter's summation of the significance of the occasion in two phrases which emphasise that God's actions amongst the Gentiles are continuous with God's earlier action at Pentecost amongst the Jews: 'the Holy Spirit fell on them [the Gentiles] just as it had upon us [the Jews] at the beginning' (11:15); and 'God gave them the same gift that he gave us' (11:17).

The fourth step (11:19-12:25) is set in Antioch and Jerusalem, and functions as a conclusion to this section of the narrative. Here, the Holy Spirit is the guiding force in two events. Barnabas, 'full of the Holy Spirit and of faith' (11:24), has missionary success in Antioch, a city which is to be crucial in sponsoring the Gentile mission (13:1-3). Agabus, a prophet from Jerusalem, predicted by the Spirit that there would be a famine (11:28), leading to the instigation of the collection— an enterprise which attempted to unite Jewish and Gentile churches in a common bond.

(3) Divine agents: In similar fashion, at each step in this pivotal section, a divine agent is active in directing the course of events. In the first step, an angel of the Lord guides Philip onto the road where he will encounter the Ethiopian (8:26). In the second step, events are initiated by the overpowering light and the divine voice to Saul (9:3-6). Parallel to this is the vision and command of the Lord to Ananias, to go and meet with Saul (9:10-16). In the third step towards the Gentiles, Cornelius sees a vision of an angel of God, and hears the command to send to Joppa for Peter (10:3-6; repeated at 10:30-33; 11:13-14). Soon afterwards, Peter sees a heavenly vision and hears a voice which he recognises as divine (10:10-16). This moment is the pivotal point in the narrative; it is this dramatic divine intervention which leads Peter to open his house to Gentiles, and thence to initiate mission amongst the Gentiles.[25] Finally, in the fourth step, an angel appears to Peter and guides him in escaping from prison (12:7-11), and an angel of the Lord strikes down Herod because of his disobedience (12:23). Thus, at each step in this section, God's plan is evident through the intervention or guidance of angelic figures.

(4) Fulfilment and necessity: These themes occur only briefly in this section. One of the scriptural prophecies which is fulfilled by Jesus is

---

[25]For a more detailed consideration of 10:1-11:18, see Squires, *Plan of God*, 116-18.

identified as Isaiah 53:7-8 (Acts 8:32-35). The theme of necessity is evident in the words to Saul, both in the general charge given to him (9:6) and in relation to his future suffering (9:16). The motif is further present in Peter's rhetorical question at the end of the third step, 'who was I that I could hinder God?' (11:17).

(5) God: God's role in this section has already been made apparent through the interpretation of portents and epiphanies, as well as through the role of the Spirit. In Samaria, it is the power of God which enables miracles (8:10); subsequently, it is the divine voice which addresses Saul (through Jesus, 9:4-6) and Peter (in a trance, 10:13-16). There are also additional direct statements about God's providence. In Joppa, it is God who declares all foods clean (10:15, 28; 11:9), thereby validating table fellowship and pointing to the Gentile mission. In Caesarea, in the only substantial speech in this section, Peter focuses on the impartiality of God (10:34-36) and the activity of God in the life of Jesus (10:37-43). This speech itself is introduced as 'all that the Lord has commanded you to say' (10:33).[26] Peter's summary of the whole incident in Caesarea reflects God's prominent role as the one who gave the gift of the Spirit (11:17) and repentance to the Gentiles (11:18). In Antioch, Luke comments—'the hand of the Lord was with them' (11:21) and 'the grace of God' was evident (11:23). In Jerusalem, Peter's release from prison was due to the church's prayers to God (12:5).

Scattered throughout this section of the narrative is a series of summaries: 8:13; 8:25; 8:40; 9:31; 11:19; 12:24. The last of these concludes this section, revealing once again that the human characters are acting out the drama of God's providence; it is the word of God which advances (12:24). This is followed by a brief geographical reference—Barnabas and Saul return to Jerusalem (12:25).

Missionary activity with a focus on Paul (13:1-21:16)

(1) Spirit: This section recounts the missionary activity of Paul and his various co-workers in towns and cities throughout Asia Minor, Macedonia and Achaia. The section begins with a commissioning scene in Antioch (13:1-3), in which the Spirit designates the key missionary personnel of this section—'the Holy Spirit said, "Set apart for me Barnabas

---

[26]At 11:1 this speech is described as 'the word of God'; at 11:12 it is the Spirit which gives this instruction.

and Saul"' (13:2). God's Spirit guides the initial journey of Barnabas and Saul; they are sent out by the Holy Spirit (13:4). As a signal of this setting-apart, the name of the central character (Saul) is changed to Paul (13:9) in the first story from this journey.

Members of the gathering in Jerusalem declare that the Spirit has guided them, when they issue a decree that 'it has seemed good to the Holy Spirit and to us...' (15:28). In Ephesus, the Spirit is active through Paul's preaching to a group of disciples of John the baptiser (19:6). Paul later tells the elders of the church in Ephesus that 'the Holy Spirit has made you overseers, to shepherd the church of God' (20:28). The general impression that the Spirit is actively guiding events is confirmed twice towards the end of this section. As he prepares to leave Ephesus, 'Paul resolved in the Spirit to go...to Jerusalem...he said, "After I have gone there, I must also see Rome"' (19:21).[27] Thus, Paul goes to Jerusalem 'as a captive to the Spirit' (20:22), aware of the prospect of further suffering because the Holy Spirit testifies this to him (20:23). Similarly, when the Judaean prophet Agabus predicts Paul's arrest, he introduces it with the phrase, 'thus says the Holy Spirit' (21:11). The theme of the Spirit's guidance runs throughout this section, indicating the continuation of divine providence throughout the missionary journeys.

(2) Fulfilment: The theme of fulfilment of scriptural prophecies is also to be found in this section. Paul interprets his missionary work in Gentile regions as such a fulfilment in his opening speech in the synagogue in Antioch. Although many Jews respond positively to Paul's preaching of forgiveness (13:43), the negative response amongst some of the Jews (13:46, 50) fulfils the word spoken by Habakkuk—'in your days I am doing a work'(13:41=Hab. 1:5). The positive response to his message amongst the Gentiles (13:48) fulfils the word spoken by Isaiah—'I have set you to be a light for the Gentiles' (13:47=Isa. 49:6). Paul is preaching to Gentiles as the accredited and appointed messenger of God. Such an interpretation of the Gentile mission is repeated by James, at the Jerusalem council. Whilst a favourable response to the gospel amongst Jews fulfils prophecy (15:16=Amos 9:11-12), the fact that 'God first looked favourably on the Gentiles' (15:14) also fulfils the prophetic word (15:17=Jer. 12:15).

(3) Divine agents: On two occasions in this section, appearances of

---

[27]For the interpretation of 'in the spirit' as a reference to the Holy Spirit, see Squires, *Plan of God*, 183; Kee, *Good News*, 38-39.

divine agents play a crucial role in the sequence of events. The first time this is narrated is soon after the split between Barnabas and Paul (15:36-41). Luke condenses the journey from Lystra to Troas (some 400 km.) into four verses (16:6-9). It is not the journey itself, but the factors which motivated this journey, which are significant; in each case a divine agent guides the travellers. First they are 'forbidden by the Holy Spirit' to travel in Asia (16:6), then 'the Spirit of Jesus did not allow' travel into Bithynia (16:7), then 'a vision [of] a man of Macedonia' pleads with Paul to come across into Macedonia (16:9). Thus, this crucial move, from Asia Minor to Europe, is validated by a threefold interjection of divine agents. Luke then adds the interpretive comment, 'God had called us to proclaim the good news' to the Macedonians (16:10). Coming immediately after the council in Jerusalem, this explicitly signals that the ongoing expansion of the church is under divine guidance.

The second occasion a divine agent appears in the narrative is when Paul is under threat from Jewish opposition in Corinth (18:5-6). The appearance of the angel to Paul (18:9-10) recalls earlier such occurrences (to Cornelius, 10:3; to the apostles, 5:19; and indeed to Zechariah, Luke 1:11-20, and to Mary, Luke 1:26-38). In this specific instance, the angel's message does not move the story on to the next phase, as is the case in the other incidents noted here; rather, the angel confirms Paul in his current activity. In this way, this epiphany functions as divine validation for the persistence of Paul throughout all of this section, preaching the gospel in the face of constant and dangerous opposition. The later epiphany at 27:23-24 performs a similar function.

(4) Miracles: When Luke summarises the report which Barnabas and Paul gave to the council in Jerusalem on their activities, he makes use of the familiar phrase, signs and wonders. Significantly, he repeats the interpretation of such deeds which has already been given (2:22; 4:30); these are 'signs and wonders that God had done through them among the Gentiles' (15:12). There are numerous occurrences of specific signs and wonders narrated throughout this section.[28]

The divine origin of these deeds is assumed, and need not be stated directly in the narrative; the exceptions are the statements that

---

[28]The blinding of Bar-Jesus in Paphos (13:9-11), healing a lame man in Lystra (14:8-10), casting out a demon from a slave girl in Philippi (16:16-18), an earthquake in prison in Philippi (16:26), healings by Paul in Ephesus (19:11-12), the overpowering of the sons of Sceva in Ephesus (19:13-16), and the raising to life of Eutychus in Troas (20:7-12).

Elymas is blinded because 'the hand of the Lord is against you' (13:11), and the Philippian slave girl recognises Paul and his companions as 'slaves of the Most High God' (16:17). Throughout the narrative, it is clear that Luke understands each one of the signs and wonders in the same way that he summarises those of Paul in Ephesus—'God did extraordinary miracles through Paul' (19:11). For Luke, these miracles are further evidence of divine providence.

(5) God: The events that take place in Gentile regions throughout this section are interpreted, in summary, as being about 'all that God had done with them' (14:27; 15:4). At the end of the section, this leitmotif is echoed by all present in Caesarea: 'the Lord's will be done' (21:14). This explicit acknowledgement of divine guidance is followed by a brief geographical note that Paul returned to Jerusalem (21:15-16), thus bringing the narrative to the next critical point.

The arrest and trials of Paul (21:17-28:15)

The narrative of this section begins in Jerusalem with Paul meeting the believers (21:17-25) and going to the temple (21:26), followed immediately by public agitation (21:27-32) and the arrest of Paul (27:33). Subsequent events all take place with Paul as a prisoner of the Romans. By contrast with the preceding section, this part of Acts has notably fewer explicit references to the theme of providential guidance. This is not to say, however, that this theme is completely out of view. As the scene moves from Jerusalem to Caesarea, Paul persists in defending himself before various authorities. Explicit references to God's direct guidance come rarely, most fully at those points in the speeches where the focus is back to Paul's conversion and commission (22:6-16; 26:12-18). Yet some of the second-level themes assume an importance in this section of the narrative.

(1) Necessity: This theme has already been clearly signalled in the previous section, when Paul stated 'after I have gone there [Jerusalem], I must also see Rome' (19:21). The geographical movement is thus interpreted as a part of the necessary plan of God. Within this section itself, this theme is picked up in the words of the Lord to Paul, 'you must bear witness in Rome' (23:11); in the words of Agrippa to Festus, 'this man could have been set free if he had not appealed to the emperor' (26:32); and in the words of the angel to Paul, 'you must stand before the emperor' (27:24). These phrases interpret the movement of

the prisoner Paul to the city of Rome as an unambiguous expression of the plan of God.

(2) Miracles and divine agents: The miracles recounted in this section serve as reminders of the ongoing providential guidance of God. Four times Paul is rescued from death; on two of these occasions, divine agents assure Paul that, despite his imprisonment, he is indeed still living out the divine plan. These reassurances serve to interpret Paul's rescue from death as a part of God's providence.

The first such incident takes place at the very beginning of this section, in Jerusalem, when Paul is rescued by the tribune from a beating by the crowd which is 'trying to kill him' (21:31-36). The next day, Paul is again saved by the tribune when he fears the violence of the crowd (23:9-10); after this, they covenant 'neither to eat nor drink until they had killed Paul' (23:12). In the midst of this, Paul receives unmistakable reassurance from the Lord himself—'keep up your courage!' (23:11). This epiphany guarantees Paul that he will fulfil his appointed task of bearing witness to God's acts (22:15), for Paul's testimony in Jerusalem will be matched by his witness in Rome (23:11).

The third time Paul is rescued from death is at a critical moment in his journey to Rome, when a storm threatens to wreck the ship (27:18-19). All aboard have given up hope of being saved (27:20). An angel of the Lord appears to Paul, reassuring him that 'God has granted safety to all those who are sailing with you', and reiterating the promise that Paul will fulfil his vocation to 'stand before the emperor' and bear witness to him (27:23-24). Like the earlier appearance, this epiphany underlines the providential disposition of events within this section of Acts. Finally, Paul is again rescued from death by the centurion, when he stops the soldiers from killing their prisoners, including Paul (27:42-44). Like the first rescue in this section, this one is simply narrated without explanation. However, the effect of the epiphanies at 23:11 and 27:23-24 has been to interpret each rescue as a working out of the divine plan.[29]

(3) Spirit and fulfilment: There is a notable absence of the motifs of Spirit and fulfilment in this section. Yet it may be that Luke intends to allude to the role of the Spirit throughout this section. The substance of Paul's speeches is the presentation of his apology, or defence (22:1;

---

[29]See Johnson, *Acts*, 399, 449. While Paul is in Malta (28:1-10), he performs miracles which are described without reference to God; but the link between miracles and divine power has been clearly established already.

24:10; 25:8,16; 26:1,2,24) whilst under arrest. In these speeches, he is able to bear witness to the gospel (22:15; 23:11; 26:16). Paul's confident defence speeches might well bring to mind Jesus' instructions to those brought before rulers and authorities—'do not worry about how you are to defend yourselves or what you are to say, for the Holy Spirit will teach you at that very hour what you ought to say '(Luke 12:11-12). Although Paul does not make any explicit scriptural quotation in these speeches (even in Jerusalem),[30] his final defence speech casts all of the events of Acts into the framework of the fulfilment of prophecy (26:23).

The section ends with two phrases which provide both a geographical and a theological summary. The geographical comment is 'and so we came to Rome' (28:14), a fulfilment of the driving force which has been explicit since 19:21 and implicit since 1:8. The theological summary is a straightforward acknowledgement of divine providence—'Paul thanked God and took courage' (28:15), in direct fulfilment of the divine exhortation to 'keep up your courage!' (23:11).

Final scene in Rome (28:16-31)

This scene is introduced with the brief geographical comment, 'when we came into Rome' (28:16). The section comprises an account of two meetings between Paul and the local Jewish leadership (28:17-22, 23-28), and a generalising conclusion (28:30-31). Paul's teaching is summarised as a testimony to three things: to the sovereignty of God (28:23, 31), to the fulfilment of scriptural prophecy in the life of Jesus (28:23), and to the fulfilment of scriptural prophecy in the failure of many of the Jews to accept the gospel (28:25-27=Isa. 6:9-10).[31] This latter prophecy is further described as a statement made by the holy Spirit through Isaiah (28:25). Luke's concluding statement depicts Paul's ongoing and unfinished activity in Rome, continuing the message of God's providential sovereignty.

---

[30]However, there are certainly scriptural allusions in the commission Paul re-counts at 26:16-18; see Isa. 6:8, 42:6; Jer. 1:7; Ezek. 2:1-3.
[31]Peterson, 'The Motif of Fulfilment', 100.

III. Conclusion

The scope of the divine plan in Acts

The above survey has demonstrated that, throughout the narrative of Acts, explicit statements about God's providential guidance are inextricably linked with a number of related themes (Spirit, divine agents, miracles, fulfilment, necessity).[32] It has also indicated that Luke used this cluster of themes to provide a comprehensive interpretation of the development of the early church: everything he recounts took place within the overarching plan of God.

The scope of this divine plan is cosmic and universal. It looks back to Jesus, encompassing the miracles he performed on earth, his death and resurrection, his exaltation to heaven, and his future role as the one who will return to execute God's judgement. It looks even further back to Israel, the nation which God guided Abraham, Joseph, Moses, David, and the prophets. Indeed, the plan of God stretches right back into the past, to the act of creation, and on into the future, to judgement at the end of history.

In the events which form the surface level narrative of Acts, this divine plan can clearly be seen at work. God's will is done in the establishment of the church in Jerusalem; the way the community serves and witnesses fulfils God's intention. God guides the expansion of the church beyond Jewish soil; the testimony to the gospel in Samaria and among the Gentiles proceeds in accord with a divine strategy. Divine providence can be seen in the life and work of key individuals: Peter (and the apostles), Stephen and Philip (and the seven), Barnabas and Paul (and other fellow missionaries). Each of these travel and testify in obedience to God's purpose. Within Luke's story the plan of God comes to a climactic moment at the end of the volume, when Paul arrives at the centre of the Roman Empire; his presence in Rome has been ensured by angelic messengers, miraculous rescues, and the guidance of the Spirit, for it is an entirely necessary outcome which fulfils Scripture.

---

[32]An additional theme which may be considered as related to these themes, is that of the word of God (4:29, 31; 6:7; 8:14; 11:1; 12:24; 13:5; 16:32; 17:13; 18:11; 19:10, 20). See the discussion below by Rosner.

The purpose of 'divine plan' language in Acts

What function is performed by this language of the divine plan? Luke
writes with his eyes fixed firmly on the situation in his own time. He
writes an account of past events because he believes that, properly
understood, these events provide a fundamental basis for living and
witnessing faithfully in his own time. The charge given to the disciples
by the risen Jesus ('you will be my witnesses', 1:8) is a charge which remains valid for all readers of Luke's work. Luke's account is an interpretation of past events, written to encourage and sustain those who
continue the witness in their own time, in a subsequent generation. To
effect this, Luke wishes his readers to understand that the events he
retells themselves bear witness to God's plan;[33] and that, in the light of
this plan, guidance of a similar nature is available to his readers as they
explore how to bear witness in their own time and own way.

Luke draws on notions of divine providence to undergird the
narrative which he presents and to interpret the events contained
within it. Such an interpretation is made in the manner of history
writers of the hellenistic period. One such writer, Diodorus Siculus,
described historians as 'ministers of divine providence' who arrange
their accounts in the light of their understanding of providence in
human events (*Bibliotheke Historike* 1.1.3).[34] Luke writes in just such a
fashion; for him, the narrative references to providence mirror the way
things happen in life. God's guidance is a literary motif which
interprets human existence. What is more, this theme has an apologetic
function in Luke–Acts (as it does in some Hellenistic histories);[35] it
strengthens the self-understanding of those who continue to bear
witness, reinforcing the idea that they are God's servants as they
proclaim the gospel to the hellenistic world and as they share in table
fellowship within mixed Jewish–Gentile communities.

The picture of the earliest Christian community which is given in
Acts 2–8 provides a model for the church in Luke's own time. It is inspired by the Spirit and faithful to Scripture; it shows the necessary
obedience to God and is guided by God. The pattern of Christian

---

[33]Thus, Johnson writes, 'his purpose is to defend God's activity in the world' (*Acts*,
7); see his discussion of Luke's apologetic purpose on 7-9, and my discussion in
Squires, *Plan of God*, 52-55, 190-94.
[34]This argument is fully developed in Squires, *Plan of God*, 15-36; see 15 for the
complete quotation from Diodorus.
[35]See *op. cit.*, 38-43, 52-55; and for a more extensive discussion of apologetic
historiography, Sterling, *Historiography*, 16-19, 378-89.

preaching which Luke advocates is to be modelled on the preaching of the apostles, as reported in the speeches of Acts. Their testimony is consistent with to the way that God has been at work in history. The centrality of table fellowship of Jews and Gentiles in the life of the church is legitimated in the pivotal section of Acts, where the move towards the Gentiles is recounted. This section functions as a validation of the inclusion of Gentiles within the church; a function which continues in the account of Paul's mission to Gentiles. The emphasis on the divine guidance of this mission, by Spirit and angels, in fulfilment of Scripture, as a necessary course of events, reinforces the view that the Gentiles belong within the community of faith. Finally, Luke offers a defence of Paul's role as a model apostle. This defence presumably reflects a context in which the significance of Paul's activities were disputed. By advocating the providential guidance of Paul's activities, Luke depicts him as an important model for a later generation of believers.

Therefore, we can conclude that the overall function of Luke's interpretation of events within the framework of the plan of God, is to offer encouragement to his readers as they live out their faith in a post-apostolic situation; to offer them a theological grounding for their missionary activity (it is an integral part of the divine plan); and to present ways by which potential criticisms can be defended by respectable means (using the language of historians who depicted history in this fashion).[36] The plan of God is an important way by which Luke nurtures and equips the church of his time for its God-given task.

---

[36]See further on this in Squires, *Plan of God*, 190-94.

CHAPTER 3

SCRIPTURE AND THE REALISATION OF GOD'S PROMISES

Darrell Bock

Summary

The use of Scripture in Acts involves five basic themes and supports the new community's claim to the heritage of God as revealed in Moses and the prophets. The realisation of the promise in Christ and the community allowed the community to claim an ancient heritage although it was a new expression of what originally was a Jewish hope. The Scripture explains Christ's position, the hope of Gentile inclusion, and the possibility of Israel's rejection. Luke's hermeneutical axioms are grounded in God's design in history and the centrality of Jesus to the plan. Luke's claim involves a promise-fulfilment perspective.

I. Introduction

'To this day I have had the help that comes from God, and so I stand
here testifying to both small and great, saying nothing but what the
prophets and Moses said would come to pass: that the Christ must
suffer, and that by being the first to rise from the dead, he would
proclaim light both to the people and to Gentiles.'—Paul as cited in
Acts 26:22-23.

The above citation is the last summary citation in Luke–Acts. It serves
as both an adequate introduction to, and summary of, Luke's use of
Scripture. It notes three central themes: (1) the message of the newly
emerged Christian teaching spans the full array of scriptural hope
from Moses to the prophets; (2) at the centre of that hope is the Christ
event, especially his death and resurrection; (3) that his vindication by
God becomes the occasion for his new appeal both to the Jews and the
Gentiles to enter into divine promise and life (light). Paul speaks as a
representative of a mission where the raised Christ speaks for God
through people such as the apostle (Acts 10:36, 42-43; Eph. 2:17). These
historically significant claims are the basis of Paul's defence before
Rome. Paul is simply playing his role in the call of God to bring the
light of God's truth in Christ to the nations (Acts 26:15-18). Luke's story
in Acts and use of Scripture travel the same highway.

New movements in the ancient world, like the emergence of 'the
Way,' often were viewed with interest but skepticism (Acts 17:18-21).
A great disadvantage of the new movement was that it lacked a history
and roots spanning the generations. The claim for heritage means
being rooted in history and legitimacy, an ancient sociological necessity for obtaining credibility, where what was older was better,
especially in making claims about what God did in history.[1] This essay
traces Luke's claim for this new movement. One way to make such a
claim was the appeal to ancient, sacred writings. The new movement
grew out of Judaism, so that is where it found its sacred roots, in her
promises. This final summary text, like many texts in Luke–Acts, does
not attempt to escape bearing the burden of citation, but reflects the
narrative's broad claim to various texts.[2] The consideration of Luke's

---

[1]On ethnography as an ancient historical apologetic genre, Sterling, *Historiography*,
103-310, 398-93. See also Berossos, Menethon and Josephus's *Antiquitates*.
[2]Other such summaries appear in Luke 24:26, 44-47 and Acts 3:22-23, 17:2-3. A
reference to Moses and the prophets also appears in Acts 28:23, but as an
introduction to a specific citation, not a summary.

broad use of Scripture should show how pervasive his appeal is.

This study proceeds in two steps.[3] First, some hermeneutical axioms reveal how Luke saw divine history and thus how he read Scripture. Also treated is current critical debate over whether Luke appeals to promise and fulfilment. Then Luke's five major scriptural themes that support his claim will be examined.

II. Hermeneutical axioms

Various themes in Luke's Gospel show his perspective. They set the historical horizon from which he works with Scripture and history. Some have questioned anew the unity and legitimacy of the designation Luke–Acts.[4] But the testimony of Luke's Gospel is crucial in setting the stage for Acts, when it comes to the use of Scripture. The question is also important, because it shows how Luke sets the table for his claim of fulfilment.

In appealing to hermeneutical axioms, I am making a case for Luke much like Richard Hays's appeal to the 'grand narrative of election and God's righteousness' as an influence for Paul's reading of Scripture, but with two major differences.[5] First, the hermeneutical appeal to these axioms is not as free and haphazard as Hays's reading argues, but serve rather as a very thought-through, fundamental claim about Scripture considered from the perspective of a prioritized theology grounded in the Christ event. Second, Hays's rejection of midrashic technique fails to distinguish hermeneutical axioms from hermeneutical techniques. The reason the early church's (and Paul's) conclusions were so different from Judaism was not because her

---

[3]For the issue of Luke's OT text in detail, see Clarke, 'Septuagint,' 66-105 and Holtz, *Untersuchungen*. Luke uses a version akin to the LXX. Holtz argues the presence of another version is evidence of a source, especially in the Twelve Prophets and Isaiah. He sees more variation in the use of the Torah and Psalms.

[4]Parsons and Pervo, *Rethinking*, argue that Luke–Acts should become Luke and Acts again, raising questions about genre, narrative, and theological differences between the volumes. On the use of Scripture, however, there is an inherent unity in the story, a point I argued for in *Proclamation*. To see a unified perspective with regard to divine design and the use of Scripture is appropriate. For detailed exegesis of Acts 2, 3, 4, 7, 8, 10 and 13, the reader can check my earlier volume. For more on Parsons and Pervo, see Marshall, 'Former Treatise', 163-82.

[5]For Hays's approach and claim for Pauline charismatic freedom, see his *Echoes*, especially ch. 5. See also comments below in the section "Scripture as Interpreter of Divine Event and Current Critical Discussion".

procedures of reading were so different from Judaism (see n. 9 below). Rather the interpretive grid, the axioms to which those procedures were applied, was the difference. Both Luke's and Paul's apparent 'revision' of the meaning of the ancient Hebrew Scriptures is really a claim that the ancient narrative, representing only promise, was incomplete without Jesus' coming. Now that he has come we can understand God's plan more clearly, because the events tied to his coming reveal the priorities and relationships in that ancient plan, in terms of issues like law, covenants, and nations. These events set new priorities, witnessed to by the Spirit, but not as a denial of the function of how older elements in revelation prepared for the promise's arrival. In this perspective, the NT writers are one.

God's design and a new era of realization

This theme emerges in Luke 1:1. The point surfaces clearly by comparing two recent translations as Luke describes his effort to compose a narrative. The RSV reads v. 1b describing his Gospel as 'a narrative of the things that have been accomplished among us', while the NRSV reads 'an orderly account of the events that have been fulfilled among us'. The NRSV is more precise. The key term is πεπληροφορημένων, referring to the presence of designed events, acts which stand fulfilled in the midst of Luke's audience. The events of Luke's Gospel are 'designed' as part of God's plan, bearing a necessity to them, as Luke 24:43-47 points out, using δεῖ while appealing both to events and Scripture. That earlier Gospel volume, according to Acts 1:1, refers to what Jesus began to do and to teach, but Acts tells the rest of that story. Even the preaching of Paul is represented as the preaching of Jesus (Acts 26:22-23). Acts 1:4 argues, the promise of the Father, that is, the enabling Spirit who would help them testify to the work of God, must be dispensed in Jerusalem (Luke 12:11-12). The Spirit's coming into the community in Acts 2 is told with appeal to a series of scriptural texts as event, sacred text, and preaching take place side by side. This combination of designed events and enabled preaching from the Spirit sets a backdrop for the appeal to Scripture. God is at work in events, revealed in Scripture and about which the Spirit from Christ makes declaration through representatives like Peter and Paul. So Paul can speak for Jesus. Luke wishes his readers to view their citations and declarations as tied to the realisation of Scripture.

The design is not just stated in general terms; it has a structure.

Four texts are crucial: Luke 7:28; 16:16; Acts 10:42-43;17:30-31. Luke 7:28 and 16:16 show how John the Baptist is, in one sense, the end of an old era.[6] As the greatest man born among women, this fore-runner prophet has a unique role in the old era. Until he came, the Law and the prophets were at the centre of God's plan. But now everything is different. The least in the kingdom Jesus brings is greater than the man who was the greatest of the old era. Now the gospel of the kingdom of God is preached. The gospel is the presence of something new and something old. The old era of expectation leads to the new era of realization. That is part of the design. To understand where the story of the new community begins, one must understand that John, as the forerunner whom Malachi promised, is part of a divine design whose roots go back to scriptural hope (Luke 1:14-17; 7:27).[7]

A similar emphasis emerges in Acts 10:42-43 and 17:30-31. Here the apostolic preaching centres on 'the one ordained by God to be the judge of the living and the dead'. Thus in Acts 10:42-43 the divine plan is mentioned first, then the reference to Scripture: 'To this one all the prophets bear witness that everyone who believes in him receives forgiveness of sins through his name'. The plan's presence is corroborated and declared in Scripture. The movement, new in execution, is old in planning. Event and Scripture are placed side by side. God's plan is what Scripture records. When Paul makes the same point to a strictly pagan audience (Acts 17:30-31), the Scripture is less explicitly present, but he still uses the plan and a biblical theology with reference to idolatry and the creation.[8] 'The times of ignorance God overlooked, but now he commands all men everywhere to repent, because he has fixed a day on which he will judge the world in righteousness by a man whom he has appointed, and of this he has given assurance to all by raising him from the dead.' What was for Jews the era of Law and prophets, for pagans was the era of ignorance, more specifically, a

---

[6]Luke 16:16 is the crux of the relationship between John the Baptist and Jesus. There are four options for βιάζεται (Marshall, *Luke*, 629-30, J. Fitzmyer, *Luke X-XXIV*, 117-18, and Bock, *Luke 9:51-24:53*, see exegesis of Luke 16:16). With Fitzmyer I have opted for a sense that sees the verb as passive and carries a sense of 'to urge insistently', but have argued that Luke sees two periods (promise–Law; fulfilment–Christ), not three (Israel, Jesus, church) as Fitzmyer does.

[7]For a correct emphasis that the beginning of the Jesus story for Luke is rooted in the early promises of the OT, see Green, 'Problem,' 61-85. The discussion as to whether that perspective represents a denial of prophecy-fulfilment as Green suggests at least for Luke 1–2, comes later in this study.

[8]Bruce, *Acts*, 333-35, shows how this speech fits Paul and the cultural realities he faced.

rejection of God's presence in the creation. A new era in the plan has come involving all nations more directly with special revelation and showing through resurrection that Jesus is the one to whom all are accountable. Acts 17:30-31 notes how fundamental the plan was in Luke's mind. Scripture addresses and establishes that the new community has rich roots connected to the living God's ancient promises.

Christ at the centre

This axiom needs little development. It is already evident in reading Luke. Whole works expound the theme, though with differing concerns.[9] But it is important to place it in proper reference to the more encompassing theme of God's plan. Christology is not the goal of Luke's use of Scripture. It is a important port of call on the way to more comprehensive claims about God's plan and the promise's subsequent realization. The literary flow of Luke's use of Scripture reveals that once Jesus' messianic and lordship credentials are established ('He is Lord of all and Judge of the living and the dead'), then scriptural attention can concentrate on how Gentiles are included and how Israel must not reject the opportunity to share in the promise. The plan argues that Jesus is Lord of all, so the gospel can go to all. Israel will miss blessing if she refuses to share in the call Jesus makes to all humanity.

Scripture as an interpreter of divine event and current critical discussion

These axioms suggest key elements in Luke's perspective towards the relationship between Scripture and event. Behind the events stand God and his plan. Expectation also existed in Judaism because of his promise in Scripture. Central to both Christian and Jewish hope was the declaration of the various covenants and the deliverance they anticipated. Most importantly, history was read by both groups in a way that looked for divine patterns of activity that signalled the re-emergence of divine design in salvific events.[10] This feature of pattern is why prophecy in Luke is not limited to directly prophetic prediction,

---

9Numerous monographs treat Luke's use of the OT for Christology. Besides my own study mentioned in n. 4, see Rese, *Alttestamentliche*; Kimball, *Exposition*, Strauss, *Davidic Messiah*.

but also includes the noting of a divine pattern or a typological-prophetic reading of the Bible. Promise for the early church included prophetic texts and pattern texts, along with appeal to covenant hope now freshly realized. The very premise behind reading history as involving promise and pattern is divine design and the constancy of God's character as he saves in similar ways at different times. Jewish imagery reusing Exodus motifs or new creation language shows how Judaism accepted this view of history. Reading history this way also fuelled Luke's perspective in seeing divine design in the events tied to Jesus. Understanding this 'pattern fulfilment' dynamic is crucial to understanding how Luke reads Scripture.

The centre of that hope involved a pivotal figure. Luke's claim is that the events of Jesus' life and ministry began the arrival of that promised era. Scripture is an interpreter of those events, explaining them and their design. At the same time, the events themselves, as unusual and unique as they are, draw one to Scripture to seek explanation. It would be wrong to view promise and fulfilment as a unidirectional activity, where a repository of texts were simply lined up with events, though that is what some critiques of reading prophecy and fulfilment in Luke have claimed for such a view.[11] For example, Soards comments,

> When one considers the function of *the past* in the speeches of Acts one finds that a prophecy-fulfilment interpretation of the scripture quotations is too restricted a perspective for understanding the role of the past, especially the scripture quotations, in the speeches. Rather than

---

[10]Two key studies on typology are: Goppelt, *Typos*, and Foulkes, *Acts of God* . For the category of typological-prophetic interpretation, see Bock, 'Use of the Old Testament in the New,' 110-12.

[11]Those who have critiqued promise–fulfilment or prophecy–fulfilment argue its approach is too unidirectional or too limiting a perspective. Note critiques by Green, 'Problem,' 66 n. 19; and Soards, *Speeches*, 201 for the following citation. Green (pp. 61, 66, 83) interchanges discussion of prophecy–fulfilment, promise–fulfilment, and prediction fulfilment. I argue that not all prophecy is unidirectional fulfilment, which is what Green's remarks may assume. Typological–prophetic fulfilment sometimes requires the fulfilling event to spot the pattern of divine design. If Green is talking about a unidirectional prophetic scheme (that excludes pattern fulfilment), then I agree with him. But prophecy in Luke–Acts is not so simple. To continue a story grounded in covenant commitment, as Green correctly argues is present in Luke 1–2, is to continue the realisation of promise, so events reveal as well as look back. One should not juxtapose as opposites the presence of redemptive story and promise-fulfilment. See also the essay by Peterson, 'The Motif of Fulfilment,' 83-104.

a mere linear prophecy-fulfilment scheme, one should see that the
past, especially the quotations of scripture, is used in the speeches to
establish the continuity of the past, the present, and even the future.

This misrepresents the prophecy-fulfilment or promise-pattern fulfilment perspective. The prophecy and fulfilment view affirms the
sociological point Soards makes. He states it with reference to time,
whereas prophecy and fulfilment has tended to state it with reference
to topic. In fact, I argued for this point about continuity by noting
Luke's purpose was 'to remove doubt by his justifying of the Gentile
mission as the way of God through Jesus the Lord despite the presence
of persecution against the church.... Anyone can now see from Luke's
account that Jesus' position is proclaimed in the Scriptures as well as
being verified both by events and his own teaching (Acts 1.1)'.[12] I also
addressed the relationship of event and text: 'We have shown that the
relationship between event and text is two-way'.[13] I discussed Psalm
110, Psalm 16, and Isaiah 55 as three good examples of this phenomena, where events helped reveal details that emerged in how the
pattern fulfilment fits in light of the Christ event. Then followed this
important critique of approaches that diminish promise-fulfilment,
while emphasizing the role of event.

In most cases, the texts used by Luke were already regarded as
either messianic, prophetic, or eschatological within Judaism. The
prophecy was not 'discovered' by the event. However, there often
came with the event a filling out of the text in line with its general
theme. Thus the exact significance of the text was revealed in the event.
To characterize this relationship between text and event as one way by
over-emphasizing either the text or the event is to fail to appreciate the
complexity of the interaction between the two elements.

In some cases, events showed how the texts lined up and how
the design worked. The various strands of christological OT use in
Luke reveal functions united in one person that Judaism placed in a
variety of eschatological figures. It was events tied to Jesus' ministry
that showed the unity of function that Luke argues for when he
discusses Jesus as the promise bearer. Most of these points are made in
Luke's Gospel, setting the table for uses of Scripture in Acts.[14] But
behind them all stand three fundamental Lucan beliefs: the events
surrounding Jesus are divinely designed; he is at the centre of God's

---

12Bock, *Proclamation*, 277. The appeal to Scripture made in this light is inherently
an appeal to the past.
13Bock, *Proclamation*, 273.

plan as the new era arrives, and Scripture helps to explain what has and is taking place. The events are recent and the era is new, but the plan is not. So goes Luke's claim to divine heritage.

How does Luke make the case? What topics make the point? Five themes fill out the picture of Luke's use of Scripture.

III. Five scriptural themes in Acts

The following list parallels one by C.A. Evans.[15] This study will first consider the five topics and then discuss their relationship and function. The list includes: covenant and promise, christology, community mission or community guidance, commission to Gentiles, and challenge and warning.

Covenant and promise

The theme of covenant and realized promise is fundamental to Luke–Acts, since it was raised as early as Luke 1:54-55 (Abrahamic), and 1:68-70 (Davidic). This emphasis continues in Acts. All the covenants of expectation, or allusions to them, appear within the speeches in Acts.

The hope of the Spirit is clearly expressed in the OT in New Covenant teaching (Jer. 31:31-34 and Ezek. 36:22-32). Peter, (Acts 2:16-39), uses another OT text that also raises this promise, Joel 2:28-32 (=3:1-5 LXX). He declares the realisation of this promise, but also indicates that 'in the last days' this pouring out of the Spirit will come. The remark alludes to Luke 24:49 and the awaiting of 'the promise of my Father', as well as to the instruction to await the Holy Spirit (Acts 1:8). Luke also makes another link. John the Baptist had indicated that the stronger one to come would baptize with the Spirit and fire, a baptism of purging within humanity. This is how one could recognize the Christ, the promised coming one, was present (Luke 3:15-17). In declaring the Spirit's arrival, not only are the last days present, but also

---

[14]The proof of this point is beyond the limits of this study. *Proclamation* showed that in first century Judaism most of the texts that the church claimed addressed Jesus were already read as promise texts. The debate was not whether the texts cited spoke about salvation or the figures involved in its drama, but whether Jesus was the fulfilment.

[15]Evans, 'Prophecy,' 171-211, esp. 209-10. His five categories are: Christological, Soteriological, Apologetic, Minatory, and Critical (of Israel).

the decisive evidence of the promised Christ's presence. This conclusion is the burden of the speech (Acts 2: 32-36), which ends with a
call to respond and participate in the promise (v. 39). Peter's audience
consisted of Diaspora Jews gathered to celebrate Pentecost, so a claim
of fulfilment would be a call to share in national hope opened up to all
by God's direction in Acts 10 (Acts 11:15-17). The call to share in promise is a call to share in a heritage rooted in Scripture.

Also noted is a tie to Davidic promise. Acts 2:30 notes God's
promise to David about a descendant to be set on David's throne. The
allusion is to Psalm 132:11, which is a commentary on the promise of 2
Samuel 7:8-16, the Davidic Covenant. The Psalm 132 citation serves to
link Peter's remarks about the fulfilment of Psalm 16:8-11b in bodily
resurrection with his remarks about fulfilment in ascension in Psalm
110:1. Peter argues that the ascension is an initial realization of a
promise made to David about one who would take up his authority at
the side of God. The realisation of Psalm 110:1 in ascension also
initially fulfils this promise to David. Because the remark involving
Psalm 132 is an allusion, it has not received as much discussion as the
three other texts cited in Acts 2, but it is an important conceptual link
in Peter's speech, as it ties Jesus' resurrection–ascension to messianic
promise. The distribution of the Spirit is evidence of the last days and
of resurrection–ascension, as well as of messianic presence and authority made available to the dispersed Jews present in Peter's audience.
Peter's speech is about christology and claims of covenant realisation.

Paul makes similar detailed claims about Davidic promise to a
synagogue audience in Pisidian Antioch in Acts 13:13-41. Here Paul's
speech reviews Israel's history up to the time of David. Then he
mentions that from this man's posterity (literally, his seed), God has
brought a saviour (v. 23). Next Paul recalls John the Baptist's promise
(Luke 3:15-17). In v. 32, Paul declares that the message about Jesus is
'the good news' about 'what God promised to the fathers'. He then
cites Psalm 2:7, Isaiah 55:3, and Psalm 16:10. The key text in this linkage
is Isaiah, where Paul says to his audience using Scripture, God gives
'to you the holy and faithful things of David'. Where Psalm 2 declares
Jesus to be the Son and Psalm 16 shows that resurrection was anticipated in the programme, Isaiah 55 shows that the promise was not
intended merely as a private commitment to David, but was made for
the benefit of the nation. Thus, Paul's usage parallels that of Peter.
Jesus' arrival is part of a divine plan; so the message of the new community is the appropriate extension and expression of Israel's promise.

The same emphasis appears in Acts 3, only now it is the promise to Abraham that is featured, as well as allusion to Moses. Here not only a note about covenant appears (vv. 24-26), but scriptural warning as well (v. 22-23), a use to be considered in detail later. The reference to Moses appeals to the promise of a prophet like Moses, an eschatological leader-prophet who delivers the people (Deut. 18:15). This remark was also anticipated in Luke 9:35, where the divine voice tells the three disciples present at the transfiguration to hear Jesus, alluding to this same passage from Deuteronomy. The Torah also points to Jesus. There can be no greater heritage claim than to take a Jewish audience back to Moses and the Torah.

The covenant promise appealed to in Acts 3 is Abrahamic. But it is tied to a more fundamental claim, namely that all the prophets after Samuel proclaimed these days (v. 24). The days in view are those surrounding the Christ's activity (vv. 18-20). Again, Scripture points to events, which in turn should drive the audience back to considering scriptural promise. When Peter makes his appeal on the basis of Abraham's promise in v. 25: 'You are the sons of the prophets and of the covenant which God gave to your fathers, saying to Abraham, "And in your posterity [literally seed] shall all the families of the earth be blessed"'.

There is a delightful ambiguity in the term 'seed'. In the original OT promise the seed of Abraham was not every physical descendant he was responsible for producing. It was Isaac over Ishmael and Jacob over Esau, before the seed came to be seen as all the descendants of the twelve tribes of Israel as descended from Jacob's twelve sons. Seed bears singularity and corporateness. Peter here focuses in on the singular seed, like Galatians 3:16, since he goes on in v. 26 to mention the one God has raised up as the source of blessing.[16] As with the speeches of Acts 2 and 13, the appeal is to one of realized promise, grounded in a claim of heritage reaching back to the nation's foundational covenant. Interestingly, where Acts 2 tied together Davidic promise and New Covenant-like hope, here the speech ties together messianic (Davidic) hope and Abrahamic promise. Thus Acts 2 and 3 together review the three fundamental covenants of promise and argue they are all fulfilled in Jesus. Jesus' ministry and the new community's message is not an attempt to break away from Israel, but a claim of the realization of her long awaited promises.

One more text probably belongs here, though it could also be

---

[16]So commentators as varied as Marshall, *Acts: Commentary*, 96, and Haenchen, *Acts*, 209.

placed in categories about christology or community mission. It is
Amos 9:11-15 in Acts 15:14-18. Here a slight distinction is noted between what the text says and how it functions in Acts. James, in citing
this text, is arguing that Gentiles belong in the community of God's
people—to take out a people for his name from the Gentiles (v. 14). In
terms of function, this text justifies Gentile involvement in the community, which is why it could be considered a text about ecclesiology.
However, the citation itself deals with the rebuilding of the fallen
Davidic house. The idea of a rebuilt Davidic house corresponds to
covenant promise as seen from the perspective of Israel's history
where the monarchy had not existed for some time. Jesus is the source
of the rebuilding effort, so that Luke's use also has christological
overtones. The Amos citation in its cited form promises that the fallen
Davidic house will be rebuilt and that the nations will be included in
its restoration.[17] So the Christ event represents the rebuilding of that
fallen house and now Gentiles are included in the promise. The placement of the text under covenant and promise is legitimate because
James cites the text to describe what the prophets promised would
happen when God completed his promises made about the Davidic
house, especially given its historical fall. How would God keep that
promise? The interesting feature is that, like Acts 3, this text addresses
the issue of blessing for the world through the presence of the one who
fulfils this text. Here, even more explicitly than in Acts 3, the claim of
heritage in terms of the unusual make-up of the newly reformed
people of God is made—that Gentile inclusion is a part of Davidic
hope. The roots of the promised multi-ethnic make-up of the new
community are ancient in origin.

---

[17]Wrapped up in the citation of Amos is the difficult question of the relationship
of this text, which reflects an LXX recension, to Amos 9:11-15 in the MT, where
inclusion of Gentiles is not mentioned, but rather the destruction of Edom. That
question is beyond my scope. However, Luke's introductory formula refers to the
prophets (plural) agreeing about the inclusion of Gentiles. Such a summary
formula in Luke often means that though no text or a few texts are noted, other
texts exist. Possible candidates include Isa. 2:2-4, Isa. 19:23-25, Isa. 49:6 or texts like
those in Rom. 15:7-13. The cited Amos recension was attractive because of its
juxtaposition of Gentile involvement with Davidic hope. On the interpretive
history of Amos 9, see Richard, 'Creative', 37-53. It is important to recall that the
LXX was a respected translation in first century Judaism. On how the MT sense
could also work, see Bruce, *Acts (Greek Text)*, 341.

Christology

Many of the texts in the covenant and promise category could also be placed here, but to distinguish the two is helpful, since christology, as the above texts show, often plays a complementary role to additional claims about God's plan. Texts noted here serve primarily a christological function.

Most of the christological texts treat activity associated with Jesus' ministry. For example, Psalm 16:10 appears twice in Acts 13:35 and as part of a larger citation of Psalm 16:8-11b in Acts 2:25-28. The passage argues for divine accreditation for Jesus, an accreditation that started in his ministry (vv. 22-24), and culminates in promised resurrection. Peter's assertion may represent a novel handling of this text, for he goes to great lengths to defend the fact that the text is not about David, who is buried. Peter argues that the immediate, bodily resurrection was predicted of the Christ (vv. 30-31). Now resurrection testifies to this promise's accomplishment and thus to Jesus as the Christ. The use of Psalm 16:10 in Acts 13 about Jesus not being abandoned to see corruption parallels the use in Acts 2:31b. This part of the citation is Luke's real concern in both texts. That Messiah would be raised was a promise of Scripture (Luke 24:43-47).

Another key activity is the ascension and session at God's right hand. This emphasis appears in the references to Jesus being seated at God's right hand from Psalm 110:1 (Acts 2:34-35; 5:31; 7:55-56). Luke prepared for this idea in Luke 20:41-44 and 22:69, where the question of why Messiah is called Lord is raised by Jesus and his assertion that 'the Son of Man (*i.e.*, Jesus) would be seated from now on at the right hand of the power of God'. Jesus claims direct access to the authority of God by sharing in his ruling authority. In Acts 2, this claim is evidenced by the distribution of promised salvific blessing, namely, Jesus' distribution of the Holy Spirit on the disciples (v. 33). Acts 5 argues that Jesus' exaltation makes him Leader–Saviour, as he offers to Israel repentance and forgiveness of sins. In Acts 7, Jesus stands at the right hand of the Father as Stephen dies. Though the meaning of his standing is debated, it is likely that he rises to welcome Stephen with heavenly vindication.[18] Regardless of the exact force, the passage does picture Jesus' current authority at God's side in heaven. Thus, in this imagery, a previously foreseen shared rule for Jesus with God is realised, a rule concentrating on the distribution of spiritual benefits to

---

[18]For the options here and a defense of this force, see Johnson, *Acts*, 139.

those who respond to Jesus' offer. Christology is present not only to describe who Jesus is, but to set forth how he functions. Luke's interest in what Jesus does reveals what God has shown him to be.

Isaiah 53:7-8 is another example (Acts 8:32-33). Here the Ethiopian eunuch asks if this passage is about Isaiah the prophet or another. The way the question is raised in v. 34 suggests that perhaps popular opinion centred on Isaiah. What is interesting about this Servant citation of Isaiah is that it does not cite the substitutionary message, but highlights Jesus' suffering. This part of God's designed programme was also noted earlier, but without OT citation (Acts 2:23). Now a text is given. Jesus suffered silently as an innocent, like a lamb led to slaughter. He was rejected and died unjustly. That summary citation reads very much like the emphasis of Luke's passion story, which highlights Jesus' innocent suffering (Luke 23:4, 14-15, 22). Thus Jesus' unjust death, taking place in the midst of rejection, is set forth in Scripture as the way of Jesus. This text became but the first that Philip would discuss with the eunuch (Acts 8:35), another example of Luke's summary appeal to Scripture where one text is cited, but others exist on the theme (Luke 24:43-47).

The remaining christological citation identifies Jesus as Son (Ps. 2:7 in Acts 13:33). An allusion to this text appeared in Luke 3:22 (also Heb. 1:5). The connection to Psalm 2 suggests that it has regal overtones. The promised ruler who conquers in battle is Son. As already noted in the covenant and promise discussion, the Acts 13 context affirms the realisation of Davidic promise, of messianic hope. The scriptural triad as a whole asserts that the promised Christ is attested to by God through resurrection, as the citation of Psalm 16:10 shows. This event demonstrates the presence of the Son (Rom. 1:3-4). A debate about this Psalm 2:7 text is whether it explains resurrection alone or is an explanation for the arrival of Jesus in history. In past debate that decision turns on the meaning of 'raising up' Jesus in Acts 13:32-33 (ἀναστήσας), an expression that by itself can refer to resurrection (using ἐγείρειν- 5:30; 10:40; using ἀνιστάναι- 2:24, 32) or to arrival on the scene of history (using ἀνιστάναι- 3:22, 26, 7:37; using ἐγείρειν- 13:22). I have argued elsewhere that the introductory formula to this passage in vv. 32-33 has three parts and that the passage uses three citations to match portions of the introductory formula (God promised—Ps. 2:7; for us—Isa. 55:3; raising Jesus—Ps. 16:10).[19] If this is correct, 'raising up' refers to resurrection as Psalm 16:10 shows, but

---

[19]Bock, *Proclamation*, 244-5.

Psalm 2:7 refers only to God's promise about a coming Son. Regardless of the view taken about 'raised up', the passage identifies Jesus as the promised Son. This speech and the other texts that have preceded it make it clear why Luke thinks Jesus is promise realised.

The use of Scripture for christology describes Jesus' career in such a way that his suffering, death, resurrection and ascension are seen not to be surprising for a Messiah. A suffering, but raised Messiah, has rich roots in Scripture.

Community mission or community guidance

This category involves three texts: Acts 1:20, 4:24-26, and 13:47. To these texts can be added the already discussed Acts 15:15-18 with its use of Amos 9. Three passages highlight the identity and function of the community's key servants (Acts 1), the call of the new community (Acts 13) and how that call is likely to be carried out (Acts 4).

Acts 1:20 combines two texts (Ps. 69:26 [69:35 Eng.] and 109:8) to make two points. First, the Psalm 69 text is applied typologically to argue that Judas has suffered the fate of an enemy of God. Second, Psalm 109 explains what the community should after Judas' judgement, namely, select a replacement. It also describes the function of the one to be selected as an overseer. Both Psalms treat the theme of how God handles those he rejects and what happens as a result. Seen in that light, their use makes sense. Despite Luke's interest in Paul, everything about the narrative mood of Matthias as one of the Twelve suggests it has Luke's approval. It is bathed in prayer, guided by Scripture, directed by Peter, and left in the hands of God. God directs the community before it launches out in mission. It is properly reconstituted, having judged one of its own as unworthy.

Acts 4:24-26 shows the disciples praying for the imprisoned Peter and John, as well as for themselves. The community responds in the face of persecution and opposition. They ask for boldness in the midst of opposition which does not take them by surprise. They cite Psalm 2:1 to note the fact that their present opposition was anticipated in Scripture—the Gentiles rage and the people imagine vain things against the Lord and his anointed. The fulfilment of this is explained in vv. 27-28. Herod and Pilate, Gentiles and the people of Israel were gathered against God's holy servant Jesus to carry out God's predestined plan.[20] Once again Scripture serves to explain events, revealing the plan about this new community. Their path of suffering is noted. Rejection should not surprise them. They simply repeat the path the anointed one walked. They are following after him.

The second text (Acts 13) describes Paul and Barnabas's mission. They warn their synagogue audience not to reject their message and cite Isaiah 49:6.[21] Their citation reveals that Jesus alone is not the light, an interesting note in view of the fact that (1) in Acts 8 Jesus had been identified as the Servant from a text in Isaiah 53; (2) the likely Jewish expectation that this text addresses the nation as a whole. Koet argues that the text asserts the mission of gathered Israel as opposed to the mission of Paul and Barnabas. To accomplish this he draws on the LXX reading for the text and then ties its reading to texts about mission in Luke 2:32 and 24:47 (note also Acts 13:47). He goes on to argue that the choice between Jesus, Paul and Barnabas, or gathered Israel as light is a false dilemma. The text's point is to challenge the synagogue audience to be a part of this light and share in the mission.

Koet has a good point, but has overstated its force. This study has already shown that taking texts as they were read by Jews is not an automatic path to understanding Luke's usage (Ps. 16 in Acts 2; Isa. 53 in Acts 8; Ps. 2 in Acts 4). More important, in our view, is the fact that the text is clearly presented as a command of the Lord given to Paul and Barnabas (v. 47a). They are describing their mission, not attempting to invite others to join them. They are explaining why they are now going to turn to Gentiles. What was true of Jesus, as one pre-eminently called to be a light to the Gentiles (Luke 2:32), is now true of them. Though only a slight difference of emphasis, I prefer to read this citation of Isaiah 49 as depicting Paul and Barnabas's mission, which is an extension of the mission of the community that sent them in Acts 13:1-2. As Acts 13:2 shows, the Spirit called them and the community

---

[20]An interesting hermeneutical aspect to this text exists. Any Jew reading Psalm 2:1 would have expected the enemy to be strictly the Gentile nations. But the new community sees the Psalm's central meaning differently. The enemy is anyone who stands opposed to the Lord's anointed. His identity is the Psalm's hub. Thus, when Jews oppose God's attested, chosen one, they fulfill the pattern of opposition found in the Psalm. A psalm of hope for the nation has become a description of the opposition of many in the nation. Scripture teaches that God's chosen way is often resisted. Acts 7 presents a much more elaborate presentation of this theme. Moessner, *Lord,* has traced this theme through Luke 9–19 and speaks of Luke applying a deuteronomistic critique of the nation. That critique, though present here indirectly, now includes Psalter texts.
[21]For a careful discussion of this text, Koet, *Five Studies,* 97-118 whose contribution is a careful consideration of these citations within the Lucan contexts in which the passages appear.

commissioned them with laying on of hands, just as the Spirit enabled the apostles as witnesses in Acts 2. Paul and Barnabas mirror that earlier community enablement as they take up the cause of witnesses to the light. It is that testifying role that probably explains why Luke presents this text. There is no invitation here, though it is indirectly implied, only a description of the function of the new community's mission as pictured in Paul and Barnabas. The citation justifies a turning to the nations, by explaining that Paul and Barnabas's call as servants of the Lord is to take the message to Gentiles and bring salvation to the uttermost parts of the earth (Acts 1:8; 26:23).

The Scripture here makes two points. The new community continues the call and ministry of the Lord as Servant. He is not Servant alone; the new community shares in his calling and identity. This use of Servant imagery parallels a more corporate understanding of the Servant, but with a twist, much like we saw in the use of Psalm 2 in Acts 4. Blessing is not a matter of heredity, but of proper response. Second, the inclusion of Gentiles in the mission of the people of God is the mission of the Servant. This emphasis fits with the use of Amos 9 in Acts 15. Gentiles are among the people of God. The claim of heritage in the promise of God is also not a matter of heredity, but of response. These points underscore that a major concern of Luke–Acts is not just the presentation of Christology to elevate Jesus and explain his suffering, but also to justify the commitment of this originally Jewish community to gathering Gentiles. Jesus is Lord of all, so the gospel can go to all—God always designed it to be so. Gentile involvement in God's plan has deep roots in God's promise. His promise is also designed for them.

Commission to the Gentiles

This section can be handled briefly, since it is anticipated by the use of Isaiah 49 in Acts 13 and Amos 9 in Acts 15 to argue for Gentile inclusion. This theme has roots in Luke 2:32 and 24:47, as well as Acts 1:8. Gentile inclusion was so innovative from a Jewish point of view, not to mention for the disciples, that God had to force its implementation using vision and radical conversion. The amount of time and repetition spent telling the stories of Paul's and Cornelius's conversion shows just how crucial this sequence is to Luke's overall purpose. Just as God testified to Jesus through resurrection, he testified to Gentile inclusion through the call to Paul and the visions he used to get

Cornelius into the fold. Here the promise of the Spirit (Luke 24:49) is reintroduced to make sure the point is not missed (Acts 11:15-18). When Peter refers to the Spirit coming on the Gentiles as he did in the beginning, Peter is alluding to the beginning of the realisation of promise that came in Acts 2, that in turn echoes the explanation of Joel 2:28-32 and the distribution of the Spirit. This kind of thematic linkage, which indirectly reintroduces OT explanation by echo, reveals how interwoven the issue of Gentile involvement is in Acts. When Paul is introduced in Acts 9 just before the Cornelius incident, a connection is implied. The role of this linkage emerges when Paul summarizes his mission in Acts 26:20 as to the Jew first and then to the Greek, showing himself going first to those in Damascus, Jerusalem, and throughout Judea, and then to the Gentiles. The interrelationship between the story of Paul and the conversion of Cornelius becomes evident in the message of Acts. He, too, is called to 'show light unto the people and to the Gentiles' (Acts 26:23). The image of Isaiah speaks not just for Peter as God's direct leading showed, but for Paul, even more explicitly as he consistently ministered successfully to them. Such a mission is the call of the new community (Luke 24:47). To be light means to carry out God's call and fulfil Scripture in taking a message of forgiveness and repentance to the nations. To be a good Jew is to seek salvation for Gentiles as well. Such an emphasis also shows how false it is to describe Luke as anti-Semitic.[22] He is simply defending what he feels the actual mission of scriptural promise is. In Luke's mind, he is arguing the case for the hope and call of Israel's promise.

Challenge and warning to Israel

That the new community is simply carrying out God's long promised commission puts the nation of Israel in an accountable position, where response, not heredity, is imperative. The remaining uses of Scripture in Acts deal with this theme.

The texts addressed to Israel take on various emphases. Some passages explain why Israel is not responding (Ps. 2:1-2 in Acts 4:25-26; Isa. 6:9-10 in Acts 28:26-27), while others warn the nation of the cost of refusal (Deut. 18:19 and Lev. 23:29 in Acts 3:22-23; Hab. 1:5 in Acts 13:41). Other texts deepen the indictment by chronicling the pattern of the nation's response, treating their current hesitation as part of an

---

22Pace Sanders, *Jews*.

ignominious history that reflects spiritual disease (Amos 5:25-27 in Acts 7:42-43; Isa. 66:1-2 in Acts 7:49-50). Some of these remarks occur in the community (Acts 4), but most are direct challenges to the nation (Acts 3, 7, 13, 28).

These texts argue that Israel, in any generation, does not have an inalienable right to promise, if she refuses to embrace God's grace. Those in the new community do not rejoice at issuing such a warning. They are not words seeking vengeance and vindication. Rather, fellow Jews plead with their neighbours to not miss God's work and risk a dangerous accountability to God (Acts 7:60; 3:24-26).

The first group of challenge texts seek to explain what God is doing, even in the midst of national rejection of Jesus. Is God not in control? The Acts 4 citation of Psalm 2:1-2 shows that these events do not catch the new community unawares. A look at how God's chosen kings are treated reveals that the 'conspiracy' between Pilate and Herod, as well as between the Gentiles and the people of Israel is not surprising. As was noted above, the community can expect suffering, but the passage also has a second function. It explains that opposition to God's anointed is to be expected, as it was predicted by the Spirit.[23] The Lord's anointed is not welcomed with open arms. This word to the community, uttered in the midst of prayer, both explains and comforts. God knows what is taking place in this opposition.

The second explanatory text comes from Paul as he addresses Jews in Rome (Acts 28:25-27). The text functions as an implied rebuke that carries an implication: Paul is free to turn to the nations, since he has shared with Israel and she is refusing. The Pauline design of to the Jew first and also to the Greek surfaces here (Rom. 1:16). Like Isaiah centuries before, Paul's call to divine renewal is falling on hard hearts, dull ears and darkened eyes. The opportunity for healing is missed. So the message goes to the nations. The interplay between Israel and the nations is always present in these citations in the latter half of Acts, showing concern for both sides of the ethnic question (so also Acts 13:41-47).

This observation about Israel-nations juxtaposition, along with the attention paid to God-fearers in Acts, may suggest that attempts to

---

23Although the Psalm 2 text in Acts 4:24-26 is applied only directly to the current situation, one suspects a reading of the Psalm like that in the midrash of Psalm 2. That Jewish exposition shows that opposition to the Lord's chosen has been strong in every period. The one twist in the Acts usage is that Israel is now among the enemies. In the Midrash, as well, the expectation was that opposition would also emerge in the end time.

argue that Acts is written primarily to Gentiles or Jews may be a false dichotomy. More plausible is an explanation that argues that Gentiles belong in the new community, and need not be Jews to fit. Perhaps Luke writes to God-fearers who had left Judaism for Christianity. These Gentiles had originally discovered God through a different route than the new community was arguing for through Jesus. Both the amount of appeal to the OT and the racial mix in the various passages suggest this point. Imagine the reshuffling of perspective that such an entry into the community required. Theophilus may have been a God-fearer who came to Jesus from Judaism, but who now wonders if he should go back.[24] Does all the Israelite rejection mean the new community is an object of divine judgement? God's heritage and promise, as odd as it sounds, rests in the new community. Even the Jews in the new community understand why Israel refuses to respond.

But the OT also confronts the nation. The second set of texts serves to warn Israel of her culpability. The use of Deuteronomy 18:19 along with Leviticus 23:29 could hardly take a more confrontational approach. After alluding that Jesus is the prophet like Moses, Peter now notes that failure to respond to this prophet leaves one accountable before God. The Lord sends prophets to his people so his message can be heard. In fact, the allusion to Leviticus shows how serious the failure is. There the OT text speaks of inappropriate worship on the day of Atonement leaving one cut off from the people, about as serious a penalty as is possible. Peter reapplies the principle of that text to the one whose offering paved the way for the new people of God. Though it might seem inappropriate or even offensive to use a liturgical text this way, the citation may be making another more subtle point as well. It may see Jesus as the prophetic martyr sacrifice that is representative of a nation, especially in light of some other clearer texts in Luke–Acts on this theme (Luke 20:19-20; Acts 20:28). If so, this becomes the third Lucan text that alludes to the theme of the significance of Jesus' death.

Regardless of the possibility of the connection to Luke's view of the cross, Leviticus warns the nation and her citizens that rejection of Jesus leaves one 'cut off' from the people of God. Peter hopes for better things, since he ends his speech with an invitation to share in God's covenant promise.

---

[24]For this suggestion that Theophilus might be a God-fearer, see Nolland, *Luke's Readers*; Jervell, 'Retrospect', 383-404, esp. 399.

The third set of texts come from Stephen's speech with its historical overview of Israel's pattern of rejection. The first citation from Amos 5:25-27 stands close to the LXX version, a point that is not surprising given Stephen is a representative of the new community's Hellenistic wing. The 'God gave them over' theme of this citation is like what Paul says (of Gentiles!) in Romans 1:24-32. In Acts, it is Jewish unfaithfulness that is presented through the words of her own prophets. The manner of citation is key, since the nation has a history of missing God's voice. Israel often turned to the worship of other gods (Deut. 4:19; 17:3; 2 Kings 21:3-5; 23:4-5; 2 Chron. 33:3, 5; Jer. 7:18; 8:2; 19:13; Zeph. 1:5).[25] Stephen's use of this Amos text argues that from Exodus to exile, the nation responded unfaithfully to God. History shows God will not stand idle in the face of this response. Stephen's remarks ultimately cause the crowd to react, when he summarizes his point in Acts 7:51-53.

The second historical text is similar in force. Isaiah 66:1-2 in Acts 7:49-50 parallels the earlier Amos citation and leads into the indicting summary of Stephen in Acts 7:51-53. The point from Isaiah is that one should not make too much of the temple. Though venerated as the house of God; the temple cannot contain him. This idea also has rich OT roots (Isa. 57:15; 1 Kings 6:11-13; 8:27; 1 Chron. 6:8; Jer. 7:1-34; Micah 3:9-11). Stephen is responding to charges that he has spoken against the temple (Acts 6:13). He is saying nothing other than what prophets said before him. By not hearing him, they are not hearing Isaiah. They are missing the point yet again, repeating their ignominious history. God is greater than a given locale. The God of heaven and earth is not to be contained in a building, even though he permitted a temple to be built. The heritage of God is not in a building, but in the evidence of the living God's activity.

These historical texts are not only a word to Israel to remember her history of failure and take pause, but remind the readers that the nation's response to God is not always correct. She repeatedly has failed to respond to God. So her rejection of the new community's message reflects error in discerning God's plan.[26]

25Polhill, *Acts*, 201.
26The only citation in Acts that seemingly falls outside these five areas treating God's plan is the rebuke of Paul at his trial appealing to Exod. 22:27-28 in Acts 23:5. Yet even the tension exhibited there appears to be a battle over who claims truly to represent the way of God. Paul's rebuke that caused another to rebuke him is not unlike Jesus' tone and warning in Luke 11:37-52. Who represents the heritage is very much in view here as well.

IV. Conclusion

The use of Scripture in Acts serves supports the new community's claim to the heritage of God revealed in Moses and the prophets. The early church argued with the Jews that a faithful response to God would mean: (1) the embracing of Jesus as the promised one; (2) the inclusion of Gentiles into the community of blessing. Failure to respond left the nation culpable. Behind these claims stood their understanding of covenant, promise and christology. Scripture also allowed the community to appreciate that her current suffering was rooted in the way of Jesus, who had travelled a similar road. History taught the sad lesson that people often rejected God's way, even in the nation of promise. Circumstances should not deflect the reader of Acts from seeing that rejection did not evidence God's judgement, but mirrored the path of rejection Jesus walked. The road that they shared was a new road, because of the coming of Christ and the new era, but paradoxically it was an old road as well, since such rejection was promised by the prophets and practised earlier by the nation. Thus for Luke history and the prophetic Scripture showed that what was taking place was no surprise. The new community had every claim of heritage to God's promise in covenant, Christ, including the suffering that came from those who rejected their message. To see that connection was to understand what being in the light meant as one walked in the darkness. Like Paul, the readers of Acts should understand they were on trial for the hope of God (Acts 26:15-18). Like Paul and the early community before him, the road might not be easy, but what God sought was faithful witness (Acts 1:7-8; 4:24-30; 28:30-31). Luke's use of Scripture in Acts underscores that the message they proclaim is the realisation of a promise that God made long ago.

CHAPTER 4

SALVATION-HISTORY AND ESCHATOLOGY

John Nolland

Summary

Luke expected an imminent parousia. For him, the kingdom of God had a present (and developing) and a climactic future dimension. The periods in salvation-history were not sharply delineated for him. The same story keeps repeating, with variations, as it moves towards its climax in the parousia. There is for Luke no causal link between the (widespread) failure of Jewish people (and especially of their leaders) to respond to Jesus or to the Christian preaching and the divine intention of taking the message of salvation to the Gentiles. To be part of the Christian movement, Luke suggests, is the only thing that makes sense as history rushes to its climax.

I. Introduction

Despite its primary orientation to the Gospel rather than Acts, the best starting point for a discussion of salvation-history and eschatology in Acts is still the pioneering study of Lukan theology by Conzelmann,[1] which identified these areas as belonging to Luke's central theological investment. The magisterial commentary on Acts by E. Haenchen[2] soon broadened the base for, and extended the influence of, the main elements of Conzelmann's views. For Conzelmann the delay of the parousia was *the* critical dilemma of later first century Christianity; and Luke's central theological agenda had been to address those needs of the church which arose out of the crisis engendered by the delay. Luke replaced eschatology with salvation-history as the central category for understanding salvation. He sought to move the focus of Christians away from an imminently expected parousia of Christ (which had failed to materialise). The parousia hope survived Luke's reformulation of Christian faith, but it did so by being moved off into the far distant future. Instead of being fervently future oriented, Christians were encouraged to focus their faith in two ways: (i) they were to look back to the time of the historical Jesus as the time in which salvation had been present in the person of Jesus—now they had from this a picture of salvation, an understanding of what the kingdom of God will be like; and (ii) they were to understand the present not negatively as delay, but purposefully as the time for Christian witness in the world. Salvation-history was to be seen as firmly segmented: first there was the period of the law and the prophets (this is the period of promise); then there is the period of Jesus (this is the period of fulfilment, when salvation is present in the person of Jesus); finally there is the period of church (this is the time for witness and suffering). Of course there was still the parousia to come, but so remote had it become that one speaks of a three-fold division of salvation-history, and not of a four-fold.

This is not the place to document the ongoing discussion that Conzelmann's work has provoked, nor to provide a fresh evaluation of his contribution.[3] It suffices for the moment to anchor the present

---

[1]H. Conzelmann, *Luke*. See also his *Outline*, 149-152, and *Acts*.
[2]Haenchen, *Acts*.
[3]If there is a consensus it would be that Conzelmann has rightly emphasised the role of salvation-history in Luke's thought, but that he was wrong to identify it as a distinctive of Lukan thought, and that, though he was right to note a delay, he has overplayed the role of the delay of the parousia in Lukan thought.

discussion in the pioneering beginnings constituted by Conzelmann's contribution and then to move on to identify and discuss the issues which are to be addressed. Our approach will be to defend a series of theses in connection with salvation-history and eschatology in Luke's thought. The concern will be to understand Acts, but at points it will be important to pursue this task by paying particular attention to features of the Gospel as well.[4]

II. Parousia hope

My first thesis is: as in the Gospel, so in Acts, Luke continued to expect the parousia within his own generation.

Somewhat optimistically, C.H. Talbert claimed in 1981 that a consensus had emerged in Lukan scholarship that Luke retained a belief in an imminent parousia.[5] What has certainly happened is that the stranglehold of a particular critical orthodoxy over the reconstruction of the historical development of first century Christianity has been broken: a crisis in the early church over the delay of the parousia is no longer considered self-evident. Parousia delay is an indisputable fact, but parousia-delay crisis is actually hard to find.

The case for a continuing expectation on Luke's part of a near parousia is largely to be made from the Gospel and will not be made in any detail here. A sketch of the Gospel materials will be offered, and this will be supplemented by such indications found in Acts.

Luke 9:27 is a straightforward statement of an expectation that the kingdom of God would come within the lifetime of some of Jesus' hearers.[6] The language of seeing the kingdom of God used here is deliberately echoed in 21:28, in Luke's version of the eschatological discourse, which makes its own statement about the nearness of the kingdom of God. Luke 21 outlines a sequence of events in an escalating pattern, beginning from the early church context and culminating with

---

[4] I understand Luke to have written the Gospel in advance of Acts to be to some extent free standing, but that both works were, at least in outline, planned from the beginning. See Nolland, *Luke 1-9:20*, xxxii-xxxiv. Though there are definite differences of emphasis between the two volumes, there is no indication that Luke has changed his mind.

[5] Talbert, 'Recent Study', 204.

[6] Support for claims made in connection with the Gospel can regularly be found in discussions of the relevant texts in Nolland, *Luke 1-9:20*; and as well as his *Luke 9:21-18:34* and *Luke 18:35-24:53*.

the coming of the Son of Man.[7] The whole sequence is expected to take place within a single generation (v. 32). In 12:54-56 it is the events of Jesus' own ministry which should make it clear to all that the flow of world history is moving rapidly towards its appointment with the judgement of God.

Luke 19:11 is often taken, in connection with the following parable, as pointing to a delay of the parousia, but here is a separation of Jesus' historical ministry from the parousia: the consummation of the kingdom of God will not come as the culmination of Jesus' minis-try,[8] but must first be preceded by Jesus' journey through death and resurrection to enthronement at the right hand of God. A similar point is made in quite a different way by the linking of 12:49 and vv. 50-53. The linking suggests that while the anticipated conflagration (of eschatological purgation and judgement) is yet withheld (*i.e.*, is not part of Jesus' earthly ministry), its purging flames are to have their anticipation in Jesus' own coming fate and in the strife and division within families to be experienced by the disciples. In this way the text points to Jesus' own expectation of an imminent eschatological dé-nouement, which is soon to come, but must be preceded by other events. The separation of the parousia from Jesus' earthly ministry is also reflected in 13:35: Jesus will be removed to heaven (via death and resurrection) from the Jerusalem that has refused to receive him; it will see him again when he comes in his parousia role.[9]

---

[7]Luke sees it all as eschatology unfolding itself in history. Note the development in Luke 21 from a beginning stage in which only Christians are affected (vv. 12-19-—we should not understand that this phase gives way to the next, only that the next is overlayed upon this one), to the first rumblings of wider dimensions (v. 9) in reports (rumours?) of wars and uprisings (perhaps far away at first, but can Jerusalem avoid being finally engulfed? [a Jerusalem perspective is adopted for vv. 5-24a]); escalation to conflicts on a national scale (v. 10); the adding in of the extra dimensions of natural disasters and signs and portents from heaven (v. 11); the engulfing of Jerusalem, heralded by the arrival a surrounding seige army (vv. 20-24a). V. 24b takes us beyond the Jerusalem perspective in suggesting that be-yond the disaster to befall Jerusalem is to come disaster for its perpetrators, indeed for all Gentile peoples. 'The times of the nations' envisages a worldwide version of that judgement visited upon Jerusalem. The heavenly bodies will provide their own dramatic accompaniment to the execution of God's judgement upon the nations (v. 25a). The picture is of people anticipating in terror the unleasing of all the destructive forces of chaos (vv. 25b-26). When all this has run its course, the Son of Man will come bringing deliverance (vv. 27-28). Indeed, every stage of this unfolding course makes its own statement that 'your redemption is drawing near' (vv. 28-32). For a recent study of the structure Luke 21 which recognises the commitment here to the nearness of the parousia, see Fusco, 'Structure'.
[8]He has not gone to Jerusalem to be enthroned there as king.

It is true that Luke fills the time between ascension and parousia with its own significance, but this is not a delay motif. Even an imminent parousia has to be waited for.[10] So the question arises: Is the time between marked only by expectation or does it have its own significance in salvation-history? For Luke this period provides opportunity for faithful service to the absent but returning monarch (19:13, 16-25; 12:42-46); and it is a time to maintain alert readiness for the return of the master (12:35-40). It would be possible to think that a delay motif has been introduced in 12:45, but that would be not to fully appreciate the dynamics of this little parable: the master's extended absence is a device to achieve a situation in which the servant is not subject to immediate check by his master. The dynamic of the story requires that the servant be given space for his true colours to emerge.

Acts does not add a lot to this picture. 3:21 opens up an interval between the exaltation of Christ to the right hand of God and the parousia restoration. But this has to do with proclaiming as Christ a Jesus who is at the moment absent. The period of his absence is a purposeful interlude: time to repent and turn to God (v. 19). The call to the Jewish people to repent is motivated by the prospect of the coming of the one who has now already been designated as Christ[11] for them (v. 20).[12] Now appointed to office, he can be expected to arrive soon. The urgency in 10:42 of the news that 'he [Jesus] is the one designated by God to be judge of the living and the dead' comes from seeing that judgement as having now become a near prospect precisely because God has now moved to establish in office the one who is to act in his name as judge. The point is much the same in 17:31: the setting of the day for judgement is an entail of the appointment of the judge.[13]

9Luke 21:8 is not warning against preaching an imminent parousia. In its Lukan context, it relates to the destruction of Jerusalem, rather than to the parousia, and it should be read as making it quite clear that Christians have no interest in following into battle a messianic war leader who declares that the time is ripe for the putting down of Jerusalem, and the imposition of a new regime; the changes in 22:68 are concerned with bringing Jesus' vindication and exaltation into prominence.
10Admittedly, by the time of writing several decades have elapsed.
11Probably through the death, resurrection and ascension sequence (*cf.*, Acts 2:36; 17:31).
12Jesus can only come and be (in a positive sense) Christ for those who are ready to receive him as Christ (*cf.*, Luke 13:35b).
13Carroll, *Response*, also argues for a imminent parousia hope in Luke–Acts.

III. Kingdom as present and future

My second thesis is: as in the Gospel, so in Acts, the kingdom of God was seen as having both a present (and developing) as well as a climactic future dimension—both in connection with Jesus.

As is the case with the first thesis, the main part of the argument belongs to the Gospel which forms an assumed background for reading Acts. Though the phrase 'kingdom of God' does not occur in Acts with the frequency of the Gospel usage, it does come seven times,[14] in five of which the phraseology provides a clear echo of the Gospel language.[15]

In the Gospel structure,[16] 4:43 both summarises and explains Jesus' preceding activity in Nazareth and Capernaum: the kingdom of God is what is happening through Jesus' ministry (cf., esp. vv. 18-19 where the anointed one brings into being what he announces).[17] Now people are encountering the rule of God in a new way in the initiatives taken by Jesus. 7:28 envisages a situation in which the 'little ones' are already in the kingdom of God, but John the Baptist is not yet in: John is in prison and not yet a participant in the new state of affairs brought about by the ministry of Jesus.[18] When the claim is made in 10:9 that 'the kingdom of God has drawn near to you', the immediate evidence of its presence is to be found in the healing of the sick that has taken place. But even in the absence of healings (in the case where there has been rejection of the messengers of the kingdom) it still remains true that the kingdom of God has made its approach in the person of the messengers who represent the extension of the ministry of Jesus himself (v. 11). In 11:20 the presence of the kingdom of God is tied to Jesus' exorcisms 'by the finger of God'.[19]

---

[14]Acts 1:3; 8:12; 14:22; 19:8; 20:25; 28:23, 31 and cf., 1:6; the titular uses of 'Christ' in 2:31, 36; 3:18, 20; 4:26; 5:42; 8:5; 9:22; 17:3; 18:5, 28; 26:23; and the other indications that Jesus is to be thought about in royal categories in 2:30; 13:23, 33; 17:7.

[15]Note the juxtaposition of εὐαγγελίζομαι and βασιλεία τοῦ θεοῦ in Acts 8:12 cf., Luke 4:43; 8:1; 16:16; the juxtaposition of εἰσέρχομαι and βασιλεία τοῦ θεοῦ in Acts 14:22 cf., Luke 18:25; the juxtaposition of κηρύσσω and βασιλεία τοῦ θεοῦ in Acts 20:25; 28:31 cf., Luke 9:2. In the linked verses, Acts 1:3 and Lk. 9:11, the verb changes from λαλέω to λέγω but the link is strengthened by the repetition of the full phrase περὶ τῆς βασιλείας τοῦ θεοῦ.

[16]The section runs from 4:14 to 4:44.

[17]εὐαγγελίσασθαι in 4:43 is an echo of the use of the same form in v. 18.

[18]John is for Luke a transitional figure: sometimes he appears alongside Jesus as his (lesser) partner; sometimes he is relegated to the pre-Jesus period. See further below.

Of course there is inevitably an element of paradox in the claim that, while the larger world goes on much as before, nevertheless the new world order of God's eschatological rule has now arrived in and through the activity of Jesus. The level of cognitive dissonance would be insufferable (paste for diamonds!) if the claim of present fulfilment were not juxtaposed with the expectation of a future kingdom of cosmic proportions. The future kingdom (the consummation of the partial present fulfilment of the hoped-for kingdom—see below) is referred to in 11:2; 13:28-29; 19:11; 21:30. G.B. Caird[20] has shown how the same sort of juxtaposition of present fulfilment and future consummation functions powerfully in the OT to set present experience into the larger context of the purposes of God in history.

Not all of the Gospel references to the kingdom of God can be satisfactorily classified as either present or future. It is not so much that they might be the one or other[21] as that the phrase takes on a comprehensive scope, designating all the blessings that are brought by the eschatological rule of God, whether seen in its present manifestation with the coming of Christ, or in its future manifestation at the time of the parousia (6:20; 12:31-32; 18:16-17). The uses in 13:18, 20 are related but different: here 'the kingdom of God' applies equally to what begins in the ministry of Jesus and to the culmination corresponding to this beginning, found in the apocalyptic coming of the kingdom of God. This usage is likely to allow not only for a beginning and an end, but also for a development (through the death, resurrection and heavenly session of Jesus; the coming of the Spirit; and the Gentile mission to the ends of the earth). 13:18, 20 throw an important light back on those texts in which the reference to the kingdom of God is to the earthly ministry of Jesus: the reference may be to what is happening in the ministry of Jesus, but it is only so in connection with a firm confidence that beyond the achievement of that ministry there is a cosmic scale culmination yet to come. Thus, 'The healings [of the ministry of Jesus] are signs [of the presence of the kingdom of God (*i.e.*, expressions of its

---

19Not to the fact of exorcisms standing alone (otherwise the same claim could as well be made for the other Jewish exorcists), but with reference also to the role of Jesus himself (note the emphatic 'I') and the implied claim that 'the finger of God' is the operative force here, that is, that the presence and power of God are here in some distinctive manner (possibly linked with the manner and not simply the fact of the exorcisms). Without kingdom language, the same idea of present fulfilment is found in 10:23-24.

20Caird, *Language and Imagery*, 199-271.

21Though this could be the case in 18:24-25, it is probably better to understand the uses comprehensively.

reality)] in the same way that snowdrops are signs of Spring. The power and reality which we meet in the snowdrop are the same ones which later, even if far more powerfully, come into prominence.'[22] The use in 9:11 may be only to the present kingdom, but it could be comprehensive.

As we turn to Acts, we note first that the exorcisms and healings which marked the presence of the kingdom of God in the ministry of Jesus do not come to a halt.[23] A palpable experience of salvation flows to the early Christians from Jesus (15:11),[24] just as it had in the time of his earthly ministry (Luke 19:9)—references could be multiplied. 'Kingdom of God' is used, if we may be guided by the links into the Gospel uses,[25] in 1:3 possibly of the present manifestation of the kingdom of God (cf., Luke 9:11), but the Acts context might favour a comprehensive sense allowing for future dimensions as well; in 8:12 primarily of the present; in 14:22 with comprehensive reference, but a future orientation; and in 20:25; 28:31 primarily of the present. Acts 19:8 and 28:23 do not have such clear links to the Gospel diction, but the use in 19:8 is likely to have the same force as that in 1:3, and that in 28:23 will not be different.[26]

IV. Repetition and escalation in salvation–history

My third thesis is: Luke knows nothing of sharply delineated periods in salvation-history; for Luke the same story keeps repeating, but in different keys and with a definite sense of escalation towards a climax represented by the parousia.

The typological element in Luke's presentation is widely recognised and its pervasiveness has been increasingly recognised.[27] At times the typology has been interpreted too woodenly as directly providing christological categories, thus leading to the claim that Jesus is a new Moses, the end-time prophet, etc. In particular instances this

---

[22]H.K. Nielsen, *Heilung*, 44-45 (my translation).
[23]There is not a perfect match with the list in Luke 7:22, but there is considerable non-specific mention of healing (2:43; 5:12, 15; 8:6-7; 19:12; 28:9) and a strong sense that this aspect of the ministry of Jesus continues on in the early church.
[24]*Cf.*, Nolland, 'Acts 15:10'.
[25]See n. 13.
[26]Note the use of πείθω in both 19:8 and 28:23.
[27]For example Jesus is likened to Elijah, Joseph, Moses, the prophets, Jeremiah, etc. In turn Peter and Paul are both likened to Jesus (as is Stephen to a lesser extent).

may be so.[28] But typological comparison can be called upon to perform a variety of different functions[29] and one needs to be wary of creating a single mould. In Luke's writings, typological likeness functions with some regularity as a kind of water-mark providing authentication that this new thing has a place in the continuing salvation-history: the hand of God is recognised by seeing that this new thing is in some way 'more of the same'.[30] By its very nature, typology places the emphasis on continuity and repetition in the unfolding of salvation-history.

One area in which Luke is at pains to explain his story in terms of 'more of the same', has to do with his explanation of the extent of Jewish rejection of the claims of Jesus and those of Christianity. Without exploring the topic in any depth here we simply note the following. Jesus' rejection in Nazareth, which functions as a 'dress-rehearsal' for his wider experience and ultimate rejection in Jerusalem is commented upon (Luke 4:24) with the proverb, 'No prophet is accepted in his own πατρίς.[31] Jesus' fate is that of a prophet. The ironic statement in 13:33, 'it is not possible for a prophet to perish outside of Jerusalem' combines the idea that Jerusalem is the heart and centre of Israel with the tradition that the Israelites have persistently rejected the prophets God has sent to them.[32] As Stephen's speech moves towards its climax we find in Acts 7:52 the provocative challenge, 'Which of the prophets did your fathers not persecute?' which is linked to a 'like father, like son' motif in v. 51. This 'like father, like son' motif is found (again in connection with the killing of the prophets) in Luke 11:47-51 and (not in connection with the killing of the prophets) is important in the final comment on Jewish rejection of the gospel message in Acts 28:25-27.[33]

---

[28]Probably only where there is a promise-fulfilment element in the thought, *e.g,* Acts 7:37.

[29]An interestingly different typology is in the account of the day of Pentecost in Acts 2. Each hearing in his own language echoes from Jewish tradition the giving of the law to all nations in their own languages (probably to offer a subtle advance justification in Jewish terms for the Gentile mission: as the word of the gospel goes out to the Jews of the world, so it should be promulgated, as the law was, to the Gentile peoples as well). See Nolland, *Luke's Readers,* 95-102.

[30]What has been termed a Lukan 'anthological style' (involving pervasive allusions to OT precedents, and to a lesser extent, to wider precedents in Jewish tradition) is particularly striking in the infancy narratives (Luke 1–2), but is evident throughout Luke–Acts.

[31]In Luke's hands πατρίς is intended to mean at one and the same time 'home-town' and 'home-land'.

[32]*Cf.,* 1 Kings. 19:10, 14; Jer. 2:30; 26:20-24; Neh. 9:26; 2 Chron. 36:15-16.

[33]The parable of the wicked tenants (Luke 20:9-16) makes an implicit link between the rejection of the son and a history of rejection of the messengers of the owner.

Any claim to a sharply segmented salvation-history in Luke's writings must deal with the boundary difficulties which are undeniably there in Luke–Acts. Where is one to make the transition from the time of promise to the time of fulfilment—when does the long-promised salvation arrive (and does it leave again)? We can begin from the notorious neglect by Conzelmann of the infancy narratives. In these narratives, in an atmosphere of joy, worship, and confession, humble representatives of the best of Jewish temple piety experience 'in embryo' the breaking in of the eschatological salvation of God. But when we reach the body of the Gospel the 'today of salvation' would seem to be marked, instead, by the period of the public ministry of Jesus (Luke 4:18-21; 19:9).[34] Taken by itself this difference is not particularly difficult to reconcile, but when it is connected with the question of whether the ministry of John the Baptist is inside or outside this period of salvation the difficulty becomes more acute. The infancy narrative perspective would incline one towards including John, but the body of the Gospel perspective would incline one towards leaving him out. Luke seems to do both! John stands alongside Jesus as (a lesser) partner in 7:33-35, and this would seem to be the overall perspective for chapter 7.[35] But within chapter 7, v. 28 clearly, and the question of v. 20 by implication, would seem to leave John outside, and in 3:16 there is a sharp separation between the time of John and the time of Jesus. On the other hand John is already one who evangelises and offers forgiveness in 3:3, 18, and he almost certainly in 16:16 is to be included in the period in which the good news of the kingdom of God is announced. Of course one can use the language of prolepsis, but it is clear enough that Luke is not marking sharp boundaries.

If it is the time of Jesus' earthly ministry which is the time of the presence of salvation, then it is difficult to understand why from as early as 9:21 Luke's Gospel is dominated by a goal for Jesus beyond his ministry. In an important sense the achievement of the career of Jesus is focused on his death, resurrection and ascension to glory at the right hand of God. Certainly the Acts accounts of the career of Jesus move very quickly over the time of his public ministry[36] and invests instead in the rejection and vindication of Jesus, with a major focus on the

---

[34]In connection with this difference of perspective note also the use of 'today' in Luke 2:11.
[35]See Nolland, *Luke 1-9:20*, 354, 143, for the suggestion that the sinful woman of 7:36-50 is understood to have found forgiveness in the first place through the ministry of John.
[36]See 2:22; 3:13; 4:10; 7:37 with v. 52; 10:37-39; 13:25 with v. 27.

resurrection and exaltation. It is not hard to see why E. Franklin[37] can claim that the ascension was for Luke the determinative eschatological event. And here we have yet another possible place to locate the decisive fresh beginning. After all, it is the exaltation of Jesus that results in the eschatological outpouring out of the Spirit;[38] it is the time of the Pentecostal outpouring of the Spirit which is identified in 11:15 as 'the beginning'; and it is the repetition of this in the case of Cornelius which identifies for Peter the (eschatological) extending of this newly achieved state of salvation[39] to the Gentiles in terms of 'repentance unto life' (11:18), acceptance by God (15:8) and the cleansing of the heart by faith (15:9).[40]

This last point of focus (on the beginning with the outpouring of the Pentecostal Spirit by the exalted Christ) takes us full circle back to the infancy period. R.E. Brown[41] is among those who have drawn attention to the important links between Luke 1–2 and Acts 1–2, not the least of which are the prominent role of the Spirit and the pervasive sense of eschatological fulfilment. Admittedly in slightly different senses, several distinct points in history have valid claim to marking the arrival of the long-promised period of salvation.

Luke seems to mark a boundary in Luke 22:35-36, but closer examination undermines even the firmness of this boundary. The immediate Lukan frame for this new instruction is surely the sifting by Satan that has just been announced in v. 31. It thus points to the Passion period as one of particular Satanic trial. In Luke's understanding, Satanic trial is episodic (*cf.*, 4:13),[42] and he would certainly have believed that there would be other periods of intense Satanic trial (no doubt the periods of intense difficulty for the church described in Acts would have been seen by him in this way). But for Luke, the church lives dialectically between total divine protection and full human

---

[37]Franklin, 'Ascension', as well as his *Christ the Lord* and *Luke*.

[38]Acts 2:17-18, 33. 'In the last days' represents Luke's addition to the quotation from Joel.

[39]The preaching of repentance and forgiveness of sins would seem in Luke 24:47 (and *cf.*, Acts 10:43) to be tied to the achievement of Jesus' death and resurrection (and by implication his exaltation), but this is not certain.

[40]Both in Acts 11:16 (*cf.*, 1:5) and Luke 3:16 the distinction between the significance of John and Jesus is characterised as: John will baptise with water; Jesus will baptise with the Spirit. It seems likely that Luke sees the Pentecostal Spirit as conferring a certain intimacy of relationship with God (Acts 2; 10:46).

[41]Brown, *Birth of the Messiah*, 242-243.

[42]Conzelmann's understanding of Jesus' ministry as a Satan-free period has not fared well in subsequent scholarly scrutiny. See Brown, *Apostasy*.

vulnerability (see Luke. 21:16, 18 and pervasively in Acts) and in its preparation for mission both the challenge of Luke 10:4 (symbolising God's provision of all else when the missionaries focused on the kingdom of God—*cf.*, 12:31) and the warning of 22:36 are pertinent.

One might be tempted to think of the ascension as marking a significant loss, and thus marking the beginning of a negative interlude. Jesus has in some sense certainly gone away (Acts 1:11) and it is likely that Luke 9:48 shows signs of reflection on the question of how one might receive and welcome Jesus in a time when he is no longer physically present. But the note struck in 24:52-53 has nothing of loss in it. The conviction is that Jesus has moved on to a larger role in which he is just as, and even more, effectively present,[43] but in a different way (or to be more exact in a series of different ways). Now he is made known to Christian disciples through the breaking of the bread (Luke 24:35); he works in response to prayer;[44] he guides through the Spirit;[45] he even makes occasional appearances from heaven;[46] but primarily he works through the use of his name.[47] The earlier state of affairs has been taken up (repetition) and transformed (escalation) in this new situation.[48]

The preceding paragraphs also show ways in which Luke's story is of things happening over again but at ever more significant levels. The day of salvation actually arrives in stages, each with their own special quality and particular contribution. Something of the interrelationship, in Luke's view, of the stages of the unfolding of salvation-history can be indicated with reference to Luke 3:3.[49] Forgiveness is offered and experienced through John's baptism, but it is also central to Jesus' ministry. There is a complex interaction between the stages of the arrival of the kingdom of God. 'Each stage depends for its effectiveness on that yet to come (though this effectiveness does not wait for the arrival of the next stage) and has its validity only in connection with an

---

[43]Effectively present, not actually present.

[44]Even through the casting of a lot (Acts 1:24-25)! 'Lord' in v. 24 will be Jesus, since he is the one whose choice of the apostles has been mentioned in v. 2.

[45]Acts 16:7 suggests that the other references to the initiative of the Spirit should be understood as concerned also with initiative of Jesus through the Spirit.

[46]Acts 7:55-56; 9:3-6; etc.

[47]Acts 3:6; 4:30; etc. In 9:34 we even have 'Jesus Christ heals you'.

[48]Because Luke is often seen as idealising the early church period, there are those who would locate the beginning of the 'negative interlude' in the post-apostolic period in which Luke is thought to be writing, but this periodisation must be imposed upon, not read out of, Luke–Acts.

[49]See Nolland, *Luke 1-9:20*, 142-143. Quoted matter is from here.

openness to, and readiness for, the next (*cf.*, Acts 19:1-7).' Forgiveness is on the basis of the exalted position of Jesus at the right hand of Jesus, but this forgiveness is anticipated in the ministry of Jesus, and even in the preceding ministry of John. 'Repentance and forgiveness are, nevertheless, not experienced identically at the various stages of this development. In the Baptist's ministry they take on distinctly the quality of readiness for the arrival of the Lord (*cf.*, Luke 3:15-17; Acts 19:4).'[50]

The theme of judgement offers another area in which to explore issues of repetition and escalation in salvation-history. Luke clearly sees God's judgement as operative (selectively) in the small scale human disasters that come along (or are delivered by the messengers of God).[51] He also sees God's judgement as operating beyond death (and prior to some ultimate judgement day).[52] And, since there is no doubt that in some way Luke sees the destruction of Jerusalem and temple anticipated in Luke 21 as a replay of the 6th century exile, we should probably understand that he also understood the judgement of God to have been operative more generally through the history of Israel. But Luke 21 pictures not just a replay, but also a movement to climax (see v. 22; *cf.*, 11:51-52), a point which is reinforced as the circle of judgement spreads to embrace the whole world.[53] We have, then, three horizons of judgement: in the unfolding of national history (or even in personal history); after the death of the individual; and in that climactic sequence of events which culminates in the coming of the Son of Man.[54] But Luke offers no systematisation about what belongs to which. We only know that what happens after death matters more

---

[50]It would be possible and worthwhile to explore in an analogous manner the continuities and developments involved in connection with Temple and Law. Chance's book, *Jerusalem*, provides some useful foundations for the temple aspect of this; and see also Larsson, 'Temple-Criticism'. On the law see also the beginning in Salo, *Law*.

[51]Luke 13:1-5; Acts 5:1-11; 13:9-11.

[52]Luke 12:5; 16:23.

[53]See outline in n. 7.

[54]It is possible that Luke does not distinguish this last from the day of judgement, but he may locate a separate final judgement phase beyond the climactic judgement in history. In the Gospel the climactic judgement in history is not particularly linked with any judgement role for Jesus (10:14; 11:31-32; but see 12:49) and the parousia of the Son of Man connotes deliverance rather than judgement (21:27-28; the nearest thing to judgement is the acknowledgment or non-acknowledgment of people by the Son of Man before the angels of God [12:8-9 *cf.*, 9:26]), but Jesus is much more clearly identified in Acts as the ultimate judge acting for God (10:42; 17:31).

than what happens before (Luke 12:4) and that what happens in national history reaches a climax as the events outlined in Luke 21 come to their completion.

Finally under this thesis we note the existence of one 'intimation' which may point to the existence of others. By 'intimation' I mean here the occurrence of an event which foreshadows an anticipated event, but is not that event itself. The obvious instance of this is found in the Transfiguration account. 'About eight days later' links Luke 9:28 with v. 27 and its talk of 'see[ing] the kingdom of God'. In the transfiguration a few chosen disciples gain a glimpse of the glory which is to be Jesus' in the kingdom of God, a glory which will only become publicly manifest at the parousia (21:27). Especially in view of Luke's deletion from 9:27 of Mark's 'come in power' (Mark 9:1), it is likely that this one clearly marked intimation may hint at a whole range of preliminary intimations of the final 'see[ing]' of the kingdom of God'. Along these lines it may also be right to see in Stephen's experience in Acts 7:55-56 another such intimation.[55]

V. Jewish unbelief not the basis for Good News to Gentiles

My final thesis is: In the unfolding of salvation-history it is wrong to establish any causal link between the (widespread) failure of Jewish people (and especially of their leaders) to respond to Jesus or to the Christian preaching and the divine intention of taking the message of salvation to the Gentiles.

The pivotal texts in which scholars have found a link between a turning to the Gentiles and Jewish rejection of Jesus or the gospel are Luke 4:24-27; 21:24; Acts 13:46; 18:6; 28:25-28.[56] So it will be necessary to explore each of these texts briefly. But it is important from the outset to note that Luke offers a programmatic statement before there is any

---

[55]Stephen's experience has sometimes been called a personal parousia, but this may be too precise an identification.

[56]Significance is sometimes also attributed to Luke 21:24. In various forms the view is propounded that the destruction of Jerusalem marks the transition from a Jewish people of God to a Gentile church: after this point the distinctive significance of Israel in the purposes of God is no more (*e.g.*, Zmijewski, *Eschatologiereden*, 217-218; Wiefel, *Lukas*, 353). But judgement is the theme in Luke 21, and it is more likely that the verse speaks of God's judgement of the Gentile nations (note the subsequent use of ἔθνη in v. 25 and the pattern of judgement upon God's people followed by judgement upon the Gentiles in Isa. 10; 13-14; 33; 4 7; Jer. 50-51; Dan. 9:26-27). See again the outline to Luke 21 offered in n. 7.

hint that Jesus will not be welcomed with open arms by his people: Simeon's words in Luke 2:32 set Jesus for the Jews and Jesus for the Gentiles, not in antithetical parallelism but in complementary parallelism; he is to be 'a light for revelation to the Gentiles and for glory to your people Israel'.[57] It is also worth noting that such a parallelism finds its reflection in the pattern of Paul's ministry in Acts. In fact we have a step parallelism which gives priority to the Jews, but which is also concerned that the gospel be made known to the non-Jewish peoples as well.[58]

Because Luke 4:16-30 is generally taken as programmatic, the attempt is often made to control the rest of the Lukan presentation from an understanding thought to have been drawn from this passage. The danger of imposition is very real. Luke 4:25-27 offers us two blessed Gentiles who gain a benefit from Elijah in one case and Elisha in the other which is missed out on by those in Israel with corresponding needs. The emphasis is on those needy people in Israel who miss out. Though vv. 25-27 have been linked to the preceding text in a variety of ways,[59] the flow of thought in the immediate context is best respected by giving the verses the following thrust: 'By your unbelief you are creating a situation parallel to that in which the prophetic ministries of Elijah and Elisha (prophets raised up in Israel and for Israel) brought no benefit to Israel.'[60] It is only in a later reading and in the context of the whole story of Luke–Acts that the blessed Gentiles gain any positive significance. In this larger perspective we may reasonably find adumbrated in the not narrowly nationalistic ministries of Elijah and Elisha the universalism which is to be the basis of the Gentile mission.[61]

---

[57]The first mention of a divided response in Israel comes soon after in vv. 34-35.

[58]*Cf.*, Paul's 'for the Jew first, but also for the Greek' in Rom. 1:16.

[59]A representative range of suggestions is encapsulated in the following paraphrases:

(i) You reject me like a prophet, and like a prophet I will bestow my miraculous benefits on those outside Israel.

(ii) Prophets are not acceptable at home, as may be illustrated from the lives of Elijah and Elisha.

(iii) Your rejection of me means that others will get the benefits, just as happened in the cases of Elijah and Elisha.

(iv) Though I am your fellow citizen, you cannot demand miracles of me any more than the people of Israel could from Elijah and Elisha.(v) Like Elijah and Elisha my prophetic calling is to minister to foreigners.

[60]A full discussion of this text may be found in Nolland, *Luke's Readers*, 32-38.

[61]See Nolland, *Luke's Readers*, 86-89, for a fuller discussion.

In the case of Acts 13:46; 18:6; 28:25-28 there can be no doubt at all that
there is a timing connection between Jewish hostility and the directing
of the mission enterprise to Gentiles in a particular location.[62] What is
in dispute is the larger significance of such a turning. A series of
considerations encourage me to see the turning as considerably less
decisive than it is sometimes thought to be.

Though the language of the turning from its first appearance
('Now we turn to the Gentiles!') could easily be seen as absolute, it is
very soon clear that as soon as Paul moves cities he starts again with
the Jewish synagogue (*e.g.*, Acts 14:1). Similarly, though the language
might suggest a total break of contact, a close examination of Acts 18
makes it quite clear that while the turning to the Gentiles is real
enough (no more preaching in that synagogue), this is not the end of
Paul's interest in reaching Jews in Corinth: he sets up operations right
next door to the synagogue (v. 7) in clear competition for the allegiance
of the synagogue congregation; and in his subsequent successful evangelism it is the conversion of Crispus, the ruler of the synagogue (v. 8),
which is subsequently singled out for special mention.[63]

The synagogue which is abandoned is without exception one
which has first produced a harvest of fresh Jewish believers in Jesus,[64]
and Luke is at pains to make it clear that it is the unbelieving Jews who
exclude themselves by their unbelief and interference with the gospel
proclamation.[65]

Often, even when it is recognised that only a more restricted
significance can be given to Acts 13:46 and 18:6, something rather more
is made of the turning in Acts 28: as the third turning it confirms and
makes final the break; coming at the end it has decisive significance;
the attached quotation from Isaiah adds its own note of ultimacy. The
translation of the final clause of v. 28 as 'they will certainly listen'
suggests a contrast between Jewish rejection of the gospel and Gentile
acceptance: from henceforth the future of the church is among the
Gentiles. Does Acts 28:20 then, take us further than 13:46 and 18:6?

---

[62]For another recent exploration of these texts see Brawley, *Luke–Acts and the Jews*,
69-78.
[63]Note also in 19:9 that, after Paul's withdrawal from the synagogue, Luke can
summarise the subsequent ministry as 'all the residents of Asia heard the word of
the Lord, both Jews and Greeks'.
[64]Corinth could be the exception (depending on the force of ἔπειθεν in 18:4), but if
so it is not an intentional exception and we note that in Corinth also there is clear
continuing interest in reaching Jews.
[65]Acts 13:45; 18:6.

First there is the question of translation. ἀκούω is used four further times in the context of Acts 28:28 (v. 22, v. 26 and twice in v. 27). In each of its other occurrences it refers to hearing and not to responding. So, surely it is best taken with the same force here in v. 28.[66] The redirection in Acts 28 comes after a mixed response from his Jewish hearers (v. 24). They have had their turn to respond. Some have responded; some have rejected. Having shown full respect for Jewish priority, Paul now announces his intention of addressing the Gentiles with his message. Neither here nor anywhere else in Acts is it that Jews reject the gospel while Gentiles accept it. The consistent pattern is of a mixed response among both Jews and Gentiles.[67]

If ἀκούω is to be translated with reference to hearing, then attention needs also to be given to how to handle the καί represented above as 'certainly'. Haenchen was quite wrong to treat the usage here as though we were dealing with a redundant καί after a relative pronoun.[68] Luke does not use καί following pronouns in any analogous way.[69] Perhaps we can keep the 'certainly': 'now that you have made your response, and particularly in the light of the failure of many of you to take up the offer, I want you to know that now the Gentiles will certainly hear, because I intend to tell them'. But it is probably better to give καί the sense 'also' and, either by treating it as an adverb modifying the whole clause, or by linking it with the preceding αὐτοί,[70] to take the whole clause as meaning 'they will hear, as well'.

66There are ninety uses of ἀκούω in Acts. Mostly it means 'hear', sometimes 'give a hearing' (2:22; 7:2; 10:33; 13:16; 15:13; 22:1, 22), a sense which easily slides into 'make a proper response to' (3:22, 23; 4:19). For senses other than 'hear' the second person predominates, with some instances of the implicit first person (10:33; 4:19). 22:22 is third person. This takes up the second person of v. 1, and 3:23 is third person, but this follows on from the second person of v. 22. This pattern supports a sense 'hear' for 28:28.

67Luke is concerned to register a large positive impact of the gospel upon both Jews and Gentiles. At times he brings this into special prominence (it is Jervell, *Luke* who first brought to prominence the question of how to account for Luke's insistance on large numbers of Jewish converts to Christianity; see also 'Church'). At other times the extent of Jewish rejection becomes more prominent, because this is something that Luke feels it necessary to comment upon: it potentially discredits the Christian movement. The mixed response among Gentiles emerges more incidentally, since it appears to have no special Lukan significance (though it helps to sustain the parallelism between Jesus for the Jews and Jesus for the Gentiles).

68Haenchen, *Acts*, 724 *cf.*, 140 n. 8.

69Nor do other NT writers.

70While καί, as 'also', normally modifies a following word it may modify a preceding word when that word stands first in its clause. See Smyth, *Grammar*, § 2881.

This best respects the principled parallelism established by Luke between outreach to the Jews and outreach to the Gentiles.

It is sometimes claimed that though Luke reports a successful Jewish mission in Jerusalem in the early chapters, he gradually moves the focus more and more onto Gentiles, with Acts 28:28 marking the final transition.[71] But this view collides sharply with 21:20 which refreshes the readers' awareness of the successful Jerusalem mission, and of the continuing relevance of Jewish Christians. Too much (by way of denoting finality) should not be made of the extra emphasis achieved from the use of Isaiah 6:9-10.[72] Stephen's speech as early as chapter 7 has much more powerfully underlined Jewish hardness of heart. Acts 28:28 as the third statement of turning is significant, but its significance is better located in establishing the pattern of outworking of the step-parallelism through which Luke sees Christian mission operating. The location at the end, in Rome, may provide some kind of symbolism of finality. If we allow that reaching Rome symbolises the gospel reaching to the ends of the earth, and in that schematic sense the completion of all Christian outreach, then there is no real problem with allowing for the possibility that this final turning symbolises the completion of all Jewish mission, but in practical terms Jewish mission is as likely to continue as is Gentile mission.

Finally we need to address the question of why Luke brings into prominence the move to Gentiles when Jewish opposition becomes sharp. I have argued elsewhere[73] that the best perspective on this feature is achieved by recognising that it takes its place within an elaborately developed apologetic. Extensive Jewish rejection of the Messiah presented by Christianity is potentially very damaging to its credibility. Luke addresses this problem in various ways, but the one that concerns us here involves incorporating the Jewish rejection into the larger shape of a success story. Luke paints an impressive picture of obstacles surmounted, apostles and missionaries who are never daunted, providential care and divine intervention. The Christian movement is indestructible: it must be of God! The very events which

---

[71]Sanders, 'Jewish People', 71, claims that in reporting Paul's mission, Luke has 'drawn a picture of *increasing Jewish hostility and opposition to the gospel*'. He would do better to claim this kind of development for the situation in Jerusalem (an initially very favourable attitude on the part of the people is turned into its opposite by misrepresentations to them; see esp. 6:11-12; 21:28).

[72]The 'progressive intensification' from 13:46 to 18:6 to 28:25b-28, claimed by Maddox, *Purpose*, 44, is not obvious.

[73]Nolland, *Luke's Readers*, 119-128.

look like Christianity's failure are themselves incorporated into the forward march of this indomitable movement.[74] The Jews, by and large, may have given up on Christianity, but Luke knows nothing of Christianity having given up on the Jews.

I conclude with a restatement of the theses. Luke continued to expect the parousia within his own generation. He sees the kingdom of God as having both a present (and developing) as well as a climactic future dimension. He does not think in terms of sharply delineated periods in salvation-history: the same story keeps repeating, but in different keys and with a definite sense of escalation towards a climax represented by the parousia. In the unfolding of salvation-history there is no causal link between the (widespread) failure of Jewish people (and especially of their leaders) to respond to Jesus or to the Christian preaching and the divine intention of taking the message of salvation to the Gentiles. Partly by means of the case that he offers for this set of theses, Luke offers a compelling picture of the Christian movement as the right and only place to be part of the presently unfolding climax of the purposes in history of the God of Israel, who is also the God of all the peoples of the earth.

---

[74]The treatment of the cross is in some ways very similar: it turns out to be Jesus' pathway to divine vindication in the resurrection and cosmic enthronement at the right hand of God.

CHAPTER 5

'SALVATION TO THE END OF THE EARTH' (ACTS 13:47): GOD AS SAVIOUR IN THE ACTS OF THE APOSTLES

Joel B. Green

Summary

This chapter takes as its point of departure the observation that salvation is the theme of Acts that unifies other textual elements within the narrative. After briefly setting the parameters of 'salvation' within the larger world of Graeco-Roman antiquity and, more especially, within the Gospel of Luke, it examines this theme in Acts with particular reference to three questions: What does salvation mean for Luke? How is Jesus Saviour in Acts? How might salvation be appropriated? In addition, attention is directed to the query, To whom is salvation available? This examination demonstrates Luke's ability to draw on notions of salvation familiar to Gentiles and Jews of the Mediterranean world in a way that also challenges, even overturns those notions. This chapter concludes that the God of Israel is portrayed in Acts as the Great Benefactor, Jesus as Lord of all, and that the salvific nature of his lordship embodies, enables, and inspires new ways for living in the world.

I. Introduction

> 'Rather, you will receive power when the Holy Spirit comes upon
> you, and you will be my witnesses in Jerusalem, in all Judea and
> Samaria, and to the end of the earth'. (Acts 1:8)

This outline of God's purpose in Acts has occasioned significant debate, especially around the location or other referent of the 'end of the
earth' to which Jesus directs his followers. Not the focus of an
equivalent amount of scholarly discussion, though related and of comparable importance, is a second question: To what are these followers
to be 'witnesses'? Distinguishing objective genitive from subjective in
the phrase, μου μάρτυρες ('my witnesses'), is unnecessary and probably impossible: those who serve God's aim in the Spirit-empowered
mission have Jesus (μου) as the content of their witness *and* they serve
as his envoys. But with what concerning Jesus will this testimony be
occupied? An answer lies close at hand in 1:22; what is needed is a
'witness to the resurrection'.[1] Closer examination confirms that such
witnesses serve as more than 'guarantors of the resurrection',[2] however, for talk of the resurrection in Acts leads regularly and immediately into the blessings available to people as its consequence.[3] For Acts,
'witness' is concerned not only with the that of Jesus and his resurrection, but also with its significance, and in Acts this significance is
developed especially in salvific terms.

This view of things has already been prefigured at the close of
Luke's Gospel,[4] where the 'things' to which Jesus' followers are
declared 'witnesses' include not only Jesus' death and resurrection,
but also the consequent offer of salvation 'to all nations, beginning
from Jerusalem' (Luke 24:49). That this witness is especially concerned
with 'salvation' is underscored again in Acts 13:47 where the phrase 'to
the end of the earth' appears again; here, substituting for the earlier

---

[1]Even closer to hand is the ascension acount in 1:9-11, with its pronounced
emphasis on witnessing Jesus' ascension βλεπόντων αὐτῶν ('while they were
watching'), ἀπὸ τῶν ὀφθαλμῶν αὐτῶν ('out of their sight'), ὡς ἀτενίζοντες ἦσαν
('as they were gazing'),[ἐμ]βλέποντες ('looking'), and ἐθεάσασθε αὐτόν ('you saw
him'). Jesus' elevated status is thus identified as a, if not the, primary subject
matter of their 'witness'.
[2]*Contra, e.g.*, Polhill, *Acts*, 85.
[3]See, *e.g.*, 2:32-33; 3:15-16; 5:30-32; 10:39-43; 22:14-16; 26:16-18. *Cf.*, Pesch, *Apostel-geschichte*, 1:69.
[4]Without prejudice concerning actual authorship, we shall refer to the narrator of
Luke and Acts as 'Luke'.

phrase, 'you will be my witnesses', are the words, 'you may bring salvation'.[5] Accordingly, Acts will be occupied with followers of Jesus who are designated and equipped as witnesses to the salvation of God, available through Jesus.

The centrality of the theme of salvation to the Lukan project[6] has already been signalled numerous times by the Evangelist. One of the most prominent of the Lukan summaries of Jesus' mission occurs immediately after Jesus announces the coming of salvation to the household of Zacchaeus: 'For the Son of Man came to seek and to save the lost' (Luke 19:10). The birth narrative introduced the miraculous and eschatological work of God specifically as oriented toward salvation (Luke 1:5–2:52). Mary celebrates 'God my saviour' (1:47); Zechariah speaks of God who 'has raised up a mighty saviour (ἤγειρεν κέρας σωτηρίας)' (1:69), so that 'we would be saved from our enemies' (1:71); the angel of the Lord announces the birth of Jesus, 'a Saviour' (2:11); and, praising God, Simeon confesses, 'my eyes have seen your salvation' (2:30). In Luke's second volume, the salvation theme is sounded in an explicit and programmatic way in Peter's sermon at Pentecost.[7] Citing Joel 2:32 (Acts 2:21: 'Then everyone who calls on the name of the Lord shall be saved') and summarizing Peter's message as a call to 'save yourselves from this corrupt generation' (2:40), this text accords privilege to the offer of salvation in missionary preaching. This scene closes with Luke's summary, 'And the Lord added daily to [the number of the fellowship] those who were being saved' (2:47).

---

[5]That is, 1:8 and 13:47 are mutually interpretive. According to its usage in, *e.g.*, Strabo (*Geography*; *cf.*, the examination of this phrase in the literature of Roman antiquity in Ellis, 'End of the Earth', 126-28; van Unnik,'Hintergrund'), ἕως ἐσχάτου τῆς γῆς ('to the end of the earth') is polysemous. We need not assume, with Ellis ('End of the Earth') and others, that Luke *must* have in mind a purely geographical connotation (*e.g.*, Ethiopia, Spain, Rome, or 'Israel'), for geography is itself a social enterprise; geographical markers such as 'Judea' and 'Samaria' (Acts 1:8) are social products that reflect and configure ways of being in the world (*cf.*, *m. Kel.* 1.6-9; Pred, *Human Geographies*; Soja, *Postmodern Geographies*). At this early juncture in the narrative of Acts, Luke has hardly provided the semantic means by which we might localize its referent. The possibilities are narrowed considerably upon reading Acts 13:47, however, with its citation of Isa. 49:6, where the more transparent sense of 'everywhere', 'among all peoples' is evident. Luke's dependence on the Isaianic eschatological vision is manifest throughout his writings (*cf.*, Seccombe, 'Luke and Isaiah'), and this further encourages our finding in Acts 1:8 a deliberate echo of the Isaianic text (*cf.*, Isa. 8:9; 45:22; 48:20; 62:11).
[6]In this essay, we assume at least the *theological unity* of Luke–Acts. On this problem, see Marshall, 'Introduction' (above).
[7]*Cf.*, Green, 'Proclaiming Repentance', 33-41.

It has long been noted that the NT vocabulary of salvation—
σωτήρ (saviour), σωτηρία (salvation), σωτήριον (salvation), and σώζω
(to save)—congregates especially in Luke–Acts, occurring 21 times in
Acts, both in narrative and speech material.[8] To these terms, others
may be added—*e.g.*, διασώζω (to save), ἐξαιρέω (to rescue), θεραπεύω
(to heal), ἰάομαι (to heal), and ὁλοκληρία (complete health)[9]—by way
of indicating not only the importance of this theme in Acts, but also its
breadth in the Lukan perspective. When, momentarily, we move to an
examination of the 'content' of salvation in Acts, we will see even more
abundantly how appropriate it is to speak of salvation as the *theme* of
Acts—that is, in narrative terms, of salvation as that which unifies
other textual elements within the narrative.[10]

In this analysis, we are working with certain handicaps. First, we
must recognize the inherent artificiality of the task of describing
Luke's understanding of salvation. In order to do so, we must turn his
narrative art into a more systematic presentation of its major theme.
Narrative is more accustomed to inviting reflection, provoking con-
templation, raising questions, but an analysis such as this one of a
narrative theme is more oriented toward explanation and assertion.
Second, this study is focused above all on the Acts of the Apostles.
Hence, we must often leave to ancillary notes what is not so ancillary
to the Lukan soteriology—namely, the important witness of the third
Gospel on this theme.[11] In addition, we will not be able to pursue as
fully as we might the degree to which Luke's soteriology is woven
with fabric borrowed from the LXX and from the wider Jewish-
Hellenistic world. What is more, we will not be able to explore a
number of related motifs which, happily, are taken up elsewhere in
this volume.[12] Nevertheless, we may address such pivotal questions
as: What does salvation mean for Luke? How is Jesus saviour in Acts?
How might salvation be appropriated? In addressing these, we will
also address the question of to whom is salvation available?

8Acts 2:21, 40, 47; 4:9, 12; 5:31; 7:25; 11:14; 13:23, 26, 47; 14:9; 15:1, 11; 16:30, 31; 27:20,
31, 34, 43; 28:28.
9διασώζω–7:10, 34; 12:11; 23:27; 26:17; ἐξαιρέω–23:24; 27:43, 44; 28:1, 4; θεραπεύω–
4:14; 5:16; 8:7; 17:25; 28:9; ἰάομαι–9:34; 10:38; 28:8, 27; and ὁλοκληρία–3:16.
10On 'theme', as distinct from, say, 'plot' or 'motif', see Prince, *Narrative as Theme*,
3-7.
11See Green, *Theology of Luke*.

II. 'The message of this salvation'

What does salvation mean for Luke? By way of addressing this question, we will first attempt briefly and at a necessarily high level of abstraction to see how this concept might have been understood in his discourse situation. What range of meaning might Luke and his first-century audience have understood by 'salvation'? What nuances were more or less taken for granted in their shared presuppositions? Then, prior to examining the evidence of Acts, we will provide a synopsis of how Luke presents 'salvation' in the third Gospel. This will assist us in our attempt to see how he might have drawn on as well as transformed wider notions of 'salvation'.

Salvation in Luke's world

In the wider Graeco–Roman world of the first century C.E., the world in which Luke writes and within which his narrative is set, 'salvation' was a semantic cousin of 'benefaction'.[13] As such, salvation had to do with the exercise of beneficent power for the provision of a variety of blessings, 'a general manifestation of generous concern for the well-being of others, with the denotation of rescue from perilous circumstances'.[14] This might include the health of the state, including its internal safety and the security of its borders; being rescued from a disaster at sea; the healing of physical malady; and more.[15]

The example of Augustus, who plays a special role in the Lukan narrative (Luke 2:1-20), is instructive. In spite of Roman reticence *vis-à-vis* the imperial cult in the early empire, Augustus permitted the

---

[12]See esp. chs. 4, 7, and 16. Outside this volume, recent studies of salvation in Luke–Acts include: Bovon, 'Heil'; Dömer, *Heil Gottes*; Flanagan, 'Salvation in Luke–Acts'; George, 'L'Emploi chez Luc', and his 'Vocabulaire de salut'; Giles, 'Salvation'; Glöckner, *Verkündigung des Heils*; Green, 'Message of Salvation'; Mangatt, 'Gospel of Salvation'; Marshall, *Luke: Historian*; Martin, 'Salvation and Discipleship'; Neyrey, *Luke's Soteriology*; O'Toole, *Unity*; Pilgrim, 'Death of Christ'; Powell, 'Salvation in Luke–Acts'; Radl, *Lukas-Evangelium*, esp. 105-11; Throck-morton, 'Σῴζειν'; Zehnle, 'Salvific Character of Jesus' Death'.
[13]Cf., Josephus *Life* 47 §244: ἐβόων ἅπαντες εὐεργέτην καὶ σωτῆρα τῆς χώρας αὐτῶν καλοῦντες; similarly, *e.g.*, Herodotus 3.12.2.
[14]Danker, *Benefactor*, 324 (with reference to σωτήρ and cognates).
[15]See MM 620-22; Danker, *Benefactor*; Foerster, 'σῴζω and σωτηρία', *TDNT* VII:966-69; *TLNT*, 3:344-49; and, more broadly (and somewhat dated), Green, *Meaning of Salvation*, ch. 4.

worship of powers operating through him—*e.g.*, peace, victory, harmony, liberty, security, et al. Augustus received such titles as 'Saviour' and was revered as the one who had brought peace to 'all the world'.[16] Thus, when Paullus Fabius Maximus, proconsul of Asia, proposed beginning the new year on Augustus' birthday, he observed:

> (It is hard to tell) whether the birthday of the most divine Caesar is a matter of greater pleasure or benefit. We could justly hold it to be equivalent to the beginning of all things...; and he has given a different aspect to the whole world, which blindly would have embraced its own destruction if Caesar had not been born for the common benefit of all.

In their decision to honour Augustus in this way, the provincial assembly explained:

> Whereas the providence which divinely ordered our lives created with zeal and munificence the most perfect good for our lives by producing Augustus and filling him with virtue for the benefaction of mankind [*sic*], sending us and those after us a saviour who put an end to war and established all things; and whereas Caesar [*sc.* Augustus] when he appeared exceeded the hopes of all who had anticipated good tidings...; and whereas the birthday of the god marked for the world the beginning of good tidings through his coming....[17]

As already intimated, however, Augustus was not the only one known as 'saviour'; this appellation fell to others as well—gods, rulers, physicians, and so on.

In Luke's 'Scriptures' (LXX), on the other hand, 'saviour' is used especially of the God who helps or delivers his people (*e.g.*, 1 Sam. 10:19; Isa. 45:15, 21; Wisd. of Sol. 4:30; 1 Mac. 4:30; Sir. 51:1). If Yahweh is not saviour, then this role is performed by his designated envoy; even in these cases divine agency remains paramount, for salvation is the coming of divine help to those in trouble. Salvation in the OT is pre-eminently defined in Yahweh's delivering Israel from slavery and, so, as rescuing Israel from the hands of its enemies, victory in battle, and security as a nation surrounded by other peoples.[18]

16Braund (*Augustus to Nero*) provides English translations of numerous inscriptions describing Augustus as son of a deity (§§2, 6, 10, 11, 13 *et passim*), progenitor of his country and/or the world (§§19-21, 28, 44 *et al.*), bringer of peace and saviour of the world (§§10, 36, 38, 44, 66, 123 *et al.*), and even referring to him as divine (§§75, 94).
17*OGIS* 2:458; ET from Price, *Rituals and Power*, 54-55.

Central to the OT notion of election and covenant is the immutable relationship between God's gracious acts of deliverance on behalf of his people and their faithful response to him as Divine Deliverer. In later periods, this relationship remains pivotal to Israel's articulation of its faith in God as the only Saviour (*e.g.*, Philo *Spec. Leg.* 1 §252). Only God would rescue his people from those who would oppress them (*e.g.*, 1 Macc. 3:18-22; 4:11; 9:46; 2 Macc. 1:11, 25; 2:17-18; 8:27; 1QM [*e.g.*, 4; 10.4-5; 14.4-5]) and protect them from the multitudinous pressures to conform to increasing foreign influences[19] and renew the covenant through forgiveness for Israel's unfaithfulness (*cf.*, Jer. 4:14; 31:31-34; 2 Macc. 7:1-42; 8:27-29; 1 Enoch 5:6).

Salvation in the third Gospel

The terminology of salvation is widespread in the third Gospel,[20] and Luke uses this and related language in a variety of co-texts to give salvation broad meaning. As outlined in the Magnificat (1:46-55), and worked out through the Lukan narrative, salvation is concerned with a fundamental redefinition of human social interaction which has its basis in the wide embrace of the graciousness of God. Salvation entails status-inversion and the reversal of conventional values as God accepts those who have otherwise been rejected. 'Human values are reversed by God not for the destruction of the wicked but for the saving of the lost'.[21] God's activity embraces the raising up of lowly persons whom Jesus encounters in the Gospel, and also of the people of Israel promised liberation from the oppressive hand of Rome; it also encompasses the bringing down of the powerful as all are invited to appropriate salvation for themselves and to serve God's salvific aim. Salvation is the coming of the kingdom of God to displace other kingdoms, and entails membership in the new community God is drawing together around Jesus.

Salvation, then, can appear in many guises. For example, the Galilean crowds see in Jesus' ability to raise a dead man to life the

---

18See O'Collins, 'Salvation', 907-10; Sawyer, 'עשׁי', 441-47.
19*Cf.*, Feldman, *Jew and Gentile*; Foerster, 'σῴζω and σωτηρία', *TDNT* VII:982.
20Σῴζω and related nouns appear in Luke 1:47, 69, 71, 77; 2:11, 30; 3:6; 6:9; 7:50; 8:12, 36, 48, 50; 9:24; 13:23; 17:19; 18:26, 42; 19:9, 10. As in Acts, however, the third Gospel employs a range of semantically related terms. On what follows, see Green, *Theology of Luke*, ch. 4.
21Johnson, *Luke*, 23.

coming of the eschatological prophet, the gracious intervention of God to bring salvation (7:16). Salvation is evident in the offer of forgiveness (1:77; 3:1-6; 7:36-50), the advent of peace (2:11; *cf.*, 1:69-70), healing and restoring the sick to their community and kin (7:11-17; 8:26-39, 40-56), the overcoming of the devil and the demonic (8:26-39; 13:10-17; *cf.*, Acts 10:38), the cleansing of the leprous (5:12-16; 17:11-19), and so on. It is important to realize the profoundly social ramifications of what may appear on the surface as (merely) spiritual or physical blessings. To be forgiven, for example, is to be (re)admitted into the community from which one has been ostracized on account of sin, just as the former demoniac and leper, in being 'saved', are restored to their families. Note, *e.g.*, how Zacchaeus, held at arm's length by the crowds as a 'sinner', is recognized and embraced as 'son of Abraham', a member of the family of God (*cf.*, 3:7-9), when salvation comes to his house (19:1-10).[22] Throughout the Gospel of Luke, salvation is represented in concrete terms—refusing any boundaries between social/communal, material/physical, and spiritual/religious.

Mary identifies God as saviour (1:47), and this is true throughout the Gospel. It is God who initiates this new chapter in the story of salvation wherein his redemptive purpose moves toward consummation (Luke 1–2), and it is God whose redemptive purpose is being served throughout Luke's narrative. Jesus is also designated saviour, of course, and that by a divine spokesperson (2:11). Ultimately, however, salvation comes from God. This Lukan emphasis is evident from the way the Evangelist has deployed the Scriptures and in the wide array of terms expressive of God's design at work in his narrative.[23] Jesus is saviour, then, as God's representative (*i.e.*, as God's Son), having been anointed for service as God's regal prophet and having embraced fully the divine aim (*cf.* 3:21-4:30).

Salvation in the Book of Acts

In a linear text like the Acts of the Apostles, what appears first influences the interpretation of everything that follows. By way of organizing our exploration of the meaning of salvation in Acts, then,

---

[22]See Green, 'Good News to Whom?', 69-72.

[23]See esp. βουλή ('purpose'), βούλομαι ('to want'), δεῖ ('it is necessary'), θέλημα ('will'), θέλω ('to will'), ὁρίζω ('to determine'), πληρόω ('to fulfil'), and προφήτης ('prophet'). *Cf.*, Cosgrove, 'The Divine ΔΕΙ in Luke–Acts'; du Plooy, 'Narrative Act'; Squires, *Plan of God*; Green, *Theology of Luke*, ch. 2.

we will take as our point of departure Acts 2, where the salvation-theme is first sounded in an overt and extended way. Acts 1 is not devoid of relevant material, and we will have occasion to look there as well as in subsequent material as we examine four motifs related to the content of salvation that surface in Acts 2.

(1) Salvation as incorporation and participation in the christocentric community of God's people. When we first encounter the community in Acts 2, it consists already of those who had followed Jesus during his earthly ministry. The word 'they' in 2:1 refers back to those 'persevering in prayer together' (1:14; *cf.*, 1:24), those 'with one mind' (ὁμοθυμαδόν);[24] in 2:1, they are ὁμοῦ ἐπὶ τὸ αὐτό (*cf.*, 1:15 [ἐπὶ τὸ αὐτό]; 14:1 [κατὰ τὸ αὐτό]), a phrase that underscores the unity and concord of the community.[25] The emphatic oneness of the community (or, its status as a kinship group) is illustrated vividly in the Lukan characterization of their economic *koinonia* (2:44-45; 4:32-5:11).[26]

That this is a community oriented around Jesus is suggested by earlier material (1:1, 21-22); by the christocentric character of Peter's address, especially the extension of the citation from Joel to include the phrase, 'everyone who calls on the name of the Lord (=Jesus; *cf.*, 2:36) will be saved'; and by the directive that people should respond to the message of salvation by being baptized 'in the name of Jesus Christ' (2:38), appropriating the blessings available through him and signalling one's allegiance to him. Subsequently in Acts Christians heal (3:6, 16; 4:10, 30; 19:13), preach (4:12; 5:28, 40), and are baptized in the name of Jesus (8:16; 10:48; 19:5); suffer for his name (5:41; 9:16; 21:13) and are those 'who call upon the name' of Jesus (9:14, 21; 22:16).

The directive to be baptized is not only to signify one's *response* to the message, however; baptism, understood in its local co-text (2:37-42), also marks one of the blessings comprising salvation.[27] Salvation is being incorporated ('added') to the number of believers. Readers of the third Gospel will not be surprised by this emphasis, for

---

[24] In Acts, ὁμοθυμαδόν refers to the single-minded harmony *either* of the company of believers (1:14; 2:46; 4:24; 5;12; 8:6; 15:25) *or* of those who oppose them (7:57; 12:20; 18:12; 19:29).

[25] *Cf.*, Luke 17:35. In the LXX, the phrase appears frequently for 'together' (יחדו, יחד; Wilcox, *Semitisms of Acts*, 93-100; Fabry, 'יחד', *TDOT* VI:43-44; *cf.* 1QS 8.19 (לכול הנוסף ליחד); CD 13.11.

[26] On this emphasis, *cf., e.g.,* 6:1-6; 9:36; 11:27-30; 16:15; Plato *Republic* 5.46.2c; Cicero, *De officiis* 1.16.51; Aristotle *Nicomachean Ethics* 9.8.1168b; Josephus *J.W.* 2.8.3 §§122-23; Bartchy, 'Community of Goods'.

[27] This motif is suggested in George, 'Vocabulaire de salut', 314-15, 319.

discipleship had already been worked out, in part, as kinship in the circle of those who follow Jesus. Nor is this emphasis extraordinary in Graeco–Roman antiquity, where status was grounded in group definition and the stress on 'belonging' was acute.

What may be surprising is the identification of those who are said 'to belong'. Acts 2 portends the expansiveness of the community of 'those being saved' in a number of ways: (1) the notation regarding people 'from every nation under heaven' present in Jerusalem in (2:5); (2) the enumeration of the countries of origin of those present (2:9-11); (3) the Joel-citation, with its emphasis on the outpouring of the Spirit on 'all humanity' (2:17) and invitation to 'everyone' (2:21); and (4) the redemptive promise for 'you, your children, and all who are far off' (2:39; cf., Isa. 57:19). Even if those present in this scene are specified as 'devout Jews' (2:5), then, the progress of the mission toward 'the nations' is anticipated (cf., 1:8; 10:1-11:18; et al.).

This move toward a multi-ethnic community is God's doing, whose salvific activity according to Luke sometimes runs ahead of the thinking and practices of those within the church. By proving himself to be the saviour of the Gentiles too—i.e., by pouring upon them the blessing of forgiveness and the gift of the Spirit—God both testifies to the authenticity of their membership in the number of God's people and confirms that 'he has made no distinction between them and us' (15:7-8; cf., 11:15-18). Jesus is Lord of all (10:43).[28]

Perhaps it is enough to say that Gentiles are included in the new community of God's people, but Luke says more. Also 'saved' are those who are set apart from normal social discourse by their maladies—e.g., lameness and paralysis (3:1–4:12; 8:7; 14:8-10), sickness and demon–possession (5:12-16; 8:7), even death (9:36-43; 20:7-12). This emphasis, which continues and parallels the healing ministry of Jesus in Luke's Gospel, reminds us that the Lukan soteriology knows no distinction between the physical, spiritual, and social; that in the larger Graeco–Roman world 'salvation' would be recognized in the healing of physical disorders (cf., the response to healing in 14:11); and that physical restoration had as one of its ramifications restoration to social intercourse.

(2) Salvation as rescue from our enemies. This second way of construing salvation deliberately borrows language from Zechariah's Song (1:68-79; esp. vv. 71, 74). The promise of divine deliverance from 'the hands of our enemies' early in Luke has seemed to many interpreters

---

[28]See Borgen, 'Cross-National Community', 229-33.

to have gone unfulfilled in Luke–Acts;[29] as a consequence, it deserves some attention in an exploration of the soteriology of Acts. Of course, at one level it is important simply to remember that narratives function in part by the interplay of anticipations (progressive discovery) and their redefinition (retrospective recovery). Hence, one must allow Luke to introduce, then alter visions of divine rescue. Can more be said?

Acts 2 contains important hints that Zechariah's vision has not been completely forgotten or waylaid. In the intertextual interplay of Joel's prophecy and its appropriation by Peter, 'salvation' has not been denuded of its apocalyptic connotations—a reminder that the coming of God signifies the downfall of those who oppose God's purpose. Acts 2:40, with its plea to 'save yourselves from this corrupt generation' also assumes a division between those who align themselves with a just God and those who are rebellious toward him (*cf.*, Deut. 32:5). Along these lines, one can also point to the use of Exodus typology to characterize salvation in 3:17-26; 7:25.[30]

Salvation as rescue from peril takes on concrete form elsewhere in Acts also. One thinks immediately of the use of the specific terminology of salvation to signify safe travel in spite of the threat of ambush (23:16-24) or storms at sea (27:31, 43-28:6). This sense is also preserved in the repeated episodes of escape from prison and mob action in Acts (*e.g.*, 5:17-21; 12:1-19; 16:19-40; 19:23-41). Clearly, the notion of 'rescue from enemies' has not been removed from Luke's soteriology.[31]

At the same time, these scenes of rescue do not report or even symbolize the deliverance from foreign domination one might expect from Zechariah's prophecy. Three observations are of interest. First, although Luke does not report the dismantling of Roman overlordship, he does narrate the relativizing of the sovereignty Rome wielded. R. Cassidy has suggested how Acts encourages in its Christian

---

29*E.g.*, Ford (*My Enemy Is My Guest*) argues that Luke establishes a revolutionary portrait of redemption in Luke 1–2 only to counter it in subsequent material; and Tannehill (*e.g.*, 'Israel in Luke–Acts') suggests that Luke guides his readers to experience the story of Israel and its messiah as a 'tragedy'—raising expectations in Luke 1–2 that go unfulfiled in the larger Lukan narrative.

30Note the significant interweaving of titles and language of deliverance in 3:13-15; 5:31; 7:35.

31It is inappropriate to relegate such uses of the vocabulary of salvation to Luke's employment of its 'profane' meaning (*pace*, *e.g.*, George, 'Vocabulaire de salut', 308-9, who sees such usage as a result of the narrative genre of Acts and its Gentile setting). The term 'profane' in this context is already anachronistic; in addition, even these instances of rescue are the outworking of God's aim.

readership an ultimate allegiance to Jesus which has as its corollary a
critical socio-political stance *vis-à-vis* the empire.[32] More subtle and for
this reason more threatening to the Roman order is the fundamental
criticism Luke lodges against the patronal ethic that served as the glue
of the empire, fixing people of all status levels within a network of
relationships of obligation and allegiance and providing divine
legitimation to the 'universal' patronage and claim of allegiance
exercised by the emperor himself.[33] For example, Acts 4:32-5:11
encourages practices that ignore status disjunctions—promoting
sharing as though all were kin while condemning in the most acute
terms those who attempt to present themselves as brokers or patrons
to the community. Second, though limited, there are passages in Acts
that portray salvation as 'life' (*e.g.*, 2:21, 28; 3:15; 13:47-48), including
eternal life or otherwise point to salvation in its future consummation
(*e.g.*, 1:11; 3:19-21). This suggests that expectations for deliverance not
fulfiled within the Lukan narrative are not necessarily thereby
negated, for the story of divine redemption continues to be written
beyond the close of Acts 28. Finally, when it is observed that, for Luke,
the real enemy from which deliverance is needed is not Rome but the
cosmic power of evil resident and active behind all forms of opposition
to God and God's people, it is plain that Zechariah's hope has not been
dashed but clarified and, indeed, radicalized. This form of salvation—
from the power of darkness, of Satan—is prominent in Acts.[34]

(3) Salvation as forgiveness of sins. Luke presents the mission of Jesus
especially in terms of 'release' (Luke 4:18-19), then develops this
concept along three lines. Typically in the third Gospel, ἀφίημι / ἄφεσις
has to do with forgiveness of sins, as in the Lord's Prayer (11:4a; *cf.*,
5:17-26). It is also clear that the 'release' made available via Jesus'
ministry is set in opposition to the binding power of Satan. Especially
in Luke 13:10-17 and Acts 10:38, healing is not only physical but
signifies wholeness, freedom from both diabolic and social restrictions, as well.[35] A third way of construing 'release' in the Lukan
narrative, also present in the Lord's Prayer, is 'release from debts'
(Luke 11:4).[36] We have already noted how 'salvation' in Acts is developed with reference to healing and to economic *koinonia*. Similarly,
salvation as forgiveness is continued in Luke's second volume. In Acts

---

[32]*Society and Politics*. See also Rosenblatt, *Paul the Accused*.
[33]*Cf.*, Green, *Theology of Luke*, 119-21.
[34]See, *e.g.*, 26:17-18; 5:16; 13:4-12; 16:16-18; 19:8-20; Garrett, *Demise of the Devil*.
[35]See Green, 'Daughter of Abraham'; Busse, *Wunder*.

2, for example, Peter promises those who undergo a repentance-baptism 'forgiveness of sins' (2:38; cf., Luke 3:3), and this anticipates the further development of a major emphasis in Acts (see 3:19; 5:31; 10:43; 13:38; 15:9; 22:16; 26:18). Indeed, 'forgiveness' can appear in balanced apposition with 'salvation' in Acts, or as a synecdoche for 'salvation'.[37] This signals a renewed/new relationship with God, of course, but also with God's people: as sin is the means by which persons exclude themselves or are excluded from the community of God's people, so forgiveness marks their restoration to the community.

(4) Salvation as reception of the Holy Spirit. Peter also promises those who respond to the message that they will receive 'the gift of the Holy Spirit' (2:38), an emphasis that will resurface repeatedly (9:17; 10:43-44; 11:15-17; 15:8). The gift of the Spirit marks persons, whether Gentile or Jew, as members of the community of God's people, and thus clarifies the status of those, especially Gentiles, who believe: God has received them into the community, quite apart from the self-understanding or strategy of that community (esp. 10:45, 47–11:15-18; 15:8). The gift of the Spirit also signifies the empowering for missionary involvement, for in Acts, the Spirit directs and empowers the mission.[38]

This brief exploration of the content of salvation in Acts has underscored how pervasive soteriology is for Acts, so that salvation can properly be called the theme of Acts. From its content we move easily into a discussion of its basis.

III. 'God has brought a Saviour'

Most now agree that, though Luke does not oppose the attribution of atoning significance to Jesus' death, the cross does not figure prominently as the basis for his soteriology.[39] Instead, Luke presents Jesus' exaltation (i.e., resurrection and ascension) as the salvific event.[40] After surveying representative evidence for this emphasis in Acts, we will

36Esler (Community and Gospel, 181-2) believes that 'release' must be taken literally, so that the holding of thousands of Jewish slaves following the Roman conquest of AD 70 provides the Sitz im Leben for this mandate. But Luke does not develop this meaning anywhere in Luke–Acts.
37See 13:26//38; 4:10-12//10:43; 10:43//11:14; 5:31; Throckmorton, 'Σώζειν', 518. This does not mean the expressions, 'forgiveness of sins' and 'salvation' are synonymous; salvation in Acts includes but is not defined narrowly as forgiveness.
38See below, ch. 16.

go on to suggest how this interpretation of Jesus' exaltation is coordinated with Luke's theology and to comment briefly on the role of Jesus' death in Luke's soteriology.

Exaltation as salvific event

Again it will be helpful to take as our point of departure material from Acts 2, for already here Luke sets forth the logic of his soteriology. In this respect, the citation from Joel 2 is paramount, as it contains at its beginning and end two central aspects of the Lukan soteriology— respectively, the universalistic reach of salvation identified above all as reception of the Spirit on the one hand, and the identification of 'the Lord' as the agent of salvation on the other. Not every detail of the Joel citation is actualized within its new context in Acts 2, but this accent on 'the Lord' anticipates the christological climax of Peter's speech in v. 36: 'Therefore let the entire house of Israel surely know that God has made him both Lord and Messiah Luke–Acts, this Jesus whom you crucified'. As Lord, Jesus is the one on whom people call for salvation. How did Jesus come to be regarded as Lord? The exegesis represented in Peter's use of Psalms 16 and 110 is crucial, demonstrating that it is via his exaltation to God's right hand that Jesus is Lord (vv. 29-35).[41] What is more, v. 33 makes plain the answer to the question arising in v. 12, 'What does this mean?' The phenomena under question are only the sequelae of the outpouring of the Spirit, itself the consequence of Jesus' exaltation. That is, a corollary of Jesus' being raised up is that he now administers the promise of the Father (*cf.*, Luke 11:13; 24:49; Acts 1:4), the gift of the Spirit,[42]*i.e.*, salvation.

Having established this nexus between the phrase 'the name of the Lord', Jesus' exaltation, and salvation, the narrator proceeds to build on this understanding in various ways.[43] For example, in the next dramatic episode, the 'complete health' of the man born lame is

---

[39]See Luke 22:19b-20; Acts 20:28. See the discussion in Green, 'God's Servant'. The significance of these texts is downplayed by Pilgrim, 'Death of Christ', who insists, *e.g.*, that Acts 20:28 is not an expression of Luke's own thought. From the standpoint of a narrative analysis, however, such a distinction cannot be drawn so carefully—*cf.*, Booth, *Rhetoric of Fiction*, 18.

[40]*Cf.*, Marshall, 'Resurrection', and his *Luke: Historian*, 169-75; George, 'Mort de Jesus'; and more recently, Tannehill, *Narrative Unity*, 2:27-40.

[41]*Cf.*, Juel, *Messianic Exegesis*, 146-47.

[42]*Cf.*, Turner, 'Spirit of Christ', 179-81.

[43]*Cf.*, Barrett, *Acts*, 1:200.

attributed to the efficacy of 'the name' (3:16); importantly, this conclusion is reached via a rehearsal of the theological significance of Jesus' being raised up (3:13-15). Later, in 4:11-12, a statement regarding God's vindication of Jesus (*i.e.*, the resurrection—*cf.*, v. 10, to which v. 11 is set in parallel) leads into a declaration of the universal significance of Jesus' name for salvation.[44]

Perhaps the clearest affirmation in Acts of the soteriological meaning of Jesus' exaltation comes in 5:30-31: 'The God of our ancestors raised up Jesus....God exalted him at his right hand as Leader (ἀρχηγός)[45] and Saviour, to give repentance to Israel and the forgiveness of sins'. This is a straightforward affirmation that Jesus' confirmation as Saviour, as the one who 'gives' repentance and forgiveness, is grounded in his resurrection and ascension.

Of course, Jesus was designated Lord and Saviour already, in Luke 2:11, and throughout his public ministry he engaged in a ministry of 'release', bringing repentance and forgiveness to Israel. Hence, it would be inaccurate to suggest that, with his exaltation, Jesus *becomes* Lord, Leader, Saviour. Rather, 'just as there are several important stages in the life of a king, from birth as heir to the throne to the anointing..., to actual assumption of the throne, so in the life of Jesus according to Luke'.[46] As the enthroned one (Messiah) and Benefactor of the people (Lord), the exalted Jesus now reigns as Saviour, pouring out the blessings of salvation, including the Spirit with whom he was anointed at the outset of his ministry, to all.

Jesus as Saviour, God as Saviour

For Luke, however, this is not the whole story. As much as it is important in his soteriology to accord privilege to Jesus' role as Saviour, it is of greater consequence to affirm that salvation is first and always from God. This is evident above all in the way Acts continues the theme begun in the third Gospel of the divine purpose at work (*e.g.*, 2:23; 3:18; 4:28; 13:27; 17:31). The fundamental narrative aim of the Lukan narrative is God's. This attracts opponents (*e.g.*, the Jewish leadership

---

44*Cf.*, Soards, *Speeches*, 46-47; Tannehill, *Narrative Unity*, 2:39-40.
45Given the parallel in 3:15 and Jesus' role here as the one from whom the blessings of salvation are available, ἀρχηγός—a lexeme with 'an extremely polyvalent spectrum of meaning' (Müller, 'ἀρχηγός', *EDNT* I:163)—apparently belongs in the same semantic field for Luke as 'Lord'.
46Tannehill, *Narrative Unity*, 2:39.

in Jerusalem) as well as helpers (*e.g.*, those who are witnesses 'to the end of the earth'). Throughout the Gospel, Jesus manifests a radical commitment to God's redemptive aim, in spite of competing agenda (*e.g.*, Luke 4:1-13; 22:39-46). As God's Son, Jesus serves God's aim and is God's agent of salvation.

God initiates salvation. What is more, even in the salvific activity of Jesus, God is the (often silent but nonetheless) primary actor. In the Pentecost address, *e.g.*, Jesus' powerful deeds are attributed to God (2:22), just as in the speech to the household of Cornelius Jesus is said to have gone about doing good and healing all who were oppressed by the devil, 'having first been anointed by God with the Holy Spirit and power, 'for God was with him' (10:38). God appointed him Lord and Messiah; God glorified him, sent him, raised him, *et al.* Though Jesus is the agent of salvation, God's redemptive plan was operative prior to Jesus' birth and subsequent to his ascension (*cf.*, 13:16-41); before Luke's soteriology is christocentric, it is theocentric.[47] Given the strength of this emphasis, it is not surprising that those who align themselves with God's salvific aim in Acts are never credited with possessing the power to minister salvation. The signs and wonders that partially constitute their missionary activity are effected by God, granted by the Lord (*cf.*, 3:12, 16; 4:10, 29-30; 5:12, 38-39; 8:18-24; 14:3, 14-15; *et al.*).

The death of Jesus and the soteriology of Acts

What, then, is the place of the crucifixion in Lukan soteriology? Among recent attempts to find a 'theology of the cross' in Luke, two are representative. First, R. Fuller has insisted that efforts to deny a Lukan interest in atonement theology are unfair; after all, statistically speaking, Luke has as many explicit references to the salvific meaning of the cross (Luke 22:19-20; Acts 20:28) as does Mark (10:45; 14:24).[48] Statistically speaking, however, this is a glaring over-statement, for Luke–Acts is not only much longer than Mark, but, in the speeches in Acts, the Third Evangelist also has many more opportunties than does Mark to outline what he regards as 'the Christian kerygma'. The most that can be said from Fuller's discussion, but this ought to be said, is that Luke neither opposes nor particularly emphasizes the salvific

---

[47]The primacy of Luke's theology is emphasized in Soards, *Speeches*.
[48]Fuller, 'Theologia Crucis'.

interpretation of the cross. Second, J. Fitzmyer has attempted to re-habilitate a soteriological interpretation for the death of Jesus by an engaging exegesis of Jesus' saying from the cross, 'Today you shall be with me in paradise' (Luke 23:43).[49] He insists that Luke portrays God's plan as coming to fruition through, not in spite of, the cruci-fixion of Jesus, that Luke portrays Jesus exercising his regal power of salvation from the cross, and that Jesus' 'transfer to paradise', from his death and burial to glory, has soteriological effect. What is missing here is any discussion of the instrumentality of the death of Jesus as a soteriological event, though Fitzmyer's essay helpfully reminds us that, to say that Luke does not accord soteriological significance to Jesus' death is not to say that Jesus' death is without meaning in redemption history.[50]

The sheer frequency of times that we read in Acts of the divine necessity (δεῖ) of the suffering of Jesus is warning enough that salvation has not come *in spite of* the crucifixion of Jesus. What is more, the specifically covenantal language employed in 20:28 (περιποιέομαι, 'to acquire'; *cf.*, Exod. 19:5; Isa. 43:21) and 20:32; 26:18 (ἁγιάζω, 'to sanctify'; *cf.*, Deut. 33:3) reminds us of Luke's record of Jesus' last meal with his disciples wherein he grounds the 'new covenant' in his own death (Luke 22:19-20).[51] Although sparsely mentioned, the salvific effect of the cross is not absent from Luke, even if it is not woven fully into the fabric of Luke's theology of the cross.[52] Luke's perspective on the suffering of the Messiah can be outlined along three interrelated lines.

We may gain our bearings by noting how Luke has staged the episode of Jesus' death in Luke 23:44-49, indicating how opposition to Jesus (symbolized for Luke in the darkness/failure of the sun [*cf.*, 22:53]) led to Jesus' death, the results of which are the repentance of the Jewish crowds and the exemplary confession of the Gentile centurion. That is, the rejection of Jesus by the Jewish leadership in Jerusalem leads to the widening of the mission to embrace all peoples, Jew and Gentile.[53] Earlier in the Gospel, we are informed (*cf.*, Luke 21:13-19),

---

49Fitzmyer, *Luke the Theologian*, 203-33.
50*Cf.*, Enuwosa, 'Η φύση τοῦ θανάτου τοῦ Ἰησοῦ'; Glöckner, *Verkündigung des Heils*; Kodell, 'Death of Jesus'; Garrett, 'Jesus' Death in Luke'; Tiede, 'Contending with God'.
51On the originality of vv. 19b-20, see Green, *Death of Jesus*, 35-40.
52One might argue that Luke thus everywhere *assumes* an atonement theology, but this does not account for his choice to emphasize much more fully and explicitly other ways of construing the significance of Jesus' death.

suffering and rejection foster the propagation of the word.[54] Similarly, in Acts, the rejection of Jesus—first, by the Jewish leadership in Jerusalem, then by some Jews in other locales (*e.g.*, 13:44-49; 14:1-18; 18:2-6; 28:17-29)—leads to the spread of the mission. The missionary program of Acts 1:8 is grounded in this: Jerusalem is the place of Jesus' passion and the first locus of hostility toward the apostolic mission, and this hostility will foster the spread of the gospel. As Luke is fond of narrating, struggle and opposition do not impede but seem actually to promote the progress of the gospel: 'It is through many persecutions that we must enter the kingdom of God' (14:22; *cf.*, Acts 6:1-7; 8:1-3,4.)

Second, this citation of the words of Paul in the narrative of Acts, set as it is in the immediate aftermath of the stoning of Paul, urges a reading of the passion of Jesus as in some way paradigmatic for all of those who follow Jesus. As C.K. Barrett has demonstrated, Jesus' words to his disciples, 'If any want to become my followers, let them...take up their cross day after day' (Luke 9:23), portend a lifetime of discipleship as cross-bearing, exemplified in the life of people like Paul in the narrative of Acts (*cf.*, 9:16). For Luke, the *theologia crucis* is rooted not so much in a theory of the atonement, but in a narrative portrayal of the life of faithful discipleship as the way of the cross.[55]

Third, in describing Jesus' crucifixion, Acts echoes the words of Deuteronomy 21:22-23:

'When someone is convicted of a crime punishable by death and is executed, and you hang him on a tree, his corpse must not remain all night upon the tree; you shall bury him that same day, for anyone hung on a tree is under God's curse'.

Acts 5:30: 'The God of our ancestors raised up Jesus, whom you had killed by hanging him on a tree'.

Acts 10:39: 'The Jewish leaders in Jerusalem had Jesus put to death by hanging him on a tree'.

Acts 13:29: 'They took him down from the tree...'.

Luke–Acts (*cf.*, Luke 23:39) accounts for four of the six uses of κρεμμάνυμι ('to hang'; *cf.*, Gal. 3:13; 1 Peter 2:24), also employed in the deuteronomic text, suggesting the formative influence of the LXX of Deuteronomy 21:22-23 on Luke's understanding of the cross.[56] No doubt in conversation with early Christian use of Deuteronomy 21:22-23 in the interpretation of the cross of Jesus, Luke thus signalled his

---

53See Green, 'Demise of the Temple'.
54See Dillon, *From Eye-Witnesses*, 210-15; Schütz, *Leidende Christus*, 109-12.
55Barrett, 'Theologia Crucis'. *Cf.*, Korn, *Geschichte Jesu*, 242-59; Carroll and Green, *Death of Jesus in Early Christianity*, ch. 4; Pilgrim, 'Death of Christ'.

awareness of the disgrace of Jesus' execution. He does not employ Deuteronomy 21:23 in order to repudiate this shame, however, but in order to acknowledge it. These allusions serve to locate Jesus' death firmly in the necessity of God's purpose. The ultimate disgrace, the curse from God, is antecedent to exaltation. The deuteronomic text is thus used in a parodic way, transforming the earlier passage beyond what one might regard as its original aim by applying it to God's Anointed One. The execution of Jesus on a cross, then, was shameful in every way, and from both Roman and Jewish points of view.[57]

These two—the cross of Jesus and the cross-bearing of those who follow him—are intimately related. In his suffering and resurrection, Jesus embodied the fullness of salvation interpreted as status reversal; his death was the centrepoint of the divine-human struggle over how life is to be lived, in humility or self-glorification. Though anointed by God, though righteous before God, though innocent, he is put to death. Rejected by people, he is raised up by God—and with him the least, the lost, the left-out are also raised. In his death, and in consequence of his resurrection by God, the way of salvation is exemplified and made accessible to all those who will follow.

IV. 'What must I do to be saved?'

The unfortunate predicament Luke faces in his narration of Acts is directly related to his presentation of the theme of salvation. All, Jew and Gentile, are called to welcome gladly the good news of divine intervention in history, but all do not, and some, especially from among the Jewish people, actively oppose the Way. It is not too much to say that the proclamation of the Christian message *demands* response in Acts, but a positive response, one in which people actually accept for themselves the gracious offer of salvation and so (re-)orient themselves around God's purpose, is not guaranteed.

The necessity of response is set forth programmatically in the narration of the Pentecost address where Peter is interrupted by his

---

56This passage from Deuteronomy does not envision crucifixion *per se*, but rather impalement of the body of the executed after death. Nevertheless, in pre-Christian times, it was already being applied to the victims of crucifixion. See, *e.g.*, Philo *Spec. Leg.* 3.152; *Post. C.* 61; *Somn.* 2.213; 4QpNah 3-4.1.7-8; 11QTemple 64.6-13; *cf.*, Schreiber, 'ξύλον', *TDNT* V:37-41; Fitzmyer, 'Crucifixion in Ancient Palestine'. *Cf.*, Wilcox, 'Upon the Tree'.
57See Carroll and Green, *Death of Jesus in Early Christianity*, ch. 9.

audience. 'Cut to the heart', they ask, 'Brothers, what shall we do?' (2:37). This is only the first of many occasions on which speakers in Acts will be similarly interrupted, though not always with such openness to the message. In 4:1 certain Jewish authorities break off the speech of Peter and John in order to arrest them. Speeches by Stephen and Paul are terminated prematurely by those who react in anger and wish them harm (7:54; 22:22; cf. 13:44-45; 26:24). Others, however, respond more positively. Indeed, at one point it is the Holy Spirit who interrupts Peter in a scene that registers dramatically the openness of Cornelius and his household to the message (10:44). The record of reactions to Paul's preaching at Athens is representative: having heard, some scoffed, others expressed their willingness to hear more from Paul, and some joined him, becoming believers (17:32-33). Such texts witness to the pervasiveness of the motif of response in Acts, while exhibiting the diversity of ways in which the message of salvation might be greeted.[58]

Why some sort of response is necessary is also clear in the Pentecost address. According to Peter, the exaltation of Jesus and the consequent outpouring of the Holy Spirit have signalled a dramatic transformation in history. Because these are 'the last days' (2:17), life can no longer be the same. To put it somewhat differently, the message of Jesus' witnesses calls for a radically different understanding of the 'world' than that held previously.[59] Within the speeches of Acts, Jewish people might hear the stories of their ancestors, to be sure, but these stories have been cast so as to encourage a reading of that history that underscores the fundamental continuity between the ancient story of Israel, the story of Jesus, and the story of the Way.[60] Israel's past (and present) is correctly understood and embraced fully only when understood vis-à-vis the redemptive purpose of God, but this divine purpose can be understood only as articulated by authorized interpretive agents—first, Jesus of Nazareth, and then his witnesses.[61] Thus, e.g., Paul's question to King Agrippa, 'Do you believe the prophets?'

---

[58]Luke marks the possibility of negative responses early on in Acts—e.g., we hear that Judas 'turned away' (Luke 22:4: ἀπελθών; Acts 1:25: παρέβη; cf. Brawley, Centering on God, 180-81) and that some Jews in Jerusalem sneered when they heard Jesus' disciples proclaiming God's mighty deeds in other languages (2:13).
[59]Our employment of the term 'world' is informed by Berger and Luckmann, Social Construction, and refers to the socially constructed way reality has been understood. Thus, the eschatological work of God in Jesus Christ has rendered obsolete old ways of viewing the world while opening up new ways in conformity with God's eternal purpose.
[60]Cf., Hall, Revealed Histories.

(26:27), concerns not simply a commitment to the prophets, but to the prophets as they have been expounded by Paul. The coming of Jesus as Saviour may signal the fresh offer of repentance and forgiveness of sins to Israel (*e.g.*, 5:31; 13:38-39), but the acceptance of this offer by Jewish people is dependent on their embracing this interpretation of God's salvific activity.[62] Greek audiences, too, are asked to adopt a new way of viewing the world. Note how, at Athens, Paul distinguishes between how God worked in the past (17:30a; *cf.* 14:16) and how he will now operate (17:30b)—a distinction that calls for repentance.

This way of construing conversion in Acts is developed in a variety of ways within the narrative itself. Late in the narrative, for example, Paul recounts his commission from Jesus, who sends him 'to open their eyes so that they might turn from darkness to light and from the power of Satan to God' (26:17-18). In this case, Luke draws on the familiar language of religious conversion,[63] but interprets it so as to situate the redemptive purpose of God within the cosmic battle whereby one kingdom gives way to the other. It is an important component of this text that Gentiles and Jews alike are regarded as in need of deliverance from darkness (*cf.*, Luke 1:78-79). Elsewhere the Christian mission can be represented as one of debate and dialogue— a battle of interpretation, as it were, as Paul calls for receptivity: 'You Israelites, and others who fear God, *listen*!...Let it be known to you, therefore, my brothers....Beware, therefore, that what the prophets said does not happen to you...' (13:16, 38, 41; *cf.*, 17:3; 19:8-10). Among Greek audiences, Paul calls for people to leave the way of idolatry and turn to 'the living God' (14:15-16). In the account of the conversion of the Philippian jailor, the question revolves at least in part around the question of allegiance: Having failed at the task of guarding his prisoners (on behalf of Lord Caesar), the jailor referred to Paul and Silas as 'Lords' (κύριοι), requesting 'salvation' from them. They directed him to place his faith in 'the Lord (κύριος) Jesus' instead, then spoke 'the word of the Lord (κύριος)' to him and his household (16:27-32). Although Luke is concerned with conversion from one form of life to

---

61*Cf.*, Green, *Theology of Luke*, 75. This points to the nature of the fundamental struggle between representatives of the Way and other forms of Judaism, but also provides a rationale for the opposition faced by Jesus' witnesses (and, we may presume, by Luke's audience as well).

62Note, therefore, the characterization of the Beroean Jews as 'more noble', as evidenced by their willingness to examine the Scriptures in light of the message of Paul and Silas (17:11).

63*Cf.*, Hamm, 'Sight to the Blind'.

another, then, he outlines no 'typical' way of understanding the nature
of that conversion.

In effect, the necessary response to the salvific message is initial
and ongoing identification with God's purpose, manifest in the Way.
Beyond this, the Lukan narrative supports no technique or pattern of
conversion.[64] It is true that two texts in particular seem to present a
paradigm of response, following as they do the direct questions, 'What
shall we do?' (2:37-38) and 'What must I do to be saved?' (16:30-34). In
the first case, though, Peter counsels his audience to repent and be
baptized. In the second the jailor is told (simply) to believe, though he
and his household respond also with hospitality and baptism. If these
texts were to be understood as establishing a pattern of response, then,
they do so poorly, since the instructions given in the one case may
complement, but certainly do not mimic, the other. If one were able to
discern an 'order of salvation' in these accounts, it would be this: God
initiates→ people hear the message of salvation→ people respond.
This is the heart of Peter's defence of the inclusion of Gentiles in the
community of God's people (15:7-11): 'God made a choice'→ 'Gentiles
hear the message of the good news'→ they become 'believers'.

To deny that Luke presents a particular pattern of response is not
to deny that some forms of response might be regarded as typical in
some sense. (1) 'Baptism in the name of Jesus' is a normal response, as
suggested by the Ethiopian's question (quite apart from any explicitly
narrated prompting from Philip), 'Look, here is water; what is to
prevent me from being baptized?' (8:36; cf., 2:41; 8:12; 9:18; 10:47-48;
16:15; et al.). Within the Lukan narrative, 'baptism' takes its meaning in
part from the ministry of John (Luke 3:1-20), with the result that it
expresses a desire to embrace God's purpose anew and to be embraced
into the community of those similarly oriented around the way of God.
(2) Repentance (or 'turning to God') is often mentioned explicitly as an
appropriate response to God's salvific work (cf., 2:38; 3:19; 5:31; 11:18;
17:30; 20:21; 26:20). Again, Luke's portrayal of this response is rooted
in his account of the ministry of John (esp. Luke 3:1-14), where
repentance is marked by behaviour that grows out of and demonstrates that one has indeed committed oneself to service in God's
purpose (cf., Luke 3:10-14; Acts 26:20). (3) That Christians are sometimes called 'believers' signals the importance of faith in Luke's understanding of salvation (cf., 2:44; 3:16; 11:17; 13:39; 14:9; 15:7; 16:30-31;

---

[64]This point is underscored in Gaventa, *Aspects of Conversion*, 52-129. *Cf.*, also
O'Toole, *Unity*, 191-224.

18:8). Indeed, another name given Jesus' disciples in Acts, 'those who call on the name' (9:14, 21), though rooted exegetically in the citation of Joel 2:32 in Acts 2:21, marks those disciples as those who believe in the name and have identified with the name of Jesus in baptism (2:38; 3:16; 8:12, 16; 9:48; 19:5; 22:16).

What is the appropriate response to the good news of salvation? Luke addresses this question with an arsenal of possibilities—*e.g.*, believe, be baptized, turn to God, listen, see, repent, and so on—but singles out no particular pattern of response as paradigmatic. God has acted graciously in Christ to bring salvation to all humanity. All humanity are called to welcome the good news, to respond with receptivity, and thus to share in that salvation not only as recipients but also as those who serve God's redemptive aim.

V. 'You and your entire household will be saved'

In this essay, however implicitly, we have tried to indicate the degree to which traditional ways of characterizing salvation in Acts have often been the product of readings by nineteenth- and twentieth-century moderns for whom individual-oriented and segregating ways of thinking have come natural. Divisions between social and ecclesial, sacred and profane, politico-economic and spiritual, material and ethereal would not have come so easy for Luke, however, as our analysis has confirmed. That Paul and Silas can speak these words, 'You and your household will be saved', to a Philippian jailor (Acts 16:31) is itself indicative of the inherent polysemy of salvation in Acts, for it suggests the absence of barriers between people and their kin groups, Gentiles and Jews, the spiritual well-being of people and their relation to the empire, and so on.

On the face of it, this expansiveness of meaning is hardly out of step with salvation as broadly understood in the Graeco-Roman world, where everyday life was not separated from the assumed divine legitimation of the Roman structures and relationships by which that world 'worked'. Nor were Luke's emphases likely to astonish persons more steeped in a septuagintal understanding of the content of salvation as Yahweh acting on behalf of his people— whether materially or with respect to forgiveness and restoration. What is of particular interest, then is how the narrative of Acts can articulate with those wider nuances, presupposed within the fabric of this socially constructed world, while at the same time challenging, even working to overturn that world.[65] The inclusion of Gentiles as full and equal partners within the community of God's people, rooted in the affirmation that God has made no such distinction (*e.g.*, 10:15, 34-36; 11:12; 15:9), would certainly have worked against the sensibilities of those who reasoned that the Jewish people shared among themselves a privileged election. The very notion that the lowly, the humiliated, those without power and privilege (among whom Jesus, not least in light of his crucifixion, must be counted) might be the recipients of divine benefaction (beginning with the exaltation of Jesus himself)—this too must have played against the sensibilities of a Graeco–Roman people for whom honour was carefully measured and rationed by long-standing, unbending canons.

    All of this is to say, though, that the God of Israel is portrayed in Acts as the Great Benefactor, Jesus as Lord of all, and that the nature of this benefaction, of this lordship, embodies, enables, and inspires new ways for living in the world.

---

[65]On the 'problem of articulation' informing this discussion, see Wuthnow, *Communities of Discourse*, 1-22.

CHAPTER 6

THE DIVINE SAVIOUR

H. Douglas Buckwalter

Summary

The pulse of Luke's christology is that of the exalted Jesus as God's co-equal. In comparing Jesus' heavenly reign in Acts with Yahweh's in the Old Testament, the parallels are pervasive and deliberate. As with Yahweh, Jesus visibly demonstrates his absolute superiority by personally revealing himself to people through his Spirit and direct self-manifestations, and by bringing to pass what he has personally communicated to them. Luke enhances this portrait of divine christology by showing that as supreme deity, Jesus, by nature, behaves toward his people as 'one who waits on tables'. The exalted Jesus never behaves beneficently for reasons of self-aggrandizement, but to minister to his people.

I. Introduction

Jürgen Roloff raises the intriguing possibility that Peter's identification
of Jesus with Yahweh in Acts 2:21 (τὸ ὄνομα κυρίου, Joel 2:32) reflects
Luke's belief in a pre-existence christology reminiscent of Philippians
2:6-11 and Hebrews 1:3-4.[1] Although Roloff does not press the point,
his suggestion touches on the pulse of Lukan christology. It raises the
possibility that Acts presents a divine christology,[2] where the exalted
Jesus as the Father's co-equal supremely reigns as Lord in heaven.
Building on the wealth of studies on Lukan christology,[3] this essay discusses what Luke's depiction of Jesus in Acts indicates about his christological beliefs concerning Jesus' divine status and its relevance to his
Jewish and Graeco–Roman audience, bearing in mind that Luke does
not record all his beliefs about Jesus.[4] His literary motives and knowledge of the christological grounding of his readers in all probability
shape the kind of christology he incorporates into his writings.

II. A survey of Luke's christology

Luke's christology is complex. Its diversity makes it difficult to reduce
to simple classifications. Scholars debate whether Luke has given it an
overall unity. Wilson argues that Luke does not integrate his christological material into any overall scheme. Its lack of uniformity comes
from Luke's non-reflective and haphazard use of christological titles
and traditions he incorporates into his writings.[5] Others contend that
Luke's christology shows a discernible unity on the basis of some leading christological scheme, portrait or description. These proposals can
be grouped under four general classifications.[6]

---

[1] Roloff, *Apostelgeschichte*, 54-55.
[2] I am indebted for this expression to Turner, 'Spirit of Christ', 168-90, as well as his
'"Divine" Christology', 413-36.
[3] E.g., Moessner, *Lord*; Bock, *Proclamation*; Danker, 'Beneficence', 57-67; Barrett,
'Christology', 237-44; '*Imitatio Christi*', 251-62; Crump, *Jesus the Intercessor*; as well
as his 'Scribal-Intercessor', 51-65; Strauss, *Davidic Messiah*; Buckwalter, *Character*.
[4] E.g., Guthrie, *Theology*, 231 argues that Luke assumes the sinlessness of Jesus in
Acts on the basis of his depiction of Jesus as 'the Holy and Righteous One' (Acts
2:27; 3:14; 4:24-30; 7:52; 17:31). Guthrie concludes: 'Since the amount of Christological material in Acts is severely limited by the author's purpose, it is not surprising
that no more is said explicitly about the sinlessness of Jesus. But there seems little
doubt that it is implied' (*ibid.*). So also Gerhardsson, *Tradition*, 54.
[5] Wilson, S.G., *Luke and the Pastoral Epistles*, 69, 79-80 *et al.*

Christologies emphasizing Jesus' humanity and exemplary functions

This relatively minor position holds that Luke concentrates on the 'man' Jesus for mainly apologetic and exemplary reasons. C.H. Talbert argues that an anti-gnostic polemic governs Luke's main christological focus and purpose in writing.[7] According to G.W.H. Lampe, Luke's distinctive christological portrait is his emphasis on the imitation of Christ. Luke illustrates through Jesus' life and ministry the sort of things that his followers can imitate (as Acts then bears out). Lampe, however, leaves his thesis largely undeveloped.[8]

Christologies emphasizing Jesus' subordinate relation to God

A more dominant position maintains that Luke deliberately subordinates Jesus to God's plan of saving history in hopes of injecting new life into a church shaken by the parousia's delay. According to H. Conzelmann, Luke replaces the expectation of Jesus' imminent return with the portrayal of Jesus as an instrument of God, both in his earthly life and in the memory of him after his death. In God's plan of salvation-history, Luke now views Jesus' death as martyrdom, his resurrection as symbolic of the believer's hope, and his life as symbolic of God's programmme of universal mission. As God's instrument, Luke does not perceive Jesus as Lord of the universe, but as subordinate to God.[9] Building on Conzelmann's thesis, E. Kränkl stresses Jesus' subordination, but in terms of a servant christology. God is exclusively the creator of the plan of salvation; Jesus functions only as its mediator. The title 'servant of God' in Acts designates Jesus as the culmination of the line of OT servants of God. The exalted Lord now stands in God's plan of salvation-history as the continuum between Israel and the church.[10]

6See further Buckwalter, *Character*, 6-24.
7Talbert, *Gnostics*; as well as his 'Tendency', 259-71.
8Lampe, 'Portrait', 160-75, esp. 167, 172-75.
9Conzelmann, *Luke*, 170-79, 184.
10Kränkl, *Knecht*.

Christologies emphasizing Jesus' function as Saviour

In countering Conzelmann's position, numerous scholars propose that Jesus' work as Saviour plays the leading christological role in Luke–Acts. Luke's belief in Jesus as God's instrument or mediator does not spring from some refashioned model of salvation-history for eschatological reasons. Rather, as I.H. Marshall and others argue, Jesus' intercessory role stems from his personal work as Saviour of the world.[11] J.B. Green asserts that Luke emphasizes Jesus' mediatorial role according to Isaiah's Servant of Yahweh and the soteriological theme of reversal. This christology, he believes, may strongly influence the substructure of Luke's entire two-volume work. Luke intends to show how Jesus as Isaiah's suffering servant embodies the idea of 'reversal' or 'transposition' in his effort to clarify the nature of salvation and discipleship. As the humble Servant of Yahweh, Jesus accomplishes God's plan by obediently giving up his life on the cross, after which he is exalted, makes available salvation to all people and so provides the model of true discipleship for his followers.[12] Frieder Schütz connects Luke's main christological concern to Jesus' passion suffering. For Schütz, Luke's emphasis on suffering in both books indicates that the readers were undergoing severe opposition from opponents of Christianity. Luke depicts a christology of the cross to give them perspective on their suffering. He accomplishes this by showing how Jesus' suffering was analogous to Luke's community. For Jesus, the cross formed an important stage leading to his exaltation; it defined what it meant for him to be 'Saviour'. For Luke's church, their suffering confirms their allegiance to Jesus and appears as the primary means by which God spreads the gospel to all nations.[13]

Christologies emphasizing Jesus' authoritative status

A major position among Lukan scholars defends christologies centering on Jesus' authoritative status as Luke's main christological concern. Here the accent is on Jesus' Lordship. F.W. Danker, for example, believes that Luke intentionally presented Jesus as a 'super-star', 'hero' or 'benefactor' from Graeco–Roman models of deities or people of

---

11*Cf.*, Marshall, *Luke:Historian*, 19, 85-86, 93, 102, 116-17, 125, 176-78.
12Green, 'God's Servant', 18-28, and 'Mount of Olives', 41-43.
13Schütz, *Leidende Christus.*

extraordinary endowment, class and merit to bridge the Jewish and Gentile religious-cultural experience. Luke details his christology of beneficence from Jesus' earthly ministry and heavenly reign.[14] D. Moessner formalizes a christological trend in Lukan studies, which sees a typological parallel between Jesus and the Deuteronomic view of Moses as presented in Luke's travel narrative. He believes that such a parallel stands at the heart of the christology of the central section of Luke's Gospel (9:51-19:44) and, though never stated outright, at the heart of the christology of Luke–Acts as well. At the core of Luke's christology, Moessner believes, is the twofold Deuteronomic depiction of stubborn Israel, a people always resisting God, and of the mediating suffering and death of his chosen prophet, who redeems Israel from their sin: as Deuteronomy depicts Moses' death outside the land as a necessary punishment for Israel's sin, so Luke depicts Jesus' death as atoning on behalf of a nation stubbornly refusing to accept Jesus' preaching of the good news of the kingdom of God.[15] E. Earle Ellis defends a messianic christology as Luke's main christological concern. Jesus appears in Luke–Acts as the means through which God brings salvation to Israel and the world. His life, death and glorification become the prototype for Christians. His mission as Messiah makes salvation universally available and provides the pattern for Christian living.[16] Taking a similar position, A.R.C. Leaney defends Jesus' kingship as Luke's governing christology. Luke portrays Jesus as a royal personality and the series of events which led to his enthronement; Luke emphasizes Jesus' kingly power to forgive sins, as experienced by his followers and proclaimed by them to others in his name.[17]

Perhaps the most common belief concerning Luke's christology sees his writing interests as closely associated with strengthening the belief that Jesus is Lord. E. Franklin maintains that Luke wrote 'to strengthen and confirm, and if need be to reawaken, faith in Jesus as the present Lord, and it was to this end that his theological interpretation was directed'.[18] Bock argues that Luke's use of OT citations and allusions reveals the christology he seeks to present in his two-volume work. He perceives Luke's main christological categories as essentially

---

14Danker, *Benefactor*; 'and 'Cultural Accommodation', 391-414, as well as his 'Beneficence', 57-67.
15Moessner, *Lord*.
16Ellis, *Luke*, 9-12, 32-36.
17Leaney, *Luke*, 34-37.
18Franklin, 'Ascension', 191-200, as well as his *Christ the Lord* , 48.

twofold, the first being subordinate to the second. From the Gospel's outset to Jesus' last days in Jerusalem, Luke stresses from OT ideas 'the foundational declaration of Jesus as a regal Messiah-Servant'; from this point onward Luke shifts his focus to OT elements suggesting that Jesus is 'a more than Messiah figure' to emphasize 'the climactic declaration that Jesus is Lord'—Luke's 'supreme christo-logical concept.'[19] Lastly, G. Voss and M. Wren argue that Luke's fundamental christological concern is to explicate Jesus' divine Sonship. For example, on the basis of an analysis of Luke 1–4, Wren believes that Luke develops in the remainder of his work the spreading acknowledgment or rejection of the foundational truth that Jesus is the Son of God.[20]

In summing up, this survey illustrates the complexity of Luke's christology: although most of these proposals are integral to the christology of Luke–Acts (Talbert and Conzelmann's are doubtful), they cannot all stand simultaneously as its leading or governing christological concern. From among these proposals, however, two common elements emerge. First, Luke describes something of Jesus' divine status, whether in favourable or somewhat diminutional terms, according to his writing purposes. Second, Luke points out that the way the earthly and heavenly Jesus behaves is instructional for discipleship. In the remainder of this essay, we shall look at the christological dimension of these points and their relevance for the Jewish and Graeco–Roman reader.

III. A deity who reigns supreme

With the two ascension accounts (Luke 24:50-53; Acts 1:9-11) and the coming of the Holy Spirit at Pentecost (Acts 2), a work that Jesus had promised he would do (Luke 24:49; Acts 1:4-5), Luke makes it clear that the exalted Jesus is for the time being physically removed from the earth and reigning alongside the Father in heaven (*e.g.*, Peter's interpretation of the Pentecost event in Acts 2:32-33 and to some onlookers to a miracle in 3:21). The language Luke uses to describe Jesus' heavenly reign in the speeches and narrative sections of Acts is important. It discloses his belief concerning the extent of Jesus' kingly reign as Lord.[21] Luke's emphasis that Jesus reigns alongside the Father

19Bock, *Proclamation*, 262, 265.
20Voss, *Christologie*, 173-5, and 'Herrn', 236-8; Wren, 'Sonship', 301-11.

in heaven raises the possibility that he depicts in Acts the exalted Jesus as present within the church in the same way that the OT describes transcendent Yahweh as immanently involved with Israel.

Transcendent Yahweh as immanent deity

The OT authors unanimously describe Yahweh as fully transcendent and distinct from creation and at the same time immanently involved with it in providentially guiding it according to his redemptive purposes. A primary way that Yahweh communicates his presence to people in the OT is by his Spirit.[22] But he also frequently appears personally and directly to people apart from his Spirit through numerous self-manifestations: in particular, the angel of the Lord, the face of God, the glory of God and the name of God.[23]

a. The Angel of the Lord. The OT so closely connects Yahweh to the angel of Yahweh that 'the line between a representative and an actual appearance of God cannot be sharply drawn'.[24] The angel of the Lord signifies God's presence[25] and a form of divine manifestation.[26] The angel of the Lord, for example, speaks in the first person as God himself (Gen. 16:10; 21:18; 22:12,16-18; Judg. 2:1-3; 6:16,18), calls himself God (Gen. 31:13; Exod. 2:6), accepts worship as God (Gen. 16:13; 22:14; Exod. 2:6; Judg. 6:22,24; 13:22) and promises to Israel his continued divine presence in the form of an angel (Exod. 23:20-21).

b. The Face of God. According to the OT, no finite being can see God's face in the fullness of its infinite glory and holiness, and live (Exod. 33:20-23). But on numerous occasions, God personally appears to people in veiled form, which the OT describes as 'God revealing his face to them'. For example, because of their encounter with the angel of the Lord, Jacob (Gen. 32:30-31; Hos. 12:3-5) and Gideon (Judg. 6:22) claim to have seen God face to face. The same is said of Moses because of his regular contact with God (Exod. 33:11; Num. 12:8; 14:14). This is also how God will deal with rebellious Israel (Ezek. 20:35). This OT

[21]See also the discussions of Bock, *Proclamation*; Strauss, *Davidic Messiah*.
[22]See further, *e.g.*, Baumgärtel, 'πνεῦμα', *TDNT* VI:362-67.
[23]See, *e.g.*, Eichrodt, *Theology*, vol. 2, 23-45; von Rad, *Theology*, 1:179-89, 239-40, 285-89; Kaiser, *Theology*, 106-7, 120-1, 133-4, 237-8.
[24]Dyrness, *Themes*, 42.
[25]Eichrodt, *Theology*, 2:24.
[26]von Rad, *Theology*, 1:287.

expression becomes, in effect, another way of describing how God has personally visited people without reservation[27] or restriction.[28]

c. The Glory of God. Within the OT the glory of God is also 'an important *terminus technicus* in describing theophanies'.[29] Moses, for example, saw God's glory pass before him (Exod. 33:18-23). Israel witnessed it in the cloud on Mount Sinai (Exod. 24:15-17; Deut. 5:24) and at the Tent of Meeting (Exod. 16:7,10; Lev. 9:23-24; Num. 14:10). God's glory filled the tabernacle (Exod. 40:34-35) and temple (1 Kings. 8:11; Ps. 63:2). Isaiah and Ezekiel saw God's glory in their visions (Isa. 6:1-4; Ezek. 1:25-28; 3:23, etc.) and at a future point in time the whole world will see God's glory (Isa. 66:18; Hab. 2:14; Hag. 2:7; Zech. 2:5). God's glory acts in the OT as 'an independent manifestation of God'.[30] It becomes 'a veritable theologoumenon of the divine presence'.[31]

d. The Name of God. In the OT Yahweh's name is interchangeable with his person and designates God himself (Exod. 3:15; Deut. 28:58; Job 1:21; Ps. 8:1-9; Isa. 30:27; Jer. 44:26; Ezek. 43:8; Amos 2:7; Zech. 14:9; Mal. 2:2). It reveals his character (Gen. 21:33; Exod. 33:19; 34:14; 1 Chron. 29:16; Ps. 124:8; Prov. 18:10; Isa. 63:16; Amos 4:13), represents his power and authority (Deut. 18:19; Ps. 118:10,26; Jer. 29:9; Ezek. 39:7,25; Dan. 9:6) and signifies his personal presence among Israel (Exod. 20:24; Deut. 14:23; 2 Sam. 7:13; 1 Kings 9:3; 2 Kings 21:7; Neh. 1:9; Ps. 75:1; Isa. 18:7; Jer. 7:12). The divine name guarantees God's presence to people in its totality,[32] without compromising his sovereign transcendence.[33] It becomes 'the side of Yahweh presented to man'.[34]

On the basis of this discussion, we have good grounds to conclude that OT theology firmly asserts that by divine initiative the transcendent creator God has personally appeared to people and made his will known to them. These divine self-manifestations indicate that at times God appears directly to people apart from his Spirit. The OT equally balances God's transcendence and immanence; it never presents one to the negation of the other. In fact, what distinguishes

---

27Jacob, *Theology*, 78.
28Dyrness, *Themes*, 42.
29von Rad, *Theology*, 1:240.
30Vriezen, *Theology*, 208.
31Jacob, *Theology*, 80.
32Jacob, *Theology*, 85.
33Eichrodt, *Theology*, 2:41-42.
34Bietenhard, 'ὄνομα', *TDNT* V:257.

God from all other 'supernatural powers' is that he visibly demonstrates his absolute superiority by personally revealing himself to people through his Spirit and direct self-manifestations, and by bringing to pass what he has personally communicated to them.

The exalted Jesus as immanent deity

Luke preserves in his writings this OT depiction of God immanently appearing to his people through his Spirit (Luke 2:26), glory (Luke 2:9; Acts 7:55) and name (Luke 13:35; Acts 15:17). But what is of considerable interest to our study is that he shows the exalted Jesus behaving in like manner. It should be noted here that Luke's heavy use of the OT suggests that even his intended Christian Gentile readers were quite familiar with it from Christian teaching and preaching.

a. Jesus and his Spirit. It is Jesus, according to Acts 2:33, who pours out the Spirit upon his followers gathered in Jerusalem. It is the Spirit of Jesus who redirects Paul to Macedonia rather than to Bithynia in Acts 16:7. This latter passage is especially revealing. The phrase 'the Spirit of Jesus' occurs in narrative comment and therefore probably reflects a Lukan viewpoint rather than a repetition of some stock phrase.[35] The Lukan phrase is unparalleled in the NT. Its closest parallels are in Philippians 1:19 'the Spirit of Jesus Christ' and Galatians 4:6 'the Spirit of his son'. Moreover, this description of the Spirit matches the way the OT commonly speaks of the Spirit in relation to deity as 'the Spirit of God/the Lord'—OT designations common to Acts as well. Peter, for example, tells Ananias, 'You have not lied to men but to *God*' (Acts 5:4), but to Sapphira he says, 'How could you agree to test the Spirit of the Lord?' (v. 9). Luke reflects here the close unity that the OT draws between Yahweh and his Spirit (*cf.*, Isa. 34:16; 63:10-14). In describing the Spirit as 'the Spirit of Jesus' in Acts 16:7, Luke indicates a similar unity. Here, the exalted Jesus sovereignly guides the mission of the church through his Spirit.

Acts also pictures Jesus as doing the same kind of work among his people as does his Spirit. Luke anticipates this phenomenon in his Gospel doublet (12:11-12/21:14-15). In the first Jesus encourages his disciples not to fear what they should say when they are hauled into court because the Spirit will inspire their words. But in the second

---

[35]*Cf.*, Marshall, *Luke: Historian*, 181.

instance Jesus uniquely refers to himself as the divine source of inspiration of the disciples' witness before their adversaries: 'For I will give you words and wisdom that none of your adversaries will be able to resist or contradict'. The expression ἐγὼ δώσω ('I myself will give') in Luke 21:15 is emphatic and draws attention to Jesus' coming heavenly work in this regard. Luke anticipates in the doublet a thorough blending of the coming ministry of the exalted Jesus and that of the promised Spirit. They both will be personally active in the church's witness. Acts bears this out. (We will discuss, however, the instances relating to Jesus under the next point below.)

Luke explicitly connects the persuasive power and authority of Peter and Stephen's preaching to the Spirit's presence. In Acts 4:8-22, Peter and John are filled with the Spirit (v. 8) and impressively bear witness to Jesus before the Sanhedrin (v. 13). In a later appearance before the Sanhedrin (Acts 5:27-40) Peter climaxes his speech with the comment: 'We are witnesses of these things, and so is the Holy Spirit, whom God has given to those who obey him' (v. 32). The Spirit actively bears witness to the gospel message as God's intended saving plan through them. Luke further comments in Acts 6:10 that Stephen spoke with faultless and uncontestable authority through the Holy Spirit. In light of Paul's filling with the Spirit soon after his conversion (Acts 9:17-19), presumably Luke intends his witness to Jesus as recorded in Acts to be understood as Spirit-inspired as well.

Thus as the Spirit's presence describes Yahweh's immanence in the OT, in a passage like Acts 2:33, where Jesus is said to have given the Spirit at Pentecost, the Spirit's presence also becomes a way of talking about Jesus' immanence.[36] Acts 2:33 and 16:7 imply that the Spirit represents,[37] if not mediates,[38] the exalted Jesus' presence and continued activity among his people. In either case, the Spirit is closely identified with Jesus; he extends the personal presence of the exalted Lord Jesus himself.

b. The visionary appearances of the exalted Jesus. Luke depicts a number of direct self appearances of the exalted Jesus to his people in Acts. For example, Acts 6:10 alludes to the exalted Jesus' personal participation in inspiring the witness of his followers. Luke mentions

---

[36]Turner, 'Spirit of Christ', 183 and n. 69.
[37]Lofthouse, 'Holy Spirit', 336; Reicke, 'Risen Lord', 162; Moule, 'Christology', 165,179; Lampe, Spirit, 72; Krodel, 'Functions', 36.
[38]Kränkl, Knecht, 180-81; MacRae, 'Christology', 161; Stählin, 'Πνεῦμα 'Ιησοῦ', 235; Turner, 'Spirit of Christ', 183.

that Stephen's enemies were unable to counter 'the wisdom or the Spirit by whom he spoke'. Luke most assuredly mentions the σοφία characterizing Stephen's witness purposefully to illustrate the fulfilment of Jesus' promise in Luke 21:15. Whether Jesus gave the wisdom through the Spirit's mediation[39] or more directly himself,[40] in either instance he is personally responsible for the wisdom that is given.

Acts 18:9-10, however, provides a clearer example of Jesus personally directing the witness of his followers. Jesus appears to Paul in a vision and encourages him in language reminiscent of OT theophany and prophetic calling: 'Do not be afraid; keep on speaking, do not be silent. For I am with you, and no one is going to attack and harm you, because I have many people in this city'. The exalted Jesus guarantees to Paul his continued personal presence with him in his witness to Jesus in Corinth. According to OT passages like Exodus 4:12, the promise of divine presence and assistance means supreme enabling, divine protective power and the possession of the divine authority inherent to it. Jesus, in effect, reassures Paul that his purposes will not fail, despite whatever opposition he may face (cf., Acts 18:12-17; also 1 Cor. 2:1-5). For Luke, the exalted Jesus behaves toward Paul here as deity supreme in power and knowledge and as one who is personally present.

The trial scenes in Acts 21:17-26:32 further support Luke's desire to demonstrate Jesus' personal participation in the church's mission. It is interesting, that as foretold in Luke 21:12-13 (cf., 12:11-12), we see in this lengthy passage for the first and only time in Acts a follower of Jesus standing trial before βασιλεῖς (Agrippa, 25:13-14, 24, 26; 26:2, 7, 13, 19, 26–27,30) and ἡγεμόνες (Felix, 23:24, 26, 33; Festus, 26:30). The inspiring work of the Holy Spirit is never mentioned or alluded to. Instead, Jesus appears as the divine agent guiding Paul's witness: 'Take courage! As you have testified about me in Jerusalem, so you must also testify in Rome' (Acts 23:11; also 22:17-21). Here again Luke shows the exalted Jesus exercising his divine prerogatives as Lord through his supreme knowledge, power and personal presence in Paul's witness. The sense here is that nothing will thwart his plan: Paul will testify about Jesus in Rome as he has already done in Jerusalem. Jesus is personally bringing to completion the work to which he has called Paul (cf., Acts 9:15-16 pars.) to the extent that in Acts 26:23 Paul

---

[39]Hengel, 'Messianischer Lehrer', 167; Pesch, *Apostelgeschichte* 1:237; Menzies, *Development*, 224-25, n. 2; Barrett, *Acts I*, 325.
[40]George, 'L'Esprit Saint', 521; Weiser, *Apostelgeschichte. 1-12*, 172; Morris, *Luke*, 324; Stein, *Luke*, 517.

can claim that it is the resurrected Christ who is, in effect, pro-claiming the gospel to the Jews and Gentiles through him. That the book of Acts ends with Paul in Rome preaching the gospel unhindered to all who would hear him (28:30-31) underscores that, for Luke, it was Jesus in fact who preserved Paul through all the difficulties he had faced from when he left Jerusalem to his arrival in Rome (23:12–28:16) and thus fulfilled the promise made to Paul in 23:11.

With Luke's description of the work of the exalted Jesus in Acts, one cannot easily dismiss the impression that he intended his readers to view Jesus' heavenly ministry as similar to Yahweh's. Yahweh providentially brought to pass through Moses his divine plan of rescuing Israel from slavery in Egypt; similarly, Jesus providentially brings to pass through Paul his divine plan of rescue in making known the gospel message 'to the ends of the earth'. The belief that Jesus' periodic visionary appearances in Acts are only secondarily relevant to Luke's christology is gravely inadequate.[41] It is precisely these kinds of passages which detail the magnitude of Luke's personal christological convictions and reassures his readers that Jesus reigns supreme.

c. The Name of Jesus. Luke's handling of Peter's use of the Joel citation at Pentecost endorses this christological perspective as Luke's. In the last verse of the citation in Acts 2:21 (Joel 2:32), Peter associates salvation in 'the name of the Lord' with the exalted Jesus.[42] The rest of Peter's sermon bears this out. Luke's use of ὄνομα in the Gospel strongly anticipates this identification of Jesus with 'the Lord' in Acts 2:21. In Luke 21:12b, Luke expands Mark 13:9b where Jesus says that his followers 'will bear testimony before Jewish and Gentile authorities *for my sake* [ἕνεκεν ἐμοῦ]' (also Matt. 10:18b) to read '...*on account of my name* [ἕνεκεν τοῦ ὀνόματος μου]'. Furthermore, in Luke 24:47 Jesus instructs his disciples that 'repentance and forgiveness of sins will be preached *in his name* [ἐπὶ τῷ ὀνόματι αὐτοῦ] to all nations'. The relation between the witness theme and the name of Jesus in these passages anticipates the christological significance of Acts 2:21. In conjunction with 2:21, these passages define the object of Christian witness—the Lord Jesus Christ—and thus supply the controlling meaning of ὄνομα in Acts. Within the book of Acts, Acts 2:21 represents the first of thirty-two times Luke uses ὄνομα with reference to Jesus' deity (only in Acts 15:14,17 is ὄνομα used of God). Salvation is always offered in the name of Jesus (Acts 2:21,38; 3:16 [2x]; 4:7-18 [5x];

41Cf., MacRae, 'Christology', 159-60; Lampe, *Spirit*, 72.
42Bock, *Proclamation*, 181-86 *et al.*

8:12) in fulfilment of all that the prophets have testified about him
(10:43; perhaps an allusion to 2:21). Believers heal (3:6; 4:30), teach
(5:28,40), baptize (8:16; 10:48; 19:5), exorcise demons (16:18; 19:13),
preach (9:27-28), witness (9:15), serve in (15:26), call upon (9:14,21;
22:16), suffer for (5:41; 9:16; 21:13; 26:9) and honour Jesus' name (19:17).

Thus, as in the OT, ὄνομα for Luke, implies transcendent deity's
personal, active and authoritative presence among his people.[43] Hans
Bietenhard observes that at times the NT inseparably links the name,
person and work of Jesus Christ with the name, person and work of
God.[44] In Luke–Acts, the link is so close that the two are nearly
indistinguishable. Within Acts, E. Schweizer rightly comments, the
name and person of Jesus are identical.[45] What believers do in Jesus'
name, or what is done to them on account of Jesus' name, is in essence
being done by or to Jesus himself. That salvation is exclusively found
in Jesus' name (cf., Acts 4:12) is powerful for Luke's first-century
readers, for in the OT this was true only of Yahweh (Isa. 43:11) and in
the NT world this would make Jesus equal to Yahweh and superior to
all other supernatural powers (cf., Eph. 1:21; Phil. 2:9-11). Luke's use of
ὄνομα makes immanent the transcendent Lord who reigns supreme in
heaven.

Although much more could and should be said of this description of Luke's christology in Acts, its strength is not only in the titles
used of Jesus but also in that the exalted Jesus conspicuously behaves
in Acts as does Yahweh in the OT. For Luke, the supremacy of
Yahweh's word according to Isaiah 55:11 is nearly as applicable to
those of the exalted Jesus in Acts: 'My word that goes out from my
mouth: It will not return to me empty, but will accomplish what I
desire and achieve the purpose for which I sent it'. And like Yahweh,
Jesus personally sees to it—as in his commissioning of Paul—that this
will be the case (cf., Jer. 1:12). To readers familiar with the OT, these
connections would have been inescapable—despite whether they
were willing to accept their possible implications concerning Jesus'
relation to the Father and, for the Gentile readers especially, to
abandon allegiance to the gods of the Graeco–Roman world. We will
discuss what this Lukan christological perspective suggests regarding
Jesus' relation to the Father in the conclusion of this essay. But before
doing so, it is necessary to look at another important element of Luke's

---

43Cf., Thüsing, Erhöhungsvorstellung, 51.
44Bietenhard, 'ὄνομα', TDNT V:272.
45Schweizer, 'Jesus Christus', TRE 16:704.

christology. It concerns his deliberate effort to show that Jesus as Saviour and Lord exercises his divine authority to his people as one waiting on tables.

IV. A deity who waits on tables

At the time of the Last Supper, according to Luke, Jesus settles a dispute among the disciples concerning greatness by contrasting two portraits of lordship (Luke 22:24-27; *cf.*, John 13:1-16; Mark 10:45). Gentile rulers, on the one hand, express their greatness in exercising their authority over their subjects and thus are called benefactors (v. 25). Luke is not denigrating the practice of benefaction.[46] Jesus seems to assume that the rulers have given 'good things' to their subjects (the disciples would, of course, be well aware of Herod's benefaction toward the Jews in building the temple, *cf.*, John 2:20; Josephus *Ant.* 15.11). Jesus probably directs his warning to the disciples in verse 26, 'you are not to be like that', against the 'self-aggrandizement' commonly sought by most benefactors.[47] Greatness, Jesus declares, should in essence express itself in service of others, not in seeking personal acclaim. Gentile rulers associate greatness with the master who sits at the table; Jesus, however, associates greatness with the servant who waits on the table. As Luke in his Gospel shows, Jesus' earthly ministry has exemplified this kind of serving behaviour *par excellence* (*cf.*, Luke 4:18-21; 7:18-23; Acts 10:38): 'Jesus has not come to be served by disciples (as one reclining at table by a waiter), but rather as one who serves and ministers to the needs of others'.[48]

But with this contrast does Luke merely intend to describe how Jesus behaved during his earthly ministry or, in a heightened sense, how he also behaves as exalted Lord? If the latter were true, for Jesus it would not be awkward for the host of the meal to act as the one who sets it on the table,[49] for divine Lordship expresses itself to its subjects in this way. In Luke 22:25-27, Jesus evidently contrasts '"the way it is" in the world' to '"the way it is" in his reign'.[50] What I would like to demonstrate here is that Luke gears the christology of both volumes,

---

[46]*Cf.*, Lull, 'Servant-Benefactor', 289-305.
[47]Fitzmyer, *Luke X-XXIV*, 1415.
[48]Fitzmyer, *Luke X-XXIV*, 1415; also, *e.g.*, Plummer, *Luke*, 501-02; Geldenhuys, *Luke*, 562; Danker, *New Age*, 349-50; Stein, *Luke*, 549.
[49]*Cf.*, Marshall, *Luke*, 814; Nolland, *Luke 18:35-24:53*, 1065.
[50]Tiede, *Luke*, 385.

in part, to redefine what benefaction means for his first-century readers with regard to Jesus as divine Lord. For the Jews, this behaviour was apparently unexpected of the messiah, nor did the Greeks and Romans normally associate such behaviour with benefactors, whether human or divine. Seneca, for example, uses the occasion of banquets to illustrate the frequent Roman mistreatment of slaves:

> For we maltreat [slaves]... not as if they were men, but as if they were beasts of burden. When we recline at a banquet, one slave mops up the disgorged food, another crouches beneath the table and gathers up the left-overs of the tipsy guests. Another carves the priceless game birds.... Another, who serves the wine, must dress like a woman.... With slaves like these the master cannot bear to dine; he would think it beneath his dignity to associate with his slave at the same table![51]

For Seneca, the issue involves the master's eating with a slave at the same table (which Seneca would like to see, and was itself nonconventional).[52] Seneca, however, does not suggest that the master switch roles and wait on the slaves![53] That deity would desire to express greatness to people in this way was apparently unknown to Graeco–Roman thinking (cf., the extreme vanity of the Roman imperial cult)[54] and perhaps to the first-century Jewish way of thinking about how the messiah would behave as well. The author of Luke–Acts orients his christology around the theme to demonstrate that such behaviour defines something of what divine Lordship means.

For example, according to Luke 12:37, Jesus asserts: 'It will be good for those servants whose master finds them watching when he comes. I tell you the truth, he will dress himself to serve, will have them recline at the table and will come and wait on them'. The context is eschatological. It refers to the second coming (v. 40). When the exalted Lord Jesus returns he will behave toward his people as one who waits on tables. Even at that time, he will not come to be waited upon, but to minister to others. The ἀμήν ('I tell you the truth') introducing the second half of the verse is for emphasis, underscoring the special importance of the saying.[55] The saying is unparalleled in the gospel

---

[51]Seneca, *Epis. Mor.* 47.5-8, trans. R.M. Gummere, Loeb 4 (Cambridge: Harvard, 1989 [1917]).
[52]*Cf.,* Bartchy, 'Table Fellowship', 796.
[53]*Cf.,* Seneca, *Epis. Mor.* 47.13-16.
[54]*Cf.,* Gill and Winter, 'Roman Religion', 93-103 and lit. cited in n. 73.
[55]Marshall, *Luke,* 536.

tradition and in all probability original to Jesus.

Moreover, as in his earthly ministry, we never see in Acts the exalted Jesus seeking personal glory or acclaim. Rather the kingly Jesus continues to express his greatness and authority to his people through acts of service and ministry. As predicted, for example, in the Gospel, Jesus gives his followers 'the words and wisdom' in inspiring their witness before their adversaries through his Spirit and directly through personal appearances (Luke 21:15; Acts 4:8; 6:10; 16:7; 18:9-10 etc.). He gives the Holy Spirit to his followers at Pentecost to empower their worldwide proclamation of the gospel (2:33). As Saviour and Prince he now gives repentance and forgiveness of sins to others (5:31; also 2:38; 10:43; 13:38-39; perhaps a similar idea is implied of Jesus in the title 'the author of life', 3:15). In language recalling Jesus' teaching in Nazareth (Luke 4:18-21) and his earthly ministry (Luke 7:21-22; Acts 10:38), Luke depicts through Jesus' name a similar ministry of the exalted Jesus in Acts: Jesus casts out demons (Acts 16:18), heals the crippled (3:6,16; 4:10) and paralytic (9:34), and proclaims 'light to his own people and to the Gentiles' (26:23). The early church's prayer in Acts 4:30, 'Stretch out your hand to heal and perform miraculous signs and wonders through the name of your holy servant Jesus' (4:30), continues to link service with the exalted Jesus.

In summary, Luke 22:25-27 presents two definitions of lordship, one human and the other divine. The disciples well know that human rulers normally do not behave in this manner. Nor were they themselves inclined to do so (v. 24)! But may not this be Jesus' point? To behave as one waiting on tables is not merely to gain access to God's banqueting table; it is to image something of the divine host.

V. Conclusion: the christological pulse of Acts

The pulse of the christology of Acts is that of the exalted Jesus as God's co-equal. Luke writes next to nothing of the divine status of Jesus in Acts.[56] Jesus is simply where he said he would be and doing the kinds of things suitable to that position. Putting the matter in perspective, Luke seems not to be concerned to write about God's divine status either.[57] He simply assumes it. As Conzelmann reasons: 'There is no theological necessity for it'.[58] In all probability, the same was true of

---

[56]So, *e.g.*, Ladd, 'Christology', 39.
[57]Schweizer, *Luke*, 91.

Jesus. Luke most likely already shared such knowledge with his readers. To conclude, therefore, with G.W.H. Lampe and R.P.C. Hanson,
that Luke does not think in terms of a personal union between Jesus
and God is inadequate.[59] It is hard to imagine that Luke could *not* have
done so. The parallels between the behaviour of the exalted Jesus in
Acts and Yahweh in the OT seem too pervasive and deliberate.

For this reason, it is arguable that Luke considered Jesus as Yahweh's co-equal[60] and co-regent.[61] What distinguishes Yahweh from
everything else is what he does and says as seen in his decreeing, preserving and providentially leading his saving plan according to his
will. In Acts, Luke describes Jesus in a similar way. The exalted Jesus
appears on equal footing with God by virtue of what he does and says
in decreeing, preserving and providentially leading his saving plan
through the church's mission to completion according to his will. Acts
describes 'the exalted Jesus as filling the role of God himself to the
church'.[62] 'For Luke Jesus acts as does the Father, and Jesus can do
what the Father does'.[63]

But Luke greatly enriches this portrait by presenting Jesus not
only as deity who is all-knowing, powerful and present, Saviour, Lord
of the Spirit, Judge of all the earth and so on, but by showing that this
kind of deity, by nature, behaves toward his people as one who waits
on tables. Luke, in this regard, appears to be re-educating his Christian
readership on benefaction. The extreme vanity of most human benefactors was no secret in the first-century world. But to Luke, what is
necessary for the readers to understand, if they are to understand
Christianity aright, is that Jesus as Benefactor must be perceived as one
who serves the food rather than as one who reclines and eats it.
According to Luke–Acts, Jesus never behaves beneficently for reasons
of self-aggrandizement, but to minister to his people. And on the basis
of the OT, it is arguable that here too 'Jesus acts as does the Father, and
can do what the Father does'.[64]

---

[58]Conzelmann, *Luke*, 149.
[59]Lampe, 'Portrait', 172,174; Hanson, *Acts*, 39.
[60]See also Fitzmyer, 'Early Church', 33.
[61]Bock, *Proclamation*, 264.
[62]Ladd, 'Christology', 39.
[63]O'Toole, 'Risen Jesus', 487.
[64]*E.g.*, the idea of deity feeding others recollects Yahweh's behaviour toward his
people in the OT (*cf.*, Deut. 10:18; Ps. 23:5; 81:13-16; 145:15-16; 146:7; Isa. 25:6). *Cf.*,
more generally Acts 11:17; 14:17: 15:8; 17:25.

CHAPTER 7

THE NEED FOR SALVATION

Christoph Stenschke

Summary

Taking our departure from recent debate on Luke's anthropology, we start with the question of the Philippian jailer and the Jerusalem crowds regarding what people need to do to be saved, and try to find clues as to why people need to be saved. Luke 1:77 links salvation to the forgiveness of sins. With this emphasis in mind we examine these two questions in their wider context: the forgiveness of sins, Luke's 'generation' and the nature of repentance. It will become apparent that for Luke people need to be saved because of a major disorder in their relationship with God.

I. Introduction

Various other contributions to this volume demonstrate the extent to
which Luke is concerned with the saviour and the salvation he brings.
It is important to inquire why this salvation is necessary. What would
Luke's answer have been, if someone had asked him for the reason
why people need to be saved? This question belongs to Luke's anthropology. In comparison to other Lukan themes studied by post-war
scholarship, Luke's anthropology in itself has received little attention.[1]
Often Luke is seen not to emphasise a distinctive view of people. His
anthropology in general agrees with that of the Synoptic Gospels (and
is thus treated in this section of NT theology or in a section on Jesus).
Sections on the theology of Acts tend to focus on the christological
development.[2] Yet some studies touching on, or devoted to, Luke's
anthropology have yielded diverging conclusions and deserve
attention:

1. In *Die Mitte der Zeit* H. Conzelmann devoted only a short section
titled 'Man as the recipient of salvation',[3] directly to anthropological
questions. At first sight nothing surprising appears: 'The message to
man reveals to him his situation, by informing him of the Judgement
to come and by revealing the fact that he is a sinner'.[4] The need of
salvation is linked to man being a sinner.

But later he comments: 'Luke vii.34 (S) again makes plain, that
sinfulness is not a characteristic of man as such'.[5] In addition, Conzelmann deems Luke's concept of sin to have a 'strong ethical colouring'.[6]
Sin is not a state but a concrete act: ἁμαρτωλός is not a general
declaration about the human situation. There are people who do not

---

[1]For survey of research see Taeger, *Mensch*, 11-18 (to 1979) and Hegermann,
Mensch (to 1992). The most recent survey of research on NT anthropology (with
strong emphasis on Paul) is Schnelle, 'Anthropologie'.
[2]This has been the traditional approach which has modern proponents, *cf.*,
Schnelle, *NT Anthropologie*, 13-43 and Stuhlmacher, *Theologie*, I.40-161 (Die Verkündigung Jesu), 161-221 (Die Verkündigung der Urgemeinde). Others see Luke's
anthropology in general agreement with other NT authors, yet would want to
allow exceptional passages, *e.g.*, Kümmel, *Man*, 87-96 excludes the Areopagus
speech. Parsons and Pervo, *Rethinking* , 89-114 emphasise strongly Acts 14, 17.
[3]Conzelmann, *Luke*, 225-31.
[4]Conzelmann, *Luke*, 227. In n. 2 he adds: 'Yet no demonstration of man's sinfulness
is attempted in any part of the preaching'. Yet several speeches stress the decided
contrast between God's intention and deliberate human counteraction. Some of
the speeches are triggered by sinful behaviour. The narrative material surrounding the speeches gives evidence for this sinfulness!

need repentance and forgiveness (Luke xv, 3ff., ...)'.[7]

2. Conzelmann's conclusion that some people do not need to repent and be forgiven has been taken further by J.W. Taeger. In brief, his conclusion is that for Luke 'Man (der Mensch) is not a salvandus, rather a corrigendus'.[8] By this he means that the need of humanity is not so profound as we find in Paul where all have sinned. For Luke there are plenty of pious people in the world who are partly ignorant of God and fall into sins and errors but who need enlightenment and perfection of their existing attitude to God rather than conversion in the usual sense of the term. Taeger's monograph is probably the most complete discussion of Luke's understanding of anthropology and sets the agenda for future study. Within the limits of this article it will not be possible to discuss it in detail, but one general remark may be helpful before we develop the subject.

Various scholars, among them I.H. Marshall,[9] have demonstrated the extent to which Luke is concerned with salvation: his Gospel is about a Jesus who 'came to seek and save that which is lost'. Unless

---

[5]Conzelmann, *Luke*, 227, n. 2. There he continues, 'Luke xiii, 2 (S) is addressed to all, not in the Pauline sense of being inescapable, but on the contrary as an appeal to individual initiative'. For the former no evidence is adduced; why the latter urge to repentance should exclude a reference to the state of man is not clear. Jesus' charge (Luke 13:1-5) shows that people don't need to be particularly bad sinners to come under divine judgement. In that Jesus calls all to repent, the stress is not on the quality or amount of morally objectionable actions.

[6]Conzelmann, *Luke*, 228 and 227, n. 2. For Conzelmann this ethical character becomes evident in Luke 13:2,4; 15:7,18; 18:3. I fail to see support for Conzelmann's claim in 18:3. 15:7 should be seen in the context of Luke's view of sinners and righteous as a whole. In 15:18 the parable's younger son confesses to have sinned against God and his father who refers to his son's *state* as his being dead and lost (15:26, 32) not to individual *deeds*. This tension demands caution (on 13:2,4 see above).

[7]Conzelmann, *Luke*, 227, n. 2. No support is given for this statement, contradicting his earlier summary, other than a reference to Schlatter, *Evangelium des Lukas*. Schlatter's treatment of the whole passage (p. 346-58) does not support Conzelmann's statement. No attention is given to the beginning of ch. 15, specifying the situation and audience or to other passages identifying the group of people Luke here refers to, *e.g.*, Luke 18:9. The chapter's third parable (vv. 11-32) indicates that the state of those who never left the father's house (or the fold) leaves much to be desired. Though they never left home they also need to return. The godly people of their dispensation are not faultless. This seems to be the thrust of the chapter. Greater care is required before such far-reaching conclusions are drawn. None of Conzelmann's eight other comments on verses of this chapter address this issue.

[8]Taeger, *Mensch*, 225 (translation mine). A summary is provided by Schnelle, *NT Anthropologie*, 8.3.

[9]Marshall, *Luke: Historian*, 77-215.

this statement (and much besides) is formal and without significance, there is some sense in which people need to be saved. Do all people need to be saved? Is their situation prior to being saved one that is better characterised as being 'lost' or as being in need of some kind of correction or improvement? Unless such terms as 'lost' are to be re-defined, and unless the apparently universal scope of the work of Jesus is illusory, then the statements made by Luke create the presumption that people in general do need to be saved. It will be our aim to discuss some basic aspects of this problem in what follows.

3. Most recently, M.C. Parsons and R.I. Pervo, in *Rethinking the Unity of Luke and Acts* have used Luke's anthropology as a test case in challenging the unity of Luke–Acts.[10] Though their treatment fails to provide that thorough comparison of the anthropology of Acts with that of Luke, which would be required to establish their case, it raises several important issues. Though they draw attention to hitherto often neglected methodological steps in studying Lukan theology,[11] their procedure, comparisons with other contemporary literature and results seem to be too dependent on a particular prior identification of the genre of Acts and on their selection of material of anthropological relevance.

Though it will not be possible in this contribution to adequately discuss and assess the above approaches and results, some issues will be raised which make us hesitant to accept the above suggestions as the definite Lukan anthropology, while certainly allowing for differences between Luke's anthropology and that of other NT authors.

Having mentioned some issues involved in Lukan anthropology, it seems appropriate to sketch some methodological points.

(a). We have to remember that we are searching for an answer to a question which Luke never directly addresses as he does the Philippian jailer's explicit question about the way of salvation. We must discover more indirect clues in the book of Acts as to the need of salvation.

(b). As we study the pages of Acts, we have to bear in mind that Luke may have already answered this question in his Gospel[12] and is not re-addressing the issue in his later work, because he is building on the foundation which he has already laid.

(c). Should neither of Luke's works with their emphasis on

---

[10]Parsons and Pervo, *Rethinking*, 84-114. See also Marshall, 'Former Treatise', 164.
[11]Parsons and Pervo, *Rethinking*, 80-89.
[12]On the relationship of both works see the recent treatment by Marshall, 'Former Treatise'.

salvation provide clues to the reason for the need for salvation, we would have to consider the possibility that Luke simply assumes a certain anthropology which underlies his own understanding of man, perhaps taken over from some source like the OT or Hellenistic ideas.

II. How and why people need to be saved

The question 'Why do I need to be saved?' is formulated in analogy to two other questions which appear on the pages of Acts. A careful look at these questions and the answers given, further clarifies issues and will serve as a convenient point of departure before we explore three themes related to our question.

1. The Philippian jailer asks his former prisoners 'Sirs, what must I do to be saved'? (16:30). His question was due to God's miraculous intervention on behalf of the missionaries. They had arrived earlier in Philippi and served a period of ministry and proclamation. Apparently the jailer was not fully acquainted with the Christian proclamation and the issue of salvation's acquisition still needed clarification. Yet the question of why he needs to be saved is not raised. Paul's answer indicates that Luke took the jailer's question as having 'soteriological' bearing.[13] Why might the jailer ask this question?

Though still in a precarious position, the jailer no longer contemplates suicide as his prisoners have not escaped. He is not asking what he must do to be saved from the dire consequences of having lost prisoners under his charge. Paul's summons allows for another reason behind the jailer's question, namely, fear of anticipated divine retribution. The jailer imprisoned men who previously demonstrated their power over the Python spirit and who have now demonstrably received divine vindication. His question is immediately related to these events: He asks 'what he, who had to sacrilegiously (*frevelhaft*) incarcerate them, as he just learned through the quake, has to do in order to "be saved" from the punitive wrath of the gods, respectively the most high God of these men'.[14] Luke is familiar with pagan concepts of divine retribution and vindication[15] and shows that salvation is

---

13For the historical and legal questions involved in the whole incident (16:9-40) see Rapske, *Paul in Roman Custody*, 115-34.

14 Pesch, *Apostelgeschichte*, II:116 (translation is mine).

15The Maltese natives make a connection between a viper biting Paul and the goddess Δίκη (28.4).

mandatory to escape God's certain judgement. Linked to human failure, judgement follows for a variety of reasons—lack of appropriate 'fruit' incurs the 'wrath to come' (Luke 3:7,9,17) or failure to recognise and receive God's messengers past and present (*e.g.,* Luke 13:33-34; 19:41-44). The judgement arriving with 'the coming of the Lord's great and glorious day' (2:20) follows the fulfilment of prophecy in the last days. Escape from certain doom is possible only by calling on the name of the Lord. People who have handed over for execution one attested by God (*cf.,* the contrast scheme 2:23-24) should dread this day.[16] Ethical failure on the personal level (*e.g.,*24:25) also incurs a coming judgement. The Jewish need for salvation goes beyond involvement in the rejection and condemnation of Jesus. The Gentiles await judgement for their failure to respond adequately to God's natural revelation (17:31).

In our case the jailer's question betrays existential fear provoked by the realisation that recent events have proven his actions to be contrary to divine will. The missionaries' answer widens the scope. Again Pesch—'The jailer now learns about a salvation in a much more comprehensive sense. It consists in the salvation which is received by faith in the "Lord Jesus"'.[17]

These considerations point to the answer to our question: Salvation is here connected to an action or state from which salvation is necessary. The answer shows that salvation has a more comprehensive scope than what is immediately related to this action or state.

Peter's confession at the beginning of Jesus' ministry is analogous to the question of the jailer and an investigation of it suggests that there may be more to the jailer's question than is found on its surface. The event(s) may have convicted him of his need of salvation. The miraculous catch of fish causes Peter to realise his own state in comparison to Jesus: 'Go away from me, Lord, ἀνὴρ ἁμαρτωλός εἰμι!' (Luke 5:8). Peter perceives a wide gap between himself and Jesus. As in the case of the jailer there is a link to a previous miracle (4:33-35, 38-39) and acquaintance with the proclamation (4:31-32). The charge to cast the net follows the end of the discourse. With his confession Peter reacts to the miraculous catch just taken (5:9). The difference between Jesus and what Peter recognises himself to be, points again to our previous observation that salvation is connected to an action or a state

---

[16]Schneider, *Apostelgeschichte* I:270 refers to the incalculable and inescapable character of this judgement.
[17]Pesch, *Apostelgeschichte,* II:116.

from which this salvation is necessary.

In addition to our reflections on what may have caused the
jailer's question, other observations can be made. The fact that the
jailer asks it betrays that he doesn't naturally have an answer in
himself. When it comes to the manner of appropriating salvation, he
pleads ignorance. Salvation cannot be accomplished by people for
themselves. The jailer asks τί με δεῖ ποιεῖν ἵνα σωθῶ. At the same
time Paul's answer shows that salvation does not just happen, it
involves a readiness to appropriate the active doing of another agent.
The jailer inquires what he must do to be saved. The answer does not
demand deeds but mental commitment. The jailer does not know what
God really requires and the way he states his crucial question may
betray this lack of knowledge. This implicit contrast of works and faith
reminds one of the Pauline discussion.[18] The jailer addresses the
missionaries as κύριοι, a word which can also mean 'Lords'.[19] Divine
undertones may be present. Again the answer is corrective—there is
only one κύριος and his name is Jesus! The missionaries proclaim, not
their own message, but τὸν λόγον τοῦ κυρίου. Following the answer's
wider soteriological scope, our question, 'Why do I need to be saved?'
could be paraphrased as 'What is wrong with me, what have I done
that I need to be saved?'

2. A question similar to that of the Gentile jailer is asked by Jews in
Jerusalem. On hearing through Peter of the decided contrast between
their having crucified Jesus and of God making him both Lord and
Messiah (2:36), the audience is 'cut to the heart' and inquires: 'Brothers,
τί ποιήσωμεν?' (2:37). In response they are charged to repent and to be
baptised so that their sins will be forgiven and they may receive the
Holy Spirit.[20] The audience recognises the need to deal with their

---

[18]Pesch, *Apostelgeschichte*, II:116: 'Within the horizon of Pauline theology it also
becomes discernible that not an 'action', but faith in the Lord Jesus is necessary for
salvation'.
[19]Says Pesch: 'His "trembling", with which he prostrates himself before the
missionaries, expresses religious fear of the men of God, whom the pagan takes to
be divine messengers—as addressing them with "Sirs (*Herren*)" can also purport'
(*Apostelgeschichte*, II:116). Moses 'trembles' at the sight of the burning bush (7:32).
Codex D reads ἔντρομος οὖσα in Luke 8:47: the woman who touched Jesus came
'trembling' and fell down before Jesus. See also Schneider, *Apostelgeschichte* II:217
and Foerster, κύριος, *TDNT* III:1051-52.
[20]Bayer, 'The Preaching of Peter' (ch. 13 below) argues 'that the initial Petrine
speeches in Acts (especially in Acts 2 and 3) set *the tone and framework* for various
other themes developed and expounded in the unfolding narrative of the Book of
Acts' (italics his). Bayer's case receives support from Luke's anthropology.

sinful counteraction of God's plan with Jesus. Salvation, not explicitly mentioned here, is linked to human failure, from which, in order to avoid these consequences, deliverance is mandatory.

Another element of the answer may further our quest. The audience is told how their sins could be forgiven. Does this charge refer to the rejection and crucifixion of Jesus, possibly seen as constituted of several acts, or are sins of a more general character in view?

The charge to the audience is extended in 2:40, as Peter exhorts them saying 'σώθητε ἀπὸ τῆς γενεᾶς τῆς σκολιᾶς ταύτης'! Is the generation present corrupted 'only' by the events surrounding the recent rejection of Jesus or is a more general characterisation of the Jews or even humankind in general in view? Do people need to be saved because they are part of a corrupt generation, which has, in its dealings with Jesus simply demonstrated this very corruption?

Further investigations are suggested by the context: (1) What exactly does Luke mean by 'forgiveness of sins', and how is this concept related to salvation? (2) Can Luke's other references to the 'generation' shed light on the 'wicked generation' here? (3) In what other context does the call to repentance appear? What sins are intended there? (4) What other clues can be derived from the second chapter prior to v. 37?

III. Forgiveness of sin

The forgiveness of sin is a Lukan stress as eight of the NT's eleven occurrences are found in Luke's pages. Of these, Luke 1:77 explicitly links this forgiveness to salvation. Zechariah predicts that John will give knowledge of salvation to his people which is to come through the forgiveness of their sins.[21] In the first pages of the Gospel Luke points out that this salvation is different in focus from the salvation of the

---

[21]'"Knowledge" has the sense of experience here; salvation is experienced in the forgiveness of sins', so Brown, *Birth of the Messiah*, 373. Brown points out (390, n. 36) how the theme of Luke 1:77 is developed in Acts 4:10-12; 5:31; 13:26, 38. Luke's other reference where salvation and forgiveness of sins are closely linked has its focus on the saviour himself (5:31): God exalted Jesus as Leader and Saviour that he might give repentance to Israel and *forgiveness of sins*. The 'work of the Saviour is said to issue in repentance and the forgiveness of sins'. Contrary to what may be expected, 'God offers not vengeance but forgiveness', Barrett, *Acts* I:290, see also 288.

OT.[22] It is not so much salvation from national and/or personal enemies but salvation from the coming judgement (see above) through the forgiveness of sins. This forgiveness of sins is closely linked to the coming Messiah: 'The dawn from on high[23] will break upon us, to bring light to those who sit in darkness and in the shadow of death, to guide our feet into the way of peace' (vv. 78-79). Salvation includes the forgiveness of sins and goes beyond this need in that it has the whole state of people in view. God graciously grants what men cannot attain themselves, as they sit in darkness, in the shadow of death and do not know the way of peace. This is why people need to be saved.

What can be gathered from Luke's other references to the forgiveness of sins? The baptism of repentance proclaimed by John is likewise linked to the forgiveness of sins, again in their most general sense (Luke 3:3).[24]

The disciples are summoned in Luke 24:47 to preach in Jesus' name repentance for the forgiveness of sins to all nations, beginning in Jerusalem. One and the same message is to be proclaimed to Jews and Gentiles alike (see Acts 26:20). The forgiveness of sins in Acts 2:38 thus should not be too closely linked with the recent events in Jerusalem.[25] Sins of a more general character are in view. Acts 5:30 again addresses the contrast between human and divine action: God exalted the crucified Jesus as Leader and Saviour that he might give repentance to Israel[26] and forgiveness of sins (v. 31). As in Luke 1:77 salvation (Jesus

22Cf., Schürmann, *Das Lukasevangelium*, I.91-92.
23The OT and Jewish background of this ἀνατολὴ ἐξ ὕψους and its Messianic reference is described by Brown, *Birth of the Messiah*, 373-74, 390-91, 661.
24Some of the sins intended can be concluded from the positive ethical instruction in Luke 3:10-14. Because Luke's emphasis is on the effects of sin and their forgiveness in the relationship of people to God, the 'social' dimension of sins appears only in passing. Yet both Luke's books provide evidence of how people's failure before God negatively affects their dealings with each other and of the 'social' bearing of God's salvation (see *e.g.*, Capper, 'Reciprocity and the Ethics of Acts' in this volume).
25Later the Athenians, certainly not directly responsible for the rejection of Jesus addressed in Acts 2, are likewise charged to repent (17:30). The reasons for their need of repentance differ and Luke enumerated them. The Jews have rejected God's revelation and (thus) the mission of Jesus; the Gentiles have perverted what has been known to them from nature, they likewise have failed: Their city is full of idols, they have failed to find God who is so close to them. God has overlooked these times of ignorance and now commands repentance. The Areopagus speech can be satisfactorily explained along these lines as the studies of Gärtner, *TheAreopagus Speech*, and more recently Külling, *Geoffenbartes Geheimnis*, Hemer, 'The Speeches of Acts' and Gempf, *Historical and Literary Appropriateness*, 112-34 and succinctly in 'Paul at Athens', have shown.

the Saviour) is linked to the forgiveness of sins. Everyone who believes in Jesus receives forgiveness of sins through his name (Acts 10:43). Sins are deemed a universal human problem. Paul proclaims in Pisidian Antioch's synagogue that, through Jesus, forgiveness of sins is offered to them—'there are many things from which you need to be justified; the law of Moses is inadequate to achieve this; the only way is the way of faith'.[27] People are in need of this liberation as they cannot achieve it for themselves. Here faith is setting free from sin, in Acts 16:31 faith saves, most likely, from sin. When the jailer is told to believe in the Lord Jesus in order to be saved, it is clear, on the basis of what has become evident thus far, namely—the strong link between salvation and the forgiveness of sins—that whatever the jailer had in mind, for Luke and his attentive reader, he needed to be saved because of his sins and from his sins.

Paul is sent to the Gentiles to open their eyes so that they might turn from darkness to light and from the power of Satan to God, so that they might receive forgiveness of sins and a place among those who are sanctified by faith in him (Acts 26:17-18). This passage takes up and summarises threads appearing elsewhere before. Two aspects emerge. First, apart from the Christian message of salvation, Gentiles, on the whole,[28] are in a dreadful state. They are seen as blind, in darkness and under the power of Satan.[29] Salvation will bring them forgiveness of sins. For Luke, forgiveness of sins is closely linked to salvation. Yet in the context of references to the forgiveness of sins there is another, more 'ontological' aspect. Salvation not only pertains to the forgiveness of individual sins, but also addresses a sinful state beyond these outward manifestations. The second aspect relevant for understand-

---

[26]For Conzelmann, *Luke*, 101, Luke means that God grants the opportunity for repentance.This explanation fails to take account of the second divine gift.

[27]Barrett, *Acts* I:650.

[28]In addition to the context which points to a generalising discussion ('your people' vs. 'the Gentiles'), this restriction seems justified in light of Luke's references to individual Gentiles interested in the Jewish faith, the positive practical consequences of this attraction and adherence (*e.g.* , Cornelius), and to instances of exemplary behaviour of Gentiles, *e.g.*, the 'philanthropy beyond ordinary measure' of the barbaric islanders of Malta (28:2). Yet Luke leaves no doubt that even more 'positive' Gentiles need salvation and need to call on the name of the Lord to be saved and to receive the Spirit (2:21; also 4:12).

[29]See Baumbach, *Verständnis*, 122-207. Satan and his dire influence on people is often described by Luke. Demonic possession is attributed to individuals among Jews and Gentiles alike. Salvation includes and often becomes impressively manifest in deliverance from this demonic influence.

ing our verses in Acts 2, is the significance of 'this corrupt generation'. The present discussion leaves us with a certain expectation of what Luke could have in mind when he reports Peter's verdict on his audience. Now we scrutinise other occurrences of the expression which could shed light on the occurrence in Acts 2:40.

IV. Luke's 'generation' and humanity in general

Altogether γενεά occurs twenty times in Luke's writings. Our focus is on those occurrences which combine 'generation' with the demonstrative pronoun or adjectives.[30] Outside the Gospel only Acts 2:40, serving as our point of departure, refers to a specific generation (τῆς γενεᾶς ταύτης), which is labelled σκολιᾶς and from which the audience is summoned to save itself.

Before we gather what Luke says about 'this generation' in the Gospel, γενεά itself deserves attention. Thus far in our references to the word we have utilised the common translation of γενεά as 'generation'.[31] Other words which can be employed allow for a wider reference of meaning. Γενεά can refer to 'family, descent', 'those descended from a common ancestor, a clan, then race, kind generally'.[32] Would Acts 2:40, with reference to Lukan theology as a whole, also allow for the more general reading 'race'? Do only the people now exhorted by Peter and charged earlier with the execution of Jesus (Acts 2:36) make up the 'corrupt generation' from which they need to be saved? Are they part or representatives of a much larger group of people or even of a corrupt humankind which is in need of salvation?

The Gospel's ten references to this specific generation are found exclusively on the lips of Jesus. 'Jesus looks upon the whole contemporary generation of Jews as a uniform mass confronting him'.[33] Five

---

[30]Büchsel, *TDNT* I:663 notes that γενεά 'is always qualified'.

[31]Even in this sense of the word the meaning in Acts 2:40 may go beyond the confines of Palestinian Jewry. In Acts 4:27 the group of those made responsible for the death of Jesus is explicitly widened beyond the confines of the Jewish religious leadership and the population of Jerusalem to include Pilate, Herod and the Gentiles. Also Büchsel, *TDNT* I: 662: 'It mostly denotes 'generation' in the sense of *contemporaries....* This generation is to be understood temporally, but there is always a *qualifying criticism*' (italics mine).

[32]*BAG*, 153. *Cf.*, Büchsel's definition (*TDNT* I:662): '"race" in the sense of those bound by common descent: ἀνδρῶν γενεή'. Luke is familiar with the concept of humankind deriving from one common ancestor (Luke 3:34, 38; Acts 17:26).

[33]*BAG*, 153. Büchsel, *TDNT* I:662 (see note 31).

occurrences appear in the eleventh chapter where 'this generation' is γενεὰ πονηρά because it asks for a sign (11:29, 2x). The Son of Man will be the sign to 'this generation' (11:30), as Jonah became the sign for the people of Nineveh. The queen of the South will judge the people of 'this generation' because they failed to listen to the one in their midst greater than Solomon (11:31). The Ninevites will condemn 'this generation' because they repented at the proclamation of their sign Jonah while the present generation fails to see the one greater than Jonah and to repent at his proclamation (11:32). 'This generation' fails to recognise the divine sign (and its signs) given to them and blindly asks for yet another sign. It is a γενεὰ πονηρά because it fails to come, to listen and to repent. Because the leadership honours the prophets of the past but fails to recognise the greater sign given to their own generation and fails to repent accordingly, 'this generation' will be charged with the blood of all the prophets shed since the foundation of the world' (11:50). Those who should know and who claimed to know failed to know and prevented others from knowing (11:52). The failure of 'this generation', though culminating in the action of killing their prophet referred to in Acts 2, is the deeper incapacity to recognise God's intention and messenger(s) and to repent. The generation's distinguishing characteristic is opposition to God.

The people of 'this generation' are compared to children who do not know what they want. They were critical of John and Jesus although both were different. In contrast to the verdict of 'this un-decided generation', divine wisdom is vindicated by her children (Luke 7:31-35).

In his first discourse on the end of the age, Jesus forewarns his disciples that he will be rejected by the people of 'this generation' before the onslaught of eschatological events (Luke 17:25).[34] Γενεά appears again in an eschatological context—'this generation' will not pass away until all things (21:32, announced from 21:5 onward, persecution of the disciples and judgement on Jerusalem) have taken place. Because of its failure to respond this generation will not escape judgement.

The people of Noah's generation (Luke 17:26) remind us that the combination of γενεά with the demonstrative alludes to familiar OT expressions: Noah is sent into the ark by God, for 'I have seen that you alone are righteous before me in ἐν τῇ γενεᾷ ταύτῃ' (Gen. 7:1). According to Jesus, Noah's generation was blind to spiritual things: While busy eating and drinking, buying and selling, planting and building, they failed to recognise Noah and his building of the ark as a sign to them. They did not repent 'and the flood came and destroyed them all' (Luke 17:27). Lot's generation did not fare better (17:28-29). Negative references to 'this generation' surface again in Psalm 11:8 LXX, where the pious psalmist confesses that God 'will protect and guard us ἀπὸ τῆς γενεᾶ ταύτης forever'.[35] God's protection is necessary as the wicked prowl on every side.[36]

Familiar OT language appears not just in the qualification of γενεά through a demonstrative, but also when γενεά is qualified by various adjectives. On two occasions Jesus directly qualifies 'this generation' in a manner which reminds us of occurrences in the OT and of that in Acts 2:40: The generation demanding a sign is a γενεὰ πονηρά (Luke 11:29). Γενεά appears without the demonstrative in Luke 9:41. On his descent after the transfiguration Jesus finds his disciples unable to cast out a spirit and addresses those present as a γενεὰ ἄπιστος καὶ διεστραμμένη.[37]

Jesus and the apostle(s) employ these expressions again

34The people in the (past) days of Noah and Lot resemble those of the (future) days of the Son of man (Luke 17:26-30). Both generations are united in their materialism, carelessness for spiritual things and in both are overtaken by thorough judgement unawares. Jesus identifies this stability in human nature. In Luke 11:47-51 the constant since the creation of the world (from Abel to Zechariah) is the rejection of God's messengers and shedding of their innocent blood. Thus the events referred to in Acts 2 are by no means surprising! The parenetic sections in the Gospel where Jesus addresses people of 'this' generation (of which the disciples are part [Luke 9:41!]), address at times similar issues (17:31). Because of this constant in people the disciples are to remember Lot's wife (v. 32): What happened to her could happen to them! What happened to the people in the day of Noah is relevant to people of this generation, it is written for their instruction, and still poses a danger. What became evident in a past generation, resurfaces again in this generation and will reappear once more in a future generation.

35The only other LXX occurrence of γενεά in the singular with a demonstative pronoun is Ps. 23:6 [LXX]. The generation there is positively described (vv. 4-6), yet the construction is different: αὕτη ἡ γενεά.

36The wilderness generation, with which God was offended (προσοχθίζω) for forty years because they were a people whose hearts went astray and who did not regard his ways is referred to as γενεὰ ἐκείνη (Ps. 94 [LXX]:10). The expression ἡ γενεὰ αὕτη may have been familiar as it also features in later Rabbinic discussion as הדור הזה (Büchsel, TDNT I:663).

37The disciples, even after their confession of him as the Messiah of God (Luke 9:20) and earlier positive references to them (e.g., Peter's reaction to the miraculous catch of fish) are included in this verdict (cf., Marshall, Luke, 391). Likewise the appearance of other positive figures in the infancy narratives, like Zechariah, Mary, Hannah and Simeon and elsewhere, e.g., the centurion in Capernaum and Joseph of Arimathea, etc., apparently does not abrogate the general verdict on the present generation.

introducing an old 'acquaintance', evoking a well-defined set of
associations. The designation has great similarity to a passage in the
Song of Moses.[38] Moses praises God's attributes ('The Rock, his work
is perfect, and all his ways are just. A faithful God, without deceit, just
and upright is he') and contrasts him with his people: 'yet his
degenerate children have dealt falsely with him, they are a γενεὰ
σκολιὰ καὶ διεστραμμένη' (Deut. 32:5). Moses questions: 'Do you
thus repay the Lord, λαὸς μωρὸς καὶ οἰχὶ σοφός?' God will turn away
from them for they are a γενεὰ ἐξεστραμμένη, children in whom οὐκ
ἔστιν πίστις (v. 20). Jesus uses an expression similar to 'that of God
when confronted by the faithless and disobedient generation in the
wilderness'[39] to chide the people of his own generation, some of whom
form his new people. The denunciation of this generation may also
allude to Psalm 77:8 LXX which presents God's great deeds and his
people's faithlessness. In vv. 5-7 God demands that the next generation
be taught the law, so that they should not be like their ancestors, a
γενεὰ σκολιὰ καὶ παραπικραίνουσα, a generation whose heart was
not steadfast, whose spirit was not faithful to God. Yet the people did
not keep God's covenant, but refused to walk according to his law.
They forgot what he had done, and the miracles he had shown them
(vv. 10f).[40]

It is noteworthy that the adjective in Peter's charge of his
audience as γενεὰ σκολιά in Acts 2:40 also 'rings bells' for the reader

---

[38]This chapter of Deuteronomy appears to be well known in early Christianity.
Quotations from it appear in Rom. 10:19; 12:19; 15:10; Heb. 1:6; 10:30 and up to
eighteen allusions have been listed.

[39]Marshall, Luke, 391. Cf.., Acts 20.30 (some within the church will speak
διεστραμμένα in order to draw off disciples after them); Lk. 23:2 and Acts 13:8.10
may echo Luke 9:41 and/or Deuteronomy 32. Josephus (Bell V.442) also employs
γενεά 'in this critical sense' (Büchsel, TDNT I, 663) in describing the moral state of
the leaders and people of Jerusalem prior to the city's capture by the Romans: '...
no age ever bred a generation more fruitful in wickedness than this was, from the
beginning of the world (μὴ γενεὰν ἐξ αἰῶνος γεγονέναι κακίας γονιμωτέραν)'.
Again Bell V.566: Jerusalem had brought forth a generation of people much more
atheistic (γενεὰν ἀθεωτέραν) than those that suffered such dire punishments as
being swallowed up by the ground (Num. 16), being overflowed with water (Gen.
6; compare 6:9 and 7:1) or being destroyed by such thunder as the country of
Sodom perished by (Gen. 19). The present γενεὰ ἀθεωτέρα compares negatively
to a variety of evil generations of the biblical past (cf. , Luke 17:26-29: 'the days of
Noah and of Lot').

[40]The last verse is noteworthy as the addressees of Jesus' chiding are his disciples
who are the witnesses par excellence. These verses of the Psalm comment on the
context of Luke 9:41.

familiar with the OT. G. Bertram's conclusion to his extensive study of σκολιός is worth quoting in full.

> In the main σκολιός in the Greek OT expresses the nature of the man who does not walk in the straightness and uprightness which God has ordained for him but who in a way which is guilty and worthy of punishment is crooked, cramped, distorted and hence corrupt.[41]

After these excursions on the addressees of Jesus' charge and the language employed by him, it is time to return to our discussion of the Gospel's references to the γενεά and to draw conclusions. Even the disciples, who fail to exorcise the spirit from the boy presented to them, can be included in Jesus' harsh estimates of his contemporaries. The occasion in this case is not the rejection of Jesus, of which the disciples cannot be accused, but rather their failure to continually believe and act according to instruction and authority received earlier and successfully practised previously (Luke 9:2, 6).

If we introduce these observations and the connotations from the OT into our quest for understanding the range of Peter's corrupt generation in Acts 2:40, we have to allow that the reference is wider than the events referred to in Acts 2:23 and point to a deeper problem with people.[42] Both the close OT parallels to Lukan usage and his choice of adjectives modifying γενεά suggest that people have a deeper problem in their relationship with God than what could be termed moral-ethical.[43] Having considered Jesus' estimate about his contemporaries, which later is shared and displayed by the apostles, we have to ask whether conclusions may be drawn from this verdict with respect to people in general, to people not part of 'that generation' in the strict sense. In Jesus' estimate are people in general 'evil, faithless and crooked' (Luke 9:41; 11:29)?

To start with, it seems quite natural that Jesus would speak about

---

41TDNT VII:406.

42If the disciples, even after the positive references to them here and earlier in the Gospel (e.g., Peter's reaction to the miraculous catch of fish) can be recipients of such a verdict, the appearance of other 'positive' figures in the infancy narratives (Zechariah, Mary, Hannah, Simeon) and elsewhere (e.g., the centurion in Capernaum or Joseph of Arimathea) does not abrogate Jesus' general verdict.

43Bertram, TDNT VII:407 comments on the σκολιά in Luke 3:5, which he takes in a metaphorical sense. The word 'expresses the ethical and social misconduct which is rooted in ungodliness and unbelief and which will vanish with the coming of the Messiah'. It has a universalistic scope: 'As all will see the salvation, i.e., the Saviour, so the setting aside of σκολιά... will take place in all mankind'. Conzelmann has overlooked this crucial origin of the moral-ethical failure.

this generation and not of an abstract humankind and its spiritual state as both verdicts employing qualifying adjectives arose from specific situations.[44] The occasions, namely the display of a lack of faith and the demand for signs are not limited to the immediate context of the verdict or to 'this (Jewish) generation'. It is also natural that when speaking about people in general, Jesus would do so with reference to his contemporaries whom he tried to call to repentance. Jesus' other verdicts on people confirm the general verdict delivered here: Jesus' verdict on generations past and future coincides with the one on this generation.[45]

This discussion has demonstrated the need to refer back to the Gospel and further beyond to appreciate the foundation of the anthropology displayed in Acts. Peter's verdict in Acts 2:40 and the investigation of the other references to the γενεά allow the conclusion that people need to be saved because they are part of one of the many generations that have failed or is presently failing before God and thus constitute a corrupt humankind.

V. Repentance

We have quickly surveyed Luke's understanding of the forgiveness of sins and his references to this (corrupt) generation in order to better understand Acts 2:38, its context which answers the question of the audience 'What must we do', and its contribution towards an answer to our question regarding why people need to be saved. We saw that salvation is closely linked to human failure, to sin from which people need to be saved. We were left wondering what kind of human failure Luke had in mind when Peter calls his audience to repent so that their sins may be forgiven (Acts 2:38-40). Is Peter addressing (1) the sin of rejecting God's Christ; (2) sins of a moral-ethical character in general; or (3) is forgiveness and salvation necessary to overcome a state of

---

[44] Both verdicts many have been intended to challenge the audience to a change of attitude! This would explain their vividness and force. More abstract reflections on humankind are found in Paul's two speeches before a Gentile audience, though both are also triggered by specific occasions in the light of which they are to be taken. Luke doesn't write a systematic presentation of the teaching of Jesus, rather he tells a story which includes his teaching. Due consideration to the form has to be paid if Luke's anthropology is to be compared to Paul's.
[45] I am not convinced by Weatherly, *Jewish Responsibility*, 99-107, who discusses recent studies of this Lukan theme and wants to limit the scope of the generation to 'the people of Jerusalem implicated in the crucifixion' (107).

people of which the first two options are but outward expressions?

It remains to examine the light Luke's four other calls to repentance (Acts 3:19; 8:22; 17:30; 26:20) and conversion shed on Acts 2:38, on the nature of the sins mentioned there, and on our question regarding why people need to be saved. Why should the addressees of these other appeals repent?

1. In chapter 3 Peter will again charge the Jerusalem audience to repent and turn to God so that their sins may be wiped out. Again the rejection and murder of Christ is emphatically mentioned in v. 14. The call to repentance and to turn to God (v. 19, not immediately follow-ing the accusation!) contains a new element—the audience needs to turn to God to overcome their sins. The plural and the further content of this address points to sins of a more general nature. 'Times of refreshment' are to come from the presence of the Lord (3:20). Here we have another benefit of salvation in addition to the gift of the Spirit[46] and another reason why people need to be saved. Jesus will remain in heaven until a universal restoration has taken place (3:21). 'The use of the word implies a creation that has diverged from the condition in which it was intended to be; it is perverted and must be put right.... Jesus as the coming Messiah will restore God's perverted world'.[47] This probably is Luke's closest reference to the 'fall', bringing about the need for restoration. God having raised his servant, sent him first to the Jews, to bless them by the servant's turning each one of them from their wicked ways (3:26).[48] People need to be saved because of their sins. God's restoration of the original order is necessary and he turns people from their wicked way in which all have embarked by giving them repentance (Acts 5:31;11:18).

2. Samaritan Simon is charged to repent from 'this wickedness of his' (8:22), namely, thinking that he could obtain God's gift with money and trying to do so. This is the only combination of μετανοεῖν with 'a specific sin and here only with that sin introduced by (the preposition) ἀπό'.[49] The construction employed (specific reference to one sin in the singular) should alert us as we study occurrences of the word in the (probably more general) plural references. The evil purpose came from Simon's heart (8:22), 'evidently here regarded as the seat of thought

---

[46]See Barrett, *Acts I*, 205.
[47]Barrett, *Acts I*, 206.
[48]Here I follow Barrett, *Acts I*, 214 who advocates this active transitive reading of ἀποστρέφειν.
[49]Barrett, *Acts I*, 415.

where purposes are entertained and plans made'.[50] Perverse thinking
(due to a lack of spiritual understanding) is sinful.
3. People should not think 'that the deity is like gold, or silver, or stone,
an image formed by the art and imagination of mortals'. But because
they have thought this way and have failed to recognise and worship
God—who actually is not far from them—there follows Paul's call to
his Athenian audience to repent (Acts 17:30). The immediate motivation for the repentance of this kind of sin is the coming judgement in
righteousness through a divinely appointed judge.

4. Paul summarises his ministry before Agrippa as declaring to Jews
and Gentiles, that they should repent and turn to God and do deeds
consistent with repentance (Acts 26:20, see also 20:21). Paul has one
and the same message for all people: Repentance in its most general
sense is needed; the Jewish sin of rejecting Jesus is not particularly in
mind. All people are away from God and need to turn to him.

In Luke's calls to repentance people are challenged to turn away
from various kinds of sin. They need to be saved from the sin of having
rejected and murdered God's Christ, from sins of a more general
nature, from the sin of lacking spiritual understanding, from the sin of
idolatry and failure to recognise and properly worship God. Admittedly, this wide reference is not yet apparent in Peter's first sermon in
Jerusalem. But by the time Paul sets out for Rome the attentive reader
has learned that people need to be saved because they are sinners
alienated from God and have no other alternative should they wish to
escape his wrath.

VI. Some clues from Acts 2 (prior to Acts 2:37)

Has Luke prepared his readers somehow for the question of the Jerusalem crowd and for Peter's answer (Acts 2:39-40)? What are the hints
that could help us to better understand both?
The witnesses of the miracle of Pentecost are devout Jews (2:5),
both from Jerusalem and afar. They entered the temple to attend the
festivities. Many of them had journeyed a long way to be present. They
are among the finest that Judaism has to offer. Yet all these observers
fail to appreciate the significance of what is happening in front of their
eyes. Some of them, recognising the extraordinary character of the

---

[50]Barrett, *Acts I*, 416.

event, modestly express their amazement while others go beyond expression of their wonder by suggesting a ridiculing interpretation (2:13), which sparks Peter's explanation of the events.

Luke presents an ironic scene. Devout Jews from many places are assembled for one of the highlights of their religious year. Yet as Scripture is fulfilled among them it is hidden from their eyes, and some even ridicule the very fulfilment. Not even the content of the apostolic utterances in their own native languages, namely 'God's deeds of power' (2:11) succeeds in pointing them in the right direction, neither does it refrain the scoffers. In addition to the guilt incurred through the rejection of Jesus (which will be directly addressed in Peter's sermon), the amazed observers need salvation from a blindness that hinders even the devout (those most likely to be familiar with the Scriptures which provided the clue to the interpretation of the event!) from perceiving the origin and significance of the event. Luke's understanding of sin contains a moral-ethical element, but also moves beyond this more readily perceptible aspect to the state of people. It remains to the newly Spirit-filled apostles to explain this origin and significance.

The contrast between divine intention and deluded human action concerning Jesus was succinctly summarised before Acts 2:36 in 2:22-24: 'Jesus, a man attested to you by God with deeds of power, wonders, and signs that God did through him among you, as you yourselves know—this man, handed over by you according to the definite plan and foreknowledge of God, you crucified and killed by the hands of those outside the law. But God raised him up...'.

Human failure and its extent has become evident. Though never a pretext for excuse, some of this failure is due to ignorance. Thus people are in need of instruction. It is God who makes known to them the ways of life and who makes them full of gladness with his presence (2:28). The Spirit had already instructed and inspired David (1:16). Since he was a prophet he had special knowledge (2:30) and could foresee things and speak of the resurrection of the Messiah (2:31). It is stressed throughout Acts that people hear and need to hear the Christian proclamation. The lack, rejection or perversion of knowledge characterising non-believers is addressed once people convert. The first item listed to which the believers were devoted is the apostles' teaching. The availability and reception of this knowledge are among the many benefits of salvation. People need to be saved in order to gain access to and receive proper spiritual insight. To play on Taeger's conclusions[51]—people need to be saved and need much correction.

VII. Conclusion

Why do people need to be saved? We have surveyed some of the
answers provided or not provided by modern scholarship on Lukan
theology and have only started to probe what Luke's answer may have
been. From the little ground we have covered of a vast Lukan field it
seems that Luke's anthropology is not as different from other NT
views of people as it has been made out to be. This study also suggests
that Luke's anthropology is entrenched in the OT. It remains desirable
to work these suggestions out in detail and to take up the questions
raised by Conzelmann, Taeger and Parsons and Pervo to gain a more
precise understanding of Lukan anthropology. It seems that people
need to be saved because of their alienation from God which shows
itself in their attitude towards him, towards themselves and their
fellow people, and which culminated in the rejection of Jesus, who had
come with a mission to seek and to save what was and is lost (Luke
19:10).

51Taeger, *Mensch*, 225.

CHAPTER 8

SALVATION AND HEALTH IN CHRISTIAN ANTIQUITY: THE SOTERIOLOGY OF LUKE–ACTS IN ITS FIRST CENTURY SETTING

Ben Witherington, III

Summary

Luke's understanding of salvation in Acts needs to be placed in its broader Jewish–Hellenistic setting in which the word-group carried this-worldly associations. This background and Luke's own wider usage help us to appreciate better the spiritual connotations of the vocabulary in Acts. Salvation has its source in God and its content is largely expressed in terms of present blessings, including forgiveness, but the future dimension is not lacking. Despite allegations that his outlook is anti-Semitic, Luke's vision is universal, embracing both Jews and Gentiles.

I. Introduction

Strange though it may seem to anyone not familiar with pagan antiquity, much of ancient pagan religion had little or nothing to do with attempts to obtain eternal life or be 'saved' in the Christian sense of the term. The 'salvation' most ancients looked for was from disease, disaster, or death in this life, and the 'redemption' many pagans cried out for was redemption from the social bondage of slavery, not from the personal bondage of sin. When a petitioner went to Delphi to ask the Pythia about important matters involving 'being saved', the questions were always about whether a person would be kept safe from some danger or be released from some disease, or be protected from death.[1] Even when the subject of salvation did come up, pagan religion, was decidedly this worldly in its focus, aims, and perceived benefits. 'Saviour'...or salvation, had to do with health or other matters of this earth, not of the soul for life eternal.'[2]

When Tacitus wrote about his father-in-law Agricola: 'Great souls do not perish with the body; your spirit will live forever', he goes on immediately to add 'what we loved and admired will never die'.[3] He clearly means that Agricola will not be forgotten, not least because of his endearing and enduring qualities which live on in those like Tacitus whom the man influenced. This was the primary form of immortality most noble pagans hoped for, perhaps also coupled with a wish to be immortalized in someone's writings. In addition, if Tacitus is thinking simply of Agricola's influence on his family (*gens*) and not of the influence of the great man on all and sundry, then he may well be alluding to the Roman concept that members of a family are closely linked throughout the generations by a spirit (*genius*) which is the guardian and embodiment of the values and achievements of the previous generations of the family.[4]

Before examining soteriology and Luke's use of the language of salvation in Luke–Acts we shall provide some further evidence for the

---

[1] J. Fontenrose, *The Delphic Oracle* (Berkeley: Univ. of Calif., 1978), 10ff.; *cf.*, Witherington, *Conflict*.

[2] R. MacMullen, *Paganism in the Roman Empire* (New Haven: Yale, 1981), 57. This is well illustrated by the famous Greek epitaph carried over into Latin as '*non fui, non sum non curo*' ('I was not, I am not, I care not') and then abbreviated '*n f, n s, n c*' (*op. cit.*, 173 n. 30). Consequently, 'The chief business of religion, it might then be said, was to make the sick well' (*op. cit.*, 49).

[3] Tacitus, *Agricola*, 46.

[4] See R. Mellor, *Tacitus* (London: Routledge, 1993), 51.

conclusion that pagan religion looked for this-worldly salvation.[5] It will be instructive to consider briefly some of the inscriptional and literary evidence that shows how the word group and its Latin equivalents were used in the newer eastern cults, such as the cult of Isis or of Mithra. This will give us some degree of insight into what pagans were looking for as they embraced these so-called Oriental cults.

II. Salvation in a Graeco–Roman mode–spared, healed, blessed

In the traditional pagan cults 'assurances of immortality prove unexpectedly hard to find in the evidence. Even the longing for it is not much attested'.[6] Among the inhabitants of Mt. Olympus there was 'no easily recognizable, universal, or at least familiar deity to name, whose followers all trusted in his power to save them from extinction'.[7] Even though it is not entirely accurate to characterize the early Empire as an 'age of anxiety' in which paganism was on the decline and becoming less vital,[8] Graeco–Roman paganism was nonetheless in need of, and in some cases looking for, a new infusion of life blood by way of participation in new cults and religions. One sees this in the enthusiasm for Mithras or Isis in the first century AD, though we know only a little of what their secret rites involved and what benefits they were thought to convey.[9] Unfortunately, Apuleius' allusive account of an 'initiation' is not as revealing as we might like,[10] but the material suggests that whatever benefits came from participating in such rites were temporary, for, when new problems and anxieties arose, the initiation must be repeated again by the same person.

It is said of Isis that she has the authority to forestall impending

---

[5]See the data amassed by W. Foerster and G. Fohrer, *TDNT* VII:665-1024; *cf.*, also J. Schneider and C. Brown, *NIDNTT* III:205-23.

[6]MacMullen, *Paganism*, 53.

[7]MacMullen, *Paganism*, 56.

[8]Against E.R. Dodds, *Pagan and Christian in an Age of Anxiety* (Cambridge: CUP, 1965), see the critique by MacMullen, *Paganism*, 64ff.

[9]The cult of Isis and Serapis was already becoming popular during the time of the Ptolemies in Egypt; see Gill, 'Behind the Classical Facade', 85-100, here 86. ; also R. L. Fox, *Pagans and Christians* (NewYork: Knopf, 1989), 64ff.; and especially MacMullen, *Paganism*, 53ff.

[10]*Cf.*, Apuleius, *Metamorphoses* 11.28.1-11.30.4. Notice that *salus*/σωτηρία refers to the freeing of Lucius from his animal form, and thereby freeing him from the power of fate (*cf.*, Book 11 in general).

death and to grant a new life *novae salutis curricula*.[11] While this does entail 'new life', it is life in this world and 'not of a different order but rather a replacement to keep things going, prolongation instead of a substitute...'.[12] Isis was also recognized to work cures, and in such circumstances σωτηρία amounted to good health, with Isis seen as Hygieia, health deified. Elsewhere devotees to Isis credit her with 'salvation from many dangers'.[13] Followers of Meter refer to her as *matri deum salutari*,[14] or as the one who saved them from captivity.[15] Mithra is lauded in the inscriptions for providing σωτηρία from water.[16] The designation σωτήρ was also common for the god of healing, Asklepius.[17] In some ways, the stiffest competition Christianity had in the ancient world was the ever expanding cult of the Emperor, with its realized eschatology, proclaiming the Emperor as the one who brought peace, safety, and prosperity to the Empire.[18] In the sanctuaries of Meter, Isis, and Mithras we often also find vows *pro salute Imperatoris*.[19] More importantly Caesar, by his patronage distributing grain, money, land, work, and because of his military exploits is seen as a saviour.[20]

It is true that people like Cicero do from time to time suggest that the mysteries, in particular the Eleusinian mysteries, have a benefit in the afterlife for at Eleusis it is shown 'how to live in joy, and how to die with better hopes'.[21] Yet even in such cases the focus is

---

11Apuleius, *Metamorphoses* 11.21.6.

12W. Burkett, *Ancient Mystery Cults* (Cambridge, Mass.: Harvard, 1987), 18.

13*Cf.*, L. Vidman (ed.) *Sylloge inscriptionum religionis Isiacae et Sarapicae* (*SIRIS*) (Berlin: 1969) 198,406,538.

14M. J. Vermaseren, *Corpus Cultus Cybelae Attidisque* (*CCCA*) (Leiden: Vol. II, 1982; III, 1977; IV, 1978; V, 1986; VII, 1977), III, 201.

15*Cf.*, Burkett, *Cults*, 139, n. 12. Notice how earlier in Xenophon, *Hist. Graec.* 5.4.26 σώζω is used to mean deliverance from judicial condemnation.

16M. J. Vermaseren, *Corpus inscriptionum et monumentorum religionis Mithriacae* (*CIMRM*) (2 Vols; The Hague, 1959-60), 568. Already in Homer frequently σώζω has the sense of saving one someone from death or destruction (*cf.*, *Il.* 8, 500; 9, 78; 14, 259) and in particular on the sea (*cf.*, *Il.* 9, 424; 10, 44). It can also be used to refer to the safe and happy return home from a voyage (*cf.*, *Il.* 9,393; Epictetus, *Diss.* 2,17, 37-38).

17*Inscr. Cretiae* I, 171, no. 24. The inscription on a stone pedestal can be seen in Cambridge at the Fitzwilliam Museum. Even minor deities like Opaon Melanthios who was worshipped on Cyprus received inscriptions of gratitude, giving thanks for the rescue ('saving') of family members (*SEG* 13, no. 588). *cf.*, T.B. Mitford, 'Religious Documents from Roman Cyprus,' *JHS* 66 (1946), 36-42, here 36-39.

18See my *Conflict*, on 1 Cor. 15 and its relationship to Imperial eschatology.

19*SIRIS* 404, 405, 535; *CIMRM* 53,54; *CCCA* 4,172.

20*Cf.*, *IG* 12, 5, 1 ,557.

clearly on the first half of this statement, and, if the afterlife is spoken of at all, it is seen as an extension of this life and not a compensation or alternative to it. Pagan religion knows little or nothing of the idea of mortification or sorrow here and now in order to have bliss in the hereafter.[22] One can hardly imagine a pagan using the formula of Paul about 'living in the world but not being of it'. Pagans sought out the help of the gods and goddesses in order to be able to better live this life to the full in safety and hopefully good health and with some wealth.

Even that most spectacular of mystery rituals the *taurobolium*, (being bathed in bull's blood), was seen as providing not a guarantee of passage to some sort of afterlife, but rather potency, virility, full life in this world, and equally importantly a shield against all evil that may befall one. This benefit, however, was apparently only good for a period of twenty years.[23] Even in the Dionysiac mysteries, as we find them spoken of in the Orphic hymns, the aim of the rites and that for which prayers are offered in the ceremonies is the provision of σωτηρία in the mundane forms of health and wealth, or for safe travel at sea, a good year or good crops, and in general a happy and pleasant life here and now.[24]

While some of these rites mentioned above seem to be aimed at overcoming the fear of death (and its obscure sequel)[25] and fear of the gradual decline of physical life and health, even this overcoming of such normal human fears amounts to a this-worldly benefit. The most the majority of pagans looked for in the afterlife was peace, the absence of suffering, sorrow, worry, and turmoil, for their shade or spirit.[26] At least one major function of the mystery rituals of Isis seems to have been to reassure a person of such an outcome.[27] Pagans were also not above resorting to various forms of magic or charms to assure the quiet and peace of their own ancestors (*cf.*, perhaps 1 Cor. 15:29).[28] 'Thus mysteries were meeting practical needs even in their promises for an

---

[21]*De legibus* 2.36.

[22]See Burkett, *Cults*, 25ff.

[23]*CIL* VI,504 = *CIMRM* 514. It is probably right to see the late inscription (from AD 376) in *CIL* VI,510 which does speak of *renatus in aeternum* through taurobolium as reflecting Christian influence, or as a late pagan attempt to co-opt the perceived benefits of Christianity while maintaining the 'traditional' pagan religions. *cf.*, MacMullen, *Paganism*, 172, n. 24 and Burkett, *Cults*, 25.

[24]*Cf.*, the listing of the inscriptions by R. Keydell in PW XVIII,1330-32.

[25]*Cf.*, Plutarch, *Non posse* 1105b.

[26]*Cf.*, *SIRIS* 464; Apuleius, *Meta.* 11.6.5.

[27]*Cf.*, Burkett, *Cults*, 26.

[28]See my *Conflict*, ad loc.

afterlife.... The initiate finally proclaimed: I escaped from evil, I found
the better. This, then must have been the immediate experience of
successful mysteries: "feeling better now"'.[29] These factors must be
borne in mind as we begin to consider what the author of Acts says
about the means, nature, and benefits of salvation.

III. Helped, cured, delivered in Luke–Acts

Luke is by no means unfamiliar with Graeco–Roman uses or earlier
Jewish uses of the σωτηρία word group. In Acts 27:34 σωτηρία is used
in its mundane sense of health, well-being, safety.[30] In several places
in both Luke and Acts σώζω is used to refer to healing, not eternal
salvation. Thus in Acts 4:9 the verb very clearly means 'healed' as the
reference to sickness shows. Perhaps healing in this text is seen as an
indicator that eschatological salvation is now available through Christ
(cf., 4:12), but 'healing' itself is not seen as either a necessary or sufficient description of what 'salvation' in Christ entails.[31] Or again, at
several points in the Gospel we find the phrase ἡ πίστις σου σέσωκέν
σε. In Luke 8:48 it surely means 'your faith has made you well' (cf.,
NRSV). The same is the case at Luke 17:19 and 18:42. More debatable
is the use of the phrase in Luke 7:50 where no physical healing is
involved. Rather a woman's sins are forgiven, and pronouncement is
made 'your faith has saved you'. Even here one could argue for a
medicinal sense, if one is thinking of the healing of the emotions by
means of the cleansing of the conscience, but in view of the association
of salvation with the forgiveness of sins elsewhere in Luke–Acts it is
perhaps better to see the more pregnant sense of σώζω here which
would include but not be limited to the concept of emotional healing.
More clearly, in Luke 6:9 Jesus is asking if it is lawful to do material

---

29Cf., Aristotle, Politics 1342a 14f. The quotations are from Burkett, Cults, 23 and 19,
to whom, along with Prof. MacMullen, I am indebted throughout this section of
the paper.
30Cf., Bruce, Acts (Greek Text), 524-25. cf., Thucydides, Hist. 3. 59. 1, and Heb. 11:7
NRSV 'it will help you to survive'.
31By this I mean that while healing may be involved, according to Luke, true
salvation after Pentecost never involves physical healing alone, and it may not
involve physical healing at all (cf., Bruce, Acts (Greek Text), 151-52). Several recent
articles have quite properly stressed that 'healing' is often what the salvation
language refers to in Luke–Acts, though, of course, forgiveness of sins is also seen
as the content of salvation elsewhere in Acts. See Carroll, 'Jesus'; Jones, 'Title';
Pilch, 'Sickness'.

good, in this case to heal or cure a person (ψυχὴν σῶσαι) on the sab-bath.[32] All these passages demonstrate very clearly that Luke knows the way σώζω/σωτηρία and the cognate terms were frequently used in the pagan world. The much more difficult question to answer is whether any of these passages demonstrate that for Luke healing is seen as an essential part of 'Christian salvation', or whether Luke is simply using the σωτηρία language in these passages in its secular sense.

In view of the programmatic speech of Jesus in Luke 4:18-27 where Isaiah 61:1-2 and 58:6 are quoted as being fulfilled, it appears to me that Luke does believe that healings, such as recovery of sight to the blind, are an important part of what the salvation that comes from Jesus entails.[33] But Luke has a more full-orbed view of salvation than these few healing passages might suggest, and clearly his main emphasis and interest lies elsewhere (see below). Perhaps one may conclude that Luke sees healing as a viable aspect but not always a necessary consequence of the 'salvation' Jesus brings. Some who are healed, are not necessarily 'saved' thereby in the fuller Christian sense of the term,[34] and some who were 'saved' were not necessarily healed thereby (e.g., Cornelius in Acts 10:34-48). This at the very least means that, on the one hand, we cannot assume that Luke's Christian use of the σωτηρία language always includes the more mundane sense of physical healing, material wealth, or preservation from danger. On the other hand, we cannot assume that his more ordinary use of the σωτηρία language always includes the Christian notion of eternal salvation.

There does, however, seem to be a larger eschatological matrix out of which Luke interprets these events of healing/salvation. Jesus was sent by God as the 'mightier one who can join the battle with Satan

---

[32]ψυχή, here as often elsewhere in the NT, refers not to the Greek idea of the soul, but to the Hebrew idea of physical life, the life principle, or in this case more generally to a human life or a living human being (cf., 1 Cor. 15:45).

[33]See also especially Luke 7:22 and 11:20. In the latter text exorcism is certainly seen as a manifestation of the inbreaking reign of God.

[34]Cf., Tabitha who was already a believer Acts 9:36-43. One may also properly wonder about examples like Luke 8:48; 17:19; 18:42. The fact that we are told in the latter two passages that these healed persons praised or glorified God for their healing does not necessarily imply that we are meant to think that they were led then and there to believe in or confess Jesus as their Lord or Saviour (in the fuller Christian sense of that latter term). Healing doesn't amount to saving in the Christian sense, for in the gospel stories Christ is not confessed or followed as a result and in the Acts story Tabitha was already a Christian.

and return those under his sway to the camp of the saved. That is to say, Jesus' healing activity is a central feature of his messianic vocation to restore God's people and usher them into the era of salvation.'[35]

It is also easy to demonstrate that Luke's view of 'salvation' is considerably broader and often different from the usual pagan sense of the term. For example, Paul is definitely viewed as a saved person yet he is not spared from imprisonment (*cf.*, Acts 16:16ff.) or excruciating suffering (Acts 14:19), though one may argue that he was delivered through or given the ability to overcome such events, even miraculously so in both of these incidents.

Luke is familiar with the concept of 'salvation' as rescue or deliverance or even protection from harm. At Acts 7:25 using the term in a sense familiar to both Jews and Greeks alike Luke speaks of God giving deliverance to or rescuing (σωτηρία) someone.[36] Acts 27:20 also falls into this category with its hope of 'rescue' from drowning. This is a sense of the term that pagans would readily understand and as we have already seen they used it in this sense when they prayed for safe passage upon the sea, or deliverance from stormy seas.

At least the first half of Luke 9:24 surely falls into the same category. Jesus is talking about those who attempt to preserve their physical lives from harm and those who by contrast even give up their life for his name sake and paradoxically find themselves in the end 'saved'.[37] Finally, in the crucifixion scene in Luke 23:32-43 we find on the lips of others the use of σώζω to mean 'rescue'. Particularly notable in this passage is the connection between Jesus being messiah and his ability to rescue self or others from harm.[38] Acts 2:40 where Peter says 'Rescue (σώθητε) yourselves from this corrupt generation',[39] might be

---

[35]Carroll, 'Jesus', 284.

[36]It will be seen that here in Acts 7:25, as often in the LXX, the term σωτηρία is not referring to some spiritual deliverance from one's own sins or their effects, but rather is speaking of actual physical rescue, in this case rescue of the Israelites from their actual bondage and state of slavery in Egypt.

[37]Unlike the first use of σώζω in this verse, the second probably does have the more pregnant sense of 'save'.

[38]Clearly enough from the use of σώζω to mean heal or deliver (see above) Luke does believe Jesus can do such things, but equally clearly since these statements are coming from Jesus' detractors it would appear that Luke is suggesting here that such a view of messiah's role is inadequate, indeed woefully inadequate, since part of what being messiah means is dying a shameful death on a cross (*cf.*, Luke 24:26). Thus the detractors seem to envision a messiah who comes and resolves all earthly dilemmas of illness, potential harm, poverty, danger, or oppression either human or supernatural. Jesus' view is portrayed by Luke as being much more complex than that, though it certainly includes some acts of healing, help, rescue.

thought to fall into this category of usage of the salvation language, but on closer inspection (*cf.*, v. 21) it appears likely that Luke has in mind the more profound notion of rescue from coming divine judgement by means of disassociation from 'this generation's' moral and spiritual darkness.

There is in addition one important text, Acts 16:30-31, which is usually thought to suggest that there must be a certain content to a person's faith response to the Good News if they are to be 'saved'. The usual way of reading this text is that when the jailor asks Paul and Silas what he must do to be 'saved',[40] he is told 'Believe on the Lord Jesus, and you will be saved, you and your household'. Notice, however, that the response of the apostles involves not just the jailor who is present and has experienced the earthquake, but also his family who appear not to be present. One must ask if Luke is really suggesting that the jailor's faith will be sufficient to 'save' in the Christian sense his whole household. If the answer to this is no, then it is very believable that what is meant is that the jailor and his house will be spared from calamity if he believes on Jesus. In this case we might translate the crucial verses: 'Sirs what must I do to be rescued (from this calamity)?' They answered, 'Believe on the Lord Jesus Christ and you will be kept safe you and your whole household'. (*cf.*, 1 Tim. 2:15). Against this interpretation is the fact that the promise of 'salvation' here is similar to what one finds in Acts 11:14 where we also hear about a person and his whole household being saved. The differences, however, in the two stories are important: (1) in the Cornelius story there is no earthquake or calamity to be delivered from; (2) not only Cornelius but also his household hear the Word and respond to it.[41]

It would be wrong to give the impression that 'rescue' or 'spare' is the main way in which Luke uses the σωτηρία/σώζω word group. To the contrary, his interests primarily lie elsewhere. For example, of the some seventeen uses of the noun forms of this word group in Luke–Acts, only Acts 27:34 clearly and Acts 7:25 possibly do not have some sort of a 'spiritual' overtones. Furthermore, it is very striking that Luke never uses the terms σωτήρ, σωτηρία or σωτήριον when he

---

[39]Though Peter is indeed appealing to the audience to repent and be baptized in Acts 2:37-42, in view of the way that he stresses elsewhere that 'salvation' is of God, not something humans do for themselves (*cf.*, below), it is best to translate σώζω here as rescue.

[40]Σώζω can surely not mean 'be healed' here, but in view of the earthquake mentioned in v. 26, one can plausibly argue that the proper translation here is 'rescued' or 'delivered' (from calamity).

relates stories about the healing of the sick or the raising of the dead, though obviously the verbal form σώζω, with the meaning 'heal', does appear from time to time as we have shown. It is as though Luke has basically reserved these nouns to refer to something of more enduring and eternal significance.

This last observation leads to another one. Luke above all the other Evangelists has a sense of and concern about historical development, about growth and change of human beings and movements (cf., Luke 2:40). This affects not only his christology but also his soteriology. As C.F.D. Moule showed, the christology of Acts is not simply identical with the christology found in Luke, but is rather a further development of it, drawing especially on the crucial events at the close of Jesus' earthly life. The ascension of Jesus leads to what has been called an 'absentee' christology, but it is also true that it leads to an exaltation christology which stresses the new roles Christ assumes as a result of the resurrection and ascension.[42] It is not accidental, I would suggest, that we find in the Gospels much more use of the mundane sense of the words for salvation than we do in Acts. This is because in Luke's way of thinking salvation in the fuller and more spiritual sense comes about because of Christ's death and resurrection, and the means of receiving the benefits of these climactic events is through the Holy Spirit, who is not sent before Pentecost to be and convey God's soteriological blessing.

[41]It can be argued that the larger sense of 'salvation' is implied in the passage, since v. 32 in fact says that the word of God was spoken not only to the jailor but to his household, and v. 33 adds that they all were baptized. Surely, however the jailor's family is not envisioned as being present in the jail, especially in view of the separation of the jail and the jailor's home (cf., v. 34). Thus, Luke has telescoped the narrative in v. 32 to include the later outcome of witnessing to the entire family. My point is that the jailor is not a potential disciple in training and thus his response in vv. 27-29 must be seen as the natural reaction of a pagan to a perceived calamity and the terror of the manifestation of the supernatural (cf., Euripides, Bacchae 443ff, 586ff.). That all the prisoners were still present and none had escaped would have brought some relief no doubt, but it surely would not entirely erase the unsettling emotional effects of an earthquake, which was often seen as a sign of God's anger in pagan thought. Of course, the apostles respond by offering the man salvation in the larger and more Christian sense of the term, which could nevertheless include rescue from potential immediate traumas and calamities such as losing one's job or even one's life because the jailor thought he had lost the inmates in his charge. Notice how in v. 23 the jailor is charged with 'keeping them safely'. See further Rapske, *Paul in Roman Custody*, 264, for a similar conclusion. *Cf.*, Marshall, *Acts*, 270-73, for a different reading of this text.
[42]See Moule, 'Christology', who points especially to the 'absentee' Christology found in Acts.

IV. The means of salvation in Luke–Acts

Luke has often been viewed as one who places the Christ event in the 'middle of time'[43] and so enunciates a theology of salvation-history, making the history of the rise of Christianity but a part of a larger drama in which God enacts his plan for humankind. This is not a fully adequate way of viewing the matter, though there is no getting away from the fact that Luke is interested in the concept of salvation and he does indeed wish to make clear that salvation ultimately is 'of the Jews'.[44] It will not do, however, to argue that Luke's concept of salvation is simply an extension of the concepts found in the Hebrew Scriptures, or that the salvation found in Christ is seen as simply an extension of the salvation referred to in the OT. The term salvation history suggests a continuum with what God did in earlier times for Israel, but it would be better to speak not of a continuum but of the final fulfilment in Christ of God's promises, particularly those found in the late prophetic literature. It is not historical development but divine eschatological intervention in and through Jesus and his followers that dictates how Luke will speak about these matters.[45] Luke's language of salvation in the Christian sense, differs with rare exception from all the earlier or contemporary Jewish literature.

For example, Luke's Christian usage of σωτηρία is significantly different from what we find in the writings of his contemporary Josephus where σώζω/σωτηρία and cognates 'are not theologically freighted terms...'.[46] Again, all the surveys of the salvation language in the Hebrew Scriptures and the LXX fully justify S.R. Driver's conclusion that salvation and deliverance in the OT 'seldom, if ever, express a spiritual state exclusively: their common theological sense in Hebrew is that of a material deliverance attended by spiritual blessings (*e.g.,* Isa. 12:2; 45:17).'[47]

43*Cf.*, Conzelmann, *Luke.*

44I have some strong reservations about the way Conzelmann set up the equation and hope to deal with this matter elsewhere. There is however no getting away from the fact that Luke is trying to place the ministry of Jesus and the Christian movement in the framework of the larger work and plan of God (*cf.*, Squires, *Plan*). Basically, he seems to see the coming of Jesus and what ensues thereafter as the fulfillment of promises God made long ago to his people in the Hebrew Scriptures. In other words, he believes that Jesus inaugurated the coming of God's eschatological dominion on earth, a fact which must be proclaimed to all as 'Good News'.

45Jervell, 'Future'.

46Foerster, *TDNT* VII:987.

Luke's language seems, however, to have some precedent in the late prophetic literature and in the Qumran material. The clearest examples seem to be those from Qumran. 1QH 15:15-16 surely speaks of eternal salvation, not merely temporal and temporary deliverance, and in 1QM 1:12; 18:11 redemption is eternal. God saves his people from temporal difficulties with a view to eternal salvation (1QH frag. 18:5), which can be contrasted to the eternal destruction of the wicked (*cf.*, 1QM 15:2).[48]

In the late prophetic material the issue is not always as clear cut. Texts like Jeremiah 46:27 or Zechariah 8:7 do speak of a future eschatological deliverance by God of God's people from foreign lands and foreigners, but here the subject is a final temporal deliverance into the Holy land, not forgiveness of sins, not conversion, not a heavenly reward, not a final resurrection. Isaiah 45:21-23 clearly enough speaks about not only Jews but all the ends of the earth turning to the Lord and being saved, but even here 'saved' seems primarily to mean being spared or rescued from God's final judgement on idolatry (*cf.*, v. 20). Isaiah 49:6 speaks of God's servant whose task it is to raise up the tribes of Jacob, restore the survivors of Israel, and be a light to the nations 'so that my salvation may reach to the end of the earth'. These Isaianic texts come the closest of any texts in the Hebrew Scriptures to what we find in the Lukan corpus, for example in Luke 2:29-32 which alludes to this last Isaianic text, or to some of the material in Peter's speech in Acts 2. What is lacking even in the most pregnant of these earlier Jewish texts is any clear association of 'salvation' with the idea of conversion, though Isaiah 45:21-23 may begin to point in such a direction.[49]

One must speak, then, of both continuity and discontinuity of Luke's use of the language of salvation with what we find in both earlier, contemporary pagan sources and earlier and contemporary Jewish sources. It is especially the frequent, almost purely 'spiritual', use of this language to refer to conversion, forgiveness of sins, cleansing of the heart and its eternal personal benefits that makes Luke's work stand out from the non-Christian sources. Also, the christocentric focus and preoccupation of Luke's salvation language makes it

---

47S.R. Driver, *Notes on the Hebrew Text and Topography of the Books of Samuel* (2nd ed. 1913), 119.

48*Cf.*, on these passages Foerster, *TDNT* VII:982-83.

49On this whole subject see J.F.A. Sawyer, *Semantics in Biblical Research: New Methods of Defining Hebrew Words for Salvation*, SBT Second Series 24, (Naperville IL: Allenson,1972).

stand apart. Among the Synoptic writers, only Luke gives Jesus the title of Saviour (*e.g.*, Luke 2:11), and it is his view that the purpose of the ministry of Jesus and his followers is to bring to fulfilment the promises of God (*cf.*, Isa. 25:9; 26:18; 45:17; 61:1), proclaiming salvation to all peoples, but especially to Israel (*cf.*, Luke 4:18-21; 7:22; 19:9; Acts 4:12; 13:46-47).[50]

Salvation in the Lukan sense of the term is something that comes from and properly belongs to God. From the early Semitic chapters of the Gospel where Simeon claims to have seen 'your σωτηρία' (Luke 2:30) to the very end of Acts where we hear that God's salvation (τὸ σωτήριον τοῦ θεοῦ) has been sent to the Gentiles (Acts 28:28) it is clear what the ultimate source of salvation is.[51] Salvation is something humans can only receive, not achieve. It must be sent to them by God. It would appear from Luke 3:6 that Luke's use of the term σωτήριον with the possessive qualifier was suggested to him from his reading of the LXX of Isaiah 40:3-5 (which he quotes at Luke 3:4-6). There we are told that 'all flesh' shall see God's salvation. But what exactly does this mean? Clearly it implies a this worldly not an other worldly manifestation of God's salvation, though equally clearly in light of the larger context of Luke 3:1-3 it would appear to have to do with something other than the immediate literal deliverance of Israel from her oppressors. John comes proclaiming 'a baptism of repentance for the forgiveness of sins' (v. 3) and it is this latter concept that Luke seems to primarily mean by the term σωτήριον, at least as it is manifest in the present.

There are only four passages in Luke–Acts where the term σωτήρ is used. In Luke 1:47 the term is clearly used by Mary to refer to God as 'my saviour' not to Jesus. The larger context lets us know that saviour here means one who scatters the proud, brings down the powerful, lifts up the oppressed, feeds the hungry, and takes away the reproach or shame of being a mother without a son in a patriarchal culture. As is consonant with the whole Semitic flavour of Luke 1–2, saviour here has its basic OT sense of the God who delivers the lowly and puts the high and mighty in their place. Yet in the very next chapter (2:11) we hear the announcement of the birth of a saviour who is messiah and Lord. This announcement in the form Luke presents it, and especially in light of the reference to emperor Augustus at 2:1, is

---

[50]See Johnson, *Acts*, 16-18.
[51]Interestingly Luke uses the term σωτήριον for salvation only at the very beginning and end of Luke–Acts.

in all likelihood meant to be seen as a counter claim to those made about Augustus. Augustus' birthday was publicly celebrated as the birthday 'of the god [which] has marked the beginning of the good news through him for the world'.[52] Furthermore, in the eastern part of the Mediterranean Augustus was hailed as σωτὴρ τοῦ σύμπαντος κόσμου (saviour of the whole world).[53] In the official propaganda Augustus' reign and public benevolences were seen as a manifestation of the favour of the gods, indeed even as a bringing in of an eschatological golden age. Tacitus by contrast, writing about a century later had a very different opinion: 'After Augustus dropped the title of *triumvir* and made himself consul...he seduced the soldiers with bonuses, the people with cheap food, and all with the sweetness of peace. Gradually growing stronger, he took over the functions of the Senate, the magistrates, and the law' (*Annals* 1, 2). Luke, while not openly criticizing Augustus as his near contemporary Tacitus did, nevertheless clearly has another opinion of who the universal saviour really is. While Luke is happy to speak of Jesus' appearance on earth as God's bringing to Israel a saviour (Acts 13:23) his view of the scope of Jesus' rulership is not limited to Israel.

Especially interesting is the fourth of the uses of the term σωτήρ in Luke–Acts, found at Acts 5:31. Here Luke's sense of the historical narrative of faith takes hold in the way he expresses his soteriology.[54] Properly speaking, Jesus does not assume the full role of Saviour and Leader prior to God's having raised him from the dead and installing him at the right hand. It is only after his death on the cross that he can offer repentance to Israel (especially for her role in what happened on Golgotha) and forgiveness of sins. It is also only then that Jesus can send the Holy Spirit which in Lukan theology is seen as Christ's agent bringing salvation to the world (*cf.*, Acts 2:33-38,47; 10:15-18). After the initial Jewish reference to God as saviour in Luke 1, the rest of Luke–Acts concentrates on Jesus as the one who fulfils that role, indeed exclusively so.

The prophecy of Joel 2:28-32 which is cited in Acts 2:16-21 ends with the promise that whoever calls on the name of the Lord will be saved.[55] But who this Lord is, is explicated in what immediately

52Priene inscription, 40-42; see W. Dittenberger, *Orientis graeci inscriptiones selectae* (*OGIS*) (Leipzig: Hirzel, 1903-1905), II, §458.
53A.H.M. Jones, *Documents Illustrating the Reigns of Augustus and Tiberius* (Oxford: Clarendon, 1949), §72. This particular inscription comes from Myra.
54On the narrative and historical framework in which Luke views salvation see my forthcoming article on 'Lord'.

follows in vv. 22ff. Jesus of Nazareth. It is thus not a surprise, since the author is a monotheist that we hear the exclusive statement in Acts 4:12 'There is salvation in no one else, for there is no other name under heaven given among mortals by which we must be saved.' Luke clearly enough believes in a universal gospel about universal salvation for all peoples (*cf.*, Luke 2:32), but the sole means of obtaining this salvation is through Jesus. He is the horn of salvation alluded to in Luke 1:69.[56] The means by which Jesus will convey knowledge of salvation to his people is said in this same canticle to be by the forgiveness of sins, a crucial association, as we shall see when we turn to the issue of the meaning of salvation for Luke.[57]

V. The meaning and benefits of salvation in Luke–Acts

We have already seen the interesting connection of forgiveness and salvation in several contexts in Luke–Acts, and also the argument in Acts 5:31 that Jesus is able to be Saviour and offer forgiveness of sins to Israel and others because of his death on the cross and the subsequent resurrection and exaltation of Jesus by God the Father. In other words, it is not accurate to say that Luke has no or at least no adequate theology of the cross, and that he does not connect it with salvation.[58] For Luke, Christ's death and resurrection are at the very heart of God's saving plan for humankind which is revealed in the Scriptures as is made evident in a text like Luke 24:45-49. This text clearly links forgiveness of sins/salvation and its proclamation with the death and resurrection of Jesus, and should not be ignored.[59]

---

[55]Σώζω here would seem to mean 'rescue', for the context speaks of the coming of the *Yom Yahweh*, the Day of Judgement from whose negative consequences those who call on the Lord will be spared.

[56]Here again in Luke 1 this canticle focuses on the OT idea of one who delivers from one's enemies. *Cf.*, vv. 71 and 74 where it becomes clear that 'saved' means rescued or delivered in this text.

[57]Foerster, *TDNT* VII:997 is absolutely right that again 'and again in Ac. the content of σωτηρία is the forgiveness of sins 3.19, 26; 5.31; 10.43; 13.38; 22.16; 26.18.' For the ways in which human beings appropriate salvation see the essay by J.B. Green.

[58]Moessner, 'Script'.

[59]That Luke does not fully explain all the other benefits or implications of Christ's death on the cross besides forgiveness of sins is a moot point. Acts 20.28 makes it clear that Luke knows of and affirms the idea of Christ's shed blood as the means by which God creates and assembles a people, an ἐκκλησία.

For Luke salvation at its very core has to do with God's gracious act of forgiving sins through Jesus which causes the moral, mental, emotional, spiritual, and sometimes even the physical transformation of an individual. We can see this already in a text like Luke 19:1-10, the story of Zacchaeus. Here we are not talking about Jesus healing the man physically, or exorcising a demon, or delivering him from his foes or from danger. Rather, the story climaxes at vv. 9-10 and we are told that 'today salvation has come to this house'. What is meant is the recovery of a spiritually lost individual by means of Jesus' gracious behaviour towards the man. Salvation is something which can happen in the present, and involves the character transformation of a human being. That such a change or conversion has happened to Zacchaeus is shown by his sudden willingness to give to the poor and pay back fourfold to those whom he had defrauded. Certainly 'salvation' for Luke has social consequences, but equally clearly it is a spiritual transformation of human personality that leads a person to see the logical social consequences of receiving Jesus.

The two texts in Acts which indicate that salvation has a future dimension are Acts 2:21 as part of the quote of Joel 2, and Acts 15:11. The former text is interesting, drawing as it does on the OT concept of the Day of the Lord (*Yom Yahweh*). Notice this day is called a great and terrible day in Joel 2:32 and more importantly what 'saved' means in that text is 'those who escape' the judgement and attendant calamity that comes on that Day. This could also be what is meant in Acts 2:21, in which case it might be best to translate the crucial phrase 'shall be delivered/kept safe/spared'. However, there is one noteworthy change in the Acts quotation of the text from Joel. Peter calls the Day the great and 'glorious' (ἐπιφανής, v. 20) day. This may suggest that the emphasis in Peter's sermon is not on the coming judgement but on the coming redemption, the positive side of the equation, in which case the translation 'saved' may after all be preferable. In any event, we are not told in any full way what this future 'salvation' amounts to. For instance, it is not here associated with resurrection. The same may be said about the other future-oriented salvation text in Acts 15:11. Salvation there is referred to as future but what it entails or what its benefits will be are not stated. This drives us back to the Gospel texts once more.

Besides Luke 19:10, Luke 18:26-27 is an important text. Here being saved (in the future) is equated with entering the Dominion of God (also in the future, v. 24). The question about the number of the saved in Luke 13:22 leads to a discussion about entering the Dominion and finally about who will be in the Dominion—Abraham, Isaac, Jacob, the prophets, and people coming from all four major points of the compass to eat in the Dominion of God. This shows that Luke knows about the messianic banquet traditions, and that he associates future salvation with such traditions. Luke 9:24b in light of this in the second reference to 'save' likely alludes to such ideas. Those who lose their lives for Jesus' namesake will be saved, that is participate in the coming Dominion of God on earth, an event triggered by the coming of the great and glorious Day of the Lord (Acts 2:20).

What we have learned from this discussion is that for Luke salvation, in the present, means the forgiveness of sins, the cleansing of the heart by the Holy Spirit and through faith. As Paul says in Acts 13:38-39 the Good News is that through the crucified and risen Jesus forgiveness of sins and indeed being set free from even sins that were not forgivable under Mosaic law is possible.

In the future, salvation means entering God's Dominion and being a participant in the messianic banquet when the Lord returns. If we may legitimately look briefly at other future-oriented texts which do not mention salvation explicitly we may expand on these conclusions. For example, one can argue that the parable of the rich person and Lazarus shows that Luke affirms that the pious person will go to heaven when they die, into intimate fellowship with the OT saints, in particular Abraham (Luke 16:19-31). Or again in the sayings material in Luke 20:35-36 a place in 'that age' is associated with a place in 'the resurrection of the dead' and being like the angels. Or again, redemption (ἀπολύτρωσις) as a future event is explicitly associated with the future coming of the Son of Man at Luke 21:27. Paul in Acts 17:31 proclaims the Day of Judgement, that Christ will be the Judge on that day, and he indicates that Christ's resurrection is the past event that assures that this other future event will transpire. When one broadens one's search it turns out to be incorrect to say either that Luke fails to affirm or has no clear concept of what salvation in the future amounts to, or to say that Luke has no clear theology of the cross or understanding of its connection with salvation. It is certainly correct to say, however, that when σωτηρία/σώζω occurs and is used in a theologically loaded sense in Luke–Acts, the large majority of the time he focuses on the present reality and benefits of salvation.

Something must be said about the suggestion that Luke's portrayal of who may and will be saved reflects anti-Semitism, or at least anti-Judaism. For instance, J.T. Sanders has argued that Luke, especially in Acts, portrays God's salvation as coming to the 'nations' (*i.e.*, Gentiles) rather than to the Jews, in view of the Jewish rejection of Jesus as saviour.[60] He believes that 'Luke's entire theology about the Jews may be seen in the Stephen episode' and his whole view of salvation is seen in the programmatic speech in Luke 4. The rejection of a mission to the Jews at the end of Acts is seen as final and what the two volumes have been pointing toward all along.[61] There are a variety of problems with these suggestions.

Firstly, there is a consistent overplaying and overvaluing of the polemics found in the Stephen speech.[62] This speech reflects forensic rhetoric, and involves defence and attack, but even so it does not negate the 'dominant tone of good will' in Acts 1–5 where the Jews are addressed and many respond to the gospel.[63] Nor does the Stephen speech prevent Luke from presenting a variety of Jews, synagogue adherents, and God-fearers as responding positively to the Good News throughout Acts right to its very end. Paul starts by preaching in the synagogue in almost every place he goes precisely because salvation is for the Jew first.

It is only when many in the synagogue reject the message that we hear the repeated statement about turning to the Gentiles (*cf.*, 13:46; 18:6).[64] Furthermore, Acts 28 portrays Paul calling the leaders of the Jews in Rome together and explaining about Jesus and the kingdom of God to them, and we are told 'some were convinced by what he said, but others would not believe' (v. 24), in other words the response was mixed, even here at the end of Acts.[65] In short, Sanders' view represents a serious distortion of Luke's view of salvation. Even in Luke 4 what the programmatic speech sets in motion is a series of mixed responses to Jesus, sometimes involving rejection by Jews as in his home town, sometimes involving acceptance and discipleship as is clear beginning in the very next chapter, Luke 5.

The point of the remarks about salvation having come to the Gentiles in Acts (*cf.*, Acts 10:45, 15:7) is not to deny that salvation is still for the Jews (*cf.*, 15:16-17, 28:24), but to justify the new and surprisingly

---

[60]Sanders, 'Salvation', 104-28.
[61]Sanders, 'Salvation', 116.
[62]See Hill, *Hellenists*, 41-101. He concludes that Stephen was not a radical critic of either the Temple or the Law, and insofar as his speech represents Luke's own views, neither was Luke.
[63]Tyson, *Images*, 125.
[64]Even after 18:6, where the remark about turning to the Gentiles is clearest, Paul returns to the synagogue again in Ephesus in 19:8-9 and we find the same mixed response as is also the case in the latter part of Acts including in Acts 28.
[65]See rightly Johnson, *Acts*, 18.

successful saving action of God among non-Jews. Luke writes as a
Gentile for Gentiles and their salvation is a matter of crucial import for
him and his audience. He must verify the new thing that God is doing,
namely that the Gentiles are and have been in the divine plan of
salvation as the Scriptures foretold (*cf.*, Acts 15:17).[66]

Luke's vision of salvation is truly universal, and that means it
must include both Jews and Gentiles—all humankind must see the
salvation of God (Luke 3:6). Human beings are called to be like Simeon
and recognize in Jesus God's 'salvation, which you have prepared in
the sight of all people, a light for revelation to the Gentiles and for the
glory to your people Israel. If we are going to talk about programmatic
remarks we would do well to begin not just in Luke 4 but already in
Luke 2:29-32.[67]

Note that the polemic against Jews who reject Jesus is tempered
by recognition that even the most heinous acts committed by Jews
which led to the crucifixion of Jesus were committed out of ignorance
(Acts 3:17). In short, the polemics in Acts, including Stephen's speech,
are a reaction to and have to do with the rejection of Jesus and of God's
salvation plan which involves both Jews and Gentiles by some Jews,
they do not have to do with any sort of total or final rejection or dis-
enfranchising of the Jews by God. They are anti-rejection remarks not
anti-Jewish remarks.

VI. Conclusions and corollaries

While modern Christianity has never been quite sure what the precise
relationship of health to eternal well being might be, it is undeniable
that the author of Luke–Acts sees the curing of diseases, the healing of

---

[66]On the 'plan of God' *cf.*, Squires, *Plan of God*.
[67]It is also important to set the whole of Luke–Acts in the larger context of Jewish
interaction with Gentiles during the Second Temple period (see McKnight, *Light*).
The first Jewish followers of Jesus in their approach to Gentiles were simply in a
more aggressive and systematic and outgoing fashion following in the footsteps of
some Pharisees and a few others who were already either seeking proselytes and
synagogue adherents among the Gentiles, or more frequently, responding
positively to enquiries from interested Gentiles. I quite agree with McKnight that
early Judaism was not in general a missionary religion, in the way that early
Christianity was, nor apparently was it a widely shared goal of early Jews to see
the Gentile world converted, but this should not cause us to overlook that there
were some precedents set in early Judaism that involved some forms of evangelistic activity. See McKnight, 116-17.

the lame, and even the raising of the dead as one of the possible
benefits of being in touch with the power available from Jesus Christ.
Even contact with an apostle's garments is seen to have this sort of
effect on some (Acts 19:11-12). Yet it is equally clear that Luke sees this
as a general benefit which can be bestowed on either Christian or
pagan or Jew, and this benefit, in and of itself, does not amount to, nor
necessarily produce conversion to, the Christian faith. As was the case
in the Gospels with Jesus, healing is something early Christians do in
passing, on the way to accomplish other tasks of more enduring value.
It is not seen as an absolutely necessary part or benefit of sharing the
Gospel in the ancient world. It is surely no accident that, as we have
seen, the noun forms σωτηρία, σωτήριον, σωτήρ do not appear in
texts where the primary subject is healing, but by contrast such
language features prominently in texts like Luke 19:1-10 where the
subject is the transformation of human character.

It is also clear, especially from the final voyage of Paul recorded
in the last chapters of Acts, but also from a variety of other texts as
well, that Christian salvation is not something that is viewed as
preventing one from suffering or experiencing disaster, though it may
be said to entail being providentially preserved through disaster if
God's plan involves the using of a particular person for some further
work of ministry thereafter. There are then some immediate, temporal,
and even physical benefits envisioned for those who come in contact
with the living exalted Christ, including especially Christians, but
clearly enough the emphasis lies elsewhere. Luke knows and
frequently uses the terms σωτηρία/σώζω and their cognates in sense
very familiar to pagans in the Graeco–Roman world to refer to healing,
delivering, rescuing, keeping safe, and preserving someone. These are
some of the purely temporal benefits of God's eschatological saving
activity. Being 'saved', however, in the pregnant sense does not seem
for Luke to carry with it any guarantees of long life, being kept safe
through trials, wealth, or perpetually good health either. Luke believes
in God's temporal providence but he does not see such intervention as
the be all and end all of the salvation that one receives by calling on the
name of Christ.

The use of σωτηρία/σώζω which stands out from the vast
majority of uses in pagan writers, from the inscriptions from the
mystery religions as well, and from the large majority of Jewish
writings as well is the purely religious or 'spiritual' use of these terms,
and especially the eternal benefits that σωτηρία carries with it in such
contexts. We do not see anything like this in the large corpus of

writings of Luke's contemporary Josephus. Normally in the OT, and in other Jewish writings as well, what salvation amounts to is the this-worldly events of rescue, deliverance from enemies, being kept safe, being kept well or being healed, and perhaps occasionally resurrection of the dead could be seen as a means of preserving someone and their family (cf., 1 Kings 17:17-24). Forgiveness of sins is of course a familiar concept in the OT but one is hard pressed to find texts where it is called salvation. The closest one gets is in the Psalms, for instance Psalm 32 where forgiveness and preservation from trouble and deliverance from danger are closely connected.

One may say that if a person with a Jewish background read Luke–Acts there would be enough overlap in the use of the σωτηρία/σώζω language with what one finds in the Hebrew Scriptures that some comprehension would surely be possible. Likewise if someone of pagan background read this work the same could be said. Where Luke's language may have caused some puzzlement is when he uses terms like σωτηρία in a more exclusively spiritual or eternal sense. Luke 1:1-4, however, suggests that the person to whom this document was written was already a Christian, one to whom such things had been explained, but needed assurance and clarification about a variety of matters.

It is striking that if one analyzes the salvation language of Luke–Acts carefully one finds the more mundane sense of rescue, heal, deliver, keep safe much more frequently in the Gospel (cf., Luke 1:47, 71; 6:9; 8:36,48,50; 9:24a; 17:19;18:42; 23:35,37,39) than in Acts (e.g., 4:9; 7:25; 14:9; 27:20,31,34), and on the other hand we find the more specifically Christian use of the salvation language more often in Acts than in the Gospel. This last fact may be put down to Luke's historical sense that the full-orbed Good News about salvation could not be proclaimed until after the death and resurrection of Jesus, since it was only when he was exalted to the right hand that it was really or fully possible to offer forgiveness in his name and on the basis of the completed Christ-event (Acts 5:30-31).

Luke knew well about salvation and health and its various and variegated forms in antiquity and he relates his discussion to such understandings. At the heart of his salvation message, however, is the new thing that God has done in Christ through Christ's life, death and resurrection which in Luke's view makes possible a sort of salvation not previously available at all and only occasionally hinted at in some of the later Jewish prophets.[68] The summary of J.A. Fitzmyer is apt when he says that salvation-history in Luke–Acts:

...is not an identification of history as salvation, but rather the
entrance of salvation into history. Luke focuses on the inbreaking of
divine salvific activity into human history with the appearance of
Jesus of Nazareth among [hu]mankind. Jesus did not come as the end
of history, or of historical development. He is rather seen as the end
of one historical period and the beginning of another, and all of this is
a manifestation of a plan of God to bring about the salvation of human
beings who recognize and accept the plan.[69]

Finally, I would add that Luke sees the coming of Christ as not just
another epoch of history but the beginning of the eschatological age
when the Dominion of God breaks into human history, and the coming
of the Spirit at Pentecost is seen as the means by which this age can be
properly proclaimed and inaugurated as the age of salvation for all
peoples as 'a light for revelation to the Gentiles and for the glory to
your people Israel' (Luke 2:32). Not the emperor, but Christ is depicted
as the means and catalyst of this greatest of all blessings, and the
benefits are seen as both temporal and eternal, unlike the largesse of
Caesar.

---

[68]The lack of discussion of salvation in its more full-orbed Christian sense and of
its importance for Luke is a surprising omission in Kee's otherwise very helpful
book on the theology of Acts (Kee, *Good News*).
[69]Fitzmyer, *Luke I-IX*, 179; see his careful discussion of Conzelmann's proposal,
ibid., 180-92.

Part II

THE CALL OF GOD

CHAPTER 9

THE ROLE OF THE APOSTLES

Andrew C. Clark

Summary

By the 'apostles', Luke generally means the Twelve, a term which emphasizes that Israel has a new leadership. The apostles function as a bridge between the ministry of Jesus and the mission of the church. They are Jesus' authorized delegates, and act as his witnesses to the Jewish people. Their first-hand knowledge of Jesus both before and after his resurrection enables them to affirm, guarantee and rightly interpret the facts about him. Paul is also an authorized witness and expounder of the significance of the gospel events. By portraying Paul as in many ways parallel to Peter, Luke emphasizes the unity of the missions to Israel and to the Gentiles.

169

I. Introduction

Scholarly discussion of the apostles has centred on the origin of the apostle-concept[1] and its different uses in the NT.[2] As regards Luke's writings, Klein argued that with Luke for the first time the Twelve are elevated to the status of apostles, the purpose being to deprive Paul of the title and to portray him as subordinate to the Twelve as a defence against Gnostic heretics.[3] Burchard, in contrast, upheld the view that Luke regards Paul as 'the thirteenth witness', and equates him with the Twelve through the terminology of 'witness'.[4] The writings of these two authors thus raise important questions about which no scholarly consensus has yet been reached. What is the significance of the concept of the twelve apostles for Luke? How does Luke relate Paul to this concept? An attempt will be made in this chapter, through a careful analysis of the evidence, to arrive at answers to these questions.

II. The twelve Apostles

The concept of 'the apostles' is clearly a key one for Luke. Whereas the term is only used once in Matthew (10:2), and once or twice in Mark (3:14; 6:30),[5] it occurs six times in Luke's Gospel and twenty-eight times in Acts. It is also worth observing that for Luke the term is always used in the plural. With the exception of Acts 14:4, 14, which will be discussed below, the term always refers to the twelve apostles.

In four of the six cases of the word ἀπόστολος in the Gospel, there is a clear collocation with the concept of the Twelve or, after the resurrection, the Eleven.[6] Luke deliberately forges a connection in the

---

[1]On this see especially Rengstorf, *s.v.* ἀπόστολος, *TDNT*, I:407-420; Gerhardsson, 'Boten', 89-132; Barrett, 'Shaliah', 88-102; Agnew, 'Apostle-Concept', 75-96.
[2]See Roloff, *Apostolat*; Schmithals, *Office*; Schnackenburg, 'Apostles'; Barrett, *Signs*; Hahn, 'Apostalat'; Kirk, 'Apostleship'; Pfitzner, 'Apostleship?'; Giles, 'Apostles'; Haacker, 'Verwendung'; Clark, 'Apostleship'; Lohmeyer, *Apostelbegriff*.
[3]Klein, *Apostel*.
[4]Burchard, *Zeuge*. See also his 'Paulus'. For a discussion of Klein and Burchard, see Maddox, *Purpose*, 75.
[5]Some scholars regard the use in Mark 3:14 as an interpolation from Luke 6:13. The external evidence for its inclusion is strong, however, and the use of the word in 6:30 without further explanation favours the inclusion of the phrase 'whom he also named apostles' in 3:14.
[6]Luke 6:13 (both words); 9:1, *cf.*, 10; 22:14, *cf.*, 3, 47; 24:10, *cf.*, 9 (in this verse the reference is to the Eleven, rather than to the Twelve).

reader's mind between the twelve special disciples and the term 'apostles'. Luke also emphasizes that they were Jesus' constant companions (Luke 8:1; 22:14, 28).[7]

These patterns continue in Acts. The connection with the initial call of the Twelve is immediately emphasized in Acts 1:2 in the mention of 'the apostles whom he had chosen'.[8] Following the election of Matthias to the 'apostolic ministry from which Judas turned aside' (1:25,)[9] it is stated that he was 'enrolled with the eleven apostles' (1:26).[10] In the next chapter Luke reinforces the identity between the concepts of 'the Eleven' and 'the apostles' by his references to 'Peter standing with the Eleven' in 2:14, and to 'Peter and the rest of the apostles' in 2:37. From now on Luke generally refers simply to 'the apostles': it is unnecessary to reinforce further their identity with the Eleven/Twelve.[11] There is, however, one final collocation between 'the Twelve' and 'the apostles' in 6:2, 6.

As for the theme of the apostles as companions of Jesus, the account of the election of Matthias makes it clear that the essential qualification for the post is that the person should be 'one of the men who have accompanied us during all the time that the Lord Jesus went in and out among us' (1:21; cf., 4:13). The close connection between the ministry of Jesus and that of the apostles is also, of course, already implied in Acts 1:1; if the Gospel is the account of what Jesus began to do and teach, then Acts must be the record of what the apostles did and taught through his enabling.[12]

7Reference is also made to the Twelve in 18:31, and to apostles in 17:5; 11:49. The reference to prophets and apostles being killed and persecuted (11:49) may be seen as previewing the sufferings of the apostles in Acts, esp. James (12:2). (In the Matthean parallel [Matt. 23:34], the reference is to 'wise men and scribes' as opposed to 'prophets and apostles'; Nolland states: 'Luke has probably introduced "apostles" here to evoke the role of the Twelve', *Luke 9:21-18:34*, 668,). Other references in the Gospel to future suffering for Jesus' disciples (Luke 12:4, 8-12; 21: 12-19) are also fulfilled in Acts.

8The verb used, ἐκλέγομαι, is the same as in Luke 6:13.

9The terms διακονία and ἀποστολή form a hendiadys. This verse contains the only use of ἀποστολή in Luke–Acts.

10Luke never actually uses the expression 'the twelve apostles'; in the whole of the NT it only occurs in Matt. 10:2 and Rev. 21:14.

11Giles points out that 'in contrast to Luke's practice in his Gospel, the Twelve are never called in Acts by the general title "the disciples"', 'Apostles', 245, Rather, Luke clearly distinguishes between the apostles and the other believers.

12On the theme of the ascended Jesus actively at work in his disciples, see O'Toole, *Unity*.

III. Peter as representative of the Twelve

In Luke's Gospel, as in the others, Peter, James and John form a special inner circle among the apostles (8:51; 9:28). Given his special place in the Gospel (*cf.*, 5:10; 9:54), it is somewhat surprising that James receives no mention in Acts apart from in the initial list of the Twelve (1:13), and in the notice of his death (12:2). The reason may be that Luke wished particularly to link Peter with John (*cf.*, already Luke 22:8). Cadbury demonstrated how fond Luke was of parallel pairs,[13] and Morgenthaler convincingly argued that the frequent pairing of believers in Luke–Acts is due to Luke's desire to follow the scriptural injunction that testimony is to be received in the mouth of at least two witnesses (Deut. 19:15).[14] This explains why Peter and John are so frequently referred to together (3:1, 3f, 11; 4:13, 19; 8:14), even when the addition of John to the phrase in question is a little unnatural (3:4; 4:19).

Peter's roles in Acts are foreshadowed in Luke's Gospel in the account of his call,[15] in his frequently acting as spokesman,[16] and in Jesus' statement of his special prayer for Peter[17] and command to him to strengthen his brothers once he has turned back (Luke 22:32). There is also an emphasis on a special appearance of the risen Lord to Peter. In 24:12 he alone of the apostles visits the empty tomb, and in 24:34 the whole company report their new conviction that the Lord has risen indeed, based on his appearance to Simon. Peter is thus portrayed as the witness *par excellence* to the fact of the resurrection of Jesus, the one whose testimony has persuasive power.[18]

In Acts the roles of strengthening his brethren and acting as a witness for the resurrection are both emphasized. He strengthens the church by his interpretation of recent events in the light of Scripture (Acts 1:16; 2:16), by his prophetic authority (4:8; 5:1-11), miraculous deeds (3:1-10; 5:14f), and teaching. In his sermons Peter consistently focuses on the resurrection of Jesus, showing that it is in accord with scriptural prophecy (Acts 2:24-31; 3:22, 26),[19] and asserts that he and

---

[13]Cadbury, *The Making of Luke–Acts*, 233-235.
[14]Morgenthaler, *Geschichtsschreibung*, vol. 2, chapter 1. See also the discussion in Trites, *Concept*, 133-135.
[15]A prominent place is given to Simon Peter in the call narrative (Luke 5:1-11); Jesus says to Simon alone that, 'from now on you will be catching people' (v. 10).
[16]Luke 8:45; 9:20,33; 12:41; 18:28. His leading role is also emphasized in the phrase 'Peter and those who were with him' (9:32).
[17]Note the distinction between the singular and plural for 'you' in Luke 22:31f.
[18]In contrast to that of the women (Luke 24:11, 22-24).

his fellow-apostles are witnesses to its reality. Both in his preaching to the people (2:14, 37), and before the Sanhedrin (5:29), however, he is clearly the spokesman of the apostles as a whole.

A distinctive role of Peter which is clearly important for Luke is that of being the first to preach the gospel to a group of Gentiles (15:7), and to acknowledge their incorporation within the church. The fact that this incident is referred to three times (10:1-48; 11:5-17; 15:7-11), as is the conversion/call of Paul, underlines its significance.[20] At the Jerusalem Council Peter strongly asserts the salvation of both Jew and Gentile alike 'through the grace of the Lord Jesus', not by Torah (15:11), a position strongly reminiscent of that of Paul (13:38f, 43).

IV. The roles of the twelve apostles

In Luke's conception the Twelve are especially related to Israel. They also have an important role within the earliest church. As regards the Jews, they function as witnesses to Jesus' resurrection. As expounders of the christological significance of the Scriptures, they provide a foundational understanding of the meaning of the life, death, resurrection and exaltation of Jesus. Peter and John, as representatives of the apostles, preach not only in Jerusalem, but also in Samaria. Peter travels more widely still, and is used to preach to a group of Gentiles, and subsequently to defend their inclusion among the people of God. In this respect he exemplifies a wider legitimizing role possessed by all the twelve apostles. These varied roles will now be discussed in turn.

The nucleus of a restored Israel

Jervell has drawn attention to the issue of the restoration of Israel, and the place of the Twelve as its nucleus.[21] Although certain of his views are open to serious criticism,[22] his attention to these previously somewhat neglected matters was salutary. The key passage is Luke 22:28-

---

[19]It is likely that a deliberate ambiguity is to be seen in the two senses of being 'raised up'.

[20]Witherup analyzes the repetitions and their variations, and argues that the 'functional redundancy' functions in four different ways to emphasize that the movement to the Gentiles is part of God's saving plan, 'Cornelius'.

[21]Jervell, *Luke*, 75-112. Murphy, *Concept*, demonstrates that the concept of 'the Twelve' was viable, widespread and multifaceted in the first century.

30. Jervell argued that 'the number twelve is significant for Luke in so far as the twelve apostles are appointed over Israel'.[23] Two questions are important in connection with these verses. First, in what sense is the verb κρίνω to be understood? The verb is capable of a wide range of meanings, and often has judicial overtones. Whereas in the parallel verse in Matthew 19:28 it seems clear that judging is in view, in Luke the possibility of a wider meaning, including exercising leadership authority, cannot be excluded. Second, should the exercise of this ruling/judging be regarded as strictly eschatological,[24] as having a present dimension, or as including both aspects? Arguments against the view that a proleptic fulfilment is in view, fail to persuade in the light of Luke's emphasis on both the apostles' table fellowship with the risen Lord (Luke 24:41-43; Acts 1:4; 10:41), and their leadership authority in Jerusalem—precisely the two elements found in Luke 22:30.[25]

Johnson has developed Jervell's position[26] by arguing that in Acts 3–5 Luke is dealing with the question of the legitimate leadership of Israel. He shows that in these chapters the present leaders of the people lack credibility and authority in the people's eyes, while the apostles have become their effective leaders.[27] The Jewish authorities[28]

---

[22]See, e.g., Turner, 'Sabbath', 114-9. Turner suggests the term 'Israel of fulfilment' for the church as the people of God, thereby 'hoping to avoid the Scylla of complete antithesis (true as opposed to false Israel; new as opposed to old Israel - language that is hard to defend from the New Testament) and the Charybdis of implying that there has been no change in the status of Israel'. It is the latter danger to which Jervell is prone; 'Sabbath' 146, n. 126.

[23]Jervell, *Luke*, 89. He also discusses (84f) the importance of Acts 1:15-26, and esp. v. 17, in connection with the need to appoint a twelfth apostle. The reference to the 'twelve tribes' in Acts 26:7 also reinforces the significance of the number twelve.

[24]Nelson, *Leadership*, 224-230.

[25]Franklin rightly emphasizes the eschatological significance of the exaltation of Jesus in connection with the apostles' role: they 'act as the rulers of the renewed Israel which is derived from the eschatological event.... The community centred upon them is the eschatological community, owing its existence to the exaltation, created by the outpouring of the Spirit, living a life of unity and controlled freedom, and waiting expectantly for its completion at the parousia', *Christ the Lord*, 97. Nelson argues that 'there is no image in Acts of the apostles on thrones', and that to see a proleptic fulfilment would 'undermine the newness of the eschatological age' and would make the Great Commission largely redundant, *Leadership*, 229f. None of these arguments has much force.

[26]Namely that 'the leaders of the people have relinquished any right to rule over the people, and the Twelve have now become the new leaders of Israel, as Luke 22:30 makes clear'; *Luke*, 94. Chance who agrees with Johnson, sees the 'others' in Luke 20:16 to whom the vineyard is given as the apostles; *Jerusalem*, 67f.

[27]Johnson, *Acts*, 79-82.

refuse to accept the obvious significance of the facts they cannot deny, that the apostles show the same remarkable boldness that Jesus displayed (4:13), and that the healing of the lame man has taken place through the name of the risen Jesus (4:15f). Their threats (4:17, 21), accusations (5:28) and floggings (5:40) prove useless in stopping the apostles from continuing to proclaim Jesus to the people as the Messiah. The people are portrayed as 'filled with wonder and amazement' at the healing of the lame man (3:9f), and so full of praise to God that the Sanhedrin are unable to punish the apostles (4:21), and the temple police are afraid to treat them with violence (5:26). The people are willing to listen to the apostles' teaching (4:2; 5:25), and hold them in high honour, experiencing many miracles by their hands (5:12ff).

In addition to this role as the effective leaders of the Jewish people, the apostles also function as the leaders of the church, at least in the early chapters. The believers devote themselves to the apostles' teaching (2:42), and lay their gifts for the needy at the apostles' feet (4:35, 37; 5:2).[29] Sapphira falls down at Peter's feet and dies, as her husband did, on hearing her judgement pronounced. Barnabas, who is clearly contrasted with Ananias and Sapphira, not only lays money at the apostles' feet, but also is named by them (4:26f), thus demonstrating his submission to their prophetic authority. When a problem arises in the community, the Twelve propose a solution, and appoint the men chosen by the community (6:2f, 6). The apostles also send representatives to investigate the happenings in Samaria (8:14) and play an important role at the Jerusalem council (15:2ff). The apostles clearly form the core of restored Israel.

Luke draws a very close connection between the apostles and the city of Jerusalem. In contrast to the other gospels, he makes no mention of resurrection appearances anywhere other than in the environs of Jerusalem.[30] The apostles are commanded not to leave Jerusalem until the Holy Spirit has come upon them (Luke 24:49; Acts 1:4). The first section (Acts 1:1–6:7) focuses exclusively on the apostles' work in

---

[28]Note that Luke stresses 'the high priest...and all who were with him (that is, the sect of the Sadducees)' as the apostles' main opponents (5:17f; cf., 4:2, 5f).

[29]Johnson comments that 'no more graphic image can be imagined for the community's recognition of the apostles' authority'; *Acts*, 91.

[30]Note that Emmaus, the destination of Cleopas and his companion, is described as 'about seven miles from Jerusalem' (Luke 24:13), and that after recognizing Jesus they both immediately return to Jerusalem (24:33), as do the apostles when Jesus has ascended into heaven (24:52). Luke also emphasizes that the Mount of Olives, the site of Jesus' ascension, was near Jerusalem (Acts 1:12).

Jerusalem. At the time of the persecution over Stephen they even stay in Jerusalem when all the other believers leave (8:2).[31] In 8:14 they are deliberately referred to as 'the apostles at Jerusalem', and after their ministry in Samaria they return to Jerusalem (8:25), where later Saul sees them (9:27). The significance of this close link between the apostles and Jerusalem may well be that Luke saw the going out of the 'word of the Lord from Jerusalem' as a fulfilment of scriptural prophecy (*e.g.* Isa. 2:1-4; Micah 4:1-5).[32] Moreover, in Jewish eschatological expectation Jerusalem was the place where not only would the salvation of God be manifest, but the people of God would be restored.[33]

The apostles are portrayed in various ways as legitimizing new developments in the expanding mission. It is they who appoint the Seven (6:3), and who send Peter and John to Samaria when they hear of conversions there (8:14). Only when these two pray and lay hands on the Samaritan believers does the Spirit come upon them (8:15-17). Similarly, it is only after Saul has been accepted by the apostles that he is then free to go in and out among the Jerusalem disciples (9:26-28). Finally, Luke emphasizes that it is 'the apostles and the brethren in Judea' who, after hearing Peter's testimony (11:1, 18), accept that God has received the Gentiles, and 'the apostles and elders' who judge that gentile believers do not need to be circumcised or to keep the law of Moses (15:5f, 22f). The crucial new developments in the growth of the early church are validated by the men who form the nucleus of the restored people of God.[34]

Following Peter's preaching to Cornelius and those assembled in his house, and his sharing of table-fellowship with the newly Spirit-filled and baptized Gentiles (10:48), a change in the apostles' role may be seen. From this point on Luke gradually marginalizes them. In 11:22 it is not the apostles (contrast 8:14) but the church in Jerusalem that sends Barnabas to Antioch. The gift sent from the church in Antioch is sent to the Jerusalem elders, not the apostles (11:30). The Jerusalem

---

[31]There is no other hint in Acts of the later tradition that Jesus commanded the apostles to remain in Jerusalem for twelve years before going out to the world (*KP* frag. 3 *cf.*, Clement of Alex. *Strom* 6.5.43; Apollonius *apud* Eusebius *HE* 5.18.14; *Acta Petri*, ch. 5).

[32]So Fitzmyer, who also comments that 'though Luke never uses the expression, Jerusalem functions for him as "the navel of the earth" (Ezek. 38:12; *cf* 5:5; *Jub.* 8:19)'; *Luke I-IX*, 168.

[33]Chance refers to Isa. 35:8-10; 2 Esdr. 13:12f, 39f; Bar. 5:5-9; Ps. Sol. 11:5-7; 4QpPs 37, III:10-11; Pes. de Rab. Kah. 20:7; b. B. Bat. 75b; *Jerusalem*, 82f.

[34]This legitimating role is clearly a unique one in the development of salvation-history; Luke does not envisage successors to the apostles in this role.

Council consists of the elders as well as the apostles (15:2, 4, 6, 22, 23; 16:4),[35] and James, who is not one of the Twelve (though *cf.*, 1:14), takes the leading role (15:13-21). After this the apostles are not mentioned again, and it is 'James and all the elders' whom Paul later visits, and whose advice he takes (21:19ff). It would seem that, as far as Luke is concerned, once the apostles have legitimized the Gentile mission they can fade from the scene.[36]

Witnesses to Jesus' resurrection

The role of the apostles as witnesses to the fact of Jesus' resurrection is clearly central for Luke.[37] This role is stressed in their commissioning (Luke 24:48; Acts 1:8), and is seen to be central to their function in the account of the choice of Matthias to replace Judas (1:21f).[38] Peter continually refers to himself and his fellow-apostles as witnesses to Jesus' resurrection in his speeches (2:32; 3:15; 5:32; 10:41; *cf.*, also 4:2, 10, 33). They are also witnesses to Jesus' deeds in the country of the Jews

---

[35]Campbell suggests that the καί may be epexegetic, but this seems unlikely; *Elders*, 163 n.61.

[36]Note also that it is only after the Cornelius episode that the report of the death of James, one of the Twelve, is given (12:2). He is not replaced for, as Barrett comments, 'death removes James from the work, but not from the number'; *Signs*, 48. The importance of the Twelve is at least partly in what the number symbolizes. Nelson suggests that 'the failure to replace James may signify the end of the apostolic transition era'; *Leadership*, 229 n.226. Schwartz points out that in Acts 'the characters in the story each have a role to play: when that role is completed, Luke's interest in them ceases'; 'End of the Line', 23.

[37]The fact of the resurrection cannot be divorced from the significance of the event, *viz.* that by it Jesus has been shown to be Lord and Messiah, and the Pentecostal phenomena give assurance of the reality of this (2:36 ἀσφαλῶς, *cf.*, Luke 1:4 ἀσφάλειαν; both verses are in the emphatic position in their respective sentences; see Dillon, 'Previewing', 224-6).

[38]Luke emphasizes that believers other than the Eleven were Jesus' companions, and witnesses of events connected with his death and resurrection. The 'women who had followed him from Galilee' (Luke 23:49, *cf.*, 8:1-3; 23:55; 24:1-10, 22; Acts 1:14) have an important role in reporting their experiences, as do Cleopas and his companion (Luke 24:13-35). Luke probably includes references to disciples other than the Eleven as present to hear these reports (Luke 24:9, 33) to emphasize that there were several suitable candidates for the position of official witness to Jesus' resurrection (Acts 1:21f). Although others might qualify, it is the apostles alone (*cf.*, 1:2f, 13) whom the risen Jesus specially commissions (1:8). The reconstituted group of the Twelve alone are to be witnesses of his resurrection (1:22). The juridicial dimensions of the witness motif are important here (*cf.* Trites, *Concept*, 128-135).

and in Jerusalem (10:39).[39] Jervell[40] is thus incorrect to deny that the
Twelve function at all as guarantors of the Jesus-tradition. Paul also
speaks of the appearances of the risen Lord to 'those who came up with
him from Galilee to Jerusalem' who are now 'his witnesses to the
people' (13:30f). We conclude that the apostles are distinctive in their
role as Jesus' authorized delegates,[41] witnesses to the reality of his
resurrection and expounders of its significance.[42]

The witness of the apostles is matched by the witness of God,
especially through the enabling of the apostles to perform signs and
wonders. There are two summary statements concerning the signs and
wonders done by the apostles (2:43; 5:12). In 2:43 the order 'wonders
and signs' is significant, because this activity of the apostles is thus
directly related both to the eschatological wonders and signs in the
passage from Joel quoted by Peter (2:19), which is programmatic for
his sermon, and to the wonders and signs in the ministry of Jesus
(2:22).[43] Just as the signs and wonders performed by Jesus represented
his attestation by God (2:22), so the similar signs wrought by Peter (3:1-
10; 4:16, cf., Luke 5:17-26; 5:15f, cf., Luke 6:40f; 9:36, cf., Luke 7:49-56)
and the other apostles attest that their message is from God. The
apostles, together with their friends, pray that God would stretch out
his hand to heal and that signs and wonders would be performed
through Jesus' name (4:30), and the shaking of the building confirms
that God is among them in power, a truth demonstrated in the

39This is presumably one reason why a member of the Twelve had to have
accompanied Jesus from the baptism of John onwards (1:21). (The main reason was
to be able to confirm that the resurrected Jesus was the same man who had
preached and healed. See, e.g., Marshall, Luke: Historian, 43).
40Luke, 78f.
41Agnew notes that many recent scholars 'tend to see both apostle and saliah as
developments of the same OT–Jewish sending convention', seen esp. in descriptions of prophetic call (cf., use of ἀποστέλλω in e.g., Exod. 3:10-15; Isa. 6:8; Ezek. 2:3
LXX); 'Apostle-Concept', 91. This convention, reflected in the legal maxim 'the one
whom a man sends is like the man himself' (Ber. 5.5; cf.,,Luke 10:16; John 13:16),
may fairly be seen to lie behind the Lucan image of the apostles.
42Dillon stresses the crucial importance of 'the Lord's revealing word of instruction' to transform 'puzzled observers into believing witnesses'; From Eye-witnesses,
292. The facts the apostles bear witness to are given their authentic interpretation
and meaning by the risen Christ (Luke 24:44-47; Acts 1:2f; see Burchard, Zeuge, 133,
135), and the apostles are thus authoritative expounders of their significance.
43See Sloan, 'Signs'. The more usual order in Acts (and all the other eight NT
references) is 'signs and wonders': 4:30; 5:12; 14:3; 15:12, though the order
'wonders and signs' is also found in 6:8; 7:36 with reference to the miracles of
Stephen and Moses, respectively.

subsequent narrative (*cf.* especially 4:33). Peter has divine insight into the sin of Ananias and Sapphira, and his words carry divine force (5:1-11). The manifest activity of God in this and other miracles results in a wholesome fear of God on the part of both the church and the Jewish people (2:43; 5:5, 11). The abundance of healings and exorcisms results in even more turning to the Lord (5:14, *cf.,* 5:12-16). The witness of the apostles is thus matched by the witness of the Holy Spirit (5:32).[44]

Authoritative teachers

Peter is the representative of the apostles, and his sermons are clearly designed to give representative examples of the apostles' teaching. The early sermons in Acts, with their application of scriptural texts to the passion and resurrection of Christ and to the carrying of the message of salvation to all peoples, correspond to the programme of the risen Lord laid down in Luke 24:27, 44-47.[45] In Peter's sermons quotations from the Torah, the Prophets and the Psalms are interpreted in a global fashion, in which the messianic significance of the Scriptures in general is taken for granted.[46]

There is a considerable stress in the early chapters of Acts on the apostles as teachers. This emerges first in 2:42, where the first of the activities to which the believers devoted themselves is the apostles' teaching. Probably 2:44-47 should be seen as an expansion of the activities listed in 2:42,[47] and in this case the meetings of the believers in the temple (2:46) would have been for the purpose of listening to the apostles' teaching.[48] In the subsequent narrative their teaching activity is frequently mentioned (4:2, 30f; 5:20f, 28, 42). In his final section of his portrayal of the witness in Jerusalem, Luke shows the apostles as perceiving their main activity as ministering the Word of God (6:2, 4).[49] Since Luke refers to the growth of the church in terms of the

---

[44]The witness of the Holy Spirit might also be seen in the way in which Peter's hearers at Pentecost are 'cut to the heart' (2:37). The boldness and powerful preaching of the apostles is a mark of the filling of the Spirit (4:13, 29, 31, 33).
[45]See, *e.g.*, Dupont, *Salvation*, 103-128, 129-159.
[46]Fitzmyer points out that in Luke–Acts as a whole there are no citations from the Former Prophets, or from the Writings apart from the Psalms, the very sections omitted in Luke 24:44; 'Use', 532f.
[47]So Peterson, *Engaging*, 152.
[48]Compare references to Jesus' teaching in the Temple (Luke 19:47; 21:37; 22:52).
[49]Prayer is also a priority, but this is 'to be understood as prayer for the propagation of the Gospel'; so Turner, 'Prayer', 73. Compare 2:42; 3:1; 4:24-31; 10:9.

growth of the Word of God (6:7; 12:24; 19:20),[50] it is evident that he sees the apostles' ministry in this respect as indispensable to the growth of the church.

To summarize, the apostles are portrayed as teachers both of the people (note λαός in 4:2, 17; 5:20; 25), and of the Christian community (2:42; 5:42 κατ᾽ οἶκον *cf.*, 2:46). Above all, they testify to the fact of the resurrection, and to Jesus as the Messiah (2:35; 3:18, 20; 4:10; 5:31, 42), on the basis of scriptural prophecies and types.

Missionaries to Israel

In contrast to Mark's Gospel, where the appointment of the Twelve/ apostles is directly related to their commission 'to be sent out to preach and have authority to cast out demons' (Mark 3:14f), the choice of the twelve apostles in Luke 6:13 is not directly related to mission.[51] They are later given power and authority over all demons and to cure diseases, and sent out to proclaim the kingdom of God and to heal (9:1f, 6). This aspect of their calling is not distinctive, however, since it is shared with the Seventy (10:9).

In Acts 1:8 the apostles are commissioned to be Jesus' witnesses in Jerusalem, in all Judea and Samaria, and to the ends of the earth (*cf.* also Luke 24:45-49). The reader might well expect that an account would soon be given of their missionary travels. While they fulfil the role of witnesses in Jerusalem, however, it is all with the exception of the apostles who proclaim the word 'throughout the region of Judea and Samaria' (8:1, 4).[52] True, Peter and John, as representatives of the apostles, both 'complete' the former work of evangelization through their prayers for the coming of the Holy Spirit, and themselves evangelize in Samaritan villages (8:14-17, 25). Peter, in the course of his pastoral visitation, also works miracles which have a considerable evangelistic impact in parts of Judea (9:35, 42; *cf.*, Luke 5:10). Generally speaking, however, the apostles are closely associated with a stationary role in Jerusalem rather than a missionary one. Peter's trip to Caesarea is the one example of a definitely missionary journey, and even in this case Peter is unsure why he has been asked to come (10:29)!

50See Kodell, 'Word'.
51Jervell comments that 'in general the apostles play a notably passive role during Jesus' earthly life'; *Luke*, 78.
52Note the allusion to Acts 1:8.

The role of being Jesus' witness to the end of the earth will in the subsequent narrative be fulfilled especially by Paul.

We may conclude by quoting Jervell,[53] with whom we agree on this point:

> In Acts the Twelve function as missionaries to the Jews. But the term "missionary" is not sufficient and may obscure their role. According to Luke the Twelve are called to proclaim before Israel that the turning point in the history of the people of God has occurred, and thereby to call the people to repentance for putting the Messiah to death. It would be more appropriate to say that Luke assigns them a prophetic role.

V. Paul and Barnabas as apostles

It is remarkable that in Acts 14:4, 14 Barnabas and Paul are referred to as apostles. Before considering various possible explanations of this deviation from Luke's otherwise consistent practice of confining the term to the Twelve, a brief survey of the dimensions of mission in Luke–Acts will be helpful.

Missions to Israel and to the Gentiles

In the programmatic prayer of Simeon (Luke 2:30-32), Jesus, who embodies God's salvation, is to be both 'a light for revelation to the Gentiles and for glory to your people Israel'. The coming of John the Baptist and Jesus is that 'all flesh' might 'see the salvation of God' (Luke 3:6). The universalism of Luke's Gospel[54] previews the missions to both Jews and Gentiles in Acts. One important example of the latter is the account of the sending of the Seventy in Luke 10:1-20. It seems likely that the number seventy deliberately recalls the traditional Jewish understanding of the seventy nations in Genesis 10 representing all peoples.[55] Nolland comments that 'Luke is fond of anticipations, and

---

53*Luke*, 93.

54On this subject, see Fitzmyer, *Luke I-IX*, 187-92.

55That some of Luke's readers understood the number to have this significance is confirmed by the fact that the manuscript evidence for Luke 10:1 is almost evenly balanced between the numbers seventy and seventy-two, representing the numbers in the MT and the LXX of Genesis 10 respectively. Metzger has shown that the two numbers are frequently interchangeable in Jewish sources; 'Seventy'.

almost certainly uses the number here to anticipate later mission to all
the nations of the earth'.[56] It is significant that Luke utilizes different
elements from the mission commission of the Twelve in Mark 6:7-13,
Luke 9:1-6 and Luke 10:1-12. He sees no essential difference in their
missions. This is confirmed by the fact that in Luke 22:35 Jesus' reference to the apostles' mission actually refers to details true only of the
mission of the Seventy, not of that of the Twelve (cf., 9:13; 10:4)! Rather
than see this as inaccuracy on Luke's part, it is preferable to regard it
as a subtle way of indicating the essential unity of the two missions.

In Acts, as has been shown, the apostles are closely associated
with Jerusalem and the Jewish people (3:12, 25f; 4:2, 8, 10; 5:12f; 20, 25;
10:42; 13:31). Their witness and teaching is crucial to the foundation of
the church among the Jews. It is not they, but ordinary believers who,
due to persecution, are scattered throughout the region of Judea and
Samaria[57] and who go about evangelizing (8:1, 4). Eventually these
disciples travel as far as Antioch, where some of them begin to speak
to Greeks also (11:19f). At Antioch Paul and Barnabas later teach and
preach the word of the Lord 'with many others' (15:35; cf., 13:1).
Neither evangelism nor teaching the word is confined to a select few.[58]
Luke, however, portrays Paul as having a distinctive role in the
mission to the Gentiles, comparable to that of Peter and the Eleven in
relation to Israel. Luke is concerned to portray the unity of his mission
with that of the mission of the Twelve (cf. 9:27-29; 15:1-35), just as in the
Gospel he emphasized the unity of the missions of the Twelve and the
Seventy. This fact is far from irrelevant to the exegesis of Acts 14:4, 14.

Acts 14:4, 14

Given Luke's otherwise exclusive use of the term 'apostles' with reference to the Twelve, it is certainly surprising that, in these two verses,[59]
he should apparently use it with reference to Paul and Barnabas. A

---

[56]Nolland, *Luke 9:21-18:34*, 549.

[57]Note the allusion here to Acts 1:8.

[58]Like the apostles, Stephen 'does great signs and wonders among the people'
(6:8), and gives a Spirit-inspired exposition of the Scriptures with prophetic
authority (6:10; 7:2-53). Philip 'the evangelist' (21:8), proclaims Christ, performs
signs and miracles, experiences the leading of the Spirit, and expounds Scripture
to lead his audience to faith in Jesus (8:5, 26-40), just as the apostles do. Even an
ordinary believer like Ananias sees a vision, and is sent by the Lord to lay hands
on Saul so that he may regain his sight and be filled with the Holy Spirit (9:10-19).

brief survey of suggested solutions to this problem may first be given, before some assessment and arguments for our preferred solution.

Perhaps a majority of scholars sees the use in these verses as indicating Luke's uncritical use of a source.[60] A variant of this view, is that Acts 14:4, though otherwise Lucan in terminology, has been influenced by 14:14 which comes from a source.[61] Many interpret the reference to apostles in Acts 14:4, 14 in the light of 13:1-4, seeing Paul and Barnabas as 'messengers of the church' (*cf.* 2 Cor. 8:23; Phil. 2:25),[62] or 'missionaries sent forth by Antioch'.[63]

Some scholars relate the designation to the 'twelve apostles' concept. Klein[64] and Schneider[65] argue that the phrase 'with the apostles' in 14:4 should be interpreted as meaning 'on the side of the apostles (*i.e.*, the Twelve)'. Others, in contrast, see the use of the term as reflecting, at least in part, Luke's acknowledgement of Paul's claim to be regarded as an apostle.[66] Marshall believes that Luke accepted that Paul and Barnabas belonged to 'a group of apostles, commissioned by Jesus, wider than the Twelve'.[67]

What assessment can be made? As regards the notion of Luke's

---

[59]There is a text-critical problem concerning 14:14. Some scholars, such as Klein (Apostel, 213) and Schneider ('Apostel') 72f, argue that the omission of 'the apostles' from the Western text implies that its presence in other manuscripts may merely be due to a borrowing from 14:4. It may be that one should explain the omission in terms of the Western editor being motivated by a reluctance to extend the title to Barnabas, who is even mentioned before Paul. A problem remains, however, to quote Barrett, *Acts*, 678, in that this 'does not explain why he also changed the plural participle into the singular, and there must therefore remain a possibility (no stronger word can be used) that the short text (and the Western text usually expands) is correct'.

[60]Roloff *e.g.*, states emphatically, with special reference to 14:4, that the use 'goes so fundamentally against his terminology that the formulation of this verse cannot come from him'; *Apostelgeschichte*, 211 (cited by Lüdemann, *Christianity*, 159). Bruce, *Acts*, 271, n. 7; 276, n. 36, thinks there may have been a travel document underlying chs. 13–14 which provided Luke with the framework of his narrative.

[61]Haenchen, *Acts*, 420, n.10; Conzelmann, *Acts*, 108; Barrett, 'Acts of the Apostles', 80.

[62]So, *e.g.*, Hahn, *Mission*, 134, n. 4.

[63]Foakes Jackson, *Acts*, 124. Note that Paul and Barnabas report back to the church in Antioch in 14:26f.

[64]*Apostel*, 213.

[65]Schneider, 'Apostel' 52f.

[66]Maddox, *Purpose*, 71; Krodel, *Acts*, 253; Jervell points out that it is no more remarkable that Luke should use the term in somewhat different ways than that the Didache should be the Teaching of the Twelve Apostles and yet speak of apostles in a different sense (*Did.* 11:3-6); 'Paulus', 379.

[67]*Acts: Commentary*, 234.

uncritical use of a source, Lüdemann has rightly emphasized that everything else in the context of 14:1-7 'has a Lucan colouring, down to individual details'.[68] This is true of vocabulary, syntax, and the typically Lucan theme of division (*cf.*, Luke 2:34f). It strongly suggests that this pericope has received close editorial attention.[69] If, therefore, Luke has retained the expression from a source, it was because he wanted to. As for the link with Acts 13:1-4, it is important to note the emphasis of the passage, which is clearly on the divine initiative: while worshipping the Lord, the Holy Spirit tells them to set apart Barnabas and Saul for the work to which he has (already) called them. The church in Antioch sends them off, but the more fundamental truth is that they are those sent out by the Holy Spirit (13:4).

What then did Luke expect his readers to make of Acts 14:4, 14? It is often neglected that in the immediate context Luke has shown Paul applying the words of Isaiah 49:6 to himself and Barnabas (13:47). He is thus claiming that they have a significant role to play within salvation-history. The phrase 'to the end of the earth' provides a clear echo of the words of the commission given to the eleven apostles in Acts 1:8.[70] It would not, therefore, be too surprising if Luke expected his readers to understand by his use of 'apostles' in Acts 14:4, 14 for Barnabas and Paul that they were fulfilling with respect to the nations the commission originally given to the eleven apostles. This verdict is supported by the clear verbal parallel, generally ignored by scholars, between 14:3 ('signs and wonders done by their hands') and 5:12 ('signs and wonders done...by the hands of the apostles').[71] Thus it is better to see the designation 'apostles' in 14:4, 14 as not merely denoting 'missionaries',[72] or even indicating an almost grudging recognition of the fact that Paul claimed to be an apostle and was recognized

---

[68]Lüdemann, *Christianity*, 159. The aorist passive of σχίζω, for example, is found in a similar context in 23:7 as well as in 14:4.

[69]The argument of Klein and Schmithals above is not persuasive, being unnatural and lacking support from the context. See also Maddox, *Purpose*, 85, n. 18.

[70]Tannehill points out that the themes of light and salvation in Isa. 49:6 also tie in with Simeon's programmatic prophecy in Luke 2:30-32; *Narrative Unity*, 2:121.

[71]Tannehill indicates other parallels between 14:3-5 and Acts 4:25-30, which support the idea that Luke is drawing a deliberate parallel between Paul and Barnabas and the Jerusalem apostles at this point; *Narrative Unity*, 2:177.

[72]*Pace* Haacker who sees Acts 14:4, 14 as merely a reference to apostles as wandering 'charismatics'; 'Verwendung', 38. There is ample evidence in the NT for a class of itinerant missionary apostles, (*cf.*, Hahn, 'Apostolat', 56-61; Schille, *Kollegial-mission*, 13; Clark, 'Apostleship', 56-60, 71f), but these verses are best seen as indicating a higher status than this.

as such by others, but a clear hint by Luke that he himself saw Paul and Barnabas[73] as playing a role similar to that of the twelve apostles.

Are there any other indications in Acts that such an interpretation is valid? It may be suggested that the parallels between Paul on the one hand, and Peter and the other apostles on the other, argue in its favour.

VI. Peter and Paul parallels

As noted above, Luke has a fondness for pairs. This concern for balance extends to parallels between characters.[74] The aesthetic and literary context is important in this connection.[75] Above all, it is helpful to relate this phenomenon to the ubiquity of a particular rhetorical technique in the ancient world, σύγκρισις (comparison). Instruction in this technique formed part of the προγυμνάσματα, the preliminary exercises in rhetorical education.[76] The technique was widely used in encomia and other forms of biography, though it was not confined to this genre.[77] The most famous use of this technique is, of course, in Plutarch's *Parallel Lives*, many of the concluding chapters of which contain carefully constructed short summaries aimed at establishing

---

73Barnabas shares with Paul in the status as well as the function of apostleship, but Luke does not see him as a leader like Peter or Paul (*cf.* Gal. 2:7-9). Pfitzner comments that 'for Luke, Paul and Barnabas form an apostolic pair. What is true for Paul is therefore also true for his companion', 'Apostleship?', 232,. Whatever the historical value of the tradition from Clement of Alexandria (*Hypot* 7; *Strom* 2.20.116; *cf.*, Eusebius *HE* 1.11.12; 2.1.1) that Barnabas was one of the Seventy, it would certainly fit well with Luke's portrayal of Barnabas as a missionary to the Gentiles. It is difficult to say whether or not Luke regarded him as having been in the group that saw the risen Lord and was personally commissioned by him, but it is quite possible (*cf.* 13:2). Paul certainly saw him in this way (1 Cor. 9:1, 6).
74Johnson, *Acts*, 10, states that 'parallelism enables Luke to draw connections between his characters and to create a dynamic tension between discrete parts of the story'. See also Tannehill, *Narrative Unity*, 1:3.
75See Talbert, *Literary Patterns*, 67-75. He argues, 70, that in the light of 'the literary, artistic and aesthetic tendencies of classical civilization ... it is not surprising to find a Greek document like Luke–Acts employing the law of duality as its architectonic principle'.
76See, *e.g.*, Clark, *Rhetoric*, 177-206; Forbes, 'Comparison', who quotes extensively from Aelius Theon, writer of a rhetorical handbook about the end of the first century A.D.
77So Stanton, 'Criticism', 77-80. On Matthew, he comments, 79f, that 'since rhetoric permeated all levels of society, it is likely that the evangelist's readers would have been far more attuned to and impressed by comparisons than are modern readers'.

the points of comparison or contrast between characters.[78]

The most obvious example of this phenomenon in Luke–Acts[79] is the comparison and contrast between Jesus and John the Baptist in Luke 1 and 2.[80] Scholars have for generations also noted parallels between the miracles, speeches and other parallel experiences in the lives of Peter and Paul.[81] These may be seen merely as one aspect of a wider parallelism between Jesus and his followers, especially Peter, Stephen and Paul.[82] There are good reasons for seeing intentional parallels between Paul and Peter, or all the apostles, which indicate something about Paul's status, not just about the likeness of both to Jesus.[83]

Miracles

The summary statements about the apostles in 2:43 and 5:12 are matched by similar statements with reference to Paul and Barnabas in 14:3 and 15:12. The contrast between the apostles' miracles done 'among the people' (5:12), and those of Paul and Barnabas performed 'among the Gentiles' (15:12) is noteworthy. Summary statements are also given in connection with the healings and exorcisms of both Peter (5:15f) and Paul (19:11f; 28:9). In both 5:15f and 19:11f the miracles are said to be unusual.[84] Every individual miracle performed by Peter has its counterpart in one performed by Paul.[85] The closest verbal points of contact are between the accounts of the healings of the two men who were lame from birth in 3:1-10 and 14:8-10.[86] In both cases those involved have to deny that the healing took place through their own divine power.[87] As regards context, both stories are placed in a

---

[78]See especially Pelling, 'Synkrisis'.

[79]For further discussion, see Berger, *Formgeschichte*, 223f, who mentions such contrasts as those between Mary and Martha (Luke 10:38-42), and Barnabas and Ananias and Sapphira (Acts 4:36–5:11).

[80]On this parallel see Brown, *Birth of the Messiah*, 248-253; George, *'Le Paralléle'*, 43-65; on 54-58 he compares it to the Peter-Paul parallel in Acts.

[81]See Praeder, 'Parallels', 23-39.

[82]See O'Toole, 'Parallels'; Moessner, 'Christ'; Johnson, *Sharing Possessions*, 58f, argues that Luke uses stereotypical prophetic imagery to describe all his protagonists as 'Men of the Spirit'.

[83]For a more detailed examination of this topic, see my forthcoming thesis, 'Paul among the Apostles in Acts'.

[84]Turner, 'The Spirit and the Power of Jesus' Miracles', 138.

[85]Compare Mattill, 'Purpose of Acts', 110f; Neirynck, 'Stories', 172-182.

[86]See Lüdemann, *Christianity*, 159.

[87]Compare Barrett, *Acts*, 664f, who sees this parallel as specially significant.

situation of gathering opposition, and as regards sequence, both follow a major speech. Each is the first healing reported for the party concerned. As regards theme, the stories echo the course of salvation-history in that salvation is sent first to the Jews, and then to the Gentiles.[88] The variety of parallels, especially the rare lexical links,[89] encourages the view that the parallels are intentional, and this suggests the likelihood that other possible parallels are also not coincidental. Other healing miracles by Peter (9:32-35) and Paul (28:7f) are recorded, again with both verbal[90] and thematic links. Both Peter (9:36-43) and Paul (20:9-12) bring back to life people who have died. Both are involved in incidents involving supernatural punishments (5:1-11; 13:8-12), in the course of which they are empowered by the Spirit (5:3; 13:9) to have insight into the hearts of those concerned (5:3; 13:10), and to discern the judgement God wishes to bring on them.[91]

Other miraculous experiences occur to both Peter and Paul. Both experience miracles of liberation (12:3-17; 16:25-34) in a context of prayer (12:15; 16:25). Each undergoes the experience of falling into a trance while in prayer (10:10; 22:17), and is addressed by an angel of the Lord (12:7f; 27:23f). Both Peter and Paul see visions which lead to their preaching the gospel to a new group (10:17-19; 16:9f).

Speeches

Both Peter and Paul give major speeches which expound the content of the gospel. The clearest similarity is between Peter's Pentecost speech (2:13-36) and Paul's speech at Pisidian Antioch (13:16-41). In addition to various verbal and thematic parallels, it is noteworthy that Psalm 16:10 is quoted in both (2:28; 13:35). In both cases the christological exposition of Scripture is related to Jesus' resurrection, mention is made of the apostles as witnesses (2:33; 13:31), and forgiveness of sins is proclaimed (2:38; 13:38).[92]

More generally, it may be noted that just as Peter is given a

---

[88] See Praeder, 'Parallels', 35.
[89] χωλὸς ἐκ κοιλίας μητρός (3:1=14:8); use of a form of ἄλλομαι together with the words καὶ περιεπάτει (3:8=14:10).
[90] Both passages use forms of the verbs κατάκειμαι and ἰάομαι.
[91] Fenton, 'Order', sees significance in the order in which the miracles are recounted, but, as he notes, there are various problems over this.
[92] Pfitzner, 'Apostleship?', 229, records six points of similarity between Acts 2:14-36 and 13:16-41.

special commission by Jesus to 'strengthen his brothers' (Luke 22:32), so Paul goes from place to place 'strengthening' disciples (Acts 14:22; 15:41; 18:23).[93] The main way Peter and Paul do this is to be understood as teaching in public and from house to house (Acts 5:42; 20:20).

Commissions

In the accounts of Paul's conversion, several highly significant statements are made about Paul. First, in 9:15f it is clear that he has a particular commission to bear witness to the Gentiles,[94] as well as to the people of Israel. The use of δεῖ emphasizes that his ministry is part of the divine plan (cf., 19:21; 23:11).[95] His call to suffer means that he will follow in the footsteps of the apostles (5:40f).[96] Second, in 22:14 Paul is said to have been 'appointed' (προχειροτονέω; the same word used of the Twelve in 10:41), to know God's will (a significant statement, for the 'will' or 'plan' of God is a key concept in Luke–Acts),[97] to see the Just One,[98] to hear his voice, and to be his witness to all men of what he has heard and seen. The expression 'witness to all men' is important because of the parallel with the description of the twelve apostles as 'his witnesses to the people' (13:31). This parallel highlights a theme which has already emerged several times, that while Peter and the other apostles are witnesses to Israel, Paul is commissioned to bring the gospel to all (22:15), and in particular, he is sent to the Gentiles (22:21). In 26:16-23 these themes are re-iterated. Paul is to be a 'servant' (the noun ὑπηρέτης recalls the reference to 'servants of the word' in Luke 1:2, meaning above all the apostles),[99] and a witness

---

[93]Pace P. Bolt, chap. 10, II, (2), b), 'his brethren' should be seen as a reference to the whole community of the disciples; compare Fitzmyer, Luke X-XXIV, 1422f.

[94]This is the first group mentioned in 9:15.

[95]See Cosgrove, 'The Divine ΔΕΙ in Luke–Acts', 168-190, who argues that Luke portrays both Jesus and Paul as creative executors of the divine plan.

[96]Rosenblatt, Paul the Accused, 17-21, argues that the juridicial appearances of Peter anticipate those of Paul.

[97]See Squires' essay, and also his Plan of God, 2, n. 5.

[98]Note that Paul is described here as seeing, not just a vision, but the risen Lord himself, just as the apostles did (contra, e.g., Dunn, Unity, 99f). Marshall, 'Resurrection', 106, comments that for Luke 'the centre of the gospel was...the resurrection, and Paul was a witness to this'.

[99]The range of vocabulary used by Luke for the concept of serving is used of both Paul (δουλεύω, 20:19; δοῦλοι, 16:17; διακονία, 20:24; 21:19) and the apostles (δοῦλοι, 4:29; διακονία, 1:17, 25; 6:4).

(26:16).[100] He is sent both to the people and to the Gentiles (26:17, 23). Finally, in 26:20 he is seen yet again to be fulfilling the commission given to the apostles, as he preaches in Jerusalem, in Judea, and to the Gentiles (*cf.*, 1:8).[101] His message (26:22f) has the same three aspects recorded in the apostles' commission in Luke 24:44-48: the passion of the Messiah, his resurrection, and the message of forgiveness for all nations, as Scripture foretold.[102]

As an indication of Luke's view of Paul's status, it is also worth pointing out the allusions[103] (26:16-18) to the call narratives of Jeremiah (1:5, 7) and Ezekiel (2:1 LXX), and to various Isaianic verses (Isa. 35:5; 42:7, 16; 61:1 LXX).[104] Paul has not only seen the risen Lord, but has been commissioned in a way analogous to the prophets, and as a result his preaching is authoritative. Notable is the frequency with which Paul's message (and his companions) is referred to as 'the word of God' or 'the word of the Lord' (13:44-49; 14:3; 15:35f; 18:11).[105] Paul can even say that his message covers 'the whole plan of God' (20:27). It is clear that while the twelve apostles guarantee the gospel facts, Paul, like them, is an authoritative expounder of their significance.[106]

100Mather, 'Paul', 23-44, suggests that these titles characterize Paul's career, and that in Acts μάρτυς is only used of those to whom the risen Christ had appeared. Schneider, *Apostelgeschichte*, I:227, comments that 'if Luke makes both the Twelve and Paul the subject of διαμαρτύρεσθαι, he thereby essentially binds together Paul's role of witness with that of the apostles'; the verb is used of apostles in 2:40; 8:25; and 10:42, and of Paul in 18:5; 20:21, 24; 23:11; 28:23.

101O'Toole, *Climax*, 82, comments that 'Paul shares in carrying out the task assigned by Christ to the apostles'.

102For Paul as an effective expounder of Scripture, compare Acts 17:1-4.

103For details, see O'Toole, *Climax*, 67f.

104Seccombe, 'Luke and Isaiah', 25, argues that many of Luke's theological categories are drawn from Isaiah. Johnson, 'Jesus', 350, relates the allusions to Isa. 42:6f, 16 and 49:6 in Acts 13:47; 26:18, 23 to their contexts in Isaiah, and argues that Paul is seen as fulfiling the commission of the Isaianic 'Servant of the Lord'. It is interesting to compare Acts 26:16 with Isa. 43:10, where God commissions Israel as both 'my witnesses' and 'my servant' (*cf.*, Isa. 41:8f; 43:12; 44:8, and the discussion in Trites, *Concept*, 35-47).

105Brawley, *Centering on God*, 154, emphasizes Luke's 'characterization of Paul as a proclaimer of the word'.

106Trites, *Concept*, 153, comments that 'the witness of the apostles guarantees both the historic facts of the life, death, resurrection and ascension of Christ, and the authoritative form of their transmission and communication'. Paul shares the second part of this function. It is perhaps worth adding, lest an unduly institutional view of the apostles be given, that, to quote Pfitzner, 'Apostleship?', 226, 'the apostles are not guarantors of the Spirit; they do not have the Spirit at their disposal, but are under the direction of the Spirit'. This is as true of Paul (9:17; 13:4, 9; 16:6-10; 19:21; 20:22f) as of Peter (4:8; 5:32; 10:19f; 11:12).

VII. Conclusion

As regards the concept of 'the Twelve', an attempt has been made to demonstrate its connection with the theme of restored Israel. To quote Giles, 'for Luke the Twelve symbolize that God in Christ is restoring Israel to what it should be.... The number twelve therefore symbolizes not a break with the past but continuity with it'.[107] Their corporate witness also points to the end time.[108]

The apostles are transitional figures who link the church with the ministry of Jesus (*cf.* 1:1).[109] Eye-witnesses (*cf.*, Luke 1:2) of the ministry (Acts 10:41), death (Luke 23:49) and resurrection (Acts 2:32, *etc.*) of Jesus, through their proclamation and teaching provide an essential foundation for the church's continuing faith and life.[110] 'Their function is to affirm, guarantee and interpret the facts about Jesus.'[111] More emphasis is given to their role of legitimizing others and their work than their own evangelism. The denotation of 'apostles', at least as far as the Twelve is concerned, is thus much more 'authorized delegates' than 'missionaries'.

As for Paul, he is an authorized 'witness to all men' (22:15). While the twelve apostles are closely associated with the mission to Israel, he is the leader in the mission to the Gentiles. Luke emphasizes the unity of these two missions. In both obvious and subtle ways he shows that Paul is equivalent to the twelve apostles, and especially to Peter, in his preaching, miracle-working power, and commissioning. He cannot share the symbolic and authenticating roles of the twelve apostles which are peculiar to them, but in terms of functioning as an authorized expounder of the significance of the Christ-event he is their equal, and as a missionary he surpasses them.[112]

107Giles, 'Apostles', 245.
108McBride, *Emmaus*, 183: 'The Church exists between two functions of the Twelve: their function as apostolic witnesses to the resurrection and their function as judges at the coming of the kingdom'.
109Nolland, *Luke 1-9:20*, 268; Conzelmann, *Luke*, 217.
110Giles, 'Exponent', 7, comments that in Acts 4:20 we read, in terms of common Jewish legal usage, that the apostles, as reliable legal witnesses, only bear witness to what they have heard and seen.... In this role they are the guarantors of the Word which brings the Christian community into existence'. Compare Eph. 2:20; 3:5; Rev. 21:12-14.
111Maddox, *Witnesses*, 28.
112Jervell, 'Paulus', 378-92, sees Paul as the *Überapostel*.

CHAPTER 10

MISSION AND WITNESS

Peter G. Bolt

Summary

In Acts, contrary to much modern usage, 'witness' refers to the activity of the twelve and Paul, and 'mission' primarily to the work of God in sending Christ to the Jew and the Gentile through the word of his witnesses. These are key themes in the narrative of Acts. By narrating the witnesses' activity and, especially, their testimony, Acts can itself be regarded as maintaining their witness. A bridge to the reader is constructed through the theme of the triumphant word, by which the reader is addressed and to which he or she may respond. A response of repentance and faith will also issue in the believer passing on the word of the witnesses.

I. Introduction

Luke draws upon 'eyewitnesses and servants of the word' (Luke 1:2).
The use of first-hand witnesses (αὐτόπται) on the one hand, and their
relationship to the word of God on the other prepares the reader at the
very outset for Acts' themes of witness and mission respectively.

　　Since modern usage of both words is much broader than that of
Acts, this essay examines (I) the relevant vocabulary, before dealing
with (II) the themes within the unfolding narrative, and, in an effort to
root the current discussion more firmly in the data, concludes with
suggestions for a more appropriate bridge between the text and the
reader (III).

II. Vocabulary

Witness[1]

μάρτυς mostly refers to the twelve (Luke 24:48; Acts 1:8; 1:22; 2:32; 3:15;
5:32;[2] 10:39, 41), in their special role as witnesses to Israel (13:31; cf.,
10:36-39),[3] having been chosen by Jesus, with him from beginning to
end and equipped with his Spirit who then bore witness alongside
them (5:32).

　　Jesus also chose Paul to be a witness (22:14-15; 26:16).[4] In no
respect inferior to the twelve,[5] he can be regarded as the thirteenth witness.[6] Chosen as a 'prisoner witness',[7] he actually takes the testimony
to 'the ends of the earth' (cf., 1:8) testifying to 'what he had seen and
heard'. When Paul calls Stephen 'your witness' (22:20),[8] it may be because Stephen had also seen the risen Lord (cf., 7:56), but, rather than

---

[1]Witness vocabulary is discussed by, for example, Casey, 'μάρτυς', 30-37; Cerfaux,
'Témoins', 157-174; Nellessen, Zeugnis; Trites, Concept; Strathmann, 'μάρτυς',
TDNT IV:474-514; Brox, Zeuge.
[2]'Those who obey God' are the apostles (cf., 29; 4:19).
[3]This has been recognised at least as far back as van Pelt, 'Witness', 832.
[4]The distinction between ὑπηρέτης and μάρτυς should not be so pressed to
exaggerate the difference between Paul and the Twelve; pace Cerfaux, 'Témoins',
160. cf., Trites, Concept, 141; Rétif, 'Témoigne', 152–56.
[5]Trites, Concept, 141.
[6]Burchard, Zeuge.
[7]Rapske, Paul in Roman Custody, 394–411. Witness and prisoner are complementary, rather than antithetical (contrast, e.g., Alexander, 'Biography', 61–62).

being part of Acts' technical usage, it may simply reflect Paul's reminiscence of Stephen testifying at his trial.[9] Unlike the thirteen, Stephen
receives no specific choice from the Lord and his speech is different in
content and purpose to theirs (see below).

μαρτυρέω[10] is used for God endorsing his word by signs and
wonders (14:3), or Cornelius' conversion by his Spirit (15:8).[11] In addition, the prophets testify to Jesus and forgiveness (10:43), and Paul, in
agreement with them, testifies to Jesus' suffering, resurrection, and
proclamation (26:22f.) from Jerusalem to Rome (23:11).

Apart from μαρτύριον of the apostles' testimony to the resurrection of Jesus (4:33), and μαρτυρία of Paul's testifying activity in
Jerusalem (22:18), Luke does not use substantives to refer to the witnesses' testimony or activity, preferring instead to narrate these things
directly.[12] Their testimony was verbal,[13] focusing upon the resurrection, or, more precisely, 'Jesus who had been raised' (cf., 4:33).[14] The
personal pronoun often designates them as Jesus' witnesses (1:8; 13:31;
22:15), in the sense both of them belonging to him, and of him being the
content of their testimony (2:32; 3:15; 23:11; 22:18). They were
witnesses to 'his resurrection' (1:22), but also 'to everything he did'
leading up to that event (10:39), including his death, and after it (10:40-
41). As such, they could testify that it was 'this Jesus' who had been
raised by God (2:32; cf., 3:15), in accordance with the prophetic witness
(10:43; 26:22), and who has made forgiveness available (5:31-32). Their
witness to 'these things' (death; resurrection; proclamation of forgiveness) fills the pages of Acts (see II).

Trites has shown that witness is a 'live metaphor' in Acts, i.e., it
has forensic overtones which would be important for the first

---

[8]This reference does not commence the semantic development of μαρτύς from
witness to martyr—Casey, 'μάρτυς', 33ff.; Brox, Zeuge; Trites, Witness, 66–67, 132.
[9]In contrast to the false witnesses (6:13, 7:58). Perhaps because he bore 'Scriptural
testimony'; Dillon, 'Easter', 254.
[10]The compound διαμαρτύρομαι is utilised for 'the solemn attestation of the
apostolic message with a view to winning converts' (e.g., 2:40; 8:25; 18:5; 20:24)
before both Jews and Greeks (10:42; 20:21; 23:11; 28:23), and for the Spirit's activity
(20:23; cf., 21:4, 11). Trites, Concept, 74–75.
[11]It also denotes approval in the eyes of others (6:3; 10:22; 16:2; 22:12), or
endorsement of another (13:22; 20:26; 22:5; 26:5).
[12]Trites, Concept, 142.
[13]Not 'words and deeds', cf., Hill, 'Spirit', 20. For this trend away from witness as a
verbal activity in twentieth-century missiological discussion, cf., Woodhouse,
'Evangelism', 13ff.
[14]Cerfaux, 'Témoins', 158–159.

readers.[15] Further study of other legal vocabulary and procedures depicted in the narrative[16] may reinforce these overtones.

Mission[17]

1. The work. If ἀποστολή retains its overtones of mission, then those designated 'apostle' are said to be engaged in 'mission service' (Acts 1:25).[18] ἔργον plays a more important role. Three times it refers to the 'first missionary journey' (13:2; 14:26; 15:38). In Pisidian Antioch, Paul cites Hab. 1:5, adding another ἔργον (13:41), referring to God's astonishing work. The citation places the 'first missionary journey' in the context of a larger work of God, for which it became a test case (Acts 15).[19] God's 'mission' to bring eternal life to the nations had begun.

2. The sending. In Acts πέμπω is used exclusively,[20] and ἐκπέμπω,[21] ἐξαποστέλλω,[22] and ἀποστέλλω[23] are used sometimes of humans sending for limited and particular purposes. ἐκπέμπω is used when the Holy Spirit sends out Saul and Barnabas to begin the 'work' of God (13:4); ἐξαποστέλλω for the Lord dispatching 'this word of salvation' (13:26) and Paul (22:21);[24] and ἀποστέλλω for sendings initiated by heavenly messengers,[25] the Spirit (10:20), God (7:34, 35), and the risen Lord (9:17; 26:17-18).

The most basic mission which stands behind these specific and

---

[15]Trites, *Concept*, ch. 9.

[16]*cf.*, Winter, 'Proceedings', on Acts 24–25.

[17]The subject is often approached from assumptions and definitions drawn from recent 'missionary' practice, rather than from a linguistic direction. See, however, Rengstorf, 'ἀποστέλλω', *TDNT* esp. I:403-404.

[18]*Cf.*, Recf., ngstorf, 'ἀποστέλλω', 446. Regarding missionaries as '...those who travel to foreign places to preach the gospel', Maddox, *Witnesses*, 16-19, cannot so identify the twelve.

[19]Some MSS include the word in the citation at 15:18, which would reinforce the point that God's work is the conversion of the Gentiles. The reader may also be meant to discern an implicit reference to the Way as the work, *i.e.*, cause/mission of God, in Gamaliel's words (5:38).

[20]10:5, 32, 33; 11:29; 15:22, 25; 19:31; 20:17; 23:30; [25:21], 25, 27. *cf.*, ἀναπέμπω 25:21; προπέμπω 15:3, 20:38, 21:5.

[21]17:10.

[22]7:12; 9:30; 11:22; 17:14.

[23]5:21; 7:14; 8:14; 9:38; 10:8, 17, [21]; 11:11; 11:30; 13:15; 15:27, 33; 16:35, 36; 19:22; [21:25].

[24]Also for the Lord dispatching an angel to rescue Peter, 12:11. See also Luke 24:49 α2 B (L) D 33 (892) *pc.*

individual ones is that of the risen Jesus. Interpreting Deuteronomy 18:15 of the raising of Jesus from the dead (3:22),—not Jesus' appearance on the stage of history (*cf.* 13:22)[26]—Peter informs the Jerusalem crowd that God has sent his Servant to Israel (26). Through listening to the preaching of the apostles, they can now listen to him. In fulfilment of the Abrahamic promise, Jesus has been sent to Israel first, *i.e.,* before he is sent to the Gentiles (25). Israel's period of opportunity is limited by a future sending from God, when he will send the appointed Christ to Israel at the time of the restoration of all things (3:20-21; *cf.*, 1:11). Between these two 'missions' of Christ, forgiveness of sins and times of refreshing will come to the repentant.

God's sending Jesus to Israel is also implied by Stephen's speech (7:51-53). It lies behind his sending of 'the word' to Israel (10:36; 13:26) and 'this salvation of God' to the nations (28:28). Through the word of his Spirit-equipped witnesses, Jesus has been and is being sent.

Conclusion

Mission and witness are integrally related. The sending of the risen Jesus is the most basic mission, which is effected by his chosen witnesses who are equipped with (Luke 24:49; *cf.*, Acts 1:4-5, 8; 2:17-21, 33), and endorsed by his Spirit (5:32). Paul, also equipped with the Spirit (9:17), is specifically sent to the Gentiles in a general sense (22:21; 26:17-18; *cf.*, 9:15-16), as well as at specific moments (13:4; *cf.*, 16:6-10, 18:9-11, 20:22, 23:11). Thus, in accordance with the Abrahamic promises, Jesus is sent, firstly, to Israel (*via* the twelve), and then to the Gentiles (via Paul).[27]

25Cornelius sends servants under direction of an angel (11:13; *cf.*, 10:5, 22, 31-33), or the Spirit (10:20). *Cf.*, the sending in response to the prophecy of Agabus (11:28-30), or the calling through a vision (16:6-10).

26The sermon contrasts Jesus' crucifixion and his resurrection. *Cf.*, Dillon, 'Easter', 248 n. 53.

27Paul has responsibility for the Gentiles in Acts, despite earlier forays by others (11:20).

III. The witnesses and their witness

The twelve witnesses

(1) Luke 24 prepares for the witness theme to follow.[28]

In the first of three main sections (1-12), the women's role is played down, in keeping with Acts' designation of the twelve as the witnesses of this stage of Jesus' career.[29]

En route to Emmaus (13-32), Jesus explains recent events according to the Scriptures. His execution had dashed the disciples' hopes (21)—hopes erected by Isaiah (*e.g.*, Isa. 40; 41:14; 43:14; 44:24-28; 52:9-10; 54; 66) and alluded to after Jesus' birth (Luke 2:25, 38; *cf.*, 21:28). Jesus counters each of the items of their concern (26): the Christ had to suffer (*cf.*, 20) and to enter into his glory (*cf.*, 22-24; and 21b *cf.*, 46). If both things are according to plan (27), then this implies that the hopes for redemption were not dashed after all.

In the third section (33-49), Jesus appears to the eleven, invites them to touch him, and then eats in their presence (36-43).[30] These incidents provide them with the evidence of the physical reality of Jesus' risen presence[31] needed for their function as witnesses (*cf.*, Acts 10:41). In language appropriate to the eyewitness, they are asked to see (ἴδετε), feel (ψηλαφήσατε) and take note (θεωρεῖτε) of what they observe. Through many such 'proofs' (τεκμήρια) across a period of forty days, they were convinced that the Risen One was the same Jesus they had served (Acts 1:3).

Reiterating that everything written about him must be fulfilled,

---

[28]On Luke 24, *cf.*, Dillon, *From Eye-Witnesses*; 'Easter'.

[29]'Perkins, 'Witnesses', 33.

[30]Although a wider group is mentioned (9, 33), the narrative distinguishes them from the Eleven (9, 10, 11-12, 33) and relegates them to the background (σύν, 33). Their mention (9) may prepare for the two who go to Emmaus (13), and/or set the Eleven's commissioning in a more 'public' context. When the eleven were not present, Jesus did not mention the necessity for proclamation, by which he later mobilises the witnesses (26, *cf.*, 45-49). Although the presence of the wider group gives some ambiguity to 36-53, Acts 1 makes it clear that it was the Eleven who were addressed by Jesus in this section (the same group is in view from 2, through to their naming in 13). In Luke 24 the Eleven were distinguished from the others because the chapter was leading up to their designation as witnesses (*cf.*, Strathmann, 'μάρτυς', 492). If the wider group were also designated as such, Acts 1, especially the election (NB 1:26), becomes nonsensical.

[31]Evans, *Luke*, 919.

Jesus opens their minds to understand the Scriptures (44-45), itemising three things (46-47). There is a scriptural necessity for the Christ (1) to suffer; (2) to rise from the dead; and for (3) repentance looking to the forgiveness of sins to be proclaimed to the nations, beginning from Jerusalem.[32] After announcing the third element, the only one still to be fulfilled, Jesus declares the disciples his witnesses and promises them ability from on high (48-49).

Neither here, nor in Acts, do the twelve receive a mission command as such (contrast Matt.28:18-20), although Paul receives one. The only sending mentioned here is that of the promised Spirit (49). Their future role is simply a consequence of the scriptural necessities.[33] These three provide the occasion and also the content of their witness ('these things'). Because they had accompanied Jesus up to the crucifixion, and eaten with him after he arose, they could testify to both his suffering and his physical resurrection. Since he had opened their minds to understand, they can proclaim both the fact and meaning of these events: Jesus died and rose again, and now makes forgiveness available through repentance, all in accordance with scriptural necessity. In Acts, the witnesses' speeches echo these three things.[34]

(2) Acts 1–2.

(a) The task (1:1-11). Recalling 'the first word', Luke mentions Jesus' many proofs of being alive (1:3, cf., Luke 24:13-43); his link with Israel's hopes for the future, here by reference to the Kingdom of God (cf., cf.,Luke 24:21); and his instruction to wait in Jerusalem for the Holy Spirit (1:4-5, Luke 24:49).

His 'second word' proper begins with the Eleven's question (1:6), which was evidently fuelled by recent events, even if its narrow-sighted nationalism ignored the expansiveness of Israel's hopes already erected by the prophets. Re-setting the agenda, Jesus reminds them that their witness role (8, cf., Luke 24:48) may begin with Jerusalem, but will take them to the ends of the earth, i.e., to the multitude of its nations (Isa. 49:6; cf., 52:10).[35] Talk of the restoration of Israel is far too narrow. They will operate within the large-scale task spreading

---

[32]Micah 4:2; Isa. 2:2 cf., 51:4-5, expected the word to go out from Jerusalem in order to gather the nations into the eschatological Zion.

[33]Kremer, 'Zeugnis', 147. These divine necessities are taken as marching orders (10:42), cf., 13:47 (see below).

[34]Dillon, 'Easter', 247-8, τούτων=all of vv. 46-7; 251-6.

[35]See Rosner's discussion, chapter 11. In this allusion to reaching the nations through his witnesses, there is a hint of Servant Christology, which will become explicit later.

out in front of the Risen Christ, which will eventually issue in the restoration of all things (cf., 3:19-26), the Kingdom of God.

(b) The Election (1:12-26). The election of Matthias forms part of the preparations for their witnessing task.[36] Replacing Judas indicates that the number of witnesses must be twelve, but why? If the number suggests a symbolic restoration of Israel[37] it does so indirectly, whereas the link with the number originally selected by Jesus is direct (1:13, cf., Luke 6:12-16).[38] It is the Lord's choice which is emphasised (1:24-26), and, if Jesus' instructions to Peter to (re-)establish his brethren— i.e., to rebuild the group—after he had recovered from his fall (Luke 22:32b) prompted the election,[39] Jesus' special concern to keep the number at twelve is further endorsed. In short, this section indicates that the witnesses had to be 'chosen beforehand' by Jesus (cf., 10:41), whether during his earthly ministry (as for the eleven, 1:2), or after his resurrection through the control of the lot (as for Matthias).[40] There may be additional overtones, e.g., the endorsement of a continued task towards Israel even after they crucified their Messiah,[41] but these should not obscure this basic notion.

Companionship with Jesus from John's baptism to the ascension was necessary (1:21-22), to enable the testimony that it was the Jesus they once knew who had been raised. Although others met this criterion, a choice was made and the twelve witnesses were complete.

(c) The Spirit (Acts 2). Although the conclusion of Peter's sermon

---

[36]Discussions of 'leadership of the church' (Tyson, 'Church', 137) and apostolic 'office' both miss the point and introduce notions of institutionalism that are foreign to Acts.

[37]E.g., Recker, 'Lordship', 178.

[38]There may, of course, be some symbolic link with Israel's tribes behind this original choice, cf., Maddox, Witnesses, 14-15. However, Luke 22:30 suggests that it is not restoration, but judgement that is in view, perhaps in terms of the gospel going to the nations (see the arguments on Hab. 1:5 below). Is this really 'restoration'? The narrative puts nationalistic notions aside (1:6ff.), in favour of a future 'restoration' on a far grander scale (3:20-21).

[39]Dietrich, Petrusbild , 173f. This suggestion should not be dismissed too quickly— pace Marshall, Luke, 822. A metaphorical sense of στηρίζω—for which Luke prefers the compound anyway (14:22 adding τὰς ψυχάς; 15:32; 15:41; 18:23)—would be entirely out of keeping with Luke (Evans, Luke, 803). The semi-literal sense needed for Dietrich is certainly possible. The LXX uses the word for 'restore to a former position', in the literal sense, (e.g., Exod. 17:12). And Luke's two other uses are literal (16:26) and semi-literal (in the translation of a stock OT phrase, 9:51).

[40]Thus there is no need to either replace apostles, e.g., after 12:2, (Pfitzner, 'Apostleship?', 227) or to establish a succession.

[41]Rengstorf, 'Election', 185. Dietrich's suggestion would reinforce this.

promised the Holy Spirit to others (2:38–39), Acts 2 focuses upon the arrival of the Spirit promised to the witnesses (*cf.*, 1:4-5, 8). Despite others being in the background (1:14-15), Acts 1 focuses upon and ends with the twelve (1:26), who are the most likely subject in 2:1. This is confirmed by the flow of the chapter. Whoever is the subject of 2:1 receives the Spirit (2-4) and a crowd comes together (5-13). This sets up two groups: those receiving the Spirit—who are all Galileans (2:7, *cf.*, 1:11)—and the crowd. The identity of the first group is revealed when Peter stands up with the eleven (2:14; *cf.*, 2:37) to address the crowd. Promising an explanation of what has gone on for 'these men' (15-16), his address provides further confirmation. When he eventually gets to this explanation, these men have become 'witnesses' (32-33), a group which has already been limited to the twelve.

Their Witness

The 'hinge chapters' of Luke–Acts have identified those chosen to be Jesus' witnesses. As former companions of Jesus, the twelve have an historically unique position, later acknowledged by Paul (13:31).[42] The narrative proceeds to show them at their task. The speeches, which provide the reader with the impression of hearing their testimony first-hand, testify to the three crucial events (Jesus' death, his resurrection, and the proclamation of forgiveness), each explained 'according to the Scriptures'.

(1) Peter at Pentecost.
Although Jesus' death was according to God's purposes (23),[43] Peter's audience, assisted by the Gentiles (23, lawless), are blamed for it. Apparently, since they included *dispersion* Jews (5-12), that Israelite generation as a whole (*cf.*, 40) is indicted for killing their Messiah. God overturned their decision by raising Jesus from the dead (24, 32-36).

Peter uses Psalm 16 to explain that Jesus had become incorrupt-ible (24-32). The allusion to Psalm 132:11 reinforces his Davidic christ-ology (30), and prepares for the exaltation to be regarded as Jesus'

42This explains the need for their endorsement as the gospel moves into new areas (8:14-25; 11:22), *cf.*, Pfitzner, 'Continuity', 38-9.
43Barrett, *Acts I*, 142: 'Why he did this, and how the predetermined event was applied to the work of salvation, requires explanation, but this passage should be noted, along with 20:28, as providing a theological framework for the otherwise uninterpreted affirmation, "You killed him, but God raised him from the dead" (*e.g.*, 3:15).'

enthronement (*cf.*, 33-36=Ps. 110:1 [109:1 LXX]). Peter's explanation is now complete: Jesus has poured out the Spirit from the exalted position of a deathless existence, in which he has been enthroned as Lord and Christ. Both these titles imply a role towards the nations. Ps. 110:1-2 implies that the Lord has taken his seat to await the overthrow of his enemies. Psalm 2 also implies that the nations will be defeated by the Christ, although amnesty is available for those who capitulate.

Peter envelops his explanation of the coming of the Spirit with reference to Jesus' exaltation with quotations from Joel 2:28-32. These pull in two directions: (1) The arrival of the Spirit upon the disciples is evidence of the arrival of the last days (17-21), for they have just exemplified the spiritual wonders promised by Joel 2:28-31. (2) Joel's promise of salvation to all who call upon the name of the Lord and who are called by him (Joel 2:32 [3:4 LXX]) promises the Spirit to a wider group (Acts 2:37-39, *cf.*, 47), in association with the forgiveness of sins. In this way, Peter's sermon moves from the coming of the Spirit on the witnesses, to the promise of the Spirit for the hearers.

Jesus, accredited by God through his miracles (22); the dispenser of the Spirit and in whose name forgiveness of sins is found (33, 38), because he is installed as Lord (21, 34-39; *cf.*, Joel 2:32), is the content of the witnesses' testimony (32).[44] Given the Davidic christology operating in the sermon, it is tempting to see Isa. 55:4 also lurking in the background,[45] a passage which promised that David would be a testimony (LXX: μαρτύριον) to the nations.

(2) Peter and the Name.

(a) In the Temple. After healing a crippled man, Peter tells the Jerusalem crowd that Jesus' wrongful killing (3:13b-15, 17) was according to the prophets (18)—no doubt especially Isaiah, who spoke of the Suffering Servant. God reversed their decision by raising Jesus, the Servant (13, *cf.*, Isa. 52:13; 26). In the resurrection, Jesus was appointed as Christ (3:20) and installed in heaven until the restoration of all things (21) and shown to be the prophet promised by Moses (22-23; Deut. 18:15).[46] Having been raised, Jesus was sent first to the Jews and then to the Gentiles in fulfilment of the Abrahamic promises (25, Gen. 12:1-2). All the prophets had looked forward to these days (24) when the Israelites would be given an opportunity to listen to the great

---

44The antecedent of the relative pronoun more naturally refers to a substantive (*i.e.*, Jesus) than a verbal activity (that God raised him).
45*cf.*, Paul's linking of Isa. 55:3 with Pss. 2 and 16 (Acts 13:32–37).
46See n. 26 above.

prophet (22-23), to repent, and so find forgiveness and refreshing (19).

As well as being identified as God's Servant, the prophet like Moses, and the Christ who will return at the restoration of all things, Jesus is also called the 'author'—ἀρχηγός, a founder of a city or a family—of life' (15). When Peter answers to the Sanhedrin for this healing, he explains that Jesus is ἀρχηγός by virtue of his resurrection/exaltation (5:31). Jesus would therefore be the founder of resurrection life. Another pointer in this direction is the concern aroused by their initial preaching that they were proclaiming 'in Jesus the resurrection of the dead' (4:2). In addition, the angelic prison visitor tells them to resume preaching the full message of 'this life' (5:20). To proclaim the forgiveness of sins is to proclaim at the same time a share in the resurrection. Because Jesus' resurrection was understood in connection with the general resurrection (cf., 26:23), to proclaim his resurrection was also to proclaim that resurrection life had arrived, for he was the 'founder of life'.

(b) Before the religious authorities. Peter explained the healing in terms of the ongoing power of the name of Jesus, the one they crucified, but whom God had raised (4:10). In support of both elements, Peter identifies Jesus as the rejected stone of Ps. 118:22 which became the capstone (11). Because Jesus' name is the only source of salvation for all humanity (12), this clearly entails the third element: proclamation which cannot be restricted to Israel.

(c) The prayer. The prayer after Peter's release (4:23-31) explicitly focuses upon Jesus' death, although his resurrection is also clearly implied. After identifying Jesus as the Christ (26=Ps. 2:2;=the Son, Ps. 2:7) and the one anointed as the Servant (27, cf., Isa. 61:1) in his earthly ministry (cf., 2:22, 10:38), the prayer parallels Ps. 2:1-2 with Jesus' death (27-28), and with the current threats against the apostles (29).

These parallels suggest that opposing Jesus' witnesses who proclaim his name, is equivalent to opposing Jesus himself (cf., 5:1-11; 5:39; 9:5; 22:8; 26:9, 14). The Psalm teaches that when the nations rise up against the Christ, they will be given to him on request (Ps. 2:8). 'The nations' who rose up to crucify Jesus, have now arisen against his name and so, just as the Psalm instructed, his witnesses 'ask' in order that the ends of the earth might become his possession. They ask for boldness, which indicates that the conquest of the nations will take place through the bold proclamation of their testimony. As they boldly speak, the Son will take possession of the ends of the earth (Ps. 2:8, cf., Acts 1:8, Isa. 49:6; 52:10; cf., Acts 2:33-36, Ps. 110:1-2). The following narrative illustrates this, as the word either converts or confounds the enemies of Jesus' name.

(d) Before the Sanhedrin. Once again before the Sanhedrin, Peter asserts that their decision to kill Jesus as one accursed of God (5:30; *cf.*, Deut. 21:22-23) was reversed when God raised him. When 'the God of our fathers' exalted Jesus to his right hand (*cf.*, Ps. 110:1-2), it was as ἀρχηγός and saviour in order to give Israel repentance and forgiveness of sins (31). Being the chosen witnesses of these three things, the apostles cannot be silenced, and the Holy Spirit also adds his witness to theirs (32).

Gamaliel's counsel indicates that opposition to the witnesses has not prevailed (33-40). As the apostles continue to proclaim that Jesus is the Christ (41-42), the reader awaits the nations to fall before him.

Stephen's indictment of the Sanhedrin

For the reader, Gamaliel's advice implied that the Sanhedrin was opposing God through opposing the witnesses. The Stephen narrative makes this explicit. Stephen is clearly distinguished from the twelve who retain the ministry of the word (6:1-7). His speech is not included on the same level as those of the witnesses, but has a supporting role. Stephen mentions Jesus' death, explaining it as a product of the same hard-heartedness which led their fathers to resist the Holy Spirit (51–53, *cf.*, Neh. 9:30; Isa. 63:10-14; Zech. 7:11-14). He does not mention Jesus' resurrection—unless implicitly in the prophet like Moses (7:37, *cf.*, 3:22-23)—but he does have a vision of the risen Lord as he dies (55-56; *cf.*, Dan. 7:13, Ps. 110:1). Similarly, his speech does not explicitly proclaim forgiveness, but he prays this for his killers (7:59-60).

However, the proclamation may be implied by the citation of Isa. 66:1-2 (49-50).[47] Isaiah 66 critiqued false religion in order to replace it with true religion—defined as a humility which trembles at God's word (Isa. 66:2, 5), listens to God when he speaks, and answers when he calls (*cf.*, 4)—and, because this has not been the kind of religion in Israel, threatened a judgement beginning with the temple (6), and issuing in a joyful renewal of Jerusalem which then went to the nations (10ff.). The authorities had accused Stephen of speaking against the temple (6:13). Stephen accuses them of not listening to God's word—which is now being proclaimed by Jesus' witnesses. The temple

---

[47]Betori, 'Luke 24:47', 117–118.

authorities have not recognised the joyful renewal going on in Jerusalem, which will soon overflow to the nations.

In terms of its narrative role, Stephen's speech is not so much a
testimony to Jesus, as a testimony against the actions of the Sanhedrin
who put him to death, and who are now opposing his name. The
witnesses bring Israel the 'word' of the promised Deuteronomic
prophet, and yet the Sanhedrin persist in the same hard-heartedness
which led to them killing 'the righteous one' (52).

The thirteenth witness chosen

(1) Conversion.

Stephen's death also introduces the one who will become the thirteenth witness (7:58; 8:1). Instead of reversing the Sanhedrin's strategy,
Stephen's death increased their persecution of the name through Saul
(8:1b-3; 9:1-2). Nevertheless, the word could not be stifled. Not only
did the persecution lead to further conversions (Acts 8:4-40; cf., 11:19-
21), but the great persecutor was himself numbered amongst them!

Saul's conversion is reported once by Luke and later, twice from
Paul's own mouth (chs. 22, 26). In the first report, the great persecutor
(8:1-3) becomes the great preacher, to everyone's disbelief (9:19-30),
and persecution leads to peace (9:31).

Paul was commissioned to carry Jesus' name to the Gentiles,
their kings and the people of Israel, a task which would entail suffering
(9:6, 15-16). Later, Paul revealed that the Lord had said that he would
be sent far away to the nations (22:17-21; 26:15-23). The risen Jesus had
chosen him as his witness with special responsibility for the Gentiles,
although this did not exclude him from preaching to his own people.

(2) Preparation.

Peter and Cornelius. After removing Paul from the action for a time
(9:30; 11:25), the narrative turns to the conversion of Cornelius. The
significance of this event is indicated by the fact that it appears three
times, being narrated (ch. 10), retold (11:1-18), and reflected upon
(15:6-8).

Peter's speech to Cornelius contains the same threefold concern
as previous speeches. It is cast as 'the word sent to the sons of Israel
evangelising peace through Jesus Christ' (36), i.e., what was promised
by Isaiah 52:7. According to Isaiah, Jerusalem's coming salvation
would be displayed 'in the sight of all the nations, and all the ends of

the earth will see the salvation of our God' (Isa. 52:10). With Cornelius' conversion, what was promised by the prophet and picked up by the programmatic Acts 1:8, begins to unfold further. Peter now realises that, if Jesus is indeed 'Lord of all' (10:36), then the conversion of the Gentiles is a necessary consequence—a realisation he will share with the other apostles (11:1-18; 15:6-8).

The word sent to Israel tells of Jesus' Servant ministry from Galilee to Judea (Acts 10:37-38), as witnessed by the twelve (39). He died as a man accursed by God (39, cf., Deut. 21:22-23), but God raised him and allowed him to be seen by his chosen witnesses, whom he instructed to testify about his appointment as judge of the living and the dead (40-42). In accordance with all the prophets, forgiveness of sins is attainable through his name to all who believe in him (43).

While Peter spoke, the Holy Spirit came upon his audience (44-48). When re-telling the events, he explained that Cornelius had wanted salvation (11:14), and the others concluded that God had granted it—even to the Gentiles (11:18)!

When the means of salvation becomes an issue (15:1, 5, 11) and the Council of Jerusalem is called, Peter's further reflection indicates that Cornelius' conversion held lessons for the Jerusalem believers in regard to the influx from the nations. After hearing from Paul and Barnabas, Peter explains that God had given his Spirit to these Gentiles to testify that they had been converted (15:6-11). To sum up the discussion, James cites Amos 9:11-12 in justification of the Gentiles coming in. In the flow of the narrative, the restoration of the fallen tent of David (16) is best understood of Jesus as the Davidic seed who has now been installed as Christ and Lord, with the Gentile influx (17) occurring as a consequence. In narrative terms, since the council flows out of the first missionary journey, the section from 9:32–15:35 reports the necessary preparations in order that the fruit of the ministry of the thirteenth witness could be duly received.

(3) Paul's witness.

(a) Pisidian Antioch. At the centre of this section (9:32–15:35), Paul's first speech (13:16-48)[48] proves to be a major turning point for Acts. It contains the familiar threefold content. Tragically, the Jerusalemites fulfilled their own prophets by killing Jesus as an accursed one (27-29). Paul's citation of Psalm 2 may also recall for the reader previous associations with the crucifixion (33, cf., 4:23-31), although here he uses

---

48For a discussion of the central section of the sermon, see Lövestam, *Son*.

it of the resurrection. God raised Jesus, who then appeared to those
who knew him before, who are now acting as his witnesses to Israel
(30–31). In the light of these events, Paul proclaims the good news that
God has fulfilled what he promised (32). Interpreted by Ps. 2:7, the
resurrection confirms Jesus as the Son of God (=the Christ), and,
interpreted by Ps. 16:10, it declares him to be incorruptible (34-38; cf.,
Acts 2:24-32). Paul enlists Is. 55:3, not because it was about
incorruptibility, but because it looked to the time when the promises
to David would be fulfilled. Since Jesus is the promised seed of David
(23), this time has dawned (34), and one of those promises, Ps. 16:10,
means that the resurrected Christ (33) has been granted an incorruptible life (34a, 35-37).

The main burden of the sermon is the forgiveness of sins, now
being proclaimed as a consequence. Paul takes pains to show that
everything about the Christ occurred for them (26, 32, 33, 38, 39).
Having stated that Jesus had come after a long period of preparation
(16-25), Paul declares that the word of salvation has now been sent to
them (26). He explains how this has come about (27-31), then returns
to the point that this word is now being proclaimed (32). The word is
then delivered: God has fulfilled his promise 'for us' by raising Jesus.
He deals at length with Jesus' resurrection (33-37), in order to explain
that this word is the logical outcome of Jesus' incorruptibility (38).
Because Jesus has been raised immortal, the forgiveness of sins, or, to
put it another way, a justification that comes simply through believing
in Jesus (39), is now being proclaimed to them as the fulfilment of
God's promise to their fathers (32).

But what if they don't accept this word? As a warning, Paul concludes by citing Hab. 1:5 LXX (41). For those familiar with the Greek
version of Habakkuk, this citation evokes several interesting connections with the story of Acts.[49] Habakkuk had cried out for salvation.
The judgement process (κρίσις) had been launched against him, but
the judge himself was 'on the take' (1:3). As a result, the law had been
disbanded and a judgement (κρῖμα) was never reached, because the
ungodly man exercised power over the righteous man (1:4). The oracle
tells the 'contemptuous ones' to look to the marvel God will work (1:5),
namely, that the Chaldeans will come and give 'him' (i.e., the righteous
man) the awaited judgement (1:6-7). Habakkuk realises that God has
appointed them to bring this judgement, but he wishes to cross-

---

[49]The following comments relate to the Greek version, which differs substantially
from the MT.

examine the discipline they bring (12). Recalling his original complaint (cf., 2-4), he asks why God is favouring the ones showing contempt (καταφρονοῦντας), being silent while the ungodly man consumes the righteous man (13). Habakkuk's 'cross-examination' concerns the timing: why hasn't judgement through the Chaldeans come yet (cf., 1:2; 2:6)? Stating that it will come, the Lord urges patience (2:3). The Lord is not pleased with the one who prevaricates under fear, but the righteous man by faith in God (or by God's faithfulness) will live (2:4).

At the least, Paul's use of Habakkuk 1:5 warns this synagogue audience against being contemptuous of the message sent to them, at the risk of seeing the nations once again used as an instrument of judgement upon Israel. On the following Sabbath, this becomes a reality. Their scoffing prompts Paul's declaration that they have judged themselves unworthy of eternal life (46, cf., 41 ἀφανίσθητε) and that he was going to the Gentiles. As the Gentiles rejoice, standing to inherit the eternal life passed over by the Jews (48), so the Jews are 'judged' by the nations. The amazing work of God (Hab. 1:5) is that the Gentiles believe, even when the people of Israel do not.

There may also be additional connections. The Sanhedrin has been indicted for wrongly putting to death the righteous one (3:14; 7:52; cf., 22:14), a decision which God overturned. The message of forgiveness has gone to them, and yet they are still contemptuous, opposing those bearing the testimony. Habakkuk, appalled at the injustice done to the righteous man (1:2-4), was promised that through God's amazing work a Gentile nation would bring the correct verdict. Despite God's vindication of Jesus in the resurrection, the Jewish Sanhedrin persisted in the wrong verdict they had passed on the righteous man. From now until its end, Acts will show an amazing work of God, that, while Jewish rejection continues, the nations pass the proper verdict upon the righteous one. Even by the time of the Jerusalem council, this amazing reversal has reached the stage where the faith of Gentiles has become a paradigm for the Jews (15:11)!

Announcing that he was turning to the Gentiles (46-48), Paul cited Isaiah 49:6. On the usual reading, this passage from the second Servant song is applied either to both missionaries,[50] or to Paul.[51] In either case, a clash between the plural ἡμῖν in the superscription, and the singular σέ in the citation,[52] and a clash with Luke's (until now)

---

[50]Bruce, *Acts (Greek Text)*, 315; Conzelmann, *Acts*, 106.
[51]Barrett, *Acts I*, 658.
[52]Schneider, *Apostelgeschichte* II:145-146.

consistent identification of Jesus as the Servant, results. If applied to Jesus,[53] although not providing a direct command for Paul and Barnabas, the citation nonetheless enjoins a course of action upon them indirectly. It is not difficult to see the same sequence as that in 26:23 (informed by the same Isaiah text) motivating Paul's change of direction here: the Christ as the first from the resurrection of the dead, would proclaim light to the people and to the nations. Through the word of salvation, Christ has gone to the people (13:26), but Isa. 49:6 also gives the Christ a mission to the Gentiles. Since that mission will be performed through the ones proclaiming the word, when the Jews oppose this word, the proclaimers simply move to the alternative mission field. This does not mean that they never speak to a Jew again, which is patently against the evidence, but it does mean that Christ's two-pronged mission guided their operations. The Christ had a mission to the Jew first and then the nations, and so Paul's strategy was clear.

(b) Gentile audiences. Following the ratification of the Gentile conversion by the Council, Paul continued his task (15:36–20:12). In this section his speeches to Gentile audiences do not mention Jesus' death, but concentrate upon the proclamation of forgiveness/repentance which flows from the resurrection. For the Lystra crowd, Paul had stressed (14:15) that repentance consisted of turning from idols to the God who has not left himself without witness (17, ἀμάρτυρος). When his preaching of the resurrection landed him before the Areopagus (17:18), Paul had opportunity to elaborate. He explained that the resurrection is God's proof to all men of Jesus' appointment as judge on the judgement day (31), and that, as a consequence, all people everywhere are commanded to repent.

(c) Miletus. Paul's address to the Ephesian elders provides Acts' fullest explanation of the death of Jesus (28): God acquired his church through the death of his Own.[54] The resurrection is not mentioned, although it lies behind the designation of Jesus as Lord (21, 24, 35). The major portion of the speech concerns the element of proclamation. Paul asks them to recall his activity amongst them: announcing and teaching whatever necessary (20), urging repentance and faith upon both Jews and Greeks (21), preaching the kingdom (25), announcing the whole plan of God (27), constantly and passionately admonishing

---

[53]Wendt, *Apostelgeschichte*, 217, apparently also takes it of Jesus; see Haenchen, *Acts*, 414 n. 5.
[54]Conzelmann, *Acts*, 175.

them individually (31), giving rather than taking (32-36). According to the Holy Spirit's warning (23, *cf.*, 21:4, 10-14), the future held prison and hardships, but Paul looks forward to completing the ministry the Lord gave, namely, to present the gospel of God's grace (24). Because people will arise speaking distortions (30), Paul commits them to God and to the same word of grace that has been the driving force of his ministry and which can both edify and provide an inheritance (32).

(d) Paul's forensic defences. Following the riot in Jerusalem, a Roman official stands Saul, the one time persecutor of the name, before his former compatriots to defend that name (22:30; 23:28). At the beginning of Acts the Sanhedrin had tried to suppress the name (4:17-20; 5:28, 40), or ignore it (5:34-40), and finally, following Stephen's indictment of them, they added their blessing to the fierce persecution mounted by Saul (8:3; 9:1-2; 22:4-5; 26:9-11). As Acts draws to a close, Rome now forces the Sanhedrin to re-examine this difficult movement which has refused to go away, and for which its former chief opponent has become its chief advocate.

Paul defends his changed life by reference to Jesus' choice of him to go to the Gentiles (22:1-21; 26:1-23), and insists that he is on trial for the resurrection. By this, he does not simply mean that he claims that Jesus rose again (25:19), but that he is on trial for Israel's hope of the general resurrection. Jesus' resurrection implies the fulfilment of Israel's hopes is under way. This claim divided the Sanhedrin (23:1-10). Paul told Felix that the same hope shared by him and his accusers, namely, that there is about to be a resurrection of the just and the unjust (24:14-16), had become the charge against him (21). Apparently, this perspective also dominated Paul's private conversation with Felix (25, *cf.*, 15f.).

Coming as something of a theological climax to the book, the fuller *apologia* before Agrippa combines the emphasis on the resurrection hopes of Israel (26:6-8) with the re-emergent threefold necessity. The prophets and Moses spoke in the hope that the Christ would suffer and rise (22-23).[55] Both these things are subordinated to the consequent proclamation, when Paul states that as 'the first from the resurrection of the dead' (*cf.*, 3:15; 5:31), Christ would proclaim light to both Israel and the Gentiles (*cf.*, 13:47). This recalls Isaiah's common image for the salvation won by the Servant, and eventually taken to the nations (Isa. 9:2; 30:26, contrast 13:10; 42:6, 16; 49:6; 50:10-11; 51:4; 53:11; 58:8, 10; 59:9; 60:1-3, 19-20).

This rather full explanation arises at a significant point in the narrative. The story is almost played out and this final great speech from Paul reminds the reader that Jesus has risen in order to proclaim light to both Jew and Gentile, and he has done this through his chosen witnesses. This theology has been the driving force for all the events portrayed.

Since Paul's defence was not just a defence of himself, but a defence of the gospel, the verdict he received was also a verdict upon this gospel—as well as the theological hopes which lay behind it and the movement now proclaiming it. Although the Sanhedrin appears to have stuck by its verdict, the Roman officials—from Gallio (18:12-17) through Claudius Lysias (23:29), Felix (24:22-27), to Festus (25:13-21; 26:24-31)—had found no fault with it all. Even the Jewish king Agrippa agreed that Paul could have been set free if he had not appealed to Caesar (26:31-32). By this means the reader is shown that Paul did not go to Rome to bear testimony for himself, but, having already repeatedly been declared innocent, he goes to Caesar in order to bear witness for the risen Christ (19:21; 23:11).

(e) Paul at Rome. After surviving a shipwreck and a viper bite, clear evidence that he was also innocent in the eyes of the pagan gods (28:1-6), Paul comes to Rome. The book of Acts closes with the apostle to the Gentiles at the centre of the empire, after reporting his 'one word' to the Jews of Rome. He had discussed the Way with them, talking about the Kingdom of God and trying to convince them about Jesus from the Scriptures (23). No further content is given, but by now we can assume that the three scriptural necessities were on the agenda. Paul's final word is an indictment of Israel's hardness of heart (26-27,=Is. 6:9-10; cf., Acts 7), and a declaration that 'this salvation of God', i.e., the salvation

---

[55]The claim that εἰ is used for ὅτι, (Haenchen, Acts, 687 n. 5, drawing attention to 26:8; so too Conzelmann, Acts, 211) requires more substantiation. Εἰ can be used for ὅτι after expressions of emotion (Jannaris, Historical Greek Grammar §1947; BAGD, 219), and possibly also after verbs of knowing, but the evidence needs to be assembled for such a usage after verbs of speaking, as here. Acts 26:8 is not particularly relevant, for it is likely that it is an attack on Sadduceean notions denying resurrection in general, in which case εἰ can be taken in its usual sense. The claim that the Jews did believe in the general resurrection (Haenchen, Acts, 684) ignores the possibility that Paul's accusers were from the high priestly groups and so (predominately) Sadducean. The usage in which εἰ expresses 'on the chance that, in the hope that', and the idea of purpose is prominent (Smyth, Grammar §2354) may be more to the point. This would mean that the prophetic hopes (i.e., as real people) are in view, rather than simply their predictions (i.e., abstracted from the people), which suits the prevailing interest in this final section of Acts.

promised by Isaiah, has been sent to the Gentiles (28). By the end of Acts, Israel has not listened to the prophet God has raised up for them (Deut. 18:15, *cf.*, 3:22-23, 7:37), but Paul promises that the Gentiles will.

But what happened to the trial before Caesar? The report of Paul's continued ministry (30-31), combined with the previous declaration of innocence by his officials leaves the reader with the impression that the trial has actually lapsed. This amounts to another declaration of innocence, albeit passively. The Sanhedrin had persisted with their verdict on 'the righteous one', apparently right through to the end. However, by the end of the book it has been made clear that the nations, right up to Caesar himself, by declaring Paul innocent through their official legal processes, had passed a different verdict upon this righteous one. God had worked a great wonder (13:41=Hab. 1:5): despite Israel's leaders persisting in their verdict, the name of Jesus had been cleared before the bar of the nations.

The book of Acts opened with the expectation that the hopes of Israel were about to be fulfilled. After the witnesses were chosen and had repeatedly established that Jesus fulfilled these hopes, Paul's forensic speeches focused these hopes on the resurrection of the dead. As the book closes, Paul is preaching the reality beyond the resurrection, *i.e.*, the Kingdom of God, and Jesus—the one who has made that resurrection life available (31, 23). Boldly and without hindrance, the message of salvation is going to the nations. And they will listen.

IV. Mission, witness and the reader of Acts

If Acts is to be used in modern discussions of mission, the connection between the particulars of the narrative to the generalities of its readers must be discussed. Often this connection is simply assumed rather than argued, but hopefully scholarship's newer sensitivity to the reader[56] will lead to better explanations of this interface. Part III is a contribution towards clarifying the bridge between the text and the reader.

Destroying some common bridges

(1) The 'Mission of the Church'. The concept of the 'mission of the

---

[56]Spencer, 'Acts', 412-14.

church' ought to be laid to rest. Acts does not present 'the Church' as an institution which is sent.[57] A particular church may send individuals to do a particular work (*cf.* 13:1-4), but the church itself is not sent. If a church does send individuals, it should do so from an awareness of the work of God in sending the risen Jesus to the nations through the word of his chosen witnesses.

(2) The reader and the witnesses. It is also inappropriate to assume that the role of the original witnesses is extended to the reader.[58] Acts does not encourage the view that the twelve ought to be regarded as 'the missionary Church *in partu*'.[59] Even if the twelve are meant to be understood as renewed Israel, it is questionable to assume that this ought to be generalised from 'Israel' to a 'regathered and restored peoplehood', to a 'renewed believing community'.[60] Because the criterion for the twelve witnesses is historical, it is by definition unrepeatable (1:21-22). The dominical choice of just this group, despite the availability of others who met the criterion, and their designation as the ones who will be witnesses for every area of the globe (1:8), also suggests an unrepeatable particularity. According to Acts, the witnesses are a part of history, and it is impossible for their role to be extended to anyone else. The twelve and Paul are chosen directly by the Lord for their task, and the fact that even those such as Stephen and Philip are clearly distinguished from them indicates that their commission is not extended to others.[61] It is not their unique commission, but the message which resulted from that commission that was preached by those beyond their circle and, by virtue of Luke's endeavours (see below), has now become the property of his readers.[62]

(3) Paul and the reader. Neither is the reader to continue Paul's role on the assumption that those who were not with Jesus from the first, like Paul, 'witnessed on the basis of their present experience with Christ.'[63] Paul is not merely a symbol for the narrative of Acts,[64] nor is he simply a bridge between the Apostles and the present, nor can his witness be generalised as 'confessional witness'.[65] Like the twelve, he was

---

[57]It deals with 'churches', as local gatherings of believers, not 'The Church'. *Cf.*, O'Brien, 'Church', 92. The notion of the church mediating salvation is also repugnant to Acts, in which salvation is 'mediated' by the word of the witnesses.
[58]*E. g.*, Maddox, *Witnesses*, 22; Kee, *Good News*, 96; Hill, 'Spirit'.
[59]Dillon, *From Eye-Witnesses*, 268; 'Easter', 242.
[60]*Pace* Recker, 'Lordship', 178, 186.
[61]*Pace* Strathmann, 'μάρτυς' and Marshall, *Acts of the Apostles*, 65-66.
[62]*Pace* Maddox, *Witnesses*, 27.
[63]Dockery, 'Acts', 429 n. 30; endorsing Talbert, *Acts*, 41-43.

specifically chosen by Jesus for a specific task. On three occasions Acts demonstrates that Paul saw the risen Lord, and heard that he would be sent as his witness amongst the nations. This can hardly be simply labelled 'his present experience', or 'confessional' in order to generalise to others. Paul's historically particular experience of the risen Lord does not become the reader's. Rather than being like the apostle to the nations, the reader is more like the nations to which he was sent. The reader is not missioner, but mission field.

(4) The Spirit and the reader. In Acts, the Spirit is promised (2:38-39),[66] and given to a group wider than the witnesses. However, we should not make too much of the fact that the witnesses' possession of the Spirit is in no way different to that of other Christians,[67] since equivalent possession does not imply equivalent roles.[68] The witnesses received the Spirit in close connection to their task, and there is no hint that this function is transferred to others in possession of the Spirit. The promise of the Spirit to others is associated with the forgiveness of sins (2:38-39; cf., 13:32, 38-39), and when the reception of the Spirit by those outside the group of chosen witnesses is reflected upon, it is in terms of them becoming believers, not witnesses (15:6-11).

(5) Paradigmatic speeches. The suggestion that the speeches form a link with the reader is closer to the point. However, this is not primarily because they are recorded as paradigms, representing what 'should be proclaimed in faithful witness by the church in [Luke's] day,'[69] but because they are testimony to what was proclaimed. Acts certainly intends their μαρτύριον to be passed on by others, but this does not make these 'others' witnesses in Luke's sense of the term.

---

[64]Maddox, *Witnesses*, makes this assertion on the basis of a comparison with the 'real Paul' of the letters. The reader of Acts receives no encouragement at all to view Paul symbolically.
[65]Strathmann, 'μάρτυς', 493–494.
[66]Whether 4:31 is a group wider than the apostles depends upon the referent to 'their own' in 4:23. Despite Pfitzner, 'Apostleship?', 215, it may indeed be limited to the apostles, as I have taken it above. 5:32, in the context only refers to the apostles (*cf.*, 5:29; 4:19).
[67]Pfitzner, 'Apostleship?', 214-15.
[68]*E.g.*, 'prophets' can be identified (11:27-28; 13:1; 15:32; 21:9, 10-11).
[69]Gasque, *History*, 356, italics added.

Constructing some better bridges

(1) The speeches as testimony. The speeches in Acts are inscribed as a permanent record of the testimony[70] of Jesus' chosen witnesses. As the narrative presents this testimony, the reader is given the opportunity to join with the minor characters who 'devoted themselves to the apostles' teaching' (2:42) and evangelised it to others (cf., 8:4; 11:19-21). The reader is not amongst the witnesses, but amongst those who hear and then proclaim their witness.

(2) Acts as testimony. Several studies have suggested that it is not just the speeches, but the entire book of Acts which operates as a witness. According to Morgenthaler,[71] Luke uses a principle of duality in order to bear witness according to the requirements of Deut. 19:15. In line with this desire, Acts faithfully records the original witnesses and so indirectly keeps their testimony alive.[72] The 'we-passages', which give the reader the impression that the narrator of the whole work was a part of the events narrated,[73] help to endorse this strategy by indicating that the author was a witness to the witnesses.[74]

Thus, a crucial strategy in achieving the author's purposes was to pass on the word of the original witnesses to his readers. Given the forensic setting of this witness, this amounts to Luke offering 'legally acceptable evidence for Christ which will be admitted as valid in the wider lawcourt of life itself.'[75] The readers stand in that lawcourt, not bearing the testimony, but listening to the testimony Acts provides.

---

[70]Trites, *Concept*, 15.

[71]Morgenthaler, *Geschichtsschreibung*.

[72]Morgenthaler, *Geschichtsschreibung*, II:7–8. His thesis is endorsed with minor critique by: Barrett, *Luke*, 36–40; Trites, *Concept*, 135; Gasque, *History*, 267–268.

[73]Alexander, 'Biography', 48, mentions the narrator stepping into the narrative temporarily. For those familiar with the device in OT narratives, such narration especially helps to establish the historical reliability of the portrayal of events, cf., Wehnert, *Wir-Passagen*. A 'fictitious we' convention is unparalleled and improbable (Maddox, *Purpose*, 7 n. 32 referring to A.D. Nock).

[74]Cf., Thornton, *Zeuge*. Given the author's interest in presenting his material as evidence against a Roman forensic backdrop, and also the Jewish forensic setting erected by the Dt. 19:15 principle, it is difficult to see why he would use first person narration if it did not reflect his own historical reminiscences. False witness was a crime in both Jewish and Roman (cf., Rapske, *Paul in Roman Custody*, 66, citing Hadrian *Dig* 22.5.3.5) settings, and was despised by our author (Acts 6:13-14; 7:58; cf., 22:19-20; 26:9-11). If he is not speaking as an eyewitness—even if he preserves the 'we' in faithfulness to his source (Porter, 'Excursus')—it would not help his case at all if this 'technique' was exposed for the fraud that it was.

[75]Trites, *Concept*, 133.

They too have the opportunity to declare a correct κρῖμα on 'the righteous man'.

(3) The triumph of the Word. The reference to the 'former word', implies that both Luke and Acts can be considered as λόγος (1:1). This is, of course, a perfectly natural way to talk of a 'treatise', but it also intersects with one of Acts' major interests, namely, the advance of the word of God.[76] By presenting the word of the witnesses, Acts continues to proclaim the word of God to its readers. By this means, Jesus continues to be sent to the nations through Acts and the advance of the word seen within the narrative can be expected to occur by means of the narrative. The nations will continue to fall before the one appointed Lord and Christ.

Mission and Witness in Acts and the Reader

The narrative does not provide the readers with a mission, in the sense of them being divinely commissioned for a particular task, but instead it presents God's mission. The third of three divine necessities has been under way since the ascension. The risen Jesus has been sent to Israel and the nations through his chosen witnesses. The key response expected from both Jew and Gentile is to listen to him. As they listen, there is a natural movement towards evangelizing the world (cf., 8:4; 11:19-21).

By recording the witness, Acts maintains that witness. As Acts presents the word of witness, Jesus and his salvation continues to go to the nations. Being members of the nations, the readers are called to listen to the word of the witnesses and to respond with repentance and faith.[77] Since that word is a message that all must hear, the believer will evangelize others, urging them to call upon the name of the risen Lord. In doing so, the readers join Luke's second word in taking salvation even unto the ends of the earth.

---

[76]Although this theme ranges more broadly, a survey of the following uses of λόγος provides a good overview: 2:22, 40-41; 4:4, 29-31; 5:5; 6:2-7, 7:22 cf., Luke 24:19; 8:4, 14, 25; 10:36, 44; 11:1, 19; 12:24; 13:5, 7, 15, 26, 44, 46, 48, 49; 14:3, 12, 25; 15:6 (as a rival) 7, 15, 32, 35, 36; 16:6, 32; 17:11, 13; 18:5, 11, 18:15 (an outsider's view), 19:10, 20; 20:2, 7, 32. In 8:21 it sums up the apostolic activity. Cf., the chapter by B. Rosner which can be regarded as something of a logical sequel to my own.
[77]This militates against too strictly dividing the intended audience into 'insider' or 'outsider'. The word is addressed to both as human beings and demands the same response, whether in an initial or an ongoing sense.

CHAPTER 11

THE PROGRESS OF THE WORD

Brian S. Rosner

Summary

The spread of the gospel message, the word of God, is a major theme and the main story-line of Acts. Luke prepares his readers for this theme in the prologue of Acts and by stressing the broad scope of Jesus' ministry in Luke's Gospel. The theme is confirmed throughout with summaries which underscore how impressive and far-reaching is the expansion, for which God is given the credit. Acts does not, however, depict triumphalistic growth since progress is consistently attended by opposition. The open-ended ending of Acts indicates that the progress of the word is ongoing.

I. Introduction

Acts narrates the progress of the gospel from a small gathering of
Jewish disciples of the earthly Jesus in Jerusalem, across formidable
cultic, ethnic, relational and geographical boundaries, to Paul's bold
and unhindered preaching of the risen and ascended Jesus to Gentiles
in Rome. Acts is unmistakably a story of missionary expansion, which
is announced in 1:8 and confirmed along the way with the so-called
progress reports. M. Hengel was right to describe Acts as 'Missions-
geschichte'.[1] I.H. Marshall states the obvious: 'the main storyline of
Acts is concerned with the spread of the message.'[2]

Virtually every commentator recognises and gives prominence
to Luke's concern with the spread of the gospel message, 'the word of
God (the Lord)',[3] to use a Lukan phrase, in Acts. For example, the
recent commentary of C.K. Barrett states that 'A quick reading of the
text confirms the picture of progressive expansion [introduced in
1:8]'.[4] In modern scholarship the progress of the gospel was perhaps
first seen as a leading theme in Acts by Hans Conzelmann in his 1954
theology of Luke–Acts, *Die Mitte der Zeit: Studien zur Theologie des
Lukas*, who saw in Acts a theology of glory, where God overturns all
opposition leading to triumphant growth.

This chapter attempts to make further progress in studying this
theme by supplementing the usual exegetical, historical and theological approaches with a missiological approach, taking full account
of the cross-cultural dimensions of Acts,[5] a rhetorical approach,
among other things considering not just what the text says but what it
does not say,[6] and especially a literary approach, looking at the way in
which Acts tells its story.[7] A final comment on method concerns
Luke's indebtedness to the Jewish Scriptures: OT background will
prove to be crucial to our interpretation at a number of points (*e.g.*,
Acts 1:8).[8] Not only explicitly but in a wide variety of subtle and
indirect ways Acts portrays the prodigious progress of the word.

---

[1]Hengel, 'Ursprünge', 25.
[2]Marshall, *Acts: Commentary*, 26.
[3]*Cf.*, 4:31; 8:14,25; 11:1; 13:5,7,44,46,48; 16:32; 17:13; 18:11.
[4]Barrett, *Acts I*, 49.
[5]See esp. Dollar, *Luke–Acts*.
[6]*Cf.*, Marguerat, 'Rhetoric'.
[7]For a survey of literature see Spencer, 'Acts' and *inter alia* Newman, 'Acts'.
[8]*Cf.*, Scott, 'Horizon' on the Table of Nations tradition, Acts 1:8 and the structure
of Acts. On the importance of the Jewish Scriptures to Acts see Rosner, 'Acts and
Biblical History'.

We shall attempt to explicate the progress theme of Acts by answering the following questions: Does Luke prepare his readers for the progress of the word that takes place throughout the narrative of Acts (section II)? Are there explicit indications throughout the book that this progress is central to Luke's purposes in writing Acts (section III)? Who is given the credit for progress (section IV)? What kind of progress is depicted (section V)? At the end of Acts has progress come to completion (section VI)?

II. Progress anticipated

Our enquiry starts by considering whether the theme in question is anticipated in the opening verses of Acts and in the 'former treatise' of Luke's Gospel.

How does Acts 1:1-11 function as the beginning of the narrative of Acts? In comparison with Luke 24:50-53, which also concerns the ascension of Jesus, Acts 1:1-11 encourages the reader to feel a part of the action by presenting most of the story in dialogue and telling the rest from the perspective of the participating disciples, rather than from that of a distant narrator. Whereas in Luke the ascension is in the form of a benediction, appropriately closing the narrative, in Acts it is presented as an invocation of God's blessing on the disciples who are commissioned to be witnesses, an equally appropriate introduction to the action to follow. Some of the main themes of Acts are introduced in 1:1-11, including the kingdom of God, the question of the status of the Jews over against the Gentiles, and especially the main story-line of Acts, world-wide mission, in 1:8.[9]

Acts 1:8 has often been understood as giving a broad outline of the structure and contents of Acts. It has been called the book's Table of Contents: the witness spreads from Jerusalem (chs. 1–7), to Judea and Samaria (chs. 8–12) and finally, with Paul (*cf.*, Acts 13:47) to 'the end of the earth' (chs. 13–28). Indeed Parsons has observed, 'most scholars see Paul's arrival in Rome as the fulfilment of Jesus' commission to his disciples to be witnesses "to the ends of the earth"'.[10] Psalms of Solomon 8:15 can be cited as support, where it is said that Pompey had come 'from the ends of the earth.' It is certainly true that

---

[9]Parsons, *Departure*. Parsons offers a full study of the two passages which supports and expands our brief comments here in great detail.
[10]Parsons, *Departure*, 157.

Rome exerts a profound influence across Luke–Acts. The decree of
Caesar Augustus in Luke 2:1-2 came from Rome and key events in the
lives of Jesus and the apostles are narrated with reference to Roman
rulers (*e.g.*, Luke 3:1; Acts 18:12).

However, the consensus view of identifying 'the end of the
earth' with Rome and seeing Acts 1:8 as outlining the course of events
in Acts does not stand up to scrutiny. As J. M. Scott points out, 'the geographical horizon of Luke–Acts is larger than the Roman Empire'.[11]
Acts 2:9-11 indicates that the book takes into view regions as far flung
as Ethiopia and Cyrenaica to the south, Arabia, Elam, Media and
Parthia to the East, the northern coast of the Aegean Sea to the north,
as well as Rome to the West. 'Every nation under heaven' is included,
to quote Acts 2:5. Furthermore, the mission reaches Rome before Paul
(18:2; *cf.*, 28:14f) and significant steps in its progress on the way to
Rome, are not mentioned in 1:8, *e.g.*, Antioch, Asia Minor and Greece.

'The end of the earth' is not, in fact, a reference to Rome. The
phrase occurs only six times in the Septuagint (Isa. 8:9; 48:20; 49:6;
62:11; Pss. Sol 1:4; 1 Macc. 3:9) and nowhere else in ancient Greek outside of writings influenced by Isaiah or Acts according to a computer
search of *Thesaurus Linguae Graecae*.[12] That Luke in using it is alluding
to Isaiah is clear from its other occurrence in Acts 13:47, which quotes
Isaiah 49:6.[13] In context Isaiah indicates that God intends to provide
salvation to all peoples. The phrase takes in the whole of the inhabited
world, denoting the ultimate limits of civilisation. Psalms of Solomon
8:15, as van Unnik pointed out many years ago, supplies no exception,
for there the reference probably means that Pompey came not from
Rome but from Spain, the furthest known point west, where he had
fought for many years prior to his travels in the East.[14]

The link with Isaiah renders unlikely the view of D.R. Schwartz
that 'the end of the earth' refers to the end of the land of Israel[15] and
that of E.E. Ellis, who opts for a specific reference to Spain.[16] R.
Brawley's contention, that the phrase has an ethnic rather than a

---

[11]Scott, 'Horizon', 523.

[12]Tannehill's search, *Narrative Unity* 2:17, missed the 1 Macc. reference. The Jewish
Scriptures also contain synonymous phrases like ἄκρος τῆς γῆς and πέρας τῆς
γῆς. These likewise denote the whole inhabited world.

[13]The Biblical and Jewish influences on Acts 1:8 are not exhausted by the link with
Isaiah 49:6; Scott, 'Horizon', argues that the Jewish Table of Nations tradition (Gen.
10) informs Luke's geography throughout Acts.

[14]Van Unnik, 'Hintergrund'.

[15]Schwartz, 'Beginning or End?'

[16]Ellis, '"End of the Earth"'.

geographical sense because Gentiles precede and follow its occurrence in 13:47 is to confuse matters with a false dichotomy (ethnicity and geography belong together).[17]

Luke–Acts certainly takes in the whole world in other places: in Luke 4:5 the devil showed Jesus 'all the kingdoms of the world'; in Luke 21:25-26 messianic signs come upon 'the world'; in Acts 11:28 the famine covers 'the whole inhabited world', and in Acts 17:6 'the whole world is turned upside down'.[18] Even permitting some hyperbole in these references, one cannot escape the impression that Acts has the widest possible geographical horizon.

Thus Acts 1:8 anticipates the vast expansion of the mission throughout Acts and beyond, a subject which we shall return to at the end of this essay, and it could well be considered the theme verse of the book. The gospel is to spread throughout the entire world. As Tannehill puts it: 'It [Acts 1:8] is an outline of the mission, but only in part an outline of Acts.[19]

In Acts 1:8 we have seen Luke's clear intention to portray the spread of the gospel in Acts and we have noted a close linkage between the opening verses of Acts and the closing verses of Luke's Gospel.[20] The question arises, does Luke's Gospel, as well as signalling geographical expansion of the Christian movement in 24:47, anticipate the universalising of the movement in ethnic and cultural terms? In other words, does Luke's Gospel prepare its readers for the inclusion of the Gentiles recorded in Acts?[21]

At first blush the search for such indications meets with disappointment, since Luke's Gospel does not have some of the more straightforward statements found in Mark, and to a lesser extent in Matthew, about concern for the Gentiles and a world-wide mission (cf., Matt 8:11; Mark 13:10; 14:9; 7:24-30—Luke omits Jesus' ministry to the Syrophoenician woman and the phrase 'to the Gentiles' in his account of the cleansing of the temple [cf., Mark 11:17 and Luke 19:46]). In fact it was Cadbury's view that Luke was the least universal of the Synoptic Gospels.[22] S.G. Wilson also concludes that Luke's Gospel is not concerned with the whole world.[23]

17Brawley, *Luke–Acts and the Jews*, 32-33.
18Cf., 17:31; 19:27; 24:5 and the places where γῆ is used in the sense of 'the earth'.
19Tannehill, *Narrative Unity*, 2:18.
20On the close relation between Luke and Acts see Marshall, '"Former Treatise"'.
21In answer to this question I have built upon Dollar, *Luke–Acts*, ch. 2.
22Cadbury, *The Making of Luke–Acts*, 254ff.
23Wilson, *Gentile Mission*, 29-56.

Maddox, on the other hand, offers a different and compelling explanation for Luke's apparent lack of interest in Gentiles, contending it

> is 'short-sighted' to deduce from [the omissions] that Luke is 'not universalistic', or opposed to the Gentiles. For one thing, unlike the other evangelists he has no need to fit into the gospel a theme which he plans to set forth in a second volume.[24]

In Luke's Gospel, Dollar notes that Luke's concern for a mission to Gentiles is made not by explicit statements but by the inclusion of material that emphasized Jesus' ministry to those considered marginal in Palestinian society.[25] Thus the Gentile mission in Acts, while not openly predicted in Luke until chapter 24, should come as no surprise to the attentive reader who is adept at finding clues and taking hints. Less skilful readers would appreciate such elements more on second and subsequent readings of Luke, in the light of having read Acts.

As our primary concern is with Acts, we shall restrict ourselves to noting briefly suggestive elements in Luke that point forward to the universalism of Acts. These include:

(1) The prophecy of Simon in 2:32, a quotation of Isaiah 42:6 (*cf.*, Acts 13:47), which indicates that salvation is in the presence of all peoples, a light for revelation to the Gentiles.

(2) John the Baptist's ministry to Roman soldiers in 2:1; 3:1,14.

(3) Jesus' reading of Isaiah 61 in the synagogue in Nazareth and his commendation of the Gentiles in Luke 4:16-30, an event described by Maddox as 'programmatic'.[26]

(4) The portrayal of Jesus as the 'friend of tax collectors and sinners' (7:34), those on the edge of Jewish society (*cf.*, esp. 5:27-39; 19:5-7).[27]

(5) The prominence of women in Jesus' ministry, from Elizabeth and Mary, through Mary and Martha, to the women witnesses of the resurrection.[28]

(6) The response of Samaritans to Jesus which forms a focus of interest for Luke (9:51-56; 10:25-37; 17:11-19; *cf.*, Acts 8:4-24), more so than for the other Gospels.[29]

24Maddox, *Purpose*, 55.

25Dollar, *Luke–Acts*, 34.

26Maddox, *Purpose*, 140.

27'Sinners' occurs 17 times in Luke and only 11 times in Matthew and Mark combined.

28On Mary in Luke 7 *cf.*, Marshall, *Luke*, 452: 'Mary's posture expresses zeal to learn (*cf.*, K. Weiss *TDNT* VI:630), and it is significant that Jesus encourages a woman to learn from him since the Jewish leaders were opposed to this.'

Long before Acts 1:8 Luke prepares his readers for the progress of the word by showing the broad scope of Jesus' ministry, which undoubtedly stood out against the narrow particularism of first century Judaism.[30]

III. Progress confirmed

It is common sense for authors to stress that which is important in their work by repetition. Luke, in Acts, adopts this practice. For example, three times he refers to Stephen's martyrdom (7:51–8:3; 9:1; 11:19), the story of Cornelius (chs. 10, 11, 15), Paul's conversion (chs. 9, 22, 26), the apostolic decree (15:20, 29; 21:25) and the turning to the Gentiles in response to Jewish rejection of the gospel (13:46; 18:5-6; 28:23-28).[31] That Acts contains a series of summaries that report the progress of the gospel is unmistakeable evidence that it is a central theme in the book.

Summaries are found in 6:7; 9:31; 12:24; 16:5; 19:20; 28:30-31, texts which report certain deeds (preaching, teaching, healing, praying), note the future-worldly character of the church (peace, unity, sharing, grace) and stress the resultant growth (multiplication, increase).[32] Many of them share certain terms and have a common syntactical

---

[29]The only other reference in the Synoptics to Samaritans is Mt. 10:5, where preaching to them is prohibited. Another possible indication of universalism is the rending of the temple veil in 23:45b, which, according to Green, 'Demise of the Temple', symbolizes not the destruction of the temple, which is still standing at the end of Luke–Acts, but 'the destruction of the symbolic world surrounding and emanating from the temple' (514). Green asks: what is the significance of the tearing of the temple curtain in Luke seen against the larger mural of the temple theology of Luke–Acts? He concludes that in Luke–Acts 'Even if the temple remains as a place for prayer and teaching, it no longer occupies the position of cultural center, the sacred orientation point for life; its zones of holiness no longer prejudge people according to relative purity. Other stories and speeches in Acts will develop the theological rationale, but in the torn veil Luke has already demonstrated symbolically that the holiness-purity matrix embodied in and emanating from the temple has been undermined' (515). Whether or not all this is signalled by the tearing of the veil, it is true that by the end of Acts the temple no longer divides humanity into insiders and outsiders; the way is opened for a mission to all people.
[30]As Dollar, *Luke–Acts*, 52 notes perceptively: 'Luke's style is to introduce a subject, then almost imperceptibly build his case until suddenly he breaks it open and almost overwhelms the reader with its importance. This can be illustrated in the way Luke brings Paul to the front of his story; 7:57; 8:1; 9:1ff; 11:26ff; 13:1ff; and in his handling of the explosive subject of circumcision (Acts 10–11 and 15).'
[31]Dollar, *Luke–Acts*, 301.

construction (an imperfect indicative verb followed by a chain of participles).[33] These texts have been the subject of much speculation, most of which has proven unconvincing.[34] They do not divide the book neatly into panels (which would be of markedly different lengths and defy logic), although they undoubtedly supply some 'rhythm' to the narrative, nor are they clues to Luke's sources (they overlap both in content and vocabulary and are general rather then specific in character).[35] Their function seems to be threefold.

First, the summaries act as transitions from one event or period of growth to the next. Cadbury writes: 'The summaries serve as... connective tissue by which memorabilia are turned into the beginnings of a continuous narrative'.[36] Barrett's comments on 12:24 could be repeated for the great majority of these texts: 'It is clear that he [Luke] is summing up the results of the narrative he has now completed before turning to the new material of the following chapters'.[37] This observation will prove to be of importance in section VI with reference to the ending of Acts, Luke's final progress report.

Second, the summaries confirm not only that progress is taking place, but that the expansion is impressive and far reaching. It is precisely because they are not specific to the episodes they close and introduce, but generalising, that we are left with the impression that Luke had much more material at his disposal. As Cadbury, suggests, the summaries 'indicate that the material is typical, that the action was continued, that the effect was general'.[38] They state implicitly what the fourth Gospel claims in John 20:30; 21:25 ('the world itself could not contain the books that would be written').

Third, in reporting progress the summaries consistently stress divine causation. Several of the texts allude back to 1:8,[39] effectively asserting the fulfilment of Jesus' commission. Most of them do not

---

[32]There is some debate over the identification of the summaries in Acts. Some would include 2:47; 4:4; 5:16; 11:24; 18:11.

[33]I owe this grammatical observation to Marguerat, 'Rhetoric', 88. On the summaries and various literary and historical matters see Cadbury, 'Summaries'.

[34]Turner, 'Chronology', 421-23 has made the intriguing suggestion that the six summaries divide the book into periods of approximately five years of growth. *Cf.*, also Filson, *Acts*, 11-14, who adopts Turner's divisions.

[35]*Cf.*, Cadbury, 'Summaries', 401: 'How far the summaries came to our author along with his materials cannot now be determined.'

[36]Cadbury, 'Summaries', 35.

[37]Barrett, *Acts I*, 595.

[38]Cadbury, 'Summaries', 402.

[39]See also Acts 26:20.

simply state that the church spread but that the word of God pros-
pered and so on. The creative force behind the notion of the growth of
the word in 6:7; 12:24; 19:20 recalls Jesus' parable of the sower in Luke
8:4-15.[40] Furthermore, the verbs to grow (αὐξάνω)[41] and to multiply
(πληθύνω) are also used to describe the rapid growth of the people of
God in LXX Exodus 1:7, a text cited in Acts 7:17-18[42] and in Genesis
9:1,7; 28:3; 35:11; 47:27; 48:4; Leviticus 26:9; Jeremiah 3:16; 23:3 (trans-
lating the 'be fruitful and multiply' formula).[43] The context for growth
is the analogous growth of Israel. In giving God the credit for progress
the summaries are in accord with much else in Acts.

IV. The author of progress

While it is true that the narrative of Luke–Acts contains some ninety-
five characters, R. Brawley observes that 'there are but four major
characters—God, Jesus, Peter, and Paul'.[44] Of these four, in terms of
action, Jesus is the centre of attention in Luke and Peter and Paul in
Acts. This observation, however, creates the false impression that God
plays only a minor and peripheral role in the two volume work.
Through a number of means Acts indicates that ultimately God is
responsible for the spread of the word.

Although on the surface human characters overcome considerable barriers to preach the message to ever-widening circles, it is God
who directs and enables them to do so. God supplies Peter with a
vision which leads him to preach to, and even enjoy table-fellowship
with, the Gentiles. God calls and commissions Paul to missionary
service and then guides him along the way. God enables Philip, to
mention a minor character, to reach Samaritans and the Ethiopian
Eunuch. We might even say, with an eye on Luke, that it is God who
sends Jesus and endows him with the Holy Spirit.

At the crucial turning points in the narrative the decisive action

---

40Cf., also Isaiah 2:1,3/Micah 4:1,2: 'In the last days...the word of the Lord will go
out from Jerusalem'.
41Kodell, 'Word', 509-10 has noted that this verb is also used in Luke 1:80 and 2:40
in summaries of growth concerning John the Baptist and Jesus.
42Tannehill, Narrative Unity, 2:82.
43Cf., Kodell, 'Word', 517: 'Luke's description of the growth of the word of God in
the summaries . . . is a result of his reflection on the parable of the sower and the
biblical tradition in which it is situated'.
44Brawley, Luke–Acts and the Jews, 110.

of God is unmistakable. This can be seen most clearly with respect to the most startling note of expansion in Acts, the 'opening of the door of faith to the Gentiles' (cf., 14:27), the credit for which is explicitly given to God in the following texts:

13:47—'the Lord has commanded [Paul and Barnabas]... to be a light for the Gentiles';

14:27—'he [God] had opened a door of faith to the Gentiles';

15:12—'They [Paul and Barnabas] related what signs and wonders God had done among the Gentiles';

28:28—'this salvation of God has been sent [a divine passive] to the Gentiles'.

The repeated occurrence of certain phrases is also revealing. The message in Acts is described as the 'word of God'[45] (see Luke 3:2-17, 5:1; 8:11; Acts 4:29,31; 6:2,7; 8:14; 11:1; 12:24; 13:5,7,44,46,48; 16:32; 17:13; 18:11), its content concerns 'the kingdom of God' (1:3; 8:12; 14:22; 19:8; 28:23,31) and 'the salvation of God' (28:28; cf., 7:25), and its progress depends upon the 'purpose', 'will' and 'plan' of God.[46] The notion that everything which occurs is in fulfilment of Scripture, which Luke–Acts assumes throughout, points directly to divine initiative.[47] When Luke notes that the church not only needs to be established, but built up, it is God who is the subject of the verb.

Brawley's list of four main characters has one glaring omission: the Holy Spirit. He regards the Spirit as 'nothing more than a convenient designation of God',[48] an overstatement that nonetheless points to their close relation. H.C. Kee's description of the Spirit as 'God's instrument in the present age' is closer to the mark.[49] To trace the activity of the Spirit in Acts is to observe the progress of the word. In Acts the Spirit is not only the agent of confirmation of community membership, of empowerment and guidance and the instrument of judgement,[50] but also the means by which God launches the good news to the end of the earth. It is no exaggeration to say that 'each successive stage of the outreach of the gospel to the wider world receives confirmation by the Spirit'[51] (see e.g. 1:8; 2:3, 38; 5:32; 6:1-3;

45Cf., Brawley, Luke–Acts and the Jews, 119: 'Luke–Acts repeatedly associates God with the word'.

46On these terms see Rosner, 'Acts and Biblical History', 79.

47See Peterson, 'The Motif of Fulfilment'.

48Brawley, Luke–Acts and the Jews, 115.

49Kee, Good News. Cf. Conzelmann,Luke, 213.

50See Kee, Good News, ch. 3

51Kee, Good News, 34.

7:51; 8:16-17, 39-40; 9:17; 10:45; 11:12,15-16; 15:8; 11:24; 13:1-2). Stephen sums up opposition to such progress as to 'resist the Holy Spirit' (7:51).

Many of the episodes in Acts reinforce the overall impression that God is at work in giving impetus to the new movement. Peter's release from prison in chapter 12 is a case in point chosen at random.[52] The way the story is told, Luke's narrative artistry, underscores what Leland Ryken calls 'the hidden or spiritual plot in the story of Acts— the mighty acts of God contending with forces hostile to the Christian gospel'.[53] Peter's plight could scarcely be worse, as depicted in 12:1-4, 6, where every detail adds weight to a sense of despair and helplessness. Yet verse 5 supplies a note of hope: 'but earnest prayer was made by the church to God for him'.[54] When Peter is rescued in 12:7-11 by God's messenger, the angel, he wanders about benumbed and it takes some time for him to 'come to his senses' (12:11). Likewise, in 12:12-17 the confusion at the prayer meeting captures comically the disbelief at the news of his rescue, for which, ironically, they had been presumably praying. All this along with the images of prison, light, and an open gate and the demise of Herod (12:23), which is as frightful as his description in 12:1-3 is frightening, convey effectively a message of the power of God over human frailty and opposition in support of the progress of the word.

V. Patterns of progress

Having noted preparation for progress (in Luke and Acts 1:1-11), and confirmation of progress (in the progress reports) and having identified the main instigator of progress (God), we are now in a position to enquire concerning the kind of progress depicted in Acts. To start we shall consider Acts section by section, looking at what might be called the plan of Acts, before making some general observations.

From one angle Acts 1–5 gets things off to a slow start. All the action takes place in Jerusalem and the movement remains thoroughly particularistic within the Jewish religious system. While an emerging leadership (2:42), separate meetings (2:46-47), membership (2:47; 5:12-13) and finances (4:32-37), and conflict with the Sanhedrin (4:1ff; 5:17ff) identify the group as distinct and increasingly separate from Judaism,

---

52On the narrative and artistic qualities of this story cf., Ryken, Words of Life, 82-87.
53Ryken, Words of Life, 87.
54'God' is emphatic by word order in the Greek; my translation refects this.

the inclusion of Gentiles is not yet on the agenda. Wilson is right to point out that all the Jerusalem audience in Acts 2, including the proselytes, were Jews (*cf.*, 5:31: 'God exalted him to give repentance to Israel').[55] Nonetheless, some elements in these chapters imply that a broader ministry is inevitable: the vast geographical references in chapter 2; 'all flesh' in 2:17; 'all that are far off' in 2:39 (*cf.*, Isa. 57:19); and 'first' in 3:26 ('God...sent him to you first'; note the context of God's promise to Abraham; 3:25).[56]

The movement of the gospel from a Jewish to a universal context occurs progressively in chapters 6–15. As Dollar notes:

> [Luke] deliberately chooses those events in the early history of the messianic movement that shows how God moved the gospel step by step from Jewish particularism to universalism. Each episode in these chapters, with the exception of chapter twelve, advances this movement in the direction of the Gentiles until the leadership explicitly announces this accomplishment in chapter fifteen.[57]

In Acts 6:1-11 the conflict between the Hellenists (Grecian Jews in Jerusalem)[58] and the Hebrews (Hebraic Jews) over the distribution of food highlights social, cultural and linguistic diversity in the church.

In the ministry of Stephen (probably a diaspora Jew; 6:8–8:3) we have 'a major turning point in Luke's story', that has repercussions through to chapter 15.[59] Conflict with the Jewish authorities comes to a head, and, in the longest speech in Acts, Stephen challenges the centrality of Jerusalem and the temple, which leads to fierce opposition and persecution scattering the movement 'throughout Judea and Samaria' (8:1; an allusion to 1:8).

The ministry of Philip to the Samaritans, who were the political and religious rivals of the Jews (8:4-25),[60] and the Ethiopian (probably a non-Jew; 8:26-40)[61] extends the gospel to other 'people groups', to use the modern missiological jargon.

In chapter 9, as in the other two accounts of Paul's conversion in

---

[55]Wilson, *Gentile Mission*, 123.
[56]Hahn's conclusion, *Mission*, 132, that such elements open up a 'world-wide horizon' perhaps makes too much of this evidence.
[57]Dollar, *Luke–Acts*, 115.
[58]They are sometimes seen as Gentiles or Samaritans.
[59]Dollar, *Luke–Acts*, 123.
[60]The Samaritans are probably not seen by Luke as Gentiles, but also not as non-Jews; see Jervell, *Luke*, 111-32.
[61]Gaventa, *Aspects of Conversion*, 104 points to his physical disability as preventing him from becoming a proselyte (*cf.*, Deut. 23:1).

Acts, it is made clear that Paul is called to preach the word both to the Jews and to the Gentiles.

In the conversion of Cornelius (9:32–11:18) Luke presents a full historical and theological justification for the universalism of the gospel, leading to the conclusion that 'to the Gentiles God has granted repentance unto life' (11:18). And in the so-called conversion of Peter we see the lengths to which God went to overcome the reluctance of Jewish Christians to preach the word to Gentiles (visions, trances, angels and the Spirit). As Dollar observes, with Peter being forced to go to Cornelius, 'Centrifugalism is supplanting centripetalism...the conversion of the messenger must precede the conversion of those who are lost'.[62]

Acts 11:19–14:28 narrates the beginnings of the first Gentile church, at Antioch, the 'third' city of the Roman Empire (according to Josephus; Jewish War 3:2:4),[63] and the initiation of the Gentile mission. Chapter 13 is particularly striking. Paul is referred to by his Gentile name, preaches his first synagogue sermon (in Acts), and, following Jewish rejection, leads a mission to Gentiles *qua* Gentiles.

The book of Acts without chapter 15 would be like a wedding ceremony without the crucial pronouncement. Everything that happens in chapters 1–14 leads up to this high point and what follows merely traces the implications of the decision. It was not uncommon in the ancient world for a piece of literature to have not only a beginning and an ending, but also a centre. Although Acts is not a tragedy, some comments of Horace about tragedies fit Acts very well:

> we look for a true beginning..., a true centre point, and a true consummation or end. Towards the central point the whole action must ascend in orderly sequence, and from it descend in an equally ordered sequence to the end.[64]

The notion of a literary centre is also known in biblical literature, with which Acts has many affinities,[65] such as 1 and 2 Chronicles[66] and some of the Psalms. The universality and progress of the word is established on the basis of the unity of the people of God. Following Acts 15 only geographical boundaries need to be crossed.

62Dollar, *Luke–Acts*, 185.
63That is, after Rome and Alexandria.
64Cited by Hitchcock, 'Drama', 16. *Cf.*, Stibbe, *John's Gospel*, 35. I am indebted to George Wieland for this reference.
65See my 'Acts anddBiblical History'.
66*Cf.*, Johnstone, '1 and 2 Chronicles'.

In Acts 15:36–21:16 Paul pursues his mission to Jews and Gentiles vigorously, moving further and further away from Jerusalem. Does Paul move away from Jerusalem only in a geographical sense, or is it the case that Jerusalem exercises less and less influence over Paul as his mission progresses? B.N. Kaye argues that Luke links Paul with Jerusalem through the presence of Silas, and that the Jewishness of Paul's ministry in Philippi, Thessalonica and Berea recedes in Athens and Corinth when Silas is no longer with Paul.[67] While it is true that in Athens Paul goes directly to Gentiles, he had already addressed a Gentile audience in Lystra in 14:8-20. Furthermore, the 'major re-direction' of his ministry in Corinth is not so much in terms of its focus as in its length (he stayed 18 months). Kaye's thesis has particular problems with the ministry in Ephesus (which he does not consider) where Paul begins as usual by preaching in the synagogue, this time for some three months, and where the mob clearly regards Paul as a Jew. Acts presents Paul consistently preaching first in the synagogues to Jews and godfearers. After Jewish rejection, he continues to preach to them (*e.g.* 18:7). He practises Jewish rituals, including circumcision (of Timothy, a Jew), a Nazirite vow and a purification rite in the Jerusalem temple. As Dollar observes, 'Paul's ministry [in Acts 15:31-21:16] is to both Jews and Gentiles with a Jewish priority which is consistent with, and represents an extension of the ministry begun by the church in Jerusalem'.[68] The progress of the word in Acts 15:36-21:16 concerns primarily geographical boundaries rather than ethnic or relational ones.

The place of Acts 21:17-28:33 in the plan of Acts as it relates to the progress of the word is not immediately apparent. Little progress is made, to put it bluntly, as Paul and the Jews are depicted wrangling before the Roman legal system. Purposes for this section have of course been proposed along the lines of an apology for Paul, and intriguing parallels with the travel section in Luke's Gospel (9:51–19:44; where Jesus goes from Galilee up to Jerusalem) have been noted. With respect to Paul's mission to Gentiles it is noteworthy that throughout chapters 21–28 both Paul's impeccable Jewishness (*cf.*, 22:3; 24:11-18; 25:8) and his ministry to both Jews and Gentiles (21:17-32; 22:21; 26:17 and the witness to those with Paul on the ship and on Malta (27:21-26; 35-36, 28:10) is stressed. The closing section of Acts says something not just about Paul but about the Christian faith: its

---

[67]Kaye, 'Silas'.
[68]Dollar, *Luke–Acts*, 259.

important (handwritten margin note)

message has a foundation in Judaism and the Scriptures and its scope is universal, going to different levels of society, not excepting rulers (two of the leading themes of the whole of Acts). These two themes intersect in startling manner in 26:22-23 before King Aprippa where Paul states that 'the prophets and Moses said [that Christ] would proclaim light both to the people [the Jews] and to the Gentiles.'

An important observation arises out of our look at the plan of Acts. The simple formulation of the gospel going from Jews in Jerusalem to Gentiles in Rome is, in one sense, misleading. We observed that the Jewish element of the mission in Acts is not removed. Acts does not replace one form of particularism (Jews alone) with another (Gentiles alone). As the book states in the second last verse (28:30), even in Rome Paul 'welcomed *all* who came to him'.

It is possible to discern not only a pattern of progress across the whole of Acts but also within the various sections. Such broad literary patterns have been noted by Newman, Talbert, Cadbury, Dibelius, Goulder and Spencer.[69] Goulder and Newman in particular contend convincingly that Acts contains a cycle of experience that is repeated several times. Witnesses are chosen by God; engage in preaching and/or the working of miracles; some respond positively, others negatively, leading to opposition and persecution; which brings about new opportunities for witness. Newman contends that 'The cycles begins in Jerusalem, grow fuller in the expansion chronicled in Judea, Samaria, Asia Minor, and Europe, and finally end with a prolonged single episode of Paul'.[70] Thus Acts is not simply a chronicle of continuous progress, but of cycles of progress and expansion. These cycles highlight the rejection and persecution which pervades Acts throughout and warn us against seeing triumphalistic progress in the book. Conzelmann's theology of glory tells only one side of the story.

VI. Unending progress

The ending of Acts is for most readers a puzzle, if not a disappointment. Why does Luke not tell us what happened to Paul, whose career he has traced for more than half the book? Many alternative explanations have been offered.[71] Scholars have suggested that the coming of

---

69Cf., Spencer, 'Acts', 388-89.
70Newman, 'Acts', 440.
71For a list of views and some assessment see Hemer, *Acts*, 383-87.

the gospel to Rome suitably climaxes the book irrespective of Paul's fate, or that Luke's readers already knew of Paul's death or release, or that Acts was indeed written to help secure Paul's release, being written as part of his defence at the trial, or that Luke intended a third book or that he ran out of room on his papyrus scroll, or that he simply did not know of Paul's fate.

Several commentators have suggested that one function of the verses in question is to indicate the ongoing nature of the progress of the word:

> the ending of Acts is truly an opening to the continuing life of the messianic people, as it continues to preach the kingdom and teach the things concerning Jesus both boldly and without hindrance. [Luke T. Johnson][72]

> The important unfinished business in this situation is for the witness of the new community to press forward. Still to be accomplished in the contemporary life of the church is the divine intention revealed to Paul and Barnabas at Pisidian Antioch midway through the narrative of Acts (13:47): "I have set you to be a light for the Gentiles, that you may bring salvation, to the uttermost parts of the earth". (Howard Clark Kee)[73]

Is there any warrant for such remarks? In both cases the above quotations are the last words in their respective volumes. Are they then simply the attempts of authors to finish their books on a pious and positive note and to provide a satisfying ending (something that, ironically enough, some would say Luke failed to do with Acts)? What is the literary function of the ending of Acts?[74] Four lines of evidence support the case for the 'unending progress of the word' reading of Acts 28:30-31: Acts 1:8, the nature of the ending of Acts as a progress report and an analysis of the verses in terms of ancient rhetoric and modern literary theory.

First, as we argued in section II, the manifesto of Acts 1:8 is not completed with the arrival of the apostle, and more importantly, the gospel in Rome. Witness to 'the end of the earth' represents a target

---

[72]Johnson, *Acts*, 476.

[73]Kee, *Good News*, 107.

[74]Siegert, 'Prose Rhythm', esp. 51-54, provides evidence that the ending of Acts is not haphazard, but purely in terms of style it exhibits, along with the prologues of Luke and Acts, a degree of rhythm which according to the conventions of ancient rhetoric one finds in carefully crafted pieces.

beyond Rome, which is not reached in Acts.

Second, as we saw in section III, Acts 28:30-31 belongs to a category of texts in the book that may be described as progress reports in which certain deeds and consequent growth are recounted. The function of such verses, we observed, was to act as transitions from one period of witness to the next. It may seem strange to close the book in such a fashion. However, at the very least it sets up the expectation that though the book has ended, the witness has not. The fate of Paul may be in doubt, but Luke leaves us in no doubt as to the fate of the progress of the message Paul preached.[75] In effect, he finishes with the subliminal message, 'to be continued.'

Third, D. Marguerat, 'The End of Acts (28:16-31) and the Rhetoric of Silence', has argued that Luke's silence on the fate of Paul, his 'suspended ending', may be compared to analogous endings in the work of Homer, Graeco–Roman poetry and historiography, including Herodotus.[76] Marguerat claims that 28:30-31, in the light of this comparative material and teaching in ancient rhetoric on the effect of silence, provides 'a portrait of the exemplary pastor, whereby the realization of the missionary agenda of the book of Acts is anticipated.'[77]

Fourth, Tannehill has applied M. Torgovnick's functional analysis of narrative closure to the ending of Acts and comes to a similar conclusion.[78] Torgovnick finds that good endings include circularity, recalling the beginning, parallelism referring to other points in the narrative, and incompletion, deliberately omitting some important elements. Although originally formed from the observation of closure in modern novels, this analysis makes good sense for Acts. Tannehill believes that the ending of Acts illustrates all three aspects. In short, it recalls the reign of God for Israel in 1:3, 6 and Jesus' commission in 1:8, providing circularity. Features parallel to earlier points include the reference to ancestral customs (28:17 and 21:28), to the hope of Israel (28:20 and 23:6; 24:15, 21; 26:6-8,23) and to turning to the Gentiles (28:28 and 13:46; 18:5-6; 19:8-9). Most important for our purposes is incompletion, which in the ending of Acts involves not only doubt about Paul's future but also about 'completion of the mission "to the end of the earth"',[79] the Lord's return and the mission to the Jews.

75Cf., Marguerat, 'Rhetoric', 8 who speaks of Acts 28:30-31 having the 'effect of duration and exemplarity', in similar fashion to the 'summaries of Acts (2:42, 45-47; 5:16; 8:3; 12:25; 15:35; 18:11; 19:8-10, etc).'

76Marguerat, 'Rhetoric', 74-89.

77Marguerat, 'Rhetoric', 89.

78Tannehill, *Narrative Unity*, 2:353-57.

In Tannehill's view:

> because God is God, hope remains that God's comprehensive saving
> purpose will somehow be realized, but there is no indication of how
> that can happen. In the meantime, Acts can only suggest that the
> church welcome those Jews who are still willing to listen and continue
> its mission to the more responsive gentile world.[80]

Thus four lines of evidence point in the same direction, to a
deliberately open-ended ending of Acts that functions to portray the
ongoing progress of the word, and perhaps even to include the readers
in the continuing task of spreading the word.[81] The approach to
narration in Acts encourages the reader to take the point of view of
those taking the witness forward. Of the four types of narrators,[82] the
'I' of the prologue, the dominant third person omniscient narrator, the
'we' narrator and the various character narrators,[83] the last two, which
do not occur in Luke's Gospel, encourage us to feel part of the action
and to see things from the perspective of the expanding early church.[84]
Acts would not be the only NT narrative to address indirectly its
readers. Hints of a similar address occur in John 20:29b ('Blessed are
those who have not seen and yet believe') and 17:20 ('I do not pray for
these only, but also for those who believe in me through their word').

N.T. Wright has asked the question of how biblical narratives
carry authority for Christians. Part of his answer fits well with what we
are suggesting for Acts.[85] Using the analogy of a play of Shakespeare,
most of whose fifth act is lost, he suggests that a fifth act could be
written by 'highly trained, sensitive and experienced Shakespearian
actors, who would immerse themselves in the first four acts' (1:140).

---

[79]Tannehill, *Narrative Unity*, 2:356.

[80]Tannehill, *Narrative Unity*, 2:357.

[81]Using a literary approach Darr, *Character Building*, comes to the same conclusion.
Cf., 53: 'through a variety of rhetorical strategies, Luke–Acts maneuvers its readers
into alignment with the "witnesses" (*autoptai* or *martyres*) who constitute the
insiders in the story. That is, the Lukan text is designed to persude the readers to
become believing witnesses'. See also 147.

[82]See Kurz, *Luke–Acts*.

[83]Eg. Peter's report to the Jerusalem church of his experiences in Cornelius' house
(11:1-18) and Paul's testimonies to the crowd in Jerusalem (22:1-22) and before
Aprippa (26:2-23), where the story is told from their personal vantage point.

[84]This of course is not their only function. Kurz, for instance, argues that the 'we'
narrater, appearing only intermittently, represents only partial support for Paul;
Paul is left alone at his trials, as third person narration resumes.

[85]See *The New Testament*, 1:139-43 and in more detail 'Authoritative'.

Acts, to adopt the model, is about the spread of the gospel and it challenges its readers to press ahead with the unfinished task.

VII. Conclusion

The theme of the progress of the word is widespread and central to the purpose of the book of Acts, being anticipated by elements in Luke's Gospel, set up by Acts 1:1-11 and confirmed throughout by the progress reports. It is, as we have seen, closely related to most of the other main strands of the theology of Acts, including the plan of God, salvation, witness, persecution, the Holy Spirit, Israel and the new people of God. It would be difficult to imagine a theme that is more comprehensive in scope.

In describing the progress of the word in Acts several general points may be made: (1) It is not progress in the triumphalistic sense that Acts portrays (*contra* Conzelmann), for opposition and persecution are pervasive and enduring; (2) the Jewish element of the mission is not removed, as might be suggested by the simple formula of the word going from Jews in Jerusalem to Gentiles in Rome; (3) God is repeatedly given the credit for progress—it is divinely ordained, planned, guided and supported expansion; and (4) the progress theme functions to include the reader in the task of spreading the word, especially with the open-ended ending of the book.

CHAPTER 12

OPPOSITION TO THE PLAN OF GOD AND PERSECUTION

Brian Rapske

Summary

The plan of an extensive witness to Jesus throughout Palestine and the Mediterranean met with frequent outside opposition, particularly from Jews, and created dissension and controversy among Christians. In a bid to assure his reader that the Christian preaching was indeed 'of God', Luke relates key moments when detractors and supporters engage in theological reflection upon events to understand what God is doing so as to embrace rather than oppose it. The Christian witness is of God because it prevails through all opposition and persecution by means of divine tokens which prepare, assist and encourage them.

I. Introduction

The early Christians declared that Jesus was indeed the Christ of promise, proclaiming his resurrection and salvation in his name. It was natural that, springing from Judaism, claiming Jews as its first converts, and seen as the fulfilment of long cherished Jewish hope, the message concerning Jesus was directed with enthusiasm to the people of God. With great intensity in Palestine and throughout the Diaspora, however, the message was opposed by many Jews and their leaders and the messengers were persecuted. Jewish Christians were treated by official Judaism as errorists to be disciplined or excluded.

As if this were not trouble enough, Jewish Christians soon discovered that believing Gentiles were being received into their community outside of keeping the law. Already increasingly marginalized within Judaism by official opposition, they were now pulled even further from their avowed home and factionalized by disagreement over this new mission initiative.

The opening of the book of Acts makes the fact of a plan to bear a worldwide witness clear (Acts 1:8). But was the plan and its development indeed the plan of God? Luke and his readers know that denial had been the response of many outside the Christian community, and uncertainty the response of numbers within it. The thesis of the present chapter is that Luke labours through Acts to demonstrate that the plan of Christian witness is of God. He describes key moments when detractors and supporters alike show an awareness that the divine intention, because it will be fulfilled, must be discerned and embraced rather than resisted. Luke also shows that the Christian witness does not prevail through resistance and hostility because of human tenacity but by divine empowerment. He describes how witnesses beleaguered by opposition and persecution are divinely prepared, assisted and encouraged to fulfil the plan.

II. Jewish opposition

Gamaliel's truth test

Gamaliel's cautionary words to an angry Sanhedrin at Acts 5:34-40 are the most 'learned'[1] Jewish reflection upon the question of the Christian message in relation to the plan of God. As the Sanhedrin debates whether to put Peter and the other apostles to death for their continued preaching, Gamaliel stops the proceedings. He reminds the Sanhedrin of two previous movements that had arisen and then quickly fell apart at the deaths of their leaders. Gamaliel advises the release of Peter and the others, and a 'wait and see' attitude on the principle that Jesus' death should be a sufficient blow to dissolve the Christian movement if it is 'of human origin' (v. 38). Though action might be taken in this case, none is really needed. That Gamaliel holds out the opposite prospect is critically important to Luke and his readers. Gamaliel is said to assert that if this movement is 'from God, you will not be able to stop these men; you will only find yourselves fighting against God' (v. 39). Sanhedral action would be both futile and perilous. Luke appears to seize upon Gamaliel's theological reflection and use it as a truth test by which he demonstrates the legitimacy of the Christian witness. His narrative argument is that because the witness has an unstoppable and overcoming character to it despite fierce opposition, it is truly of God.

Luke's reader has already been notified of the motive underlying the apostles' intransigence. Earlier forbidden to speak and teach in the name of Jesus by an angry Sanhedrin because it wants to 'stop this thing from spreading any further' (Acts 4:17), Peter and John refuse to obey using these words, 'Judge for yourselves whether it is right in God's sight to obey you rather than God' (4:19).[2] It is an unstoppable compulsion for them (4:20). On their second appearance before the Sanhedrin, the reason for their refusal to obey is stated more clearly and forcefully, 'We must obey God rather than men' (5:29). Additionally fortified by a miraculous release from prison and an angelic command to publicly preach (5:19f.), they declare that their sense of compulsion is a matter of the divine necessity (δεῖ).[3]

Convinced by Gamaliel's counsel, the Sanhedrin releases the apostles after a severe flogging and a warning that the previous ban on all preaching still holds. Luke is able to argue persuasively through the narrative that the Christian witness has been divinely mandated by relating that the apostles' response to the punishment is an immediate

---

[1]Note the careful mention of Gamaliel's credentials at Acts 5:34.

[2]This response, however closely it conforms to similar sayings outside the NT, must surely spring from the dominical warning to fear God and obey him rather than bowing to human threats and opposition (Luke 12:4f., 8f.). *Cf.*, Socrates (Plato, *Apol.* 29.D) with Acts 4:19 and 5:29. For discussion, see Lake and Cadbury, 'Acts', 4:45; Bruce, *Acts (Greek Text)*, 155; Haenchen, *Acts*, 251; Conzelmann, *Acts*, 42.

[3]See Cosgrove, 'The Divine ΔΕΙ in Luke–Acts', 186-90, for a discussion of the divine initiative.

joy[4] at being counted worthy to suffer disgrace for the name of Jesus
and that thereafter the good news concerning Jesus Christ is cease-
lessly and extensively preached and taught so that the number of
disciples continues to increase (Acts 5:42; 6:1). Stephen next bears a
powerful and unstoppable witness (v. 6f.). The Synagogue of the
Freedmen cannot 'stand up' (6:10) to the power and Spirit by which he
speaks. Though Stephen is killed and a great persecution is unleashed,
Luke can relate that 'those who had been scattered preached the word
wherever they went' (8:4), including Philip whose fruitful ministry is
next related (8:4-8, 12-14, 26-40). The Christian witness, because it
grows in the face of official Jewish opposition, is the plan of God.

Saul opposes the plan of God

Luke lays out Saul's persecuting activity as an exact case of what Gamaliel has warned against. As principal official agent of the high priest(s)
(Acts 9:1; 22:5) and Sanhedrin (22:5), Saul pursues Jesus' disciples not
only in Jerusalem (7:58; 8:1-3; 9:1, 21; 22:2-4; 26:10) but also to foreign
cities (9:1f., 14, 21; 22:5; 26:11f.). He goes into synagogues and from
house to house, beating them and trying to make them blaspheme
(22:19; 26:11), imprisoning them (8:3; 9:21; 22:4, 19; 26:10), and seeing
to their conviction on capital charges in Jerusalem (9:1; 22:4; 26:10).[5]
Three times in Luke's narrative (9:3-19; 22:6-21; 26:12-18), the reader is
told how Saul is divinely compelled to realize that he is resisting the
irresistible plan of God in persecuting the followers of Jesus.

      Luke tells how Saul fell to the ground at the flashing of a heaven-
ly light and heard a voice speaking to him in Aramaic in solemn divine
cadences[6]—'Saul, Saul, why do you persecute me?'. To his reverent
request for introduction,[7] the voice replies, 'I am Jesus whom you are
persecuting'.[8] Jesus stands on the continuum between identification (a
'heavenly spokesman and representative')[9] and identity ('organic and

---

[4]Cf., Acts 13:52; 16:25 and the dominical instruction at Luke 6:23.
[5]Further, Hultgren, 'Paul's Pre-Christian Persecutions', 97-111.
[6]The double vocative Σαούλ Σαούλ recalls Gen. 22:11; 46:2; Exod. 3:4; 1 Sam.
3:10. Cf., Luke 8:24; 10:41; 22:31; 2 Esd. 14.1; 2 Bar. 22.2.
[7]Τίς εἶ, Κύριε; Saul does not at first know that the speaker is Jesus, but the voice
is a heavenly one, therefore κύριος should be rendered 'Lord' rather than simply
'Sir'. So Bruce, Acts (Greek Text), 235; Marshall, Acts:Commentary, 169f.; Longenecker, 'Acts', 371.
[8]Cf., Acts 22:8: 'I am Jesus of Nazareth....'.
[9]Marshall, Acts: Commentary, 169.

indissoluble unity')[10] with his persecuted followers. If the Pauline epistles can be taken as giving insight,[11] Jesus' words should be understood as much closer to an assertion of radical identification. The 'I am' of the heavenly speaker probably also recalls to a shocked Saul the ineffable name of God.[12] These words must first have carried Saul into a dark grief. Every abuse, imprisonment, flogging and execution of Christians had in fact been an assault upon the Righteous One himself. In Jesus' self-identification, Saul now knows that he has set himself against the plan of God. Luke records that the voice also said, 'It is hard for you to kick against the goads' (Acts 26:14). This refers not to pangs of conscience in Saul but 'the futility of his persecutions of the Way and the inevitability of his conversion...'.[13] Resisting the plan of God cannot be successful, only painful; and in the end, God's will prevails.

Later, as a prisoner in Caesarea, Paul can relate to King Agrippa, 'I was not disobedient to the vision from heaven' (Acts 26:19). Immediately after his vision (9:20), Saul engages in indefatigable and fruitful witness despite the early distrust of believers and the hostility and violence of opponents. Moreover, the church, with its arch persecutor overcome during the very course of his opposition, grows both spiritually and numerically in the ensuing time of peace (9:31). The plan's compelling quality and hence, its divine origin, is thus confirmed to the reader through the triple record of Saul's conversion and call and through the accounts of his missionary labours.

III. Christian opposition

First opposition to the Gentile Mission

Peter's preaching of the good news to the Gentile Cornelius and his household was at once momentous and deeply troublesome to the early church. Luke's careful and extensive description of events clearly

---

10Longenecker, 'Acts', 371.
11See Gal. 6:17; Col. 1:24. *Cf.,* 1 Cor. 6:15; 8:12; 10:16f.; 12:12ff.; Eph. 1:23; 4:4, 12, 16; 5:23; Col. 1:18, 24; 2:19. For other Lukan indications of radical identification, Luke 10:16; Acts 1:1; 4:23-30.
12Conzelmann, *Acts,* 71: 'The question is formulated in view of the ἐγώ εἰμι, "I am," of the one who appears in the vision'.
13Squires, *Plan of God,* 177. For discussion of the provenance of this saying, see Lake and Cadbury, 'Acts', 4:318f.; Haenchen, *Acts,* 685.

suggests not only how significant the internal opposition was at the time, but also that it was a matter of continuing interest and concern for Luke's readers. Was the Gentile mission an aberration needing correction, or a 'new thing' of God to be embraced? A negative report concerning Peter's action quickly spreads, Luke relates, 'so that when Peter went up to Jerusalem, the circumcised believers criticized him and said, "You went into the house of uncircumcised men and ate with them"' (Acts 11:3). The reference to their circumcision does not identify the disputants as part of a 'circumcision party'. They are simply Jewish Christians. If the reference to 'the apostles and the brothers throughout Judea' at Acts 11:1 is in some sense an antecedent, Peter has run foul of the grassroots membership of the church and its apostles and elders. Haenchen cannot be right in asserting that the sharpness of the opposition has been blunted in the text to criticism over the matter of Jewish/Gentile commensality;[14] indeed, the interposition of the terms 'circumcised' and 'uncircumcised men' suggests that the Gentiles' status as believers is under question.

Before the gathered church, Peter explains 'everything...precisely as it had happened' (Acts 11:4). Peter's orderliness (cf., Luke 1:3) and completeness of description is augmented significantly for the reader by Luke's prior description of the events, replete with extensive repetition. The divine initiative through vivid communications is strongly emphasized. Four times it is reiterated that Cornelius saw an angel of God who commanded him to send for Peter (Acts 10:3-7, 22, 30-32; 11:13f.). Jewish Christian sensibilities in the reader would be addressed as Luke notes that Cornelius' piety motivates the divine initiative in the first instance (10:4, 31). Mention of Cornelius' piety elsewhere (10:2, 22, 25) also helps the apostle and Luke's reader along. Peter himself receives ample divine communication. He first receives a vision—twice fully described (10:10-16; 11:4-10) and once alluded to (10:28)—in which something like a sheet is lowered from heaven filled with unclean animals and he is commanded three times to kill and eat. The Spirit immediately thereafter instructs Peter to go with the three men whom Cornelius has sent (10:19f.; 11:12).

It is significant that the preaching was not a 'freelance' operation but fully apostolic[15] and that Peter is not simply led, but 'driven', to acknowledge and embrace the unfolding plan of God. Twice it is noted that, as a proper Jew should, and perhaps as many times as he is

---

14Haenchen, *Acts* 354, 359.
15Bruce, *Acts (Greek Text)*, 265; Haenchen, *Acts*, 360.

encouraged, Peter staunchly refuses to accede to the command to kill and eat (Acts 10:14; 11:8). The Spirit must soothe Peter's alarmed Jewish sensibilities about going with Gentiles (10:20; 11:12), and on his arrival in Caesarea, Peter registers his keen awareness of the legal implications of his presence among the Gentiles even as he indicates his growing acquiescence to heavenly instruction (Acts 10:27f.).

The Holy Spirit's coming upon Cornelius and the others in a manner strictly comparable to Pentecost is the final and most compelling indication of the new divine initiative (Acts 10:44-46; 11:15). That this should happen just as Peter 'was starting to speak' (Acts 10:44; 11:15) makes it clear that the action is all of God and not attributable to apostolic eloquence.

The reader learns that all these events are suitably witnessed by the Joppa Christians who have accompanied Peter—six men[16] called 'circumcised believers' and 'brothers' (Acts 10:23, 45; 11:12). Peter's appreciation of the implication of what God has done is indicated to these Jewish Christian brothers thus: 'Can anyone keep these from being baptized with water?' (10:47; cf., 8:36). The answer is an unequivocal 'No'; the Gentiles are just as much believers as any circumcised Jewish Christian. There is room for neither Jewish nor apostolic opposition, only acquiescence and embrace. Later he stands, a church leader and apostle, before the gathered Jerusalem church and puts the question in even more personal terms when he exclaims, '...who was I to think that I could oppose God!' (11:17). Peter cannot, either on personal merit or by his own strength, stand against the Gentile mission because it is God's new initiative in the plan. Neither, the text implies, can nor should the church.

When the Jerusalem church and its leadership heard Peter's report, 'they had no further objections and praised God, saying, "So then, God has even granted the Gentiles repentance unto life"' (Acts 11:18). Does Luke attest to the church's unanimous embrace of this new phase in the plan of God? Marshall offers that 'it is not clear how far the church at Jerusalem was prepared to follow Peter's lead. We should not take verse 18 to imply that the church at Jerusalem forthwith entered zealously into a mission to Gentiles; indeed, it never seems to have done so...'.[17] While Luke does not indicate that there remains any question concerning what God has begun to do, he also

---

[16]Bruce, *Acts (Greek Text)*, 258 describes this as 'a wise precaution...in view of the criticism which his action would inevitably incur'.

[17]Marshall, *Acts: Commentary*, 198.

indicates that the mission to the Gentiles was far from a majority
undertaking. The Hellenistic Jews who had been connected with
Stephen, theologically daring as they were in other matters, nevertheless tell the message 'only to Jews' (11:19) in Phoenicia, Cyprus and
Antioch. A minority of Hellenistic Jews from Cyprus and Cyrene,
however, go to Antioch and begin to speak 'to Greeks also' (11:20).
These mission thrusts are universally assessed by Luke in terms of a
divinely given success; 'the Lord's hand was with them' (11:21) and a
great number of people 'believed', 'turned' and 'were brought to the
Lord' (11:21, 24).

Pharisaic Christian opposition to the Gentile Mission

The church at Antioch and its missionaries began to prosecute a
vigorous and broad mission. Saul and Barnabas, sent out by Antioch
at the behest of the Spirit, preach to Jews, God-fearers, and Gentiles.
Despite the opposition and persecution of jealous Jews and their
Gentile allies in various places, the preaching also meets with broad
success (Acts 13:43, 48f.; 14:1, 21). Returning to Antioch, Saul and
Barnabas report 'all that God had done through them and how he had
opened the door of faith to the Gentiles' (14:27). In the flush of this
divinely given success, however, internal opposition arises.

   Men from Judea arrive in Antioch and begin to proselytize
among the believing Gentiles, asserting that they cannot be saved
apart from circumcision (Acts 15:1). The dispute that erupts in the
Antioch church is intense (στάσις: 15:2; cf., 19:40; 23:7, 10; 24:5).
Though it cannot be said who exactly the Judean teachers were from
Acts 15:1, their teaching was most ardently approved and publicly
supported by Christian converts who still belonged to the party of the
Pharisees (15:5).[18] At the Council of Jerusalem, it is they who assert the
absolute necessity (δεῖ) of circumcision for Gentile believers.

   Noting a considerable earlier debate in the proceedings, Luke
moves for his reader's benefit to what he considers the determinative
contributions in the discussion. The focus there is once again upon the
divine initiative and its implications. Alluding to the Cornelius episode, Peter states that it was the divine choice that he be the first to
preach to the Gentiles and see them come to faith. It was the divine
knower of hearts who showed his acceptance of them by giving the

---

18Sanders, 'The Pharisees in Luke–Acts', 143 n. 7.

Holy Spirit just as he had to the Jews. God had made no distinctions. The basis of salvation for Jew and Gentile alike was the grace of the Lord Jesus and not law keeping (Acts 15:7-9, 11). Peter characterizes the Pharisaic insistence on circumcision as a matter of opposing the plan of God when he asks, 'Now then, why do you try to test God by putting on the necks of the disciples a yoke that neither we nor our fathers have been able to bear?' (15:10). Bruce observes, '…to impose conditions on believers over and above those which God has required is to stretch his patience or invite his judgement'.[19]

After briefly noting for the reader Barnabas' and Paul's account concerning 'the miraculous signs and wonders God had done among the Gentiles through them' (Acts 15:12) and James' demonstration from scripture (Amos 9:11f.) that a Jewish and Gentile mission had long been the expressed intention of God, Luke describes James' conclusion: 'It is my judgement, therefore, that we should not make it difficult for the Gentiles who are turning to God' (Acts 15:19). A letter is to be drafted stipulating minimal ritual requirements for Gentiles to observe in the interest of Jewish/Gentile fellowship. Luke indicates that this policy met with a unanimous agreement (15:22, 25). It is of more than passing interest, however, that while the letter vigorously embraces the Gentiles (15:23), it also vigorously dissociates the senders from the actions of the circumcision advocates (15:24).

James writes that, 'It seemed good to the Holy Spirit and to us not to burden you with anything beyond the following…' (Acts 15:28) and then notes the minimal requirements. The reader is not explicitly told what the Holy Spirit's approval consisted in. Because the letter does not require or even mention circumcision and the ritual requirements are not a test of salvation for the Gentiles, the church would have had confidence that, consistent with the reports of God's earlier actions, it was attuned rather than opposed to the will of the Holy Spirit. In any event, the order of mention shows the church to be subordinate to the will of the Spirit in this matter. Subsequently, the letter is warmly received by Antioch and other mixed congregations (15:30f.; 16:4) and Luke is able to relate that, out of this turmoil, the churches were 'strengthened in the faith and grew daily in numbers' (16:5).

---

[19]Bruce, *Acts (Greek Text)*, 336.

Jewish Christian opposition to Paul

The final indication of significant opposition within the church relates
to Paul's last visit to Jerusalem with the collection from the churches of
the Diaspora. Paul delivers a full report to James and the Jerusalem
elders of the success God has given to the Gentile mission (Acts 21:19).
While the leadership's praise to God is unequivocal, a grave concern is
expressed. The apostle is told that, over time, a significant proportion
of the Jewish population of Jerusalem have become followers of Jesus
and they are all zealous for the law. James states, 'They have been informed that you teach all the Jews who live among the Gentiles to turn
away from Moses, telling them not to circumcise their children or live
according to our customs' (21:21).

Whatever the source of the false report,[20] James' words implied
that many Jewish Christians were inclined to believe the worst of Paul.
Cullmann is probably right to describe the Jewish Christian stance at
this point as 'extreme distrust, not to say open hostility'.[21] The strategy
James recommends to meet the false accusations is intended not only
to confirm Paul as a law abiding Jew but also to ensure harmony within the Jerusalem church. James' mention of the Jerusalem Council's
findings for Gentiles in this context (21:25) is curious.[22] It is not a mere
aside or an unrelated issue, but represents James' awareness of where
the root of the false report concerning Paul lies and what may ultimately be at stake. The concern seems to be that a dispute will rebound
negatively on the Gentile mission's continuing legitimacy. The broad
principles and arrangements for Gentile mission may have been clear
to most; however, their implementation in many particular cases (the
circumcision of Timothy being one, 16:1-3), could easily create serious
Jewish Christian misunderstanding. An explosive controversy over
Paul held the threat of setting many in a stance of opposition to the
divine will regarding the terms of Gentile inclusion in the church.

An explosion did occur. Paul is accused at the temple by some
Asian Jews of the capital crime of bringing a Gentile into the forbidden

---

[20]Two possible sources present themselves: (1) Jewish Christians hostile to the
Gentile mission and bent on eliminating its principal spokesman (*cf.*, Acts 11:2;
15:1, 5), or (2) unbelieving Jews, on the assumption of the continued rich
interchange between them and Jewish Christians (*cf.*, Acts 2:46; 3:1; 5:12f., 20f., 42;
21:23f., 26-28; 24:18).
[21]Cullmann, 'Dissensions', 90.
[22]Jervell, *Luke*, 195, speaks of the 'peculiar' mention of the apostolic decree at verse
25 and that it is 'bound up with Paul's relation to the law and Israel'.

precincts. A riot ensues which Luke describes as both voluble (Acts 21:28, 34, 36; 22:22f.) and violent (21:27, 30f., 34f.; 22:23). Were Jewish Christians in this seething, hostile mass lending their voice to the cries for Paul's death? The pattern of daily attendance of great numbers of Jewish Christians at the temple,[23] when taken together with the indications of a universal hostility to Paul at that moment (21:28, especially vv. 30f.), render this likely. Moreover, Luke's silence concerning the reaction of the Jerusalem church to this disaster, when earlier he consistently indicates to his reader the Jerusalem church's solidarity with its leaders in times of severe opposition (4:23-31; 8:1-3; 12:5, 12-17),[24] also tells in favour of a Jewish Christian rejection of Paul. While Paul's arrest created its own ministry opportunities (23:11), nothing positive can be said of the Jerusalem church here. This very silence suggests that the Jerusalem church, at least in part, was not reconciled to the plan of God. It is only as Paul is spirited off to Caesarea that the reader is again told of 'friends' (24:23: presumably missionary colleagues and the church there) who undertake his material care and assist him in continuing ministry.[25]

IV. How the persecuted fulfil the plan of God

What made the Christian witness so compelling and unstoppable? Many who heard and resisted it were, no doubt, inclined to attribute its spread to mere human tenacity or stubbornness. Luke notes that the Christian witness was not only divinely conceived but also divinely executed (1:8). He discloses that the irresistible character of the witness was due to divine preparation, assistance and encouragement of the witnesses.

Divinely commissioned

Must Christian witnesses expect persecution? Jesus, during his earthly ministry, forewarned his disciples that faithful witness would generate trouble and persecution.[26] Luke is at pains to demonstrate in Acts

---

[23]Passages cited *supra*, 8 n. 20.

[24]*Cf.*, Acts 24:23; 27:3; 28:14f. for Lukan indications of later church support for the prisoner Paul.

[25]On Paul's effective ministry in Caesarea and the support of the Caesarean church in the enterprise, see Rapske, *Paul in Roman Custody*, 171f., 320f., 357.

that Jesus' prophetic words have been significantly fulfilled in the experience of his disciples.[27] They are delivered over to synagogues (Acts 6:9; 9:2, 21; 22:19) and thrown into prisons (4:3; 5:18-23; 8:3; [9:2, 21]; 12:4-10; 16:23-37; 21:33-28:31). They appear before kings (12:1-4; 25:13-26:32) and governors (13:6-12; 18:12-17; 23:33-24:26; 25:1-26:32). Persecution comes from Sanhedral officials (Acts 4:1-20; 5:17f., 27-40; 9:1f.; 21:30[?]; 23:10), members of synagogues—whether directly or through the power of Gentile surrogates—(6:9-14; 9:20-23, 29; 13:45, 50; 14:1f., 5, 19; 17:5, 13; 18:12f.; 20:3), a Jewish king (12:1-3) and Gentile private citizens (16:19-22; 19:23-38).

In Acts, moreover, Luke furnishes his reader with a record of additional divine indications and apostolic catechesis to the effect that persecution will be a certainty for Christian witnesses. The vocational aspect of Paul's own experience of suffering and persecution has been considered elsewhere.[28] Suffice it to summarize here. At Acts 9:15f. the Lord tells Ananias that Paul has been radically subordinated to the Lord's own exclusive use. Paul's witness will engage the Gentiles and their leaders as well as the people of Israel and will be characterized by varied and multitudinous sufferings that bear the full divine authorization (δεῖ).[29] Paul tells the Ephesian elders at Miletus that in city after city the Spirit has repeatedly indicated for him 'prison and hardships' (Acts 20:23) in Jerusalem. The next verse discloses that Paul has not mistaken the communications as warnings. His witness will be fulfilled through incarceration and its related distresses. Twice again, at Tyre (21:4) and Caesarea (21:10f.), Paul receives predictively clear but motivationally neutral prophecies that he will be imprisoned in Jerusalem. Despite the powerful pleading of men and women sensitive to the Spirit, he is not deflected. When the believers at Caesarea say, 'The Lord's will be done' (21:14), this is a 'positive affirmation of the will of God'.[30] Luke's reader learns that Paul's imprisonment is expressive of the divine will and his obedience to it.

The linkage between faithful witness and severe persecution found in dominical prophecy and heavenly communication also

---

26Luke 6:22f.; 9:1-6; 10:1-16; 12:4-10; 12:11f.; 21:12-19; 22:35-38.
27Further on the theme of prophetic fulfilment in Luke–Acts, Frein, 'Narrative Predictions', 22-37 but especially 31-33 in relation to Jesus' disciples.
28Rapske, *Paul in Roman Custody*, 398-411.
29*Cf.*, Cosgrove, 'The Divine ΔΕΙ in Luke–Acts', 177 n. 25. See further, Tiedtke and Link, 'δεῖ', *NIDNTT* II, 664-66; Grundmann, 'δεῖ, δέον ἐστί', *TDNT* II, 21-25.
30Conzelmann, *Acts*, 178. So also Schneider, *Apostelgeschichte:* II:305; *pace* Lake and Cadbury, 'Acts', 4:269.

emerges in apostolic catechesis for Luke's reader to note. Paul's first missionary journey, affirmed from first to last as the Spirit's 'work' (13:2; 14:26),[31] is both broadly fruitful (13:12, 43, 48; 14:1, 21) and troubled. The Jews, out of jealousy (13:45),[32] blaspheme the message and initiate community disturbances (13:50; 14:2, 4f., 19) which lead to expulsion (13:50), life-threatening plots (14:5) and Paul's stoning (14:19). When the apostles return to strengthen the disciples and encourage them in the faith, they instruct them: 'We must go through many hardships to enter the kingdom of God' (14:22). Persecution is not the exclusive preserve of apostolic witnesses as the first person plural makes plain; it is the lot of all believers. Entry into the kingdom of God,[33] here construed 'in its futurist sense, not in that of "realized eschatology"',[34] comes through a course of life filled with troubles. Moreover, the apostles affirm that this relationship is forged out of the divine necessity (δεῖ).

Divinely emboldened

The persecution of witnesses is an acknowledged certainty within the plan of God. But disciples are not left to work up an iron resolve of their own accord or to bear witness unassisted. Luke instructs his reader that, in fulfilment of the dominical promises,[35] Christian preaching compels because it is emboldened by filling with the Holy Spirit. Disciples both answer and spark opposition by their inspired speech. Peter, already indwelt by the Spirit at Pentecost, is 'filled with the Holy

---

31The term ἔργον forms an *inclusio*.
32The jealousy of the Jews in the Diaspora (Acts 13:45; 17:5; *cf.*, 5:17) was not solely on account of the numbers of converts but what those numbers represented. They raised serious questions regarding the acceptable terms for inclusion and constituted a diminution of power for the ruling élites in the Jewish community. Significant numbers of conversions from among the God-fearers would have diminished Jewish standing and protection within the Gentile community, particularly when converts were, or had connections with, the Gentile ruling élites (Acts 13:49f; 14:5; 17:4, 12).
33 *Cf.*, Acts 1:3; 8:12; 19:8; 20:25; 28:23, 31.
34Williams, *Acts of the Apostles*, 173.
35Jesus promised that his disciples would have no need to worry about the content or form of their speech when they were called to make a defense (Luke 12:11f.; 21:14). At Luke 12:12, Jesus promises that the Holy Spirit will instantaneously instruct as to the divinely required words; at Luke 21:15, Jesus promises that he himself will give his disciples 'a mouth and wisdom' to speak so that opponents are confounded.

Spirit' (Acts 4:8) as he and John speak to a hostile Sanhedrin. Despite being 'unversed in the learning of the Jewish schools'[36] and without apparent interest in public affairs[37] in the estimation of their auditors, they demonstrate a remarkable ability in confident theological/ forensic disputation. The 'boldness' (Acts 4:13) here described is a matter of compelling erudition and liberty of expression in the threatening context. The Sanhedrin is astonished in the face of the apostles' words and unable to speak against the crippled man's miraculous healing (Acts 4:13f.; cf., Luke 21:15). On Peter's and John's return, the gathered church prays, asking the Lord to permit it to do works of power and to speak his word 'with great boldness' (4:29). The petition is answered by a fresh endowment of the Holy Spirit so that the believers can publicly proclaim the word of God 'boldly'; i.e., with power and fearless confidence (4:31).

Stephen is opposed by the members of the Synagogue of the Freedmen in heated argument, but they cannot stand against the wisdom[38] and the Spirit by which he speaks (Acts 6:10). They drag him before the Sanhedrin on false charges. When they observe that his face is 'like the face of an angel' (6:15) this does not mean that Stephen is transfigured.[39] Rather, his demeanour reflects 'confidence, serenity, and courage'[40] in anticipation of bearing witness—in short, Stephen's expression suggests divine inspiration.

Healed and filled with the Holy Spirit (Acts 9:17), Luke writes that the newly-converted Paul became 'more and more powerful' (9:22) in his preaching.[41] He compellingly proves in the synagogues that Jesus is the Christ despite Jewish incredulity and eventual hostility (9:23). Barnabas confirms Paul's true discipleship to an anxious and fearful Jerusalem church by the facts of the vision and how in Damascus he had 'preached fearlessly in the name of Jesus' (9:27). Heedless

---

36So Bruce, Acts (Greek Text), 152. Probably not 'illiterate' owing to the high literacy rate among Jews of the first century A.D. Further, Longenecker, 'Acts', 300, 307; Hanson, Acts, 78.

37So Marshall, Acts: Commentary, 101; Bruce, Acts (Greek Text), 153; Lake and Cadbury, 'Acts', 4:44. Haenchen, Acts 218 n. 1, suggests ἰδιώτης may either designate the layman as distinct from the expert or be synonymous with ἀγράμματος in the sense of "unlearned", "man of the people"'.

38Contra Haenchen, Acts, 271, the wisdom is not religious but divine.

39Contra Lake and Cadbury, 'Acts', 4:69; Haenchen, Acts, 272. The reader is not being strongly encouraged to recall such passages as Exod. 34:29-35 (cf., 2 Cor. 3:18); Judg. 13:6; Esth. 15:13; or Luke 9:29.

40So Longenecker, 'Acts', 337.

41 Cf., Metzger, Textual Commentary, 365.

of his own safety, Paul boldly and energetically bears witness in debate with the Hellenistic Jews in Jerusalem until he is spirited away by fellow Christians in response to death threats (9:28). Here too inspired boldness both sparks and answers opposition.

Elymas the Jewish sorcerer opposes Paul and Barnabas by trying to turn the proconsul of Cyprus away from the faith. 'Filled with the Holy Spirit' (13:9), Paul speaks a powerful prophetic word against Elymas who is struck blind for a time. The proconsul is amazed and becomes a believer.

The gospel proclamation at Pisidian Antioch is attended by such considerable positive response that it results in a filling; only here it is the Jews, who are 'filled with jealousy' (Acts 13:45) and begin to contradict and blaspheme the message. Paul and Barnabas give bold and effective reply (13:46). The word of the Lord spreads extensively, but opposition grows. While the apostles are persecuted and expelled, their disciples are 'filled with joy and with the Holy Spirit' (13:52)—presumably equipped to spread the word and meet further opposition (cf.,14:22).

Paul and Barnabas next preach in Iconium and a great number of Jews and Gentiles come to believe. Opposition is stirred up by the Jews among the Gentiles; nevertheless, the apostles spent considerable time there. Relying upon the Lord,[42] they speak fearlessly (Acts 14:3) concerning God's grace and their message is confirmed by miraculous signs and wonders. The city becomes severely polarized and certain Jews and Gentiles lay a plan to stone them. As at Pisidian Antioch, success, boldness and opposition here stand in a reciprocally escalating relationship. This answers the perceived difficulty of opposition leading to a long stay.[43] While the apostles eventually flee of their own accord, it is to further the preaching of the good news (14:7).

Luke also speaks of fearless, open speech at Acts 18:26 and 19:8. The first instance describes Apollos' preaching in the synagogue at Ephesus. Apollos knows only the baptism of John and what ensues at Acts 19:1-6 suggests that while Apollos' preaching springs of deep conviction concerning Jesus, it does not reflect the liberty and boldness of Spirit-inspired speech. His ministry in Achaia, however, is irresistible and must be accounted Spirit-inspired, though the characteristic terminology is not present (18:28). Paul stays at Ephesus for three

---

42So Zerwick and Grosvenor, *Grammatical Analysis*,1:397; Moule, *Idiom Book*, 50.
43*Cf.*, Lake and Cadbury, 'Acts', 4:161 and the discussion in Bruce, *Acts (Greek Text)*, 318; Moule, *Idiom Book*,162f.; D.J. Williams, *Acts*, 244f.

months preaching in the synagogue about the kingdom of God. His reasoning in discourse and persuasion is fearlessly unrestrained (19:8). Here again, the forceful preaching sparks Jewish obstinacy and blasphemy. Paul's subsequent ministry is characterized by instruction and extraordinary miracles of healing and exorcism. Conversions throughout Asia are extensive enough to adversely affect the economic interests of trades that service the pagan cult of Artemis (19:9-20, 26f.) and lead to a Gentile attempt at lynch justice (19:23-41). It is unsuccessful.

Acts closes with Paul under house arrest in Rome, preaching the kingdom of God and teaching about the Lord Jesus Christ to all who visit him. Luke tells his reader that he did this 'boldly and without hindrance' (Acts 28:31). One might at first think that 'unhindered', a pre-eminently legal term[44] connoting the freedoms granted in the conditions of Paul's keeping and reflecting official Roman benignity, removes this passage from consideration. However, Paul has proclaimed the good news concerning Jesus and met with sufficient official Jewish opposition for him to have turned to the Gentiles (28:24-28). Moreover, it is to faithful witnesses who have been delivered into prison that divinely inspired utterance is promised (Luke 21:12). van Unnik writes that 'the opposite to παρρησία clearly is "to be ashamed", of course in the tribulations and even danger of death'.[45] Confinement and binding, both of which Paul experiences at Acts 28:16-30, carry profound shame implications.[46] What Luke indicates to his reader as Acts closes is that Paul is not silenced by the opposition of official Roman Judaism nor intimidated by his personal circumstances. Rather, Paul engages all and sundry in the confident speech that God gives him.

Boldness, the reader discovers in Luke's account, is not something naturally found within the persecuted witness; it comes through the Holy Spirit's filling. The reader is instructed by a multiplicity of examples that the disciple pledged to fulfil the divine plan can rely upon the Spirit for boldness of speech and be able to carry on through the negative effects of opposition and persecution.

44So MM, 20.
45van Unnik, 'The Christian's Freedom', 475.
46See Rapske, *Paul in Roman Custody*, 283-312. The connection is also made in the canonical Pauline epistles (1 Thess. 2:2; Phil. 1:20; Philem. 8; Eph. 6:19f.).

Directly assured and helped

God ensures the success of his plan in the time of persecution, Luke further indicates to his reader, by giving his witnesses assurance in visions and making them fruitful through helping miracles. At Acts 4:23-31, in the face of Sanhedral threats, the Jerusalem believers gather to pray for assistance to continue their witness. After they pray, the building in which they are gathered is 'shaken' (4:31). In the OT, earth-quake frequently denotes the presence and action of God.[47] Here, the quake is an assurance that the sovereign Lord is near to his people and that he immediately assents to their petition for help. Universal filling with the Holy Spirit and ability boldly to speak the word (v. 31) are given.

The briefly described miraculous release of the apostles[48] from prison at Acts 5:18f. also both assures and assists. The agent of release is an 'angel of the Lord'. Longenecker writes that this expression is 'the LXX term for the Hebrew "Angel of Yahweh" (*mal'ak YHWH*), which denotes God himself in his dealing with men (*cf.*, Exod. 3:2, 4,7; passim)'.[49] While there is, in the act of release itself, an affirmation of the divine sympathy for the apostles' plight, this is not the sole end. The angel commands the disciples to fulfil the plan of God. They are to continue to bear a public and complete witness—to stand in the temple courts and declare 'the full message of this new life' (Acts 5:20). The release and command inspire the disciples to fearless obedience (5:25, 42). In a climate of popular support (5:26) and official hostility (5:27-40), the witness bears much fruit (6:1).

Stephen, out of a superabundant filling with the Holy Spirit (Acts 6:5; 7:55; *cf.*, 6:8), receives a vision of the open heaven just before he is stoned. He sees Jesus, 'standing at the right hand of God' (7:55f.). Marshall writes that Stephen

---

[47]So Exod. 19:18; Ps. 114:7; Isa. 6:4; Ezek. 38:19f.; Joel 3:16; Amos 9:5; Hag. 2:6; but note 1 Kings 19:11f. *Cf.*, Ovid, *Metam.* 15.669-72; Virgil, *Aen.* 3.88-91.

[48]Hanson's remark that this is 'an extremely vague and casual angelic deliverance, which we can hardly take as serious history' (*Acts*, 85) overlooks entirely the prospect that its brevity may reflect the author's desire to invest more space and detail in depicting Peter's release. One might, on the other hand, argue that the angel's instructions to the apostles and the officials' confusion in the miracle's aftermath at Acts 5 actually make it a *more full* account than Acts 12 where, outside of 'mundane' instructions to Peter, the angel is mute and only two verses are devoted to the officials' reaction!

[49]Longenecker, 'Acts', 319. Bruce, *Acts (Greek Text)*, 170 speaks of 'an extension of the divine personality'. *Cf.* Luke 1:11; 2:9; Acts 7:30, 38, 53; 8:26; 12.7, 11, 23.

sees Jesus in his role as the Son of man; he sees him as the One who
suffered and was vindicated by God (Lk. 9:22), *i.e.*, as a pattern to be
followed by Christian martyrs, but also as the One who will vindicate
in God's presence those who are not ashamed of Jesus and acknowledge their allegiance to him before men (Lk. 12:8). This probably
explains why the Son of man was seen to be standing, rather than
sitting at God's right hand (2:34). He is standing as advocate to plead
Stephen's cause before God and to welcome him into God's presence.[50]

Stephen, who has borne unequivocal witness through persecution, is
now extended the comfort of a visionary expression of the unqualified
divine satisfaction and approval. The defender of the faith is himself
now defended.

Luke's account of Peter's imprisonment at Acts 12, in relating the
details of the security arrangements made (prison, soldiers and chains)
and the elaborate description of Peter's progress to freedom (sentries
and gates), emphasizes to the reader not only the divine interest but
also the extraordinary power which may be directed in service of the
persecuted witness. Acts 12:5 is not likely to be the 'essential lesson of
the story'[51] though the reader is being challenged that the time of
persecution, when prospects could not be more bleak, should also be
the time for earnest and sustained prayer. The miraculous release,
Luke notes for the reader, is a matter of complete surprise to those
involved. Peter, befuddled and passive with sleep so that he must take
instructions to get dressed, has 'no idea that what the angel was doing
was really happening' (12:9; *cf.*, v. 12) until he finds himself alone in the
street. He first assumes a vision, not a release. The servant girl Rhoda
leaves Peter standing outside the locked door in her joyful rush to tell
the praying church. The gathered believers, moreover, incline to
theorize that the girl has become unhinged or has received a visitation
from Peter's angelic *alter ego* announcing his demise (12:15).[52] They do
not assume Peter's release.

Peter's categorical affirmation when he comes to himself that
'the Lord sent his angel and rescued me from Herod's clutches and

---

[50]Marshall, *Acts: Commentary*, 149. Further in this regard, Bruce, *Acts (Greek Text)*,
210 and the sources there cited.
[51]So Marshall, *Acts: Commentary*, 208.
[52]Bruce, *Acts (Greek Text)*, 286: 'The angel is here conceived of as Peter's spiritual
counterpart, capable of assuming his appearance and being mistaken for him, like
the *Avestan fravasi*'. *Cf.*, Gen. 48:16; Dan. 3:28; 6:22; Tob. 5:4-16; Jdt. 13:20; Matt.
18:10; Heb. 1:14; Rev. 2–3.

from everything the Jewish people were anticipating' (Acts 12:11) is perhaps the true focus. The Lord cares for his beleaguered witnesses and powerfully helps them when they and their supporters are help-less. But to what end? The reader must draw inferences from the text as Peter does not resume his earlier prominent role in Luke's account. While the venue to which Peter departs is undisclosed (12:17), his brief later appearance and vigorous advocacy of Gentile inclusion on the sole basis of the gospel at the Jerusalem Council (15:7-11) assure the reader that his rescue is to a continuing and controversial witness for the Lord Jesus; not a life of quiet ease.

The earthquake at Philippi and its attendant results, as at Jerusalem, is an expression of the divine interest and help. As the imprisoned Paul and Silas are praying and singing hymns to God, 'suddenly there was such a violent earthquake that the foundations of the prison were shaken. At once all the prison doors flew open, and everybody's chains came loose' (Acts 16:26). The prayers and hymns are not for deliverance but have a praise and witness aspect to them.[53] This means that the earthquake vindicates the truth of what is prayed and sung about God. The reader learns that it also triggers connections in the pagan jailer's mind which Paul and Silas, severely injured and humiliated as they are, exploit for gospel witness. The jailer and his household are converted and baptized (16:30-34). The divine action powerfully facilitates mission, not escape or release.

On several occasions, a beleaguered Paul receives divine assurance. At Corinth Paul's witness results in Jewish opposition and blasphemy. Turning to the Gentiles must have significantly increased that hostility, not only because his mission was generally fruitful, but because he was using the God-fearer Titius Justus' house next door to the synagogue and had claimed Crispus the synagogue ruler and his household among his first converts (Acts 18:7f). In these circum-stances, Paul has a vision in which the Lord says, 'Do not be afraid, keep on speaking, do not be silent. For I am with you, and no one is going to attack you, because I have many people in this city' (18:9f.). The call not to fear may reflect Paul's anxiety about continuing to witness in an increasingly hostile context. The command to tenacious-ly continue preaching and teaching is grounded in the pledge of the Lord's abiding presence and protection. Paul must rely upon the vision's assurance to know that the Lord is with him through troubles. He is not categorically promised that he will not be attacked (cf.,18:12-

---

[53]Rapske, *Paul in Roman Custody*, 337-39.

16); rather, he is assured that he will come to no harm.[54] Paul must keep preaching even under what may look like serious threat. He is, finally, encouraged with foreknowledge of the success that the gospel will have in Corinth (cf.,13:48); the Lord has many people there and they will come to him through Paul's witness.

After a particularly hostile confrontation with the Sanhedrin in Jerusalem, the Lord appears to the prisoner Paul and tells him, 'Take courage! As you have testified about me at Jerusalem, so you must also testify in Rome' (Acts 23:11). The reference to Jerusalem relates to Paul's experiences and activities subsequent to his arrest a few days before;[55] specifically, his witness to the Jerusalem mob from the steps of the Fortress Antonia and to the Sanhedrin (22:1-21; 22:30–23:11). The Lord is pleased with Paul's obedience to the divine will[56] in Jerusalem; a sense of completion is implied. The way ahead is also laid out for Paul as his earlier Spirit-inspired conviction about going to Rome receives a direct and emphatic reconfirmation (δεῖ: cf.,19:21). The reason segment of the assurance ('as...so') suggests that not only the fact of witness in Rome, but also the character of it will be comparable with the Jerusalem witness; i.e., as Paul has been a witness in chains before hostile groups and authorities in Jerusalem, in similar fashion he will further the plan of God in Rome.

V. Conclusion

It would have been difficult enough to confirm God's way to willing hearts in pleasant circumstances. But Luke had a more onerous theological task. Out of the record of the Christian witness' spread in a climate of deep and often violent hostility, Luke must demonstrate that 'the Way' was, and is, the plan of God. From official Jewish theological reflection upon Christian witness Luke draws the principle that if it is of God, it will be invincible. By this measure, he shows that through opposition, threats of many kinds and even death, the expressed choice of Christian witnesses is to obey God. Moreover, in troubles, the vigour of their witness only increases, as does the extent of its geographic spread and capture of followers. Within this

[54]So Bruce, Acts (Greek Text), 394; Longenecker, 'Acts', 485; contra the NIV.
[55]It is doubtful that the witness referred to here relates primarily to Paul's much earlier preaching in Jerusalem at Acts 9:28f. as suggested by Munck, Acts, 225.
[56]Δεῖ καί would appear helpfully to reinforce the sense of divine necessity in the witness at Jerusalem.

theological framework, the triple record of Saul's conversion and call stands out. Through a vision of the risen Lord, Saul's persecutions are exposed to be futile and self-harming resistance to the plan. That plan is vindicated as divinely ordained when its most ardent persecutor is shown to have become at once its most ardent missionary advocate.

The expansion of the Christian witness to Gentiles poses a challenge for the church rightly to discern the hand of God. Luke shows how Peter, with proper Jewish reticence, shares in or, better, is divinely drawn through and observes the unfolding of the plan in the events of Cornelius' conversion. In affirming what he sees and bowing to its implications, Peter both bears witness to the plan and vindicates its divine origin to companions and reader alike. The first reaction in the Jerusalem church to news of Peter's behaviour, however, is criticism. While Peter's account to them results in a Jewish Christian acknowledgement of the Gentile mission in Jerusalem, it does not universally engage them in that mission; not even in its most 'progressive' quarters. Despite this, Luke can report that the now broader Christian witness continues to advance. The attempt by certain Jewish Christians to require circumcision of the Gentile converts in Antioch reveals continuing resistance to the divine plan. At the Jerusalem Council the divine initiative is reviewed historically, in recent missionary advances, and scripturally. The resulting letter embraces the Gentiles, censures the minority Jewish Christian action, and establishes minimal ritual requirements of the Gentiles in the spirit of the divine initiative. Luke is still able at this point to tell his reader of the plan's further vindication through numerical growth. But the circumstances leading up to and following Paul's arrest appear to allow Luke no room to encourage his reader. Jewish and Roman actions do tend to swallow the issue, but Luke's indication of hostility in the church toward Paul before his arrest and the telling silence after imply a substantial grassroots Jewish Christian dissociation from the Gentile mission and, hence, the plan of God.

Luke informs his reader that the Christian witness is irresistible not only by virtue of its divine conception but also by its divine execution. First, believers are divinely steeled to stand by indications of the close connection between witness and persecution. Trouble should not surprise or stop the witness because dominical prophecy, heavenly communication, and apostolic catechesis all herald its divine necessity. For Paul, persecution and particularly imprisonment have a vocational dimension. Second, witness in effective teaching and preaching is irresistible because it is divinely emboldened by special fillings of the Holy Spirit. Fillings and boldness may simply 'come' or may be petitioned for. Luke gives examples where these fillings spark severe persecution owing to mass conversions or empower the witness to answer persecutors. There is, at times, a reciprocally escalating relationship between success, filling/boldness, and persecution.

Finally, Luke instructs the reader through his narrative that the unstoppable character of Christian witness arises out of direct divine intervention on the believers' behalf. Through such tokens as earthquakes, miraculous releases from prison and visions, the Lord gives both his people, and his plan which they pursue, an unqualified, 'Yes'. By such divine actions, the petitions of persecuted believers are assented to, they are preserved in their lives, and in their deaths they are defended, their anxieties are assuaged, witness opportunities are created, and the sure future prospects in fulfilment of the divine plan are foretold.

CHAPTER 13

THE PREACHING OF PETER IN ACTS

Hans F. Bayer

Summary

Judging from the literary function of the Petrine speeches and observing the fact that Peter arises in Acts 1–9:32 as spokesperson of the collective, apostolic witness group it becomes apparent that Peter's Pentecost and Temple speeches play a significant role in laying the theological foundation for the unfolding narrative of the Book of Acts. Peter arises as a prophetic repentance preacher along the lines of Old Testament calls to return to the God of the Fathers. At all stages of Peter's preaching this call implies the inclusion of Gentiles, a fact which is expressly stated in Acts 10. Salvation is made possible on account of God's sovereign initiative by sending Jesus the Messiah, Lord, servant and prince of life. It is Jesus who sends the Holy Spirit and shapes the present and future hope of God's work of restitution, commencing with forgiveness of sins and peace with God.

I. Introduction

Under the influence of contemporary literary analysis, biblical scholarship increasingly engages in historical and theological investigation only subsequent to the analysis of larger literary units.[1] This general approach promises to yield far more adequate results than the hitherto widely practiced atomistic dissection of texts for the purpose of historical and/or theological investigation.

In the following contribution we shall apply this general approach to our specific task by briefly investigating the literary context of the reported Petrine speeches and the emerging portrait of Peter, prior to focusing on some characteristic motif-historical and, above all, theological features of the Petrine speeches themselves.

As we proceed, the Pentecost and Temple speeches of Peter (Acts 2:14-36, 38-39, 40b; 3:12b-26) as well as the Petrine speech before Cornelius (Acts 10:34-43, 47) will be our main focus, while other speeches attributed to Peter will be considered as appears appropriate.[2]

II. The context of the Petrine speeches and the emerging portrait of Peter

Contextual analysis of Peter's speeches

Some thirty years ago, Ridderbos identified the following notable elements regarding the literary function of Peter's speeches within the unfolding narrative of Acts:[3] (1) The speeches serve as important contributions to the literary structure and development of thought. They explain (and illustrate) what is being narrated.[4] (2) The speeches fit into the various social and geographical settings alluded to in Acts 1:8,

---

[1]Note this same approach to Acts in the volumes of A1CS.
[2]The following texts have been considered: Acts 1:16-22; 2:14-40; 3:6; 3:12-26; 4:8-12; 4:19f; 4:24-30; 5:3f; 5:29-32; 8:20-23; 10:14; 10:26; 10:34-43; 10:47; 11:5-17; 15:7-11.
[3]Ridderbos, *Speeches*, 1ff.
[4]More recently it has been argued convincingly that inversely the narrative illustrates what the speeches convey. There exists indeed a close reciprocity between narrative and discourse. Taking the Temple-speech as an example, we observe that it does not only function as a response to the healing of the lame but also interprets the healing as an example of the active and present work of the risen Lord. Hamm goes even further and claims that the narrative of the healing explains the speech to a certain degree. *Cf.*, Hamm, 'Acts 3:12-26,' 199-217, 205.

demonstrating by select samples how the message spreads from Jerusalem to the end of the earth, adapting to the respective circumstances along the way. (3) The speeches themselves display a principal structure (*cf.*, esp. Peter: Acts 2:14-36,38-40; 3:12-26; 10:34-43; Paul: 13:16-41), thereby implying the unity of message proclaimed in the early stages of Christianity.[5] On a literary level therefore, the speeches 'interact' with the aim of the narrative in a reciprocal and explanatory fashion, they exemplify the spread of the message and they point to a continuous and enduring core of that message in various settings. As we relate the elements (1) and (2) identified by Ridderbos to results of recent studies on Luke–Acts, we note that the basic observations of Ridderbos' study are generally confirmed and further developed by such studies as those of Talbert, Hamm and Tannehill.[6]

Greater divergence exists on Ridderbos' point (3), particularly through the work of such scholars as Wilckens and Schneider, who, generally following Dibelius, view the similarities among the speeches in Acts as evidence in support of Lucan composition.[7] Regardless of these opposing views on point (3), it must be conceded that Luke intended to give the impression that the message was proclaimed with an abiding core shared by all preachers in Acts, allowing at the same time for unique emphases to surface at appropriate points.

Beyond these general factors pertaining to the entire book of Acts, we must now ask more specifically how the initial Petrine speeches in Acts, especially the Pentecost and Temple speeches, interact thematically with the entire narrative of Acts. To formulate an answer to this question, we briefly consider the theme of eschatology in the initial Petrine speeches of Acts as a test-case.[8]

5It is Soards' merit (*Speeches*, 296 and *passim*) to have emphasized 'repetition' in the speeches as a unifying element in Acts. Among the repeated themes he finds 'witness', 'God's sovereignty' and the 'centrality of Christ'.

6See esp. Tannehill, 'Functions', 400-401 and n. 4.

7The possibility of Lucan composition of the speeches must be considered. However, there are sufficient points of dissimilarity between the respective speeches to suggest that Ridderbos is handling the evidence essentially in a responsible manner. Ridderbos' historical explanation of the literary phenomenon is never seriously entertained by Wilckens, *Missionsreden*, 3rd ed., *passim*. We hope to address this complex question elsewhere, investigating Wilckens' hypotheses in detail. *Cf.*, similar to Wilckens, Schneider, *Apostelgeschichte, passim* and Schneider's discussion of Acts 10:34-43 ('Petrusrede,' 253-279) in which he argues with Wilckens and Conzelmann that the speech in Acts reflects Lucan composition and lacks decisive evidence for a kerygmatic structure going back to the Gospel of Mark (a view upheld by Stuhlmacher, Guelich, and others).

8*Cf.*, for further on the following Bayer, 'Eschatology,' 237-241 and below, II.2.1.

We observe that eschatology does not claim a dominant place in the ongoing narrative of Acts. It is important to note, however, that the theme of eschatology is prominent in the first three chapters of Acts. Looking at Acts as a whole, the outpouring of the Holy Spirit[9] and the unfolding message among Jews and Gentiles[10] is viewed as fulfilled (or in the process of being fulfilled) eschatological prophecy. Only the anticipation of the Parousia with related events remains as an element of future expectation.[11] However, as surely as the outpouring of the Holy Spirit and the mission among the Gentiles has come (or is coming) about, the Parousia will occur.[12] While Luke does not frequently and explicitly return to the eschatological perspective in the course of the unfolding narrative after chapter 3, it is quite clear that this perspective nevertheless determines the eschatological framework in which the ensuing events are perceived.[13] Considering the theme of eschatology as a test case, we see that the foundation laid in the Petrine speeches within the initial three chapters of Acts sets the tone of the eschatological framework for the entire book.

Building on Ridderbos' three observations concerning the general function of the speeches in Acts, it is our additional hypothesis that the initial Petrine speeches (Acts 2, 3) set the tone and framework for other themes developed and expounded in the unfolding narrative of Acts (*e.g.*, christology, pneumatology, ecclesiology, soteriology).

Here, however, we must limit ourselves to identifying some significant themes attributed to Peter (particularly in his speeches in Jerusalem) and allow this volume to confirm or question our stated overall hypothesis regarding the thematic significance of the initial Petrine speeches for the entire book of Acts.

What we glean from these above-mentioned literary factors is a heightened sense of alertness in analyzing the addresses of Peter as significant keys for understanding the overall message of Acts.

---

[9]See Ezek. 36:25ff; Isa. 31:31-34; Joel[LXX] 2:28-32; Zech. 1:3-6; Mal. 4:5-6; 1QS 55:20f; T.Levi 8:14; T.Benj 9:2; *cf.*, Luke 3:16. *Cf.*, Giles, 'Present-Future 2', 12.

[10]Isa. 49:6; *cf.*, Luke 21:24; 24:47.

[11]*Cf.*, Acts 1:11; 2:17 and 3:20. *Cf.*, Bayer, 'Eschatology', 239, n. 22. I noted there that besides expectations of restoration, the resurrection of the dead (Acts 4:2; 17:32; 24:15; 26:3) and final judgement (Acts 4:23; 10:42; 13:41; 17:31; 24:25) are essentially tied up with the Parousia.

[12]Giles, 'Present-Future 2', 18 observes: '...the death and resurrection of Christ has made future realities present possibilities'.

[13]*Contra* Conzelmann, *Mitte*, *passim*; Vielhauer, 'Paulinismus', 9-27, Wilckens, *Missionsreden*, *passim*, and others who deny Luke a vital expectation of the parousia on the basis of questionable redaction-critical premises.

The portrait of Peter as spokesman of the collective, apostolic witness[14]

Common to all favourable and exposing information we possess about Peter in the Gospels and Acts is the notion that he is the spokesman for the disciples/apostles in interacting with Jesus as well as bearing witness to Jesus' death and resurrection.[15] The fact that Peter is identified as a spokesperson of the initial post-Easter apostolic witnesses may have consequences for historical and theological investigation. As mentioned above, many critical studies such as those by Wilckens, Plümacher and Smith, identify Peter's speeches more or less as Lucan compositions. They claim this primarily on account of literary and theological similarities observable between Peter's and Paul's speeches and on account of apparent Lucan terminology and a literary proximity to comparable Graeco-Roman speeches.[16] On the other hand, conservative studies such as those by Ridderbos appear to confine the initial speeches more or less to Peter himself,[17] overlooking the fact that Peter speaks in the early chapters of Acts for, and with, other apostles.

The evidence suggests that Luke intended to give at least the impression that what Peter said was representative of the collective apostolic group (cf., Acts 2:14; 2:37; 2:42; 3:4; 3:12; 4:7f.13; 4:19; 4:24ff; [cf., 4:32]; 5:2f; 5:29; 6:2; 8:14ff). It is all the more interesting and significant to note that starting with Acts 9:32,[18] and concluding with Acts 15:7-11, Peter functions much more as an individual (see e.g., Acts 11:1, Acts 15:6), albeit still amidst other believers (e.g., Acts 10:45, 11:12, Acts 15:6). We can say that Stephen, Philip, Paul and Peter (as missionary to the Gentiles and contributor at the Jerusalem Council), appear and speak out much more as individuals. Luke thus emphasizes that what Peter said in the initial stages of the early church (Acts 1–9:32, until he works as a missionary outside of Jerusalem) is what all the apostles said and what the apostles said is what Peter

---

14The significant theme of 'witness' in Acts has frequently been investigated; cf., recently, Soards, Speeches, 283ff and 302, n. 14.

15Cf., the careful, albeit in many points unconvincing study of Smith, Controversies, passim.

16We hope to address this problem elsewhere in detail; cf., Soards, 'Speeches in Acts', 65-90.

17So also too simplistically Foakes Jackson, Peter, 75. Consequently, Foakes Jackson cannot make sense of the presence of John with Peter in Acts 3, ibid., 78.

18With a preliminary ending at 12:19.

said.[19] The fact of corporate and collective witness (*cf.*, Acts 1:22: μάρτυρα τῆς ἀναστάσεως αὐτοῦ σὺν ἡμῖν γενέσθαι ἕνα τούτων) arises as a significant factor in the initial phases of the account. Peter's function as responsible speaker of the corporate apostolic group and the fact that his addresses are public (and are thus cast in general terms) obscure from the outset characteristic features and narrow the margin of Petrine idiom in Acts 1–9:32.[20]

       According to Luke then, we are not so much to identify idiomatic Petrine elements in the initial Petrine speeches and statements in Acts 1–9:32 as much as we are to view them as collective, apostolic witness establishing the foundation for the rest of Acts.

III. Peter as a preacher of repentance and salvation

Peter as a preacher of repentance

Peter as spokesperson for the collective, apostolic witness arises as a prophetic preacher of repentance in Jerusalem (see esp. Acts 2:38,40; 3:19b; 5:31b and implicitly Acts 8:22; 10:42f; 15:8). Together with other

---

[19]This may be a better explanation of the evidence than what Foakes Jackson, *Peter*, 80 presents by stating that not so much a person as an impersonal 'mouthpiece of ideas' is encountered in the early chapters of Acts, thereby implying that Luke stood on feeble historical ground in recounting these early stages of the Christian church. In his recent study on Peter as the 'apostle of the whole church', Perkins argues that 'Peter is clearly the central character among the apostles in Jerusalem. He is usually the spokesperson for the group. However, he does not enjoy supremacy over the other apostles.' (Perkins, *Peter*, 95). As with many authors before him, Perkins does not, however, distinguish the *initial* phase of corporate witness (with Peter as spokesperson) from later phases of individual witness (including Peter). In his analysis of 2nd century data on Peter, Perkins makes the interesting observation that Peter figured for Gnostic and orthodox Christians as 'the spokesperson for the understanding of Christian truth held by the majority of Christians' (Perkins, *Peter*, 159).

[20]It is at the point of Peter's mission to the Gentiles (Acts 10–11) that Foakes Jackson suddenly sees the 'real' Peter emerging from the Lucan account (as well as his *Peter*, 84f). Foakes Jackson engages in a correct diagnosis but fails to convince in his interpretation of the facts. The fact that Peter in Acts gradually fades out of this spokesman function and emerges more clearly as an individual, may explain the phenomenon that he does not figure as greatly in the later writings of the Apostolic Fathers (with the exception of Papias) and Apologists as he does in apocryphal writings of the second century. Differently Smith, *Controversies*, 214. On Peter in apocryphal writings, *cf.*, Perkins, *Peter*, 151-167.

prophetic preachers (cf., Stephen in Acts 7:2-53 and Paul in Acts 13:16-41), he calls his fellow Jews to return to God in the light of his sovereign work through Jesus.

In his recent work on the relationship between Christianity and Judaism in the first century A.D., Dunn states in general terms what we will attempt to demonstrate in specific terms concerning Peter's preaching in Jerusalem. Dunn states: 'Christianity began as a movement of renewal breaking through the boundaries first within and then round the Judaism of the first century'.[21] This notion echoes Schlatter's 1927 observation regarding Peter in Acts: 'Das letzte Ziel des Apostels [*i.e.*, Peter; H.F.B.] war nicht das, eine Christenheit neben die Judenschaft zu stellen, sondern aus der Judenschaft die Gemeinde Jesu zu machen.'[22] At least during the initial stages of witness in Jerusalem, repentance and belief in Jesus was preached within the ancient Jewish and prophetic framework of calling the chosen people of God to return to the God of the Fathers. This long-established motif has been extensively researched by Steck.[23]

While we cannot present in detail the interesting (and yet at times unconvincing) theses developed by Steck, it is of great import that the well-established OT and inter-testamental tradition of prophetic speeches of repentance (cf., esp. Jer. 3:12-16; 7:3-25; 14:6f; Ezek. 18:30; Zech. 1:3; 7:8-10; Mal. 3:7) clearly re-emerges in Peter's speeches. As can easily be demonstrated, the speeches of Peter in the early chapters of Acts aim at repentance (2:38; 3:19; 5:31) and exclusively call Jews to return to the God of their Fathers. Steck emphasizes that the main purpose of these speeches is the 'Rückkehr des in Verfehlung und Schuld stehenden Volkes in das mit Erwählung und Bund gesetzte Gottesverhältnis'.[24] Steck thus draws the plausible conclusion that these speeches are not so much 'mission-speeches' as they are prophetic calls to Israel on account of the recent and mighty works of God.[25]

21Dunn, *Parting*, 258f; italics in the original.
22Schlatter, *Geschichte*, 53f.: 'It was not the ultimate intention of the apostle to place Christendom besides Judaism, but to bring forth from Judaism the church of Jesus.' [H.F.B.]
23Steck, *Israel*, *passim*. Cf., more recently Moessner, *Lord*, 296-307 and *passim*, who focuses on Luke's central section in the Gospel, asserting that Jesus is portrayed as the Prophet-like-Moses and that Peter, Paul and Stephen arise in that same framework. Cf., Rosner, 'Acts and Biblical History', 71 and n. 31-33.
24Steck, *Israel*, 268: 'Return of the people to the covenantal relationship with God from a state of sin and guilt'. [H.F.B.]
25Steck, *Israel*, 268.

The essential pattern of this prophetic call consists of pointing (1) to the unfaithfulness of Israel, followed by (2) a reference to God's patience, (3) a possible reference to the rejection of God's prophets,[26] and (4) often a culmination in the call to repentance. Within this speech pattern, biblical prophecy may be adduced. Depending on the response of the audience, punishment with ultimate final judgement or restitution with eventual salvation ensue.

Steck documents this recurring, and at times varying, pattern spanning from the OT and the inter-testamental period through the Gospels and Acts to Rabbinic Judaism as well as some Apostolic and post-Apostolic Fathers. Steck notes: 'Eine jahrhundertelang lebendig gebliebene Vorstellungstradition..., deren theologische, traditions-geschichtliche und traditionskritische Bedeutung für das palästin-ensische Spätjudentum, aber auch für das palästinensische Urchristen-tum nicht leicht überschätzt werden kann'.[27]

On account of Steck's investigation of the recurring theme of prophetic repentance speech to Israel it is not compelling to claim that Luke must have composed these Petrine speeches. The origin of prophetic, and now Christ-centered repentance speeches (the God of the Fathers is always the initiator) is conceivable at any stage in early Christianity. Based on its long history and the current deeds of God the form and content of the prophetic repentance speech 'lies in the air', so to speak. Moessner demonstrated that the same motif and self-understanding is to be found in the preaching of Paul as 'preacher of eschatological repentance to Israel', when addressing Jews (cf., esp. Acts 13:40-46; 18:6; 28:25-28).[28] The motif-historical evidence outlined above suggests the simultaneous use of this motif by various early Christian preachers, including Peter (esp. as speaker of the collective apostolic witness), Stephen, Philip[29] and Paul.

Within this general framework of the long-established prophetic repentance speeches, Stephen's and Paul's speeches to Jews (Acts 7, 13) display a certain shift of emphasis from the centrality of repentance so dominant in early Petrine preaching to a lengthy review of past dis-

[26]See Luke 6:22f; 11:47ff and 13:34f regarding general references to the violent end of repentance preachers.
[27]Steck, *Israel*, 318: 'The theological, tradition-historical and tradition-critical significance of an enduring and vital traditional conception for Palestinian Judaism and also for early Palestinian Christianity cannot easily be over-estimated.' [H.F.B.]
[28]Moessner, 'Paul in Acts', 101-103.
[29]Cf., Spencer, *Portrait*, 273f.

obedience and resistance to God's messengers (*cf.*, Stephen's speech) and affirming Jesus as Messiah (Paul's Pisidian Antioch speech).

Luke, in fact, takes up the long-standing tradition of chronicling prophetic calls of repentance in Israel, beginning with the repentance preacher John the Baptist,[30] continuing with Jesus[31] and concluding with Peter, Paul and others. Since the well-established phenomenon of repentance preachers can surface at any time in Israel (esp. in Jerusalem!), the Lucan report of the Spirit-filled and prophetic witness Peter (*cf.*, Acts 2:1-4) captures the motif-historical and historical potential of the times. We may therefore legitimately ask: What is to be expected of witnesses trained by Jesus to be repentance preachers (Luke 9:2; 10:5ff par; Matt. 10:23) other than to call Israel to repentance in the light of the accomplished deeds of God in Christ?[32] While Wilckens denies that Jesus ever linked his own rejection with that of his disciples,[33] there is sufficient evidence to show that the followers of Jesus await the potential rejection in line with prophetic preachers of repentance of old (*cf.*, Mark 10:25-45).[34] Luke thus presents speeches which convey in content the milieu and horizon of OT, inter testamental as well as the Baptist's and Jesus' prophetic repentance speeches.[35]

Taking into consideration that the death and vindicating resurrection of Jesus as well as the outpouring of the Spirit were preached as recent eschatological events, unprecedented 'fuel' for a renewed emergence of prophetic repentance speech to Israel on account of the renewed work of God among his people was at hand.[36]

---

[30]*Cf.*, Luke 3:3 pars; Luke 3:7-9; 3:17. *Cf.*, Jos.Ant. 18.5.2 and IQS 8,13-16; 10,20.

[31]*Cf.*, Mark 1:15; Luke 11:37-54; 12:32; 13:34f; 15:3ff; 19:42-44; 21:8-36.

[32]*Cf.*, also 1 Thess. 2:15f. See the informative overview in Wilckens, *Missionsreden*, 200-208.

[33]Wilckens, *Missionsreden*, 204. *Cf.*, however, Luke 6:22f; Luke 11:47f,49ff.

[34]See Bayer, *Predictions*, 54-61.

[35]Wilckens did modify his view somewhat from the second to the third edition of his *Missionsreden*. Nevertheless, Wilckens could not fully accept the notion that the motif-historical evidence presented by Steck was sufficiently conclusive to demonstrate that Luke's report in Acts reflected historical fact. Wilckens did accept, however, that the pattern of these repentance speeches did stem from a pre-Lucan source. We may recount Kähler's verdict of 1873, focusing on the Temple-speech in Acts 3:12ff: 'Sachlich hat die "neuere Kritik" nichts gefunden, was an dieser Rede anstößig wäre; sie hält sich so vollkommen innerhalb des Kreises eines echten jüdischen Christentums, sie lebt und webt so völlig in den Anschauungen eines messiasgläubigen Juden, ... daß allerdings eine meisterliche Mimik oder eine Höhe historischer Objektivität bei dem Erfinder vorausgesetzt werden müßte, wie sie ihresgleichen kaum finden möchte.' (Kähler, 'Reden', 516; *cf.*, similarly Wilcox, 'Foreword', 216).

(1) Peter as 'solemn witness.'
The fact that Peter arises as a prophetic repentance preacher within the context of the collective, apostolic witness is corroborated by a solemnity of speech. We note an emphatic and solemn tone of speech in 2:14 (ἀποφθέγγομαι) 2:21; 2:29; 2:36; 4:10; 10:34.[37] There is further an extended and particular self-awareness as μάρτυς 1:22 (of the resurrection); 2:32; 3:15; 5:32; 10:39; 10:41.[38] As such, Peter's obedience to God far surpasses his respect for man 4:19; (cf., 5:4); 5:29.[39]

(2) The eschatological perspective of Peter as spokesman of the collective, apostolic witness.
Turning now to the eschatological perspective extractable from the Petrine speeches, we note that an extreme near-expectation[40] is equally avoided as a vital expectation of the Parousia is alive and well.[41] The eschatological perspective in the Petrine speeches contains the expectation of Christ's Parousia in the context of fulfilled (the outpouring of the Spirit) and yet anticipated salvation-historical events (e.g., times of refreshment and restitution). The Petrine speeches do not operate primarily within simple time-frames of near, or far, expectation.[42]

As we have already mentioned above, the eschatological framework in Acts is substantially shaped by the Petrine speeches in Acts 2 and 3. The Pentecost speech announces the present realization of a significant end-time event. The Temple speech focuses on past/present and future eschatological events:[43] it affirms that the past death and resurrection of Jesus is God's sovereign work. Looking at the present and future, the Temple-speech connects the call to present repentance of the Jewish audience with the fulfilment of future end-time events all centered in the resurrected, living Christ.[44]

---

[36]Cf. similarly 1Sa. 12:6f.
[37]Cf., Soards, Speeches, 83.
[38]A total of 13 times in Acts. It is noteworthy that Paul's reference to 'witness' in Acts 13:31 points away from himself to the original, collective group of apostolic witnesses; in Acts 22:15 and 26:16 Jesus declares Paul as 'witness'; in Acts 22:20 Paul calls Stephen a 'witness'; Paul never refers to himself as 'witness' in Acts.
[39]See also Peter's emphasis that God is impartial 10:34 (cf., 1Pet. 1:17).
[40]Pace Foakes Jackson, Peter, 77. Taking the Pentecost speech as an example of 'primitive Christian preaching', (ibid., 77) Foakes Jackson detects only near-expectation features in the speech. According to Foakes Jackson, even the Temple-speech is marked by temporal near-expectation, ibid., 79.
[41]Cf., Gaventa, 'Eschatology', 27ff, regarding an overview of current positions on Lucan eschatology.
[42]Cf., Bayer, 'Eschatology', 243-45, 249f.
[43]Carroll, Response, 137ff.

It is partially on this basis that Carroll correctly questions whether Luke's report actually compensates for the supposed delay of, the Parousia[45] by apparently focusing on present fulfilment (Luke 17:20f; Acts 3:22f).[46] Indeed, the event-centered eschatology contained in the collective apostolic witness of the Pentecost and Temple-speeches may have influenced Luke's perspective. Consequently, the 'today' of repentance, faith, salvation and the undiminished expect-ation of the Parousia express, according to Luke, the view of the early apostolic witness. Carroll further observes that Luke is far less creative here than e.g., Grässer held. Carroll highlights those pericopes which point to a continued near expectation (cf., Acts 2:16-21; Luke 21:29-36)[47] while simultaneously stressing outstanding salvation-historical events (with a potential delay-factor) expected before the end (cf., Acts 3:18ff).[48] Carroll rightly notes that Luke focused more on sequences of events than on time-frames.[49] We have argued elsewhere that this Christ-centredness of the early apostolic eschatology resolves the ap-parent tension between near-expectation on the one hand (Pentecost speech) and the contingency of yet remaining salvation-historical events on the other (Temple speech). This unique eschatological per-spective extracted from the Petrine speeches in Acts 2 and 3 is viewed, once again, as a collective, early apostolic, Christ-centered witness.[50]

In conclusion, Peter as the representative of the collective witness-group arises as a solemn prophetic preacher of repentance, holding eschatology in a Christ-centered tension between the extremes of near-expectation and far-expectation.

44Cf., Soards, Speeches, 279, who asserts that the passion of Jesus inaugurated the unfolding of the final events of God's rule.

45See Aune, 'Significance,' 87-109 who concludes: 'We found no evidence to suggest that the so-called problem of the delay of the Parousia was in fact perceived as a problem by early Christians' (ibid., 109).

46Carroll, Response, 166. Carroll argues against Conzelmann and others.

47See also Marshall, Luke, 781; Soards, Speeches, 279.

48See Carroll, Response, 166f. See also Marshall, Luke, 783, who rightly considers it to be a false '...assumption that Jesus did not expect an interval before the Parousia'. Cf., also Bayer, Predictions, 244-249.

49See e.g., Luke 12:35-48 and Acts 1:6-8. Cf., Carroll, Response, 165. The certainty of the sudden coming of Christ (Luke 21:34f) constitutes the foundation of Luke's portrayed future expectation. See Luke 17:22-37; 21:24ff.34-36; Acts 1:6ff; 3:19-26; see further Acts 10:42 and 17:31. Regarding near-expectation, see Luke 18:1-8; 21:32.

50Bayer, 'Eschatology', 249f.

Peter as a preacher of salvation

While the theme of repentance holds prominence in the initial
speeches of Peter, his message never turns into a pronouncement of
irreversible judgement.[51] On the contrary, his call to repentance is
innately connected to the offer of salvation in terms of receiving
'forgiveness of sins', being 'welcome to God' and receiving 'peace'.[52]
This message breaks through the initial confines of a particularly
Jewish horizon (Acts 2, 3) and assumes universal dimensions (Acts 10).

(1) The universality of the message.
Peter's Pentecost speech does already contain an implicit reference to
salvation for all mankind (2:21, 39), while the addressees are clearly
Jews. The same can be observed for Peter's Temple speech. Πρῶτον
(3:26) also implies that God's salvation will go beyond the boundary of
Palestinian and Diaspora Judaism. But the speech at Cornelius' house
contains explicit (and implicit) statements concerning the salvation of
Gentiles. Above all, Acts 10:34f (cf., 10:45 and 11:18) refers to the fact
that among παντὶ ἔθνει are those who are δεκτός (welcome) to God
(cf., 10:28). This is complemented by the statement that Jesus is πάντων
κύριος (10:36) and that the prophets predicted forgiveness of sins to
πάντα τὸν πιστεύοντα in Jesus (10:43).[53]

Within this general framework we observe the following particular aspects: (1) Peter makes emphatic references to ἄφεσις (cf.
ἐξαλείφω) τῶν ἁμαρτιῶν 2:38; 3:19; 5:31; 10:39; 10:43 (cf., 1 Pet. 2:7,10;
1 Pet. 3:21).[54] While the propitiation of Jesus' sacrifice is not mentioned
explicitly, it is clear that salvation is in the name of Jesus (4:9-12; 10:36).
(2) Peter refers explicitly to being 'saved' (cf., to turn from this wicked
generation: 3:26) [2:21] 2:40; 4:9,12; 11:14 (cf., 15:11). (3) Repentance
among Jews sets off 'times of refreshment' and 'restoration of everything prophecied' (3:19-21). We have seen that 'times of refreshment'
constitute divine interventions, 'which would relieve and refresh from
this world's bonds and burdens...',[55] while 'restoration' refers to God

[51]Peter's differentiated accusation of the Jewish authorities/audiences (2:36; 3:13f;
4:10; 5:30) including the 'ignorance motif' (3:17; cf., 17:30 and 1 Pet. 1:14) further
support this fact.
[52]Note Peter's frequent but not unique reference to καρδία, 2:36 (cf., 2:26f; 2:37);
5:3f; 8:21f; cf., 15:8f: cleansing of the heart (see 1 Peter 1:22).
[53]Cf., Soards, Speeches, 83 and 183, n. 179.
[54]Cf., Paul in 13:38. In 26:18 Jesus pronounces to Paul that he will proclaim
forgiveness of sins to the Gentiles. Cf., Soards, Speeches, 87.
[55]Bayer, 'Eschatology', 245.

bringing Jews and Gentiles to himself and accomplishing all his purposes with them.[56] (4) Salvation is related to being welcomed, and
accepted, by God (10:34f) and (5) includes 'peace' with God (10:36).

In conclusion, Peter subscribes to a traditional form of prophetic
repentance speech which clearly holds out various aspects of salvation
offered by the covenant God to both Jews and Gentiles.

IV. Peter as a preacher of Christ:[57] The christology of the collective, apostolic witness with some Petrine emphases.

The Jesus-kerygma is reported as witness to the deeds and words of
Christ and serves the purpose of showing that Jesus is Christ and Lord
as fulfilment of Scripture, calling those to repentance who hitherto
have not honoured the affirmation and vindication of Christ by the
God of the Fathers.

We have suggested that Peter's initial speeches are to be viewed
as expressions of a collective, apostolic witness. Even christological
particularities are predominantly reflections of the collective, apostolic
witness, which Peter, as spokesman, conveys. Within this framework,
we encounter prominent emphases which might well allow a glimpse
of Peter himself, despite the fact that Paul and others are recorded to
have spoken similarly. This may be especially the case (1) when these

---

[56]Bayer, 'Eschatology', 247f.

[57]Regarding OT usage in Luke–Acts cf., Bock's contribution in this volume as well
as Bock, 'Use of the Old Testament in Luke–Acts', 494-511; Bock, *Proclamation*; see
further Rese, 'Funktion,' and Rese, *Alttestamentliche Motive*. Peter arises as an
authoritative, prophetic interpreter of God's revealed word by applying it
unequivocally to concrete situations (cf., the Pentecost and Temple speeches). In
the Pentecost speech we notice the tendency to actualize the LXX text, bringing its
message directly to bear on the situation of Pentecost. Elsewhere the citations from
the OT attributed to Peter show both a clear respect for the literal sense as well as
the tendency to apply these passages legitimately to Christ for lack of any more
fitting application (cf., the case of Pss. 16:8-11 and 110:1, which cannot be applied
to David). The speech at Cornelius' household contains, in accordance with a
different audience, no direct reference to the OT (cf., however, 10:43). The reference
to Ps. 118:22 in Acts 4:11 is esp. noteworthy as a possible Petrine element. Considering the citation of Ps. 118:22 in 1 Peter 2:7 it becomes evident that the focus on
divine vindication in Acts 4:11 draws on one part of the total spectrum of meaning
of Ps. 118:22. Jesus refers to the aspect of divine judgement and vindication in
Mark 12:10f pars, echoed in 1 Peter 2:7 where Ps. 118:22 marks the climax of
citations in 1 Pet. 2:6ff (cf., Selwyn, *Peter*, 33-36; 268-277). In contrast, Paul does
combine Isa. 8:10ff with Isa. 28:15ff (cf., 1Peter 2:6ff) in Rom. 9:33 without, however, referring to Ps. 118:22.

emphases continue beyond Acts 1–9:32 into Acts 10–15; (2) wherever the Petrine epistles corroborate expressions identified in Acts.[58] We shall point to these as we identify the christology in Peter's speeches.

Titular christology

Of particular importance in Peter's speeches are the titles κύριος[59] and χριστός.[60] Since these two titles have been investigated extensively elsewhere[61] it remains to be stated from our vantage point that they function as the central factor of the collective, apostolic witness. Acts 2:36 stands out as the key statement on christology, combining these two major titles in one expression. While this is by no means germane to the collective, apostolic witness there is good reason to understand the earliest apostolic witness as a major catalyst of these titles.

Beyond these two titles the following 'simple' christological concepts must be noted:[62] (1) Son of David (2:29-31; cf., Paul 13:23); (2) Jesus of 'Nazareth' (3:6; 4:10; cf., 10:38); (3) παῖς[63] (3:13, 26; 4:27,30); (4) ἅγιος καὶ δίκαιος (3:14cf., 4:27,30; 7:52; 22:14); (5) ἀρχηγὸς[64] τῆς ζωῆς 3:15 (cf., 5:31); (6) ἀρχηγὸς καὶ σωτήρ (5:31); (7) Prophet-like-Moses (3:22; cf., 7:37);[65] (8) κριτής (10:42 cf., Paul: 17:31; 1 Peter 4:5), and (9) σωτήρ (5:31 cf., Paul: 13:23). After considering factors of narrative christology we shall return to some of these terms (cf., III. 3.) in order to elicit christological emphases of the collective, apostolic witness.

---

[58]References to 1 Peter are drawn from Selwyn, *Peter*, 33-38, entitled '1 Peter and St. Peter's Speeches in Acts'. Selwyn argues that the evidence points to a literary independence and commonality of person writing in 1 Pet. and speaking in Acts: 'The connexion ... is not literary but historical: the common ground lies in the mind of St. Peter who gave, and was known to have given, teaching along these lines and to a great extent in these terms.' It is perhaps in these documentable details that we find the characteristic Peter emerging from the collective witness of the early church. Therefore it is too quick to speak of Lucan theology and christology here, as *e.g.*, Schneider, *Apostelgeschichte*, I:334, does.

[59]Cf., esp. 2:36 and 10:36 ('Lord of all').

[60]Cf., among many instances 2:36; God as κύριος: 2:39; 3:22 and frequently.

[61]See the concise, informative overview by Schneider, *Apostelgeschichte*, I:331-335.

[62]Cf., Soards, 'Speeches in Acts', 73 and n. 22.

[63]Here we might encounter Petrine idiom.

[64]Here we might encounter Petrine idiom.

[65]Cf., 1QS 9,10f and 4QTest 5-7 concerning the Messianic expectation of a prophet-like-Moses.

Narrative christology

Complementing titular christology, the following narrative elements are noteworthy: According to Peter, the ministry of Jesus extends from John the Baptist (Acts 1:22) through his death and resurrection (1:22; 2:23; 2:32; 3:15; 4:10; 5:30; 10:38ff; as fulfilment of Scripture: 2:31; 3:18; cf., 13:33ff),[66] ascension (ἀνελήμφθη, 1:22), glorification (3:13) and exaltation (2:33; 5:31) to his pouring out the promised Holy Spirit (2:33; cf., 11:16) and continuing activities of mercy (3:6,16: healing; 3:20: times of refreshment; 3:21: restitution of all that has been prophesied) and culminates in his Parousia (3:20) and judgement of mankind (10:42).[67]

Within this overall perspective some explanatory details surface: (1) Christ was affirmed by God's powerful display of signs and wonders (2:22; 3:26; 10:38) and enthroned as Lord and Christ (2:36),[68] despite rejection (2:36; 3:13ff). (2) It was God's plan to give Jesus into the hands of lawlessness (2:23) to achieve his goal of providing salvation.

It is at this point that we observe a particular Petrine concentration on God's sovereign will. Soards and others are correct in stating that this theme is assumed and prominent throughout Acts.[69] Nevertheless, it is clearly highlighted in Peter's speeches. The sovereign and initiating will of 'the God of our Fathers' (3:13,18; 4:24; 11:9), is particularly expressed in—and through—Jesus (2:22ff; 3:13,15,18 [his Christ], 20f, 26; 4:12, 27f[70]; 10:38, 40, 42).[71] The theme of God's foreknowledge and fore ordination recurs repeatedly.[72] As the condition for the resurrection,[73] Jesus was not left in Hades, his flesh did not see corruption 2:31 (cf., 2:27 and 1Pet 3:18). Rather, Jesus appeared to a

---

[66]Cf., Lövestam, Son, passim, regarding the fact that Psalm 2:7, Isaiah 55:3 and Psalm 16:10 (see also Acts 2:30f) are all cited in Acts 13:33-35 as references to Jesus' resurrection.

[67]Cf., also Schneider, Apostelgeschichte, I:334.

[68]Ποιέω in 2:36 means enthronement; cf. context as well as Luke 4:18-21; 9:35; Acts 2:22 and Mark 3:14. Contra Zmijewski (Apostelgeschichte, 147) who pits this section against 'Lucan' tradition, which affirms that Jesus is Lord and Christ prior to exaltation, cf., Luke 2:11. Acts 2:36 'bezeichnet hier also das "schöpferische" Handeln Gottes an Jesus, vor allem sein Auferweckungs- und Erhöhungshandeln', ibid., 147. Zmijewski does not explore the 'both-and' possibility implied by ποιέω: already Lord and Christ prior to exaltation, enthroned and affirmed as such at the point of exaltation.

[69]Soards, Speeches, 273.

[70]Cf., Soards, Speeches, 276.

[71]Cf., similarly, Schneider, Apostelgeschichte, I:334 and Soards, Speeches, 85.

chosen group of witnesses (10:40) and was exalted (2:33; 5:31). This is so, because God is 'with Christ' (10:38; *cf.*, 2:22).

Particular to the Petrine speeches is finally the fact that the Holy Spirit is send as a promise (2:39; *cf.*, 2:33: the Holy Spirit is poured out by Jesus) and gift (λήμψεσθε τὴν δωρεὰν του ἁγίου πνεύματος; 2:38; 8:20; [10:45]; 11:17; [15:8]). We note that there are no further references to this in Acts. Again, the God of the Fathers is the initiator.

The Temple speech in Acts 3 as the focal point of early apostolic christology

A unique combination of titular and narrative christology is found in the so-called Temple speech recorded in Acts 3.[74] The following features are noteworthy: (1) The 'God of our Fathers' affirms Christ. This repeated emphasis is crucial for Peter's Jewish hearers. Paired with this assurance is the fact that the initiative for recent events in Jerusalem lies with their God.[75] Upon the foundation of this recurrent and combined theme Peter builds his Christ-testimony in a rhetorically sensitive manner by pointing first to the present deeds of Christ (vv. 12,13a,16), before reviewing past events (vv. 13b-18), and outlining future deeds of Christ (19-21) following the repentance of Jewish listeners. We find here a confluence of Christ's functional and ontological uniqueness. (2) While we encounter primarily functional christology in v. 13 (the present activity of Christ), we observe in vv. 14-15 titular christology. Jesus is identified in a unique way as the Servant (vv. 13 and 26) as well as the Holy and Righteous one (v. 14).[76] The attributive descriptions 'the Holy one'[77] and 'the Righteous one'[78] could allude to a variety of OT concepts.[79] Jesus is viewed in terms of particular purity and devotion to God, perhaps as God's messianic

---

[72]*Cf.*, 2:22f: ἀποδεδειγμένον (only twice in Acts) ἀπὸ τοῦ θεοῦ; *cf.* 2:36; 4:28; 10:41f (*cf.*, 1 Pet. 1:2,20!); 15:7 (*cf.* 1 Pet. 1:1 and 2:9). The fact that OT Scripture as prophecy is being fulfilled (1:16; 1:20; *cf.* Ps. 118:22 in 4:11; *cf.* 1 Pet. 2:7) and that even the Patriarch David is identified as a prophet (1:16; [*cf.* 2:16,18]; 2:29; 2:30f; [*cf.* 4:25]) points in the same direction of God's foreknowledge and fore ordination.
[73]The reference to God raising Jesus appears to be more generic to Acts: 'The God of the Fathers raised Jesus whom you put to death' (ὁ θεὸς τῶν πατέρων ἡμῶν ἤγειρεν Ἰησοῦν, ὃν ὑμεῖς διεχειρίσασθε κρεμάσαντες ἐπὶ ξύλου: 5:30) 2:24,32; 3:15,26; 4:10; 5:30; 10:40; (*cf.* 10:29-33; re: for Paul, *cf.*, 13:30, 33f, 37; 17:31).
[74]For more details, see Bayer, 'Eschatology,' 241-43.
[75]See the divine initiative in vv. 13, 15, 18, 20, 21, 22, 25 and 26.
[76]*Cf.*, Luke 23:47; Acts 7:52; 22:14.

Servant (*cf.*, Acts 4:27,30; Isa. 53:11b). Jesus' unusual position is further accentuated by the term ἀρχηγός (v. 15). The question of the actual identity of Christ is crystallized by the antithetical statement of τὸν ἀρχηγὸν τῆς ζωῆς and ἀπεκτείνατε: The head[80] of life has been killed. Alongside with narrative and ontological descriptions of Jesus we find the challenging—and for Jewish hearers, offensive—reference to Jesus as the object of faith (v. 16). For a Jewish audience this comes dangerously close to identifying Christ as God.[81]

In conclusion we note that everything Peter as apostolic witness reports from the past, present and future points to the fact that Christ is preeminent, if not God. As such, he shapes the present and future salvation or perdition of mankind.

V. Conclusion

On the literary level we are alerted to the fact that the Petrine speeches hold significant keys to the interpretation of the unfolding narrative. We submit the hypothesis that the initial speeches in Acts set the stage for the entire unfolding narrative. While this hypothesis has to be further verified by other studies in this (and other) volume(s), we do suggest that the corporate and collective thrust of the speeches in Acts 1–9:32 (with a focus on Acts 2 and 3) supports that notion. Studying the theology of Peter's speeches leads to the following conclusions:

Initially (Acts 1–9:32), Peter functions as spokesperson of a collective group of apostolic witnesses. His message is, broadly speaking, similar to that of other witnesses as presented in Acts while at times, particular emphases are visible.

---

[77]It can be a reference: (1) to God: *e.g.*, Isa. 6:3 and frequently; (2) to the king of Israel: *e.g.*, Ps. 89:19; (3) to the ransomer: Isa. 47:4; (4) to Elisha the prophet: 2 Kings 4:9; (5) to Aaron, the priest: Ps. 106:16.

[78]It can be a reference to God: *e.g.*, Ps. 129:4. *Cf.*, the 'righteous' Son of Man in 1 Enoch 46:3. The righteousness of the messiah is mentioned in Isa. 32:1. The righteousness of the Servant is mentioned in Isa. 53:11b.

[79]*Cf.*, for further detail, Bayer, 'Eschatology,' 241-243. The connection between the terms 'the Holy one' and 'the Righteous' is found in Isa. 5:16 with reference to God.

[80]Ἀρχηγός may convey the meaning of source or origin, but it is more likely that 'leader' or 'head' is implied here. Note the proximity of this usage to Acts 5:31 (the functional usage of 5:31 suggests the meaning of 'leader/prince' in conjunction with 'saviour').

[81]*Cf.*, Peter's reference to Christ as judge of the living and the dead before a Gentile audience, 10:42; *cf.*, 1 Peter 4:5.

Peter arises as a prophetic and solemn repentance preacher in accordance with the pattern of OT and inter-testamental repentance speeches. The motif is widespread and fits especially well into the earliest stages of apostolic witness to Jews in Jerusalem. This rich OT and inter-testamental motif is taken up by Peter in such a way as to hold out the hope of salvation within the call to repentance. The acts of God through Christ occurred for the purpose of bringing the chosen people back to God. While the initial speeches (Acts 2, 3) contain indirect allusions to the inclusion of Gentiles in this act of reconciliation, Peter in Acts 10 states explicitly that this is so. Salvation includes, among other aspects, forgiveness of sins, acceptability to God, peace with God, times of refreshment and eventual restoration of all that has been prophecied throughout the ages.

Peter combines narrative and (partially unique) titular christology. It converges on the eminence of Christ and thus on Christ-centered pneumatology and eschatology with event-sequences taking precedent over time-sequences. Peter consequently avoids the extremes of near-or far-expectation and derives his anticipation of further events exclusively from God's future plan with Christ.

Particular Petrine emphases within these broadly sketched theological perspectives include the focused reference to the sovereign work of God the Father, unique titular christology such as Jesus as παῖς and ἀρχηγός, Christ-centered eschatology and 'classical' repentance preaching.

CHAPTER 14

THE SPEECH OF STEPHEN

Heinz-Werner Neudorfer

Summary

Stephen and his circle, the so-called Jerusalem 'Hellenists,' belong to the most important and most unknown groups of early Christian history. Stephen's speech is the longest speech in Acts. Its character is ambiguous, both defensive and missionary. Many historical, literary and theological questions have been raised. The chapter tries to show that the speech fits well into its actual historical and literary context, as soon as it is regarded in a really historical way—and not from the standpoint of a historical theory. Its theological theme is stressed in this contribution. The author tries to point out the main motifs which are the 'proprium' of Stephen's speech such as Stephen's characterization of Israel's history as a history of revelation and salvation tending towards Jesus, the positive evaluation of the Jewish Diaspora situation as an occasion of living with God, the primitive christology, the 'contrast formula' concerning an inner-Jewish potential of conflict which existed long before there were Christians, and the concept of the Jerusalem Temple in connection with a kind of 'Temple-ideology' which even Jeremiah had condemned. As a whole, for Luke Stephen's speech is a contribution to Paul's struggle against the Judaizers who at the time of Paul's (first) Roman custody were still a danger for Christian communities. The background of the speech is shown to be the early Christian Hellenistic milieu, the most important theological elements of which are reflected by Stephen, as their 'chief theologian'.

I. Introduction

Modern study of Stephen's speech (Acts 7:2-53) must take into account three main areas of inquiry: the historical, the literary and the theological dimension of the text.[1] The three areas are closely related. The historical question must be asked ever since doubts were raised as to whether the speeches were actually delivered by the historical characters at all, and if so, whether they were delivered in the manner in which Luke recorded them. What is more, these doubts have turned into a new scholarly consensus, prepared by scholars like M. Dibelius, E. Schweizer and U. Wilckens, and formulated by W.G. Kümmel: 'The speeches in Acts are therefore composed by the author, even though he may have used new or traditional sources in some cases'.[2] Increasingly it was concluded that the different speeches in Acts, which amount to about one third of the number of verses in the work, do not display specific characteristics which make them dependent and unique according to form and content. Rather, they presumably can quite easily be detached from the situations and contexts in which they appear in the present text; thus, it is concluded, they are common-places rather than specific reactions to specific historical situations. If this verdict is applied to Stephen's speech, it would mean that it is not an apology, as the unaware reader would assume when looking at the context of Acts 6:13–7:1. It is not a defence speech in which the accused tries to answer the accusations mounted against him. Rather, and we again have a difference of opinion, it is a missionary speech or a typical sermon spoken in a synagogue, as it might have been preached in any synagogue, possibly without any Christian background whatsoever.

The literary question is closely connected with the historical problem: The basic problem is to identify the correct literary form of Stephen's speech and discern its formal links and connections of content with the surrounding material.[3] At the same time, it is important to focus on its compositional function within the framework of Acts as a whole. Besides, the possibility of editorial activity must be kept in mind.[4] This latter area of inquiry, however, brings the theological question into the picture. What are the roots of the theological statements in Acts 7 in tradition history? What is their theological

---

[1]Cf., Haenchen's three problems (idem, Apostelgeschichte, 280-281).

[2]Kümmel, Einleitung, 136.

[3]Here, also, divergent scholarly opinions exist; concerning the assumption that the speech in Acts 7 does indeed react to the accusations mounted against Stephen, cf., Scott, 'Speech', 93.

meaning and significance in the context of early Christianity? Finally, the last question brings the inquiry back to the historical dimension of whether it is possible to derive information about the theological stance of the 'Hellenists' (Acts 6) and their representative Stephen.

II. Context and meaning of Stephen's speech

Stephen was stoned to death around the year 31/32 AD,[5] that is, only 1–2 years after the presumed date of Christ's death on 7 April 30.[6] The nascent Christian movement probably had reached the point where it had its greatest influence among ordinary Jews, while the majority of the political and religious leaders within Judaism clearly distanced themselves. The crisis related with the neglect of the Hellenistic widows seems to have been overcome when Stephen got into conflict with other Jews. This conflict was located in the milieu of the Hellenistic Diaspora synagogues in Jerusalem, from which Stephen probably originated himself, but with which he got into conflict through his missionary activities. Due to his spiritual and intellectual abilities, his opponents were unable to contradict him convincingly. Thus juridical means to convict him were sought. This led to the apparently over-hasty summoning of the Sanhedrin. Stephen was accused of acting in opposition to 'this holy place and the law'. False witnesses testified and accordingly accused him of respective utterances. The high priest in his function as chairman of the law court gave the defendant opportunity to defend himself. In my opinion it is historically plausible that Stephen would have been granted the right to speak, no matter whether the situation narrated in Acts 6–7 reflects an act of lynch-law or a more or less legal, if hasty, proceeding.

A survey of the status of Stephen's speech in early Christianity reveals that it played a special role as a document of early Hellenistic Christians.[7] To begin with, its central position in the tradition process within nascent Christianity needs consideration. The cosmopolitan city of Antioch, where a considerable number of Christians settled

---

[4]To mention but a few studies, see J. Bihler, *Die Stephanusgeschichte*, MThS 1,16 (München: Hueber, 1963); R. Storch, *Die Stephanusrede Ag 7;2-53* (Ph.D. thesis Göttingen, 1967); S. Légasse, *STEPHANOS. Histoire et discours d'Étienne dans les Actes des Apôtres*, LeDiv 147 (Paris: Les Éditions du Cerf, 1992).

[5]Riesner, *Frühzeit*, 56, 286.

[6]Stuhlmacher, *Theologie*, 55-57; Riesner, *Frühzeit*, 52.

[7]*Cf.*, also Neudorfer, 'Urchristentum'.

after their expulsion from Jerusalem (Acts 11:19-20) appears to have been a centre where early Christian traditions about Jesus were treasured. According to the prologues in the Gospels, it was the home of Luke, the author of Acts,[8] and it was here, in particular, that the Apostle Paul received some of the 'raw material' for his own theology,[9] as he mentions explicitly in several places (e.g.,1 Cor. 15:3a; 11:23a?). Again, it was here that the Christian community assumed such a characteristic shape that, for the first time, it became necessary to distinguish them terminologically from the Jewish community.[10] The decisive formation of the message of Christ in the Greek language happened here, in Antioch (if it had not already begun in Jerusalem).

In addition, the tradition about Jesus had already been translated into Greek in Jerusalem, so that the considerable number of Jews in the Diaspora could understand it. As M. Hengel has shown, many Jews from Palestine mastered the *lingua franca*. This circumstance, however, does not render the bilingual work of the (Diaspora) Jews redundant. They had been using the Greek Septuagint all their lives and felt comfortable with it. The translation of the tradition about Jesus could not be achieved by a purely mechanical process; rather, sophisticated theological transformations were necessary. Furthermore, a missionary concept was developed in order to reach the Diaspora Jews present in Jerusalem with the message of Jesus, the Messiah. There were good reasons why it was the 'Hellenists' in particular who developed a keen interest in missionary activity.[11]

Another characteristic aspect of Acts is the fact that its outline is

---

[8]According to Kümmel, *Einleitung*, 116, the first reliable source is *Eusebius* (*idem*, h.e. 2:4:6); he rejects the early sources, the anti-Marcionite prologues to the Gospels; *cf.*, also Neudorfer, 'Lukas', 9.

[9]*Cf.*, Stuhlmacher, *Theologie*, 141, 161, 180-182, 284-286.

[10]Acts 11:26.

[11]Acts 11:19-20; the reasons for the development of this interest are related to their biography. Since they had grown up as part of a minority group among gentiles, they did not consider gentiles as abominable people who were to be avoided as much as possible. Rather, the environment in which they grew up furthered manifold relationships, even friendships, between pagans and Jews. This explains why their communities of such synagogues had open doors for gentiles. It is necessary, however, to note the wide spectrum of attitudes in these diaspora synagogues. They included strictly nationalistic and religiously narrow members (presumably the family of Saul of Tarsus may be included here), as well as extremely liberal Jews, who adapted to the surrounding culture to such an extent that one of them could give his daughter the name of the pagan goddess Diana, as a tombstone from North Africa shows; see also Neudorfer, *Apostelgeschichte*, 1, 135ff.; on the 'Hellenists' and early Christian mission, *cf.*, Hengel, 'Ursprünge'.

arranged according to several principles which display different structural characteristics. The basic structure arises from the basic chronological sequence in which Luke reports the incidents. He draws attention to this organising principle in the prologue to his two works, Luke and Acts (Luke 1:1-4). This outline is complemented by a second grid which focuses on geographical criteria. This geographical structure follows the Great Commission given by Christ (Acts 1:8b), as Luke sets out to show its fulfilment in his book. From the outset, Luke emphasises in his two works how the gospel prompts human beings to act and become mobile.[12] Luke uses Stephen's speech to show this same motivating power with regard to examples taken from the OT. Vocabulary used in the speech, *viz.* the verbs ἐξέρχομαι (v. 7), (ἐξ-) ἀποστέλλω (vv. 12,14,34,35) and ἐξάγω (vv. 36,39), as well as the noun ἔλευσις (v. 52), supports this thesis. These words imply a movement away from a given point. Is it possible that Luke chose these words deliberately in order to communicate to his Jewish readers that they should become more flexible, ready to leave some of the traditional positions inherited from their forefathers? This conclusion becomes even more likely when due attention is paid to the fact that composite words with the prefix οικ-, which semantically imply a *stabilitas loci*, are generally used in a less positive way. It is not without reason that J.J. Scott can point out several connections between Acts 7 and world mission:

> 'Thus Stephen's speech provides a theological basis and mandate for the world mission of the people of God, for an expansion of Christianity that seeks to bring all peoples, nations and languages under the domain of the suffering, glorified, ruling son of man/ Messiah.[13]

Although less conspicuous, religious criteria provide a third structuring principle next to the chronological and geographical criteria already mentioned. In the course of his works, Luke will proceed to report how the gospel of Christ reached out beyond the narrow circle of Judaism via the Jews of the Diaspora, the 'Hellenists', (who were looked down upon by many Jews) and the Samaritans (who from a historical point of view were only partly considered to be Jews) and finally reached the gentiles. While the summary outline in Acts

---

[12]This motif is particularly prominent in the opening chapters of Luke's Gospel (chs. 1–2).
[13]Scott, 'Defense', 140-141.

1:8b and Peter's sermon in Acts 2 can be considered as basic theological introductions of the concept of the mission to the gentiles, the
reports about the 'Hellenists' from Acts 6 onwards describe the first
actual steps of the mission to the gentiles. Luke programmatically
places Stephen's speech at the beginning of this second block in his
Acts of the Apostles. It presents a sophisticated attempt to challenge
the assumption of Jewish salvific exclusivity which tried to be sensitive
to the Jews. Apart from its forensic character, the sole purpose of
Stephen's speech is, looking back, to take up problems which were
perceived to be controversial, even divisive, namely the position of the
followers of Jesus with respect to the temple, the cult and the law, and
at the same time point ahead by introducing the following reports of
the mission in Samaria,[14] at the same time providing crucial arguments for the subsequent discussion within the early church about the
incorporation of gentile Christians as part of the covenant people Israel
(Acts 11:1-18; 15). We may consider this last point as an important
aspect of the development within early Christianity. In its own way,
Stephen's speech is a Lucan contribution to the arguments between the
apostle Paul and the 'Judaizers', for this controversy had not yet been
resolved at the time Acts was written, presumably during the early
sixties. Possibly this controversy was revived through Jewish nationalistic tendencies, which ultimately led to the Jewish War. Luke uses this
speech of Stephen to provide arguments which ultimately were directed against Jews and Christian Judaizers.

In Acts 7 Jewish animosity against Christians reaches its climax.
Kilgallen points out the 'atmospheric changes' in the first chapters of
Acts, from the early benevolence of the Jews towards the early church
towards an open animosity and the attempt to extinguish it.[15]

> 'The Stephen speech, in its harshness, does bring to mind the rejection
> of Israel. Luke-Acts, we believe, has a nuanced understanding about
> the time when this rejection occurred. It is a time very close to the
> moment of Stephen's speech.' (51)

In it Luke clarifies the connection between the Jewish animosity and
the church's explicit confession of faith in Christ, including the confession of his deity (v. 56). It is only in response to Jewish animosity

---

[14]'Shechem' occurs twice in v. 16. This suggests that it was emphasised, presumably because it is meant to be an allusion to Abraham's acquisition of a grave in
Shechem, contrary to LXX and Masorah. The 'city in Samaria' presumably refers
to Shechem.
[15]Kilgallen, *Speech*, 111–112.

that the mission to the gentiles took off. In his book Luke demonstrates that ultimately it was the Jews themselves who triggered the mission to the gentiles; for they were not prepared to accept the (Hellenistic) Jewish Christians in their midst, *i.e.*, in their community life and their community of faith (Acts 8:1,4; 11:19ff.). The task of Stephen's speech is to show why the mission to the gentiles ultimately came about.

III. Stephen's speech as an 'historical review' in the context of Jewish literature

There is a whole range of texts in the biblical literature and in Jewish writings that display formal parallels with Stephen's speech. Already in the OT we can find historical reviews (*e.g.*, Deut. 26, Josh. 24, Neh. 9, Jth. 5, Pss. 78, 105, 106, 136, Ezek. 20). P. Dschulnigg differentiates between two types of historical reviews in the OT: the 'aretalogical historical review' and the 'paraenetic historical review', allowing, however, mixtures of these types.[16] According to him, Acts 7 constitutes 'an almost pure form of that type of historical review in which Israel is charged with wrong-doing'.[17] Nevertheless, it must be borne in mind that those who speak here do not abandon their basic solidarity with their people, despite their harsh criticism. This assumption may also be true for Stephen's speech, as the analysis of inclusive and exclusive statements in the speech shows (see below). The closest parallels in the OT are Psalms 78 and 106, and in particular Ezekiel 20. Ezekiel's speech —a quite extensive example—originated around 591 BC. It constitutes God's response to a question of the elders of Judah and concentrates on the repeated disloyalty and disobedience of Israel in the course of its history, thus focusing on the topic of the 'law'. Israel's behaviour is contrasted with the Lord's conduct and his holiness. This is achieved by quoting different formulae which originated in the covenant concept (*e.g.*, Ezek. 20:19, 41-42).

The closest parallel in the NT is Paul's sermon in Antioch in Pisidia (Acts 13:16b-41 [17-22]). The apostle starts with the election of the patriarchs, the time in Egypt and in the desert. He touches upon the time of the judges, of Samuel and Saul. He mentions David, but then immediately moves on to his descendant Jesus Christ and his rejection by the Jews in Jerusalem. The temple does not play a role in his speech.

---

[16]Dschulnigg, 'Rede', 197.
[17]Dschulnigg, 'Rede', 198.

A non-biblical parallel in early Jewish literature worth mentioning is Josephus' first speech in front of the besieged Jerusalem (BJ 5:376-419). O. Michel writes with respect to Josephus' two speeches:

> Both priestly speeches are attempts to save the people, the city and the temple. They are committed to a particular understanding of righteousness which consists of two parts (...). Both speeches provide an in-depth analysis of the particular historical occasion. Despite the apparent assumption that the threatening situation could still be changed, however, they are mile-stones on the way to catastrophe.[18]

In this speech the ark of the covenant[19] and the temple[20] play a certain role, which should not be surprising in the light of the priestly background alluded to by Michel. Josephus considers the wickedness of the Jews as the real reason for the military invasion of the Romans.[21] He considers their present violation against the temple and against the law as even worse than it had been during the first Roman invasion under Pompey.[22] Thus a destruction of the temple is always considered as a consequence of the people's sin rather than primarily the result of an enemy's attack. Josephus criticises the temple as a place where abominable sins are committed[23] and arrives at the conclusion that God could not possibly continue to inhabit a house defiled to such an extent.[24] Nevertheless, he still envisages the possibility of salvation for the people, the city and the temple if Israel confesses its sin and repents.[25] Michel writes:

> Josephus alludes to cultic motifs related to Zion theology, as well as demands already raised by the prophets. However, he develops them in a very particular way in order to suit his paraenetic purposes. He uses the examples from Jewish history which he mentions in a two-fold manner. On the one hand, he uses the form of prophetic reproach, for he argues that the Jews have made the temple a place for battle and have outraged God (Jewish War 5:377-378). He himself, he stresses, was thus forced to speak about the 'works of God' before unworthy ears. On the other hand he finishes his speech by offering

---

[18]Michel, 'Reden', 958.
[19]BJ 5:385, 389.
[20]Esp. BJ 5:402ff.
[21]BJ 5:395.
[22]BJ 5:397, 411.
[23]BJ 5:402.
[24]BJ 5:412-413.
[25]BJ 5:415.

God's grace like an arbiter. The Deity is easily reconciled to those who confess and repent (5:415). The speech finally concludes with an appeal to renounce stubbornness and to have compassion with the temple, even with their own destiny.[26]

Both similarities and dissimilarities between Stephen's speech and the speech of Josephus are obvious. Both use incidents from Israel's past to achieve their ends. The difference, however, lies in the fact that Stephen, the martyr, intends to convince his audience of his own point of view at the beginning of his speech, but completely looses the hope that this might be achieved at the end of his speech. While Stephen ends in reproach and accusation (Acts 7:52-53), Josephus, the politician, offers the people the possibility of a new start. Although he demands a theologically significant response (realisation of guilt, confession and repentance), he factually suggests political and military action, namely the surrender of the city to the Roman besiegers. In general, both stress that the temple has been defiled: whereby Stephen bases his statement on theological principles, while Josephus takes recourse to historical considerations based on the conduct of the Jews.

IV. Theological motifs and building-blocks in Stephen's speech

Israel's history as salvation history and revelation history that is open to an interpretation with reference to Christ

(1) The speech opens with God's history with Israel's forefather Abraham in the form of his self-revelation (in a theophany). The technical term εἰδέναι in its different forms occurs throughout the speech (7:2,[26]30,35,44,55) and comes to its almost ecstatic climax in the formula θεωρεῖν (v 56), which links the original revelation of God to Abraham with Jesus' present revelation to Stephen in the form of a climactic *inclusio*. The fact that the phrase θεὸς τῆς δόξης ὤφθη (v. 2) is repeated in chiastic sequence in the phrase εἶδεν δόξαν θεοῦ (v. 55) demonstrates that this is no coincidence. Through these literary devices Luke signals that what happens to Stephen is in God's control, it happens according to the divine plan. At the same time, Luke

---

[26]Michel, 'Reden', 962.

indicates that revelation history has not come to an end, as was the opinion in contemporary Judaism. No, revelation history is happening now and its subject in the divine δόξα is now the υἱὸς τοῦ ἀνθρώπου together with the θεός (v 59). Stephen's prayer is now not only addressed to the κύριος JHWH, but also κύριος Ἰησοῦς (v 59).

(2) The pattern of 'promise–fulfilment' belongs to the realm of salvation historical thought. Right at the beginning of the paragraph dealing with Abraham (7:5) appears the technical term ἐπαγγέλλομαι together with the land promise. The latter concept is taken up explicitly at the beginning of the paragraph on Moses, which employs the fulfilment motif (7:17).[27] In both instances this corresponds with the other technical term πληροῦν, in each case linked with the temporal expression of 40 years which is significant in the concept of salvation history (7:23,30). Other figures employed, such as the numbers 2 (vv. 13,29), 3 (v. 20), 12 (v. 8) also show that 'holy' history is in focus.

The author of the speech sees the historical events described as expressive of God's salvific and generous activity. God helps Abraham in the apparently hopeless situation of childlessness and gives him the 'inheritance' (7:5) and the 'covenant of circumcision' (7:8); he saves Joseph 'out of all his calamities' and gives him 'grace and wisdom before Pharaoh' (7:10); he lets Moses be saved from the water (7:21) and grants the people σωτηρία (through Moses; 7:25) and λόγια ζῶντα (7:38). These three (Abraham as ancestor, Joseph and Moses as redeemers), however, had to endure a fundamental threat to their existence. This means that it was God's intervention on their behalf which made them into what they became for Israel. And this same pattern is now claimed for Jesus/or Christ: and what is more, God did not confirm his ministry by simply saving him out of the threat of death, but by delivering him from death itself and by raising him to sit at his right hand (7:55f.).

The 'Diaspora' as an opportunity to live and die with God

Next to this introduction to a christological message via extensive[28] allusion to incidents known to the Jews from the past, the positive description and evaluation of the non-Israelite land and (to a considerable degree) its inhabitants is conspicuous as well. God

---

[27]The term καιρός (7:20) also belongs to the vocabulary employed with respect to salvation history.

intervenes there as well, and there in particular, *e.g.*, in Mesopotamia (7:2), in Haran (7:2,4), in Egypt,[29] in Midian (7:29), on/at Sinai (7:30, 38), at the Red Sea (7:36). While there is 'great need' in Canaan (7:11), grain, and thus salvation, can be found in Egypt (7:12). It is the Egyptian king who recognises Joseph's potential and puts him in an appropriate position (7:10), while his own brothers sold him into slavery (7:9). It is the Egyptian princess who discovers Moses and adopts him (7:21), which in effect means that she makes him into an Egyptian. In contrast to early Jewish tradition, which makes Moses into a teacher of the Egyptians,[30] Stephen's speech includes an explicit reference to Moses' Egyptian education.

It is in this context that σοφία is mentioned (7:22; *cf.*, Acts 6:3,10).[31] Thus it is an Egyptian to whom Israel owns its deliverance out of Egypt, which is the fundamental historical event leading to its existence. What is more, it is emphasised that God was with Joseph in Egypt (7:9); furthermore, the location where God appeared to Moses was 'in the desert at Mount Sinai', that is, outside Canaan, and this place is explicitly called γῆ ἁγία (7:33). Thus it is not the extraneous circumstances that make a place holy, but God himself sanctifies it. In addition, it is well-known that during NT times many Jews of the Diaspora longed for Jerusalem. This yearning was to be fulfilled for them when they grew old and returned to live in the 'Holy Land' in order to be buried in Jerusalem, where the Messiah was expected to appear. In contrast to this custom, Stephen's speech spells out that Abraham bought a tomb in Shechem, that is, in Samaria. This is where he and the other patriarchs were buried. This location deviates from the information given in the masoretic text as well as the LXX.[32]

---

[28]According to Dschulnigg, 'Rede', 197, the part dealing with Moses deals with 'the normative period which reflects on Israel's history', 'the decisive period of Israel's foundation', which forms an essential part of the historical review, while sections dealing with the patriarchs or later periods up to Solomon are only rarely employed. Dschulnigg writes: 'Against this background we may judge that the elements in the historical review in Acts 7 do not pose a serious problem' (ibid.).

[29]The toponym and ethnonym together occur no less than fifteen times (16 times if 7:18 is included)!

[30]So Pesch, *Apostelgeschichte*, with reference to Artapanus 3:6-8.

[31]Pesch points out that a reference to the education of Moses in Egypt is missing in Exod. 2, but also points out the (Hellenistic) Jewish traditions about it, which apparently existed, as Philo, *Vit Mos* I:20-23, and Josephus, *Ant* 2:232-237, show.

[32]It is not necessary to treat further incongruities between Acts 7 and the OT passages, which have long been recognised in critical scholarship (*cf.*, Acts 7:4 with Gen. 11-12!); *cf.*, among others, Richard, 'Acts 7'.

According to Genesis 25:9f., Abraham was buried in the cave which he
had bought near Hebron. According to Genesis 33:19, it was Jacob who
bought land near Shechem from the sons of Hamor, the father of
Shechem, but he also was buried in the cave near Hebron (Gen. 50:13).
It was Joseph who was buried in the field near Shechem which Jacob
had bought (Josh. 24:32). According to later Jewish tradi-tion,[33] his
brothers were also buried there. However one may evaluate the data
historically, the fact remains that the burial-place at Shechem was
deliberately employed in Stephen's speech. Its significance is to
demonstrate that those who are buried outside Jerusalem because they
remained in the Diaspora have no disadvantage with respect to the
resurrection (for this was the whole point of being buried in Jerusalem). It may be presumed that, in doing so, Stephen touched upon a
subject that was debated among contemporary Jews of the Diaspora.
According to him, Palestinian Jews have no advantage over them.

Christology

Usually commentators emphasise the fact that no specifically Christian contents occur in Stephen's speech; they do not appear until the
actual martyrdom (7:55f,59f.). This is basically true, but several important factors need to be taken into consideration.

(1) The most clear christological component is the mentioning of the
previously announced ἔλευσις τοῦ δικαίου (7:52).[34] Similar to the
'Son of Man' (7:56),[35] the title ὁ δίκαιος is a designation for Jesus
current among early Jewish Christians (Acts 3:14;[36] 22:14). It probably
continues a tradition at home in Jewish apocalypticism, in which the
messiah was expected as 'the Righteous One' or as 'the Suffering
Righteous One'.[37] These ideas were probably connected with the
identical designation of God as the 'Righteous One' frequent in the OT,
and particularly with Isaiah 53:11[LXX], a text which was frequently
interpreted as messianic. The title 'Son of Man' in all likelihood goes
back to Christ himself. The title κύριος, on the other hand, was

---

[33]Cf., Jub 46:9-10; Josephus, Ant 2:199-200; TestXII.
[34]Cf., Scott, 'Defense', 135-136.
[35]Cf., Marshall, *Ursprünge*, 63-81.
[36]Here it is combined with the 'pattern of contrasts' and the denial motif!
[37]Schneider, δίκαιος, esp. I:783; references: äthHen 38:2; 53:6; see also Billerbeck 2,
289-290, Wisdom of Solomon 2:12*-20; 5:1-7.

probably coined by Greek speaking Jewish Christians (in Jerusalem/ Antioch?). There are other allusions in the corpus of the speech itself.

(2) In the paragraph from 7:35-39, which is a relatively free composition by the author, the relationship between Moses and the people is expounded. Moses is called ἄρχων καὶ λυτρωτής. Λυτρωτής (Hebrew: go'el) is *hapax legomenon* in the NT, but other forms of the same root can be found in other NT texts with prominent christological impact. In Luke's Gospel, Zechariah praises the birth of Jesus, because through it God will work λύτρωσιν τῷ λαῷ αὐτοῦ (Luke 1:68); the prophetess Hannah, also in the complex of the birth stories about Jesus, proclaims Jesus to all who wait for the λύτρωσις Ἰερουσαλήμ (Luke 2:38); Jesus himself refers to his offering of his own life as λύτρον (Mark 10:45 par.); the disciples Jesus met on the road to Emmaus had hoped that Jesus would be λυτροῦσθαι τὸν Ἰσραήλ (Luke 24:21). In the letter to the Romans, Paul quotes a traditional source which probably originated from Stephen and the Seven (Rom. 3:24f.), which talks of the ἀπολύτρωσις ἐν Χριστῷ Ἰησοῦ. Is it possible that 'Saviour'[38] also is an old title which the early Christian community applied to Christ?

(3) The designation ἄρχων occurs at two other locations (7:27,35a). In the first instance, it occurs in conjunction with δικαστής in the quotation from Exodus 2:14 which expresses the rejection of Moses by the Israelites, which conspicuously is employed twice. The second time it appears in combination with ἀρνέομαι (7:35), which, in the framework of the so-called contrast scheme, played an important role in the early dialogue between Jews and Christians (Acts 3:13f.); here it serves to provide a link to the rejection of Christ by the Jews—one more evidence for the fact that Stephen's speech is a contribution to the discussion with Jews or Judaizers.

(4) The 'prophet like me' which God would send to Israel (Deut. 18:15) was applied to Christ in early Christianity. Peter quotes this passage extensively in this way in Acts 3:22ff.

(5) The demonstrative pronoun ουτος occurs frequently in the passage (5 times), each time at the beginning of a sentence and very likely in conscious contrast to its derisive usage in 7:40 (quotation) and 6:14,

---

[38]Foerster, 'σωτήρ', *TDNT* VII:1016, in connection with Acts 3:15; 5:31; 13:23, writes: 'The parallel between σωτήρ and λυτρώσις, as well as the addresses of the speeches, suggest that Jewish messianic hopes are in focus, but the salvation does not consist in the liberation from Roman rule, but rather in the forgiveness of sins'.

where opponents use it with the same meaning when delivering their allegations. In the wider Acts context, however, it is reminiscent of christological texts (*e.g.*, Acts 4:11; 6:14; 9:20,22; 17:3).

The 'Pattern of Contrasts' in Stephen's speech

(1) In Acts 2:36; 5:30; 10:39f. we find the so-called 'pattern of contrasts' in its short form. Early Christians used it to counter the Jewish argument that Christ as crucified religious seducer was under God's curse (Deut. 21:22f.).[39] The basic structure is clear: 'You (Jews) have... but God has....' In substance, the same pattern occurs in Stephen's speech: Joseph had been 'sold' to Egypt by his brothers, the patriarchs, but God 'was with him and delivered him out of all his calamities' (7:9f.). Moses had been 'disowned' by Israel and rejected as ἄρχων καὶ δικαστής, but God sent him to them as ἄρχων καὶ δικαστής (7:35). Apparently this is evidence of typological exegesis with respect to the archetypal figures of Joseph and Moses, but this only made sense in connection with a corresponding contemporary (anti-)typos. This is where Christ enters the picture, who was rejected by Israel, but confirmed as redeemer by God. In this sense, the 'pattern of contrasts' is closely related to Christ as redeemer figure, and by applying it to Joseph and Moses, the author makes the theme of redemption his main emphasis.

(2) The pericope on Moses contains a high frequency of the verb ἀδικεῖν (7:24,26f.). Subjects of the verb are Jews. They wrong each other (ἀλλήλους v 26). The same kind of behaviour is displayed by Jacob's sons against Joseph and by the Israelites against Moses. Luke also employs the catchword ἀδικεῖν in Paul's apology before the governor Felix in Acts 25:10. The apostle explains Ἰουδαίους οὐδὲν ἠδίκησα ὡς καὶ σὺ κάλλιον ἐπιγινώσκεις. This leads to the conclusion that Stephen wants to point out that inner-Jewish conflicts and 'wrong-doing' are not unique to his present context, his own debates being part of them. At any rate, Paul and the Christian community cannot be accused of being opposed to Judaism *per se*.

(3) The change from 'we' to 'you' and from 'your' to 'our', beginning at v. 4 and persisting to the end of the speech. From a sociological viewpoint, two groups are opposed to each other. Who is who? A more

---

[39]*Cf.*, Stuhlmacher, *Theologie*, 191.

precise analysis of ἡμεῖς and ὑμεῖς, including the personal and possessive pronouns derived from the two terms (neglecting the forms occurring in OT quotations) results in the following picture. In the main corpus of the speech, the speaker identifies himself (and the group to which he belongs) to a high degree with his audience, which consists of his accusers. Nevertheless, he differentiates himself from his audience at two significant points. The first is near the beginning of the speech, when he mentions the land in which Abraham once lived as μέτοικος and where 'you (the audience) are now living' (7:4). The second is in the final part of the speech, where he attacks his audience (7:51-53). Here he consistently addresses them in the second person plural and emphasises their descent from their forefather's rebellious generation.[40] This shows that ἡμεῖς always designates the Jewish people as a whole, while ὑμεῖς designates those Jews who were born and lived in Palestine. In Luke's terminology, they are the 'Hebrews', his accusers and his audience. This highlights the contrast between the two Jewish groups, as has long been recognised in the study of Acts. Stephen, not surprisingly, identifies himself with the Jews of the Diaspora, the 'Hellenists'.

The οἶκος-Motif

The οἶκος-motif plays an important role in Acts 7. This is not surprising, as the opponents accuse Stephen to speak against τὸν τόπον τοῦτον, and Isaiah 66:1 [MT] mentions 'this house'. The noun proper occurs six times; as well, the following composite constructions occur: κατοικεῖν (7:2,4,47) μετοικεῖν (7:4,43), πάροικος (7:6,29) οἰκοδομεῖν (7:47, 49). This overview reveals the multi-dimensional quality of the οἶκος-motif. On the one hand, it becomes clear that the reference is indeed to the temple in Jerusalem; on the other, life outside the promised land is in focus. At the same time, the Hebrew word points to the fact that the genealogical aspect of the family clan is also important here. The root οἶκ- obviously encompasses much more than just the temple in Jerusalem. 2 Samuel 7:5,11, an important text for Jewish temple and royal ideology, establishes a clear connection

---

[40]Richard, 'Character', 265: 'The controversial shift between "our/your fathers" is really understood in the light of the positive/negative character of the speech'. The section dealing with Joseph he considers as an especially polemical part of the speech.

between the temple and the family clan of David (at least in MT; LXX translates v. 11 with the opposite meaning!). In the speech, David's desire to build a σκήνωμα for the sanctuary is contrasted with Solomon, who built an οἶκος, for this resulted in the establishment of the cult in Jerusalem. This consequence must have been a cause of contention for the Jews of the Diaspora.

V. Concerning the theological roots of Stephen's speech

In another context I have tried to identify the essential characteristics of the theology of early Christian 'Hellenists'.[41] It may prove helpful to mention these characteristics before trying to determine the 'theology' of Stephen's speech, so that the two may be compared. Those traditions which were passed on in the 'Hellenistic' circle and are still extant in Paul's letters should also be included here. This comparison may reveal whether the speech in its essential traits is indeed a genuine documentary evidence for the theology of the 'Hellenists'.

The 'Hellenists' in Acts

Including the other reports about the 'Hellenists'[42] in Acts results in the following picture of their theological emphases:[43]
   1. The 'Hellenists' obviously were driven to missionary activity among non-Jewish people.[44]
   2. They thought within the framework of salvation history.
   3. The Holy Spirit,[45] spiritual gifts and ecstatic experience played an important role.
   4. They had a reluctant attitude towards the temple (cult) and the law.
   5. Their statements reflect an early stage in the development of christology.
   6. Baptism was important.

Comparing these six traits with the results obtained in the analysis of

[41]Neudorfer, Stephanuskreis, 331ff.
[42]This can be seen especially in the reports about Philip (Acts 8) and the missionary activity of the Hellenists which had been expelled from Jerusalem (Acts 11:19-21).
[43]Neudorfer, Stephanuskreis, 334.
[44]Cf., Scott, 'Defense', 140-141.
[45]Cf., Hengel, 'Jesus und Paulus', 193-199.

Stephen's speech leads to the following interesting observations:
(1) There is a surprisingly high interest in and a positive evaluation of
non-Jews and countries outside Palestine in Stephen's speech. God's
revelations outside Canaan play an important role.
(2) The influence of salvation history in Acts 7 is clearly evident.
(3) The activity of the Holy Spirit is not mentioned, but this is not
surprising, as the speech mainly focuses on a review of Israel's history
in the OT. Nevertheless, the Jews are accused of resisting the Holy
Spirit's activity (7:51). Instead, we encounter the appearance and
activity of angels (7:30, 35, 38). But it must be remembered that the
emphasis on them goes back to Luke rather than Stephen, at least in
part (6:15; 7:53). Most important, however, is the emphasis on the fact
that Stephen is endowed with the Holy Spirit (6:5, 10; 7:55, 59). The
catch-word θεωρεῖν (7:56) points to an ecstatic experience.
(4) While a critical attitude towards temple and cult may be observed
implicitly and explicitly, the law is only mentioned in passing and in
an exclusively positive manner. It consists of 'living words' (7:38), is
received from angels (7:38,53; see Gal.3:19), but nevertheless rejected
by Israel (7:53). There is no explicit criticism of the law in Stephen's
speech. Yet this may be due to the fact that the speaker follows the
sequence of the accusations mounted against him (6:13, 14) in his
apology, so that in the end he does not get the opportunity to address
the second accusation.
(5) The title ὁ δίκαιος (7:53) corresponds to an early stage in the
development of christology (see above). This is also true concerning
the employment of Deuteronomy 18:15, which must have been one of
the main OT texts which were used to describe Christ's significance.
According to Stuhlmacher, the 'pattern of contrasts' also belonged to
the earliest interpretations of Christ's death.[46] This means that all
essential elements of 'Hellenistic' theology can be found in Stephen's
speech.

Alexandria?

The question remains as to whether it is possible to give more details.
Possibly a connection between the theology's origin and the port of
Alexandria can be made. Here lived the religious philosopher Philo, a
contemporary. Some of the motifs and exegetical methods employed

---

[46]Stuhlmacher, *Theologie*, 191.

in Stephen's speech were also present in his works. The link between Stephen and Philo would be strengthened if it could be shown that Stephen also came from Alexandria,[47] as some scholars since H. Grotius maintain.[48] But ancient sources supporting this assumption are missing. On inscriptions, the name Στέφανος occurs only in Italy. A sixth century Armenian manuscript mentions the assumption that Philo belonged to those Jews of the Diaspora who had disputed with Stephen (Acts 6:9).[49] Although this is probably a mere speculation,[50] there are several observations supporting a connection between Acts 7 and Philo: the Greek bible common to both, typological exegesis, the high regard for Abraham and Moses, the latter of which can acquire almost divine character in Philo, the relatively weak interest in Palestine,[51] the unique occurrence of the catchword σοφία in Acts 6ff., etc. On the other hand, differences must not be brushed aside. Ultimately, Philo's thought is historical, and this does not correspond with the salvation historical framework in the review of the OT in Acts 7. Joseph is evaluated differently in the two traditions, for he is the epitome of a bad politician for Philo.[52] Above all, Philo lacks any messianic expectation. All this shows that further research is necessary and relevant in this area. In connection with the links between Acts 7 and the Letter to the Hebrews, the hypothesis of a relationship with Alexandria seems to be the most likely explanation, and it is worth pursuing. L.W. Barnard has extended the assumption of a connection between Alexandria and Acts 7 into the post-apostolic period by comparing Stephen's speech with the Letter of Barnabas (which he dates to the second decade of the 2nd century, written in Alexandria).[53] He arrives at the conclusion that the author of the letter has directly applied Acts 7 in his own situation, which is why he used it in his letter.

---

[47]Cf., Neudorfer, *Stephanuskreis*, 146, 252.

[48]Cf., H. Grotius, *Annotationes in Acta 2* (Paris, 1646), on Acts 6:1 and 6:5.

[49]This may be found in English translation in Runia, *Philo*, 5; see there for further references.

[50]Runia, *Philo*, 60: 'pure fantasy'.

[51]Sandmel wrote concerning Philo: 'It cannot be over-emphasized that Philo has little or no concern for Palestine', (Sandmel, *Philo*, 116).

[52]Written communication by Dr. Helmut Burkhardt, Grenzach.

[53]Cf., Barnard, 'Saint Stephen'.

'Hellenistic' traditions as 'bridges' to Pauline theology

The (bilingual) members of the 'Hellenistic' part of the early Christian community in Jerusalem (Acts 6:1ff.) transmitted important parts of the Jesus tradition, which had originally been passed on in Aramaic, into the Greek *lingua franca*. This was necessary because it is more than likely that the majority of this group didn't know Aramaic. Their mother tongue in the Diaspora, as is well known, was Greek.[54] Since the early Christian community had a missionary orientation, it was necessary that 'the new faith was understood intellectually with reference to its main aims and contents..., that is, it needed theological reflection and the (systematic) development of its teaching.'[55] These traditions mainly consisted of (the Lucan or Pauline version of) the Lord's Supper,[56] the atonement formula in Romans 3:25-26[57] and the christological formula in 2 Corinthians 5:21.[58] Other important theological terminology (such as the designation of Jesus as κύριος? *cf.*, Acts 7:59f.) may also go back to this group. From here lines of contact can be traced to Pauline theology. Only a few can be mentioned here: thought within the framework of salvation history, the close link with the OT, the contrast between outward circumcision and circumcision of the heart (Rom. 2:25-26; 4:10-12; Eph. 2:11; Col. 2:11; 3:11), undermining the law.

Samaritan background?

We reject the assumption that a theology influenced by a Samaritan bias underlies Acts 7, despite some parallels.[59] The emphatic employment of Shechem may be explained alternatively on the basis of Jewish sources. If a Samaritan influence is presumed, it would remain unexplained why the historical flashback extends up to Solomon, thus going beyond the Pentateuch, which was favoured by Samaritans. Also, the omission of some favourite Samaritan topics would need

---

[54]Hengel in particular has demonstrated this in several studies.
[55]Stuhlmacher, *Theologie*, 161.
[56]Ibid., 141.
[57]Ibid., 193-94.
[58]Ibid., 195.
[59]Richard comments correctly: 'The Samaritan evidence is but one segment of the textual picture which prevails in Acts 7' (idem, 'Acts 7', 207); *cf.*, also Mare, 'Acts', and Richard, 'Acts'.

explanation. Stemberger has demonstrated parallels from Jewish exegetical tradition for the majority of the speech, reaching the conclusion that only the burial of the twelve patriarchs is a purely Samaritan tradition. In conclusion, the assumption of a Samaritan background to Stephen's speech is not very likely.

VI. Conclusion

This study examined historical, literary and especially theological problems related to Stephen's speech. The following statements may summarise the results of the investigation:

1. The example of Stephen's speech reveals Luke as a writer who uses speeches in a literary manner, similar to Thucydides. In doing so he uses reliable information and traditions and displays great skill in incorporating this speech also into the context of his work.[60]

2. Historical and theological arguments suggest that the speech in Acts 7 was indeed made by Stephen in a similar fashion, albeit in a more expanded version. Luke has adapted it in several places to suit his literary goals. He has established links between it and its literary context to incorporate it as a part of the over-all scheme of his two works. Another reason why Luke has used Stephen's speech was that he wanted to use it as a support for Paul in his controversies with the Judaizers, which still continued at the time of his composition (even more so after the developments in Palestine in the early sixties!).

3. The main source from which Stephen's speech drew was the OT. The theological background of Stephen's speech was probably provided by early Christians who were deeply grounded in the Hellenistic Judaism of the Diaspora (possibly in Egypt). These Christians were involved in a controversy with Palestinian Judaism, and saw a great advantage in the 'gentile' land and its inhabitants, which it used as a theological argument for a Christian mission among the gentiles.

4. The coming of Christ and his life were interpreted in the light of the OT, which is astonishing at this early stage (approx. 31–32 AD). The speech opens a door for Paul's theology and his mission among the gentiles. It opens perspectives which have been pursued by Paul, and which only he developed in full.

---

[60]For a different opinion, see Pesch, *Apostelgeschichte*, I:244.

CHAPTER 15

THE PREACHING AND DEFENCE OF PAUL

G. Walter Hansen

Summary

The narrative frames Paul's speeches to establish their value as the word of God and to make the resurrection of Christ their focal point. The mission speech to Jews (Acts 13) presents the resurrection as the fulfilment of scriptural promises and the basis of forgiveness and justification. The speeches to Gentiles (Acts 14, 17) overturn popular piety by the use of classical traditions and the announcement of judgement by the risen Jesus. The defence speeches (Acts 22-28) exonerate Paul as the faithful teacher of Israel by virtue of his adherence to the hope of Israel fulfilled in the resurrection of Christ.

I. Introduction

Paul's speeches present a brilliant array of theological themes. Since some of these themes (*e.g.*, divine providence, christology, fulfilment of prophecy, and salvation-history) recur with such regularity in the speeches, they are often taken as major points in outlines of Lukan theology.[1] But reconstruction of the theology of Acts must move beyond lists of recurring themes in the speeches. To understand the place of the speeches in Lukan theology it is necessary to pay close attention to the connection between the speeches and their narrative contexts. In Luke's tapestry the speeches are tightly interwoven into the fabric of the entire narrative. The speeches are events in the narrative structure and function as both causes and effects in the narrative sequence.[2] For this reason, Gaventa rightly insists that 'an attempt to do justice to the theology of Acts must struggle to reclaim the character of Acts as narrative'.[3]

This chapter pays special attention to the bi-directional connection between Paul's speeches and their narrative contexts. The speeches gain their meaning from their narrative framework; they also provide a theological foundation for the narrative. When we focus on the link between the speeches and their narrative contexts, two prominent features of Lukan theology emerge. First, the interplay between the speeches and the narrative discloses Luke's theological evaluation of the speeches. We will seek to explicate how the narrative is constructed to prove in different ways for different audiences that Paul's speeches are the word of God. Second, the interaction between speeches and the narrative clarifies the theological focal point of the speeches. Though several themes are repeated in the speeches, one theme is highlighted by the narrative setting for the speeches. This study explores how Luke has interwoven the speeches and narrative to make the resurrection of Christ the focal point in Paul's speeches to non-Christian audiences.[4] Different implications of the resurrection are developed in different narrative contexts.

Four types of speeches by Paul are reported in Acts: a mission speech to Jews (13:6-41, 46-47); mission speeches to Gentiles (14:15-17;

---

[1]Soards, *Speeches*, 183.

[2]Gempf, 'Public Speaking', 259-303

[3]Gaventa, 'Towards a Theology of Acts', 150.

[4]Paul's message to the elders of the church (20:18-35) is the only one of his speeches directed to a Christian audience. Interestingly, it is the only one that omits any reference to the resurrection.

17:22-31); a farewell speech to elders of a church (20:18-35); defence speeches to Jews and Romans (22:1-21; 23:1-6; 24:10-21; 25:2-11; 26:2-29; 28:17-28). Our focus here will be Paul's missionary preaching and his defence speeches.[5]

II. Mission speech to Jews

Summaries of Paul's preaching in Damascus and Jerusalem are reported: 'he began to proclaim Jesus in the synagogues, saying, "He is the Son of God"' (9:20); 'proving that this [Jesus] is the Christ' (9:22); 'speaking out boldly in the name of the Lord' (9:28). But in this account of Paul in the synagogue of Antioch of Pisidia, 'he has found his own voice within the story of the Church'.[6] His speech is a major event in the narrative of his first mission.

Theological evaluation

The narrative of the mission of Paul and Barnabas in Acts 13 begins with the report that 'they proclaimed the word of God in the synagogues of the Jews' (13:5). The impact of that event was so great that the proconsul, Sergius Paulus, wanted to hear 'the word of God' (13:7). He believed 'for he was astonished at the teaching about the Lord' (13:12). At this early stage in the narrative of Paul's mission, the reader is prepared to expect dramatic results from the proclamation of the word of God.

When Paul and Barnabas visit the synagogue in Antioch, they are invited by the leaders of the synagogue to speak a 'word of consolation to the people' (13:15). Paul responds by first telling the Jewish story of God's acts of salvation which reached a climax when God 'according to the promise brought to Israel a Saviour, Jesus' (13:23). Then Paul prefaces his proclamation of the gospel with a direct address to his audience: 'to us the word of this salvation has been sent' (13:26). Luke reports that the result of the proclamation of the word was so great that 'the next sabbath almost the whole city gathered to hear the word of the Lord' (13:44). When some Jews opposed what was spoken by Paul, he informed them that it was necessary for 'the word

---

5See Towner in this volume on Acts 20.
6Rosenblatt, *Paul the Accused*, 33.

of God' to be spoken first to them (13:46). But since they rejected the word, Paul told them that the Lord had given his mandate for the Gentile mission through the prophetic word of Isaiah: 'I have set you to be a light for the Gentiles, so that you may bring salvation to the ends of the earth' (13:47). The narrative informs us that when the Gentiles heard this, 'they were glad and praised the word of the Lord and believed' (13:48). Luke summarises the result of Paul's speech in Pisidian Antioch with the comment that 'the word of the Lord was being spread through the whole region' (13:49).

Of these references to the word of God, six are found in the narrative context for Paul's speech and two are found on the lips of Paul. This constellation of eight references in Acts 13 to the 'word of God' rivets our attention on a major theme in Luke–Acts: the productive power of the word of God as preached by Jesus and his witnesses. Throughout Luke–Acts the message of Jesus and his witnesses is 'the word of God'.[7] The crowds who came to Jesus heard 'the word of God' (Luke 5:2). When the early church in Jerusalem was filled with the Holy Spirit they spoke 'the word of God' with boldness (Acts 5:31). The twelve refused to 'neglect the word of God in order to serve tables' (Acts 6:2). After the conversion of Cornelius and his household, the report went out that 'the Gentiles also had received the word of God' (11:1). Luke summarises the action at key points in his narrative in Acts with the assertion that 'the word of God kept on spreading' (6:7; 12:24; 19:20). Just as Jesus explained in his parable of the sower and the seed Luke 8:8),[8] Luke demonstrated by his narrative in Acts that the word of God has the inherent power to multiply a hundred-fold when it is received by good hearts. This emphasis on the productive power of the word of God sets the stage for Paul's proclamation of the word of God in Antioch in Pisidia.

When we examine the content of Paul's speech, we can discern two reasons why his message is considered by Luke to be the word of God: (1) his message presents an exposition of Scripture and (2) his message proclaims the testimony of witnesses to the resurrection.
(1) Exposition of Scripture: Paul's message (a) begins with a summary of Jewish history laced with allusions to key OT texts, (b) claims that those who executed Jesus were fulfilling 'everything that was written about him (13:29), (c) quotes three OT texts (Ps. 2:7; Isa. 55:3; Ps.16:10)

7Fitzmyer, *Luke I–IX*, 1.157.
8Robinson ('On Preaching the Word of God', 132) notes that in Luke this parable is not a parable about parables (so Mark), it is 'about the preaching of the Christian church'.

to explain the significance of the resurrection of Jesus, and (d) concludes with a warning in the words of Habakkuk 1:5. In his response to Jewish rejection of his message, Paul quotes Isaiah 49:6 to validate his Gentile mission.

The pattern for this use of Scripture in Paul's opening speech in his mission can be observed in Jesus' address in the synagogue in Nazareth (Luke 4:18-20) and in Peter's Pentecost address (Acts 2). All three inaugural addresses either begin, or end, with a Scripture quotation which validates the mission that is beginning.[9] There is also a correspondence between the three references to David in Paul's speech and the Davidic references in other speeches in Acts: Peter (1:16; 2:25-34);[10] the prayer-speech of the community (4:25); Stephen's speech (7:45-46); James (15:16). In these respects, Paul's exposition of the OT is 'representative of the main line of the church's official teaching'.[11]

In Paul's speech the quotations from the prophets and psalms are viewed as authoritative: 'everything that was written' must be fulfilled (13:29). The actions of everyone connected with the cross were prescripted by the prophetic word. The mission of the church is likewise directed by the prophetic word (13:47).

(2) Testimony of eyewitnesses: Paul's message is also viewed as the word of God because he faithfully proclaims the testimony of witnesses to the resurrection of Jesus (13:31-32). The testimony of these witnesses is the good news that Paul announces. 'Luke is at pains in Acts to contextualize Paul's activity within a movement happening in the Jerusalem Church and enunciated by its chief spokespersons'.[12]

So the authoritative status of the word proclaimed by Paul is the same as the words quoted by Paul from the psalms and the prophets and testimony proclaimed by Paul from apostolic witnesses. The word of God is not only the promise given by the psalmists and the prophets, it is also the fulfilment of the promise proclaimed by Paul.

The recipients of the word of God are first of all the Jews. The priority of the Jews is emphasised throughout the speech: 'to us the word of this salvation is sent out' (v. 26); 'we preach to you the good news of the promise' (v. 32); 'God has fulfilled this to our children' (v. 33); 'let it be known to you, brothers' (v. 38); 'it was necessary that the

9Tannehill, *Narrative Unity*, 2:160.
10Ellis, 'Midrashic Freatures in the Speeches of Acts', 306: 'we may observe the pesher pattern in a number of Old Testament quotations in Acts 2 and Acts 13, all of which are eschatologically applied to the present'.
11Rosenblatt, *Paul the Accused*, 33.
12*Ibid*. 34.

word of God should be spoken to you first' (v. 46). The restoration of the Jewish people through the power of the word of God is the first priority and first stage in the narrative structure of Acts.[13]

When the Gentiles hear that the word of God is also for them, they 'praised the word of the Lord' (13:48). The narrative stresses that it is the word of God which is praised, not Paul. It is the word of God which has the regenerative power to produce eternal life in believers (13:48). The narrative of the 'acts of the apostles' is in fact a narrative of the acts of the word of God,[14] for it is the word of God which is the source of the power for the apostles and the effective cause of all that happens through the apostles.

Theological focal point

Paul's sermon in the synagogue confirms and expands major Lukan theological themes, such as salvation-history, promise and fulfilment, and the people of God. But we can see from the narrative setting for this speech that Luke's own primary concern is the significance of the resurrection of Jesus for those who hear. The sermon is an event which pulls the audience into the effective orbit of the resurrection event so that those who reject the message are judged 'unworthy of eternal life' (13:46) and those who believe it are 'destined for eternal life' (13:48). Luke's only reference to 'eternal life' in Acts (cf., Luke 10:25; 18:18, 30) in his narrative of the impact of Paul's speech sends us back to the speech to investigate how the speech produces this result. When we study the speech from the perspective of its aftermath, we can see how 'eternal life' follows naturally as a consequence of the central emphasis of the speech on the benefits of the resurrection of Jesus for those who believe.[15] This emphasis on the resurrection of Jesus is secured by demonstrating that it is (a) the ultimate climax of salvation-history, (b) the fulfilment of the promise, (c) the basis for forgiveness and just-ification, and (d) the amazing work of God.

(a) The climax of salvation-history. The speech begins with a survey of the mighty acts of God in the history of Israel: choosing the

---

13See Jervell, *Luke*, 43: 'The mission to Jews is a necessary stage through which the history of salvation must pass in order that salvation might proceed from the restored Israel to the Gentiles.'
14See Schubert, 'The Final Cycle of Speeches', 16: 'the story of the proclamation of the word of God'.
15O'Toole, 'Christ's Resurrection', 371.

ancestors, making Israel great in Egypt, leading them out, putting up
with them in the wilderness, destroying their enemies, giving them the
land, giving them judges, giving them Saul, removing him, and raising
up David to be their king (13:16-22). To take this opening section as
simply a rehearsal of Jewish history unrelated to the rest of the
sermon[16] misses the way that this recounting of God's acts moves to a
climax: 'God brought to Israel a Saviour, Jesus' (13:23). But even the
entrance of Jesus as the Saviour of Israel is not the ultimate climax of
this account of God's acts. The zenith point in this history of God's acts
is only reached when 'God raised him from the dead' (13:30). A
striking parallel between the history of Israel and the story of Jesus
points to the resurrection of Jesus as the goal of salvation-history.
When the people 'requested a king' (ἠτήσαντο βασιλέα—13:21), their
action led to the tragedy of Saul whom God removed (13:22a). But God
reversed this tragedy when he 'raised up David (ἤγειρεν τὸν Δαυίδ)
for them to be their king' (13:22). Similarly, when the Jewish leaders
asked Pilate (ἠτήσαντο Πιλᾶτον—13:28) to have Jesus killed, their
action led to the tragedy of the cross. But God reversed this tragedy
when he raised Jesus (ὁ δὲ θεὸς ἤγειρεν αὐτόν) from the dead. This
parallelism has not been observed because most outlines divide the
speech into three parts based on the threefold direct address in verses
16, 26, and 38.[17] This division is warranted from a literary point of
view. But from a historical point of view, the history of God's acts on
behalf of Israel led to and is inextricably linked with the goal of that
history: 'he brought to Israel, a Saviour, Jesus, as he promised' (13:23);
'God raised him from the dead' (13:30).

The link between the introduction of Jesus as the *Saviour* and the
introduction of the kerygma as 'the word of *salvation*' also points to the
resurrection of Jesus as the goal of salvation-history. The cross is not
viewed as a salvific act; it is simply presented as the criminal act of the
residents of Jerusalem and their rulers (13:27-29) who unwittingly
fulfilled Scriptures when they requested Pilate to execute Jesus. The
good news is that God reversed this tragedy when he fulfilled his
promises by raising Jesus (13:30-33). Salvation is offered by Jesus the
Saviour on the basis of his resurrection.[18] Resurrection is the
culmination of salvation-history.

(b) The fulfilment of the promise. In 13:23 we read that a promise

16Dibelius, *Studies*, 166.
17See Pillai, *Apostolic Interpretation*, 1-3; deSilva, 'Paul's Sermon', 34-35.
18Marshall, *Luke: Historian*, 169.

is fulfilled by God's provision of Jesus, the Saviour, the seed of David, to Israel. It appears that the promise in view is the Davidic promise of 2 Samuel 7:12 LXX: 'I will raise up your offspring after you (καὶ ἀναστήσω τὸ σπέρμα σου μετὰ σέ), who shall come forth from your body, and I will establish his kingdom.' If the next use of the word 'promise' (13:32) is interpreted in connection with 13:23, then the fulfilment referred to by the phrase 'raising Jesus' (ἀναστήσας Ἰησοῦν—13:33) could be understood as 'sending Jesus' to Israel, not raising Jesus from the dead. Certainly the verb 'raising' (ἀναστήσας) has this meaning of 'sending' in the quotation of Deuteronomy 18:13 in Acts 3:22 and 7:37: 'The Lord your God will raise up (ἀναστήσει) for you a prophet like me from among your brothers.' Bruce argues along this line of interpretation that 'the promise of v. 23, the fulfilment of which is here described, has to do with the sending of the Messiah, not His resurrection'.[19] Arguments for this interpretation point to (1) the absence of the phrase 'from the dead' in verse 33; (2) the parallel with 'He raised up David (ἤγειρεν τὸν Δαυίδ) to be their king' (13:22), and (3) the possibility of a two step sequence of 'raising Jesus' in the sense of sending him (13:33) and 'raising him from the dead'— ἀνέστησεν αὐτὸν ἐκ νεκρῶν (13:34).[20]

There are good reasons to take the phrase 'raising Jesus' in 13:33 as a reference to the resurrection of Jesus. (1) The focus of the immediate context (13:30-31, 34) is resurrection from the dead. If 'raising Jesus' (13:33) is a reference to Jesus' earthly life there seems to be an awkward break in the train of thought.[21] (2) It is more likely that the same word, 'raising' (ἀναστήσας, 13:33; ἀνέστησεν, 13:34), would have the same meaning in the same context, rather than two different meanings. (3) The verb 'to raise' (ἀνίστημι) is used by itself in Acts 2:24, 32 without the phrase 'from the dead' to mean resurrection from the dead. (4) Bock argues that 13:32-33 is a three part introduction to the three scriptural citations that follow: first, the reference to 'the promise to the fathers' (v. 32a) fits with the citation of Psalm 2:7; second, the reference to the 'fulfilment to the children' introduces the citation of Isaiah 55:3; third, the reference to the 'raising of Jesus' points to the citation of Psalm 16:10. Although this neat arrangement of the text appears to be somewhat contrived, the way that the chain of citations introduced by 13:32-33 builds towards the proclamation of

19Bruce, *Acts (Greek Text)*, 269 (1st ed.).
20See Bock, *Proclamation*, 244, for discussion of alternative interpretations.
21O'Toole, 'Christ's Resurrection', 366.

the resurrection of Jesus (13:35-37) supports the view that the phrase 'raising Jesus' (13:33) means resurrection from the dead. In that case, the fulfilment of the promise (13:32-33) is the resurrection of Jesus from the dead. The specific contents of the promise fulfilled by the resurrection of Jesus are given in Psalm 2:7, Isaiah 55:3, and Psalm 16:10.

Psalm 2 was interpreted messianically in the context of Judaism. God's promise of a Davidic heir to the throne (2 Sam. 7:10-14) was linked with this ideal, poetic description of God's Son.[22] In the context of Paul's speech, Psalm 2:7 is cited as a prophecy of the resurrection of Jesus. His resurrection demonstrated that he is the Son of God depicted in this Psalm.[23] Bock argues that 13:34a should be taken in connection with Psalm 2:7 as the explanation for the designation of Jesus as God's son. 'Because Jesus was the incorruptible Son promised in Scripture, he must be raised.'[24] It seems better, however to see the phrase 'by raising Jesus, as also it was written in the second psalm' (13:33a) as the introduction to the quotation of Psalm 2:7 (13:33b) and 13:34a as the introduction to the citation of Isaiah 55:3. This interpretation observes the parallelism between the two references to the resurrection (13:33a and 34a) which introduce the two citations (13:3b and 34b). First, the resurrection (ἀναστήσας᾽ Ἰησοῦν) demonstrates that Jesus is the Son of God promised to David (Ps. 2:7); second, the resurrection (ἀνέστησεν αὐτόν) demonstrates that the 'holy and sure things promised to David' (τὰ ὅσια Δαυὶδ τὰ πιστά—Isa. 55:3) are available *to us* (Δώσω ὑμῖν).

Isaiah 55:3 is a promise to exiled Israel that God will renew his eternal covenant with David and his people will experience the 'holy and sure blessings promised to David'. The introduction to the citation emphasises that *'because* (ὅτι) he raised him from the dead no longer to return to corruption' the holy things promised to David (τὰ ὅσια Δαυίδ) are sure and certain (τὰ πιστά). The point of quoting Isaiah 55:3 is that Jesus' resurrection guarantees certain 'holy things' for the audience; the benefits of the resurrection are secured *for us* because this son of David is incorruptible since God raised him from the dead.[25]

The concepts of incorruptibility ('no more to return to corruption') and 'holy things' provide a twofold link between the quotation of

---

224QFlor
23Contra Bruce (*Acts*, 276 [1st ed.]) who takes it to refer to the baptism of Jesus.
24Bock, *Proclamation*, 249.
25Dupont, 'ΤΑ ῾ΟΣΙΑ ΔΑΥΊΔ ΤΑ ΠΙΣΤΑ', 111. Kilgallen, 'Acts 13:38-39', 492: 'One can understand why *ta hosia Dauid* can be characterized as *ta pista*, for it is by His raising Jesus to incorruptibility that the *ta hosia* merits the description *ta pista*.'

Isaiah 55:3 and Psalm 16:10. The inference made in 13:34a that the
resurrection entails incorruptibility is now demonstrated by the quotation of Psalm 16:10 in which incorruptibility is the point of the text:
'You will not let your Holy One experience corruption'(13:35).[26] The
next verses focus on the deliverance from corruption to prove that the
Psalm applies not to David who saw corruption but to Jesus who did
not see corruption because God raised him up (13:36-37). Thus, the
resurrection secures the indestructibility of the 'holy things' (τὰ ὅσια)
and the 'Holy One' (τὸν ὅσιον). The indestructible Holy One is the mediator of the indestructible holy things by virtue of his resurrection.[27]

(c) The basis of forgiveness and justification. The nature of the
'holy things' guaranteed by the resurrection of the 'Holy One' are
explained in 13:38-39. Kilgallen presents evidence to interpret the 'holy
things' to be 'forgiveness of sins' (13:38) and justification (13:39).[28]
Paul's speech leads to this conclusion, 'indicated by the collocation of
scripture texts, that the Davidic holy one, who is both the result of the
covenant with David and faithful to God, is the one who mediates
holiness which involves forgiveness of sins and justification'.[29]

The offer of 'forgiveness of sins' in the conclusion of Paul's
speech fits with a common theme in the preaching of the church. In
Acts, the phrase 'forgiveness of sins' is found three times in Peter's
speeches (2:38; 5:31; 10:43) and twice in Paul's speeches (here and
26:18). This element in the preaching of Paul fulfils what the conclusion of Luke's Gospel anticipates: 'forgiveness of sins is to be proclaimed in his name to all nations' (Luke 24:47). The offer of justification,
found only here in Acts, contains echoes of familiar Pauline concepts:
law of Moses, faith, justification. Yet, this formulation of justification
by faith in Paul's speech led Vielhauer 'to point out striking differences
from the statements in Paul's letters'.[30] Vielhauer claims that forgiveness of sins and justification are never associated by Paul in his letters.
But his claim is refuted by this connection in Romans 4:5-7 where Paul
explains the justification of the ungodly (Rom. 4:5) by quoting from
Psalm 32: 'Blessed are those whose iniquities are forgiven'.[31] Vielhauer
asserts that the expression of justification by faith in Paul's speech
means 'only partial justification, one which is not by faith alone, but

26Bock, *Proclamation*, 255.
27Kilgallen, 'Acts 13:38-39', 494.
28*Ibid*. 498-501.
29*Ibid*. 502.
30Vielhauer, 'On the 'Paulinism' of Acts', 41.
31Barrett, *Acts*, 651.

also by faith'.[32] In other words, justification by faith supplements justification by law. But his assertion fails to see that the phrase 'from everything from which you could not be justified by the law of Moses' more naturally means that justification by the law is impossible; justification comes only by faith.[33] Kilgallen says that 'nowhere in the Pauline writings does one ever find a combination of the terms used in Acts 13:38b-39'.[34] But the three terms ('justified', 'from', 'sins') referred to by Kilgallen are combined in Romans 6:7 (δεδικαίωται ἀπὸ τῆς ἁμαρτίας). True, the use of the preposition 'from' (ἀπο) with the verb 'to be justified' (δικαιωθῆναι) in Acts 13:38 (and Rom. 6:7) conveys the meaning 'is set free from' (NRSV) rather than the typical Pauline forensic sense.[35] But the basic contrast between justification by law and justification by faith expressed here in Paul's speech is found in Paul's letters (Gal. 3:11).[36] Luke has provided a fairly accurate summary of Pauline soteriology at this point.[37]

Paul's offer of forgiveness of sins and justification emphasises the mediation of Jesus by the double use of the pronoun 'this one' in 13:38-39 (διὰ τούτου ... ἐν τούτῳ).[38] They point back to the immediate context where Jesus is the 'Holy One' who did not see corruption because God raised him from the dead (13:35-37). Forgiveness of sins and justification are benefits of Jesus' resurrection mediated through him to all who believe in him. Since he is God's Holy One by virtue of the resurrection, he is the mediator of the 'holy things' promised to the exiled nation of Israel (13:34), but now made universally available to everyone who believes (πᾶς ὁ πιστεύων, 13:39).

(d) The amazing work. After the offer of forgiveness of sins and justification, Paul's speech ends with a warning (Hab. 1:5). The warning directs the attention of the audience to a *work* which God is *working*, a *work* (note the threefold repetition) which they will not believe even though it is told to them. Some have thought that this work must refer to some kind of judgement; in the original context it referred to the destruction of the nation by the Chaldean invasion; in the context of the Jewish audience it refers to judgement for rejecting the gospel ('since you reject it, you judge yourselves to be unworthy of eternal

---

32Vielhauer, 'On the 'Paulinism' of Acts', 41.
33Haenchen, *Acts*, 412, n. 4; Marshall, *Acts: Commentary*, 228.
34Kilgallen, 'Acts 13:38-39', 503.
35Barrett, *Acts I*, 650.
36Pillai, *Apostolic Interpretation*, 66-67.
37Longenecker, 'Acts', 426.
38Kilgallen, 'Acts 13:38-39', 504.

life'—13:46).[39] Pillai, however, identifies the 'work' with the resurrection of Jesus for three reasons.[40] First, the entire speech focuses on
God's saving acts in history culminating in the ultimate act of raising
Jesus from the dead. Second, the temporal location of the work, 'in
your days' points to a recent event. Third, the work should be the
object of faith, but it is not believed. The resurrection of Jesus is
presented as the object of Christian faith in Acts.

This line of interpretation fits in well with our findings that the
resurrection of Jesus is the goal of salvation-history, the fulfilment of
the promise, and the basis of forgiveness and justification. The
resurrection of Jesus is the work of God which includes within it the
benefits of forgiveness of sins and justification. Indeed, the 'resurrection of Jesus is not merely an event in the past, but a permanent
deed, which, though already fulfilled, still extends into the future as a
hope. The object of this hope is the eschatological triumph of the
believer, who will be raised in glory, while the unbelievers, the scoffers, "wonder and perish"'.[41] For this reason, Luke links the speech to
the narrative with his double reference to 'eternal life' (13:46, 48).
Building on the implications of the resurrection of Jesus developed in
Paul's speech, the narrative informs us that believers are destined to
eternal life and unbelievers have forfeited eternal life. The central
proclamation of the message that God raised Jesus from the dead is the
foundation for the hope that through the mediation of Jesus God will
also raise everyone who believes in him.[42]

Furthermore, the narrative after the speech enables to see how
this universal offer of the benefits of the resurrection of Jesus to
'everyone who believes in him' is the foundation of the Gentile
mission. Paul and Barnabas quote Isaiah 49:6 as a command given 'to
us' (13:47). But the singular pronoun 'you' is found in the citation. De
Silva explains that 'Paul and Barnabas continued the work of Christ by
presenting him as the 'light' to both Jews and Gentiles'.[43] By preaching
the 'word of salvation' (13:26) about the risen 'Saviour' (13:23, 30, 33,
37), they 'bring salvation to the ends of the earth' (13:47).

39Bruce, *Acts*, 279.
40Pillai, *Apostolic Interpretation*, 71-73.
41*Ibid.* 73.
42O'Toole, 'Christ's Resurrection', 371.
43deSilva, 'Paul's Sermon', 48.

III. Mission speeches to Gentiles

Examination of the narrative contexts for Paul's hurried remarks to superstitious barbarians in Lystra and his reasoned address to sceptical philosophers in Athens enables us to observe Luke's theological evaluation and focal point for these speeches.

Theological evaluation

(1) Paul's preaching at Lystra.
The narrative of Paul's mission in Lystra begins with the healing of a man lame from birth. As a result of listening to Paul preaching, he had faith to be healed (ἔχει πίστιν τοῦ σωθῆναι—14:9). And at Paul's command to stand up, he sprang up and walked. The narrative leaves no doubt that Paul's word produced saving faith and conveyed God's healing power. The verbal parallels between this healing and the healing of the lame man by Peter (3:1-8) are obvious: both lame men are 'lame from birth'; both Peter and Paul 'look intently at' the lame man before the healing occurs; both lame men 'walk about' when they are healed.[44] These parallels indicated that Paul's preaching has the same prophetic quality as Peter's; both speak the word of God with power.[45]

Not only is Paul identified with Peter by Luke's narrative construction, he is also identified with Hermes by Luke's account of the crowds' response to the miracle. 'They shouted in the Lyconaian language, "The gods have come down to us in human form!" Barnabas they called Zeus, and Paul they called Hermes, because he was the chief speaker' (14:11-12). Martin shows how this misidentification, though it was scandalous from the perspective of the apostles, Barnabas and Paul (14:14), served the purpose of Luke.[46] Luke's characterisation of Barnabas and Paul fits with classical Greek traditions about Zeus and Hermes. Since the time of Homer, Zeus and Hermes were portrayed as patrons of ambassadors and guarantors of the veracity of

---

[44]The Western text bring the two accounts even closer by adding the words 'I say to you in the name of the Lord Jesus' before Paul's command (cf., 3:6) and the words 'immediately he leaped up' after his command (cf., 3:7-8). Bruce calls this 'a pietistic addition which makes the parallelism with ch. iii more complete', (Bruce, *Acts (Greek Text)*, 281).

[45]Johnson, *Acts*, 251.

[46]Martin, 'Gods or Ambassadors of God? Barnabas and Paul in Lystra', 152.

their speeches. Hermes was depicted as the messenger of his father, Zeus, 'the leader in speaking', 'the bringer of good news'.[47] Because Paul was 'the chief speaker' (14:12) who 'brings good news' (14:15), he was appropriately identified as Hermes. Even though this was a misidentification, it was still a useful way for Luke to provide a kind of indirect legitimisation of Paul's preaching to a Hellenistic audience. If Hermes was the messenger-god in Greek traditions, then Paul was like him, though, of course, far superior to this mythological figure since he was the messenger of the living God.

Ovid's similar story told early in the first century[48] is also within the orbit of classical Greek traditions regarding Zeus and Hermes.[49] In Ovid's account, however, the gods, Zeus and Hermes, are mistaken for mortals, while in Acts mortals are identified as gods. In both stories hospitality is extended to strangers. Ovid describes how Zeus and Hermes disguised as travellers were turned away from a thousand homes until finally an elderly couple, Baucis and Philemon offered the travellers food from their meagre resources. Similarly, Luke's account tells how Paul and Barnabas were rejected in Antioch and Iconium until they were finally given an extravagant welcome as gods in Lystra. Though the pagans in Lystra misunderstood the identity of the 'apostles' (14:14), their openness to the preaching of the apostles demonstrated that God had indeed 'opened a door of faith of the Gentiles' (14:27). Luke's account sets forth the hospitality of these Gentiles as exemplary, even though misguided. Apostles should be given an extravagant welcome. The hospitality offered in Ovid's account was the occasion for the disguised gods to reveal their true identity and receive worship. The apostles revealed their own true identity in Luke's account by their vehement refusal to be worshipped as gods. In this way Luke's narrative establishes not only the uniqueness of the living God over against the worthless superstitions of pagan idolatry (14:15) but also the trustworthiness of the apostles as faithful messengers of that living God. 'Paul and Barnabas did not play to the gallery, posing even as "divine men"'.[50]

(2) Paul's preaching in Athens.
Luke's narrative setting for his synopsis of Paul's Aeropagus address

47See the documentation in Martin, 155.
48Both stories are set in the same region where inscriptions associate Zeus and Hermes. See Hansen, 'Galatia,' 393.
49*Metamorphoses* 8.611-725.
50Winter, 'In Public and In Private', 129.

contributes to his theological evaluation of the speech in at least five ways.

(1) His description of Paul's initial response to idolatry in Athens indicates the motivational impetus for the speech.[51] Because Paul was 'deeply distressed to see that the city was full of idols' (17:16) his speech proclaimed the transcendence and providence of the one true God (17:22-28) and demanded repentance for idolatry (17:29-30) in the face of certain judgement (17:31). This connection between Paul's own spiritual revulsion against ubiquitous idolatry in Athens (17:16) and his call to repentance (17:29-30) places his speech on the same level as the Jewish prophets' denunciation of idolatry and the opposition of early Greek philosophers to the worship of idols.

(2) Luke's depiction of Paul's enraged reaction against idolatry in Athens (17:16) also provides the context for the appeal in his speech to a Stoic poet for support in his refutation of idolatry (17:28). Aratus, a Cilician poet (c. 315-240 B.C.), acclaimed that 'It is with Zeus that every one of us in every way has to do, for we are also his offspring'.[52] From their own poet's insight that we are God's offspring, the Athenians should have known that 'we ought not to think that the deity is like gold, or silver, or stone, an image formed by the art and imagination of mortals' (17:29). Balch reviews the evidence that 'some early Stoics, in theory but not in practice, held the view expressed in Acts 17:29'.[53] Plutarch, for example, lampooned Zeno, the founder of Stoicism, for this contradiction between the theory and practice of Stoics: 'it is the doctrine of Zeno's not to build temples of the gods, because a temple not worth much is also not sacred, and no work of builders or mechanics is worth much. The Stoics, while applauding this as correct, attend the mysteries in temples, go up to the Acropolis, do reverence to statues, and place wreaths upon shrines, though these are works of builders and mechanics'.[54] Balch argues that later Stoics abandoned even the theoretical opposition to images in their rapprochement with popular piety. For example, Dio Chrysostom's Oration 12, delivered at the end of the first century, presents a reasoned defence of images.[55] No doubt this accommodation with idolatry in the first century reflects

51Gärtner, *The Areopagus Speech*, 45: 'a pointer for the reader that a subject of fundamental importance is to be treated...a hint of what the speech is to attempt'.
52*Phaenomena* 5; also found in Cleanthes (c. 331-233 B.C.), *Hymn to Zeus* 4.
53Balch, 'The Areopagus Speech', 68.
54Plutarch, 'Stoic Self-contradictions', *Moralia* 1034B.
55Balch, 'The Areopagus Speech', 71.

the force of the imperial cult. Endorsement of popular piety must have been seen as necessary for survival in the imperial period.[56] According to Balch, 'Acts pictures Paul presenting the ancient, authentic, philosophical opinion' against the defence of images by contemporary Stoics.[57] In an aside to the readers, Luke comments that the contemporary Athenians were more interested in satisfying their insatiable curiosity for something new (17:21) than in protecting venerated traditions. It is Paul who calls the Athenians back to their philosophical roots by quoting their own poets to them. As Malherbe puts it, Luke's narrative achieved 'a subtle turning of the tables: the pagan philosophers who question the apostle do not themselves hold to the legitimating tradition; it is Paul who does'.[58] So Luke's picture of Paul's rejection of popular religious pluralism aligns Paul with the orthodoxy not only of Jewish faith but also with classical orthodoxy in Greek philosophy.

(3) Paul's connection with early Greek philosophers is strengthened by the way that Luke weaves several allusions to Socrates into his narrative. Like Socrates, Paul engaged in dialogues (διελέγετο) 'in the *agora* (ἐν τῇ ἀγορᾷ) every day with those who happened to be there' (17:17).[59] Also like Socrates, he was charged with proclaiming 'foreign divinities' (Ξένων δαιμονίων, 17:18).[60] So like Socrates, Paul was put on trial to give account of his 'new teaching' (17:19).[61] Luke indicates the favourable reception which the Aeropagus address should receive from his readers in the Greek world by this association of Paul with Socrates.

(4) By his account of contrasting reactions to Paul's teaching before and after the speech, Luke gives the Areopagus address a specific place in the context of Greek philosophical positions. On the one hand, the Epicurean philosophers mocked Paul with the derogatory name,

---

56Winter, 'In Public and In Private', 140-41.

57*Ibid.* Balch's position needs to be modified somewhat by the obervations of Attridge and Winter that there was accommodation to popular piety even in classical Stoicism. See Attridge, 'The Philosophical Critique of Religion under the Early Empire', 59-72; Winter, 'In Public and In Private', 138-139.

58Malherbe, *Paul and the Popular Philosophers*, 152.

59Plato, *Apology* 17: 'If I defend myself in my accustomed manner, and you hear me using words which I have been in the habit of using in the *agora*'; *Apology* 23: 'I go about the world, obedient to the god, and search and make enquiry into the wisdom of any one, whether citizen or stranger'.

60Plato, *Apology* 24 BC: 'Socrates is a doer of evil, who corrupts the youth; and who does not believe in the gods of the city, but has other new divinities (ἕτερα δὲ δαιμόνια καινά) of his own.'

'babbler' (σπερμολόγος, 'seedpicker', 17:18). 'Seedpicker' was local slang for a gutter sparrow, one who picked up scraps in the market, a worthless vagrant, or one who traded second-hand scraps of philosophy.[62] The term expressed disdain for a plagiarist of the ideas of great teachers.[63] On the other hand, the Stoic philosophers were confused by the newness of Paul's concepts (17:19-21).[64] They thought Paul was advocating strange divinities (Ξένων δαιμονίων), probably taking *Iesous* (Jesus) and *Anastasis* (resurrection) as 'the personified and deified powers of "healing" and "restoration"'.[65] They sought to know more about Paul's teaching by taking him to the Areopagus.

This same contrast of responses to Paul is found after the speech: 'some mocked; but others said, "we will hear you again about this"' (17:32). It is reasonable to suppose that Luke deliberately continued his contrast between the Epicureans and the Stoics by describing these different responses after the speech. The Epicureans who mocked Paul before the speech also mocked him afterwards. Likewise the Stoics who wanted to know more before, were open to hear him again after. Some even 'joined him and became believers, including Dionysius the

---

[61]Scholars debate whether the Areopagus refers simply a place, the Hill of Ares, or to the administrative body named after this place (see Hemer, 'Paul at Athens', 341-350). Some take 17:19 as a description of an arrest and formal trial: 'They arrested him (ἐπιλαβόμενοί τε αὐτοῦ, see the use of this term for arrest in Luke 23:26; Acts 16:19; 17:6; 18:17; 21:30) and brought him[for trial] before the Areopagus council'. So Tannehill, *Narrative Unity*, 2:216: 'the speech fits better if Paul is addressing not only the philosophers but also an official body that has responsibility for the city, including it religious facilities' (216). Luke seems to indicate that Paul was addressing the Areopagus as a governing body by his parallels with the trial of Socrates (Haenchen, *Acts*, 527), by Paul's remarks which appear to hold his audience responsible for religious conduct in the city, and by the reference Dionysius, the Areopagite (17:34). Gärtner (*The Areopagus Speech*, 65) suggests that Paul faced 'an informal inquiry by the education commission' of the Areopagus Council. *Cf.*, Dibelius, *Studies*, 67-68; Conzelmann, 'The Address of Paul on the Areopagus', 219.

[62]Dio Chrysostom (*Discourse* 32.9) uses this term in an interesting sketch of those who stand 'at street-corners, in alleyways, and at temple-gates, pass around the hat, and play upon the credulity of lads and sailors and crowds of that sort, stringing together rough jokes and much *babbling* (σπερμολόγιαν) and that rubbish of the marketplace'.

[63]Gärtner, *The Areopagus Speech* 48: 'a term of abuse, whose approximate meaning is one who goes about the streets and markets picking up words of wisdom from great teachers, and then passes himself off as such an one' .

[64]Isocrates (*Antidosis* 83) describes the orators dilemma: 'If they repeat the same things which have been said in the past, they will be regarded as shameless babblers, and if they seek for what is new, they will have great difficulty in finding it'.

[65]Bruce, *Acts*, 351.

Areopagite, a woman named Damaris, and others' (17:33).

　　Luke's portrayal of a divided reaction to Paul's preaching occurs again in Acts 23:6-10. In his trial before the Jewish Sanhedrin, Paul caused a division between the Pharisees and Saducees by deliberately siding with the Pharisees in his affirmation of the 'hope of the resurrection of the dead' (23:6-7). Neyrey has argued that Luke developed this parallel between these two episodes to clarify Paul's own position: just as he took the side of the Pharisees against the Saducees in Jerusalem on the issue of the resurrection, so he took the side of the Stoics against the Epicureans on the issue of theodicy.[66] In the Areopagus address Paul develops his theodicy by proclaiming attributes of the 'unknown God'. This God is the transcendent creator of all things and is therefore not dependent on anything made by human hands (17:24-25). The true God is the benevolent administrator of all nations since he set their times and places (17:26). God is the just judge of all people; he has fixed the day of judgement and appointed the judge (17:30-31). These affirmations about the 'unknown God' proclaim the God of Scriptures,[67] but they also present God in terms of common Stoic theology.[68] A standard outline of Stoic arguments 'on the nature of God' is presented by Cicero in his work, *De natura deorum*: 'first they prove that the gods exist; next they explain their nature; then they show that the world is governed by them; and lastly, they care for the fortunes of mankind'.[69] 'It must be concluded', says Winter, 'in seeking to understand Paul's approach to Stoic views held by his audience, that he may well have consciously used the traditional outline of the Stoics on *De natura deorum*'.[70] There were also some points of convergence with Epicurean philosophy: God is living, knowable, and not dependent on man-made temples or gifts.[71] But the Epicureans denied the traditional Stoic belief in God's providence and God's final judgement after death.[72] Since Epicureans denied that God

---

[66]Neyrey, 'Acts 17, Epicureans, and Theodicy', 121.
[67]See Gärtner, *The Areopagus Speech*, 203-228.
[68]Conzelmann, 'The Address of Paul on the Areopagus', 221: 'The author takes advantage of a convergence between the Bible and Hellenism'. Winter, 'In Public and In Private', 135: 'Paul had found a very helpful bridge between Stoicisim and the Old Testament in his speech'.
[69]Cicero, *De Natura Deorum* II.4.
[70]Winter, 'In Public and In Private', 136.
[71]See Winter, 'In Public and In Private', 136-138. On the basis of these points of agreement with Epicureanism, Winter rejects Neyrey's thesis that Luke portrays Paul on the side of the Stoics against the Epicureans (138).
[72]Neyrey, 'Acts 17, Epicureans, and Theodicy', 125.

was judge and affirmed that death is final, they 'were known by their opponents in terms of stereotypes, especially the stereotype of those who deny providence and theodicy'.[73] Apparently, Luke structured his narrative to reflect this contrast between the Stoics and Epicureans. Whereas Paul's speech agrees with Stoic doctrines of the providence and judgement of God, it contradicts the Epicurean denial of these doctrines. So the Epicureans mocked Paul, while the Stoics were open to hear more. Luke evidently wanted to show that Paul's preaching was rejected by the Epicureans in Acts 17 and the Sadducees in Acts 23. As Neyrey suggests, 'If mockery and dismissal come from groups who can be shown to be wrong, that in itself is further confirmation of the correctness of what they mock and dismiss. Comparably, to find common ground and perhaps endorsement from groups generally considered the guardians of the basic tradition (Stoics and Pharisees) can only transfer that approbation to the new group of Christians as well. They are not mavericks'.[74]

(5) Luke indicates his perspective on Paul's preaching in Athens by using his standard terms for evangelistic preaching: in the narrative we learn that Paul was 'telling the good news (εὐηγγελίζετο) about Jesus and the resurrection' (17:18).[75] In the speech a synonymous term is used: 'this I proclaim (καταγγέλλω) to you' (17:23).[76] Both these are linked with 'Jesus', 'Christ', and the 'word of God' as the content of preaching throughout Acts. We may conclude that Luke was defining the nature of the preaching, both in the narrative and in the Areopagus address, to be orthodox, apostolic preaching by his use of these terms.

Dibelius, however, suggests that there is a divergence between the narrative and the speech.[77] Jesus and the resurrection are the main themes of the preaching in the narrative. But, says Dibelius, 'the main ideas of the speech, knowledge of God and God's relationship with man, are Stoic rather than Christian'.[78] 'We can only conclude', according to Dibelius, 'that the Areopagus speech is a Hellenistic speech with a Christian ending'.[79] Dibelius's conclusion that 'the speech is alien to

---

[73]*Ibid*. 124.

[74]*Ibid*. 134.

[75]The last of 14 occurences in Acts of this verb (εὐαγγελίζω) for evangelistic preaching about Jesus (see Acts 5:42; 8:4, 12, 25, 35, 40; 10:36; 11:20; 13:32; 14:7, 15, 21; 15:35; 16:10; 17:18).

[76]I proclaim (καταγγέλλω) occurs in Acts 3:24; 4:2; 13:5, 38; 15:36; 16:7, 21; 17:3, 13, 23; 26:23.

[77]Dibelius, *Studies*, 67.

[78]*Ibid*. 63.

the New Testament'[80] is the result of his failure to see its Jewish background. Haenchen has pointed out—'Dibelius has underemphasised the Old Testament components of the Areopagus speech'.[81] Gärtner's conclusions point in the opposite direction from Dibelius. He shows that 'the criticism of idolatry follows the pattern often found in Old Testament and Jewish texts'.[82] He draws attention to the close parallels between Stephen's polemic against temple service and the Areopagus address. Stephen's assertion that 'the Most High does not dwell in temples made with hands' (ἀλλ' οὐχ ὁ ὕψιστος ἐν χειροποιήτοις κατοικεῖ, 7:48) is repeated by Paul: 'the Lord of heaven and earth does not live in shrines made by human hands (οὗτος οὐρανοῦ καὶ γῆς ὑπάρχων κύριος οὐκ ἐν χειροποιήτοις ναοῖς κατοικεῖ, 17:24)'. 'In the Areopagus speech, the censure is directed against the Gentiles, but the fault found with their temple cult is the same as that implied in Stephen's speech, namely, a consignment of the Almighty to a temple built by men.... It is probable that in this connection, we are dealing with a Christian "catechetic" tradition.'[83] This recognition of the use of Jewish and Christian traditions in the speech enables us to see the basis of Luke's theological evaluation of the speech as a model of Christian evangelism (εὐηγγελίζετο) and proclamation (καταγγέλλω) in a Gentile context. Even though there are important points of contact with Stoic philosophy, as we have observed, the entire speech has a solid Jewish-Christian foundation.

Theological focal point

(1) Paul's preaching at Lystra.
To frenzied worshippers in Lystra, Paul and Barnabas announced the 'good news' (εὐαγγελιζόμενοι ὑμᾶς, 14:15) of Jewish monotheism. To Jews the gospel proclaims 'Jesus is the Christ'; to Gentiles it begins by saying, 'God is one and has not left himself without witness'.[84] Their demand that the superstitious crowds 'turn from these worthless

79Ibid. 58.
80Ibid. 63.
81Haenchen, Acts, 528.
82Gärtner, The Areopagus Speech, 250; See pages 203-228 for numerous links with the Jewish polemic against idolatry, including references to Ps. 115: 5; Isa. 31:7; 37:19; 66:1-2; 2 Kings 19:18.
83Gärtner, The Areopagus Speech, 209.
84Bruce, Acts (Greek Text), 283.

things to the living God' is based on the character of God: God is the transcendent Creator of all things (14:15), the benevolent administrator of all nations (14:16), and the generous 'witness' to his own goodness through the gifts of rains, abundant harvests, and joy (14:17).

    Although this speech seems more like Jewish preaching of the shema, 'Hear, O Israel, the Lord our God the Lord is one' (Deut. 6:4), than Christian preaching of salvation through Christ, there are two hints that Luke's narrative was designed to point discerning readers to Christ. The first implicit pointer to Christ is found in the narrative prelude to the speech. The parallel between the lame man healed by Paul and the lame man healed by Peter would bring to the reader's mind Peter's announcement that 'this man is standing before you in good health by the name of Jesus Christ of Nazareth, whom you crucified, whom God raised from the dead' (4:10). Second, the command in the speech to forsake idolatry is related to a turning point in history. The claim that God allowed all the nations to follow their own way in the past (14:16), implies that a change has taken place in the present. Although the speech contains no explicit reference to Christ, 'it is hard to believe that it was not meant to point to Jesus Christ and his work as the divine climax of history'.[85] After reading the Areopagus address, the reader would then see clearly that the abridged reference in the Lystra speech (14:16) to God's plan for the nations in the past needed to be completed by the announcement of the resurrection of the God-appointed judge of the nations in the present (17:30).

(2) Paul's preaching at Athens.
The narrative of Paul's proclamation of 'Jesus and the resurrection' in the market-place (17:18) sets the agenda for the Areopagus address.[86] He was brought before the council of the Areopagus to give account of himself for preaching these strange deities. But Paul turns the tables: he warns the Athenians of impending judgement for their idolatry and builds his address toward the announcement of the day of judgement.[87] The introduction (17:22-23) frees Paul from the accusation of promoting alien gods in Athens and provides him with a point of contact for his proclamation of the unknown god.[88] Praise for Athenian

---

[85]Longenecker, 'Acts', 436.
[86]Conzelmann, 'The Address of Paul on the Areopagus', 220: 'The entire address presses toward the focal point of its theme, formulated as: Jesus and Anastasis.'
[87]See Zweck's rhetorical analysis of the speech ('The Exordium of the Areopagus Speech', 97).
[88]Zweck, 'The Exordium of the Areopagus Speech', 102.

religiosity leads to a focus on one example of their religious practices—their altar dedicated to the unknown god. Ironically, Paul's proclamation of this god leads to a condemnation of their religiosity.

The main arguments of the speech (17:24-29) building on the common ground of Jewish, Christian and Hellenistic sources, make a case for the nature of the one true God and a case against idolatry. Refutations of idolatry (vv. 24b, 25a, 29) place the Athenians under judgement for 'the objects of your worship' (v. 23; cf., v. 16). Although the purpose of God's providential care for all nations (vv. 25-26) was that they would 'search for God' (v. 27), Paul offers no encouragement that they have found God through their religious practices. Far from affirming their religious pluralism, Paul draws attention to their failure by the phrase 'perhaps grope for him and find him'. The optative mood of both verbs puts the outcome in question. And the meaning of 'grope' portrays a blind man feeling around in the dark.[89] The concessive expression that follows, 'though indeed he is not far from each one of us', only serves to emphasise the tragic failure of the blind groping in the dark. Even though God is so near and desires to be found, he is not found by this blind groping.[90]

True, the Athenians' own poets have expressed insights into the nature of God. The point of their insights that 'in him we live and move and have our being' and that 'we are the offspring of God' (17:28) is that since we are like God, God is like us, the true God is the living God (17:29a); therefore, 'we ought not to think that deity is like gold or silver or stone, an image formed by the art and imagination of mortals' (17:29b). Despite the insights of their own poets, however, the Athenians have been living in 'times of human ignorance' (17:30). They were wrong to think that God lived 'in shrines made by human hands' (v. 24); they were wrong to think that God needed gifts made by human hands (v. 25); they were wrong to think that different nations were under the patronage of different deities (v. 26);[91] they were wrong to think that the living God who is the source of our life could be like an inanimate idol (v. 29). Since in all these ways the theology of the Athenians is judged to be wrong, the speech cannot be taken as a positive evaluation of natural theology. Interpreters who find a positive view of natural theology in this speech[92] miss the force of

---

[89]Bruce, *Acts (The Greek Text)*, 337.

[90]Marshall, *Acts: Commentary*, 288: 'This groping takes place despite the nearness of God to men, of which Paul goes on to speak, and it may indicate the sinful failure of man to find God to which Romans 1:20f. point'.

[91]Winter, 'In Public and In Private', 142.

Paul's arguments against the idolatrous religiosity of the Athenians.

The conclusion (17:30-31) of all these arguments against the idolatry of the Athenians is the call to repentance in the face of impending judgement. Though God has graciously 'overlooked' their past ignorance (v. 30), they are not innocent.[93] Though God has postponed judgement, he has set a day for judgement, established a standard of righteousness for judgement, appointed a man to be the judge, and verified his appointment of that man by raising him from the dead (17:31). The entire speech has been aimed toward this announcement: a man raised by God from the dead will be the judge of the world. Placed under judgement by the Athenians for preaching alien gods named Jesus and the resurrection, Paul now warns them of judgement by the risen Jesus for worshipping alien gods. The resurrection of Jesus from the dead is proof (πίστις) provided by God to all of the certainty of future judgement. Fortunately, advance notice of this future judgement gives time for repentance in the present.

The narrative postlude to the speech keeps the attention on the resurrection as the theological focal point of the speech (17:32). In Aeschylus's account of the founding of the court of the Areopagus by the city's patron goddess Athene, a statement by Apollo denies the resurrection: 'Once a man dies and the earth drinks up his blood, there is no resurrection'.[94] Evidently, at least some of the members of the Areopogas council reasoned that they had the right to pass judgement in the present, since there would be no judgement in the future. Their ridicule of Paul's announcement of the resurrection expressed their judgement. Others, however, were open to learn more. And at least one member of the court was converted by Paul's 'proof' provided by the resurrection.

IV. Defence Speeches

Acts 21–28 portrays Paul defending himself against accusations of the Jews before Jewish and Roman authorities. His defence speeches[95] are about fifty percent of all his speeches in Acts.[96] This clearly indicates that defending Paul is a major purpose of Acts. But Luke's reasons for defending Paul are still the subject of much discussion. Is Luke's

92Dibelius, *Studies*, 60; Vielhauer, 'On the "Paulinism" of Acts', 36; Soards, *Speeches*, 98.
93Against Dibelius, *Studies*, 56.
94Aeschylus, *Eumenides*, 647.

defence of Paul a defence of Christianity against Roman judgement,[97] a defence of the Gentile mission and Gentile church against Jewish attack,[98] a defence of Paul against charges of apostasy from the Jewish faith,[99] a model for persecuted Christians to follow in their defence,[100] a portrayal of Paul as a competent Graeco–Roman rhetor[101] and moral philosopher,[102] or some combination of all the above? Our analysis will attempt to clarify Luke's theological evaluation and theological focal point of Paul's defence speeches by examining the interplay between the narrative context and the speeches.

Theological evaluation

In Luke's narrative of Paul's last visit to Jerusalem, he sets the stage for Paul's defence speeches by describing two misconceptions about Paul.

---

[95]Luke uses the term 'defence' (*apologia*) in noun and verb form 7 times (22:1; 24:10; 25:8, 16; 26:1, 2, 24). Rhetorical analysis of these speeches demonstrates their forensic structure and style. See Winter, 'Proceedings', 333; Veltman, 'The Defense Speeches of Paul in Acts', 257.

[96]Paul's mission speeches (Acts 13:16-41, 46-47; 14:15-17; 17:22-31; 20:18-35) total 49 verses; his farewell speech to the Ephesian elders (20:18-35) is 18 verses; his defence speeches (22:1, 3-21; 23:1, 3, 5-6; 24:10-21; 25:8, 10-11; 26:2-23, 25-27, 29; 28:17-20, 25-28) total 73 verses.

[97]So Haenchen, *Acts*, 630: 'the burning question for Luke and the Christians of his time: can Chritianity be understood in unbroken continuity with Judaism? If that is possible, then the Christian doctrine can be recognized as an inner-Jewish αἵρεσις and hence as a *religio quasi licita*'.

[98]Conzelmann, *Luke*, 147: 'the question still remains, how it is that the Gentile Christian church does not keep the Law and yet stands within the continuity of redemptive history'. Conzelmann suggests that Luke demonstrates the continuity with Jewish faith 'by emphasizing the agreement about one central dogma, the doctrine of general resurrection' in Paul's defence speeches (148).

[99]Jervell, *Luke*, 165: 'according to the charges and rumors, Paul is a false teacher in Israel. . . . the main point is not what Paul teaches Gentiles, nor is it that he preaches to them; rather, it consists in what he teaches Jews'.

[100]Dibelius, *Studies*, 213: 'when, in the five trial scenes examined here, Paul always says the same thing in his defence, it is because the author wants thereby'. commend to the Christians of his day the use of such themes in their own defence."

[101]Winter, 'Proceedings', 333: reading Paul's defence speeches 'in the light of the advice given in the handbooks on forensic speeches, especially the works of Cicero and Quintillian, shows that those in Acts 24–26 follow the conventions recommended in the handbooks'.

[102]Malherbe, *Paul and the Popular Philosophers*, 163: Luke 'represented Paul as speaking in language derived from discussions by and about the moral philosophers of his day'.

First, he is accused of being a teacher of apostasy to Jews in the Diaspora. James and the elders inform him of rumours that he is teaching Jews living among the Gentiles to forsake Moses, circumcision, and the customs (21:22). When some Jews find him in the temple they shout: 'Fellow Israelites, help! This is the man who is teaching everyone everywhere against our people, our law, and this place: more than that, he has actually brought Greeks into the temple and has defiled this holy place' (21:28). These accusations of teaching apostasy (ἀποστασίαν διδάσκεις) to Jews everywhere may well include an indirect attack on Paul's Gentile mission since Paul's offer of salvation to Gentiles would have been viewed as a negation of the cardinal doctrine of the election of Israel.[103] The second misconception about Paul is that he is a revolutionary. The Roman tribune, surprised by Paul's use of Greek, asks him, 'Do you know Greek? Then you are not the Egyptian who recently stirred up a revolt... ?' (21:37-38).

These two misconceptions about Paul prepare the way for two themes in the defence speeches: (a) Paul's identity as a Pharisee who is faithful to the law and customs of the Jewish people and (b) Paul's identity as a Roman citizen who is completely innocent under Roman law of all charges brought against him.[104] In his first defence speech Paul's description in Hebrew of his first class Jewish training at the feet of the great rabbi Gamaliel, where he was 'educated strictly according to our ancestral law, being zealous for God' (22:3) serves as the introduction to his conversion story. After that speech Paul's declaration that he was born a Roman citizen greatly impresses the Roman tribune, Claudius Lysias, who paid for his citizenship (22:25-29). In his second speech before the Sanhedrin, Paul strongly affirms his Jewish identity: 'I am a Pharisee, a son of Pharisees' (23:6). Luke then proceeds to underscore Paul's Roman citizenship and his innocence under Roman law in Lysias's letter to Felix (23:26-30). In Paul's third speech before Felix, he affirms his Jewish orthodoxy: 'I worship the God of our ancestors, believing everything laid down according to the law or written in the prophets' (24:14). In Paul's fourth speech before Festus,

---

103Against Jervell, *Luke*, 165: 'the main point is not what Paul teaches Gentiles, nor is it that he preaches to them; rather, it consists in what he teaches Jews'. But what Paul taught the Gentiles had implications for the Jews.
104Tajra, *Trial*, 61: 'As a Pharisee, Paul stands well within the mainstream of Judaism, he is therefore not the ringleader of a heretical, illegal or subversive sect. Paul's Roman citizenship plays a key role in his case. It allows him to make his appeal to Caesar which transforms the nature of his case and which enables him to come to Rome, the goal of Acts and the goal of Paul.'

he declares his innocence: 'I have in no way committed an offence against the law of the Jews, or against the Temple, or against the emperor' (25:8). In Paul's fifth speech before Agrippa, he reasserts his Jewish identity: 'I have belonged to the strictest sect or our religion and lived as a Pharisee' (26:5). After the speech Agrippa declares Paul's innocence under Roman law: 'this man is doing nothing to deserve death or imprisonment' (26:30-31). When Paul met with the Jewish leaders in Rome, he began his conversation (28:17-18) by refuting the charge of apostasy from Jewish law ('though I had done nothing against our people or the customs of our ancestors') and the charge of any violation of Roman law ('the Romans wanted to release me'). Since the speeches are all in the 'I' style[105] and relate uniquely to Paul's identity as a Pharisee and a Roman citizen, it seems clear that Luke's primary purpose is a personal defence of Paul's Jewish orthodoxy and legal innocence under Roman law.

It is not difficult to see how this purpose for the trial section (Acts 21–28) relates to the mission section (Acts 13–20) of Luke's biography of Paul. If Paul were rejected on the basis of his apostasy from Jewish law and his guilt under Roman law, then his Gentile mission and the Gentile church planted by that mission would be seriously undermined. As Jervell says, 'if the greatest segment of the Christian church stems from a Jewish apostate, then the church is not the restored Israel and likewise has no right to appeal to Israel's salvation.... Luke's concern is the struggle for the right of citizenship in the people of God, and it is in this context that the problem of Paul must be solved'.[106] So he portrays Paul as the faithful, orthodox teacher of Jewish doctrines. Paul's church is rooted in Jewish faith since Paul never taught anything but the Jewish faith.

Luke's struggle is also for the right of Christian citizens to be granted legitimacy in the Roman empire since their Christian religion is a faithful expression of the Jewish faith. He repeatedly draws attention to the uniquely Jewish nature of the accusations against Paul. The Roman officials, much like Gallio in Corinth (18:14-15), all state that Paul was only 'accused of questions of their law' (23:29), but is innocent under Roman law. Paul expresses his gratitude to King Agrippa that he can evaluate the Jewish accusations because he is 'especially familiar with all the customs and controversies of the Jews' (26:2-3). O'Toole points out the significance of Agrippa in this trial: 'The real

---

105Schubert, 'The Final Cycle of Speeches', 4.
106Jervell, *Luke*, 174.

importance of Agrippa II lies in the answer to the question still in the reader's mind: was Paul found guilty because the Roman officials did not understand the Jewish religion and so could not see where his guilt lay?'[107] Agrippa is presented as one Roman official who clearly understands the intricacies of the Jewish religion and on the basis of that knowledge emphatically declares Paul's innocence: 'This man could have been set free if he had not appealed to the emperor' (26:32). The point is that the accusations against Paul only have to do with intramural Jewish debates—they cannot be the basis for any judgement under Roman law. It is precisely because Paul is such a faithful adherent to Jewish doctrines, that his church should be granted the privileges of a *religio licita* already granted to the Jewish religion.

Evidently, Luke wrote for Christian readers who were threatened by Jewish neighbours and Roman authorities because of Paul.[108] Since Paul had been rejected by the Jewish people and executed under Roman law, his adherents faced a real problem. In the world around them, Paul's words were devalued to the level of apostate teaching and criminal speech. Luke presents a theological evaluation of Paul's defence to answer this double threat. Paul spoke not as a criminal and apostate, but as a faithful teacher of Israel and as a respected Roman citizen. More than that, as we shall see in the next section, Paul spoke as faithful witness to the resurrection who was personally commissioned by the risen Lord. Therefore, Paul's word must be accepted as the word of the Lord.

Theological focal point

Luke demonstrates the continuity between Paul's affirmation of Jewish orthodoxy and his witness to salvation in Christ by keeping the focus of the defence speeches on the resurrection. Luke repeatedly reminds his readers that Paul was really on trial for his belief in the resurrection: 'I am a Pharisee, a son of Pharisees. I am on trial concerning the hope of the resurrection of the dead' (23:6; 24:21; 26:6; 28:20). So from Luke's perspective the Jewish charges against Paul were not the primary cause for their attack. What they really objected to was Paul's proclamation of the resurrection of Christ. As Luke had already stated in Acts 4:2, the Jewish leaders were enraged because the apostles 'were

---

107See O'Toole, *Climax*, 34.
108Jervell, *Luke*, 177.

teaching the people and proclaiming in Jesus the resurrection from the dead'. Paul's defence speeches emphasise that belief in the resurrection of Christ is the hope of Israel, the fulfilment of the law and prophets (24:14-15), the fulfilment of the promise given by God to the fathers of Israel (26:6), the hope of the twelve tribes of Israel, the goal of all Jewish worship (26:7), and just what the Prophets and Moses said was going to take place (26:22). 'Belief in the resurrection is thus the distinguishing mark of Israel.'[109] Far from being a teacher of apostasy, Luke portrays Paul as the one true teacher of Israel by virtue of his faithful witness to the resurrection of Christ. In this, Luke draws attention to two aspects of Paul's witness to the resurrection of Christ.

First, Luke repeats Paul's conversion story twice in the defence speeches (22:4-16; 26:12-18) to emphasise that Paul's witness to the resurrection was commissioned and empowered by the risen Lord Jesus. We can see the development of this emphasis in Luke's careful revision of Paul's conversion story.[110] In Paul's first account of his conversion, he receives his commission through Ananias (22:12-16). The benefit of referring to Ananias in this speech before Jews in Jerusalem is seen in Paul's description of him as 'a man who was devout by the standard of the Law, and well spoken of by all the Jews' (22:12). Thus, Paul's commission was given to him by one who had not broken with his Jewish roots. The Jewish flavour of the commissioning through Ananias is also expressed by the traditional messianic title, 'Righteous One' (22:14).[111]

In this speech in the temple precincts, Paul relates how he received confirmation of the commission delivered through Ananias by a vision of the Lord in the temple who commanded him, 'Go! For I will send you far away to the Gentiles' (22:21). The parallels with the commissioning of Isaiah in the temple (Isa. 6) would have been obvious to devout Jews and should have proven his credentials as a great prophet like Isaiah. But in fact the message that Jesus was alive and appearing in a vision in the temple threw them into a frenzy of throwing off their cloaks and tossing dust in the air (22:22-23).

When we turn to Acts 26 and read Paul's retelling of his conver-

---

109Jervell, *Luke*, 170.
110Hedrick, 'Paul's Conversion/Call', 432: 'The differences and "contradiction" among the three accounts are to be explained by Luke's literary technique.' Hedrick gives a complete account of the differences between the three accounts in Acts and suggests that the changes were both theologically and stylistically motivated, but he does not draw out the theological motivations for Luke's redaction.
111Haenchen, *Acts*, 629; Longenecker, 'Acts', 526.

sion story before Agrippa, we find that he makes no mention that his commission came through the mediation of Ananias or through a vision in the Temple. Instead the entire commission is received on the road to Damascus directly from the risen Lord. Other changes heighten this revised version of the commissioning of Paul: not only a bright light (22:6), but a light brighter than the sun (26:13) surrounded not only Paul (22:6), but all those with Paul (22:13), so that not only Paul (22:7), but all those with Paul (26:14) fell to the ground. All of these changes draw attention to the exalted position of the one designated as Lord (26:15). Paul's use of the title 'Lord' for Jesus poses a direct contrast to Caesar who was given the same designation by Festus before Paul's speech (25:26).[112] In a setting where King Agrippa and Bernice had been welcomed with great pomp and ceremony (25:23), Paul described the incomparable majesty and glory of the risen Jesus who had commissioned him.

When Paul recounted the words of Christ (26:16-18), he was claiming that he had experienced what the prophets of Israel had experienced when they were commissioned by the Lord of Israel (cf., Isa. 6:9; Jer. 1:10; Dan. 10:11). He was appointed by the Lord to be his servant and witness (26:16) to the Gentiles (2:17). He was sent to do the work of the Lord: to open the eyes of the blind (26:18) was the work which Jesus had been sent to do (Luke 4:18) and which he accomplished (7:22). In this climatic retelling of his conversion story, Paul makes no mention of his own blindness (cf., 9:8; 22:11). Instead he is the one who is commissioned to open the eyes of the blind. The goal of opening the eyes of the blind is deliverance from darkness to light and from Satan to God, forgiveness of sins, and inheritance with all sanctified believers in Christ (26:18). All of this is the work of Christ: he came 'to shine upon those who sit in darkness and the shadow of death' (Luke 1:79; Acts 26:23); he delivered all who were oppressed by the devil (Acts 10:38); he forgave sins (Luke 5:20; 7:48; in Acts forgiveness is by faith in the risen Christ: 2:38; 5:31; 10:43; 13:38); and by the 'word of his grace' (the proclamation of the risen Christ) God gives 'the inheritance among all those who are sanctified' (Acts 20:32). All of this work of Christ is available to those who have faith in Christ (26:18).

What Luke has done in this speech is to merge Jesus' mission with Paul's mission. Paul continued the mission of Jesus. Paul was the link between Jesus and the church established by his mission. Not only was Paul's mission a continuation of the mission of Jesus because Paul

---

112O'Toole, *Climax*, 65.

did the work of Christ, but also because Christ did his work through Paul: Christ was raised from the dead 'to proclaim light both to the Jewish people and to the Gentiles' (26:23). O'Toole offers this helpful comment: 'Actually, Paul preaches to the Gentiles; the resurrected Christ has from the Father a mission which Paul performs. What Paul does can be predicated of Christ. So, the resurrected Christ cannot only be said to be in heaven; he is with and in Paul proclaiming light'.[113]

The second aspect of Luke's portrayal of Paul's witness to the resurrection is the divisive consequence of his witness. Paul's obedience to the heavenly vision (26:19) of the risen Christ in the pursuit of his Christ-given and Christ-empowered mission resulted in Christlike suffering: Jews seized him in the temple and tried to put him to death (26:21). The terms used here are used in the description of Christ's suffering (Luke 22:54; Acts 5:30). Since Paul's mission was the same as the mission of Christ, Jews rejected Paul just as they had rejected Christ. This rejection had been predicted by Christ (22:18) and by the Holy Spirit through the prophet Isaiah (28:25-27). In the final scene in Acts, there is a division between the Jews persuaded by Paul's proclamation of Jesus and 'others who would not believe' (28:23-24). This division brings to conclusion a major theme of Luke–Acts: the mission of Christ continued by the apostles and Paul brought restoration for repentant Israel and judgement on unrepentant Israel.[114] Luke's clear presentation of this sharp division in Israel excludes Paul's accusers, not Paul, from the true people of God. 'Paul, not his accusers, has the right to speak on behalf of the people and to represent Israel.'[115]

V. Conclusion

Acts ends with Paul in prison 'preaching the kingdom of God, and teaching concerning the Lord Jesus Christ with all openness, unhindered' (28:31). This conclusion is consistent with Luke's narrative of Paul's preaching and defence: it presents both the irresistible success of the word of God and the unavoidable suffering of one who preaches it. The success of the word of God is evidence that Jesus Christ is the risen Lord. Suffering for the word of God is the cost of identification with Christ in the world.[116]

---

[113]O'Toole, *Climax*, 119.
[114]Moessner, 'Paul in Acts', 96-104.
[115]Jervell, *Luke*, 171.
[116]Evans, 'Speeches in Acts', 302; Gaventa, 'Towards a Theology of Acts', 156-157.

Part III

THE RENEWING WORK OF GOD

CHAPTER 16

THE 'SPIRIT OF PROPHECY' AS THE POWER OF ISRAEL'S RESTORATION AND WITNESS

Max Turner

Summary

Part I first elucidates the main points of Lucan pneumatology on which scholarship appears to be agreed, then highlights the areas of dispute which are addressed in subsequent parts. Part II argues that the Holy Spirit in Acts can be understood exclusively as a Christianised version of the (Jewish) 'Spirit of Prophecy'. Part III indicates that Luke regards this gift as granted (normatively) in conversion-initiation, and Part IV attempts to explain why this is so by showing that for Luke the 'Spirit of prophecy' is not merely an empowering for mission, but a charismatic presence of the Spirit which the evangelist understands as necessary for the 'salvation' of Israel (= her messianic restoration). A concluding part offers brief remarks on the relation of this account of Luke's pneumatology to the more general aims of this volume.

I. Introduction

This introductory part of the article first summarises the main points of Lucan pneumatology on which scholarship appears to be agreed,[1] then highlights the areas of dispute which we shall address in subsequent parts. Part II argues that the Holy Spirit in Acts can be understood as a Christianised version of the (Jewish) 'Spirit of Prophecy'. Part III indicates that Luke regards this gift as granted (normatively) in conversion–initiation, and Part IV attempts to explain why this is so by showing that, for Luke, the 'Spirit of prophecy' is necessary to what the evangelist understands as the 'salvation' of Israel. A concluding part offers brief remarks on the relation of our account of Luke's pneumatology to the more general aims of this volume.

Areas of consensus on Lucan pneumatology

H. von Baer[2] set the agenda for subsequent scholarship, both methodologically (as a forerunner of redaction criticism) and in his intent to discover the specifically Lucan view of the Spirit. On the following points later research has done little more than to offer minor corrections and variations to his pioneering work.

(1) The essential background for Luke's pneumatological material is Jewish and deeply rooted in the OT. Von Baer maintained, especially against H. Leisegang, that Luke did not draw any significant traits of his conception of the Spirit from Greek mysticism, nor from Mantic prophetism.[3] The Spirit is not mere 'substance' but the presence,

---

[1]Constraints of space forbid a formal review of the *Forschung*. For an account of the development of scholarship see Turner, 'Significance' or *idem. Power*, chs. 1–2. For other types of survey of the literature see *e.g.*, Dubois, *De Jean-Baptiste*, iii-xx; Bovon, *Luke the Theologian*, ch. 4; Menzies, *Development*, ch. 1, and Mainville, *L'Esprit*, 19-47.

[2]*Geist.*

[3]Leisegang argued that Philo's conception of the prophetic Spirit provided a bridge between Greek concepts of πνεῦμα and those in the Church (*cf., Geist*). His second monograph attempted to derive virtually all the pneumatological material in the Synoptic Gospels from Hellenism, *cf.*, his title: *Pneuma Hagion: Der Ursprung des Geistesbegriffs der synoptischen Evangelien aus der griechischen Mystik*. For analysis and criticism of the latter see (*inter alios*) von Baer, *Geist, passim*; Barrett, *Spirit*, especially 3-4; 10-14; 36-41; Turner 'Significance', 134-42. For criticism of his understanding of the Spirit in Philo see von Baer, *Geist*, 27 (n. 18); Verbeke, *L'Evolution*, 236-60, and Isaacs, *Concept*, 28, 29, 54-8, 60-61, 141-2.

empowering and saving activity of the God of Israel himself, the self-revealing extension of his person and vitality into history. In maintaining an OT background to Luke's pneumatology, however, von Baer was also affirming a contrast with the more developed and distinctively Christian Johannine and Pauline portraits of the Spirit. The Spirit in Luke–Acts has often since been considered 'Old Testament' in character both in the range of broadly charismatic activities attributed to the Spirit and in the language used to describe them,[4] although it would almost certainly be safer to characterise the language and ideas as 'early Jewish Christian', as it is usually recognised that Luke's material also reflects distinctive Inter-Testamental Period (ITP) understandings of the Spirit and significant Christian developments.

(2) The Spirit is the uniting motif and driving force within the Lucan salvation history, and provides the legitimation of the mission to which this leads. One of von Baer's central arguments against the alleged Hellenism of Luke's pneumatology was that the diverse manifestations of the Spirit in Luke–Acts all combine to serve this distinctively Jewish motif. In Luke 1–2, the Spirit brings about the birth of the Messiah who is to redeem Israel (1:32-35), affords prophecies relating to the saving events about to unfold (1:42-43, 67-79; 2:25-32), and empowers the Elijianic forerunner who prepares the way of the Lord (1:15,17). In Luke 3–4 the Spirit then comes as Jesus' messianic empowering for the redemptive mission, while Pentecost brings a parallel endowment for the Church's mission, over which the Spirit remains the initiator (*cf.*, esp. Acts 2:4; 8:29; 10:19, 44; 11:12; 13:2,4 *etc.*), the driving power (Luke 24:49; Acts 1:8; 4:31; 9:17,31), the guide in significant decisions (16:6,7; 19:21; 20:22-23), and the legitimator of the whole endeavour, especially at its most delicate points (*cf.*, 5:32; 8:17-18; 10:44-45,47; 11:15-18; 15:28).[5] For von Baer these different activities of the Spirit divided salvation history into three sharply distinguished epochs (each characterised by its own distinctive type[s] of activity of the Spirit)[6]—(1) the OT/time of promise terminating with Jesus' baptism,[7] (2) the period of Jesus' ministry during which he alone is empowered (*cf.*, 4:14, 4:18-21) by the Spirit (John the Baptist having

---

[4]So especially Lampe, 'Holy Spirit', 159-200; George, 'L'Esprit Saint', 513-15; 528-29; Chevallier, 'Luc', 1-16; Mainville, *L'Esprit*, esp. 323-332.

[5]*Cf.*, Shepherd, whose (broader) thesis is that the function of the Spirit in Luke's writings 'is to signal narrative reliability' and so to provide the confirmation of the Gospel throughout Luke–Acts (*Function*, 247 and *passim*).

[6]See esp. *Geist* 111, but also the majority of Part 1 (43-112).

effectively been removed from its commencement by the notice in
3:19-21, and the epoch concluding with Jesus' ascension and the redactionally high-lighted 'Spiritless' interregnum of Acts 1:12-26),[8] and
(3) the period of the church empowered for witness by the Pentecostal
Spirit. The significance of this periodisation has proved more
contentious.

(3) For Luke, the Spirit is largely the 'Spirit of prophecy'; in Acts especially as an 'empowering for witness'. Von Baer saw that the Spirit was
essentially the 'Spirit of prophecy' in each of the 'epochs', though in
different ways—mainly as oracular speech in Luke 1–2; as the unique
messianic endowment to proclaim eschatological liberation and God's
reign (and to effect these with words of power) in the ministry of Jesus,
and the power of inspired witness to Jesus in the period of the Church.
In connection with the third of these, von Baer drew attention to Luke
24:49 and Acts 1:8 (gateway redactional texts into Acts) which above
all characterise the Spirit as the power to witness;[9] to Peter's Pentecost
speech which programmatically describes the promise of the Spirit to
all Christians as the gift of the 'Spirit of prophecy' promised by Joel
(2:17-18, 33 and 38-39), and to the way the narrative of Acts repeatedly
associates the Spirit with witness, if in different ways.

(a) As a gift that is God's own witness to the gospel especially towards
Jews (2:33-36; cf., 5:32); (b) as God's witness to those who are his
people, i.e., through the gift of the Spirit he attests to them as his own
(esp. 15:8; cf., 5:32);[10] (c) as the mediator of confident assurance of the
Gospel testimony to the believer;[11] (d) as the inspiration to give
witness (esp. 4:31);[12] (e) as providing charismata which make the
content of the witness more dramatic and effective (including e.g.,
signs and wonders alongside the preaching, but also charismatic
wisdom enhancing the speech event and other forms of inspiration
empowering them); (f) as part of the content of the witness (Acts 2!)

---

[7]Von Baer can also speak of 1:35 as the beginning of the new epoch in which 'der
Geist Gottes als Wesen des Gottessohnes in dieser Welt erscheint' (Geist, 48).
[8]Geist, 79-85.
[9]Geist, 84.
[10]Cf., Kee, Good News, 35-36.
[11]According to von Baer the Spirit in Acts 2 provides the robust assurance (going
beyond mere 'faith') of Jesus' exaltation as Christ and Lord (Geist, 99).
[12]Geist, 102-103. Von Baer himself would include Luke 12:10 under this motif
(blasphemy against the Spirit being taken as refusal to bear the testimony to Christ
that the Spirit prompts (Geist 137-45)), and this has been widely accepted; but, per
contra, see Turner, 'The Spirit and the Power of Jesus' Miracles', 142-43, esp. n. 46.

and (g) as the Lord of the witnesses (guiding, encouraging, *etc.*).[13]

In continuity with von Baer, the major works on Lucan pneumatology have increasingly emphasised Luke's tendency to portray the Spirit as the 'Spirit of prophecy', even if they have drawn quite different conclusions from it.[14]

(4) Correspondingly Luke shows relatively little interest in the Spirit as the power of the spiritual, ethical and religious renewal of the individual. Gunkel had argued the Spirit in the primitive community reflected in Acts was naked supernatural power (especially of miraculous speech, such as prophecy and tongues), and discerned simply by cause and immediate effect, not in terms of the inspiration of less 'charismatic' activities furthering some divine plan and or working towards some theological goal. As the charismatic 'Spirit of prophecy' the Spirit might thus be expected to have little or no bearing on ordinary Christian life.[15] Von Baer pointed out the weaknesses of such a portrait. The miraculous speech in question for Luke was mainly witness to Christ and the Spirit was evidently the driving power of the Church's mission, and of salvation-history more generally. It seemed to follow that the Spirit might be discerned behind virtually all Christian witness, not merely in the most blatantly supernatural events of it. By analogy, the Spirit who gave the charismatic *paraklesis* (9:31) and joy (4:33; 13:52) and fear of the Lord (5:1-10) which built up the church, should also be traced behind the more general community life of the congregations depicted in the summaries (esp. 2:42-47; 4:32-37).[16] Again, in contrast to the *religiongeschichtliche Schule*'s assertion that there was little of significance in common between the religious life of Jesus and that of earliest churches, von Baer (with Büchsel) maintained that for Luke the Spirit was the power of Jesus' life of sonship (Luke 1:35; 3:22), and equally of that of the Church.[17] But von Baer agreed

---

[13]Hence the Spirit cannot be reduced to Gunkel's 'naked supernatural power' (see von Baer, *Geist*, 103-104; 184-92).

[14]Most notable in developing von Baer's emphasis are the contributions by Lampe, 'Holy Spirit', Schweizer, 'πνεῦμα, κτλ., *TDNT* VI:389-455'; Haya-Prats, *El Espíritu*; *idem*, *L'Esprit*; Stronstad, *Charismatic Theology*; Menzies, *Development*, and Mainville, *L'Esprit*. In two works Shelton has developed the concept of the Spirit as the power of witness, though without clearly relating this to the Jewish concept of the 'Spirit of prophecy' (Shelton, '"Filled"' and *Mighty*). On these see Turner, '"Empowerment"?'.

[15]See Gunkel, *Wirkungen* (ET *Influence*, esp. 1-71), and on him Turner and Menzies (as at n. 1).

[16]*Geist*, 185-92.

that the evidence in favour of these conclusions was relatively fragmentary: *i.e.,* he conceded Luke showed relatively little interest in the Spirit's role in the religious renewal of the individual. The Spirit is portrayed first and foremost as charismatic empowering. There have since been those who have deemed the 'little interest' to be effectively none (*e.g.,* Schweizer and Menzies), but the careful study of Haya-Prats (himself rather closer to Gunkel than to von Baer at points) has shown this to be premature.[18] Others (most notably J.D.G. Dunn)[19] have attempted to make new covenant life of sonship by the Spirit (and correlative experience of the kingdom of God) central to Luke's pneumatology, but this too has required revision.[20]

(5) Luke's pneumatology develops beyond Judaism in giving the Spirit Christocentric functions. If Luke's pneumatology owes much to the Jewish conception of the 'Spirit of prophecy', he goes beyond any usual Jewish ideas (a) in making the Spirit the chief witness to the Christ event (the charismatic preaching centres on this), and (b) in casting the exalted Messiah as the one who 'pours out' this Spirit in God's place as his own executive power (2:33), and as the one who becomes present and known to the disciple *in* the Spirit (*e.g.,* in visionary and other charismatic experiences), and extends his influence through them.[21] The 'Spirit of the Lord' has thus effectively become the 'Spirit of Jesus' too (*cf.,* 16:6-7), and Jesus has become significantly identified with 'the Lord' of Joel 2:28-32 [3:1-5 LXX/MT] upon whose name one is to call for salvation (by baptism 'in the name of Jesus Christ', [*cf.,* Acts 2:21,33-36,38-39]).[22] Von Baer was careful to note that Luke–Acts does not go as far as to make the Spirit 'the Paraclete' (*i.e.,* the personal presence of Jesus as Advocate/Revealer when Jesus himself is withdrawn through the ascension), nor does Luke present the Spirit quite as clearly as Paul does as the 'Spirit of Christ' who both mediates personal union with the heavenly Lord and radically stamps the believer with his eschato-logical sonship. But von

---

[17]*Geist*, 16-20.
[18]*L'Esprit*, ch. 6.
[19]Especially *Baptism*, chs. 2–9.
[20]Dunn himself has subsequently charged Luke with almost complete disregard for the experience of eschatological sonship mediated by the Spirit (*Jesus*, 191). His more recent contributions accept that for Luke the Spirit 'is indeed pre-eminently the Spirit of prophecy' ('Baptism', 8; *cf.,* earlier *Jesus* 189-91; *Unity*, 180-84).
[21]*Geist*, 39-43; 80-85; 99; 174.
[22]*Geist*, 93-94. *Cf.,* Stählin, '"Τὸ πνεῦμα'Ιησοῦ"'; Turner, 'The Spirit of Christ', *idem,* '"Divine" Christology', esp. 413-24, 434-36.

Baer perceived that Luke has important elements of these more developed conceptions, and several have attempted to tease out further this aspect of Luke's thought.[23]

Areas of continuing disagreement about Lucan pneumatology

There is sharpest disagreement on the following (closely related) questions. (a) Was the Spirit in Acts Joel's 'Spirit of prophecy' alone (or some broader gift based in other OT promises of the Spirit), and what range of charismata and effects are attributable to this gift? (b) How did Luke relate the Spirit to conversion-initiation? (c) Was the Spirit for Luke merely a *donum superadditum*[24] of charismatic empowering or did the Spirit also have soteriological functions? We shall treat these seriatim in the following sections.

II. The Spirit as the 'Spirit of Prophecy' in Acts

(a) Does Acts imply that the Spirit given to all Christians is the 'Spirit of prophecy' promised by Joel? Two lines of evidence secure an unequivocally affirmative reply to this question. First, the nature of the gift of the Spirit promised to Christians in 2:38-39 is clear enough—it is Joel's gift of the Spirit of prophecy. His audience will hardly expect Peter to be speaking of any other gift of the Spirit when he has so carefully explained Pentecost in terms of fulfilment of Joel (*cf.*, 2:15-21,33). When Peter states that all those who are baptised receive the 'gift of the Holy Spirit', what he says continues to refer back to the

---

[23]*Cf.*, Stählin and Turner (as previous note). Mainville (*L'Esprit* 333 (*cf.*, also 337)) can even describe the Spirit in Acts as 'the presence of Jesus when Jesus is absent', thereby consciously evoking Raymond Brown's own description of the Johannine Paraclete and applying it to the Spirit in Acts (though see the qualification in n. 17). MacRae admits the pneumatology of Acts is the biggest challenge to characterisation of Luke–Acts as portraying an 'absentee Christology' ('Christology', 151-65). O'Toole and others have made a convincing case that it is precisely texts such as Acts 18:10 (with *e.g.*, Luke 21:15; Acts 2:14-38; 5:31; 9:4-5 (22:7; 26:14), 9:34, etc.) that most truly represents Luke's Christology, which is rather one of soteriological omnipresence, and the chief means of that saving presence is the Spirit (*cf.*, O'Toole, *Unity*, esp. chs. 2–3; also his essay 'Risen Christ', 471-98). *Cf.*, Buckwalter, *Character and Purpose* (esp. 211-31), and his essay in this volume.
[24]*I.e.*, a 'second' grace, or enabling, distinct from the gift of salvation and granted subsequent to it.

wording of Joel 2:28-32 [LXX 3:1-5].

> Thus his affirmation that this ἐπαγγελία ('promise'; cf., 2:33) is offered
> 'to you and to your children' takes up and reaffirms Joel's promise
> that the Spirit will be poured out 'on your sons and daughters' (2:17c).
> When Peter then insists that the promise is to 'all' called by God (cf.,
> καὶ πᾶσιν: 2:17b), the basis for his claim lies in Joel's assertion, 'I will
> pour out my Spirit on *all flesh*' (2:28a [3:1a]), and the amplifying
> phrase τοὺς εἰς μακράν ('to all those who are far off') draws on Joel
> too (LXX 3:4; MT 3:8)). Finally, the assertion that the gift will be given
> to everyone 'whom the Lord our God calls to him' alludes to the last
> words of Joel's oracle (2:32 [3:5b]: 'whomsoever the Lord calls'), not
> cited earlier by Peter.

Peter thus draws on the wording of Joel's prophecy not merely
for the basis of the universality spoken of, but, consequently, for the
very nature of the promised gift itself.

Second, in the rest of Acts the Spirit is consistently portrayed as
the source of the very gifts Judaism regarded as proto-typical to the
'Spirit of prophecy':[25]

> (a) The Spirit is thus the author of *revelatory visions* and *dreams*:
> programmatically at 2:17, but also specifically at Acts 7:55-56 (and
> Luke would probably trace such vision/dream guidance as 9:10-18;
> 10:10-20; 16:9-10 and 18:9-10; 22:17-18,21; 23:11 to the Spirit (cf., the
> specific mention of Spirit in these contexts, 10:19; 16:6-7)[26]

> (b) The Spirit gives *revelatory words* or *instruction* or *guidance*: 1:2; 1:16
> (=OT); 4:25 (=OT); 7:51 (=OT); 8:29; 10:19; 11:12,28; 13:2,4; 15:28; 16:6-
> 7; 19:21; 20:22,23; 21:4,11 and 28:25 (=OT)

> (c) the Spirit grants *charismatic wisdom* or *revelatory discernment*: Luke
> 21:15 and Acts 5:3; 6:3,5,10; 9:31; 13:9 and 16:18

> (d) the Spirit inspires *invasive charismatic praise, e.g.,* the tongues on the
> day of Pentecost: 2:4; 10:46; 19:6, and

> (e) the Spirit inspires *charismatic preaching* or *witness* (Acts 1:4,8; 4:8,31;
> 5:32; 6:10; 9:17) or *charismatic teaching* (9:31; 13:52 and 18:25(?) *etc*.)—
> the former is not strictly anticipated in Judaism, but it is an obvious

---

[25]*Cf*., Turner, 'The Spirit of Prophecy and the Power of Authoritative Preaching',
66-88 (esp. 72-76 for typology of gifts prototypical to Jewish views of 'Spirit of
prophecy'). A more detailed account is available in Turner, *Power*, chs. 3–5.
[26]*Contra* Haya-Prats (*L'Esprit* §4).

extension of the Jewish concept of the Spirit as the Spirit of prophecy (combining some of the above), and derives from pre-Lucan Christianity.[27]

Along with the specific references to the Baptist's promise (1:5; 11:16) and references to believers receiving this gift of the Spirit (specified explicitly as Joel's gift at 2:17-18, 33; 38-39 and as 'the same Spirit' at 10:44,45,47; 11:15; 15:8),[28] the above include nearly all of the references to the Spirit in the book of Acts.[29] Luke then evidently regards 'the promise' made to believers to be a christianised version of Joel's 'Spirit of prophecy': (*contra* Dunn and J. Kremer) he does not synthesise some more composite 'promise of the Spirit' by adding other OT prophecies of the eschatological Spirit (such as Ezekiel 36) alongside Joel's.[30] In that sense Acts 2:14-39 is genuinely programmatic for the pneumatology of Acts.

(b) The conclusion that Luke's pneumatology is based in Jewish conceptions of the 'Spirit of prophecy' has become the basis for the claim that Luke could therefore not attribute either miracles or the ethical life of the community to the Spirit (especially Schweizer and Menzies).[31] This, however, needs to be challenged. The most widely read Jewish literature, the biblical translations (LXX and Targums), made virtually no attempt to distance the Spirit from miracles.[32] The same writings can at times even strengthen the conception of the Spirit (understood as the 'Spirit of prophecy') as the power of the righteous life (*e.g.*, when *Targum Pseudo-Jonathan* renders Gen. 6:3 'Did I not put my holy spirit

---

[27]See Turner, 'The Spirit of Prophecy and the Power of Authoritative Preaching', esp. 68-72, 87-88.

[28]Other reference to believers receiving the Spirit are 8:15,16,17,18,19 and 19:2,6.

[29]We are left with only eight occasions that do not immediately fit the categories of gifts we would regard as prototypical of the Spirit of prophecy: (1) Acts 5:3,9 referring to Ananias and Sapphira 'lying to' and 'testing' the Holy Spirit by their deceit; (2) Acts 6:5 and 11:24, ascribing charismatic 'faith' to the Spirit, and 13:52 similarly charismatic 'joy'; (3) 8:39 which speaks of the Spirit snatching Philip up and transporting him away; (4) 10:38, referring to Jesus' own anointing with Spirit and power, and (5) 20:28 where the Spirit is described as appointing overseers. These can all, nevertheless, be understood as pertaining to activities of the Spirit of prophecy: see Turner, *Power*, ch. 13, esp. §2.2.

[30]On this point, against Dunn, 'Baptism', 21-22, see Menzies, 'Luke and the Spirit', esp. 131-33.

[31]Schweizer ('πνεῦμα, κτλ.', 407-409) made the claim but with no independent analysis of Judaism; Menzies, (*Development*, chs. 2–5) attempted to substantiate Schweizer's claim by showing ITP writers were reticent to attribute miracles or ethical effects to the Spirit.

[32]See Turner, 'The Spirit and the Power of Jesus' Miracles', 132-34.

in them that they might perform good deeds?' (*cf.*, also *Neofiti*, and compare translations of Isa. 11:1-4; 44:3; Ezek. 36:26, etc.). Within the variety of other ITP Jewish writings there is also ample further evidence that miracles of power could be attributed to the Spirit/Spirit of prophecy,[33] and that the same Spirit might have considerable religious/ethical effects.[34] Of perhaps special importance is the trajectory of broadly 'messianic' expectations built from the davidic figure in Isaiah 11:1-9 (*cf.*, 1 Enoch 49:2-3; Psalms of Solomon 17:37, 18:7; 1QSb 5:25; 4Q215; 4Q252; 4Q285; 4QpIsa[a] 3:15-23; *Test. Levi* 18:7, *etc.*). The Spirit of prophecy which brings him charismatic wisdom and understanding is simultaneously 'the spirit of knowledge and of the fear of the Lord' (so a considerable religious/ethical influence on him; one which 1 Enoch 62:1-2 can sum up as 'the Spirit of righteousness') and the source of the 'might' which enables him to effect Israel's eschatological liberation, cleansing and restoration. Luke (following his sources) has sketched his portrait of the Messiah partly against such a background.

> Luke 1–2 is redolent with hopes for a *Davidic Messiah* who will redeem Israel and transformingly restore her, making her a light to the Gentiles (*cf.*, 1:32-33,35; 68-79; 2:25-26, 29-35, 38). Luke uses traditional material which traced Jesus' conception as the 'holy' Son of God to the Spirit (a work of power with no little religious ethical/import!) and combined this with an allusion to Isaiah 32:15, and hence to the Spirit as the source of Israel's renewal (1:35). In 2:40-52 he uses a further messianic tradition to depict Jesus as full of wisdom and aware of his unique sonship and consecration to God's purposes. Jesus' reception of the Spirit on the occasion of his baptism (3:21-22) must then be understood as bringing Jesus a new nexus of activities—not (*contra* Dunn) 'eschatological sonship', which has been more than fully assured by 1:35 (and displayed in 2:40-52), but empowering for the messianic task. The voice from heaven alludes to Psalm 2:7 and Isaiah 42:1-2 and so interprets the coming of the Spirit upon him as the enabling to fulfil the task of the royal Messiah and of the prophetic Isaianic Servant-Herald, and Luke builds on both motifs. It is as the messianic Son and Isaianic Servant-Warrior (*cf.*, Isa. 49:24-25/Luke 11:20-22) that he represents Israel in a replay of the Exodus/wilderness testing of the nation (4:1-13). With the Spirit's aid (as 4:1 redactionally implies) Jesus overcomes Satan in the contest situation,

---

[33]See Turner, 'The Spirit and the Power of Jesus' Miracles', 134-36; *idem. Power*, ch. 4.

[34]*Cf.*, Turner, 'The Spirit of Prophecy and the Ethical/Religious Life', esp. 169-86.

and returns to Galilee 'in the power of the Spirit' (4:14) to proclaim and effect Israel's release in terms of fulfilment of the hopes then associated with Isaiah 61 (Luke 4:18-21). Luke's main source in 4:16-30 had already presented Jesus as the Isaianic soteriological prophet announcing Israel's messianic Jubilee and New Exodus, and Luke used this (and the obvious thematic connections with Is. 42:1-7) to fuse his royal and Mosaic-prophetic-Servant christologies.[35] From the perspective of this passage and its associated hopes Jesus is empowered by the Spirit to free Israel from her 'slave-poverty', 'exile-captive' and 'blind' estate and lead her along the wilderness way towards restored Zion. The task includes miraculous healings and exorcisms for the former were traditionally associated with the New Exodus (and also coming to be linked with the Messiah: *cf.*, 4Q521) and the latter were readily explained as part of Israel's release from her spiritual enemies (*cf.*, 11QMelchizedek). Similar hopes are echoed in Luke's one description of Jesus' ministry in Acts (10:36-39).

If Luke has taken over and even reinforced such Jewish and Jewish-Christian ideas of the Spirit of prophecy on the Messiah,[36] the burden of proof rests on the shoulders of those who claim that Luke's understanding of the Spirit as the 'Spirit of prophecy' would inevitably have precluded his associating the Spirit with the miracles in Acts or with the religious ethical transformation of the community depicted there. We shall revisit this question in section IV.

III. The gift of the Spirit and conversion–initiation

This has been a major battleground in several wars. Acts has proved to be the Waterloo for those campaigning for a Confirmationist position —that the Pentecostal gift of the Spirit is normally conveyed by laying on of apostolic/episcopal hands subsequent to conversion (Thornton, Dix, Adler), or a Sacramentalist one—that the Pentecostal Spirit is normally conveyed by the water rite of baptism (Lampe and Beasley-Murray).[37] The positions advocated at present are: (1) Acts has no consistent norm, but reflects a diversity of sources and/or practices

---

[35]*Cf.*, Turner, 'Jesus and the Spirit'; also 'Holy Spirit'; *idem. Power*, ch. 9; Strauss, *Davidic Messiah*, 263-304.

[36]Turner, 'The Spirit and the Power of Jesus' Miracles', argues (against Schweizer and Menzies) that Luke reaffirmed the tradition that Jesus worked miracles by the messianic 'Spirit of prophecy' upon him. But *cf.*, Menzies, 'Spirit and Power', and, for rejoinder, Turner, *Power*, chs. 6–9.

(*e.g.*, Quesnel);[38] (2) the norm is a conversion–initiation pattern in which conversional repentance/faith is crystalised in baptism, and the Spirit is received in connection with the whole process (so Dunn),[39] or (3) the norm is that the Spirit is given subsequent to conversion and 'salvation' (*i.e.*, as a *donum superadditum, e.g.*, of prophetic empowering for mission: so Stronstad, Mainville, Menzies). The evidence supports the second of these in so far as (a) 2:38-39 paradigmatically associates the gift of the Spirit with conversional faith and baptism, (b) the only passage which postpones the gift of the Spirit to a point discernibly later than Christian baptism is Acts 8:12-17, and 8:16 implies this was exceptional (the notice would be redundant if the Spirit were normally given subsequent to baptism), and (c) the paradigm of 2:38-39 must be assumed for the numerous occasions (before Acts 8 and beyond it; *cf.* especially 2:41; 8:36-38; 16:15, 33; 18:8 *etc.*) where people are explicitly said to come to faith, or to be baptised, but where reception of the Spirit is not mentioned (*i.e.*, the reader is to assume such conversional faith and baptism is met with the gift of the Spirit unless, as in 8:16, it is stated otherwise).

> Acts 19:1-6 has often been taken as a counter-example, but it is probably not. In sharp contrast to Apollos, who was a Spirit-inspired preacher of Jesus although (like the disciples of Jesus) he had experienced only the baptism of John (18:24-28)—if he could still be taught the way 'more accurately' this notice can hardly mean he was resubjected to Christian baptism or topped up with the Spirit[40]—the twelve 'disciples' at Ephesus have *not* heard of the gift of the Spirit, and *are rebaptised*: *i.e.*, Paul treats them as those in the process of conversion.[41] What 'news' do they 'hear' (19:5a) from Paul that becomes grounds for their baptism? It can hardly be that John preached repentance and a coming Messiah (if they had not professed *that*, Paul could hardly have assumed they were true Messianic 'disciples' in the first place); the only other item of information in 19:4 is that *Jesus* is the

---

[37]See especially Lampe, *Seal*, and Dunn, *Baptism (passim); cf.*, also Bovon, *Luke, the Theologian*, 229-37, under the heading 'The Holy Spirit and the Laying on of Hands'. Price, 'Confirmation' argues for a Confirmationist theology of the Spirit in Acts on the ground that the Spirit in Acts is a *donum superadditum*.

[38]Quesnel, *Baptisés*, with good review of previous adherents. *Cf.* also Haya-Prats and Shepherd. For critique of Quesnel see Turner, *Power*, ch. 12, §2.2.D.

[39]*Baptism in the Holy Spirit*, chs. 4–9; similarly Montague, 'Fire'.

[40]*Contra* Shepherd, *Function*, 228-29.

[41]These crucial distinctives render improbable Menzies' view that the Ephesian disciples are converts of Apollos, and as fully Christian as he is (see *Development*, 268-77. A similar position is held by Kim, *Geisttaufe*, 212-38).

Messiah they were hoping for. But if that was the *novum* they 'heard', little wonder they were subsequently 'baptised into the Lord Jesus'; they were not yet fully *Christian* disciples. For whatever reason Luke has portrayed them as 'almost' Christians up to 19:4,[42] the point remains that *the Spirit is then granted as usual as part of their conversion-initiation package —no significant 'delay' is implied between 19:5 and 19:6* (and Paul's question in 19:3 presupposes the Spirit is *normally* given in connection with Christian baptism: *i.e.*, where baptism has not led to this gift one *must* question the baptism).

What does this say about the nature of the gift of the Spirit in Acts? Von Baer argued (against Gunkel) that if the Spirit was given to all and at conversion then it was unlikely that the gift was conceived of purely as a charismatic empowering.[43] It is to the issues that we now turn.

IV. A *Donum Superadditum* or a soteriological necessity?

We have noted in I.(3) above there is general agreement that the gift of the Spirit in Acts is above all a prophetic empowerment to witness to Jesus. This has usually been interpreted in one of two ways: (a) scholars in the classical Pentecostal tradition (especially Stronstad and Menzies)[44] have inclined to argue that Luke understands the Pentecostal gift to the disciples in parallel to Jesus' Jordan experience, and so exclusively[45] as a *donum superadditum* empowering mission (Luke 4:18-21/Luke 24:47-49; Acts 1:8; 2:11),[46] and the disciples' Pentecostal experience has then been taken as paradigmatic for all believers; (b) Haya-Prats and Mainville have argued for a charismatic endowment serving more wide ranging (including ecclesiastically orientated) ends.

---

[42]For due criticism of the unlikely explanations of Käsemann, Wilkens and Wolter, see above all Barrett, 'Apollos', and Menzies, *Development*, 268-70.

[43]*Geist*, 190-192.

[44]Stronstad, *Charismatic Theology*, 51-52; Menzies, *Development*, 198-207; but *cf.*, Shelton, *Mighty*, chs. 10–11.

[45]For the 'exclusively' see Stronstad, *Charismatic Theology*, 12; Menzies, 'Luke and the Spirit', 119 and 138-39.

[46]The parallels Luke provides between Jordan and Pentecost have long been observed: see esp. von Baer, *Geist*, 85; Talbert, *Literary Patterns*, 16; Chevallier, 'Luc', 5; Stronstad, *Theology*, ch. 4; O'Reilly, *Word*, 29-52; Russell, 'The Anointing', 47-63; Aker, 'New Directions', 108-127; Mainville, *L'Esprit*, 285-86, 291; Menzies, *Development*, 201 (n. 2), 206-207.

1. The Spirit exclusively as empowerment for mission? This interpretation is certainly too narrow to be sustained, and the argument
from the parallels with Jesus' case may prove a double-edged sword.[47]
To be sure, Luke highlights the gift of the Spirit to the apostles as an
empowering to witness (Luke 24:47-49; Acts 1:8), but that is because
the expansion of the witness is a major plot in Acts, and the twelve
(especially Peter) are the leaders in this (at least as far as Acts 15).
Similarly, the immediate co-text perhaps focuses the gift of the Spirit
to Paul (9:17) as empowering for mission, but if this is so (and it is not
explicit) such an emphasis would be perfectly understandable in the
light of the fact that it is Paul's mission that will dominate Luke's
account from chapter 13 onwards. One hardly needs to assume that
Luke thought the gift was granted these leaders as missionary
empowering alone. Neither Judaism nor early Christianity prepared
for such an idea. Nor would it be comprehensible why Luke should
think such a gift universal and normatively given at conversion (see III
above):

> Luke evidently does not believe that all converts immediately go out
> to preach like Paul in Damascus (9:20): rather, according to Luke's
> paradigmatic summary in 2:42-47, they receive instruction, and share
> in the table fellowship, worship, and communal life of the church. By
> and large in Jerusalem it is not the company of believers in general but
> the apostles who preach, work signs, and have 'the ministry of the
> word of God' (6:2: cf., 4:33). In this they are joined by some specially
> endowed people like Stephen (cf., 6:8,10) and Philip (8:5-40, cf., 'the
> evangelist' (21:8)), or, on one unusual occasion, by a household of
> 'friends' of Peter and John (4:23,31). The tale is similar beyond Acts 8.
> Luke may well have believed a majority of Christians became in-
> volved in different types of spoken witness but (perhaps surprisingly)
> he nowhere explicitly states that the rank-and-file of the church (far
> less immediate converts) actively spread the word. Rather this seems
> to be left to people like Philip, Paul, Barnabas, John Mark, Silas,

---

[47]Dunn, *Baptism in the Holy Spirit*, chs. 3–4, presses the same parallels to prove the
disciples only enter the new covenant and eschatological sonship at Pentecost. But
the argument from parallels need careful analysis. The many parallels between
Jesus' journey towards suffering in the fifth and final part of Luke and that of Paul
in the fifth and final part of Acts hardly mean their sufferings are of symmetrical
theological import. In the case of the Jordan/Pentecost parallels the argument is
'double-edged' because Jesus comes to Jordan as the very impress of the Spirit
(1:35) while the disciples have no corresponding experience. One might then argue
Pentecost must include not merely an empowerment parallel to Luke 3:22 but also
the component of Jesus' experience derived from Luke 1:35 which they lack.

Timothy, Apollos, *i.e.*, evangelists and their co-workers (of whom no doubt Luke knew far more than he has named: *cf.*, 8:4;[48] 11:19-20, *etc.*).

Nor is there any suggestion that the Spirit given to the Samaritans, to Cornelius' household, or to the Ephesian 'twelve', is exclusively an empowerment for mission, and, in fact, Luke does not explicitly associate any of these parties with evangelistic activities of any kind.[49] Finally, this view needs to turn a blind eye to a whole series of pneumatological texts in Acts that clearly have little or nothing to do with missionary empowering, but where activities of the Spirit serve the spiritual life of the church (or of individuals within it). For a consideration of these we must turn above all to Haya-Prats' research.

2. The Spirit as the charismatic empowering of the church. Mainville and Haya-Prats while recognising that for Luke the Spirit is above all the driving force of the mission, nevertheless admit this is not the whole story. Most notable amongst the many texts that have virtually no direct evangelistic significance, and, rather, evidently speak of actions of the Spirit for the benefit of the church herself, are 5:3,9 (Ananias and Sapphira's sin is a lying to the Spirit; implying the Spirit monitors the holiness of the church); 6:3 (those endowed with wisdom from the Spirit are appointed to serve tables in the context of a dispute); 11:28 (Agabus' prophecy of famine allows the Antioch church to arrange relief) and 20:28 (the Spirit appoints leaders to the church). A number of other texts relate to purely personal prophecies (*e.g.*, those of warning to Paul in Acts 20:23; 21:4, 11). Admittedly, some charismata that benefit or direct the church also have secondary missiological significance. As well as clarifying relations between Jews and Gentiles within the church, the decision prompted by the Spirit in Acts 15:28 probably made mission to the Gentiles easier; similarly, churches that live in the fear of the Lord, and with the comfort of the

---

[48]Acts 8:1 generalises that 'all' were scattered, and 8:4 that 'those who were scattered went about preaching the word', but the latter does not repeat the 'all' of 8:1, and in no way suggests that 'each' preached the word; merely that, as a result of their going out, the word was spread (by some).

[49]Stronstad, Shelton and Menzies have variously argued that (1) the laying on of hands that bestows the gift (8:17 and 19:6) is an ordination for mission, (2) the gift to Cornelius' household is accompanied by the same prophetic outburst of witness to God's great deeds that served the evangelism of Acts 2, and so marks the Spirit as endowment for evangelism, and (3) the later summaries speak of the growth of the church in Samaria, Caesarea and Ephesus, and so identify the Spirit given to the groups concerned as empowerment for mission. But each of these arguments appears to be special pleading: see Turner, '"Empowerment"?', 114-17.

Spirit, may expect to attract converts (9:31), just as churches encouraged and challenged by charismatics like Barnabas (11:24) would. And missionaries who by God's grace become 'filled with joy and the Holy Spirit' even when they are rejected (13:52) are undoubtedly thereby refreshed for the next bout of mission. But these are secondary missiological effects, sometimes suggested by the connections in Luke's narrative; they are not evidently the primary purposes of the charismata in question. Luke, like the rest of Christianity, evidently thought the Spirit was also for the benefit of those in the Church, not merely to empower her to draw outsiders into her ranks.

Haya-Prats has also devoted special attention to the question of whether the Spirit has a role in the everyday life of the Christian.[50] Here he tends to agree with Gunkel. Luke considers repentant faith expressed in baptism to bring 'salvation' in the form of forgiveness of sins, and Jesus is 'present' to the community in and through his 'name'. The Spirit is given to those who have received all this, and so as a *donum superadditum*. If the Spirit occasionally fills a person with 'wisdom' (Luke 21:15; Acts 6:3), 'joy' (13:52; *cf.*, Luke 10:21) or 'faith' (6:5; 11:24) these are exceptional and powerfully charismatic intensifications of ordinary Christian virtues. The Spirit is not required for the ordinary level of Christian faith, joy and wisdom because for Luke these fall within the range of unaided human possibilities. Haya-Prats also then agrees with Gunkel that nothing in the summaries of the church's new life (2:42-47; 4:32-37) is directly attributable to the Spirit, but admits that as these are immediately preceded by the Pentecost and 'Little Pentecost' accounts it is possible that Luke understood the Spirit as the inspiration in part of the moral and religious life described in them.[51] This last admission is probably an understatement. The narrative tension of expectation of an 'Israel of the Spirit' is carefully built up from Acts 2:1 to 2:38-39. Yet the summary of conversions and the life of this community (2:40-47) has not a single mention of the Spirit. This device requires the reader to resolve the tension with the assumption that it is the unmentioned advent and charismata of the promised Spirit that is responsible for the overall dynamic of the new community. This, of course, might be resisted by those who think the 'Spirit of prophecy' has nothing to do with ethical renewal, but such an assumption appears to rest on a serious distortion

---

[50]*L'Esprit*, ch. 6.
[51]*L'Esprit*, 156, 162. See the more positive narrative-critical arguments of Shepherd, *Function*, 167, 170-73.

of the evidence (see II (B) above). In a Jewish environment, 'charismatic wisdom' (the second most common gift attributed to the 'Spirit of prophecy' in Judaism) would precisely be expected to give the dynamic renewed understanding of faith that might then flow into (*e.g.,*) charismatic teaching which addresses others and/or might promote joyful obedience and worship/thanksgiving in the charismatic and those addressed alike (*cf.*, already Sir. 39:6 for several of these elements combined).[52] In this light the cases of those described as 'full of' the Holy Spirit and wisdom, joy or faith above should be regarded as exceptional only in degree rather than in the kind of working of the Spirit. The same Spirit of prophecy would be expected to explain the strong sense of God's (and Christ's) transforming presence in the community. Any Jew hearing Peter's promise of the eschatological 'Spirit of prophecy' (2:38-39) to be granted universally could reasonably expect the Spirit thenceforth to be the power of the community's religious and ethical renewal. I suggest the burden of proof lies on the shoulders of those who claim Luke did not so think.

This raises the question whether Luke implies that this charismatic 'Spirit of prophecy' is simultaneously a soteriological necessity, the power by which Israel's own restoration is wrought.

3. The Spirit as the charismatic power of Israel's restoration? We have noted that Luke's portrait of the Messiah of the Spirit is set against the background of hopes for Israel's restoration (see II above). It is probable that the Baptist's promise that the coming one will baptise with Holy Spirit and fire (Luke 3:16-17) also belongs with this scenario, and develops Jewish reflection on Isaiah 4:4 and 11:1-4. The Baptist himself has sifted Israel in preparation for the Messiah who will finally cleanse Zion through a righteous fiery and purgative rule empowered by the Spirit.[53] For Luke, Jesus' ministry inaugurates this. It is an appeal to all sectors of Israel (including 'the sinners') to participate in the transformation of Israel, and to become a community of reconciliation based in what Borg has called a 'paradigm of mercy',[54] inspired and enabled by God's reconciling presence in liberating power (=the king-

---

[52]*Cf.*, also (in addition to texts at II(B) above): *e.g.*, 1QH 7:6-7; 9:32; 12:11-13; 13:18-19; 14:12-13, 25; 16:6-12; Philo *Gig.* 55 and *passim*; *T. Simeon* 4:4; *T. Benj.* 8:1-3, *etc.*

[53]*Cf.*, Turner, *Power*, ch. 7. Against Menzies, *Development*, ch. 7, the point of Luke 3:16 cannot be that the Messiah will merely 'sift' Israel through his Spirit-empowered word: as Webb has shown ('Activity', 103-111) the Messiah comes with *the shovel* to cleanse the floor where the sifting of wheat and chaff has already been performed.

[54]Borg, *Conflict*.

dom of God).[55] This, for Luke (like much Judaism), is what 'salvation' is all about: its content is not merely 'forgiveness of sins' and assurance of future bliss (things already presupposed by nomistic Judaism). The divine forgiveness awaited is more specifically the one that will remove the divine chastisement of Israel evinced in her oppressed and sorry estate; and the salvation hoped for is correspondingly a deliverance and messianic rule that frees her to serve God without fear in holiness and righteousness as a community of 'peace' (cf., Luke 1:68-79).[56] To a limited extent this salvation is made present by Jesus amongst his followers, through his Spirit-empowered acts and teaching (cf., especially 4:18-21),[57] but the events of the Passion precipitate a radical change. For Conzelmann the Passion, of course, means the return of Satan, and a future in which 'salvation' is reduced almost to a memory of the past 'Satan-free' period of the ministry and to a hope for the eschaton. Per contra, Franklin has rightly observed that Luke 19:11-27; 22:14-30; 23:42-43; 24:49 (etc.) all anticipate that through the Passion God's transforming reign through his messianic king will be intensi-fied, rather than weakened. Answering to this, Acts 2:33-36 asserts Jesus' elevation to the supreme place of kingship and power, the throne of David's 'Lord' at God's right hand. This, as both Franklin and Mainville have stressed, is the climax of Luke's christology and soteriology; the fulfilment of the promise in Luke 1:32-33.[58]

But how is this restorative Davidic rule over the house of Jacob (so Luke 1:32-33) to be implemented from the heavenly throne? And how is the 'salvation' begun by Jesus in the ministry to be continued

---

[55]For similar conclusions reached by different approaches see e.g., Meyer, Aims; Lohfink, Jesus, cf., also Hurst, 'Ethics', 210-222. These are attempts to discuss the 'historical Jesus' but Luke provides some of the best evidence and builds a similar portrait in his redaction. Marshall and York have shown the great degree to which the 'bi-polar reversals' anticipated in the Magnificat are seen to be fulfilled in Jesus' ministry and teaching, and in the life of discipleship to which these point (Marshall, 'Magnificat'; York, Last).

[56]Cf., Wright, The New Testament, part III (Judaism) and 373-83 on Luke. So also Stalder, 'Heilige Geist'.

[57]Conzelmann used the framework of von Baer's three epochs to argue 'salvation' was all but limited to this period; Dunn, (Baptism, chs. 3–4) used the same framework to argue the disciples only began themselves to experience salvation after Pentecost. Against the former see e.g., Marshall, Luke: Historian; Franklin, Luke, 13-26 and 249-61. Against the latter see Turner, 'Jesus and the Spirit', esp. 29-34; idem. Power, chs. 6-9, 11. Menzies, Development, chs. 6, 8, 9.

[58]Franklin, 'Ascension', 191-200; idem, Christ the Lord, 29-41; idem, Luke, 249-61. Mainville argues Acts 2:33 is the literary and theological key to the whole of Luke–Acts (L'Esprit, passim). Cf., Turner, Power, 290-303.

and intensified amongst the disciples? Luke 24:47-49 and Acts 1:3-8 provide only one possibility: *viz.* the one means by which Jesus had already inaugurated that salvation; namely the Spirit, now poured out as the Messiah's executive power (Acts 2:33). The same 'Spirit of prophecy' which will enable the Twelve and the community around them to fulfil the destiny of Isaiah 49:6 as a light to the nations (Luke 24:47), bringing the message of salvation to 'the end of the earth' (Acts 1:8; *cf.*, 13:47), will thus also be the power to raise up Jacob and restore the preserved of Israel (*cf.*, Isa. 49:5-6). Accordingly, Luke redactionally identifies 'the promise of the Father' (1:4) with the Baptist's logion; Jesus will now 'baptise' them 'with Holy Spirit' as John promised (1:5 —and the question in 1:6 shows the disciples rightly perceive this concerns the cleansing/restoration of Israel, and so even possibly her promised 'rule' over the nations (*cf.*, Dan. 7).[59] And this Spirit is to 'come upon them' 'from on high' (1:8; *cf.*, Luke 24:49)—clear allusion to Isaiah 32:15 (LXX) and to the promise of the restoration of Israel (32:15-20) through the Spirit. In short the redactional gateway texts into Acts suggest the gift of the Spirit is not merely empowering to witness, but that the varied activities of the Spirit of prophecy in the individual and in the congregation will together also constitute the purging and restoring power of God in the community which effects Israel's transformation/salvation.[60] The latter line of thought is developed at a number of points in Acts.

(1) The Pentecost account (2:1-13) quite deliberately echoes Jewish accounts of the Sinai theophany (it is close to, though not dependent on, Philo's,[61] and Jesus is exalted to God's right hand not merely as the Davidic Messiah, but (as in the Gospel) as the Mosaic Prophet (*cf.*, 3:18-

---

[59]John's promise evidently cannot be reduced to an assurance that the disciples will be empowered to witness and so to sift Israel (as Menzies takes it): the emphatic 'you' (will be baptised) includes them (along with the rest of Israel) as the objects of Jesus' messianic purging of Israel. For this broader restorationist view of Luke's concept of John's promise, see Kim, *Geisttaufe*; Turner, *Power*, chs. 7, 10-11, 13.

[60]See also Tiede, 'Exaltation'; Kim, *Geisttaufe*.

[61]The attempt by Menzies (*Development*, 235-41) to dismiss Moses/Sinai parallels from this scene appears to be somewhat tendentious, for the alternative theophanic parallels he offers lack precisely the most important parallels to Sinai that Acts 2 affords: they do not concern an event on earth before the assembled people of God, nor do they come at a redemptive-historical turning point for Israel, nor do they follow an ascent of Israel's redeemer to God, nor involve miraculous speech reaching all nations! For more balanced assessment see Wedderburn, 'Traditions', 27-54; Kim, *Geisttaufe*, 157-68, 242, and *cf.*, Turner, *Power*, ch. 10 §1.4.

23). It is especially as the latter that he ascends on high to receive a gift of foundational importance which he gives to his people (2:33-34; cf., Exod. 19:3; Ps. 68:18 [esp. the Targum rendering]; Josephus Ant. III.77-78, etc.) at the beginning of a decisive new phase of 'Israel's existence, and amidst theophanic phenomena strikingly reminiscent of Sinai.[62]

(2) The life of the community depicted in the summaries (Acts 2:42-47 and 4:32-35) matches both the salvation hoped for in Luke 1–2 and the main thrust and goal of Jesus' preaching—an Israel of reconciliation led by the Twelve as a community which is free of oppressors, which without fear joyfully worships God, serving him in holiness and righteousness, and from which poverty and hunger are banished by the caring rich.[63] To what should the sudden emergence of this 'fulfilment' of Jesus' hopes be attributed if not to the Spirit by which he extends his rule over Jacob and purgingly 'baptises' Zion? There is no need, of course, to assume the Spirit performs such activity other than as the 'Spirit of prophecy'.[64] The Spirit experienced in the charismatic teaching of the apostles and other prophetic figures, in the charismatic praise of the community, and in spiritual wisdom granting joyful grasp of the Gospel and its implications (perhaps thereby motivating the caring love for the poor), would together be adequate to explain the evident 'enthusiasm' and the sense of God's transforming presence in the congregation.

(3) The idea of the 'cleansing' or purging of Israel inherent in the Baptist's promise then emerges most prominently both in the Ananias and Sapphira incident (cf., 5:3,9) and in the Cornelius episode. With respect to the latter, it can be no accident that the one time when the Baptist's promise that Jesus will purge/cleanse Zion with Holy Spirit is 'remembered' is 11:16, in the midst of questions about whether Gentiles can be 'clean' (the focus of Acts 10). Their participation in the Spirit of prophecy shows that Cornelius' household has a part in the 'Israel' the Messiah is cleansing/restoring by the Spirit and thus they are readily admitted to baptism, and Peter can later refer to God as having 'cleansed their hearts by faith' (15:9).

> This whole incident, which initially took Peter and the church by surprise, apparently led to some reinterpretation of Israel's hope. In

---

[62]See Dupont, 'Ascension', 219-28, and Turner, 'Spirit of Christ', 174-79.

[63]See Seccombe, Possessions, 200-209; York, Last, 62. For 'salvation' as participation in the restored community, and rescue from oppressors, see Joel Green's essay (§§2.3.1-2.3.2) in this volume.

[64]Contra, Shepherd, Function, 167, see Turner, Power, ch. 13.

3:19-26 national restoration of Israel around the Messiah as (together) Abraham's seed was expected eventually to lead to the universalising of the blessing promised in Gn. 22:18. But in 15:14-18 the argument appears to be that Israel's restoration is in principle complete (merely to be extended further into the diaspora) and accordingly it is the hour for the eschatological influx of Gentiles. The hopes of Luke 1-2 have largely been fulfilled (if in surprising fashion).[65]

It is difficult to dismiss Luke's 'Spirit of prophecy' as a *donum superadditum*. It is certainly much more than an 'empowering to witness'; the same gifts of the Spirit that fuel the mission (charismatic revelation, wisdom, prophecy, preaching and doxology) also nurture, shape and purify the community, making it a messianic community of 'peace' conforming to the hopes for Israel's restoration. Without this gift there could be no *ongoing* experience of the 'salvation' the disciples experienced in Jesus' ministry, and certainly no deepening of it (something similar would have had to be said of the Samaritans if they had been left by Philip and the apostles without the Spirit granted in 8:17). For Luke the charismatic 'Spirit of prophecy' is very much the power and life of the church, and so probably of the individual too (hence the close association of the gift of the Spirit to conversion-initiation). It is the means by which the heavenly Lord exercises his cleansing and transforming rule over Israel as much as the means by which he uses her as the Isaianic servant to witness his salvation to the end(s) of the earth (1:8; 13:47). In this Luke's understanding of the Spirit is not so distant from that of either Paul or John as is regularly assumed.[66]

V. Conclusion: Luke's pneumatology and the theology of Acts

What does Luke's pneumatology tell us about his theological en-

---

[65]*Cf.*, Jervell, *Luke, passim* (especially 41-74) and Turner, *Power*, esp. 306-15, 418-27. If Luke anticipates some further landslide of Israel to faith—of which there is little sign—it would be into the transformed Israel of the Spirit he knows in the Church, the one fashioned and ruled by the Messiah on David's throne at God's right hand, not a Temple-and-Torah-centred national Israel ruled by the Messiah seated in Jerusalem. Against those claiming Luke expects a more literal and Zionistic fulfilment of Luke 1-2 see Räisänen, 'Redemption', 94-114.
[66]See Turner, 'The Spirit of Prophecy and the Ethical/Religious Life,' 186-90, for development of this comparison; also Hui, *Concept, passim*, for the relation of Luke's pneumatology to Paul's.

deavour? His portrayal of the Spirit of prophecy as the charismatic
power of Israel's restoration under her Davidic Messiah/Mosaic
prophet appears to be ideologically motivated,[67] *i.e.,* Luke attempts to
explain and so to legitimate the Church in the light of her founding
moments (and this explains much of the allegedly OT character of his
pneumatology).[68] Far from attempting to persuade the reader that the
church finds its true identity when it leaves Israel and Judaism behind
(as J.C. O'Neill argued),[69] Luke wishes to maintain that she is the
fulfilment of the promises to Israel. His exclusion of those who fail to
give heed to the Mosaic Prophet from the nation of Israel (3:22-23) and
his apparent belief that the promises of Luke 1–2 are largely fulfilled
by Acts 15 in the Church supports this, and in addition suggests he
writes (like the author of the Fourth Gospel) at a time when Christianity is still actively competing with (hellenistic) Judaism for the claim to
be God's 'Israel'.[70] Far less clear is whether Luke also attempts to
challenge (*e.g.,*) an institutionalising church of his own day with an
idealised portrayal of her charismatic beginnings. That he believed the
'Spirit of prophecy' was still available to all believers is barely in doubt
(*cf.,* Acts 2:39!), and he may have anticipated his account would encourage greater dependence on the Spirit. Only in question now is
whether there is sufficient evidence to show that Luke knew of a non-
charismatic sector of the church which he sought to correct and
'strengthen' (so Kim).[71] The one passage which affords the clearest
glimpse of the church of Luke's day (Acts 20:25-35) envisages a
number of problems, but a waning of the Spirit does not appear to be
amongst them.

---

[67]We use 'ideology' to denote a construal of the community's symbolic universe
intended to justify the community over against some other group. For the
background of such a usage of 'ideology' in social sciences, and the perceptive
application of it to Mark's gospel, see Watts, *Influence*, 243-46.
[68]So Chevallier, 'Luc', part II.
[69]O'Neill, *Theology of Acts*.
[70]*Cf.* Kim, *Geisttaufe*, 243-44.
[71]The attempt by Kim (*Geisttaufe*, 209-38) to interpret the Ephesian 'twelve' as a
cipher for non-charismatic (Markan?) Christian groups of Luke's day is by no
means the easiest solution to the difficulties of 18:24–19:6 (on which see above).

CHAPTER 17

THE NEW PEOPLE OF GOD

David Seccombe

Summary

A stage by stage examination of Acts reveals the new people of God emerging as a deliberate theme, such as can only be accounted for by the supposition that it was one of Luke's purposes to show how the focus of God's saving plan had moved from the racially determined Jewish community to a non-racial world-wide fellowship composed of Jews, Samaritans and Gentiles. The way in which the author has presented his message makes it probable he was writing in a situation in which synagogue and church were in tension, with the synagogue in the ascendant, and where mission to Jews and Jewish sympathizers was in progress.

I. A revolutionary transformation

In three decades from AD 30 to 60, the notion of 'the people of God' was transformed within early Christianity from a community largely limited to the racial descendants of the patriarch Jacob, with its focal point the God of Abraham and the land of Israel, to a multiracial world fellowship also focused on the God of Abraham, but also on the Messiah Jesus enthroned as King at his right hand. As a result of this change world history turned into a radically new direction. Our main witness to how this revolution took place is The Acts of the Apostles. What it shows is that the change in the idea of the people of God lagged behind the reality itself. Shortly after the death and resurrection of Jesus a great movement of faith out into the Gentile world began, which not all of its participants fully understood. Luke saw it as a mighty, Holy Spirit driven act of God, the latest in a succession of salvation events by which God was bringing about his kingdom in the world. Acts is structured to allow a theological understanding of this transformation and of the new people of God itself, to emerge naturally from the sequence of events it records. To see this is to go a long way towards discerning one of the major purposes of the book.

Such a revolutionary transition from racial community to multiracial world fellowship naturally provoked opposition. It continues to generate questions for us today. The persecution of Jews by a nominally Christian country in our generation has raised in acute form the question of the true relationship of Christian and Jew. 'True' may seem a strange adjective; I use it to indicate the relationship between Christian and Jew which is consistent with the canonical form of Christianity—the teaching of Jesus and the apostles. For those who see their Christian obedience in terms of faithfulness to this canon this question is more than academic. In this respect Acts has become something of a 'storm-centre,' seen by some as anti-Jewish, and by others as the friendliest book in the NT to Jews. J.T. Sanders concludes: 'he (Luke) comes to the opinion that all Jews are equally, in principle at least, perverse...the world will be much better off without them...' According to Sanders, Luke's polemic against them is 'the leaven within Christianity and within western society against which we must all and eternally be on guard'.[1] On the other side, J. Jervell argues that Luke–Acts is written by a Jew, or from the viewpoint of Jewish Christians, at a time when Jews were a valued minority in the church. Luke's

---

[1]*Jews*, 317; and see 'Jewish People', 51-75; also Cook, 'Mission', 102-23.

seemingly anti-Jewish statements are directed at unrepentant Jews and have nothing to do with anti-semitism.[2]

A question with such far-reaching implications must necessarily concern us in this study. The fact that careful scholars come to such opposite conclusions means the issue is complex. Our approach will not be to cite proof texts, but to observe how 'the new people of God' emerges as a theme in Acts, and to inquire into its implications for Christian–Jew relationships. There are also other important issues, which must also concern us: Did the transition from Jewish community to multiracial fellowship proceed according to the inner nature of Israel's faith and Jesus' ministry, or was it a historic 'accident'? Who belongs to the new people of God, and how is membership determined? What is the nature and status of the new community and what is its destiny?

II. Israel's restoration begins

The first concern of the small band of disciples gathered in the upper room was to reconstitute the twelve-fold apostolate, ruptured by the defection of Judas. Peter cites only scriptural necessity as the reason for replacing Judas, but this begs the question what the necessity related to. In the light of Jesus' promise to the apostles that they would 'sit on thrones judging the twelve tribes of Israel' (Luke 22:30), and their question to him at the ascension about the restoration of Israel (Acts 1:6-8) it is hard to imagine that Luke did not intend his readers to see it in connection with Israel's restoration and the twelve-fold foundation of its community (see Rev. 21:14).[3] A strong interest in the 'restoration of Israel' is apparent in the writings of Luke.[4] James' declaration that God had returned to rebuild the fallen tent of David so that the Gentiles might seek the Lord (Acts 15:16f.) shows that Luke saw the restoration of Israel not as something to be effected only at the parousia, but as actually in progress.[5] Perhaps the 120 gathered in the upper room are also symbolic in this regard (Acts 1:15). If we are right in this reading of Luke's motive, we may venture to suggest even at this early stage that a doctrine of final rejection of Israel is most unlikely.

[2]*Paul*, 26-51; also *Luke*, 41-69. For a recent summary of the debate see Sanders, 'Who is a Jew?', 435-443.
[3]Further, Jervell, *Luke*, 82ff.
[4]Luke 1:33,54,68ff; 2:25, 32, 38; 24:21; Acts 3:19-21.
[5]Further, Kaiser, 'Promise'.

III. The remnant of Israel

With the foundation of a restored Israelite community in place, the events of the day of Pentecost unfold. The miracle of languages reminds us of the scattering of Babel and God's promise that he would one day 'change the speech of the peoples to a pure speech' (Zeph.3:9). It may well have reminded Jewish readers of the legendary proclamation of the Law to the seventy nations in the time of Moses.[6] Yet, however strong may be the overtones of a gathering of the Gentile nations, at the surface level the story is told very strictly in terms of the gathering and conversion of the scattered Jews and proselytes of the Diaspora. The 'Jews and proselytes' of Acts 2:10 refers not just to the visitors from Rome, but to the whole sweep of nations from Persia to Rome.[7] Peter thus stands to address a representative gathering of Jews and circumcised converts to Judaism from Israel and all the lands into which they have been scattered. He speaks to them as 'Jewish men' (Acts 2:14) and 'Israelites' (Acts 2:22) and 'the whole house of Israel' (Acts 2:36). His manner of address strongly affirms their membership of the chosen people of God.

However, he also reminds them of a scripture which declares the salvation not of all Israel, but a remnant: 'For in Mt. Zion and in Jerusalem there shall be those who escape, as the Lord has said, and among the survivors shall be those whom the Lord calls' (Joel 2:32). This saved remnant numbers 'everyone who calls on the name of the Lord' (Acts 2:21), and in 2:36 Peter concludes that this Lord to be called upon for salvation is the Jesus, 'whom God has made both Lord and Christ'. Accordingly, in words that recall the preaching of John the Baptist, he urges his hearers to repent and be baptised, and to save themselves from 'this crooked generation' (Acts 2:38-40). Thus membership of Israel is not enough. The axe is laid at the tree of each person's life. Only the truly repentant remnant of the people, who call on the name of the Lord Jesus will survive. Nevertheless, the promise of salvation through Jesus, and therefore the offer of membership in this remnant people of God, was made to everyone who heard the message and 3000 believed and were gathered that day 'into one place' (ἐπὶ τὸ αὐτό) (Acts 2:44, 47). Thus we learn of a division within the historic people of God, such as Luke has previously intimated in Luke 2:34.

---

[6]SB II, 604. Pentecost may already have become the celebration of the giving of the Law, as in later Judaism (SB II, 601f.).
[7]The 'Cretans and Arabians' of Acts 2:11 appear to be an afterthought of the author who missed them as his eye swept the world from East to West.

The curious phrase ἐπὶ τὸ αὐτό which has already occurred in Acts 1:15 as a circumlocution for church (ἐκκλησία), indicates the adding together of these converts, through their believing, to the one hundred and twenty to form a coherent people. It is Luke's way of depicting the coming into being of the new people of God, at a stage in the narrative where he is not ready to use the natural word ἐκκλησία. Their distinctiveness and separateness is also underlined by their baptism, which, here and throughout Acts is acknowledged as the normal way people cross the visible line into membership of the church. Acts 10:44-48 and 16:31 make it clear that baptism itself was not determinative of Christian identity, but a sacramental sign.

Peter extends the promise of salvation to the families of those who heard 'and to all that are far off, everyone whom the Lord our God calls to himself' (Acts 2:39). His audience might naturally hear this allusion to Isaiah 57:19 as emphasizing the inclusion of Jews scattered in distant lands, but the readers of Acts, particularly Gentiles, are surely intended to note that they too are included (cf., Eph. 2:13, 17). The remnant people, though brought together by repentant acknowledgement of the Messiah Jesus, is to be bounded ultimately by the predestinating will of God (cf., Acts 13:48). Perhaps this is the reason the children of those who believe receive particular mention.

IV. A Messianic people

The notion of a division within the people, and of a people within the people, is expressed even more strongly in Peter's second address. Moses foretold the coming of a prophet who must be followed at pain of being cut off from the people (λαός) (Acts 3:22-23). The term λαός (people) is used to signify the historic people of God, never Gentile peoples, until they are welcomed among the people of God (Acts 15:14). Thus Peter makes an enormous assertion: henceforth the boundaries of the true people of God will be determined within Israel by allegiance to the prophet Jesus. This is what the Scriptures had always intended. God will remove from his people those who decline to acknowledge the appointed King. The people of God is a messianic community, as in intention it always was. Nevertheless, Luke does not withdraw from the Jewish people as a whole its elect status. He charges them with killing 'the Prince of Life', but concedes that it was 'in ignorance' (Acts 3:15, 17; cf., Acts 17:30). Despite their crime they are still the 'sons of the covenant' and the 'seed of Abraham' (Acts

3:25); the Christ is theirs (Acts 3:20) and has now been sent 'first to you to bless you in turning every one of you from your wickedness' (Acts 3:26). Sanders sees this as a second chance after their killing of Jesus, which was refused, and is therefore past history by the time Luke writes.[8] It is just as natural, however, to read it as an appeal to Jews of his day, whom Luke still hoped might turn. Nowhere in Acts does he explicitly revoke Israel's elect status (*cf.,* Rom. 11:28).

V. Leadership of the new people

The first official attempt to suppress the nascent movement represents a clash of views over the real leadership of the people of God. The Jewish rulers gather together (compare Acts 4:5 with 4:26) disturbed by the growth of the new community. Luke tells us that at this point it numbered about 5000. Peter, as is his custom, addresses his audience in a respectful and inclusive manner, 'Rulers of the people (λαός) and elders' (Acts 4:8). Nevertheless, they crucified the Messiah, whom God has now raised to be the chief stone in the building. We must not overlook the importance of this image, of which the leaders were reminded only a few weeks previously by Jesus himself (Luke 20:9-19). They, the builders of the nation (its rulers) found Jesus too difficult to accommodate to their structure and rejected him. God, however, has reversed their decision and made him the key stone, that is, the ruler. Thus Peter is not announcing a new religion, but a new leader of the people. 'No other name under heaven is given...by which we must be saved,' (Acts 4:12) he adds, for Israel's salvation had always been the task of its God-appointed judge or king.

Because there is a fundamental crisis relating to the leadership of the people, the gathered believers respond in the words of Psalm 2, which depicts an attack of the rulers of the world on God's anointed king. Had Luke continued the quotation he might have implied that just as the continuance of individuals among the λαός hung on their acceptance of Jesus, so too the rulers remained legitimate rulers amongst God's people only if they refrained from rebellion against 'the Lord's anointed'. He does not take such a step, though he unmistakably asserts the ultimate authority of Jesus. If we were to

---

[8]Sanders deals with apparent signs of favour towards the Jews with the thesis that they are given a second chance because they murdered Jesus, and are only finally rejected when they also reject the gospel. 'Jewish People', 59ff. While this may be true of individuals, it is unproven with regard to the whole people.

extrapolate we might be approaching some sort of differentiation between church and state, but this is not Luke's concern.

We may reflect at this point that just because 'the people' is now defined in its membership and its leadership by attachment to Jesus, there is a newness about it which justifies our use of the non-biblical term 'new people of God.' It is not meant to suggest by this that it is new in the sense of not existing before. It is clear that Luke and the apostles see it comprised of patriarchs, prophets and saints of old, as well as recent believers. Perhaps 'restored people of God', or 'remnant people' would have been better terms. Nevertheless it is true that there is a newness now that the king is revealed and exalted and calling for people's allegiance. Some such designation is required when we consider that we now have two distinct communities, both of them entirely Jewish, acknowledging different leaders and different principles (though the Christians are not denying a limited jurisdiction to the High Priest).

Luke intends to pursue the theme of opposition a considerable distance. However, he creates a break between the first two attacks by a second and fuller description of the quality of life of the new community.

VI. God in their midst

The two descriptions of the life of the early Christian community in Jerusalem (2:42-47; 4:32–5:16) have a common form and purpose.[9] They are intended to show that God was truly amongst this people. Their leaders were empowered to perform signs and wonders (Acts 2:43; 4:33; 5:15f.), and fear, such as commonly accompanies the presence of God, fell upon the believers and those around them (Acts 3:43; 5:11,13). The story of Ananias and Sapphira emphasises the holiness of the infant church which God was zealous to defend—much as he had in the early days of the Israelite community.[10] The degree of fellowship among the community of believers and the generosity of their sharing, evidenced the grace of God among them and signalled, particularly to Luke's hellenistic readers, the presence of something remarkable happening in Jerusalem. He uses evocative language

---

[9]Further, Seccombe, *Possessions*, 199ff.
[10]The main similarity is to the story of Achan (Josh. 7), but one thinks also of Num. 15:32ff; 2 Sam. 6:6ff.

suggesting the attainment of unattainable Greek ideals of true friend-ship. Jewish readers would note that the community was loyally attendant at the temple, surrounded by miracles, and full of prayer and praise. Surely this is the true people of God, Luke wishes his readers to conclude.

The prominent role of the apostles, particularly in the second community description, sandwiched as it is between two accounts of ineffective opposition on the part of the Jerusalem leaders, is also worth pondering. Nowhere does Luke hint at any ambitions to authority beyond the believing community. Nevertheless, Peter works wonders, disburses the people's gifts, dispenses judgement, and is sought out and honoured by the multitudes, in every way appearing as a true leader of the people.

VII. Condemnation of Israel's rulers

The second attack is motivated, according to Luke, by sectarian jealousy: 'the party (αἵρεσις) of the Sadducees...filled with jealousy' (Acts 5:17). We are surely correct to discern here an echo of the common dismissal of the Christian movement in the fifties and sixties of the first century as 'the sect (or party) of the Nazarenes (Acts 24:5,14; 28:22; cf., 15:5; 26:5). Luke is unhappy with such a perception and is preparing to deal it a hard blow. For the moment he is content to quietly undermine the opposition by a reminder of the 'sectarian' character of the Sadduceeism to which most of the priestly elite belonged.

At the second hearing Peter again declares Jesus to the leaders, this time as 'Prince and Saviour' (Acts 5:31). Their opposition hardens but not to the point of outright rejection. Gamaliel urges caution and in Acts 6:7 we learn that many priests subsequently became obedient to the faith. Luke will relate one more incident of opposition before he virtually closes the book on the rulers.

Stephen's story is told (1) because he brings official opposition to its climax; (2) because his speech places the new people of God in its true salvation-historical contex; and (3) because Stephen paves the way for Paul. There are some curious aspects of the story which re-quire close inspection.

Stephen appears to the Sanhedrin as an angel. For us this has unfortunate iconic connotations, but to Luke's original readers it was probably intended to signal that Stephen stood as the messenger of

God in the highest council of the people.[11] It has often been observed that his speech makes a poor defence; that he appears to break off mid-way into an outburst against his accusers. The reality is that he, the accused, brings God's accusation against the leaders, that they are a 'stiff-necked people, uncircumcised in heart and ears,' persecuting the prophets, and now murdering the Righteous One (Acts 7:51-53). They underline the truth of this judgement by killing him.

Some would read this as an ultimate or penultimate rejection of the Jewish people as a whole,[12] but that is to read more into the speech than is there. Certainly it is a serious judicial condemnation of the rulers, who along with all the other charges, are exposed as non-keepers of the law. (Acts 7:53) But even so it is not a condemnation which makes repentance impossible, for the young Saul is at that very moment walking onto the stage.

VIII. A creed for the people of God

Stephen's speech reads like an 'I believe in the historic people of God.' God appeared to our father Abraham, called him to the Land, and promised it to him and his seed. God gave them the covenant of circumcision. God rescued his people by the hand of Moses, was amongst them through the angel of his presence, gave them his word, revealed the pattern of the tabernacle, and allowed Solomon to build 'a habitation for the God of Jacob'.

However, entwined with this creed are matters every Jew must consider. Again and again God appeared to his people and blessed them when they were outside the Land. Once and again the people resisted the leader God had appointed to rescue them, just as now they are opposing Jesus. The people refused the worship ordained by God through Moses and turned to Aaron (the High Priest!) to give them a more tangible cult. Their worship, though Mosaic in form, became idolatrous in spirit, and is in danger of continuing so if they fail to acknowledge that God and his purposes transcend the temple.

---

[11]SB II, 665f. give various examples from Jewish sources in which men's faces appear like angels'. The most obvious example was Moses, whose face shone as a result of his being in the presence of God.

[12]O'Neill, *Theology of Acts*, 83. *Cf.*, Kilgallen, *Speech*, 112. Haenchen thinks the diatribe is directed at the Jews, who in Luke's time were the Christians' 'irreconcilable enemies', and for whom repentance was 'a merely theoretical possibility', (*Acts*, 289f.).

In his concluding accusation, Stephen associates the rulers with
the uncircumcised spirit and hardness of heart of their forebears. They
are not the people of God in truth, but only in form, though never does
Stephen deviate a hair's-breadth from the orthodoxy of Moses and the
fathers of the OT. Clearly God will take his people from the midst of a
hardened and rejecting people as he has always done.

The most significant aspect of Stephen's speech for our theme is
Acts 7:37-38:

> This is the Moses who said to the Israelites, 'God will raise up for you
> a prophet from your brethren as he raised me up.' This is he who was
> in the church (ἐκκλησία) in the wilderness with the angel who spoke
> to him at Mt. Sinai.

With circumlocutions such as ἐπὶ τὸ αὐτό, Luke has avoided the
loaded word ἐκκλησία in the early part of Acts, no doubt because he
wanted first to establish its true significance.[13] In his own day
ἐκκλησία and συναγωγή were at loggerheads, the church being seen
by its opponents as a 'sect' (αἵρεσις). Luke has called the Sadducees an
αἵρεσις (5:17) and will use the same term of the Pharisees (15:5). Later
Paul will query its appropriateness for the Christian movement
(24:5,14). With Stephen's significant use of ἐκκλησία Luke makes it
clear why. In calling themselves ἐκκλησία the Christians were claiming
their oneness with the congregation which gathered in the presence of
God at Sinai. Having established its true connection Luke proceeds to
use ἐκκλησία without restraint throughout the rest of Acts. Once again,
therefore, we must demur at any interpretation which sees the
newness of the new people of God as novelty. There is ever only one
people, because there is but one God. The people who assembled
before him at various points in history and who yielded him the trust
of their hearts are bound together as one ultimate assembly, the one
flock which, Paul will later say, God 'bought with his own blood'.
(Acts 20:28)

Looking back over the ground, we see that Luke has described
the formation of a new people from within the old people, and has
identified the former with the original Mosaic community. It is still
exclusively Jewish. Once again Luke's picture is hard to square with
rejection of the entire Jewish race.

---

[13]He introduces it in an ambiguous manner in 5:11: it could refer to the meeting or
to the whole Christian community.

IX. Assembling the outcasts

One wonders whether Luke may not be hinting in his double use of διασπείρεσθαι in 8:1,4 (cf.,11:19; 1 Pet. 1:1) the beginnings of a Christian *diaspora*. If so, it becomes paradoxically the means of a further gathering together of the scattered people of God. Philip proclaimed Christ to 'the city of Samaria'. If we follow the majority text, the city of Sebaste must be referred to. The reason for referring to it by an obsolete name[14] was probably to underline its connection with the lost northern kingdom and the lost sheep of the house of Israel. Multitudes of men and women are baptised including their erstwhile divine man, Simon the magician. But there is no pouring out of the Holy Spirit.

The gift of the Spirit is withheld until the apostles in Jerusalem send Peter and John, who pray for them and lay their hands upon them. These actions indicate acceptance and solidarity. The original church in Jerusalem is acknowledging the Samaritans as members of the people of God. This is no small step towards a people who were regarded as apostate 'untouchables.' R.B. Rackham comments on 8:12: 'The Kingdom [they preached] was neither the Jewish ecclesia, nor the rival Samaritan ecclesia, but a new ecclesia, which bore the name of Jesus, who had been anointed as its Messianic king or Christ.'[15] Had the Samaritans entered into full Christian experience without the blessing of Jerusalem the possibility was there of separate, even rival Christian communities developing. Is it possible that God withheld his Spirit to ensure there did not spring up two 'denominations', a Jewish and a Samaritan? Accordingly, the gift of the Spirit becomes the mark of the unity of believers in the body of Christ. The story of Simon the Magician is added, no doubt for its intrinsic historical interest and for what it says about the demise of magic before the gospel, but also to re-emphasise the importance of every individual's heart before God. Without genuine repentance and a true heart there is no entry amongst the people of God, no matter what the apparent outward response or the sacramental symbols. Peter and John return to Jerusalem preaching in Samaritan villages along the way. On the Christian side of the fence Jew and Samaritan are now one people.

At the beginning of this chapter I spoke of Christianity as a world-wide non-racial fellowship compared to the community of Israel. The appropriateness of that can now be seen. It is possible to

---

[14]Bruce, *Acts (Greek Text)*, 183 (2nd ed.).
[15]*Acts*, 114.

speak of the wider Christian 'community' in a loose sense, but, insofar as Jewish and Samaritan Christians had no common physical focus such as the Jews worldwide enjoyed in their temple, but only a common faith in Jesus, expressed in mutual acceptance and a sense of brotherhood, 'fellowship' seems a better description.

Philip's next assignment is to evangelize a eunuch of the court of the *Candace* of Ethiopia. (8:26-39) It is sometimes difficult to know how far to go in seeing significance in an author's details. Luke draws attention to their meeting in a desert place (8:26). Says Isaiah, 'Let not the eunuch say, "Behold I am a dry tree". For thus says the Lord: 'To the eunuchs...I will give in my house...an everlasting name....' (Isa. 56:4f.). God appears to be gathering the outcasts, according to his promise. It is a mistake to see this man as a Gentile. He is an Ethiopian (αἰθίοψ, 'burnt face'), but has been to Jerusalem to worship, so is presumably a proselyte. However, his emasculate condition would have barred him from sharing fully in the worship of the temple. He stands next to the Samaritans in Acts representing the circumcised worshipper of Israel's God who is nonetheless not fully acceptable. At the sight of water the eunuch asks a critical question, 'What prevents me being baptised?' Luke employs such rhetorical questions to stir his readers to agreement with the divinely led expansion of the boundaries of the people of God.[16] Had the eunuch asked what prevented him entering the temple, he would have been reminded of his physical imperfection. Nothing hinders his full inclusion amongst the people of Jesus and he goes on his way rejoicing.

X. Gentile breakthrough

The gospel has come now to Jews, Samaritans and outcast converts to Judaism. The next step is to the Gentiles. Luke has signalled their approach in Acts 2:39 and 3:25. Now comes the conversion of Saul and his appointment as 'a chosen instrument of mine to carry my name before the Gentiles and kings and the sons of Israel.' (9:15) It is one of the ironies of history that the first impulse towards a Gentile mission was the wave of persecution unleashed by Saul, and that he should then become the great missioner to the Gentiles.

It was the exodus of believers from Jerusalem following the death of Stephen which led to certain Cypriot and Cyrenaean Jews

---

[16]10:47; 11:17

speaking to Gentiles in Antioch with dramatic results (11:19-21). Luke holds back this report, however, until he has established the legitimacy of Gentile conversion. This he does by interrupting Paul's story to bring Peter back into the picture for the solemn purpose of validating the breakthrough of the gospel into the Gentile domain.[17] A significant proportion of Acts is now devoted to a detailed account of the conversion of Cornelius and the explanation of its significance before the Jerusalem elders (Acts 10:1-11:18).

Peter's reaction to being told to eat unclean animals is understandable. He was no Pharisee, but even an ordinary Jew was scandalised by the thought of the contamination attendant on eating defiled food. Social intercourse with Gentiles carried the same stigma. If there was any thought at this stage in the apostles' minds of a mission to the uncircumcised it certainly did not include joining them in table fellowship prior to their baptism, circumcision and cleansing. But Peter is told not to call common what God has cleansed and the scene is twice repeated. An unusual feature of the whole incident is the way Peter is called to attend on Cornelius in his home. A Gentile might acceptably approach a Jew out of doors to hear his message and perchance decide to become a proselyte. The Pharisees had an active missionary program (Matt.23:15). We have the story of the Capernaum centurion who, considerate of Jewish custom, declined to pressure Jesus to come to his home. (Luke 7:2-10) In Peter's case, the situation is divinely orchestrated to bring him into the Centurion's house to declare the gospel, in the midst of which, the Spirit comes to demonstrate God's acceptance.

The importance of this should not be overlooked. Peter says it is unlawful for a Jew to 'associate closely' (κολλᾶσθαι–10:28) with people of other races. By entering Cornelius' house he is doing precisely that, especially when the invitation is extended to 'remain for some days' (10:48). When, later on, he is criticized it is precisely at this point: 'Why did you go to uncircumcised men and eat with them?' (11:3) Thus more is achieved here than the conversion of a Gentile. Close association and table fellowship are established, implying brotherhood in a radically new people of God.

In this respect Luke's play on the word διακρίνω (10:20; 11:2,12;

---

[17]It is hard to suppress the feeling that the two examples of Peter's ministry in 9:32-43, besides their historical interest in charting the progress of the gospel among the Jews along the coastal plain, and besides bringing Peter to Joppa for his next 'divine appointment' are also intended to spotlight his incredible Christ-likeness at a moment when his authority is decisive to Luke's argument.

cf., 15:9) is noteworthy. The Jews prided themselves in their law-given ability to make accurate moral distinctions. διακρίνω is a key word meaning 'discriminate', 'make distinctions' or 'judge between right and wrong'. Blended into their moral understanding were the many fine distinctions which needed to be made on the basis of the laws of purity. In Acts 2:46 the Jerusalem Christians 'partook of food in gladness and ἀφελότης of heart.' ἀφελότης denotes their lack of questioning and scruple about whom they were eating with and whether their food was *kosher*, for table fellowship was a problem even amongst Jews. In 10:20 the Spirit tells Peter to go to Cornelius' house 'discriminating with respect to nothing' (μηδέν διακρινόμενος). In 11:2 the circumcision people criticised him (διεκρίνοντο), *i.e.*, they made moral distinctions at his expense. In 11:12 at the inquiry Peter repeats the Spirit's instruction to him to go 'discriminating with respect to nothing.' The counterpart to this is God's refusal to show favouritism to any one race (*cf.*, Rom. 2:11) and the fact that people who fear him and do right are acceptable (δεκτός, *cf.*,Luke 4:19) regardless of their nation (Acts 10:34f.). 'Acceptable' evidently implies more than acknowledging that someone in some manner belongs; with God it means intimate relationship, and it appears to be his intention that this should also be reflected in fellowship amongst his people.[18]

Peter concludes his explanation with a rhetorical appeal, which Luke intends also for his readers: 'Who was I that I could withstand God?' The critics were silenced and conceded that God had granted repentance and life to the Gentiles (11:17f.). The way Luke presents this, shows that his concern is wider than mere membership; it embraces the character of the emerging people and their interrelationships.

Luke moves at once to record the large number of Gentiles who had believed the preaching of the refugees from Jerusalem. The Jerusalem church sent Barnabas to Antioch to investigate, and he is able to report 'the grace of God' (11:23), so confirming the reality of these disciples' faith and the presence of God among them (*cf.*, Acts 4:33). The decision to send famine relief to their Judaean brothers is a demonstration of the κοινωνία uniting the two communities (11:27-30).

---

[18]This explains Paul's strong reaction to Peter's withdrawing from table fellowship with Gentiles in Antioch (Gal. 2:11ff.)

XI. Severance of church and synagogue

Following the destruction of yet another attempt to destroy the church, this time on the part of Herod, Luke begins what is to be his major preoccupation for the remainder of Acts: the mission of Paul. Material pertinent to the theme of the new people of God now becomes more sparse for the simple fact that, apart from the renewed attack from the circumcision party in chapter 15, and its settlement, Luke has developed the theme almost as far as he needs to go. Of course the rest of the book evidences the continual growth of the Christian movement, but it is told more from the viewpoint of the expansion and growth of the word of God than of the development of a community, though the two are correlates. What we are shown, in some detail, is the pattern of Jew-Gentile mission which Paul appears to have pioneered. One wonders whether this was not still so controversial at the time Luke wrote that it was part of the purpose of Acts to defend it. We generally assume that what Paul was doing in the West others were doing southwards and eastwards. We are then surprised by the absence of any documentation of these missions. But may it not be that Paul was a pioneer, and his approach unique? May it not also be that Luke is presenting it not simply as something that happened, but as much an act of God as the exodus and Jesus and Pentecost?[19] Could Luke be arguing that this is the way mission should be, and not only mission, because the mission grows out of an implicit ecclesiology?

Paul's pattern, wherever possible, was to begin in the synagogue, and only when this became unworkable as a base, to move to other premises. In doing this, he follows a conviction, shared by Luke, that God's covenant with Israel required it.[20] However, it would also have been a very natural thing for Jews belonging to a predominantly Jewish church to hope that other Jews might join them in what they saw as a biblical mission. The Jerusalem eldership's hostility need not have been the norm for other Jewish communities.[21] Only as the mission proceeded did it become increasingly apparent that it was.

According to Luke, the Jews were provoked to jealousy by the attention of the crowds to Paul's message and came out in opposition. The synagogue officially dissociated itself from the new movement,

---

[19]This is implicit in Paul's application of Isa. 49:6 to his own activity (Acts 13:47).
[20]Rom. 1:16; 15:8; Acts 3:25f; 13:46.
[21]Matera points out that in this speech (and throughout Acts) responsibility for Jesus' death is attributed not to all Jews, but to the Jerusalemites and their leaders, and that Luke's intention is to warn others against rejection. ('Responsibility').

forcing it to base itself elsewhere. Paul's words, 'It was necessary that
the word of God should be spoken first to you. Since you thrust it from
you and judge yourselves unworthy of eternal life, behold we turn to
the Gentiles' (13:46), are easily read in the light of a later period as a
final rejection of the Jews in favour of a new Gentile 'Israel', the church,
but nothing in the Acts context requires this, for a few lines later Paul
is again in a synagogue, at Iconium (14:1ff.).[22] Moreover, one must ask
why in this speech (and in others) Luke should so emphasize Israel's
elect status and its role as the theatre of God's saving work if it is his
understanding that all this has now been cancelled. Does it not sound
like an appeal to Jews? Surely, then, Luke means the speech to be read
and heeded by Jews and Jewish sympathizers among his own contemporaries. It is evident from the scriptural support Paul adduces for
his final action that his concern (and Luke's) is to justify his turning to
the Gentiles.

No scriptural justification is given for turning away from the
Jews, presumably because none was needed. It was neither theologically motivated, nor final, but forced on Paul by the attitudes of that
group of Jews. Paul had probably hoped that the synagogue as synagogue might accept his message, in which case it would become the
local church-synagogue, headquarters of missionary work amongst
the Gentile population, and a living witness to the saving, reconciling,
power of Christ.[23] Instead, he must shake the dust from his feet as
witness against them that they have ceased to be numbered amongst
the people of God, who are no longer delineated by virtue of their
membership in Jacob's family, but by their foreordination to eternal
life and their subsequent belief (13:48). Galatian Christianity was thus
forced to develop outside and away from the synagogue and the main
Jewish population. This would become a repeating pattern. Luke was
presumably unable to show us a case of a synagogue naturally evolv-
ing into a church, or he surely would have done so. Nevertheless, he
makes it clear (he is emphatic) that many Jews and proselytes responded positively and presumably joined with the newly converted
Gentiles[24] to form the church.

---

[22]Further, Tannehill, 'Rejection by Jews,' 83-101.

[23]In 13:47 Paul assumes the mantle of the Servant of Yahweh. The Servant vocation
was not restricted to Messiah alone; it was a calling meant to be shared by Israel.
That Paul and Luke should have wished that the Gentile mission should proceed
from a Jewish church is in accordance with their reading of the Scriptures: Acts
15:15-18.

XII. The culture of the new people of God

It is somewhat surprising to find the issue of circumcision raised a second time, and another long chapter devoted to it. This means that more than 10% of Acts is devoted to this question. However, the issue in chapter 15 is not the same as chapters 11 and 12. The concern there was to justify evangelism towards and fellowship with uncircumcised Gentiles. Such people soon become a fact of life in the churches. The question which then arose was their obligation towards the law, the need to be circumcised being uppermost. The fact that circumcision is singled out suggests that requirements for existing in covenant relationship with God were uppermost in the minds of the Jewish antagonists. The *Torah* required every descendant of Abraham to be circumcised or be 'cut off from his people' (Gen.17:9-14). The issue therefore, becomes whether salvation is to be found only within Israel, defined by its covenant of circumcision, or whether the nations which are promised blessing through Abraham (Gen.12:3) may find it within their own people. In modern terms this amounts to whether Gentile Christians were to be required to adopt Jewish culture as part of their obedience to Christ and as a condition of salvation. Had this been the way of it, an enormous stumbling block would have been placed in the way of the Gentile mission, and the preoccupation of the believer would have been shifted from 'the grace of the Lord Jesus' (15:11) to the considerable burden of keeping the law (15:4). Even more serious, the Pauline mission to that point would have been declared invalid, and its converts 'unsaved'. The new people of God would simply be an Israel enlarged by many proselytes.

Luke tells the story in such a way as to represent the proponents of circumcision as a small group within the church, emanating from the 'sect' of the Pharisees (15:5), and the Gentile mission as something which enjoyed the support of many Christian Jews. By including it Luke is able to rehearse the evidences of God's authorship of this expansion of the boundaries of his people. Paul and Barnabas bring joy to the brethren all along the way to Jerusalem as they report the conversion of the Gentiles. In Jerusalem they are welcomed by church, apostles and elders (15:2-5). At the ensuing debate Peter reminded the

[24]Acts 13:44 can only mean that the word has spread beyond the Jews, proselytes and God-fearers to the idol-worshipping Gentiles. Jervell's view (in 'Church', 11-20) that Acts does not include these latter among its candidates for salvation, and that Paul only preached to God-fearing Gentiles cannot be sustained (see 14:11-18; 16:16ff; 17:16-31; 18:10; 19:19, 23ff. and Sanders, 'Who is a Jew?' 443-451).

other apostles and elders that God had already given his testimony on
this question by giving the Holy Spirit to those who believed, making
no distinction (15:9). To seek now to yoke the Gentiles to a law that not
even Jews had been able to keep would be to provoke the Lord by
questioning what he had already settled. Paul and Barnabas then
recounted the evidences of God's work through them among the
Gentiles, and James summarised and supported the general conclusion from Scripture: the house of David has now been restored so that
the nations may seek the Lord. The implication drawn from this
scripture, in the light of the *de facto* existence of 'saved' Gentiles, is that
they may seek the Lord as Gentiles from within their own culture, and
not by becoming Jews. The covenant with Israel does not determine
the full boundary of the eschatological people of God. Christ's people
will number men, women and children of 'all peoples, nations and
languages'.

The only requirements made by the Council were that Gentile
Christians should refrain from a few practices which were abhorrent
to Jews. The only reason given for them is the existence of Jews in
every city (15:21). They should be taken, therefore, as a further affirmation of the Jew–Gentile fellowship which was emerging in the Pauline
churches, even if they are related to the laws applicable to the resident
alien (Lev.17-18).[25]

The leadership of the early church at this point appears to have
clarified its mind fully on the nature of the new people of God, and no
obstacle remained to the spread of Christianity to the ends of the earth.
One of the great strengths of Christianity is in every age has been its
adaptability to any culture, the basis of which was hammered out at
the Jerusalem Council.

XIII. An appeal to the Jews

In pursuit of our theme we come finally to Paul's meeting with the
Jews in Rome. Because they form a striking conclusion to Acts, his
words have been rightly seen as a key to understanding the author's
outlook on the Jews and the continuing people of God. It is surprising
that no record is given of Paul's meeting with the churches in Rome,
though there were a considerable number of believers in the city, many
known to him, whom he had previously intimated his desire to visit

[25]Further see Fitzmyer, *Luke the Theologian*, 175ff.

(Rom. 1:15). Haenchen's insinuation that Luke deliberately suppressed the fact of an existing Christian community in Rome is false; he even has them come out to welcome Paul.[26] All the more odd, then, that the book concludes with Paul's audience with and final speech to the Jews.

It is a commonplace of interpretation of Acts that Paul's quotation of Isaiah 6 and his concluding comment indicates the termination of any mission to the Jews in favour of a Gentile Christian church, to which is transferred all the covenant privileges of Israel. Frequently this view goes hand in hand with a dating of Acts late in the first century at a time when Christianity was predominantly Gentile.[27]

But would Luke want to subject Gentile readers to yet another appeal to the Jews at the conclusion of his work? Surely it makes more sense if it is Jews and Jewish sympathizers he is wishing to address. That some of the Roman Jews were convinced (28:24) ill accords with excising them finally from the people of God. Indeed, on almost every occasion when Jews have been addressed in Act some, and sometimes many, have believed. Luke's final statement that Paul welcomed all who came to him is equally difficult to square with such a conclusion.

The period AD 70–90 is a most unsuitable setting against which to try to make sense of the ecclesiology of Acts. The destruction of Jerusalem and its temple made it easy for anyone wishing to advance a case for Christianity as a new people of God. One wonders why the author of Acts would be bothered with the kind of arguments he marshals if he was writing with its memory. That his Peter or his Paul should never even warn of it in their speeches (which Luke is alleged to have invented) is extraordinary. He could have advanced no more powerful argument for God's displeasure with Judaism and the legitimacy of Stephen, Paul and the new people of God than by drawing attention to the destruction of Jerusalem. His silence on this is as perplexing as his silence on the end of Paul and Peter, unless he wrote before any of these things had eventuated.

The serious respect which the author clearly has for Judaism, and his passionate concern to establish the validity of the new people of God, particularly the legitimacy of Gentile Christianity, presupposes its novelty and fragility over against a Judaism with strength and unquestioned antiquity. This was the situation from the middle of

---

[26] Acts 28:15; Haenchen, Acts, 103.

[27] E.g., Haenchen: 'It is in Rome itself that stubborn Israel is subjected to one last appeal—and dismissed...' (Acts, 102; cf., 729). Esler, Community and Gospel, sees that Acts defends the legitimacy of Christianity for the sake of Jews and God-fearers joining the church, but places this in the post-70 era.

the first century to the outbreak of the Jewish War in AD 66. It is most unlikely that Judaism presented much threat to Gentile Christianity outside Israel itself for a long time after the disgrace of the great war. That Luke should devote such a proportion of Acts to establishing the freedom of Gentile believers from circumcision and Jewish law bespeaks a time when circumcision had some kudos in the wider world. We have observed the author framing rhetorical questions to his readers to judge for themselves on matters relating to the acceptance of outsiders and Gentiles into the ranks of the people of God (Acts 8:36; 11:17). What relevance could these have had when Gentiles were in the ascendant in the churches? That he should wish to represent the ἐκκλησία as in genuine continuity with God's salvific acts in Israel's history over against the priestly aristocracy, the Sanhedrin and the 'sects' of Sadducees and Pharisees presumes a situation in which church and synagogue are in deep rivalry with the synagogue in the ascendant. This is as it was pre-66, not post-70.

Luke's preoccupation with God-fearers, from which Jervell draws the conclusion that Paul never preached to pagans, is better explained if they are seen to be significantly represented amongst the people to whom Luke wishes to speak. The existence of a significant class of Gentiles drawn towards Judaism and the synagogue, who might be genuinely perplexed by the rival claims of Christians and Jews, is also a fact of the pre-war period, but is most unlikely for a long time afterwards.

Thus there are weighty considerations arising even from a narrow consideration of this one theme which favour our placing Acts before the outbreak of the war, and which drive us in a different direction when we come to interpret the final chapter of Acts.

Read against the background I have suggested, Acts 28 can be understood in a way which is in harmony with the rest of Luke–Acts and which makes perfect historical sense. The interface between church and synagogue in the early sixties was still fluid. Luke wishes still to win the undecided God-fearers and also Jews. It is for this reason that he concludes Acts with an audience with Jews in Rome and not with a meeting with the church. By the time he writes the pattern of eventual rejection of the gospel by the official Jewish community has become the norm. It is not the case, therefore, that he entertains any immediate hopes of the whole nation being won over, or even of whole synagogues. On the contrary, he anticipates general Jewish rejection with a positive minority response, but a much more favourable reaction from Gentile adherents of the synagogue. Paul reminds the

Jews of Isaiah's estimate of their hardness of heart: 'The Holy Spirit was right in saying to your fathers through Isaiah the prophet, "...You shall indeed hear but never understand... for the heart of this people has been made dull...".' (28:25-27). Does this indicate a final rejection of the Jewish people? It is a passage Jesus himself used to explain what would be the general Jewish response to his ministry, but also to stir up the attention of the remnant to whom it had been given 'to know the mystery of the Kingdom of God' (Luke 8:10 par.). Is it likely that Luke would intend his readers to place a different construction on the passage in Acts 28? Is it not better seen as Luke's way of saying, 'Do not imagine that the unbelief of the majority of Jews is evidence of the falsity of Christianity; Isaiah himself (and Jesus) said it would be so'. It is also a powerful appeal and warning to 'those who have ears to hear.' It is common in Acts for such speeches to end with such grave warnings (see 7:51ff; 13:40ff.), and they cannot all indicate a final rejection of all Jews. As for claiming this passage as evidence of Luke's anti-semitism, one would need also to accuse Jesus, Mark, Matthew and Isaiah.

Paul's exhortation concludes with the words, 'γνωστὸν οὖν ἔστω ὑμῖν ὅτι τοῖς ἔθνεσιν ἀπεστάλη τοῦτο τὸ σωτήριον τοῦ Θεοῦ. ῀αὐτοὶ καὶ ἀκούσονται (28:28). The RSV ignores the καί and translates the final sentence, 'They will listen,' implying a contrast between Jewish and Gentile response and creating an impression that Luke is announcing the end of the Jewish mission. But as Nolland[28] has shown 'they *too* will *hear*' is a better translation, which rather than jettisoning the Jews maintains the parallel observed throughout Acts that the gospel always comes first to the Jew and then to the Gentile. What Luke wishes to emphasise in the concluding sentences of Acts is not that the mission to the Jews is over, but that the mission to the Gentiles is a God-intended unstoppable fact. Thus his final description of Paul has him for two whole years welcoming 'all who came to him preaching the kingdom of God and teaching about the Lord Jesus'. Any exclusion is expressly denied.

In the sixties Judaism and the synagogue were powerful forces throughout the Empire. The churches were essentially struggling Jewish institutions[29] with a growing Gentile following. When Christianity emerged again into the light of day in the nineties and early

---

[28]Nolland, *Luke's Readers*, 106ff.
[29]Jervell is undoubtedly correct in observing that Jewish Christians were predominant in influencing the church pre-70 (*Paul*, 26-51).

second century, it was a predominantly Gentile movement with a minority of Jews. The period AD 70–90, about which we know very little, witnessed this transformation. It must have been a period of Gentile Christian advance, unhindered by a now seriously demoralised Judaism. No doubt it succeeded as well as it did partly because of the weakness of Judaism in the twenty years after the war, but also partly because of the powerful theological foundation laid by Luke and others.

XIV. A partial hardening of Israel

The development of our theme in Acts has ruled out the idea that the Jews have been rejected. Luke's church is always Jew and Gentile. This is not to say, however, that Luke does not acknowledge a judgement upon national Israel. Such is clearly indicated at many points in his Gospel,[30] and is tacitly acknowledged in Acts in Paul's final quotation of Isaiah 6. Luke does not say explicitly, as Paul does, that 'a partial hardening has come upon Israel' (Rom. 11:25), but in leaving us with Isaiah 6 he leads us to the brink. Always what we see in Acts is partial hardness and partial acceptance. Startlingly absent from Acts are warnings of national overthrow, though these are common in the Gospel of Luke. Does Luke still hold out the possibility that Israel might turn and disaster be averted, or did the apostles regard it as inevitable, but its repetition unconducive to evangelizing Jews?

Acts never makes the inclusion of the Gentiles a theological consequence of the rejection of Christ by the majority of the Jews, though they are so often connected that we are left wondering. Nor does it develop a positive theology of the jealousy stirred by the sight of the Gentiles in numbers becoming heirs to their blessings, becoming an instrument of Jewish salvation. Luke records the jealousy, but in his day it was the driving force of persecution. Nevertheless, in the light of Paul's interest in the possible role of jealousy in winning the Jews (Rom. 11:14) it is intriguing that the motif is there in Acts. Unlike Paul, Luke does not verbalise a scenario in which Israel as a whole will turn to Christ (Rom. 11:15, 16, 23, 25-31), but in his many expressions of hope in Israel's redemption (*e.g.*, Luke 24:21; Acts 1:6-7) he certainly creates the expectation. Luke and Paul do appear to be at one in seeing a connection between the turning of the nation Israel to Christ and the

---

[30]Luke 13:1-9, 34f; 19:11-27, 41-44; 20:9-18; 21:20.

Parousia. (Acts 3:19f; Rom. 11:12, 15) Reading Acts and Romans 11 side by side, one is struck by many suggestive similarities. The interesting thing is that Acts appears the more primitive, setting out the grist from which Paul has milled his extraordinary theology of the destiny of Jew and Gentile.

XV. The new people of God

Sufficient evidence of Luke's interest in the 'new' people of God has emerged from our investigation to justify our concluding that it must be rated as one of his major purposes in writing. He appears to place it within the context of 'the restoration of all things spoken by the mouth of his holy prophets', which, of course, includes the restoration of Israel. Accordingly, in the first half of Acts we are shown the establishment of a renewed Jewish church. Luke draws our attention to its prophetically prescribed twelve-fold leadership, the determination of its membership by the electing call of God and by each individual's belief in Jesus as 'Lord and Christ', and the many evidences of the attendance of God upon the new community.

In a series of attacks on the community's leaders by the established leadership of the Jews the claim of Jesus to be the true leader of the true people of God emerged, and we were brought to the point where, as the apostles grow in Spirit-led authority, God declares his judgement against the Jerusalem leadership. However, nowhere in Acts did we discover any concern to assert any administrative jurisdiction on the part of Christians over non-believers. Luke's concern transcended 'secular' politics.

In many places we saw Luke insisting on the continuity of the new people with elect Israel of the Scriptures. He rebuts the charge that 'the Way' is a party or sect like the Pharisees or Sadducees. On the contrary, it is the very same ἐκκλησία that accompanied Moses in the wilderness. In various speeches God's salvation acts in Israel's history are brought forward to show that what happened with Jesus and what is now happening in the church is part and parcel of the one great divine movement. The true people of God now, as always, are those who are aligned with that movement; those, therefore, who refuse to obey the prophet Jesus will be cut off from the chosen λαός.

As the gospel radiates forth from Jerusalem it encounters and embraces Samaritans, 'outcasts', and finally Gentiles. We saw that Luke's interest touched not only their conversion and recognition, but reached out to embrace them in the Christian fellowship. Though Acts displays minimal interest in any ecclesiastical system, it binds the Samaritans and Gentiles in close friendship to the original Jerusalem church. Specially noteworthy is Luke's interest in the table fellowship between Jewish and Gentile Christian, which was such a sticking point for many Jews, but which underlined the reality of the unity of these peoples in the one people of God.

Luke pays so much attention to the legitimacy of fully accepting the Gentiles as brother saints, and without their being circumcised, that we were forced to conclude that he wrote with this as a major concern, implying that he wrote into a situation in which the acceptance of Gentiles on Pauline terms was still controversial. The new people of God, as Acts shows it develop, is neither a renewed Jewry expanded by an inflow of proselytes, nor a Gentile 'new Israel' from which the Jews have departed, but a 'church of nations' (Gen. 28:3; 35:11; 48:4) from all peoples, the Jews included and first, and also the Gentiles. Believing Gentiles belong as heirs of Abraham's promise of blessing for the nations, not by being melded with the Jews through circumcision, but by being blessed with the gift of the Holy Spirit on the gracious initiative of God, and by their simple acknowledgement of Christ. Their cultural identity is preserved.

The new people are sometimes called ἅγιοι emphasising their identity with the old people of God, sometimes μαθηταί indicating their spiritual identity with those who literally listened and learned from Jesus, and sometimes ἀδελφοί indicating that, transcending all ethnic, cultic and social differences, they are one new people, brothers and sisters to each other, and also to the human Lord Jesus.

The unpleasant fact that Christianity was spurned by Jewish officialdom and failed to capture the synagogues is admitted throughout Acts; indeed, its progress is distinctly and emphatically charted. Nevertheless, it is seen to be in accordance with the Scriptures and the pattern of Israel's history. The notion of a partial hardening of Israel is hinted at, though not spelt out or theologically constructed.

The picture of the church as a fellowship of Jews, Samaritans and Gentiles is maintained to the end of Acts. The book closes with an appeal to Jews and their sympathizers to embrace Jesus and the kingdom, and with a severe warning against unbelief. If, at the present time, the majority of Jews refuse salvation, and if many Gentiles receive it, the plan of God is entirely uncompromised.

CHAPTER 18

THE WORSHIP OF THE NEW COMMUNITY

David Peterson[1]

Summary

In broad terms, Luke portrays Christian life and ministry as the way to worship or serve the God of Israel under the New Covenant. More specifically, such worship is the expression of faith in Jesus as Messiah and Lord. The doctrine of a new temple is not enunciated, though it is clear from the sermons in Acts that the resurrected Christ fulfils this Jewish ideal. He becomes the new point of contact between heaven and earth, pouring out the Spirit on disciples in Jerusalem and through their testimony becoming the means by which the nations are drawn to share the blessings of the End time. Within this framework of thought, what Acts says about early Christian gatherings takes on particular significance.

---

[1] A modified version of Peterson, *Engaging*, 136-165, reprinted with the permission of the publishers.

I. Introduction

It is remarkable that common terms for worship are rarely used by
Luke and that only once is such terminology applied to the activity of
a Christian meeting. Of course, Acts has much to say about the prayer,
praise and mutual ministry of the earliest churches. The distinctiveness of these activities can be measured by viewing them against
the background of contemporary Jewish and Graeco–Roman alternatives. Fundamentally, however, the theology of worship in Acts must
be established on other grounds.

An obvious starting point is an investigation of the role of the
temple and associated themes, particularly in the light of the apostolic
sermons. When the risen and glorified Jesus is proclaimed as the
source of life and blessing for Israel and the nations, the implication is
that he is to be the eschatological centre of true worship. As the focal
point of God's plans for Israel in the End time, Christ fulfils and replaces the temple and the whole method of approach to God associated with it. The message for Gentiles is not in the end very different:
a relationship with the living and true God is to be found by turning
from idols to serve the living Lord Jesus. By the Spirit-inspired preaching of the gospel, the ascended Lord draws people from every nation,
race and culture to himself. As in the OT, a genuine engagement with
God depends on the word of the Lord.

II. The earliest disciples and the temple

Continuing associations with the temple

The geographical, theological and literary centrality of Jerusalem and
the temple in Luke–Acts is widely acknowledged.[2] In the Gospel, the
temple appears as the place of divine revelation. Luke begins and ends
his infancy narrative with an important revelation in the temple (Luke
1:5-22; 2:41-50) and records that the prophecies of Simeon and Anna
about Jesus were also given in the temple courts (2:25-38). With these
narratives, Luke makes the point that the godly in Israel acknowledged Jesus and saw their piety leading inevitably to him. Jesus' final

---

[2] *Cf.*, Chance, *Jerusalem*. I have outlined the theological significance of the temple
in the OT and Jewish inter-testamental works in *Engaging*, 42-8.

visit to Jerusalem and the temple is then the focus of the lengthy central section of this Gospel (9:51–19:46). Following his much abbreviated account of the cleansing of the temple (19:45-6), Luke indicates that Jesus adopted the temple court as the place for propagating his own teaching about God and his purposes (19:47-8; cf., 21:37-8).

The third Gospel also emphasizes that the temple was 'a house of prayer' for Israel (19:46, cf., 1:8-10; 2:27-32, 36-8; 18:10-14) and thus concludes with the disciples returning to Jerusalem after the ascension of Christ, where they 'stayed continually at the temple, praising God' (24:53). While it is true that Luke betrays a predominantly positive view of the temple, it is overstating the case to argue that the Evangelist avoids making the temple the object of God's wrath.[3] Acts continues to portray the temple as a place of revelation. Most obviously, the disciples met regularly in the temple courts to teach and encourage one another (Acts 2:46; 5:12) and to give public testimony to the gospel about Jesus (3:11-26; 4:2; 5:42). This was not simply for the practical reason that the temple was a place where crowds could be easily addressed but because the disciples, like their master, wanted to take the word of salvation to the centre of Judaism itself. Later, the Apostle Paul received an important vision in the temple. However, this experience actually led him away from the temple (22:17-21), so that he could preach the resurrected Christ as the centre of true worship for all nations (e.g., 17:16-33).

The temple also remained for a while a place of public prayer for Christians. As well as meeting 'house to house', where they ate together and praised God as the community of the Messiah (2:46-7), the earliest Christians apparently went up to the temple at the set hours of prayer (3:1), continuing their association with the traditional practices of their religion (cf., also 21:20-6; 22:17-21).[4] Since 'the ninth hour' (3 p.m.) was the time of the afternoon sacrifice, the most natural way to read Acts 3:1 is to suppose that the disciples participated in the prayers associated with the burnt offering and incense at that time (cf., Exod. 29:38-43).[5]

This may at first seem strange, considering the indications in Jesus' teaching that he would somehow replace the temple in the plan

---

[3]Weinert, 'Temple', 87, artificially isolates the temple from what Jesus says about the fate of Jerusalem in Luke's Gospel. In reality, Luke does not 'spatially or theologically distinguish the temple from the city (Jerusalem)' (Giblin, Destruction, 58-9).

[4]This is the most satisfactory understanding of the plural ταῖς προσευχαῖς ('the prayers') in 2:42. Cf., Falk, 'Jewish Prayer Literature', 268-276.

and purpose of God.[6] Apart from the fact that the implications of his
position must have taken some time to be worked out, there are other
factors to be considered. As a group of pious Jews, aware of the fulfilment of Israel's hopes in the person and work of the Christ, they perceived that their fundamental task was to bear testimony to Jesus
before their fellow Israelites and so become the means by which other
Jews might be spared in the coming judgement and share in the blessings of the messianic era (cf., 3:17-26). Acts suggests that they were
aware of being distinct within their generation, the beneficiaries of the
New Covenant (cf., 2:38-41).[7] On the one hand, it was logical for them
to meet separately, to express their new-found relationship with God
through Christ and to strengthen one another in the role given to them
by God. On the other hand, if they were to function as the faithful
remnant, the servant community called to bring Israel back to God (cf.,
Isa. 49:5-6), they could not immediately disengage themselves from the
temple and separate themselves from the traditional practices of their
religion:

> The remade Israel does not turn aside from the old which still has
> claims upon her. The relationship is still open-ended. Though there
> may be little positive hope that Israel as a whole will repent, the
> relationship is not closed and Christianity has not turned aside from
> its source.[8]

By preaching in the temple, the Jerusalem Christians related Jesus
most closely to Jewish hopes about the End time. The messianic redemption had been accomplished. Christ had poured out the promised Spirit on the disciples in Jerusalem and made them witnesses to
him as the heavenly Lord. In him the blessings of 'the last days' were

---

[5]Josephus (*Ant.* 14.4.3) indicates that public sacrifices were offered in the temple
'twice daily, in the early morning and *about the ninth hour.*' If the early Christians
had wanted to make a complete break with the Jewish sacrificial system they
would have had to absent themselves from the afternoon sacrifice.
[6]*Cf.*, Peterson, *Engaging*, 80-107.
[7]Although the New Covenant is not mentioned by name in Luke's second volume
and Jer. 31:31-4 is not cited, Luke 22:20 suggests that we should look for indications
of the fulfilment of that prophecy in Acts. The language of Acts 2:38 is particularly
suggestive in this regard, with its offer of the forgiveness of sins. The promise of
the Holy Spirit relates to Joel 2:28-32, which parallels in sense the prophecy of Jer.
31:34 that 'they will all know me, from the least of them to the greatest.'
[8]Franklin, *Christ the Lord*, 78. The idea that they were the servant community is
suggested by the allusion to Isa. 49:5-6 in Acts 1:8. *Cf.*, Rosner, 'The Progress of the
Word', ch. 11.

being realized (2:1-39). However, since the early preachers focused on Jesus as the only source of eschatological salvation, and warned of divine judgement against those who rejected this gospel, the temple became the place where they experienced opposition and arrest (4:3; 5:25-6, cf., 21:27-30). Preaching about the centrality of the exalted Christ in God's plans for Israel suggested that he was a replacement for the temple, the law and the whole structure of worship associated with it. Such a message inevitably led to the exclusion of Christians from the temple and in due course also from the synagogues.[9]

The radical teaching of Stephen

Luke does not record the charge of the false witnesses at Jesus' trial nor mention any claim to destroy the temple and rebuild it when he presents the mockery of those who witnessed the crucifixion (Luke 23:35).[10] In his account of the trial of Stephen, however, he notes the accusation that he spoke 'against the holy place and against the law', claiming that 'this Jesus of Nazareth will destroy this place and change the customs Moses handed down to us' (Acts 6:13-14, cf., v.11).

As in the case of Jesus, the witnesses were apparently called false because they misrepresented what Stephen said. He seems to have taught that Jesus was the one in whom the law and the temple found fulfilment, predicting that judgement was coming upon Jerusalem because of its failure to acknowledge this. Luke uses the story of Stephen to summarize the rejection of the gospel by Jerusalem as a whole and Stephen's speech explains why this happened: 'Jerusalem preferred to remain with the Temple and to regard that as the final mark of God's favour, rather than let it lead them to Jesus to whom it pointed'.[11]

---

[9]'The fact of Jesus brings meaning to the Temple, but it also emphasizes its inability to make the Abrahamic covenant a reality unless it leads to him' (Franklin, *Christ the Lord*, 102). Note Franklin's helpful exposition of Peter's speech in Acts 3, showing how extensively Jesus is portrayed as the one in whom the covenant promises are confirmed for Israel.

[10]The evangelist may have wished to emphasize the responsibility of the political leaders for Jesus' death or to avoid any suggestion that Jesus himself wished to destroy the temple. McKelvey, *New Temple*, 86-7, suggests that Luke delayed recording this charge until Acts 6 because he wished to make the point that the judgement on Jerusalem and its temple 'is suspended till the gospel, duly fulfilled in the gift of the Spirit, has been offered and rejected, *i.e.*, till the first stage of the dominical commission ("you shall be my witnesses *in Jerusalem*") has been executed'.

Stephen responds to his accusers with counter-accusations, based on an interpretation of Israel's history (7:1-53) and set within the framework of an apocalyptic vision of Jesus the Son of Man, who is observed 'standing at the right hand of God' (7:55-6). This vision may be a way of asserting the readiness of the Son of Man to act in judgement against apostate Israel. Alternatively, it may be contrasting Jesus' 'place' in heaven with the temple as a nationally delimited 'holy place' in Jerusalem. Christ's heavenly and universal rule suggested the end of the temple as an expression of God's special relationship with Israel, since God's glory and purposes for the nations are clearly bound up with the glorified Christ.[12] Stephen makes no specific reference to the charge that he was 'against the law', beyond accusing Israel of being disobedient to the law and hostile to Moses (7:35-39). The climax of this disobedience has been the rejection of Jesus as 'the Righteous One', sent by God (7:52-3). Most of the speech responds to the charge of being 'against the temple', as Stephen asserts that the temple has been the focal point of Jewish disobedience.

Some scholars have argued that Stephen's speech was an attack on the building of the temple itself, viewing its erection as a declension from God. 'Better in his eyes is the Meeting-Tent in the desert where God and His folk may ever be on the move, than a material building which attempts to "localize" God—an attempt hopeless from the start, as the very builders realized (1 Kings 8:27).'[13] But it would be more accurate to say that the speech is an attack, not upon the temple itself, but 'upon an attitude which assigned permanence and finality to it. It is a discussion of the Jews' attitude to it in the light of their rejection of the Christ.'[14] Stephen is asserting that the promise to Abraham finds its ultimate fulfilment not in the law given to Moses nor in the temple

---

[11]Franklin, *Christ the Lord*, 102-3.
[12]*Cf.*, Giblin, *Destruction*, 110 note 14. For alternative views of the significance of Stephen's vision see Barrett, 'Stephen and the Son of man', 32-8; Crump, *Jesus the Intercessor*, 176-203.
[13]Cole, *New Temple*, 40. Simon, 'Saint Stephen and the Jerusalem Temple', 127, argues that 'the building of the Temple by Solomon seems to stand on the same plane as the making of the golden calf'. For Simon this means that Stephen's stance on the temple is different from Luke's (*cf.*, Simon, *Stephen and the Hellenists*, 24-6).
[14]Franklin, *Christ the Lord*, 105. Reference to the temple as (a house) 'made with hands' (7:48, χειροποιήτοις, *cf.*, Mark 14:58) comes close to Stephen's description of the idol that was made in the wilderness (7:41). Franklin rightly notes, however, that 'the question here is not one of worship, and so of idolatrous activity, but rather of a man-made institution which, by seeking to express some claim upon God, limits the divine freedom and so impairs the divine transcendence'.

but in Jesus to whom everything in the OT points.

Stephen's speech, therefore, has a very important function in the narrative of Acts. It shows that the expulsion of the earliest Christians from Jerusalem and the temple was the result of their preaching of Christ, which raised fundamental questions about the permanence and sufficiency of the institutions of Judaism. It also provides a theological introduction to Luke's narrative of the Gentile mission, by reaffirming that the Lord of heaven and earth cannot be tied to a single place (7:48-50, citing Isa. 66:1-2) and that Jesus as Son of Man has been exalted to the right hand of God. Devotion to the temple must not halt the advance of the divine plan for the people of God, which focuses on Jesus the glorified Messiah, who is Lord of all (cf., 10:36).

The narrowness of attitude which Stephen opposed comes to the fore again most dramatically with the later arrest of Paul. Even though he was engaged in traditional purification rites at the temple, some of his Jewish opponents from the province of Asia seized the opportunity to accuse him publicly (21:26-30). Here the issue was not simply the supposed presence of his Greek friends in the sanctuary but the way he preached to Gentiles (cf., 26:20-1). His teaching seemed to undermine Jewish beliefs about the centrality and permanence of the law and the temple in God's purposes.

The OT had spoken about the nations going up 'to the house of the God of Jacob', to learn from him so that they might 'walk in his paths' (Isa. 2:3). The theme of the Gentiles making a pilgrimage to Zion is clear in a number of OT prophecies (e.g., Isa. 60; Micah 4:1-3; Jer. 3:17-18). But the earliest Christian preachers indicated that the nations would find God in Jesus Christ. This was their testimony as the renewed Israel, as those who acknowledged the fulfilment of God's purposes for Zion in the Messiah and his people. The temple and the law were God's provisions for Israel until the dawning of the messianic era. Cultic regulations and other barriers to fellowship between Jews and Gentiles were being removed by God himself, so people from every nation could be united in his service (e.g., Acts 10:9-48; 15:1-35).

The coming of the Spirit and the preaching about Christ

Stephen's defence is designed to point Israel away from the temple to the resurrected and glorified Son of Man. Stephen may well have been the most radical exponent of this theme, but his focus on the exalted Lord Jesus is consistent with various other examples of preaching to

Jewish audiences in Acts (*e.g.*, 2:14-36; 3:12-26; 4:8-12; 13:16-41). Israel must be renewed by responding appropriately to the message about Jesus.

Peter's Pentecost sermon (2:14-40), with its application of the prophecy of Joel, is widely recognized as being programmatic for Acts as a whole. Joel 2:28-32 predicts that, 'before the coming of the great and glorious day of the Lord', God will pour out his Spirit on all flesh, and all will prophesy. Whereas the Spirit especially designated and empowered the prophets and other leaders of the people under the Old Covenant, God promised that all his people would be possessed by the Spirit in the last days. Joel's prophecy corresponds to some extent with Jeremiah's promise that all God's people would know him and obey him in a new way (Jer. 31:31-4). It also parallels to some extent Ezekiel's vision of the Spirit as 'the life-principle of a nation which truly knows the LORD and is inwardly his people' (Ezek. 36:26-7; 37:14; 39:29).[15] The Spirit is the 'organ of communication' between God and his people, guiding them and giving them power to witness to their Lord.[16] The coming of the Spirit is another way of talking about the coming of God to dwell amongst his people, to fulfil the ideal of the temple and to transform their lives by his presence (*cf.*, Ezek. 40–48). Acts goes on to show how the Spirit-indwelt community came to include believing Gentiles along with the Jewish disciples of Jesus (10:44-8; 11:15-17; 17:32-3).

Peter's sermon proclaims that the witnesses of Jesus' resurrection have received from the exalted Lord the promised Holy Spirit (2:32-3). Consequently, these are 'the last days' (2:16-17), and Jesus is the Lord upon whom everyone must call in order to be saved from the coming judgement of God (2:21,33-6; *cf.*, 22:16). The mode of the Spirit's bestowal on the Day of Pentecost corresponds to the missionary vocation of the disciples: his coming is indicated by the gift of prophetic speech and 'tongues' for the purpose of proclaiming the gospel to people from every nation. Those who repent and call upon Jesus as Lord and Christ, being baptised 'in the name of Jesus Christ', are promised that their sins will be forgiven and that they themselves will receive the gift of the Holy Spirit (2:37-9). In this way they will share in the benefits of the New Covenant and participate in the new community of the people of God.

---

[15]Lampe, 'Holy Spirit', 162. Lampe gives further references to show how the bestowal of the Spirit was a primary characteristic of the age of final redemption in Jewish expectation.

[16]*Cf.*, Turner, 'Spiritual Gifts', 7-64 (esp. 14-15, on 'the Spirit of prophecy' in Acts).

Thus, the Spirit in Acts is the witness to the fact that Jesus lives and is 'the present Lord'.[17] Spirit-inspired preaching about Jesus is the way in which his power and authority are made known and people are enabled to respond to the great saving events of his death, resurrection and ascension. In this way they may engage with the ascended Lord himself. As we shall see, Paul's preaching to Gentiles expresses the same truth in different terms. In the perspective of Acts, the glorified Lord Jesus is the new point of contact between heaven and earth for people of every race without distinction. The focus is not so much on his redemptive work as a fulfilment of the sacrificial system but on the idea that God's glory and kingly power are supremely expressed in Christ.

'Name' theology in Acts

The name of Jesus Christ represents his divine authority and his continuing power to grant the blessings of salvation (*e.g.*, 2:38; 3:6, 16; 4:10, 12; *cf.*, Luke 24:47). In 3:6, Peter 'releases the very power of healing through utterance of the name of Jesus Christ'.[18] Healing does not take place because the right formula is pronounced but because Jesus is openly acknowledged as the only source of help and salvation. The deeper significance of that name is explored in Peter's sermon (vv. 12-26). 'It is precisely the Jesus who came, as God's fulfilment of the hopes of Israel, who was crucified, was raised and vindicated, whose name has done this'.[19] In simple terms it was the exalted Lord Jesus who healed the lame man. But the name of Jesus continues to be the focus of Peter's thinking because he knows that the salvation promised by Joel and other eschatological prophets (*cf.*, Joel 2:32 in Acts 2:21) is for those who call upon the name of Jesus Christ (*cf.*, Acts 2:38). The healing of this man is a pointer to the saving power of Jesus in the widest sense (*cf.*, 4:10-12).

Since 'calling upon the name of the LORD' was a distinguishing mark of Israel in the ancient world, it was extremely provocative for the apostles to claim that Jesus was the one on whom to call for

---

[17]Franklin, *Christ the Lord*, 46.

[18]Haenchen, *Acts*, 200. *Cf.*, Bietenhard, *TDNT* V:277-8, and Ziesler, 'The Name of Jesus', 28-32.

[19]Ziesler, 'The Name of Jesus', 34. In Ziesler's words, 'the healing by the name is thus "gospelised" (of course in Luke's simple sense), and gospelised still in terms of the name'.

salvation. Furthermore, the name of God was associated with God's presence at the sanctuary, where he chose to encounter his people and where the authorized worship of Israel took place (*e.g.*, Deut. 12:5-11; 1 Kings 8:28-30; 9:6-7). In the temple context of Acts 2–4, focus on the name of Jesus signifies that the worship of Israel is being 'recentralized' and 're-mobilized' in the person of the Messiah.[20]

III. The challenge to the Gentile world

The gospel's encounter with pagan cults

From the time of Alexander the Great (356-323 B.C.), Greek culture and its religious notions and practices had continued to have the most pervasive influence on the Mediterranean world. No official Greek religion appeared such as was known in Babylonia, in Egypt, in Rome or among the Jews. Many local 'cults' were transported to new sites by missionary efforts or were copied by other communities. New cults were practised alongside older cults, sometimes being fused with one another in the course of time. Polytheism is essentially tolerant of all faiths. Thus, throughout the Roman Empire, religion was essentially the result of the fusion of local traditions and elements common to the wider world of Greek thought and practice.

Paul's encounter with paganism in Lystra is dramatically presented in Acts 14:8-18. Here the local Lycaonian cult appears to have identified its gods with Zeus and Hermes, to make its deities more understandable to the classical world.[21] The theme of worship is at the heart of Luke's brief account of Paul's preaching, as in the more substantial proclamation at Athens (17:22-31). The call to turn from the futility of pagan worship (v. 15, τούτων τῶν ματαίων) is represented as 'good news' (εὐαγγελιζόμενοι). Primarily this is because of the liberating truth that there is one living and true God, who created and sustains all things. Luke's editorial note (v. 18) suggests that Paul was unable to continue with his message and proclaim Christ in this context.

---

[20]Perry, 'No Other Name', 90-5, argues that authentic worship in Israel is restored among those who see mighty works done in Jesus' name, repent and receive forgiveness in his name, gather in his name to hear the apostles' teaching about him, and pray in his name. *Cf.*, Buckwalter, 'The Divine Saviour', ch. 6.
[21]Gill and Winter, 'Roman Religion', 84-5.

Apart from the explicit mention of local cults in Lystra and
Athens, Paul's contact with other cults is implied by the record of
places visited and certain details in the narrative. D. Gill has argued
this particularly with reference to local cults at Paphos (13:6-12) and
Ephesus (19:23-7) and B. Winter has proposed that an encounter with
the authorities over the imperial Roman cult is suggested by Acts
18:12-17.[22]

Paul's preaching in Athens

Although Paul was clearly familiar with the beliefs and practices of
paganism, Luke records that in Athens he was particularly distressed
'to see that the city was full of idols' (17:16). His reaction was twofold.
As was his custom, he turned first to the synagogue and reasoned with
the Jews and God-fearing Greeks, presumably preaching Jesus as the
Christ and showing how the Scriptures had been fulfilled in his death
and resurrection (cf., 13:16-41; 17:2-4). However, he also dialogued in
the market-place daily with 'those who happened to be there'. Paul
may well have employed some of the argument detailed later in the
chapter, but those who heard him were convinced that his message
was essentially about 'Jesus and the resurrection' (v. 18). In other
words, Paul was not simply engaged in apologetics or pre-evangelism.
He apparently saw that the preaching of Jesus and the resurrection
was the key to persuading those who were given over to idolatry.

For all that, some of his listeners categorized him as yet another
preacher of 'foreign gods' or strange powers (ξένων δαιμονίων, v.
18).[23] Such novel teaching had to be examined by the experts in the
court of the Areopagus, an ancient institution exercising jurisdiction in
religion and morals in Athens (vv. 19-20). Paul's defence carefully
weaves the themes of ignorance and worship together. He notes the
extent of their religious feeling, as indicated by the many objects of
their devotion (σεβάσματα), but insists that the altar dedicated 'to an
unknown god' is a pointer to their ignorance of the true God (vv. 22-
3). When the text of the following verses is closely examined, it is clear
that he puts forward a number of OT perspectives about the character

---

[22]Gill and Winter, 'Roman Religion', 87-103.
[23]When Paul spoke about 'Jesus and the resurrection' it is possible that they
understood him to be speaking about 'the personified and divinized powers of
"healing" and "restoration"'. Cf., Bruce, Acts, 330-1.

and purpose of God, the foolishness of idolatry, and human responsibility in relation to God, without actually quoting scripture (vv. 24-
29).[24] The true God cannot be accommodated in human sanctuaries
and have his needs met by those who would serve him (θεραπεύεται,
v. 25),[25] since he is the creator of all things.

Each part of the carefully worded statement in vv. 24-5 attacks an
important presupposition of paganism. Furthermore, God's ordering
of nature and history is designed to provoke men and women to 'seek
him and perhaps reach out for him and find him' (vv. 26-7). The
characteristic response of humanity has been the lie of idolatry, even
though it is totally illogical and has often been acknowledged as such
by pagan poets and philosophers (vv. 28-9). Such 'ignorance' of God is
actually culpable. In the framework of teaching about the judgement
of God against all false worship, Paul then introduces again the theme
of Jesus and the resurrection (vv. 30-1).

The apostle's conclusion is that Gentiles can seek God and find
him by turning in repentance from their idolatry and believing in the
resurrected Jesus. By implication, this is to offer acceptable worship to
'the living and true God' (cf., 1 Thess. 1:9-10).[26] Such preaching about
the resurrection from the dead and the need to acknowledge the divine
kingship of Jesus inevitably led the early Christians into direct conflict
with the pluralism and relativism of the Graeco–Roman world.

IV. Homage and service under the New Covenant

Luke's use of traditional terms for worship is limited, but revealing.[27]
A brief survey of the relevant texts confirms the view already outlined,
that a new theology of worship is being enunciated in Luke–Acts, with
Jesus at its centre.

---

[24]Cf., Bruce, Acts, 334-5. The essential content of the speech is biblical, 'but the
presentation is Hellenistic', 341.

[25]The θεραπεύειν word-group regularly conveys the notion of cultivating the
favour of the gods by sacrifice. Consequently, it is rarely used in a religious sense
in the LXX and is only used in that way in Acts 17:25 in the NT. The religious
application of the terminology is common in Greek inscriptions and papyri (cf.,
Beyer, TDNT III:128-9).

[26]On the preaching of the resurrected Christ as the centre of true worship for the
nations, cf., O'Toole, 'Paul at Athens', 185-97.

[27]I examine the meaning and application of such terms in the OT and Greek literature in Engaging, 55-79, before proceeding to an analysis of their use in the NT.

Homage to the ascended Lord

Luke generally restricts the important term προσκυνεῖν ('to bend over, pay homage, worship') to a quite technical usage, applying it to those engaged on a pilgrimage to honour God in the temple at Jerusalem (Acts 8:27; 24:11, *cf.*, John 12:20) or to the practice of idolatry (Acts 7:43, adapting Am. 5:26). On one occasion, however, he uses it to describes a response to the exalted Christ. When Jesus was taken up into heaven, the disciples 'worshipped him' and then returned to Jerusalem with great joy, where they stayed continually at the temple, praising God (Luke 24:52-3).[28] Perhaps Luke reserved the term for this climactic moment to indicate that this was at last the real recognition of Christ by the disciples.[29]

This passage highlights the paradox of early Christian worship then presented in the early chapters of Acts. Prayer and praise were offered to the glorified Jesus while adoration continued to be offered to the God of their ancestors in the context of the Jerusalem temple.

As the earliest disciples proclaimed the exalted Christ and called upon their fellow Israelites to acknowledge him as the giver of the Spirit (Acts 2:33), 'the author of life' (3:15), and their only saviour in the coming judgement (4:12), they were, in effect, summoning them to worship Jesus, as they themselves had done. Yet Luke did not go on to employ προσκυνεῖν in Acts to describe either initial acts of homage and devotion to Christ or the content and purpose of regular Christian gatherings. Such terminology was presumably not applied to Christian meetings in Acts or the Epistles because of its particular association with the rites of paganism or with the Jewish cult centred at Jerusalem.

The confession of Jesus Christ as Son of God, Lord and Saviour, was at the very heart of the earliest Christian preaching (*e.g.*, Acts 2:36; 5:42; 9:22; 10:36; 1 Thess. 1:9-10; Col. 1:28; 2:6-7). Such confession was also the essential response to that preaching required from those who joined the apostolic group and were baptised 'in the name of Jesus

---

[28] Although προσκυνήσαντες αὐτόν is missing from Western texts, this reading is well attested and should be accepted. Criticism of the 'Western non-interpolation' approach to textual criticism is aptly made by Metzger, *Textual Commentary*, 163-6 (2nd ed.).

[29] So Fitzmyer, *Luke X-XXIV*, 1590. Note, however, the significant response of Simon to Jesus in the narrative of Luke 5:1-11. Luke regularly records that people 'fell down' before Jesus as a gesture of respect, associated with supplication or gratitude (5:8, 12; 8:28, 41, 47; 17:16).

Christ' (*e.g.*, Acts 2:38; Rom. 10:9-13; Heb. 3:1; 4:14). Its centrality to the
Christian life is further suggested by various indications in the Pauline
letters of primitive credal statements (*e.g.*, Rom. 1:3-4; 10:9-10; 1 Cor.
8:5-6), and possibly some hymn fragments (*e.g.*, Col. 1:15-20; Phil. 2:5-
11), celebrating 'the elevation of Jesus to a position of transcendent
status and a uniquely close connection with God'.[30] Some of these rem-
nants of early church tradition may take us back to Palestinian congregations and to Christians whose native language was Aramaic, as
with the untranslated Aramaic prayer 'Maranatha' ('Our Lord [or O
Lord] come!' 1 Cor. 16:22).

Prayer to Jesus as Lord was offered by Stephen (Acts 7:59-60), in
a way that is striking when compared and contrasted with the prayers
of Jesus to the Father (Luke 23:46, 34). Ananias also prayed to Jesus as
Lord (9:10-17, where v. 17 shows that the 'Lord' addressed was Jesus)
and designated the followers of Jesus as those who call on his name
(9:14; *cf.*, 22:16). Again, it is most likely that Jesus is the Lord addressed
in prayer by the disciples in 1:24.[31] Paul is represented as calling upon
him as Lord on the Damascus road (9:5; 22:10; 26:15-18) and in a subsequent vision in the temple (22:17-21).

As Jesus Christ was acknowledged to be the unique agent of
God's saving purposes and the Son of God at his right hand, he became
an object of devotional attention in a way that was characteristically
reserved for God alone in Jewish tradition. This did not begin at a later
stage, under the influence of pagan thinking, but amongst the first
circle of Palestinian Jewish Christians. It was an extraordinary development within the Jewish monotheistic tradition, which did not
destroy the fundamental notion of belief in one God. In short, it was
'an unprecedented reshaping of monotheistic piety to include a second
object of devotion alongside God'.[32] Such devotion to Christ was not
restricted to prayer or praise, but is presented as a pattern of daily
obedience to the exalted Lord, thus distinguishing Christians from
every other contemporary religious group.

---

[30]Hurtado, *One God, One Lord*, 95. *Cf.*, Martin, 'New Testament Hymns', 37-49,
France, 'The Worship of Jesus', 17-36, and Hengel, *Jesus*, 78-96.
[31]'In view of the fact that in 1:2 the same verb is used of Jesus choosing the apostles,
it is more probable that he is the one addressed here.' (Marshall, *Acts: Commentary*,
66). *Cf.*, Bruce, *Acts*, 47.
[32]Hurtado, *One God, One Lord*, 100. Against those proposing that the worship of
Christ was a late development, resulting from the impact of Graeco–Roman thinking on Christianity, see esp. Hurtado, 93-100. He argues persuasively that such
devotion was a direct outgrowth from, and indeed a variety of, Jewish traditions.

Serving the Lord

In the 'Song of Zechariah' we are told that the whole purpose of the messianic redemption is to enable God's people to worship or serve him (λατρεύειν αὐτῷ/, Luke 1:74). As in the book of Exodus, God has come to save his people in a mighty way, to fulfil the terms of the covenant he made with Abraham. This time he has used the Messiah as a 'horn of salvation', to set his people free from fear of oppression by their enemies, so that they might serve him appropriately. The salvation on view is experienced by means of the forgiveness of sins (v. 77), recalling the promise of Jer. 31:34. The service that this makes possible is nothing less than a lifestyle of 'holiness and righteousness before him all our days' (v. 75).

Zechariah's prophecy establishes a theological framework within which to understand the work of Christ and the life of the early church. When the messianic salvation is proclaimed, those who respond to the gospel are empowered by the Spirit to serve God as he desires. The life of the community depicted in the summaries at Acts 2:42-7 and 4:32-5 particularly highlights what it means to serve God in holiness and righteousness, as the renewed Israel.

Luke later has the Jews at Corinth charge Paul with persuading the people to worship or fear God (σέβεσθαι τὸν θεόν) 'in ways contrary to the law' (Acts 18:13), referring to the whole way in which Paul taught that the Gentiles could be related to God. Similarly, he has Paul describing his Christian life and ministry in the broadest possible terms as a way of worshipping or serving the God of Israel: 'I worship (λατρεύω)the God of our fathers, as a follower of the Way, which (the Jews) call a sect' (24:14; *cf.*, 27:23). The context suggests that Paul had found the way to serve God that fulfilled the Law and the Prophets. Even though some regarded Christians as merely 'a sect' (αἵρεσις) of Judaism, they preferred to designate themselves as 'those of the Way' (9:1; 19:9, 23; 22:4; 24:14, 22).[33] Their 'worship' was a pattern of life with Jesus at its centre.

Paul also describes his ministry of preaching and teaching about the Lord Jesus at Ephesus as a way of 'serving the Lord' (20:19, using the verb δουλεύειν). Since such traditional worship terms were used

---

[33]Marshall, *Acts: Commentary*, 168-9, suggests that behind this term lies the concept of 'the way of the Lord/God' (18:25-6) as the 'way of salvation' (16:17), and notes parallels in the literature of the Qumran Sect and other religious groups. *Cf.*, Ebel, *NIDNTT* 3:935-943.

with a narrowly cultic reference in other contexts (*e.g.*, 7:7,42), it is clear that they were being adapted to express something quite different in Christianity. The notion of worship was certainly not restricted by Luke to what the early Christians did when they met together.

There is only one context in Acts where the language of worship is specifically applied to the activity of a Christian gathering. In Acts 13:2 the prophets and teachers of Antioch are said to be 'worshipping' or, more literally, 'serving' the Lord (λειτουργούντων...τῷ κυρίῳ) and fasting, when the Holy Spirit calls for the sending forth of Barnabas and Saul on their first missionary journey. The verb λειτουργεῖν and related words were regularly employed in the LXX in a technical sense, to describe the priestly service of the God of Israel (*e.g.*, 2 Chron. 11:14, Joel 2:17, Ezek. 45:4, *cf.*, Luke 1:23; Heb. 10:11). This terminology was not used to describe the worship or service of the Israelite nation as a whole but only the ministry of priests to God, as accredited representatives of the nation, and of Levites to priests. Later Jewish literature indicates some movement towards a general figurative application of these words.[34] The terminology is certainly being used in a transformed sense by Luke.

The meeting on view in Acts 13:2-3 could have involved the whole church, but it is also possible that it was 'a small prayer fellowship of leading men'.[35] Many commentators take v. 2 as a reference to prayer,[36] since v. 3 speaks about prayer and fasting. If this is correct, Luke will be highlighting corporate prayer as the 'cultic' activity which replaces the sacrificial approach to God which was at the heart of Judaism. It is possible, however, that Luke means that 'these prophets and teachers were carrying out their appointed ministry in the church'.[37] In other words, the ministry of prophecy and teaching, which was exercised by those especially gifted for the benefit of other believers in the congregation, was a specific way of serving or worshipping God under the New Covenant. If the service of God involved a certain lifestyle and ministry in everyday contexts, it also had a definite expression when Christians gathered together.

---

[34]*Cf.*, Wisdom 18:21 and Daniel 7:10 in particular and note the application of the more general Hebrew word for 'service' (עבדה) to prayer by the Rabbis (R. Meyer, *TDNT* IV: 225).

[35]Strathmann, *TDNT* IV: 227. *Cf.*, Schweizer, *Church Order*, 73, 172.

[36]So Haenchen, *Acts*, 395-6, Reicke, 'Reflections', 195, and Marshall, *Acts: Commentary*, 215.

[37]Bruce, *Acts*, 245 (my emphasis). *Cf.*, 1 Clement 44:3 and Didache 15:1.

V. The character and function of early Christian gatherings

Two summary passages in the early chapters of Acts suggest that Luke was presenting something of an 'apology' for the Jerusalem church to his readers (2:42-7; 4:32-7).[38] The new community was not a break-away movement from Judaism, nor merely one of several sects within Judaism, but the true people of God, the renewed Israel where his Spirit was powerfully at work. Elsewhere, Luke only touches on aspects of what believers did when they met together, or emphasizes historical events to which the activities of a gathering were something of a backdrop (*e.g.*, 13:2; 20:7-11).

Acts 2:42 provides a brief summary of the activity of the first group of Christians, where we are told that 'they devoted themselves to the apostles' teaching and to the fellowship, to the breaking of bread and to prayer'. Some commentators regard the four elements specified in this verse as a primitive liturgical sequence, implying that their meetings regularly involved instruction, [table] fellowship, then the Lord's Supper and prayers.[39] However, 2:44-7 appears to be an expansion on this initial summary and some of the things mentioned there clearly took place at different times and in different places. Luke is giving a description of the ministry of these disciples to one another in a variety of contexts, not simply telling us what happened when they gathered for what we might call 'church'. Here is a brief portrayal of their community life as a whole.

In 4:32-7 many of the same details are presented in a different order and in an expanded form. The alarming narrative about Ananias and Sapphira follows (5:1-11), with another summary of the way God was powerfully at work to bless those in Jerusalem and beyond (5:12-16). This whole sequence shows the holiness of the Christian fellow-ship, apart from the observance of dietary or purificatory rites so common in Judaism, and demonstrates that 'God is near to, and jealously guards the new community, which is his own possession'.[40]

---

[38]Seccombe, *Possessions*, 215-18. See note 45 below for the particular relevance of this apologetic to Hellenistic readers. In more general terms, the early chapters of Acts are designed to show how prophetic expectations are first fulfilled in the renewed community in Jerusalem.

[39]So, Jeremias, *Eucharistic Words*, 118-22, followed by Marshall, *Luke: Historian*, 204-6, and *Acts*, 83. Haenchen, *Acts*, 191, argues strongly against this position, asserting that 'the activities paired with καί represent detached and self-contained units.' Moule, *Worship*, 18-19, argues positively for the view that vv. 44-7 expand on v. 42.

The centrality of teaching

Luke uses a strong verb in 2:42, 46 (προσκαρτεροῦντες, 'devoting themselves to')[41] to stress that the earliest disciples were pre-occupied with and persevered in the activities he lists. Their first pre-occupation was with the apostolic teaching. Meeting together in the temple courts (2:46) appears to have been for the express purpose of hearing the apostolic preaching (cf., 3:11-26; 5:21), though there were also opportunities for teaching in the home context.

We may surmise that these earliest converts desired to be encouraged in their faith but also to identify with the public preaching of the gospel to their fellow Israelites as an act of testimony to its truthfulness. Apostolic instruction continued to be at the centre of church life later in Gentile contexts (e.g., 11:25-6; 18:11; 19:9-10; 20:7-12, 20-1, 28-32; 28:30-1). B. Blue has rightly pointed out that there were two different spheres in which the early communities operated, the public and the private, each requiring facilities to accommodate their different needs.[42] Luke draws attention to the central importance of the apostolic word in both public and private spheres.

The expression of Christian fellowship

The κοινων- words in Greek normally mean 'to share with someone in something' above and beyond the relationship itself, or 'to give someone a share in something'.[43] The terminology is used in a number of NT contexts to refer to the joint participation of believers in Christ (e.g., 1 Cor. 1:9) or the Holy Spirit (e.g., 2 Cor. 13:14) or their share in the demands and blessings of the gospel (e.g., Phil. 1:5). Common participation in Christ necessarily leads to a mutual fellowship amongst members of the Christian community (e.g., 1 John 1:3).

At first glance, τῇ κοινωνίᾳ in the absolute sense (literally, 'the sharing') in Acts 2:42 refers to the sharing of material blessings described in vv. 44-5.[44] There we are told that 'All the believers were together and had everything in common (κοινά). Selling their possessions and goods, they gave to anyone as he had need'. Yet this sharing

[40]Cf., Seccombe, Possessions, 213. Earlier in the same chapter Seccombe outlines the parallels between Acts 2:42-7 and 4:32–5:16.
[41]Cf., Grundmann, TDNT III: 618.
[42]Blue, 'Jewish Worship', ch. 23.
[43]Cf., Hauck, TDNT III: 804-9.

was clearly a practical expression of the new relationship experienced together through a common faith in Christ (*cf.*, vv. 38-41). This is affirmed in a later passage, where a similar statement about sharing their possessions is prefaced by the words 'all the believers were one in heart and mind'. (4:32-7). Luke highlights their unity in several contexts by the use of the word ὁμοθυμαδόν ('together', 1:14; 2:46; 4:24; 5:12). That relationship brought a certain sense of responsibility to one another. The sharing of goods came to include the distribution of food to the needy in their midst (*cf.*, Acts 6:1-2) and was certainly not restricted to formal gatherings of the believers. It may be best, therefore, to give κοινωνία its widest interpretation in 2:42, including within its scope 'contributions, table fellowship, and the general friendship and unity which characterized the community.'[45]

It is important to note that this sharing of property and possessions was voluntary and occasional. The need of that first community of disciples in Jerusalem was related to the physical and social environment in which they found themselves. Their progressive isolation from unbelieving Israel must have made the economic situation of many very precarious. Here was no primitive form of 'communism', but a generous response to particular problems in their midst (2:45; 4:34-5). The examples given in 4:37; 5:4 show that people did not dispose of their whole estate but only certain portions of it. Believers continued to maintain their own homes and used them for the benefit of others in the church (*e.g.*, 12:12). There was no rule about the common ownership of property such as was found amongst the men of the council of the Qumran Community.[46]

---

[44]So Moule, *Worship*, 18-19. He suggests that this is more appropriate in the flow of the argument than alternative interpretations, such as 'the fellowship of the Holy Spirit' or 'the fellowship of the (sacramental) bread and wine'. Hauck, *TDNT* III:809, summarily dismisses the suggestion that it can signify 'the community of goods.'

[45]Seccombe, *Possessions*, 204. Seccombe argues from the use of κοινωνία in Hellenistic literature that Luke's description of the common life, meals, and material sharing of the Jerusalem church was designed 'to commend Christianity, or perhaps the church itself, to people for whom κοινωνία was a supreme virtue.' (200-209)

[46]Even though Capper, 'Community of Goods', 324-56, has argued that the activities recorded in Acts are close in form to the more widespread *Essene* practice of community of goods, he makes some important qualifications (340-1).

Eating together

'The breaking of (the) bread' (τῇ κλάσει τοῦ ἄρτου) in Acts 2:42 most obviously refers to the common meals shared by the earliest disciples in their homes (v. 46). They met 'by households' (κατ' οἶκον) and they met 'daily' (κατ' ἡμέραν), perhaps particularly because of the physical needs of many in that community. The literary and non-literary evidence shows that domestic residences continued to be the venue for Christian gatherings in Gentile contexts until the fourth century.[47]

Some commentators argue that the expression in 2:42 is a technical term for the Lord's Supper and that this was already separated from the ordinary meals of the Jerusalem Christians in some way.[48] 'To break bread' in other contexts, however, describes an ordinary meal in terms of the Jewish custom of initiating the meal by breaking a loaf and distributing bread to all present (e.g., Luke 24:30, 35; Acts 27:35). To 'break bread' was to eat together. The adoption of this term as a title for the Lord's Supper is not formally attested until the second century AD (cf., Didache 14:1; Ignatius, Eph. 20:2). When Luke mentions in Acts 2:46 that they were 'breaking bread in their homes', he goes straight on to say (literally) 'they were partaking of food with glad and sincere hearts'. The language implies that they were eating food to sustain physical life. What is the ground for giving the expression a different meaning in v. 42?

It might be argued that the reference to the meeting of the Christians in Troas 'on the first day of the week' in order to break bread (κλάσαι ἄρτον) is a pointer to a formal Sunday gathering for the purposes of the Lord's Supper (20:7).[49] But Paul's discussion with them occupied their attention until after midnight and again after the meal, suggesting that it was a very unstructured and informal meet-ing. When Luke mentions that Paul finally broke bread (perhaps on behalf of everyone present), he adds 'and when he had eaten, he engaged in

---

[47]Blue, 'Acts and the House Church', 119-222. Blue, 'Jewish Worship', ch. 23, has also shown how the synagogue practice of table fellowship provides a significant background for the development of Christian activity in this regard.

[48]Jeremias, Eucharistic Words, 120-1, takes 'the fellowship' of Acts 2:42 to refer to the fellowship meal (called the Agape) and 'the breaking of bread' to refer to 'the Eucharist' which had become separated from the meal proper. However, as noted above, this is an illegitimate narrowing of the meaning of κοινωνία in the context. Marshall, Last Supper, 127, rightly proposes that here and in 1 Cor. 11:17-34 'the Lord's Supper proper took place in the context of a fuller meal held by the congregation'.

[49]Cf., Marshall, Acts: Commentary, 325; Foerster, TDNT III:1096.

much further conversation until dawn' (v. 11). It is really quite artificial to suggest that the meal by which Paul satisfied himself after such a long time was somehow distinct from 'the breaking of bread'. Since Christian meetings were largely held in the context of private homes, it is natural that they expressed their fellowship in terms of eating together.

In my judgement, therefore, 'the breaking of bread' in Acts cannot be taken to refer to a liturgical celebration distinct from the everyday meals that believers shared together. Such meals were doubtless 'full of religious content because of the recollection of the table fellowship which Jesus had with his followers during his earthly ministry'.[50] The reality of Christian fellowship was expressed from the earliest times in the ordinary activity of eating together. Furthermore, these meals were presumably given a special character by the fact that they were sometimes associated with teaching, or prayer or praise. Perhaps the grace at the beginning or end of the meal focused particularly on the person and work of the Lord Jesus, reminding the believers of the basis of their fellowship in him. In this way, a meal could be given the same sort of significance that Paul wished to ascribe to the community suppers at Corinth (1 Cor. 10:16-17; 11:17-34).[51]

Eating together was a way of expressing the special relationship which believers had with one another in Christ and the special responsibility to one another involved in that relationship. These meals may well have been informal expressions of what was later more structured and organized.

Prayer and praise

Christians in Acts are portrayed at prayer in a variety of contexts. In the earliest chapters, they are found praying at the temple and in

---

[50]Behm, *TDNT*, III:730. He argues that Acts 2:42,46 'has nothing to do with the liturgical celebration of the Lord's Supper', (731) but says that the meal in 20:11 'within the context of the Pauline mission' must be the cultic meal described by Paul as the Lord's Supper in 1 Cor. 11:20. It is unlikely, however, that Luke would use the same expression in two similar contexts quite differently.

[51]Moule, *Worship*, 20, rightly argues that 'it is not in the words "the breaking of the loaf", but in their context that one must look if one is to detect any further significance in what the Christians did together at their meals'. Moule, 21-6, ably challenges the distinction made by some scholars between a primitive Palestinian fellowship-meal and a sacramental, Hellenistic 'Eucharist'. *Cf.*, Peterson, *Engaging*, 215-18.

homes, but not in Palestinian synagogues. After Jesus' ascension, the disciples 'all joined together constantly in prayer' (1:14), specifically praying on one occasion for guidance concerning the appointment of a twelfth apostle (1:24). After the Pentecost account, we are told of their continuing participation in the set times of prayer at the temple, presumably in the company of other Jews (2:42, cf., 2:46; 3:1). But their eating together in households involved 'praising God' (2:47) and must also have involved prayer in the strict sense of petition.[52]

A meeting to give thanks for deliverance from persecution and to pray for effectiveness in gospel ministry is given great prominence in 4:24-30, where the point is made that such prayer plays an integral part in the advancement of God's word and saving purpose (v. 31). Luke later highlights leaders' meetings to pray for those beginning a new ministry (6:6; 13:3; 14:23), a church meeting to pray for the release of Peter from prison (12:5, 12), and numerous other examples of individual or corporate prayer. In such contexts, the prayer was 'occasion-specific and group-specific'.[53]

VI. Conclusion

A new theology of worship is enunciated in Luke–Acts, with Jesus at its centre. Luke first demonstrates how the temple at Jerusalem 'played its predicted role as the venue of the eschatological fulfilment and then gave way to the new salvation which is not confined to a particular topographical location'.[54] The exalted Lord Jesus is presented as effectively the new point of contact between heaven and earth, fulfilling the role of the temple in God's purpose. As such, he becomes an object of devotion in the early churches.

From another perspective, Christian life and ministry is viewed as the way to serve God under the New Covenant. Christ is the one

---

[52]The use of the definite article and the plural in the expression 'the prayers' (ταῖς προσευχαῖς) in 2:42 suggests that the reference is to *specific prayers* rather than to prayer in general (NIV, 'to prayer'). I am not persuaded by the argument that 2:46a and 47a both primarily concern the temple (cf., Falk, 'Jewish Prayer Literature', 271-3).

[53]Falk, 'Jewish Prayer Literature', 276. Cf., Turner, 'Prayer', 72-5; Crump, *Jesus the Intercessor*, 237-241.

[54]McKelvey, *New Temple*, 84. Against Cole, *New Temple*, 48-9, McKelvey, 89-90, does not think that David's fallen and rebuilt 'tent' (σκηνή) in the quotation from Amos 9:11 in Acts 15:15-18 can be taken to mean that the resurrected Christ is the new temple.

who makes possible the forgiveness of sins and the outpouring of the Spirit predicted by the prophets, so that God's people are liberated to serve him in a new way. Such worship finds particular expression when Christians gather to minister to one another in word or deed, to pray, and to sound forth God's praises in teaching or singing, but it is not to be restricted to these activities. In effect, ministry in the public sphere becomes the means of inviting people to call upon the name of Jesus and participate in the blessings of the new community. Ministry in the private sphere is then an expression of the relationships engendered through faith in Christ and an exercise of the responsibilities entailed through membership of the church.

While Acts suggests some parallels between Christian meetings and the activities of the synagogue, it must be stressed that Luke presents the community life of the earliest Christians in terms that set it apart from Pharisaical Judaism, with its focus on the study and application of the Law. Only a very general correspondence between certain features of the synagogue and Christian gatherings may be discerned from Luke's evidence.[55] Again, although parallels might be drawn with the Qumran community, there is nothing of the monastic lifestyle, with its focus on ritual and moral regulations, in Luke's presentation of early Christianity. Rather, there is an awareness of being the community of the End time, loosed from the strictures of Judaism, focusing on Jesus and the prophetic Scriptures, having its own distinctive forms of prayer and praise, relating to one another and serving one another in everyday contexts such as the household.

---

[55]For the possible influence of synagogue services on Christian liturgical development, cf., Beckwith, 'Jewish Background', 39-51, and Daily and Weekly Worship. But cf., Falk, 'Jewish Prayer Literature', 277-301.

CHAPTER 19

THE CHRISTIAN AND THE LAW OF MOSES

Craig L. Blomberg

Summary

A flurry of recent research on the Law in Luke–Acts has supported an understanding of Luke as interested in promoting a Law-keeping form of Christianity. Careful analysis of each reference in Acts germane to this topic, in sequence and in context, does not support this conclusion. Instead, Luke's major redactional concern is to show how Christianity increasingly broke away from its Jewish roots. Scripture is important not as Law to be obeyed but as God's Word which is fulfilled in Christ.

I. Introduction

Just over a decade ago, interest in the Law in Luke–Acts was almost non-existent. The only book-length works on the topic had been those of J. Jervell and S. Wilson, who both seemed to overemphasize Luke's interest in a law-keeping Christianity.[1] I had tried to defend this criticism in a short survey of the relevant texts, as did M. Turner in a discussion of Sabbath-keeping in the NT.[2] Those surveys observed that Luke often portrays Jesus and the early church as law-abiding, but that his more dominant redactional interest lies in the progression of the gospel away from exclusively Jewish concerns to a law-free, Gentile Christianity. That should then make the former portrayal all the more likely to be historical, since it functions in part at cross-purposes from Luke's major theological interest.

Since 1984, however, interest in the Law in Luke–Acts has compounded almost annually, with a substantial majority of studies supporting a more conservative understanding of Luke's perspective.[3] Most notably, M. Klinghardt argues that Luke sees Jewish Christians as required to keep much of the Law (esp. almsgiving), even for salvation, while Gentile-Christians must keep that part of the Law intended for them (the Apostolic Decree).[4] K. Salo comes to similar conclusions by a different route and is more forthright about the resulting incoherence: Luke wants to unite Christian Jew and Gentile in table fellowship but fails, being unable to demonstrate how to preserve this unity if not all want to obey the dietary laws.[5] Shorter studies echo these themes.[6] The extent of their effect is well-illustrated by the continuing popularity of Jervell's numerous articles[7] and at least one

---

[1]Jervell (*Luke*) saw Luke as the most conservative writer in the NT in this respect. Wilson (*Luke and the Law*) found law-keeping and law-free aspects but believed that the former predominated.

[2]Blomberg, 'Law'; Turner, 'Sabbath'.

[3]Important exceptions include Downing, 'Freedom'; *idem*, 'Law'; Seifrid, 'Jesus'; *idem*, 'Messiah'; and Weiser, 'Gesetzes- und Tempelkritik'. Maddox (*Purpose*, 36-39) and Syreeni ('Exegesis') find Luke contradictory and incoherent.

[4]Klinghardt, *Gesetz*. Most of Klinghardt's case rests on an interpretation of Luke 16:16-18 (difficult verses for any interpreter), Luke's redactional omissions (always problematic arguments from silence), a playing down of the significance of Acts 13:38-39 and 15:10-11, and a convoluted interpretation of the Apostolic Decree.

[5]Salo, *Law*, alleging that most of the redaction in Luke's Gospel comes in chs. 1–2, not 3–24.

[6]E.g., Esler, *Community and Gospel*, 110-30; Räisänen, 'Freiheit', 63; Koet, *Five Studies, passim*.

[7]Another anthology has been collected: Jervell, *Paul*.

Acts commentary that adopts his perspective uncritically throughout.[8]

This 'pro-Jewish' trend in Lucan studies extends to a massive literature, almost all of it in the last decade, on Luke's attitude toward the Jews as a whole and in particular toward their leaders, especially the Pharisees.[9] Similar recent interest has surrounded Luke's view of the temple and Jerusalem.[10] In each case, the majority of studies has concluded, implausibly in my opinion, that Luke was more concerned to stress continuity with Judaism than discontinuity.[11] Some have suggested that 'Luke' was himself a Jew or at least a God-fearer.[12] F. Bovon marvels at this shift of opinion and attributes it to two sources: a commendable post-holocaust zeal not to offend Jews that unfortunately can lead scholars to see early Christianity as less of a 'break-away' movement from Judaism than it really was, and a widespread disregard of the major studies of the 1960s and 1970s on the topic.[13]

Another key distinctive of most of these pro-Jewish studies and of all of the pro-Torah interpretations of Acts is that they lack consistent narrative-critical analysis. That is to say, they jump around exegeting isolated texts apart from their larger contexts and the narrative flow of the plot of the book.[14] This short essay, though limited to Acts, tries to remedy this situation by progressing through Luke's entire second volume sequentially.[15]

---

[8]Schille, *Apostelgeschichte*.
[9]See esp. Brawley, *Luke–Acts and the Jews*; Tyson, *Luke–Acts*; Wills, 'Depiction'; Vanhoye, 'Juifs'; O'Toole, 'Reflections'; on the leaders, Carroll, 'Pharisees'; Powell, 'Leaders'; Gowler, *Host*.
[10]See esp. Bachmann, *Jerusalem*; Weinert, 'Temple'; Chance, *Jerusalem*.
[11]For more balanced exegesis, see Weatherly, 'Jews'; Darr, *Character Building*, 87-126; and Walker, *City*.
[12]E.g., Willimon, *Acts*, 87; Salmon, 'Insider or Outsider?', 76-82; Karris, *Luke and Acts*, 41.
[13]Bovon, 'Luke–Acts'. For an example of that earlier, more balanced consensus, see Richardson, *Israel*, 160-65; and much of the literature cited throughout Blomberg, 'Law'. I limit my interaction with secondary literature in this essay largely to more recent works *only* because I have already thoroughly covered that earlier ground.
[14]Unlike the works of Darr, *Character Building*; and Tannehill, *Narrative Unity*, vol. 2, which, tellingly, come to far less positive conclusions about Luke's continuity with Judaism.
[15]Omitting the Gospel could skew results but could also avoid the fallacy of attributing pre-Pentecostal trends to post-Pentecostal redactional interest. For a survey of the relevant data in Luke, see Blomberg, 'Law', 54-62.

II. Analysis

An overview of the entire book of Acts may help chart the right course from the outset. Luke discloses his outline primarily through three textual clues: (a) the epitome of the contents in 1:8 (the progression of the gospel from Jerusalem to the uttermost parts of the earth); (b) the six summary statements about the spread of the gospel at the end of each 'panel' (6:7; 9:31; 12:24; 16:5; 19:20; 28:31); and (c) the numerous parallels between 1:1-12:24 and 12:25-28:31, suggesting a twin focus on Jewish and Gentile Christianity in general, and on Peter and Paul in particular.[16] A reasonable outline for Acts, therefore, might well proceed as follows:

I. The Christian mission to Jews (1:1-12:24)
    A. The church in Jerusalem (1:1-6:7)
    B. The church in Judea, Samaria, and Galilee (6:8-9:31)
    C. Further advances in Palestine and Syria (9:32-12:24)
II. The Christian mission to Gentiles (12:25-28:31)
    A. Paul's first missionary journey and Jerusalem Council (12:25–16:5)
    B. Wide outreach through further missionary journeys (16:6–19:20)
    C. To Rome *via* Jerusalem (19:21-28:31).[17]

This very structure highlights Luke's concern to show the transformation of an exclusively Jewish sect into a major, empire-wide religion and suggests that the burden of proof will be on anyone alleging that Luke is promoting a Torah-centric Christianity. This hypothesis must be tested against the relevant textual details, in sequence and context.

The Church's earliest days

In Acts 1, Jesus commands the disciples to wait in Jerusalem for the promised Spirit to empower them for centrifugal witness to the ends of the earth, and then he ascends into heaven (vv. 1-11). It is unlikely

---

[16]On which, see esp. Talbert, *Literary Patterns*, 23-26.
[17]Klein, Hubbard, and Blomberg, *Interpretation*, 346; Longenecker, 'Acts', 234. *Cf.*, Smend and Luz, *Gesetz*, 137: Acts begins in the temple and ends in Rome. Thus Luke shows how the gospel expands from Jewish to Gentile circles, so that 'the Gentile mission is for Luke a Law-free Gentile mission'. See also Rolland, 'L'organisation', 81-86.

that γή in v. 8 can be limited to Israel or preclude Luke's seeing at least a provisional fulfilment of this mandate with Paul's arrival in Rome at the end of the book.[18] But it does make it highly likely that the mission envisaged will go beyond exclusively Jewish audiences or concerns. In Luke 24:44-48, Jesus has already insisted that this universal mission incorporate a Christological interpretation of the Scriptures and embrace πάντα τα ἔθνη (v. 47). So, as Betori explains,

> If Christian preaching in Jerusalem shows itself from the outset to be directed, in form and in content, to the pagan world, it becomes impossible to see in the church of the earliest days an entity which is bound up with the law. . . . It can be said that, seen in this light, Luke's effort is precisely to tone down, within the limits set by respect for historical facts, the 'Jewish' aspects of the first community.[19]

The disciples may still be wondering if their mission merely reconstitutes 'true Israel' (1:6). Jesus corrects that misunderstanding in v. 8.[20]

So they wait (1:12-14), interpret the OT typologically to replace Judas (vv. 15-26), and receive the Spirit at Pentecost (ch. 2). Although their first audience may have been exclusively Jewish, it represented people 'from every nation under heaven' (2:5).[21] The thrust of Peter's preaching is the fulfilment of Messianic prophecy in Jesus and the events of the day (vv. 17-21, 25-28, 34, 35) and the need to repent and be baptized in Jesus' name (v. 38). No word appears anywhere about obedience to the Law; the whole point is that what Jews who thought themselves faithful have been doing thus far is inadequate. If Luke intends Mosaic typology, as in the rabbinic tradition that Sinai and Pentecost coincided,[22] he says nothing whatever about it. And the end of Peter's sermon contains clear hints that his message is not limited to Jews. Representatives of the entire Jewish world are listening and included in 'you and your children' (v. 39); 'all who are far off... whom the Lord our God will call' surely include Gentiles, too, as the rest of the book will confirm.[23]

The fledgling three thousand member church (v. 41) begins to

---

[18]*Contra*, respectively, Schwartz, 'Beginning or End?'; and Ellis, '"End of the Earth"'. *Cf.*, esp. Bruce, 'Church', 659-61.

[19]Betori, 'Luke 24:47', 119.

[20]Barrett, *Acts. I:* 76: 'Luke uses the question to underline the non-nationalist character of the Christian movement.'

[21]All English Bible quotations are from the NIV unless otherwise indicated.

[22]For references, see Bruce, *Acts*, 50, n. 5.

[23]*Cf.*, Fitzmyer, *Luke the Theologian*, 192; Polhill, *Acts*, 117.

gather regularly (vv. 42-47). Their public meeting place in Jerusalem is the temple courts (v. 46), and on at least one occasion some assemble at 3 p.m. (3:1), the hour of the afternoon sacrifices. Does this mean that Luke saw them as still devoted to the temple cult? While it is unlikely that the disciples of Jesus would have so quickly abandoned the sacrificial system, it is doubtful if this is Luke's emphasis. Not one word of the text ever refers to the sacrifices, and what is mentioned adequately accounts for the references to temple and time. (1) The temple courts were the only place of adequate size in Jerusalem for so large a public gathering (note the contrast between 'temple courts' and 'homes' in 2:46). (2) It was an optimal site for witness and proclamation, as the unfolding events of chapter 3 demonstrate (see esp. v. 11). (3) 3p.m. was also one of the fixed times of prayer, which is mentioned in the text (3:1), and which all would have participated in (vs. only a few who offered sacrifices on any given day).[24] Pesch and Schneider are correct: 'According to Luke, "the temple for the Christians is not a place of sacrifice, but, as for Jesus, a place of teaching and prayer" (cf., Luke 19:46f; Acts 2:46)'.[25]

The reference to the temple in 3:1 is entirely introductory and subordinate to the miracle narrative which ensues (vv. 2-10), merely explaining why the disciples happened to pass by this beggar. One verse in Peter's subsequent sermon suggests a Jesus-Moses typology (3:22, quoting Deut. 18:15). But the whole point of the reference is not to call Peter's listeners to the Law but to Christ: 'you must listen to everything he [Jesus] tells you'.[26] A second reference to Scripture again foreshadows the Gentile mission—'through your offspring all peoples on earth will be blessed' (v. 25; cf., Gen. 22:18, 26:4)—despite the salvation-historical priority of beginning with the Jews (v. 26).

Nothing germane to the issue of the Law appears in 4:1–5:42, although there is more fulfilment of prophecy (4:11, 25-26). If anything, the confrontation with 'official Judaism' that occupies these chapters sets the stage for the church moving beyond the confines of Jerusalem. Even Gamaliel's providential intervention to free the arrested apostles (5:34-39) rests on spurious logic and fails to prevent

---

[24]Cf., Kliesch, *Apostelgeschichte*, 57. Indeed, Luke may even see hints here of the early church as an *alternative* to the temple cult; cf., Mussner, *Apostelgeschichte*, 27; Schmithals, *Apostelgeschichte*, 39.

[25]Pesch, *Apostelgeschichte*, I:37; quoting Schneider, *Apostelgeschichte*, I:299. Barrett (*Acts*, 178) argues that this overlooks 21:26, but Paul's scheme there backfires and functions *negatively* in Luke's narrative.

[26]Cf., Arrington, *Acts*, 41.

their flogging (v. 40).[27]

In chapters 6–7, the dispute between the Hebrews and Hellenists leads to the appointment of seven 'deacons', all apparently Hellenists, and to the persecution and subsequent dispersion of Christians, stimulated by the ministry and martyrdom of perhaps the most outspoken Hellenist leader, Stephen. The Jewish leaders accuse him of blasphemy against Moses and God (6:11) and of speaking against the holy place and the Law (v. 13). More specifically, they charge that he claimed that Jesus would 'destroy this place and change the customs Moses handed down' to them (v. 14). Luke calls these latter two charges 'false' (v. 13), but this hardly proves an intent to promote Stephen as a paradigm of law-abiding Christianity: (1) Many false statements are partly true but exaggerate or distort the truth.[28] (2) That is precisely the case with v. 14a—Jesus did predict the temple's destruction elsewhere in Luke's writing (Luke 21:5-28) but did not say that he would destroy it.[29] (3) Elsewhere in Luke, too, Jesus portends a clear change with respect to Mosaic traditions, most notably the Sabbath (Luke 6:1-11) and the dietary laws (11:37-41).[30] (4) V. 11 is not designated as false witness, yet its themes clearly overlap with those of vv. 13-14.[31] (5) Above all, 7:1 has the high priest explicitly ask Stephen about the truth of the charges against him, and by the logic of the Sanhedrin, he clearly indicts himself!

There are those who claim that in this lengthy speech (7:2-53) Stephen never really replies to the question put to him. L. Johnson is right to remark that 'these readers who object that the greater part of the speech is beside the point simply show that they have not grasped what the point is'![32] A number of commentators concur and highlight two central themes: the temple is not necessary for worshipping Yahweh; the unbelieving Jews, not Christians, are the true lawbreakers.[33]

Of course, Stephen would deny that any of this is blasphemy,

---

[27]See further Darr, *Character Building*, 116-20.
[28]Cf., Bruce, *Acts*, 126; Williams, *Acts*, 125.
[29]Cf., Faw, *Acts*, 89; Larsson, 'Temple-Criticism'.
[30]Blomberg, 'Law', 58-60.
[31]If Luke wanted the label less ambiguously to cover both references, he could have put it first or in both vv. 11 and 13-14.
[32]Johnson, *Acts*, 120.
[33]Marshall (*Acts: Commentary*, 131-32) makes each of these themes even more specific: the Jews have mistakenly thought that God dwelt in his temple and have consistently disobeyed the Law and rejected the deliverers God sent to them. Kilgallen ('Function', 173-93) sees the main idea of the sermon reflected entirely in the second of these points, as indicated by its climactic position in vv. 51-53.

because these are divinely orchestrated changes to the Mosaic economy. For those who do not accept the early Christian perspective on Jesus, this logic will utterly fail to convince. Stephen is stoned, and the early church has taken another step away from its Torah-centred roots. The attention Luke devotes to the whole Stephen affair (6:8–8:1), the detail with which he recounts just his speech alone—the longest in Acts (7:2-53)—and the significance of the persecution which his stoning unleashes (dispersing Christians throughout Judea and Samaria, 8:1), underline how devoted Luke is to stressing this next stage in Christianity's progressive departure from its nationalistic Jewish heritage.

From Jew to Gentile

Chapters 8–9 offer various vignettes of the church 'moving out'. Philip preaches to Samaritans (8:4-25) and to a ritually impure 'eunuch' (vv. 26-40). Saul is commissioned to preach to Gentile as well as Jew (9:1-31), with the former in the emphatic first position in Christ's call (v. 15).[34] No less than the Hebrew apostle, Peter, leaves Jerusalem to travel to Lydda and Joppa (9:32-43), even staying in the home of one Simon the tanner, whose trade rendered him unclean.

The next key stage in the early church's self-understanding occurs in 10:1-11:18, with the thrice-narrated conversion of Cornelius. The attention Luke devotes to the episode makes plain that he is no conservative but committed to stressing how the church increasingly freed itself from the Law.[35] The main point is clearly Peter's recognition that the dietary laws no longer applied for Gentile or Jew in Christ and that the major barrier to table fellowship between Jew and Gentile was obliterated. God's threefold command to eat the unclean animals of the heavenly vision (10:9-16) leads to stunning conclusions: Peter deduces that no person is unclean (v. 28), that God accepts people of every nation who fear him and do right (vv. 34-35), and that therefore the gospel should be preached to Cornelius (vv. 36-43). God dramatically confirms Peter's deductions by sending his Spirit on the centurion and his companions before he finishes preaching (v. 44). The sceptical Jewish Christians in Jerusalem finally agree: 'So then, God has even granted the Gentiles repentance unto life' (11:18). No

[34]Williams, *Acts*, 172.
[35]On this repetition, see esp. Witherup, 'Cornelius'.

stipulations about obeying any law ever appear as a prerequisite for this 'life'.

Completely subordinate to this major theme are two references to Cornelius as pious. In 10:2, he is introduced not only as a centurion from the Italian Regiment, to make clear his Gentile origins, but also, with his family, as 'devout and God-fearing', regularly giving alms and praying. The reference (v. 3) to the vision he saw one day at 3 pm undoubtedly implies he was in prayer at that time (recall 3:1-2). This explains how Cornelius the Gentile came to be praying to the true God of Israel and thus received the angelic message; it implies nothing about the need for Christians to follow the Jewish Law.[36] The reference to Cornelius' respect among the Jewish people in 10:22 is even more incidental, inserted merely to curry Peter's favour, because Cornelius' emissaries do not yet know that Peter will be unusually well disposed toward them as Gentiles. From Luke's perspective these narrative asides also heighten the parallels between this centurion and the one whose servant Jesus healed in Luke 7:1-10.[37] But in that episode, Jesus praises the centurion's faith precisely by contrasting it with the faith he has seen in Israel (v. 9). These are not pro-Torah sentiments here! Obviously, Cornelius was no raw pagan, but he sets the stage for the full-fledged Gentile mission soon to begin.[38]

That mission first centres on Antioch (11:19-30); then Luke closes the first half of his book with events back in Jerusalem (ch. 12). Paul's missionary journeys now proceed in earnest (chs. 13–14). In his travels, Paul regularly seeks out a Jewish audience first, but sooner or later meets with rejection. Then he turns to the Gentiles, among whom the gospel meets with the greatest success (cf., 14:27). Luke's Paul effectively contextualizes the kerygma for each setting (contrast 13:16-41 with 14:15-17), but not once does he so much as hint at obedience to the Law as a part of the gospel message.

In fact, the one reference to 'the law of Moses' that does appear (13:39 [Gk., 38]) refers to its inability to provide forgiveness of sins.

---

[36]Indeed, one can almost make the case for the exact opposite—that the new table-fellowship created among Jewish and Gentile Christians replaces temple cult. See Elliott, 'Household'; but cf., also the critique by van Aarde, 'Houses'.

[37]See the full list of parallels in Schmithals, *Apostelgeschichte*, 104-5.

[38]Jervell defies credibility by arguing that Luke's portrayal of Cornelius as the paradigm Gentile convert implies that virtually all other Gentile converts in Acts were God-fearers, too (in Jervell, 'Church', 11-20). For critique, see Sanders, 'Who Is a Jew?' In fact, the *only* way Ἕλλην can mean God-fearer in Acts is if it is qualified, as 17:4 shows. Cf., Seifrid, 'Jesus', 42.

There is, of course, a grammatical ambiguity here: ἀπὸ πάντων ὧν οὐκ ἠδυνήθητε ἐν νόμῳ Μωϋσέως δικαιωθῆναι might imply that the Mosaic Law could provide forgiveness for some but not all sins, though even this would not necessarily imply that Christians were meant to obey the Law to obtain that forgiveness. But it is more likely that ἀπὸ πάντων and ὧν οὐκ ἠδυνήθητε are parallel, and that the text should be translated, '... through [Jesus] is proclaimed the forgiveness of sins from everything, *i.e.*, from which the Law of Moses could not justify.[39] (1) This is a standard use of a preposition followed by an object and relative pronoun which it governs (*cf.*, in Acts as recently as 13:2).[40] (2) Luke's theology elsewhere consistently attributes forgiveness of all sins exclusively to the grace of the work of Christ (*e.g.*, Luke 1:77; 3:3; 4:18; 15:11-32; 18:9-14; Acts 2:38; 4:12; 5:31; 10:43; 15:11; 16:30-31; 26:18). (3) Paul's use of the OT in this immediate context refers back to a verse in Habbakuk that forms part of that prophet's larger discussion of justification by faith (13:41, citing Hab. 1:5; *cf.*, Hab. 1:4, 2:4).

(4) Attempts to make sense of Paul's preaching in Acts 13 on the 'partial justification' theory prove singularly incoherent. For example, Klinghardt argues that this part of vv. 38-39 is not Paul's major point and that Romans 6:7 provides a grammatical parallel.[41] But Paul's use of δεδικαίωται ἀπό refers to full justification in Christ, and Kilgallen has surely demonstrated that 13:38-39 is the climax of Paul's sermon.[42] Salo claims that the contrast between ἐν νόμῳ Μωυσέως and ἐν τούτῳ (referring to Christ) compares 'while being a Jew' with life 'as a Christian', and that being in Christ, while necessary for salvation, does not imply any change in the Law.[43] This is an entirely unnatural interpretation of a text that, on any reading, refers at least to the partial inability of the Law to perform what non-Christian Jews expected it to do. Surely it is best to follow a substantial consensus of commentators that see Acts 13:38-39 as actually one of the most Pauline statements in the entire book.[44] Even Jervell concedes that the clearest evidence for his position does not emerge until Acts 15 and later.[45]

---

[39]*Cf.*, Barrett's paraphrase (*Acts I*, 650): 'There are many things from which you need to be justified; the law of Moses is inadequate to achieve this; the only way is the way of faith.'

[40]Zerwick, *Greek*, 8, citing this text.

[41]Klinghardt, *Gesetz*, 99-109.

[42]Kilgallen, 'Acts 13,38-39'.

[43]Salo, *Law*, 217.

[44]See Buss, *Missionspredigt*, 126. *Cf.*, Weiser, *Apostelgeschichte 1-12*, 336; Kliesch, *Apostelgeschichte*, 99; Krodel, *Acts*, 242.

[45]Jervell, *Paul*, 13-25.

The Apostolic Council

If there is virtually no support in Acts 1–14 for Luke's interest in promoting a Law-observant Christianity, what of chs. 15–28? Acts 15:1 does introduce a controversy without precedent in the book: some Judeans came to Antioch teaching circumcision (and therefore law-keeping in general, cf., v. 5[46]) as a requirement for salvation. Yet every other detail Luke describes in this narrative (vv. 2-29) demonstrates how keen he is to reject this position.

First, Luke stresses the welcome Paul and Barnabas, who had rejected the 'circumcision party's' claims, received both in Phoenicia and Samaria and among the apostles and elders in Jerusalem (vv. 2-4).[47] Second, Peter endorses Paul's position without qualification (vv. 6-11). Indeed, his words in vv. 10-11 reflect a theology of grace vs. law entirely worthy of the Paul of the epistles.[48] J. Nolland has correctly argued that 'yoke' and 'bear' in v. 10 need not imply that Peter, or Jews more generally, had agonized under an insufferable hardship with the Law.[49] But in a context in which the apostles are trying to remove a difficulty (v. 19) and a 'burden' (v. 28) from Gentiles wanting to become Christians, Luke may well intend a more negative sense.[50]

Third, James, potentially the most conservative speaker at the council, endorses both Peter and Paul robustly (vv. 13-18).[51] He supports Peter's testimony (v. 14), which affirmed that Jew and Gentile are both saved by grace, apart from the Law. His quotation of Amos 9:11-12, largely following the LXX, makes it clear, *against* the MT,[52] that Jew and Gentile are united on equal terms. Contra Jervell, λαός in v. 14 does not establish the Gentiles as a separate 'associate people' of God following the laws of the Old Testament appropriate for them.[53] Rather, the indefinite use of λαός for Gentiles should be translated just

---

[46]Because circumcision was the last step toward keeping the whole Law that many adult male God-fearers refused to take. The existence of God-fearers in the time of Acts is now well represented by Murphy-O'Connor, 'God-Fearers?'.

[47]Cf., Weiser, '"Apostelkonzil"', 158.

[48]Cf., Refoulé, 'discours'. Salo (*Law*, 243) and Klinghardt (*Gesetz*, 109-13) fail utterly to account for this inconsistency in their hypotheses.

[49]Nolland, 'Acts 15:10'.

[50]So also Johnson (*Acts*, 263), citing Gal. 5:1 and Luke 11:46 as parallels; and Schneider (*Apostelgeschichte*,II:181, n. 62), citing Luke 14:27 and Acts 9:15.

[51]Notwithstanding the attempt of Riesner ('Speech') to link 'Simeon' of v. 14 with the temple prophet of Luke 2.

[52]On this discrepancy, see most recently van de Sandt, 'Explanation'.

[53]Jervell, *Luke*, 41-74.

as 'people' (without the indefinite article in English), with a focus on God's initiative in electing them even as he did the Jews (*cf.*, 18:10).[54] Luke's point, then, will parallel 26:18b, in which Paul refers to the Gentiles receiving 'forgiveness of sins and a place among those who are sanctified by faith in me'.

Fourth, the provisions of the Apostolic Decree are established as an alternative to the Judaizers' request that Gentiles be made to obey the Law of Moses. V. 24 explicitly distances the Council from the circumcision party; it seems incredible to imagine that the provisions of the Decree would implicitly affirm that party's claim. But that is precisely what a wide swath of interpreters allege. The most common opinion is that the four stipulations correspond to laws found in Leviticus 17–18 enjoined of aliens in Israel as well as Jews. Thus, it is argued, Luke envisages Gentile-Christians keeping that part of the Mosaic Law originally intended for them.[55] At times, this argument is strengthened by appeal to rabbinic traditions about pre-Mosaic, 'Noahic' laws, incumbent on all peoples (*cf.*, b. Sanh. 56a-b).[56] These perspectives, however, seem untenable.

To begin with, the narrative flow of vv. 19-29 runs in an opposite direction. As already noted, the council is trying to make things easy for Gentiles (vv. 19, 28); complete abstinence from idol meat, as a legal requirement, would *not* have been simple, as later debates in Corinth demonstrate (see 1 Cor. 8:1-11:1).[57] V. 21 can be read as implying that the Mosaic Law is widely known in Gentile lands, so that its injunctions for Gentiles should come as no surprise. But the grammar is more naturally taken as implying that because Jews are scattered all about the Graeco–Roman world, their sensibilities should be taken into account and not unnecessarily offended.[58] V. 23 explicitly limits the addressees of the decree to Gentile believers in Antioch, Syria and Cilicia, apparently the regions in which the trouble had started. 'It seemed good to the Holy Spirit and to us' (v. 28a) is a remarkably casual introductory formula for a legal injunction and grounds the

---

[54]See, respectively, Dahl, 'People'; and Dupont, 'Un peuple'.
[55]*E.g.*, Haenchen, *Acts*, 450; Simon, 'Decree', 459-60.
[56]*E.g.*, Stählin, *Apostelgeschichte*, 205; Catchpole, 'Decree'.
[57]On which, see Blomberg, *1 Corinthians*, 159-206.
[58]See Blomberg, 'Law', 66. One could just possibly agree with Schwartz ('Futility', 279) that 'James means that it would be wrong to impose Mosaic law upon converts to Christianity, for experience show that only a few would be willing to accept the worship of the true God under such a condition,' though this seems a less likely interpretation.

decision in the council's deliberations themselves, not in any text of
Torah. 'Requirements' (v. 28b) can refer to legal stipulations but just as
easily to desirable customs.[59] 'You will do well to avoid these things'
(v. 29) again makes the Decree sound far too optional if Mosaic
authority was being invoked for a mandatory set of rules for salvation
or Christian living.[60]

In addition, every attempt to see the four abstentions of v. 20 as
more than *ad hoc* advice on how not to offend certain Jews fails to
explain the selection of this particular list of items. There are numerous
other prohibitions in the Law for the alien in Israel (*cf.*, Exod. 23:12;
Lev. 16:29; 20:2; 22:10, 18; Num. 15:30; Deut. 16:11, 14; 26:11). Deuteronomy 31:12 even suggests that in some way the sojourner was
expected to obey all the Law. The Rabbinic list of Noahic commands
is broader, too (including, *e.g.*, laws of social justice and refraining
from blasphemy, robbery and eating meat out of a living animal).
What is more, it is difficult to match the prohibition against 'strangled
things' (πνικτός) with anything in either written or oral Torah. The
usual linkage with animals killed in the wild (Lev. 17:13-15) or with the
possibility that strangled animals wouldn not have their blood properly drained proceeds by inferences not likely to have come to mind
unless one was already hunting for references to strangled animals in
these passages.[61] Πορνεία, too, is not normally limited to the forms of
incest proscribed in Leviticus 18.[62]

Wilson's attempt to link the four restrictions with pagan idolatry
is an improvement, but by his own admission again works least well
with πνικτός[63] and fails to explain why only these expressions of
idolatry would be prohibited.[64] Klinghardt reverts to the interpretation based on restrictions for the sojourner in Jewish territory but then
eliminates all commands except those accompanied by a particular

[59]Wilson, *Luke and the Law*, 82.
[60]*Cf.*, further Tannehill (*Narrative Unity*, II:192), who follows Danker ('Reciprocity', 52-54): 'you will do well' implies that 'you will earn the good will of the requesters, to be demonstrated in future relationships'.
[61]See esp. Wilson, *Luke and the Law*, 84-94.
[62]*Ibid.*, 88. *Cf.*, the discussion of broad and narrow interpretations of πορνεία in another controversial context, often tied in with Acts 15, in Blomberg, 'Marriage', 176-78.
[63]Wilson, *Luke and the Law*, 94-102. *Cf.*, also Dickinson, 'Theology'.
[64]See the critique by Wedderburn, '"Decree"'. Wedderburn's modification of Wilson (πνικτός as the pagan practice of offering a sacrifice in its entirety to a deity or to ward off the demonic), however, requires implausible stages of redaction (and misunderstanding) within Acts and the early church.

'cutting off' formula: *karath* in the *niphal* with *'ish* or *nephesh* as subject and followed by *min* plus an object (*cf.*, Lev. 17:9, 14; 18:29).[65] But what evidence is there that any ancient Jew actually adopted such a criterion and what likelihood that anyone would ever have thought of it unless one was already looking for features shared by the prohibitions of Leviticus 17–18? The same questions cast doubts on Callan's modification of Klinghardt's view (noting that even the latter's elaborate formula can be found outside of Lev. 17–18), which restricts the stipulations of the Decree to laws for the *ger* that are introduced by the formula 'any man' (*'ish 'ish*) and 'followed by the warning that the violator of the law will be cut off from the people'.[66] Far better to conclude with Weiser:

> The *result with respect to the contents* of the Apostolic Council is the insight that the Mosaic Law as a code of customs does not come to have foundational significance either soteriologically or ecclesiologically. It is not a salvifically necessary presupposition for baptism and does not constitute Christian life. It does not serve as a religious constitution for Christianity but appears according to Luke as 'a cultural phenomenon'.[67]

The Apostolic Council thus settles the debate over a Torah-observant form of Christianity by opting for freedom from the Law.

Paul's subsequent mission

Near the outset of his second missionary journey (15:36-18:22), Paul circumcises Timothy (16:3), and Luke immediately adds that as they travelled they promulgated the Apostolic Decree (v. 4). It is strange to read of this circumcision so quickly after the Council, on anybody's interpretation of the Decree, since the one thing clearly resolved in Jerusalem was that circumcision was unnecessary for salvation. And it is even more striking that a reminder of that resolution should come, by implication, in the very verse after Timothy is circumcised. But Luke offers an entirely adequate explanation: Timothy is half-Jewish (and would have been treated as a Jew), his uncircumcised state is

---

[65]Klinghardt, *Gesetz*, 186.
[66]Callan, 'Decree'.
[67]Weiser, '"Apostelkonzil"', 166. *Cf.*, Smend and Luz, *Gesetz*, 155, n. 206; Cheung, 'Analysis', 150.

well-known (and therefore scandalous), and Paul wants to avoid unnecessary offence when they witness to Jews (v. 3).[68] He will later write that to those under the Law he became 'as one under the Law', though not considering himself permanently bound by its mandates (1 Cor. 9:20). And from a literary perspective, v. 3 enables Luke to correct in advance the criticism levelled in Acts 21:21.[69] V. 4, then, may well reflect his way of signalling that freedom in Christ cuts both ways: Jewish Christians are welcome to follow Jewish ritual so long as it does not become a legal requirement (*cf.*, Rom. 14:1-15:13).[70] Verses 3-4 also bring closure to the issue which initially led to the Council and mark off 15:1-16:4 as a literary unit.

Paul's travels resume as does his pattern of preaching first to Jews, when possible, but quickly finding himself rejected and left to concentrate on Gentiles. The controversy about the Law seems over. Nothing germane to Torah-obedience appears in any of Paul's preaching throughout the rest of his missionary journeys (16:6–20:38). If anything, the Jewish leaders consistently appear as his opponents; the Roman rulers, as his (unwitting) rescuers (esp. in Philippi and Corinth). The only possible exception to a uniformly Law-free gospel in these chapters is Luke's extremely passing reference to Paul's getting a haircut in Cenchrea, 'because of a vow he had taken' (18:18b).

What was this all about? The best guess is that he was ending a temporary (usually 30-day) Nazirite vow (*cf.*, Num. 6:1-21).[71] Josephus speaks of such vows as a customary form of prayer or thanksgiving for preservation from illness or other affliction (*War*, 2.15.1; *Ant.*, 19.6.1). Paul had enough to be concerned about throughout his ministry to make this traditional expression of his Jewish piety very natural. Yet Numbers 6:14 prescribes sacrifices after the completion of the vow, including a sin-offering. Was Paul planning to offer these? Luke says nothing of him going to Jerusalem on his return to Palestine; he heads to Syrian Antioch instead (18:22). One later rabbinic tradition suggests that some time prior to the mid-second century, some Jews abandoned the sin-offering as part of the vow-completion ceremony (p. Ned. 1.36b [1.1.11]).[72] So the inference that Paul still believed in and practiced temple sacrifices as part of a Torah-centric Jewish Christianity is

---

[68]See esp. Bryan, 'Look'; *contra* Cohen, 'Timothy'. Even more implausible is Walker, 'Timothy–Titus'.
[69]Pervo, *Paul*, 55.
[70]*Cf.*, Tannehill, *Narrative Unity*, II:190. Krodel (*Acts*, 298-99) adds that Gal. 5:11 may reflect a criticism of this flexibility on Paul's part.
[71]Wikenhauser, *Apostelgeschichte*, 216; Marshall, *Acts: Commentary*, 300.

tenuous in the extreme. If Luke had wanted to make this point, he surely could have expressed it more directly!

Why then does he refer to this vow at all? In part because it explains Paul's stopover at Cenchrea, and Luke is scrupulous about giving the details of Paul's itineraries throughout all his missionary journeys.[73] He probably also wants to prepare the way for 21:23-24, to explain the Jerusalem Christians' request on that occasion. If Paul was known for practising this particular form of Jewish devotion, then the later scheme to support four men ending vows in Jerusalem could be seen as more reasonable.

That brings us to chapter 21. The only other passage in all of Acts directly relevant to the question of whether Luke envisaged any early Christians as having to keep the Law involves the dilemma Paul faces at the end of his third journey. Hearsay and rumour have distorted the picture of what he teaches (v. 21),[74] and the leaders of the Jerusalem church want Paul to demonstrate that he himself is 'living in obedience to the law' (v. 24b). So they insist that he join in the purification rites of four temporary Nazirites and pay their expenses (vv. 23-24a).[75] But James' proposal does not necessarily determine Luke's theology. Paul is Luke's protagonist, particularly in chapters 13–28. Still, Paul acquiesces with the request, though without a word to express his opinion on the matter (v. 26).

What does Luke think of all this? Again it is unlikely that he was promoting obedience to the Law: (1) As in 18:18, one cannot be sure that the original prescriptions of Numbers 6 were even followed. (2) Paul's behaviour may not have had its intended effect; just because he obeyed this law did not mean that he kept all the Law, and even support for Nazirite vows could be perceived as more of a charitable act than a legal requirement.[76] (3) James and his companions immediately remind Paul about the Apostolic Decree (v. 25), as if to reassure him that they are not reneging on their earlier commitment to allow

---

[72]For the diversity of first-to-third century Jewish casuistry concerning such vows, see the entire Mishnaic tractate *Nedarim*.

[73]See already Lake and Cadbury, 'Acts', I:230.

[74]The charge that Paul was teaching Jews *not* to circumcise their children goes beyond what the Paul of the epistles could endorse—cf., Gal. 5:6, 6:15, and 1 Cor. 7:19.

[75]Marshall (*Acts: Commentary*, 345, n. 1) lists the three possible legal contexts: (1) the men had contracted ritual uncleanness and Paul can share in the purification without having shared in the defilement; (2) Paul is unclean for having travelled in Gentile territory, so he needs purification too; and (3) this is the end of a Nazirite vow for Paul as well.

[76]Bruce, 'Church', 658, n. 54, citing Jos. *Ant.*, 19.294 (=19.6.1).

him to promote his law-free gospel under ordinary circumstances.[77] Certainly in Acts 15 no one ever spoke of Paul having to prove that he kept the Law. The Jerusalem church leaders may well have realized that their ploy did not prove Paul to be thoroughly Torah-observant, but they could hope it would at least appease his harshest critics.

By far the most important reason for doubting that Luke as narrator approved of the church's scheme, however, comes in vv. 27-36: the entire plan disastrously backfires. Precisely by going into the temple at the time of the appropriate offerings, Paul is mistakenly accused of unlawfully bringing a Gentile with him (v. 28).[78] This provokes a near-riot and another Roman rescue of Paul, though in the form of his arrest. God, of course, will work even through Paul's imprisonment (chs. 22–28). But it is exactly that providential direction which will occupy Luke's attention. The references to Christian adherence to Jewish ritual serve merely to introduce a much larger and quite different theme that is Luke's true interest.

Paul the Prisoner

The rest of Acts thus centres on Paul in prison, his various defense speeches, and his ill-fated trip to Rome. Here the prophetic role of Scripture, already abundantly illustrated with numerous specific uses of the OT throughout Luke's writing,[79] is generalized and highlighted. Paul is on trial for 'the hope of Israel' (28:20; cf., 26:6), which is specified as belief in the resurrection of the dead, and particularly of Jesus (23:6; 24:21).[80] These repeated references clearly reflect a strategy by Paul to offset the offence of his Gentile ministry (cf., 22:21-22; 26:23) and to divide the Sanhedrin. To this end, and only to this end, Paul calls himself a Pharisee, since the Pharisees believed at least in a general resurrection on the last day (23:6).[81] He proclaims that he believes 'everything that agrees with the Law and that is written in the Prophets' (24:14), but Luke has made plain, from at least Luke 24:47 on,

---

[77]Cf., Polhill, Acts, 449.

[78]See esp. Kurz, Luke–Acts, 102: 'With irony, [the narrator] shows again how human plans can be overturned: the very action that Paul undertakes to make himself more acceptable to the Jews is the action that leads to their seizing him.'

[79]On which, see esp. Bock, Proclamation. Cf., Dillon, 'Prophecy'.

[80]On the close tie between these two concepts, see Haacker, 'Bekenntnis'. Mussner (Apostelgeschichte, 10) sees a threefold reference in Israel's hope—the promise of Messiah, resurrection from the dead, and forgiveness of sins, all fulfilled in Jesus.

that the whole of Scripture speaks of Jesus. This christological
interpretation of the OT does not leave either Decalogue or ritual law
unchanged (recall Jesus' treatment of Sabbath and kosher laws in Luke
6 and 11) and climaxes in Acts 26 with Paul's insistence that the
prophets and Moses predicted Jesus' suffering, resurrection, and the
church's witness to both Jew and Gentile (see esp. vv. 22-23).[82]

The main point in all of Paul's protests is that he is innocent of
any crime against Jews or Romans (25:8). He also believes that his
religion is the true fulfilment of Jewish hopes,[83] but that is a far cry
from claiming that he (or Luke) promotes a Torah-observant Christianity. Luke's main purpose is to clear Paul of the charges against him,
whether because he is defending the church directly to Rome, Rome to
the church, the church to Judaism, or some combination of the three.[84]
Paul's appeal to Caesar may indicate a desire (by both Paul and Luke)
to move Christianity out of its Jewish matrix and allow it to be heard
at the highest legal and political levels of the Roman empire.[85]

The only datum in Acts 22–28 not immediately amenable to
these purposes is Paul's impetuous interchange with Ananias the high
priest in 23:1-5. At first glance, Paul appears contrite over his blunt
talk: 'Brothers, I did not realize that he was the high priest; for it is
written: "Do not speak evil about the ruler of your people"' (v. 5). Is
Paul so bound to a command from the Pentateuch (Exod. 22:28) that he
can reverse his position so quickly? Five considerations render it
improbable.

(1) V. 1 employs a distinctive verb for living as a Hellenistic
citizen (πολιτεύω) and takes no advantage of a splendid opportunity
for Paul to affirm his adherence to Torah. (2) Paul's outburst in v. 3

---

[81]Cf., Darr, *Character Building*, 123: 'Given Paul's desperate situation, the reader
will take these words about his membership in the Pharisaic party with a grain of
salt. In any event, the emphasis of Paul's claim seems to fall on his affiliation
through heritage ("a son of Pharisees"), not on the status of his present
membership.' Again, 'this is all a clever, irony-laden ploy consisting of partial
truths'. Contrast 24:24-25, where Paul contextualizes his message quite differently
for Felix and Drusilla. It is true that Paul is also aligning himself with certain OT
expectations of resurrection, but this is not his primary purpose, because in each
case he neither cites nor alludes to Scripture, while the larger narrative flow
stresses the ineffectiveness of his ploy in persuading his Jewish antagonists.
[82]On which, see esp. O'Toole, *Climax*.
[83]Cf., Bruce, 'Apologetic', 389: 'The gospel, for Luke, is the crown and climax of
Israel's faith: that is the dominant emphasis of these apologetic speeches.'
[84]For these options, see Marshall, *Acts of the Apostles*, 33-34.
[85]See esp. Tajra, *Trial*.

stems precisely from the impotence of the Law to generate proper high-priestly behaviour in this situation. (3) Paul's charge against Ananias, however tactless, is absolutely true (*cf.*, the climax of Stephen's speech in 7:51-53) and is never retracted. (4) Paul's anathemas in his epistles, even against professing Christians, are equally pointed and never withdrawn (*e.g.*, Gal. 1:8, 9; 2:11-14; Phil. 3:2). (5) V. 5a makes eminently good sense as bitter irony. Paul would then be lamenting sarcastically, 'I did not think that a man like this who flaunts the Law in front of the Sanhedrin could be the high priest.'[86] V. 5b could form part of Paul's irony as well, but it is also possible that this half-verse should be punctuated not as Paul's words, but as Luke's follow-up explanation (*cf.*, his similar parenthesis in v. 8).[87]

Acts closes with one final account of Paul, at last in Rome, preaching first to Jews, but, upon failing to receive a sufficiently enthusiastic reception, turning to Gentiles (28:17-31). Many central themes reappear: Paul's innocence (v. 17), Christianity as the hope of Israel (v. 20), the Christological focus of the OT in general (v. 23), and an appeal to a specific prophecy to account for the disappointing response Paul's preaching elicits (vv. 26-27; citing Is. 6:9-10). As the final story in the book, however, this episode carries climactic force. If one cannot legitimately derive a once-for-all rejection of the Jews from this passage, one at least is left with a strong sense of the discontinuity of Paul's preaching from Judaism.[88] Luke has one last great opportunity to portray Paul as observing the Mosaic commandments, but he takes no advantage of it. Instead, he closes with the unifying message of both his volumes: the bold and unfettered preaching about Jesus and the reign of God (v. 31). Luke 24:47 and Acts 1:8 have been fulfilled, at least provisionally;[89] the task of carrying Christianity forward devolves in large part to Gentile believers.

III. Conclusion

Luke does not present the Mosaic Law as playing a major role in the life of a Christian, Jew or Gentile. He faithfully records various incidents within early Jewish Christianity in which believers did continue

---

[86]Krodel, *Acts*, 424. *Cf.*, Arrington, *Acts*, 228; Faw, *Acts*, 248; Williams, *Acts*, 385.
[87]*Cf.*, Delebecque, *Les Actes des Apôtres*, 110.
[88]For balanced assessments, see Tannehill, 'Rejection by Jews', 83-101; Marguerat, 'Rome'.
[89]Kliesch, *Apostelgeschichte*, 159.

to obey parts of the Law, including its temple ritual. In no instance is this his primary focus, however; careful narrative criticism demonstrates that these details serve merely to introduce or explain larger parts of Luke's story which promote different themes. In fact, Luke's theological and literary emphases consistently highlight how the fledgling church increasingly broke away from its Jewish roots, however reluctantly or unevenly. When disputes with Judaizers erupted, the spokesmen for all the other parties represented at the Jerusalem Council agreed on a compromise that left Paul's law-free gospel intact: Gentile Christians should avoid unnecessarily offending Jewish brothers and sisters, and Jewish Christians were free to practice their traditional piety, but no one was required to obey any command of the Law for either salvation or Christian discipleship, apart from its fulfilment in Christ. This agreement was honoured even during the turbulent, closing days of Paul's time in Jerusalem. Through it all, Luke presents Christians as justified and nurtured by the grace of Christ alone.

CHAPTER 20

MISSION PRACTICE AND THEOLOGY UNDER CONSTRUCTION (ACTS 18–20)

Philip H. Towner

Summary

Luke's account of the Pauline mission in Corinth and Ephesus reflects a development in mission practice—prolonged periods of ministry in each city independent of the synagogue and in spite of continued opposition—that coincides with or grows out of the theology of a universal mission and inclusive people of God. Paul's dialectical calling, with its obligations to reach both Jews and Gentiles and its implications for God's inclusive people, finds fulfilment as the demands of theology are realized in the formation of churches made up of Jews and Greeks on the Antioch model.

I. Introduction

The Corinth–Ephesus period reported in Acts 18–20 marks a high point in Luke's portrayal of the Pauline mission. One factor in this is, of course, the mission's success (18:8; 19:10). But the narrative also reveals some unique developments in mission practice and theology. For the first time we read of extended periods of mission work, which lead to the establishment of churches in two significant cities, Corinth and Ephesus. Before Acts 18, Luke chooses memorable or significant events to characterize Paul's visits to various places (Cyprus, Perga, Pisidian Antioch, Iconium, Lystra, Derbe, Macedonia, Philippi, Thessalonica [3 weeks], Beroea, Athens). Yet generally the impression is of relatively brief visits. This does not mean that he did not actually spend extensive periods of time in some cases, or that the accounts of his travels are exhaustive. But in comparison it appears that in Luke's presentation a certain amount of emphasis falls on this latter stage.[1] In the transition in the narrative which follows in the trip to Jerusalem, Paul becomes the prisoner-witness.[2]

Most agree that one of the major literary and theological concerns of Acts is to chart the history of faith and salvation and that the progress of the Christian mission is central to this task.[3] As for a Lukan history of faith, the gospel is universal and salvation is for all (cf., Luke 2:32).[4] As for Christian mission, the role of Paul in opening up the whole world to the gospel is crucial to the Lukan narrative. At his conversion and calling he is set on a paradoxical course of ministry designed to reach the whole world. Luke makes his mission central to the fulfilment of God's salvation plan. The question we want to try to answer from a Lukan perspective[5] is whether this universal mission theology has influenced the way in which the task of mission was carried out.[6]

It is indeed unique developments in the missions in Corinth and Ephesus that suggest the question ought to be asked, and we will

---

[1]Cf., Tannehill, Narrative Unity, 2:221ff.
[2]Weiser, Apostelgeschichte, 216-217.
[3]Cf., Rosner, ch. 11 in this volume.
[4]Cf., Witherington, ch. 8 in this volume.
[5]Paul's own thinking runs along similar lines: e.g., for the inclusive people of God: see Gal. 3.28; 5:6; 6:15-16; 1 Cor. 12.13; 10:32; Rom. 12:4. For Paul's calling to both Jews and Greeks, see 1 Cor. 1:22-25; 9:19-21. For the inclusive gospel, see Rom .1:16; 3:9, 19, 21-31; 4:11, 16; 5:12, 18.
[6]The question is not a new one; cf., Riesner, Frühzeit, 1-30; Hengel, Jesus, 50.

concentrate on the record of ministry there. However, several factors
must be considered if the contribution of this section in Luke's presentation is to be appreciated. First, it is difficult to understand Paul at this
stage in isolation from the Paul who entered Luke's picture in the
earlier chapters. Second, the level of thought about mission practice
and theology reached in Corinth and Ephesus must be seen in relation
to earlier patterns and developments. Third, the recent reading of
Luke's literary intention in the Corinth–Ephesus section as being to
emphasize the Ephesus mission as the 'climax of universalism' in
distinction from the Corinth mission requires evaluation. These factors
suggest an agenda. First, we will put Corinth–Ephesus into perspective by considering certain aspects of background and Pauline mission
history. Second, the mission work in Corinth and Ephesus (Acts 18–
19[20]) will be examined. Third, the relationship between these two
episodes will be considered in light of recent scholarship. Finally, the
Corinth-Ephesus stage will be considered as the culmination and
resolution of Paul's calling and mission.

II. Formative events and patterns

Paul's twofold call

The very similar situations which develop in Corinth and Ephesus,
and which lead to developments in mission practice and theology, in a
sense originate in Luke's account of the dawning of Paul's missionary
self-awareness. We will observe in the event of his conversion and
calling that the missionary agenda set for him contains two contradictory items. As his ministry proceeds, they will create tension, but he
nevertheless consistently applies himself to the achievement of each,
and a kind of dialectical process is evident.[7] Ultimately, in Luke's
reflection on the Pauline ministry these antithetical elements in his
calling eventually reach a stage of resolution as theology and developments in mission practice come together to yield a new entity.[8]

    This 'dialectic' goes back to the twofold nature of Paul's calling
to the Gentiles and to the Jews (9:15) which Luke interprets along the
lines of several OT prophetic backgrounds. 13:46-47 allows a point of

---

[7]The use of the model here is much less ambitious than that of certain nineteenth-
century scholars; cf., Gasque, Criticism, 21-95.

entry. In this text we learn of the sense of obligation to preach to the Jews 'first' (*cf.*, 3:26) which the pattern of visiting the synagogue satisfies, even if that pattern was conditioned more out of practical realities than theology.[9] The symbolic protest which follows the Jews' rejection of Paul and Barnabas described in v.51 occurs again in 18:6. In the later passage the pattern of rejection by the Jews recurs, and in Paul's response something of the reasoning of his sense of obligation to the Jews may emerge from an OT allusion. The response, as with 13:44ff. and 28:26ff., is to declare that he is turning to the Gentiles, and as in 13:51 this is accompanied by the graphic protest-gesture of shaking off dust from the clothing (from the feet, 13:51; *cf.*, Luke 9:5; Mark 6:11; Luke 10:10-11; Matt. 10:14).[10] Here the added phrase τὸ αἷμα ὑμῶν ἐπὶ τὴν κεφαλὴν ὑμῶν (*cf.*, 20:26) is reminiscent of the statement in Ezekiel 33:4, which suggests the possibility that Luke characterizes Paul's ministry in terms of the 'watchman': The watchman is charged to speak to Israel; it is an obligation, and failure to carry it out carries grave consequences.[11] Whether or not Ezekiel's watchman is in mind (the concept of blood-guiltiness is certainly wider spread), the thoughts of fulfilling an urgent obligation (to proclaim the gospel to the Jews) and transferring responsibility (καθαρὸς ἐγώ) to someone else are clearly in view.[12] The obligation as in 13:46 is to preach the word of God to 'you' first. Thus Paul is oriented towards one of the items on his mission agenda—the Jewish one—out of a sense of responsibility (*cf.*, 1 Cor. 9:19-21; Rom. 9).

13:47 supplies an interpretation of the Gentile orientation. Here the command of the Lord (οὕτως γὰρ ἐντέταλται ἡμῖν ὁ κύριος) which directs the Paul-Barnabas mission is shaped in terms of the Servant's calling in Isaiah 49:6—τέθεικά σε εἰς φῶς ἐθνῶν τοῦ εἶναί σε εἰς σωτηρίαν ἕως ἐσχάτου τῆς γῆς. The importance of the OT prophetic images in the Pauline self-understanding as the apostle of

---

[8]Paul's literary interests are different, but the sense of paradox is the same. Romans 9–11 reveals something about the paradox and the way it figures in Pauline mission thinking. What drives him to the Gentiles is an eschatological understanding that the Gentiles must first be reached before the consummation of all things which includes the salvation of Israel. 'The salvation of the Jews, too, will only be furthered by an intensive world-wide mission to the Gentiles' (Hengel, *Jesus*, 52).

[9]See especially Hengel, 'Synagogeninschrift', 145-83, esp. 170-72; *cf.*, Kim, *Origin*, 61-62.

[10]SB I. 571; Schneider, *Apostelgeschichte* II:147-48.

[11]Tannehill, *Narrative Unity*, 2:223;

[12]*Cf.*, Pesch, *Apostelgeschichte* II:148; Böcher, *EDNT* 1:38.

the Gentiles (Rom. 11:13), especially the Isaianic Servant model, is well known.[13] Luke's record corresponds to this Pauline picture. The same background is to be understood in Paul's statement in 18:6: ἀπὸ τοῦ νῦν εἰς τὰ ἔθνη πορεύσομαι (13:46; 28:28). What should not be missed, however, is that the Servant passage (49:5-6) defines the Servant's mission as one that is to the nations and to the tribes of Jacob (τοῦ συναγαγεῖν τὸν Ιακὼβ καὶ Ισραήλ, v. 5; τοῦ στῆσαι τὰς φυλὰς Ιακὼβ καὶ τὴν διασπορὰν τοῦ Ισραὴλ ἐπιστρέψαι, v.6). This corresponds to both Luke's and Paul's two-faceted interpretation of the Pauline mission.

Elements in 18:9-10 suggest that Jeremiah's call possibly also figures in Luke's interpretation of Paul's position (cf., 26:17; Gal. 1:15).[14] This word from the Lord to Paul, which contains a renewal and reminder of his calling (see below), employs language that is reminiscent of the calling of Jeremiah to be the prophet to the nations (Jer. 1:5-8, 19). The verbal links consist of μὴ φοβοῦ (Jer. 1:8; Isa. 41:10), λάλει (Jer. 1:7), ἐγώ εἰμι μετὰ σοῦ (1:8). Additional allusions include the promise of rescue (Jer. 1:8; cf., Acts 26:17), the awareness of a calling εἰς τὰ ἔθνη (Jer. 1:5) and opposition from the Jews (Jer. 1:18-19).

Thus Luke presents the two dimensions of the Pauline mission in terms of obligation and OT promise. The calling of the Servant in Isaiah and of Jeremiah (if it is in mind) provide a basis for holding together the two orientations in Paul, though in his ministry they are clearly in conflict. Up until this point, the two prongs of Paul's mission consciousness present him in the course of his preaching with a situation of polarization, an either/or. Luke makes it clear that some Jews come to faith; but it is also apparent that the two groups, Jews and Gentiles, are dealt with on separate terms. Furthermore, it is thematic that in one city after another the predictable first rejection by the Jews generally leads to a rather hasty departure—until the Corinth–Ephesus stage of ministry is reached. The tension created by the two focal points of Paul's ministry remains unresolved. It is in fact heightened somewhat in that the Antioch experience of Jew-Gentile unity in Christ seems to be non-repeatable.[15]

---

[13]See Riesner, Frühzeit 207-213; Holtz, 'Selbstverständnis', 321-30; Kim, Origin, 91-99; Hengel, Jesus, 51-52; Munck, Paul, 24-35.
[14]Cf., Holtz, 'Selbstverständnis', 324-25; Munck, Paul, 26-30.

Antioch as a model church

The church which was planted in Antioch among both Jews and Greeks[16] (11:19-26), authenticated by Barnabas and to which Barnabas brought Saul to minister for a year, undoubtedly provided a situation in which Pauline mission thinking was stimulated.[17] From the perspective of Luke's literary and theological depiction of the Pauline ministry, it is an essential influence. Antioch was a large densely populated city, capital of the Roman province which included Syria and Cilicia, with a significant Jewish community (*cf.*, Josephus, BJ 2.560; 7.45).[18] In it the mission of the early church to the Jews, which predominated in Jerusalem and Judaea, took a decided turn towards the Gentiles; and the second decisive stage of the early church's expansion is reached: Jews and Gentiles (mainly God-fearers)[19] shared a new status based neither on ethnic nor traditional religious differences, but on faith in Christ (15:7, 11). Corresponding to the new status is the new term, Χριστιανοί (11:26), that describes the new category.[20]

Luke describes Paul as sent out from this church. Once sent out, he and Barnabas target strategic cities, and presumably seek to replicate the Antioch church model.[21] But the pattern of Jewish rejection and hasty departure in his subsequent ministry apparently makes extended stays in the cities difficult; if replicating the Antioch church model was the goal, it was an elusive one.

Antioch influenced the Pauline mission in another equally important way. Acts does not reveal specifically whether or to what

---

[15]It is interesting to compare how the Thessalonian correspondence, which predates Corinth–Ephesus (perhaps sent from Athens; 1 Thess. 2:17; 3:1; Acts 17:10-15; see discussion in Simpson, 'Thessalonians', 935-36) addresses the church as a group of Gentile converts (1 Thess. 1:9); Jews are opponents who hinder the preaching of the gospel to Gentiles (2:14-16). There is a sense of continuity with the church in Judaea (2:14), but no emphasis on the transcendence of old barriers— Jew/Greek. There is a sense of excitement that Gentiles are coming to faith, and this could be linked to OT promises, but there is no indication that Antioch has been replicated.

[16]For the reading "Ελληνας, see Bruce, *Acts (Greek Text)*, 272; but see Barrett, *Acts I*, 550-551) for "Ελληνιστάς of non-Jewish Greek speakers.

[17]See Taylor, *Paul* 88-95.

[18]See discussion in Liebeschuetz, *Antioch* 40-41, 92-95.

[19]*Cf.*, Hengel, *Jesus*, 72-73.

[20]*Cf.*, Barrett, *Acts I*, 556-57; Hengel, *Geschichtsschreibung*, 87-88 (ET: *Earliest Christianity*, 103); Xeres, 'Χριστιανοί', 211-225, esp. 212-216 (brought to my attention by C. Stenschke); Weiser, *Apostelgeschichte*, 163; Schneider, *EDNT* 3:478.

[21]*Cf.*, Campbell, *Elders*, 166-67.

degree Paul's Antioch experience shaped his theology of God's people. From Luke's presentation (11:21-26), we should probably assume that it is meant to be so understood. The crisis that developed over Jew-Gentile relations through outside interference (15:1ff.; Gal. 2) and the resolution reached by the Jerusalem Council, together form a turning-point in the mission practice of Paul: the Antioch experience has been re-authenticated;[22] from this point on Luke has Paul separating from Barnabas, coming out from under the direct authority of the Antioch church and thinking of mission in more far-reaching terms (16:9).[23]

An early pattern

A pattern or strategy for Paul's ministry is clearly discernible from the time of the first mission trip. As is well known, it consists of going first to the synagogue upon entering a city to preach to the Jews (13:5, 14; 14:1; 17:2, 10, 17). While this often yielded some good results in the form of the conversion of some Jews and Gentile God-fearers, the next step in the sequence was generally opposition and rejection by the Jews (13:45; 14:2, 19; etc.). This in turn leads to ministry to the Gentiles. The programmatic statement in 13:47, in which Luke describes Paul's application of Isaiah 49:6 to his own ministry, presents this develop-ment as a salvation historical one (cf., Rom. 9–11). In that early exper-ience with Barnabas in Pisidian Antioch the die had been cast. Luke depicts Paul as attempting to fulfil an obligation to preach first to Jews (see above) and then to the Gentiles. Generally, however, the next step in the face of opposition was one of flight. Extended ministry in any one place was apparently out of the question; the Antioch ideal seemed out of reach.

R.C. Tannehill is right to describe Paul's mission during this period of time as 'synagogue-based'.[24] Paul's practice of going first to the synagogue should be understood not as a Lukan literary device for presenting a view of salvation history (though the writer uses it to good effect), but rather as historical reality.[25] It represents the situation that Paul was presented with at the time of his calling, and the

---

[22]See the discussion in Taylor, *Paul* 88-122.
[23]Hengel, *Jesus*, 50. The Antioch experience(s) almost certainly stimulated Paul's theology of the people of God (Acts 15:1ff.; Gal. 2; cf., Taylor, *Paul* 88-139).
[24]Tannehill, *Narrative Unity*, 2:222.
[25]See discussions in Marshall, *Luke: Historian*, 184-85; Hengel, *Jesus* 53-54; Kim, *Origin* 60-62.

situation in which he began to work out the implications of that twofold calling. Certainly for Paul's ministry the synagogue would have had its practical advantages, but the picture Luke presents emphasizes its limitations: Jews and Gentile 'God-fearers' had to be evangelized within the Jewish community and pagan Gentiles, more or less, on the run.

Churches, nevertheless, were successfully planted. Mission strategy provided for the upbuilding of the new converts through return visits (instruction, encouragement) and the appointing of leaders (14:21-28; 16:4-5; 18:23). The house church had already become an essential feature of the Pauline church (16:15, 40).[26]

III. Modification of the pattern and developments in Corinth and Ephesus: Acts 18-19(20)

Mission practice and the outworking of theology

Acts 18–19(20) reveal developments in Pauline mission practice which cannot be separated from the Lukan understanding of Paul's self-awareness and presentation of the mission up to this point. It is worth exploring in some greater detail how the pattern of ministry already established is modified at this stage.

(1) Corinth (18:1-17). At the outset, it appears as if Paul's pattern of ministry will recur. He establishes the synagogue as his preaching base (18:4). Paul's initial efforts in the synagogue of Corinth are summarized in the typical twofold way. First, we are told of the Jews' eventual opposition to Paul (v.6), which led to the announcement that he had fulfilled his obligation to the Jews and the repetition of his 'turning to the Gentiles' statement. Second, Luke explains that this preaching yielded powerful results: an influential Jewish family, that of Crispus the ἀρχισυνάγωγος, received baptism along with 'many of the Corinthians'.

Opposition, however, forces a move from the synagogue. This in itself is not completely unprecedented. 18:7 tells of Paul's relocation to the house of the Greek God-fearer, Titius Justus. Yet the reader is led to believe that the apostle's instinct was to depart from the city. This is

---

[26]*Cf.*, discussions in Campbell, *Elders* 141-75; Banks, *Community*; Meeks, *Christians* 29-30, 75-77; Murphy-O'Connor, *Corinth* 153-61.

at least one of the implications to be drawn from the word of the Lord to Paul:

εἶπεν δὲ ὁ κύριος ἐν νυκτὶ δι᾽ ὁράματος τῷ Παύλῳ, Μὴ φοβοῦ, ἀλλὰ λάλει καὶ μὴ σιωπήσῃς, διότι ἐγώ εἰμι μετὰ σοῦ καὶ οὐδεὶς ἐπιθήσεταί σοι τοῦ κακῶσαί σε, διότι λαός ἐστί μοι πολὺς ἐν τῇ πόλει ταύτῃ (vv.9-10).

This word functions in several ways. First, in this situation of pressure and uncertainty, the word provides a reminder and a confirmation of Paul's calling to ministry. The initial μὴ φοβοῦ and the following ἐγώ εἰμι μετὰ σοῦ correspond to the OT pattern of the calling and exhortation of the prophet (cf., Jer. 1:8; Isa. 41:10, 13; 43:5; 49:2; Josh. 1:9).[27] But this does not mean that the word of comfort and encouragement is unrelated to the current stressful situation. The word is possibly structured as a chiasm:

Command A Μὴ φοβοῦ,
Command B ἀλλὰ λάλει καὶ μὴ σιωπήσῃς,
Reason A₁ διότι ἐγώ εἰμι μετὰ σοῦ καὶ οὐδεὶς ἐπιθήσεταί σοι τοῦ κακῶσαί σε,
Reason B₁ διότι λαός ἐστί μοι πολὺς ἐν τῇ πόλει ταύτῃ.

According to the narrative sequence, the word perhaps intends to prepare Paul for the event about to be narrated (vv.12-17). It may also refer more generally to the opposition from the Jews already in progress, which that later event will epitomize.[28] In either case, the language suggests that the circumstances are to be viewed by Paul from the perspective of his calling.

Second, the word instructs or directs concerning the course Paul's ministry is to take (cf., 16:6-10; 22:21). As Luke reports it, such events typically feature in the taking of new steps in the expanding evangelistic mission (cf., 13:2; 16:6-10; 20:22-23). However much the Acts depiction corresponds to the experience of Paul, it is at least noteworthy that Luke's report confirms the impression given by Paul that this type of 'direction' was not unusual in his experience (cf., Gal. 2:2).[29] In this case, the instruction is to be understood against the background of Paul's experience up to this point, which has been to

[27]Cf., Pesch, Apostelgeschichte II:149; discussion in Long, "Call" 494-500.
[28]Schneider, Apostelgeschichte, II:251; Tannehill, Narrative Unity, 2:223-224.
[29]For the purposes of the 'occasional revelation' in Paul's ministry, which includes direction, see Bockmuehl, Revelation 144; Aune, Prophecy 248-62.

depart when opposition arises. The command λάλει καὶ μὴ σιωπήσῃ
thus also implies logically the instruction to 'stay in Corinth'. This is a
noticeable development in mission practice, which Luke connects with
a revelation from the Lord.

Third, the basis of the ministry command included in the word
(λάλει καὶ μὴ σιωπήσῃς) is a theology of the people of God: διότι
λαός ἐστί μοι πολὺς ἐν τῇ πόλει ταύτῃ. (18:10). The language takes
up the theme introduced in 15:14: ὁ θεὸς ἐπεσκέψατο λαβεῖν ἐξ
ἐθνῶν λαὸν τῷ ὀνόματι αὐτοῦ.[30] James' quotation is drawn from
Exodus 19:5 (ἔσεσθέ μοι λαὸς περιούσιος ἀπὸ πάντων τῶν ἐθνῶν
ἐμὴ γάρ ἐστιν πᾶσα ἡ γῆ; cf., Exod. 23:22; Deut. 7:6; 14:2); Luke
credits James with an innovative application as he has applied the
covenant-forming statement to the inclusion of the Gentiles in a way
different from the original. In Exodus the λαός consists of the Hebrews
whom God has drawn out from the rest of the nations (ἀπὸ πάντων
τῶν ἐθνῶν expresses separation); James' rearrangement of the material
implies that members from all the nations shall become God's people
(ἐξ ἐθνῶν indicates source).[31] In both James' speech and in 18:10, λαός
refers to the people of God but is no longer an exclusive reference to
Jews as it tends to be, when conveying theological meaning (sometimes λαός may stand for ὄχλος in a general sense),[32] elsewhere in
Luke's gospel and Acts.[33] In the use of εἰμί and the first person pronoun (μοι) there continues to be the sense of a chosen people belonging
to God, only now it includes Gentiles as well as Jews without distinction.[34] As Luke develops it, the theological concept of a universal
people of God (Jews and Gentiles without distinction) begins to
assume a definite though still theoretical shape through the Peter/
Cornelius encounter; it is implicit in the account of Antioch that
theology and practice have come together. Here, through the revelation from God, Luke links the concept to the Corinth mission. Mission
experience and developments in mission practice are closely bound up
with theology; the historical experiences characterized by opposition,
dissonance, paradox and divine revelation finally lead to a breakthrough which enables a nascent theology to be implemented in

---

[30]The concept of a people prepared by God for his own possession is expressed in
various ways in the NT (cf., Eph. 1:14; Titus 2:14; 1 Pet. 2:9).
[31]Cf., Dahl, 'People' 319-27; cf., Tannehill, Narrative Unity, 2:187.
[32]This is debated; see H. Frankemölle, EDNT 2:340-42 and note 33 below.
[33]See Flender, Heil 119-22, 121; Dahl, "People" 324-25; Frankemölle, EDNT 2:341-
42; Dupont, 'ΛΑΟΣ' 47-50; Jervell, Luke 41-74.
[34]Tannehill, Narrative Unity, 2:187.

practice. In Corinth, adjustments in mission practice allow Paul to plant a church which, as earlier in Antioch, may transcend old categories and barriers: the people of God whose sole basis is the gospel about Jesus the Messiah.[35]

This leads to the final point—that Luke links a definite development in mission practice to the Corinth mission. First, Paul remains in the city for an extended period of time (18:11). Second, he carries out his ministry in a neutral (or Gentile) setting, the house of Titius Justus, which was, however, in the closest proximity to the synagogue (συνομοροῦσα τῇ συναγωγῇ, v.7). In this way, the orientation of the ministry shifts from the synagogue to something broader which does not exclude access to Jews. From this vantage point, the message is directed to both Greeks and Jews, but extended ministry is not dependent upon Jewish receptivity.

(2) Ephesus (18:18-19:10). The same development generally recurs in Ephesus. Luke records an initial brief visit to the city (18:19) during which Paul again begins the work in the synagogue. Following the intervening trip back to Jerusalem and Antioch and the return through the Galatian region, he resumes the ministry in the synagogue of Ephesus (19:8). This second more prolonged period of ministry (three months) meets with the typical response of rejection and resistance from the Jews. Some believed. Again, he sets up in a neutral (or Gentile) location (taking the disciples out with him), the lecture hall of Tyrannus, which is followed by the statement that he continued in this way for an extended period of two years (v.10; cf., 20:31). There are some differences when the ministry in Ephesus is compared with Corinth: among others, there is no formal announcement of a turn to the Gentiles and no word from the Lord is recorded.

The Corinth-Ephesus episodes: disunity, unity, complementarity

(1) The argument for disunity. The differences alluded to above in the Corinth–Ephesus accounts figure prominently in two recent attempts to assess the significance of Corinth and Ephesus for an understanding of developments in theology in Acts. Both R.C. Tannehill and F. Pereira argue that Luke has presented developments in Ephesus in a way that is unique and distinct from those in Corinth;[36] Luke links the

---

[35]Lohfink, *Sammlung* 58-61.
[36]Tannehill, *Narrative Unity*, 2:230-240; Pereira, *Ephesus*.

'climactic' emergence of a truly universal understanding of God's people and a mission to the world specifically to the Ephesus mission.

(a) The first element of comparison is the scope of the respective missions. Tannehill and Pereira suggest that the separation from the synagogue and the turning to the Gentiles in Corinth (18:6-7) imply that the λαὸς πολύς to which the Lord refers, whatever it might mean in principle, is both historically in this city and still conceptually (theologically) made up almost exclusively of Gentiles, or that Paul's Corinthian ministry is strictly to the Gentiles. Thus although a new development in mission practice is apparent, at this point Jews and Gentiles will continue to be dealt with on separate bases, and an inclusive people of God has not yet developed.[37]

The reasoning behind this conclusion runs as follows. First, Paul announces explicitly that he is turning to the Gentiles (v.6). This statement is lacking in the Ephesus report because the ministry that follows opposition there is not, in contrast to Corinth, exclusively directed towards Gentiles.[38] Second, summaries of results verify this conclusion. Luke does not say that Paul in Corinth preached to Gentiles and Jews as he does in 19:10 (which stresses the point; Ἰουδαίους τε καὶ Ἕλληνας). Furthermore, the explicit reference to 'Corinthians' in the summary of results given in 18:8, meaning Gentiles in the city (cf., similar references in 17:22; 19:28, 34), is held to indicate that the emphasis is on a Gentile mission and Gentile conversion in Corinth.[39]

(b) The second point of comparison is the separation from the synagogue. Essentially, it is the way in which Luke describes Paul's departure from the synagogue and move to the lecture hall of Tyrannus that suggests a more decisive step.[40] The additional note, ἀφώρισεν τοὺς μαθητάς (19:9), indicates the formation of a separate religious community out of those who had formerly belonged to the synagogue, an action which poses a serious threat to the Jewish community.[41]

Thus Tannehill and Pereira argue that the Ephesian episode (18:18-19:22) is the climax in Luke's account of Paul's missionary ministry.[42] In some respects (Paul the Apostle of the Holy Spirit and the

---

[37]So Tannehill, *Narrative Unity*, 2:235; Pereira, *Ephesus* 153.

[38]Tannehill, *Narrative Unity*, 2:234-35; Pereira, *Ephesus* 151-53.

[39]Pereira, *Ephesus* 150-53; Tannehill, *Narrative Unity*, 2:234-35.

[40]On the meaning of ἡ σχολὴ Τυράννου and what might be implied about the nature of the Pauline mission movement from it, cf., discussion of views in Meeks, *Christians* 82-83 and notes.

[41]Tannehill, *Narrative Unity*, 2:234, 236; cf., Pereira, *Ephesus* 131-32.

miracle worker; the climactic farewell to the Ephesian elders) this is undoubtedly true. The same factors, however, are also capable of providing evidence of the unity or complementarity of the two episodes.

(2) The argument for unity and complementarity. There are connections between the Corinth and Ephesus episodes which bind them together and suggest that they should be held together to understand developments in mission practice in relation to a theology of the inclusive people of God. (a) Although it is possibly incidental, the accounts are connected by persons mentioned—Paul, Aquila and Priscilla, Apollos. In fact, the account of Apollos' meeting with Aquila and Priscilla in Ephesus (18:24-26) and subsequent trip to Corinth (18:27-19:1) forms a transition between these two stages of ministry (19:1) and indicates a substantial link between the two churches. (b) The accounts are connected by the development of a new mission strategy out of the old pattern: preaching first to the Jews in the synagogue (18:4, 19; 19:8) is followed by extended ministry outside of the synagogue. Moreover, in each case the opposition of the Jews (18:6; 19:9) causes departure from the synagogue which is necessary for the new development of an extended ministry in the cities (instead of leaving) from a neutral base (18:7; 19:9). In fact on this score Corinth and Ephesus seem identical. Given the change in Paul's circumstances following Ephesus, it hardly seems cogent to argue, as Pereira does, that because afterwards (in Acts) Paul does not preach in synagogues, it is the Ephesus mission, in distinction from Corinth, which reflects a decisive break from the synagogue.[43] (c) The episodes are connected in a complementary way by further accounts of united opposition, in the one case instigated by Jews, in the other by Gentiles (18:12-17; 19:23-41). (d) The theological 'climax' reached in Paul's speech to the Ephesian elders in 20:17-35 reflects the convergence of ideas from the Corinth and Ephesus episodes.

The rest of the factors cited by Tannehill and Pereira will be evaluated in the same order as they were presented above.

(a) Scope of respective ministries: turning to the Gentiles. In 19:8-9, as earlier in 13:45-47 and 18:4-7, the pattern of opposition in the synagogue followed by the decision to preach outside the synagogue recurs. In the earlier incidents Paul states decisively that he is turning to the Gentiles, but this is absent from the Ephesian episode. Is this omission a telltale clue that the climax of universalism has been

---

[42]Pereira, *Ephesus*; Tannehill, *Narrative Unity*, 2:230-240.
[43]Pereira, *Ephesus* 132.

reached in Luke's account of Ephesus, that here *for the first time* the
ministry that follows is consciously not exclusively to the Gentiles?
This seems an unlikely conclusion to draw. First, this amounts to an
argument from silence. Second, as an argument for 'development' it is
weak, for the repetition of the similar 'turn to the Gentiles' language in
28:25-28 is then not easily explained (γνωστὸν οὖν ἔστω ὑμῖν ὅτι τοῖς
ἔθνεσιν ἀπεστάλη τοῦτο τὸ σωτήριον τοῦ θεοῦ· αὐτοὶ καὶ
ἀκούσονται, v.28). As it occurs in each setting it is undoubtedly to be
understood as a programmatic statement; the point is, this program of
a mission to Gentiles which does not exclude the Jews 'first' (however
paradoxical it might seem) apparently continues (26:17).

Salvation summaries (18:8; 19:10) are thought to demonstrate the
development of universalism specifically in Ephesus. In the case of
Corinth, Luke indicates that the move from the synagogue does not
mean that Jews and God-fearers are no longer preached to. First, it is
significant that Luke includes the information about Titius Justus's
house that it was alongside the synagogue: συνομοροῦσα τῇ
συναγωγῇ (v.7). This location at least suggests Jews and God-fearers
would continue to have (and perhaps could not easily avoid) access or
proximity to the gospel, but not by virtue of their being members of the
synagogue.

Second, the probability that this new base of operations is in the
house of a Gentile who had aligned himself with the synagogue, a
'God-fearer', may be significant.[44] R. Pesch suggests that this is a sign
that Paul is in open competition with the synagogue to win the hearts
of the Gentile hearers.[45] But from a Lukan perspective, the emphasis
may lie more on the symbolic change in the place of teaching God's
word.[46] In any case, not only the proximity of the house but also the
religious status of Titius Justus as a God-fearer, who would have been
an adherent in some sense of the synagogue community, suggest
continuity despite the break.

Third, Luke makes a point of including the reference to the conversion of Crispus, the ἀρχισυνάγωγος and therefore a Jew who
would have been influential in the synagogue,[47] and his whole family

---

[44]Most accept that such a category did exist, but for the debate and the idea that it
is a literary device created by Luke to show the Gentiles have replaced the Jews as
God's people, see (in addition to the commentaries) Kraabel, 'God-Fearers', 113-
26; Gager, 'Jews', 91-99; Wilcox, 'God-Fearers', 102-22; *cf.*, with Siegert,
'Gottesfürchtige', 109-64; Overman, 'God-Fearers', 17-26.
[45]Pesch, *Apostelgeschichte*, II:149.
[46]Weiser, *Apostelgeschichte*, 273.

(v.8). We are not told specifically how this came about, but the inference to be drawn from the passage is that it was a result of Paul's preaching. This comment is placed after the statement that Paul had moved out of the synagogue. Whether or not the arrangement of the passage is sequential (though this seems the most natural way to read it), the comment is a part of the salvation summary statement and not to be separated from the statement about the conversion of 'many of the Corinthians' which the attached clause supplies: Κρίσπος δὲ ὁ ἀρχισυνάγωγος ἐπίστευσεν τῷ κυρίῳ σὺν ὅλῳ τῷ οἴκῳ αὐτοῦ, καὶ πολλοὶ τῶν Κορινθίων ἀκούοντες ἐπίστευον καὶ ἐβαπτίζοντο.[48] Luke apparently indicates that Paul's message preached from this new location influenced both Jews and Gentiles.

Fourth, the attack that follows in vv.12-17 indicates that Jews continued to be influenced after Paul's departure from the synagogue. The Jewish charge is that Paul was inducing people to worship God in a way contrary to the law (παρὰ τὸν νόμον ἀναπείθει οὗτος τοὺς ἀνθρώπους σέβεσθαι τὸν θεόν).[49] It would be special pleading to see in this a reference exclusively to Paul's ministry in the synagogue. Consequently, we are compelled to conclude that Paul's continuing ministry in Corinth, from a neutral location (which abutted the synagogue), influenced both Gentiles and Jews. 'Corinthians' may be a reference to Gentiles in the city, but it seems very likely that the membership of the Lord's λαὸς πολύς cannot be so limited. The salvation summary statement of 19:10 (ὥστε πάντας τοὺς κατοικοῦντας τὴν 'Ασίαν ἀκοῦσαι τὸν λόγον τοῦ κυρίου, 'Ιουδαίους τε καὶ ''Ελληνας.) is more sweeping in terms of numbers and geography, but

---

[47]The office was apparently not limited to one individual (cf., 13:15; 18:17). Matters of status and function and the relevant sources are thoroughly discussed in Brooten, Women Leaders, 15-33 (5-14 for the argument that women too held this office); cf., Schürer, History II:433-36.

[48]Pereira's argument (Ephesus 151-52) that the use of the aorist verb in the case of the description of Crispus' conversion and the imperfect verbs in the case of the Corinthians' conversion indicate Crispus' conversion is the result of previous events (i.e., preaching in the synagogue), while the Corinthians' conversion is to be linked to Paul's subsequent ministry outside of the synagogue is possible but not demanded by the text. Crispus' response could well be set out here as the first of a good many conversions.

[49]For the view that the Jews have in mind the Roman law or that a deliberately ambiguous reference is made, see Bruce, Acts (Greek Text), 396; Conzelmann, Acts 153. The monotheistic perspective of v.13 and conclusion of Gallio about the issues involved (v.15) suggest, however, that the Jewish concern is not ultimately with Paul's actions in relation to Roman law but in relation to the Torah (see Tannehill, Narrative Unity, 2:226-27).

not in terms of the categories of people involved.

From the location outside of synagogue and from the permanent base, the mission reaches Jews and Greeks, realizing in practice the theology embodied in the divine statement λαός ἐστί μοι.

(b) Separation from the synagogue. First, it is possible that the phrase ἀποστὰς ἀπ' αὐτῶν ἀφώρισεν τοὺς μαθητάς in 19:9 does not indicate that Paul took the drastic (symbolic and threatening) step of separating members of the synagogue who had become Christians. The disciples in view could have been with Paul from an earlier point (cf., 19:1).[50] But even if this is the indication, the decision made in Corinth to move to the house, which was adjacent to the synagogue, of Titius Justus, who had been linked to the synagogue as a God-fearer, would hardly have been much less provocative (cf., 18:13).[51] In fact Luke's inclusion of the account of the united Jewish attack would seem to underline this point. It may be that the Jewish complaint centered on the synagogue's loss of Gentile God-fearers to the new message,[52] but again, the reference to the conversion of Crispus the ἀρχισυνάγωγος and his household suggests caution in making such a distinction.

Consequently, the indications seem to point instead to parallel (or complementary) developments in these two important centres of Pauline Christianity. The two episodes, connected by the story of Apollos and the disciples of John the Baptist, form two parts of a last stage of Paul's pre-imprisonment missionary ministry in Luke's account. In each case, there is the decision to separate from the synagogue and continue ministering for an extended period from a neutral location. In each case, Jews and Gentiles come to faith. Mission practice has taken a turn that allows the theology of an inclusive people of God to be worked out. But there are other indications that Corinth and Ephesus are two parts of a whole

(c) Opposition. The description of the opposition that each prolonged period of mission activity provokes links these two episodes together. Jewish opposition is first seen in each city in connection with

---

[50]Sanders, Jews 391 n. 36. On the other hand, if the defence which the Jewish Alexander later tried to make before the crowd (19:33) was intended to dissociate the synagogue from Paul and Judaism from the disruptive movement, and if this is a reflection of conclusions reached by Jewish leadership earlier (19:9), then Paul's action may not have shocked the Jewish community to an unusual degree.
[51]Cf., Pesch, Apostelgeschichte, II:148-49.
[52]The description of Titius Justus is σεβομένου τὸν θεόν; the charge of the Jews against Paul relates to his influence on Jewish worship—σέβεσθαι τὸν θεόν (18:13). A connection may be implied. Cf., Tannehill, Narrative Unity, 2:227.

Paul's preaching in the synagogue. But Luke records united acts of opposition in each case.[53] In Corinth, it is a Jewish front which drags Paul before Gallio the proconsul (18:12-17). Gallio's indifference becomes a backdrop for Luke's emphasis on Jewish opposition.

In Ephesus, the prolonged Pauline mission (Ephesus may have been a base for wider travel, cf., 19:21-22; 1 Cor. 16:5; 2 Cor. 13:1-2[54]) was having similar effects on the Gentile population. The source of the problem was apparently the conversion of many who turned completely and dramatically from the practices associated with pagan worship (e.g., 19:17-20). A silversmith named Demetrius is credited with predicting the implications of this development both in terms of the effect on the economy and on the religion of Ephesus (vv.25-27). His galvanizing influence over his fellow artisans and eventually many more produced a hostile protest against Paul.

Other Lukan themes might be present,[55] but the most obvious point is that the united opposition results from the prolonged missions in Corinth and Ephesus. The gospel is presented as a threat to Judaism and Gentile paganism. The effects are felt on religious, economic and social-cultural levels. There is no attempt to hide this fact. Moreover, the implication that might be drawn is that this is the pattern of the world-wide mission—preaching to the whole world which yields results in terms of conversion and continued opposition from both Jews and non-Jews. This seems to be a pattern that continues throughout Acts. But this pattern is best observed if the Corinth–Ephesus episodes are seen as a unity, two complementary episodes which illustrate a mature stage of development in Pauline mission practice and theology.

(d) The farewell speech (20:17-35). Luke's account of Paul's farewell speech[56] functions in Acts as a conclusion to the free ministry of Paul, and in Luke's record may also serve as a kind of paradigmatic conclusion to and interpretation of the effectiveness of the Pauline mission.[57] In it Paul explicitly affirms the inclusive gospel and people of God which embrace both Jew and Greek without distinction. It signals a coming together of mission practice and theology.

---

[53]Cf., ὁμοθυμαδόν, 18:12; οὓς συναθροίσας, 19:25; φωνὴ ἐγένετο μία ἐκ πάντων, 19:34.

[54]See discussion in Riesner, Frühzeit 189-94, 285.

[55]E.g., the apparently helpful intervention of two government officials may have apologetic value of some sort.

[56]Cf., Hansen, ch. 15 in this volume.

[57]E.g., Roloff, Apostelgeschichte 300-301; Tannehill, Narrative Unity, 2:252-61.

The structure of the speech has been extensively examined.[58]
Quite apart from the parenetic significance it has for the listening
elders and later church, it reveals an awareness of the resolution of the
dilemma of Paul's call in the missions in Corinth and Ephesus. (1)
Paul's message is characterized by repentance to God and faith in
Christ (v.21) and by grace (vv.24, 32). By this time, such descriptions
assume the universal thrust in Paul's mission. But the inclusive scope
that developed in Paul's ministry is seen most clearly in the speech in
references such as the summary 'I testified to both Jews and Greeks'
(v.21) and the statement that Paul announced 'the whole purpose/
counsel of God' (v.27). Announcing πᾶσαν τὴν βουλὴν τοῦ θεοῦ, as
Tannehill correctly argues,[59] must, on the basis of the connected
disclaimer from guilt which precedes (διότι μαρτύρομαι ὑμῖν ἐν τῇ
σήμερον ἡμέρᾳ ὅτι καθαρός εἰμι ἀπὸ τοῦ αἵματος πάντων, οὐ γὰρ
ὑπεστειλάμην τοῦ μὴ ἀναγγεῖλαι; v.26-27a), be understood as a
reference to the message of salvation. In that disclaimer 'all' provides
a perspective that is missing from its use in connection with preaching
to Jews in 18:6, but only because in the later summary the preaching to
Jews and Gentiles is viewed holistically, not because the Paul depicted
in Corinth had not yet conceived of a universal people of God. The
λαός of God defined in 18:10 is equally in view in 20:28 in the expressions 'the whole flock' and 'the church of God' (παντὶ τῷ ποιμνίῳ; τὴν
ἐκκλησίαν τοῦ θεοῦ; v.28). The reflection here is backwards on a
mission and obligation to 'all' (cf., 22:15) which has been fulfilled.

But its fulfilment is not to be found simply in the Ephesus
mission.[60] First, the concept of the inclusive people of God in relation
to Pauline mission practice is explicitly in view at least as early as 18:10
(the theology is implicit much earlier). Although 'Jews and Greeks' in
20:21 may present a parallel to 19:10, the language used to describe the
formation of 'the church of God' (τὴν ἐκκλησίαν τοῦ θεοῦ, ἣν
περιεποιήσατο; v.28) reveals a link with the λαὸς τοῦ θεοῦ theme
developed in 18:10.[61] In each case, God's unique claim to 'ownership'
of this people is underlined (cf., Isa. 43:21).[62] The term ἡ ἐκκλησία τοῦ
θεοῦ, which occurs only here in Luke and on the lips of Paul (cf., 1 Cor.
1:2; 10:32; 15:9; 2 Cor. 1:1; Gal. 1:13; 1 Thess. 2:14), accentuates the

[58]See Tannehill, *Narrative Unity*, 2:252-53 and notes; Pereira, *Ephesus* 199-202.
[59]Tannehill,*Narrative Unity*, 2:257. But Cf., Dupont, *Milet* 119-125, for the view that
the broader ethical implications of the gospel for Christian living is meant.
[60]Contra Tannehill, *Narrative Unity*, 2:257; Pereira, *Ephesus* 205-207
[61]See notes 26-28 above; Lohfink, *Sammlung* 90-92.
[62]Cf., Weiser, *Apostelgeschichte* 322-23.

inclusive idea in the earlier term by conveying the notion of geographical universality.[63] Second, the inclusive ministry is evident in both Corinth and Ephesus, as observed above. Third, Paul's reference to 'the plots of the Jews' (v.19) refers first to 20:3 (where Corinth might be included[64]) and suggests a reference in the speech wider than Ephesus which may include the united effort made against Paul in Corinth (18:12-17). Fourth, Paul's reference to self-support and work with the hands (v.34) recalls the early stage of work in Corinth (18:3), though it may well also apply to his practice in Ephesus.[65] Thus while the setting of a final meeting with the Ephesian elders provides Luke with an appropriate concluding scene for his description of this stage of Paul's mission and the progress of the gospel, the picture of development in the Pauline mission and thought conveyed in this scene reflects back on both Corinth and Ephesus—and beyond.

IV. Conclusion

I began by suggesting that developments in the Pauline mission reported by Luke must be seen from the perspective of Paul's calling. In the record of that event, we found what might be described as a paradoxical or dialectical 'job description'; an obligation to preach to the Jews and to go to the Gentiles. We have seen that this twofold calling finds a practical resolution in Corinth and Ephesus, as extended ministry outside of the synagogue, but not excluding Jews, is linked to a theological concept of the inclusive people of God. Thus the Lukan development of the Pauline mission in this section of Acts offers a reflection of how theology in a context of specific circumstances influenced the development of practice so that the goal of theology, an inclusive people of God, might be realized: (1) the circumstances include preaching, opposition and the break from the synagogue; (2) this combination occasions the revelation from the Lord which adjusts Paul's missionary practice; as a result (3) the Antioch church model is replicated.

---

[63]See Thrall, *II Corinthians* 1: 89-93.
[64]See Riesner, *Frühzeit* 206-207; Schneider, *Apostelgeschichte*, II:294, n. 18.
[65]The reading in D (Τυράννου τινὸς ἀπὸ ὥρας πέμπτης ἕως δεκάτης) may reconstruct fairly enough a situation in which Paul would have worked at his trade up until 11:00 a.m., while Tyrannus (assuming he was a teacher and not simply the owner of the building) taught; from 11:00 onwards the typical schedule of rest allowed Paul the use of the building. See further the commentaries.

The farewell speech (20:17-35) provides another window through which to glimpse the resolution of this paradoxical calling. As it summarizes and concludes Paul's free mission, it links together mission theology and development in mission practice in Corinth and Ephesus. Jews and Greeks must be (and are being) reached. An inclusive gospel is affirmed; its proclamation has formed an inclusive people. It is in the formation of this people of God, whose basis is not race but solely the grace of God, that the dialectic of Paul's mission is resolved. Yet it is resolved only in part, or rather each historical representation of 'the church of God' is a partial fulfilment of the ultimate resolution. For in practice the obligation to preach to Jews and Greeks and the dangers of hostility and rejection from both Jews and Greeks continue (*cf.*, 22:21; 23:6; 26:17; 28:23ff.). The tension is renewed. In Luke's presentation of this process in which Paul has been caught up, the missions in Corinth and Ephesus contribute the circumstances which lead to precedent-setting developments in mission practice and which enable the demands of a theology to be met: old paradigms and barriers are transcended in the inclusive church of God.

CHAPTER 21

ISRAEL AND THE GENTILE MISSION IN ACTS AND PAUL: A CANONICAL APPROACH

Robert Wall

Summary

One of the principal roles of Acts in the New Testament is to introduce the author and subject matter of the Pauline letters. In particular, Acts defines Israel as a congregation called by God and constituted by those who call upon the name of the Lord Jesus for their salvation. Against the critical consensus, still framed by Vielhauer's negative verdict, we contend that this definition of a spiritual Israel agrees with Paul's response in Romans 9– 11 to the most controversial aspect of his ministry: that God's election of Israel is neither conditioned upon Jewish ethnicity nor annulled by membership of converted Gentiles.

I. Introduction

The Canonical approach to Acts

This chapter considers the theology of Acts in its canonical rather than historical *Sitz im Leben*. As such, it may well appear out of place in a volume dedicated to constructing the theology of Acts in its first-century setting. I.H. Marshall indicates as much in his introductory essay, where he admits to the importance of reflecting upon the theological argot of Acts in its 'canonical context', but then sets aside this interest as secondary to the primary interests of the current volume. Indeed so. Yet, it seems useful to include in this volume a study that considers the theology of Acts in relationship to the theology of the NT, if only to offer a few modest suggestions of a complementary, perspective by which the thematic interests of Acts, already considered by other contributors, can be 'thickened' in importance for the current interpreter.

In discussing a canonical approach to the theology of Acts, we acknowledge at the outset the importance of historical investigation for our fuller project. In doing so, however, the point to underscore is that the biblical theological task is not exclusively an historical problem but concerns the very nature of Scripture's role in the ongoing life of the church. That is, Scripture taken all together bears 'objective' witness to God's revelation in the history of both Israel and Jesus from Nazareth, and functions therefore both to nurture the church's theological understanding and to guide its responsible life as God's people in the world. In this way, the study of Acts in its historical setting is theologically important for current readers since its narrative of Christ's immediate successors within earliest Christianity nurtures a normative (although partial) understanding of God and how God relates with humankind within history.

Significantly, the author of Acts understood his Scripture in precisely this way. Indeed, any determination of his theological or pastoral intentions must carefully attend to the use of canonical Scriptures in his composition, where biblical citations and allusions help to construct a theological framework for a fuller understanding of the history he narrates. In this regard, the current reading of Acts as Scripture is guided by how the author of Acts read his Scripture as the context for interpreting the sacred history he narrated.

The hermeneutic of the canonical process is also concentrated by this same idea of Scripture: the church's preservation and eventual canonization of Acts to its trustworthy witness to the word of God and continuing usefulness in forming the church's theological understanding. The properties of this process left behind in its canonical product yield important clues about the role the church intends for Acts to perform within the NT, whether or not it is precisely the same as the author intended for his first readers (see below). Only when Acts is read in complementary relationship with other biblical witnesses, rather than in isolation from all others or in conjunction only with Luke's Gospel or in disjunction from Paul's letters, can its theological conception of faith and life be more fully envisaged and appreciated.

Finally, then, the determination of a book's meaning is logically related to the nature of its assumed referentiality, whether the interpreter's primary methodological interest is historical, compositional or theological. In locating the book of Acts in its biblical setting for study, the interpreter elevates the theological significance of its own intercanonical relationships with collections of other biblical books that form Scripture's full witness to God. No one disagrees that Scripture's theology is at the very least the sum of its various theologies; however, our point is to underscore more keenly their synergy so that the whole is actually greater than the mere sum of its parts when factoring in the theological importance of these intercanonical relationships that are fixed by the final form of the NT canon.[1]

The unity of Acts and the Pauline corpus within the New Testament

This present study explores a canonical approach to a single thematic interest in Acts—that of God's universal salvation. Our purpose is illustrative and suggestive of an overarching orientation to the subject matter of Acts, which may well expose other layers of meaning when additional thematic interests are considered. In keeping with our methodological interest in Acts, the following discussion supposes the interpretive importance of certain canonical markers (especially final literary form, placement within the NT, and title) that indicate the role Acts performs within the NT: Acts both concludes the narrative of Jesus contained in the fourfold Gospel and introduces the apostolic advice found in the multiple letters, especially the Pauline collection.

---

[1]These various methodological interests are developed in Wall and Lemcio, *Canon*.

By following these canonical markers the interpreter of Acts is oriented to its narrative as programmatical for understanding the theological subject matter of the writings that precede and follow it within the NT canon.[2]

If one of the roles that Acts performs within the NT is to introduce the letters of the NT, we presume that the narrative of Acts will yield clues to the deeper logic of the Pauline letters, beginning with Romans. In fact, the first placement of Romans within the letter canon and the formidable history of its interpretation, rather than a matter of its mere length, envisage its strategic importance in organizing the entire Pauline witness to the gospel of God. Further, the significant parallels between Luke's concluding biography of Paul in Acts 28:14-31 and Paul's opening autobiographical statement in Romans 1:1-15—the first from Paul in his corpus—underscore certain perceptions of his authority as an exemplar and transmitter of normative Christianity. The importance of this biblical interplay between the Paul of Acts in Rome, where his Gentile mission is summed up and legitimized, and the Paul of the Pauline corpus in Romans, where his apostolic self-understanding is introduced into the NT and defended, illumines a theological conviction rather than historical circumstance: Paul is the authorized carrier of the word of God, whose writings have ongoing significance for the formation of the people of God.[3]

In particular, the present chapter is concerned with the nature of the theological controversy provoked by Paul's Gentile mission—a controversy that centres his entire biblical witness: whether God's election of Israel as covenant partner has been annulled by the Gentile mission. In my view, a primary value of Romans is its provision of Paul's own substantial and mature response to this very controversy, which in turn frames the theology of his NT collection of letters. In this regard, then, one role of Acts within the NT is to supply a narrative setting that deepens our understanding of the very controversy found at the epicentre of Paul's theological conception.

A canonical approach to the theology of Acts will tend to shift primary attention from the presumed unity of Acts and the third Gospel to the presumed disunity of Acts and the subsequent collection of Pauline letters. Modern Acts criticism has supposed, with a few notable exceptions, that the portrait of Paul in Acts is not worth very much as a resource for constructing the life or understanding the

---

[2]For a discussion of this particular point, see Wall, 'The Acts of the Apostles.'
[3]Wall and Lemcio, *Canon*, 142-60.

theology of the historical Paul.[4] We will not argue that a uniform theology or christology exists between the Lucan and Pauline Pauls; nor that both Pauls have the same persona or follow a common chronology—although modern critical scholarship has surely exaggerated these differences. We will suggest, however, that the intercanonical relationship between their different theologies and portraits, Lucan and Pauline, form a complementary and even simultaneous whole. According to a canonical approach to biblical theology, these two distinctive voices are congregated within the biblical canon to form a normative and synergistic whole to effect the most effective biblical witness to God's revelation in Christ Jesus. On this basis, we can only presume at the outset of our study that the careful consideration of the role of Acts and its theological conception within the NT, and then of the significance of its intercanonical relationships, will 'thicken' the overall contribution that Acts makes in nurturing a fully Christian understanding of God and God's relations with humankind.

II. Israel and the Gentile mission in Acts

Few disagree that the extended citations from Joel 3:1-5 (LXX) in Acts 2:17-21 and from Amos 9:11-12 (LXX) in Acts 15:16-17 play a major role in organizing the narrative of Acts and its theological subject matter: each is cited by successive leaders of the Jewish mission (Peter, James) in order to interpret two watershed events of earliest Christianity (Pentecost, Jerusalem Synod); and both texts provide ample biblical justification for Luke's account of the movement of God's universal salvation from Jerusalem to Rome. These two texts are also important for organizing the entire composition as a narrative commentary on Scripture. The narrator of Acts appears to be 'canon conscious'[5], whose narrative envisages a particular understanding of the OT that closely links the biblical history of Israel with the events of earliest Christianity as a single movement of God's promised salvation to its fulfilment. Luke's 'canon consciousness' does not merely validate a 'Christian' interpretation of these events; rather, the reader of Acts is led to

---

[4]Vielhauer contends that the Lucan *Paulusbild* is a distorted picture of the historical Paul and his theological programme has been especially influential during the modern period; 'On the "Paulinism" of Acts', 33-50. Even though current Acts criticism considers the details of Vielhauer's view anachronistic, many still follow his essential claim that the Paul of Acts does not well approximate the Paul of history; *cf.*, Lentz, *Portrait of Paul*.

assume in advance that the narrated events are related and made explicable by Scripture, under the rule of the Spirit, as the word of God.[6] This particular quality of the composition seems similar to midrashic literature, if only vaguely, since its author exegetes earlier texts by means of narrative augmentation and application.[7]

D. Boyarin's study of the intertextuality of midrash extends this point.[8] The Evangelist's narrative style is similar to the midrashist who (like Boyarin) employs biblical texts, inherently gapped and dialogical, which he then naturally 'slips' into as principal conversation partner in order to complete their meaning for his readership, whether to respond to their theological confusion or to their spiritual testing.[9] The Evangelist's repetition of catchwords and phrases from cited texts throughout the entire narrative suggests a sustained dialogue between himself and biblical prophets, between his narrative and Scripture, that is characteristic of midrashic literature. In this sense, the activity of God within history, as narrated by Acts, determines how we should understand the biblical prophecy, not the reverse. The two extended citations of Scripture that organize the narrative of Acts are not merely apologetical ('proof-from-prophecy'), then, but are integral to its intended theological meaning.[10]

---

[5]The idea of 'canon consciousness' as a characteristic of midrashic literature is introduced by Seeligmann, 'Midrashexegese,' 151-54. Seeligmann's point is that most biblical writers viewed their canonical literature, even though its limits were not yet fixed, as exercising a special role in religious discourse, including the writing of texts. That is, the selection, wording and ordering of narrative literature envisages the often subtle synthesis of a writer's Scripture into his text, which then functions as an interpretation of sacred texts employed.

[6]*Cf.*, Jervell, *Paul*, 122-37.

[7]For Lucan narrative as midrashic, see Evans and Sanders, *Luke and Scripture*, 13.

[8]Boyarin, *Intertextuality*, 1-21, which supplies the methodological support for his understanding of midrashic literature. Although he does not consider intertextuality as a feature of midrashic literature, Hays contends for a similar reading of Pauline letters in his important *Echoes*.

[9]So Fishbane, *Torah*, 16-18.

[10]Evans has demonstrated the importance of the Joel citation for Acts: its use is not ad hoc but functions to explain the xenolalia at the Pentecostal coming of the Spirit and to provide a biblical backdrop for Peter's programmatical sermon. In fact, for Evans this critical speech is 'an acting out of the prophetic message of the prophet Joel' (*Luke and Scripture*, 217). Further, the Joel text is 'a major contributing element to the Evangelist's understanding of the gospel' (*Luke and Scripture*, 220), supporting especially its pneumatological (power for preaching and performing the word of God) and soteriological (universal salvation) aspects.

Acts 2:22–15:12 as a narrative commentary on Joel 3:1-5 (Acts 2:17-21)

From this literary perspective, we view the first half of Acts as a narrative commentary on Joel 3:1-5 (LXX; Acts 2:17-21). The formal division of this narrative unit is bracketed off by the parallel verses of Acts 2:22 and 15:12. In 2:22, Peter addresses the Jews in Jerusalem about 'Jesus of Nazareth, a man attested to you by God with (1) mighty works and wonders and signs (2) which God did (3) through him (4) in (Israel's) midst'. By the time the narrator relates in 15:12 that another assembly of Jews in Jerusalem 'listened to Barnabas and Paul as they related what (1) signs and wonders (2) God had done (3) through them (4) among the Gentiles', the shift of speaker from Peter to Paul and the more shocking change of object from Jews to Gentiles correspond to a particular interpretation of the Joel prophecy envisaged by the narrative of conversion of the intervening chapters.

The repetition of the 'signs and wonders' catchphrase in the inclusio, as well as its use in the intervening narrative (*cf.*, Acts 2:19, 22, 43; 4:30; 5:12; 6:8; 7:36; 8:6, 13; 14:3; 15:12), is rhetorically important as a 'marker' that envisages a reflexive dialogue between Luke's narrative and the cited prophecy. By following the signs and wonders, the reader not only better understands the full meaning of the Joel prophecy but this expanded understanding of its meaning in turn supplies an effective explanatory model for making meaning of the narrative itself. In this way Luke employs Joel's rather disturbing prophecy as the theological subtext of his narrative. According to its prophetic calculus, the signs and wonders are 'poured out' by the Spirit at the dawning of 'the great and manifest day, when all who call upon the name of the Lord will be saved'.

The first two uses of 'signs and wonders' indicate God's sponsorship of Jesus's messiahship (2:22) and that of his apostolic successors (2:43). The reference to those of the apostles in 2:43 is interesting because it is prefaced by note of the 'fear (that) came upon every soul' without any record of an antecedent circumstance likely to produce such fear. In narrative context, however, 'fear' seems an accompaniment of the apostolic 'word' (2:41): when accompanied by signs and wonders, the apostolic word is received as the divine word and so 'feared' as the measure of God's eschatological verdict (2:40). Likewise, 'when Ananias heard these words [of Peter], he fell down and died. And great fear came upon all who heard of it' (5:5). The narrative pattern is followed here too, when they accompany the apostolic word

and produce fear as a result (5:12). In this latter case, God's execution
of Ananias is a prolepsis that the proclaimed word carries the prospect
of divine retribution for any who deny its truth. Finally, the reference
to them in introducing the Stephen story (6:8) prepares the reader for
his speech, where they link the ministries of Moses (7:36) and Jesus—
the 'prophet-like-Moses' (7:37; cf., 3:22)—in leading Israel into God's
salvation (7:35). The refusal to follow Moses and then Jesus, despite the
signs and wonders, results in Israel's spiritual disaffection and divine
judgement.

Stephen's martyrdom provokes the persecution that drives the
diasporic Jewish believers out of Israel into Samaria in beginning the
next stage of the church's appointed mission (cf., Acts 1:8c). In Acts 8:4-
5, Philip 'preaches/proclaims the word/Christ' to 'multitudes [who]
with one accord gave heed to what was said when they heard him and
saw the signs which he did' (8:6; cf., 8:13). In this case, 'signs and
wonders' and 'amazement' accompany the word of God and confirm
by allusion to prophetic witness (=Joel) that the 'last days' have
arrived, when the eschatological 'Day' of the Lord's salvation is at
hand for a people outside of Israel. Likewise, since the signs and
wonders of the Spirit also announce the prospect of divine rejection for
refusing the gift of salvation, the story of Simon is logically added to
the narrative: he who first 'believed Philip as he preached good news
about the kingdom of God and the name of Jesus Christ' (8:12) and was
'amazed' by 'signs and great miracles' (8:13), then imperilled his own
salvation by supposing its attainment is a matter of greed rather than
grace (8:14-23).

The catchphrase seems to progress to its fullest explication in
14:3 where the Gentile mission of Barnabas and Paul is summed up as
'speaking boldly for the Lord who bore witness to the word of his
grace, granting signs and wonders to be done by their hands'. Here
again, signs and wonders authenticate the proclamation of the word of
God, but now among Gentiles. The division within the city resulting
from the evangelistic crusade (14:4) recovers the missionary meaning
of the original judgement motif in the Joel text: they are harbingers not
only of God's salvation-creating powers but also of the spiritual crisis
which is provoked by the preaching of God's word about the Risen
Jesus. The choice the audience must make, whether for or against God,
issues in either salvation or judgement—an eschatological option that
once belonged exclusively to the Jews but has now been extended to
include even pagan nations. Thus, the final reference to 'signs and
wonders' in Acts 15:12 within the context of the Jerusalem Council

carries the cumulative force of this entire preceding narrative of Gentile mission: the fact of their occurrence among Gentiles supplies evidence in support of a universal salvation.

Likewise, the repetition of 'call' (ἐπικαλέω) in Acts is also a gloss on the Joel prophecy, whose importance in Acts is deepened by these two additional reasons: (1) 'calling' is a verbal idea common to both the Joel and Amos citations, suggesting their integral importance for the whole of Acts; and (2) it is this verbal idea of 'calling' that concentrates Paul's argument in Romans 9–11, providing important linguistic evidence for the very intercanonical conversation between Acts and Paul for which this chapter contends. The importance of the 'calling' motif in Acts is underscored by an important difference between the 'calling' of Joel and the 'calling' of Amos. According to Acts 2:21 (Joel 3:5), 'calling' (ἐπικαλέσηται) is an idiom of human conversion, while in Acts 15:17 (Amos 9:12), 'calling' (ἐπικέκληται) is an idiom of divine election. In both passages, 'calling' is linked to 'the name of the Lord'; however, in Joel the active 'calling' is directed to 'the name of the Lord' while in Amos the passive 'calling' is determined for those that seek the Lord 'by my name', that is, by the action of the Lord God who, according to James's declaration, 'take(s) out of (the Gentiles) a people for his name' (15:14). In this second use, God is subject of divine calling, while in the first case, the Lord Jesus is the object of humanity's call to conversion. Finally, the result of human 'calling' upon the Lord Jesus, according to Joel's prophecy, is salvation (=conversion); whereas, the result of divine 'calling' of Gentiles, according to Amos's prophecy, is the restoration of eschatological Israel (15:16). The importance of these differences for determining the whole and integral meaning of 'calling' in Acts and in relationship to Romans 9–11 will be teased out below.

In its prophetic setting, Joel's 'calling upon the Lord's name' is the language of prayer, and those 'calling' upon the Lord are pious believers. This original sense of 'calling' is reflected in Acts in the story of Stephen, when at death he 'calls' to the Lord Jesus to 'receive my spirit' (7:59). Even so, in the messianic dispensation of God's salvation, Stephen's petition is to the Messiah rather than to God, since the Risen Jesus is now principal agent in the work of divine judgement and deliverance. Stephen, filled with the Spirit of Jesus, calls on him to receive what belongs to him, trusting that Jesus is in a position of exalted authority and so able to enact that deliverance from eternal death. 'Calling' involves, then, both a sense of identity with Jesus and a confidence in Jesus's heavenly authority.

The clearest sense of 'calling' in Acts, however, shifts its meaning from the petitions of pious believers to the conversion of non-believers: 'calling' upon the Lord Jesus now means to profess saving trust in him. In this light, we note the intriguing allusion to the Joel formula 'call upon the name of the Lord' in the narrative of Saul's conversion to Christ and his call to the Gentile mission in 9:13-22. In their crucial exchange, Ananias and the Lord define Saul's mission ironically: rather than bringing more suffering to 'those calling upon your name' (9:14), as Ananias fears, Saul will 'bear my name' (9:15) and will 'suffer for my name' (9:16), as the Lord instructs. Ananias's protest is then repeated by the Jews in Damascus in response to Saul's proclamation of Jesus as 'Son of God' (9:20): 'Is not this the man who harassed those who called upon this name?' (9:21). The Lord's words about Saul are quickly fulfilled. The point we make here is not to exploit this episode for its value in introducing Paul's future ministry; rather, it is to simply note that Luke's narrative alludes to the Joel formula in conjunction with Paul's commission: the fulfilment of Joel's prophecy will be realized by his ministry of the word which brings either salvation or judgement to those who hear it.

Clearly, ἐπικαλέω is closely tied to the change in the referent of the formula, 'name of the Lord,' in Acts. What Moule calls a 'free interchange between Jesus as Lord and God as Lord' exhibits considerably more complexity, ambiguity, and movement.[11] By the time James cites Amos in 15:17, the narrative has unequivocally posited Jesus as the convert's 'Lord' and the 'name' on which the convert calls for salvation. When the formula is first used in the Joel citation, the reader may well assume the identity of 'Lord' to be God, in keeping with the original context, or perhaps intentionally ambiguous at first reading. Yet, clearly Luke's Peter interprets 'Lord' as that status given Jesus by God (2:36). Indeed, while Luke may use the single term 'Lord' ambiguously throughout Acts, the idioms 'name of the Lord' or 'my name' refer only Jesus. 'Name of the Lord' is actually used only two times—in the Joel citation and in the Damascus Road epilogue (9:29), where reference is to Saul who 'preached boldly in the name of the Lord' (9:30). Earlier, Jesus speaks in the first person to Paul and to Ananias about his name. The immediacy and persuasiveness of direct discourse add dramatic force to the mention of Jesus's name in this episode. Ananias refers to those 'who call upon thy name' (9:14) and the Lord responds that Saul 'is a chosen instrument of mine to carry

---

[11]Moule, 'Christology', 161.

my name before the Gentiles' (9:15). Significantly, in a subsequent tell-ing of the Damascus road christophany, Paul recounts how Ananias exhorted him to 'rise up and be baptized, and wash away your sins, calling on (Jesus's) name' (22:16). Here, Luke picks up the language of Joel to confer upon Paul the legitimacy of his salvation.

More important for this discussion is the significance of the 'name' of the Risen Jesus to animate the powers of the coming age. The account of the healing of the lame man in Acts 3–4 especially focuses on the objective meaning of the 'name,' where it evinces a certain power that leads to healing/salvation (3:6, 16; 4:10-12) and also to conflict/judgement (4:17-18). Calling upon Jesus's name is to have 'faith in his name' (3:16) whereby the lame are converted (3:8) and made 'whole' (3:16; cf., Luke 4:17) in witness that the promise of the holy prophets is now fulfilled (e.g., Joel; cf., 3:21) now that Jesus has been enthroned as Lord and Christ.[12] Therefore, the apostles teach in the 'name' of Jesus (4:17-18), signs and wonders take place by mention of this 'name' (4:30) and salvation from sins result from mention of the 'name' (10:43). In this light, the 'name' of Jesus is part of a larger arsenal used to facilitate the church's universal mission; and these various references to the 'name of Lord/Jesus' all gloss the 'calling' formula of Joel to suggest to the reader that the church's mission intends to provoke the calling upon the Lord's name simply because it infallibly results in salvation.

In similar fashion, the meaning of the saving result of conversion takes on discrete layers through interaction with various narrative contexts. In its original context, the prophetic formula 'whoever calls on the name of the Lord shall be saved ($\sigma\acute{\omega}\zeta\omega$)' refers only to pious Jews who have separated themselves from the nations, who face certain judgement on the day of the Lord. Peter's subsequent exhort-ation, however, picks up this phrase from Joel to revise the point originally scored: a true Israel salvation is actually 'from this crooked generation' (2:40), who evidently are those who now stand under God's curse. In this effort at theological gerrymandering, the borders of eschatological judgement have been redrawn to mark out those saved as belonging to a remnant community of Jewish converts, who are separated not from other gentile nations but from those who are 'crooked' within Israel—probably an allusion to the description of disobedient Israel (Deut. 32:5; cf., Luke 9:41; 11:29). The population of this 'crooked generation' becomes increasingly clear as the narrative

---

[12]Tannehill, Narrative Unity, 2:53-54.

unfolds, when rulers of the Jewish people (4:26), the disciples Ananias and Sapphira (5:10), and the prophet Bar-Jesus (13:11) all are recipients of divine judgement. In this way, the borders of 'true' Israel are no longer drawn in ethnic or national terms, but in spiritual terms to include all who 'call upon the name of Jesus' and exclude 'this crooked generation' who reject the word of God.

The next layer of meaning builds this same point more gradually. According to 2:47, 'the Lord added to their number day by day those who were being saved,' which include 'all who believed' (2:44) 'in the name of Jesus Christ for the forgiveness of sins' (2:38). With some grammatical distance, salvation is from sins and those saved are believers in the 'name of Jesus Christ.' The meaning of salvation in 4:9-10, takes up this theme when Peter asks the rulers whether 'we are being examined today concerning...(the) means by which this man has been saved.' In this setting, σῴζω carries a double meaning, referring to the lame man's healing and to divine forgiveness, both of which bear witness to the resurrection. Peter's response underscores the formula's multivalence: 'there is no other name under heaven given among men by which we must be saved' (4:12)—the name of Jesus heals and forgives those who call upon his name, which in turn deepens our understanding of Joel's prophecy.

Peter later recounts the Cornelius episode to critics in Jerusalem, telling how the angel had told Cornelius that he (Peter) 'will declare to you a message by which you will be saved...' (11:14). But in the subsequent re-telling of Cornelius's conversion, this message is deleted, so that Peter merely says, 'As I began to speak, the Holy Spirit fell on them just as on us at the beginning' (11:15). What this contraction does is leave virtually no space between the saving message and the Spirit's proof of saving—not unexpected, then, is Peter's conclusion, 'If then God gave the same gift to them as he gave to us when we believed in the Lord Jesus Christ' (11:17). The lack of distance between salvation offered the Gentile and salvation confirmed speaks to the centrality of God's activity and thus of salvation as a gift, now given to the Gentiles.

The pivotal events narrated in Acts 15 consolidate the meaning of 'salvation.' When opponents to the Gentile mission insist that without circumcision 'you cannot be saved' (15:1), no new argument comes forth to refute their claim. The whole narrative to this point in Acts supplies evidence that required no addition commentary. Peter merely summarizes a past episode (Acts 10:1–11:15), concluding that 'we believe that we shall be saved through the grace of the Lord Jesus, just as (Gentiles) will' (15:11). How far this articulation has come from Joel's picture of being saved, and yet one is not shocked when it appears. The adumbrations of this clear statement of divine grace appeared as layered nuances throughout the intervening narrative.[13]

Acts 15:13–28:28 as a narrative commentary on Amos 9:11-12 (Acts 15:16-17)

Keeping in mind the midrashic quality of Acts defined earlier, the second half of Acts functions as a narrative commentary on Amos 9:11-12 (LXX; Acts 15:16-17). The formal division of this narrative unit is bracketed by the parallel verses of Acts 15:13 and 28:28. In 15:13, James introduces his citation and interpretation of Amos with the exhortation, 'listen (ἀκούσατε) to me!'. Acts then concludes with Paul's speech in Rome to the city's Jewish leadership, resulting in an internal squabble (= Jewish rejection) anticipated by the preceding narrative.[14] In response to this final rejection of his message, Paul expresses a third time (cf., 13:46; 18:5-6) his resolve to turn to the Gentiles since 'they will listen' (ἀκούσονται) (28:28). The intervening narrative of Gentile conversion (those who 'listen' to the word of God) and of Jewish rejection, only confirms and expands the meaning of the Amos prophecy.

What then is the meaning of the Amos prophecy in Acts? Perhaps apropos of narrative literature, the depiction of theological crisis and reflection follows from the fact of experience: the experience of conversion requires the Jerusalem Council to settle the theological conception which undergirds the church's mission. What informs James's use of Amos, then, is the concern to provide theological justification to the fact of Gentile conversion by 'calling upon the name of the Lord Jesus.' On this experiential basis, James can argue that 'the prophets agree with this (experience)' (15:15).

Sharply put, the debate provoked by Gentile conversions narrated by Acts is whether God's salvation is universal and whether the 'true' Israel is identified by humanity's response of faith to the preaching of the gospel. For the first time in Acts the theological principle is explicated that non-Jews may be enrolled among the people of God. James now appeals to another Scripture (Amos 9:11-12) to explain that the testimonia of Peter and Paul merely agree, as it must, with Scripture: Gentile conversion does not annul God's promise of a

---

[13]For development of this point, see C. Wall, 'Narrative Commentary'.
[14]Cf., Tannehill, Narrative Unity, 2:354-55.

restored and redeemed Israel, but rather expands it; nor does faith
(rather than Torah observance) as the condition of Gentile conversion
contradict God's plan of salvation, but rather confirms it. The second
half of Acts provides a narrative that supports and explains this
theological consensus reached at Jerusalem.

Once again, there are a few intriguing allusions to the first part
of the Amos citation (15:16) that facilitate a more reflexive reading
between the two. For example, the promise that God 'will rebuild the
tent (σκηνήν) of David' is picked up in 18:3 where Paul's occupation
is described as a 'tentmaker' (σκηνοποιός).[15] The irony of this narrative detail is clear: Paul is actually God's appointed 'tentmaker' by
whose Gentile mission the Davidic/Messianic kingdom is reconstituted and restored according to Scripture (cf., Acts 1:6). In this same
sense, the crucial repetition of the word for a 'rebuilt' Israel, ἀν-
οικοδομέω, is picked up in the closing exhortation of Paul's Farewell
Speech to the Ephesian elders, where his preaching of the word of God
'builds' (οἰκοδομέω) up a true Israel (20:32; cf., 9:31). Further, the
οἶκος-family is a favourite of Luke's and well represented in the
second half of Acts. For example, the familiar story of the conversion
of the Philippian jailer (16:16-34) posits salvation in his οἶκος (16:31-34;
cf., 16:15). Here in this profane city, which is occupied by demons and
policed by trouble-makers, God calls out Gentiles to rebuild the 'house
of Israel' (2:36; 7:42) through a proclamation of the word of God
(16:17). God's promise of a restored Israel is not annulled by the
Gentile mission but rather confirmed by it.

More to our point is the second part of the Amos citation (Acts
15:17), where the LXX's departure from the MT allows Luke to use it
midrashically in support of 15:14, where James concludes that God is
'tak(ing) out of (the Gentiles) a people for his name.'[16] This phrase
combines two important Lucan catchwords—the term for 'people'
(λαός), which Luke uses for the 'people of God' or Israel (cf., Acts 2:47;

[15]My student, P. Haury, first called this linguistic connection to my attention.
[16]So Johnson, Acts, 265-73. The LXX changes in the vocalization of the MT Amos,
so that the reference to a 'remnant of Edom (edom)' now becomes 'the rest of
humankind (adam)' and its corresponding verbal idea changes from 'possession'
(yirshu) to 'seek' (yidreshu). Luke adds the object of humanity's search, 'the Lord',
and changes the tense of the following verb, ἐπικαλέω, to perfect passive, 'have
been called' to make even more abrupt the shift from the active voice of the Joel
citation. The result is a citation that now can interact well with the dramatic
conclusion James reaches in 15:14, while at the same time interacting with the
concluding phrase of the Joel citation, 'all who call upon the name of the Lord will
be saved', and with the first half of Acts which interprets it.

3:23; 4:10; 5:12; 7:17, 34; 12:11; 13:17, 24), and 'name' (ὄνομα), which to this point in Acts typically refers to the Lord Jesus, rather than the Lord God, as the object of humanity's call of conversion—a gloss on Joel's 'all those who call upon the name of the Lord' (Acts 2:21; see discussion above). Given these subtexts, then, James's point becomes even clearer: the elect Israel that God calls to salvation is reconstituted by 'all those who call upon the name of the Lord'.

The use of 'name', which links 15:14 with 15:17, also joins together the different images of 'calling' found in the two critical citations from Joel and Amos. Here, James shifts the focus of 'calling' from Jesus to God: it is God who 'takes out a people for his name', even as it is the Lord God who speaks in Amos 9:12 of 'Gentiles who have been called by my name'. That is, James is 'discoursing on God's choice of a "people for his name"' rather than on the restored Israel's choice for 'the name' of the Lord Jesus.[17] Appropriately, the verbal form of ἐπικαλέω also shifts in Amos LXX from its active to perfect passive voice, indicating God's effective calling of a people into Israel. That is, humanity's 'call of conversion'—the theological interest of the first half of Acts in commentary on Joel's prophecy of humanity's call—has given way to God's electing 'call to conversion'. The fact of the historical experience of conversion requires a substantial rethinking of the doctrine of divine election: that God has also called Gentiles into eschatological Israel because of their faith in the name of Jesus. The plan of God's universal salvation requires this sort of partnership between a God who calls a people out the world for salvation, and a people who respond to God's call by calling upon the Lord's name for their salvation. This more rounded theological conception, already introduced into the narrative by Peter's first missionary speech on Pentecost (see the use of προσκαλέω with the phrase κύριος ὁ θεός ἡμῶν in 2:39), requires the second half of the narrative for its full exposition.

In the second half of Acts, ἐπικαλέω is almost always used of Paul's appeal to Caesar for legal deliverance (25:11, 12, 21, 25; 26:32; 28:19). If we understand these various occurrences (and the episodes they appear in) as a gloss on the thematic divine call, then two programmatical impressions follow. First, Luke's story of Paul acknowledges the importance of national citizenship for the ministry of the word (cf., 22:28; 23:27). Naturally, one who is identified by his national citizenship will 'call' upon the nation's ruler to insure his well-being.

---

[17]Johnson, *Acts*, 265.

Indeed, Paul's call to Caesar ameliorates Paul's political crisis, so that the very call itself constitutes deliverance from Jewish death plots. In this use, ἐπικαλέω functions as an allegory of the believer's call on the name Jesus for deliverance from sins and eschatological judgement. Luke takes Israel's call to the Lord in Joel and through the course of the Acts narrative defines this term as a universal prerogative to identify with the One who has ultimate authority over one's soul.

Second, the second half of Acts, and indeed Luke's story of Paul, focuses on his missionary journey to Rome, the city at the mythical centre of the profane world. Paul's appeal to the Caesar complements well the outworking of God's plan for Paul to preach the word of God in Rome (19:21; 23:11; 27:24), which is then realized at narrative's end when he enters the city (28:14, 16). If viewed in reflexive relation to the Amos ἐπικαλέω, these various appeals to the Caesar along with God's plans for a mission in Rome nurture a more radical understanding of divine election: that God intends to call a people out of even Rome at the very centre of the profane universe. This conclusion, more than any other perhaps, intensifies how universal God's salvation is.

III. Israel and the Gentile mission in Romans 9–11

Our purpose in this section of the chapter is not to provide a detailed exegesis of Romans 9–11, nor a thematic treatment of the Pauline notion of 'calling' but to consider Paul's use of 'calling' (ἐπικαλέω/ καλέω/κλῆσις) language in Romans 9–11 against the backdrop of Acts. Few deny anymore the importance of Israel's definition (or 'redefinition') as the elect people of God for organizing the set of core convictions that undergird Paul's mission and writing. Since this passage, and indeed the 'calling' motif, deals specifically with this issue, its importance for understanding the whole of Pauline theology is rarely contested. In Dahl's apt phrase, 'the inner unity of Paul's mission and theology is nowhere more obvious'.[18]

Indeed, most detect signs of wear when studying Romans 9–11: Paul no doubt needed to rehearse these same controversial arguments on many occasions, so carefully crafted and well rounded is this written response to the Romans. The principal theological controversy was provoked by his definition of divine election,[19] a fundamental of

---

[18]Dahl, *Paul*, 86.
[19]See Wright's helpful summary in *The New Testament*, 259-68, 456-58.

Jewish belief which Paul had apparently adapted to help interpret the history and experience of the Gentile mission. According to Paul, the mercies of divine election are realized even among those Gentiles who respond to the word of God in faith. Perhaps the author of Acts had heard Paul's argument not a few times[20], and so was familiar with its subject matter and midrash-like appeals to Scripture in support of his conclusions. Perhaps Luke had even heard Paul use the 'calling' motif in a way similar to its use in Acts, in both texts to define God's universal salvation and to defend Paul's Gentile mission.[21] In any case, the intercanonical relationship between Acts and Romans supposes that the narrative of God's universal salvation found in Acts supplies an authorized context for a fuller understanding Paul's programmatical apologia of the Gentile mission found in Romans 9–11. This is so whether or not Luke himself wrote in support of Romans or to introduce a proto-collection of Pauline letters already in circulation. From the perspective of the biblical canon, their common 'calling' motif links these two compositions together within the NT in a reflexive dialogue that deepens the reader's understanding of the entire Pauline corpus and its theological subject matter. In this sense, the question Paul responds to in Romans 9–11, whether the results of his Gentile mission have annulled God's promise of Israel's salvation, now depends equally upon Acts for its full answer.

There is a sense in which the deeper logic of a theology of Acts differs from that of the Pauline corpus, although this may be one result of different literary genre. An historical narrative will tend to privilege the fact of experience as the setting or occasion of theological reflection, even as Pauline literature tends to privilege core theological convictions as the setting for religious experience. In Acts, theological reflection responds to the pentecostal experience of universal salvation, whereas in Romans theological reflection on the nature of God's electing mercy (9:6-29) requires in turn a particular construal of conversion (9:30–10:21). In Romans, faith is first of all measured by the subject matter of what one believes (orthodoxy); and the crisis that occasions the writing of his letters, including Romans, is first of all a theological crisis. Thus, in Romans, once the ideas of divine election are clarified, the praxis of mission is not only intelligible but rational.

---

[20]Although much disputed, Fitzmyer argues that Luke was a companion of Paul, that the we-materials of Acts are from his personal diary, and that he has a good sense of Paul's theology and missionary idiom; so *Luke I-IX*, 47-51.
[21]Whether the Evangelist actually knew of any of Paul's letters remains debated; see Wenham, 'Acts'.

A final preliminary observation, made here without much comment. In Romans 9–11, Paul's argument moves between an ethnic and spiritual Israel. While he contends for a 'true' Israel whose membership is conditioned upon profession of faith in Christ, his theological project is nevertheless bracketed by expressions of lamentation (9:1-5) and hope (11:25-32) for an ethnic Israel, still loved by Paul for the sake of his ancestral religion. There is, however, no such ambivalence in Acts (*cf.*, Acts 28:23-8): a 'true' Israel of God is reconstituted by those Jews and Gentiles of various kinds from various places who through various missions all become converts to the same message about Messiah Jesus. If Romans 9–11 tends to blur an authentically Pauline definition of Israel, then the narrative of Acts brings it to even sharper focus within the NT: the 'true' Jew is one who repents and believes the gospel.

God's 'Call' to Conversion

Paul's use of καλέω/ἐπικαλέω in settling the theological controversy provoked by his Gentile mission is crucial.[22] In making his first point about God's covenant with an elect people, Paul brackets off and redefines divine mercy (in 9:14-23) in terms of the 'calling' motif (κληθήσεται/καλοῦντος in 9:6-13 and in reverse order ἐκάλεσεν/κληθήσονται in 9:24-29). In the first passage, the motif is used to link God's choice of Isaac (9:7) and then Jacob (9:11) to underscore the freedom of divine sovereignty: God freely is merciful on those whom God alone 'calls' (9:12). The Israel of divine election, then, is defined by 'promise'—a 'spiritual' Israel—rather than by ethnic or national identity (9:6-7), or 'because of works' (9:12). The use of καλέω is especially strategic in 9:12 where Paul sets forth the fundamental thesis of his entire theological conception: the borders of a true Israel are set 'not because of works but because of God's call.' Curiously, Paul does not indicate here on what grounds God extends the call to be saved. However, the justification project, implicit in Romans, is made explicit in Acts where God's merciful call of Gentiles into salvation is predicted by Scripture itself (rather than by the systematic [and extra-biblical] ideas of predestination or omniscience).

---

[22]Paul always uses καλέω for divine calling and ἐπικαλέω for humanity's response, whereas Luke employs a biblical text (Amos) that uses ἐπικαλέω but carries the same theological freight.

In the other bracketing passage, where he again argues for the freedom of God to freely elect a true Israel, Paul finally makes clear that God has called Gentiles to be 'vessels of mercy' (9:24). The subsequent appeal to Hosea 2 found in 9:25-26 supplies a new and more radical ingredient to Paul's understanding of divine mercy which includes Gentiles as objects of God's call. In its prophetic setting, Hosea's notion of divine calling was directed toward the people of the Northern Kingdom: even though their spiritual disaffection had alienated God, they were still considered children of promise and in the future would be restored by God's mercy. By dynamic analogy, Paul equates the Gentiles with the ten tribes of the Northern Kingdom: Gentiles who were 'not my people/not loved' are now those 'I call "my beloved"/called "children of the living God"'.

What is less clear is why Paul retained the prophet's reference to 'the very place' (9:26) where God's mercy finds those formerly excluded from the promise of blessing. Virtually every modern commentator assumes that Paul had in mind the same 'place' Hosea had in mind, namely Jerusalem, perhaps even to agree with the Jewish expectation of an eschatological pilgrimage of the nations to the holy City to help inaugurate the messianic kingdom. Even though this conviction is perhaps implicit elsewhere in Romans (so 11:25-32; 15:29?), it seems unlikely to be the case here given Paul's rather emphatic reversal of the prophetic formula of universal salvation by mentioning Gentiles before the Jews (9:27-29) instead of 'to the Jew first and then to the Greek' (so Rom. 1:14-16). Nor does Fitzmyer's verdict seem right that 'there really is no need to try to specify the "place", which just happens to be part of the quotation',[23] since Paul has already telescoped and revised his Hosea citations. Why wouldn't he have edited out this reference to 'place' if superfluous to his argument? In light of our canonical approach, the identity of this place where a Gentile people are called 'children of the living God' is brought to clearer focus in a reflexive conversation with Acts, where the 'place' of divine election is not Jerusalem but Rome (see above)! Such a placement of divine mercy radically redraws the borders of a true Israel to include even those found in Rome at the very centre of a secular universe where people most definitely are not God's people.

---

[23]Fitzmyer, *Romans*, 573.

Humanity's 'call' of conversion

In responding to the claim that the deeper logic of the Gentile mission supposes that a merciful God has annulled the promise of salvation to Israel, Paul demonstrates from Scripture that in fact God calls forth a spiritual Israel that includes Gentiles. He now shows that membership within this Israel requires 'faith' (9:30), not 'works' of the law (9:32). In making his programmatical point in 10:4, Paul contends that with the completion of Messiah's earthly ministry a new dispensation in the history of God's salvation is inaugurated, which 'ends' ethnic Israel's privileged status under the law (cf., 3:2). Whether 'kinsfolk by race' (9:3) or Gentile, 'every one who has faith may be justified'. Paul's harsh indictment of ethnic Israel in Romans 9–11 does not envisage his rejection of Torah but rather the Jewish rejection of Jesus's earthly ministry as messianic—an emphasis made more emphatic by relationship to Acts, which narrates the history of Jewish rejection of the gospel. If Christ is the object of faith, the practical question remains: what is the nature of this faith that justifies anyone who believes?

Paul's handling of various OT texts in 10:5-13 intends to define the mode of this faith by which anyone can become members of true Israel.[24] Most commentators rightly concentrate the Pauline definition of faith by 10:9—with a verbal confession that 'Jesus is Lord' when coupled with an inward conviction that God has already confirmed the truth of this confession by raising Jesus from the dead. The result of this confession of faith, then, is that 'you will be saved'.

What is of equal importance in this definition, however, is Paul's assertion that this Christian confession of faith in the Lordship of Jesus (10:9) is evoked by the preaching of the 'word of faith' (10:8). It is this proclaimed gospel that supplies the subject matter that is now 'on your lips (i.e., that 'Jesus is Lord') and in your heart (i.e., that 'God raised him from the dead')'. Yet, this missionary calculus remains severely gapped; from Romans, we still know very little about the mode of Paul's preaching ministry that elicits confessions of faith in Christ from new converts. In this light, the role that Acts performs within the NT is to fill in this gap with provision of a narrative of Paul's preaching ministry. The very nature of narrative vivifies theological ideas in order to render them in ways that enhance comprehension and application. Without Acts, the practical importance of Paul's assertion that justifying faith responds to the proclaimed gospel may very well

---

[24]So Dunn, *Romans 9-16*, 599-618.

be imperilled: Acts compels us to think of Paul's theological concept-ion as a 'fact' of history. Further, the theology of Acts complements Paul's argument here by noting that the Spirit of the Risen Jesus empowers the preaching of the word and engenders its hearing, which results in the response of faith.

Of special importance in this regard, of course, is Paul's use of the 'calling' (ἐπικαλέω) motif in 10:12-14, especially his citation of Joel 3:5 (LXX) in 10:13 which repeats Luke's use of the same Scripture in Acts 2:21. From the perspective of the NT, the narrative commentary of this text in Acts 2:22-15:12 (see above) provides a inner-biblical backdrop against which the reader of Romans better understands its importance in 10:13. For example, Acts and Romans both define humanity's 'call upon the Lord' as a confession of faith in response to the proclamation of the word of God. Acts confirms the controversial result that 'there is no distinction between Jew and Greek' in the new dispensation of salvation. Acts agrees with Paul that the 'Lord' to which Scripture bears witness and on whom both Jew and Greek must call is none other than the Risen Christ. Acts describes more concretely what Paul euphemistically refers to as the 'riches' of salvation that Christ (through his Spirit) bestows upon the convert, whether as heal-ing from sickness or forgiveness from sin. Finally, Acts underscores the force of Paul's contention that all humanity is responsible to freely 'call upon the name of the Lord Jesus' for salvation as the appropriate and even logical response to a God who has freely called all humanity into a true Israel.[25]

---

[25]This essay is dedicated to Professor P. Moessner in celebration of his installation as Professor of NT Language, Literature and Exegesis at Columbia Theological Seminary (Decatur, Georgia, USA).

CHAPTER 22

SOCIOLOGY AND THEOLOGY

Stephen C. Barton

Summary

Comparatively little work has been done so far on the social-scientific interpretation of Acts. This may be because questions of historicity and theology have been the dominant concerns of interpreters, or because the material in Acts is not susceptible of social-scientific analysis. In spite of several grounds for caution, it is suggested that the models and methods of the social sciences have a legitimate role to play in deepening our understanding of the world behind the text (the world of the author), the world within the text (the narrated world of characters, intentions and events), and the world in front of the text (the world of the reader). Two major examples of recent social-scientific analysis of Acts are considered, and the essay concludes with a theological reflection on the contribution of social-scientific interpretation to the ongoing task of reading Acts as part of Christian scripture.

I. Prolegomena

The starting-point for a discussion of sociology and theology in Acts has to be, Is there anything to talk about? This might appear a rather defensive way to begin, but there is a problem, and it can be expressed in a number of ways.

First, if the evidence of the history of scholarship is anything to go by, sociological or social-scientific exegesis of Acts is almost a non-starter. M. Powell's recent, competent survey of 1991,[1] has chapters on issues like genre and purpose, composition history, theology, Acts as history, and Acts as literature. But matters sociological barely get a look in, and when they do they are introduced within categories of a quite different kind, like 'Ecclesiology' or 'Church and State'. This itself illustrates one of the major factors which has given impetus to the development of sociological exegesis generally: a perception that interpretation of the NT has for too long been carried on within predominantly doctrinal horizons to the neglect of other approaches to the text—approaches which may themselves have important doctrinal implications. As yet, however, sociological approaches in Lucan studies have attracted relatively little attention, even though Luke–Acts as a text comprises about one-quarter of the NT as a whole.[2]

A second and related aspect of the problem is the dominance in scholarship of issues to do with the historicity of Acts. Put briefly, the agenda here focuses on questions like, Is Acts theology masquerading as history or a special kind of history in its own right? This then leads to investigation of Lucan historiography in the light of the historiography of his day, and/or to consideration of whether Acts can be used by modern historians for the purpose of reconstructing the history of the early church. Among the issues usually hidden here are old chestnuts like what to make of Luke's unabashed supernaturalism, the extent to which Luke gives an idealized portrayal of church life in apostolic times, how to explain the differences between the Paul of Acts and the Paul of the letters, and so on. None of these issues is unimportant, but the massive investment of energy in ploughing these well-worn furrows of inquiry—often along the now arguably rather outmoded lines of, Did it happen like this or not?—appears to leave

---

[1]Powell, *Acts*.

[2]Confirmation of this surprising lacuna comes from Garrett's substantial article of 1992, 'Sociology'. The seminal works she discusses are works on the 'Jesus movement', Paul, 1 Peter and Matthew. No examples are discussed of sociological work done on Luke–Acts.

most interpreters too exhausted or distracted to try approaching old texts and old problems in new ways.

In passing, it is worth asking why the interpretation of Acts has been dominated by this kind of agenda, not least in Britain and the United States. The answer is likely to involve quite a complex task of historical and cultural analysis in its own right, a task which could well be illuminated by perspectives from the sociology of knowledge. For the claim of advocates for social-scientific interpretation is that it has the potential for illuminating, not only the ancient sources, but also the reasons why the sources have been read in certain ways.

In this particular case, the dominance of the historical agenda in the reading of Acts can be linked plausibly with the following factors: (a) the rise to pre-eminence since the Reformation and the Enlightenment of historical criticism as the culturally dominant way of engaging in the scientific exegesis of the Bible; (b) the strong ecclesiastical/ doctrinal interest in the historical veracity of the apostolic witness, in relation to which the narrative of Acts is of obvious importance—for instance, in the area traditionally known as 'church, ministry and sacraments'; (c) the particular Protestant (including Pentecostalist) interest in the testimony of Acts to the church in apostolic times, prior to (what is often seen as) the dimming of the original vision represented by 'Early Catholicism'; (d) the success and growth of archaeology as a major historical discipline able to fill out or even verify the 'historical geography' of the world of the early church; and (e) the long-running epistemological debate, rooted partly in British empiricism and positivism, over how to make sense of claims about the supernatural of which the Book of Acts is full. In this light, it is hardly surprising that 'Acts as history' has for a long time—and perhaps rightly so—been such a dominant concern.[3]

A third aspect of the problem has to do with the nature of the Acts material itself. Some, like E.A. Judge and A. Malherbe, would argue that Acts is amenable to interpretation as a source for the social history of early Christianity, but not for interpretation using the tools of the social sciences.[4] The data just is not there for controlled social-scientific inquiry. What is more, the tools of the sociologist are just too blunt and the problem of the incommensurability between the etic ('outsider') categories of the sociologist and the emic ('native')

---

[3]For a very useful survey of Acts scholarship, see Gasque, *History*. On the broader issues of hermeneutics and cultural history, see Frei, *Eclipse*; Louth, *Mystery*; and Morgan with Barton, *Biblical Interpretation*.

[4]See Judge, 'Social Identity'; Malherbe, *Social Aspects*.

categories of the sources is insuperable.[5] In a very percipient article on this very point, written in response to the appearance in 1983 of W. Meeks's, *The First Urban Christians*, S. Stowers states the issue thus:[6]

> Scholars [of early Christianity] have appropriated modern scientific theories and models, facilely assuming commensurability on many different levels. The debate in the philosophy of science, and a parallel debate in the philosophy of history, should warn us to be skeptical about the applicability of modern models to antiquity.... Most social scientific schemes of description and explanation embody peculiarly modern assumptions about values, beliefs and social structures. The historian must be able to analyse and evaluate theories and methods thoroughly enough to discern when fundamental assumptions will produce distortion if applied to antiquity.

Such warnings have to be taken seriously. But it may be the case that certain kinds of scepticism about the validity of sociological interpretation work with too rigid a view of how sociological analysis proceeds, or with expectations about social-scientific method and its applicability which social scientists themselves do not share or, yet further, with anxieties about the ideological and even anti-religious bias of the social sciences which are by no means a necessary con-comitant of the discipline.[7]

On the other hand, there are those who are enthusiastic about sociological exegesis and who steer clear of Acts on quite different grounds. A case in point is R. Scroggs who, in 1975, published a seminal essay on 'The Earliest Christian Communities as Sectarian Movement', in which he uses the sociology of sectarianism to bring certain features of early Christianity into sharper focus. Astonishingly, however, a text which ostensibly bears testimony to the early church (the Acts of the Apostles) is swept aside in favour of texts (the gospels) which ostensibly concern an earlier, non-ecclesial period altogether. He says by way of attempted justification: 'The book of Acts, which purports to tell the history of the church, is of little use for our pur-pose'. In a footnote, he adds peremptorily: 'It is late, tendentious, and offers few traditions that can be sociologically evaluated'.[8] So whereas

---

[5]On the distinction between etic and emic approaches and their hermeneutical implications, see Brett, *Biblical Criticism*, 16-17.

[6]Stowers, 'Early Christianity', 151.

[7]For further discussion of these issues, see Holmberg, *Sociology*; and Elliott, *Social-Scientific Criticism*, esp. 87-100.

[8]Scroggs, 'Earliest Christian Communities', 1-23; quotations from p. 8 and n. 26.

in Judge's estimate, Acts is good for history but not for sociology, in Scroggs's view it is good for neither history nor sociology! However, Scroggs's scepticism is quite illogical and deeply at odds with the very enterprise he himself wishes to promote.[9]

This is not to deny that there are legitimate grounds for caution in the sociological exegesis of Acts. Two essays are especially noteworthy in this respect. Both raise the important question whether it is at all possible to use Luke–Acts as a mirror of what we call, often with disarming vagueness, 'the Lucan community'. The first essay is by L.T. Johnson, himself the author of a monograph on Luke–Acts and a commentary on Acts.[10] In his essay,[11] Johnson makes a number of important points. First, not even in the interpretation of Paul's letters —Romans, for example—has there been unqualified success in drawing inferences about the social situation of his addressees: 'The study of Paul's letters reminds us that even in documents of a genuinely occasional nature, not every element in the document is determined by the place, the people, or the occasion.'[12] Second, with reference this time to the gospels, how justified is the assumption that the pastoral and theological concerns of an evangelist are determined by a situation of crisis among his readers? As Johnson says, 'Reading everything in the Gospel narratives as immediately addressed to a contemporary crisis reduces them to the level of cryptograms, and the evangelists to the level of tractarians.'[13] In regard to Luke–Acts in particular, Johnson argues that the difficulties of mirror-reading are even more acute: the author's identity is unknown; the addressee is an individual not a church; due weight has to be given to the influence of the tradition and to Luke's professed intention to write an historical account; due weight has to be given also to the differences between Luke's two volumes, differences which complicate attempts to 'read off' the community from the text; and there is the additional complicating factor of the evidence of literary artifice in Luke's writing: 'Given a fairly intricate and intelligible literary structure... our *first* assumption with regard to individual parts within that structure should not be that they point to a specific community problem, but that they are in service to the larger literary goal of the author'.[14]

---

[9]For further critique of Scroggs's essay, see Barton, 'Early Christianity', 140-162.
[10]Johnson, *Literary Function*; as well as his *Acts*.
[11]Johnson, 'Lukan Community'.
[12]'Lukan Community', 89.
[13]'Lukan Community', 90.
[14]'Lukan Community', 92.

The other essay along these lines is D. Allison's more recent piece, 'Was there a "Lukan Community"?'[15] If anything, he is more doubtful of the possibility of finding Luke's community than Johnson, and justifies his doubt on five considerations. (a) The reticence of scholars to say what they mean by 'community' means that we do not really know what we are looking for.[16] (b) If the author of Luke–Acts was the companion of Paul, as early tradition attests (Col. 4:14; 2 Tim. 4:11), it is likely that his identity was not bound up with any one church but instead with the church universal, a supposition which fits well with the universal evangelistic outlook of Luke–Acts itself. (c) We cannot safely assume that Luke belonged to one group in particular if he was an itinerant missionary; and Luke's thorough-going interest in journeys and itinerant preachers suggests that he was. (d) Luke's prologue (1:1-4) makes no mention either of a particular community or of a communal crisis which explains why Luke has written. On the contrary, it is formulated in 'frustratingly general terms' and gives good reason for inferring that 'its author anticipated that Luke–Acts would enjoy wide circulation' beyond the bounds of any single audience.[17] (e) Related to the preceding, the difficulty of establishing Luke's purpose and the diversity of scholarly proposals about Luke's purpose may be indicative of the writer's translocal concerns and his relative independence of any particular Christian group.[18]

There can be no doubt that these two essays raise important questions about the viability of drawing inferences from Luke–Acts about 'the Lucan community'. In a sense, these kinds of questions are similar to the ones scholars of an earlier generation raised about form criticism. So we will have to bear them in mind in our discussion of the Acts material in this essay. But it needs to be said also that sociological

---

[15] Allison, 'Lukan Community?'.

[16] Confirmation of this comes in the recent essay by Moxnes, 'Social Context'. After acknowledging that the problem of moving from text to social situation 'has not so far been solved' (p. 379), he goes on to question whether we ought to talk of 'community' or 'communities', and comes to the conclusion that the 'tensions' reflected in the text 'are so general in character that they can be found in a number of Hellenistic cities in the eastern part of the Roman Empire'!

[17] 'Lukan Community?', 66.

[18] Cf., also Riches, 'Communities', 233-234: 'By contrast with the two other Synoptic Gospels, Luke's work raises a fundamental question as to whether we should relate the Gospel and its author to a particular congregation or indeed to a particular place. ...Luke's parish seems to be a wider one than that of either of the other two Synoptic evangelists, and his concerns are those of the emerging church with its various settlements scattered across the empire.'

exegesis of Acts is not limited to reconstructing the community behind
the text. There are all kinds of realities within the narrative world[19] of
the text itself which have a social or cultural dimension—clean and
unclean food, healing miracles, almsgiving and communalism, charismatic manifestations, the exercise of authority, experiences of conflict
and persecution, and so on—and the disciplines of philology, history
and literary criticism may be insufficient on their own to understand
what these things mean. Furthermore, to the extent that 'the Lucan
community' behind the text continues to be a legitimate object of
scholarly speculation, alongside the Matthean, Marcan, Johannine and
Pauline 'communities', then social scientific methods will have an
inevitable and necessary part to play.

In more general terms, though, we need to indicate at a fundamental level what justifies the use of the social sciences in the interpretation of Luke–Acts. Are the kinds of difficulties outlined above an
insuperable obstacle to such an enterprise? I myself think not, and
would argue instead that since reading Acts responsibly requires a
reading which is sensitive to history, there can be no *a priori* exclusion
of methods and models of a social-scientific kind which have the
potential for deepening our historical sensitivity. If historical analysis
focuses on diachronic relations, on relations of cause-and-effect over
time, social-scientific analysis focuses on synchronic relations, on how
the meaning of an event is affected by the relation of one social actor to
another within the complex web of culturally-determined social
systems and patterns of communication. Whereas historical analysis
tends to focus on the particular (persons, events and institutions), the
social sciences focus more on the typical, conventional, tacit, taken-for-
granted dimensions of life in society. Put otherwise, the social sciences
make possible what cultural anthropologist C. Geertz calls 'thick
description' in interpretation[20]—whether of the world behind the text
(the world of the author), the world within the text (the narrated world
of characters, intentions and events), or the world in front of the text
(the world of the reader).

This kind of 'thick description' is made possible by the asking of
a different set of questions to those traditionally asked by historians.
H. Kee has grouped these in seven categories: boundary questions,
authority questions, status and role questions, ritual questions, literary

---

[19]For a useful social-scientific study of one aspect of Luke's 'narrative world', see
Moxnes, 'Social Relations'.
[20]See Geertz, *Interpretation*, 3-30.

questions with social implications, questions about group functions, and questions concerning the symbolic universe and the social construction of reality.[21] Putting such questions does not run counter to historical analysis. Rather, it aids historical awareness by opening up other dimensions of the reality to which the text testifies. The two approaches are complementary. As another anthropologist, J. Pitt-Rivers puts it: 'To understand the past is like understanding another culture'.[22] There is, in my view, no reason in principle why this should not apply to the interpretation of the Acts of the Apostles.

Social-scientific criticism also makes possible what Meeks calls 'a hermeneutics of social embodiment'.[23] In other words, it offers a corrective to the strong tendency to 'theological docetism' in certain circles—the assumption that what is important about the NT is its 'theology' abstracted somehow from its literary and socio-historical setting. This is a particularly strong temptation in the interpretation of Acts, since Acts itself reflects a pervasive 'theology of the word' and gives enormous prominence to the witness, preaching and teaching of the apostles.[24] All the more important, then, to learn with the help of the social sciences that beliefs and doctrines help constitute systems of communication and patterns of identity and action within a society. As such, they are cultural artifacts which shape and are shaped in turn by the societies and groups which develop them and pass them on. Scroggs made the point well in his 1978 address to the Paris meeting of the *Studiorum Novi Testamenti Societas*:

To some it has seemed that too often the discipline of the theology of the NT (the history of *ideas*) operates out of a methodological docetism, as if believers had minds and spirits unconnected with their individual and corporate bodies. Interest in the sociology of early Christianity is no attempt to limit reductionistically the reality of Christianity to social dynamic; rather it should be seen as an effort to guard against a reductionism from the other extreme, a limitation of the reality of Christianity to an inner-spiritual, or objective-cognitive system. In short, sociology of early Christianity wants to put body and soul together again.[25]

---

[21]Kee, *Knowing the Truth*, 65-69.
[22]Pitt-Rivers, *Shechem*, 169.
[23]Meeks, 'Social Embodiment'.
[24]See further, Marshall, *Luke: Historian*, 157-187.
[25]Scroggs, 'Sociological Interpretation', 165-166.

II. Sociology and theology in Acts: two case studies

One of the most comprehensive attempts to 'put body and soul together' and to fill the lacuna in the interpretation of Luke–Acts mentioned at the outset is P. Esler's monograph, *Community and Gospel in Luke–Acts*.[26] In company with redaction criticism, Esler does not see Luke as a disinterested recorder of the story of Jesus and the early church. Nor, however, is Luke to be seen as some kind of armchair theologian 'who ponders over purely religious questions before issuing forth from his scriptorium to enlighten his fellow-Christians as to the correct attitude which they and their community should adopt to their social and political environment.'[27] Rather, Luke's is applied theology from the start, motivated by strong social and political interests and written for a specific, historical community whose needs are as much material as they are spiritual.

Using a method he calls 'socio-redaction criticism', which attempts to combine redactional and sociological analysis, Esler argues that Luke–Acts is best interpreted as written to provide legitimation for a Christian community whose relations with both the Jewish synagogue community and the wider Gentile society were fraught with the inevitable tensions arising from the Christian group's sectarian status. Luke's theological narrative is taken in a strongly functionalist way: it legitimates and justifies the beliefs and practices of his group over against those of alternative social worlds which have been left behind at conversion. So Luke's motivation is not purely theological; and H. Conzelmann's attempt to explain Luke's interest in history as a solution to the theological and religious problem of the delay of the parousia is rejected.[28]

The picture of Luke's community which emerges is a fascinating one. Contrary to the widely-held view that Luke's audience was Gentile, Esler argues that many in Luke's group were converts from Judaism or Gentile God-fearers. The new solidarity between Jews and Gentiles thus formed included the practice of table-fellowship. The reason for Luke's particular interest in table-fellowship was to legitimate Jew-Gentile commensality in his community and to maintain Jew-Gentile cohesion in the face of strong opposition from synagogue Jews and Jewish Christians who saw the practice as a threat

---

[26]Esler, *Community and Gospel*.
[27]*Ibid.*, 1.
[28]*Community and Gospel*, 67.

to the identity of the Jewish *ethnos*. An essential 'sectarian strategy' adopted by Luke is to defend the practice by appealing to (and re-writing) history. The great apostles, Peter and James, together with the Jerusalem Church, are portrayed now by Luke as giving their backing to Jew-Gentile table-fellowship. The prominence in Acts of the Cornelius episode and of the Apostolic Council is due more to Luke's strategy of legitimation than to what may have happened historically.

A similar interpretation is placed upon other major themes of Luke–Acts: the status of the Jewish law, the place of the temple, attitudes to poverty and wealth, and attitudes to Roman imperial authority. Esler argues that, in each case, Luke's writing betrays strong social and political concerns which reflect both the socially and religiously mixed character of his community and its vulnerability as a sectarian group to pressures from outside. In the chapter on 'The Poor and the Rich', for example, he argues that Luke developed a specific theology of poverty in order to address the problems of social stratification and economic disparity which threatened the fellowship. His criticism of 'spiritualising' and 'individualising' interpretations is severe:

> The ingrained disregard among scholars for the social and economic setting of Luke–Acts, and their corresponding enthusiasm... for its alleged spiritual and individualistic approach to salvation, originate in a clear middle-class bias. Generations of scholars, in their seminaries and universities, have been so successful in making Luke's message on possessions palatable for bourgeois tastes that its genuinely radical nature has rarely been noted.... That the Lucan Gospel imposes on the rich an indispensable requirement, quite at odds with the social values of their own society, to provide the destitute with food and other necessities of life in this world sounds the death-knell over all such interpretations of his theology as, affected by middle-class bias, present salvation as a reality reserved for the individual in the after-life.[29]

The importance of Esler's contribution at the level of Lucan interpretation generally deserves to be acknowledged, especially given the dearth of work of this kind a decade ago. He has offered a sociological interpretation powerful enough to constitute a comprehensive advance on redactional approaches which have stayed with the conventional interest in 'Luke the theologian'. The sect typology of B. Wilson and the model of sect development opened up by H. Richard

---

[29]*Community and Gospel*, 170, 199.

Niebuhr are used to significant effect to bring to our attention plausible social and political interests which lie behind and shape Luke–Acts. Also, he has drawn sharp attention to the social location in which most scholarly interpretation of Luke–Acts has taken place and to its possible effects on how we read this material.

But I would wish to express a number of reservations as well. To take the last point first, it is not clear to me with what justification Esler correlates a 'spiritualising' interpretation with 'middle-class bias'. It is, in fact, notoriously difficult to make correlations between ways of seeing and socio-economic location. There is also a certain irony in Esler's position, to which he seems to be oblivious. For the criticism he offers applies *ipso facto* to what he himself has written. It must also relativise what Luke has written, if Luke too is a person of some culture (*i.e.*, 'middle class'), as is commonly held.

Second, Esler's heavily functionalist interpretation is open to serious question.[30] For a start, it goes against the grain of Luke's own stated purpose. Instead of being an account of the past in order that his benefactor, Theophilus, may know the truth, Luke's writing becomes a coded address to a sectarian community, providing legitimation for its alternative identity and lifestyle over against its parent body Judaism. Luke says he is doing one thing. In fact, we know better: he is doing something else which our special methods allow us to decode. Now, it may indeed be the case that the truth which Luke is seeking to commend to Theophilus does have strong countercultural aspects and implications. His work is, after all, a written testimony concerning a massive, new revelation of the divine in recent history, and the call for a thoroughgoing repentance and conversion pervades both volumes.[31] But the attempt to correlate each major theme of Luke's testimony with the needs of a hypothetical community of sectarian hue seems to take us, not only beyond the evidence, but also against the grain of what is said. The effect is reductionist. The text becomes a cypher for the needs of Luke's community (or of the modern reader) instead of being allowed to be what it claims to be: a testimony to a revelatory truth of universal significance.

Finally, there is an important issue about the status and adequacy of the sect-church typology with which Esler has chosen to work. To summarize points I have made elsewhere,[32] it is vital to ask:

---

[30]For an excellent discussion of the general issue, see Stowers, 'Early Christianity', 149-181.
[31]See further, Barton, *Spirituality*, 77-83.
[32]Barton, 'Early Christianity', esp. 152-159.

Is this typology so wedded to the problems of modernity and so prone to ideological manipulation that it lacks the necessary affinity with the subject-matter to which it is being applied? Does the typology contain an implicit anti-Judaism, by casting Judaism as the monolithic, static, unreformed 'church' from which the Christian 'reform movement' separated and became a 'sect'? Do not such types, approximate and ideologically loaded as they are, generate as many problems as they solve? We are forced, I think, to reckon with the possibility that the sect-church typology is too blunt as a tool of analysis. No doubt, it serves a purpose if a blunt tool is required (as is often the case in NT interpretation) but then it must be laid aside.

As my other case-study of a major social-scientific attempt to 'put body and soul together' in the interpretation of Luke–Acts, I refer more briefly to the volume of essays edited by J. Neyrey, entitled, *The Social World of Luke-Acts. Models for Interpretation*, published in 1991.[33] There are thirteen essays, divided into three parts. What may be useful here is a summary of the contents followed by several reflections.

The first part is headed, 'social psychology'. In the second essay under this heading, anthropological insights into honour and shame as basic values in Mediterranean antiquity are used to throw light both on Luke's characterization and on the conflictual nature of many of the encounters and relationships he depicts. This meshes well with an essay on first century personality as 'dyadic' rather than individualistic, where Mediterranean cultural anthropology is used to suggest that, in the world of antiquity, a person's sense of identity was more a question of group membership (Who do I belong to?) than of individual introspection (Who am I?). This helps to make sense of Luke's preoccupation with matters like genealogies, kinship, ethnic identity, gender, marital status, place of origin, membership of a group or party, and so on. It also helps to make sense of the strong communitarian ethos of Luke's ethics. This is complemented later by an essay on patron-client relations which uses the sociology of patronage in conjunction with historical studies of patronage in the Roman Empire to explore the extent to which Jesus and the first Christians challenged and transformed traditional patronage structures and practices along with their harmful social manifestations.

In the second section, on 'social institutions', a pair of essays on (respectively) the city and the countryside in Luke–Acts throws into much sharper relief than before the critical inter-relationship between

---

[33]Neyrey, (ed.), *Social World*.

the teaching and practice of Jesus and the apostles on the one hand, and the politics, religion, economics and kinship patterns of their cultural milieu on the other. A subsequent essay on Luke's counter-posing of the institutions of temple and household contains a similar thrust. In another essay to do with the interpretation of the many accounts of sickness and healing, a major corrective is offered to what is called 'medical materialism' or 'medicocentrism' in much con-ventional Lucan interpretation. This is done by means of the applica-tion of work in medical anthropology which enables the healings to be interpreted in relation to health-care systems which are more consonant with a first-century point of view.

Finally comes a third group of essays which addresses issues of 'social dynamics'. One of these uses Mary Douglas's theories about 'natural symbols' to show how Jesus and the apostles subverted the symbolic order of Judaism (based on purity) in favour of a new order of things expressed in a reformed purity system which was inclusive rather than exclusive. Analysis of important rituals and ceremonies in Luke–Acts which embody and enable this new order constitutes the subject-matter of the last two essays. With respect to ceremony, particular attention is drawn to the all-pervasive motif of meals, table-fellowship and hospitality in the light of the anthropology of food and commensality. *Inter alia*, the significance of the episode involving Peter and Cornelius in Acts 10–11 is illuminated in a new way.[34]

In a number of respects, this is a more successful work than Esler's, although it is unfair to compare a monograph with a multi-authored collection of essays. Nevertheless, it is worth noting that none of the thirteen essays appears to make use of the church-sect model. In addition, rather than attempting to explain the textual data, where the danger is always that the data is explained away (in relation to a hidden social function), the emphasis in the essays is more on providing models that help us understand the data better at the surface level of the text. Significantly, all the models used are drawn from the discipline of social (or cultural) anthropology. This, together with the fact that the various contributors refrain from trying to do too much with the particular model each adopts, means that there tends to be a greater degree of 'fit' between the textual data under examination and the model being used to understand it. In my opinion, future work on sociology and theology in Acts will be very well served by the Neyrey collection.

---

[34]*Social World*, 378-382.

III. A theological postscript

By way of drawing this discussion to a close, I would like to touch on
a question gaining increasing prominence in biblical and theological
studies in certain quarters.[35] It is the question, what is the significance
for Christian theology of social-scientific attempts of the kinds I have
surveyed to put body and soul together again in Acts interpretation?
To put it another way, how does social-scientific interpretation affect
the ongoing process within the church of reading Acts as Scripture?

The first point to make in response is that, in essence, this is no
different from the question about the theological significance of historical criticism. As indicated earlier, social-scientific interpretation of
Acts is part of the larger task of learning, in a controlled and responsible way, how to read Acts with due historical sensitivity. Given both
that Luke-Acts is historical narrative and that Christian truth includes
claims about the life of Jesus and the early church, it is inevitable and
necessary that the best available critical tools be used in the ongoing
attempt to comprehend the astonishing realities to which the text bears
witness. The fact that such critical tools may have a genealogy linking
them in part with Enlightenment rationalism, atheism and the hermeneutics of suspicion is reason for circumspection but not for retreat.
Even scepticism and atheism, so Christians must believe, have their
part to play in the difficult vocation of coming to the true knowledge
of God,[36] a knowledge mediated in part by Christian Scripture.

Following this, perhaps the main point is that social-scientific
interpretation of Luke–Acts is important theologically because it helps
fill out our picture of the impact of the Spirit of God in and through
first, Jesus the Son of God, and subsequently, the Spirit-inspired
apostles and the communities of believers brought into being by their
testimony. This impact was such as to affect people in a thorough-
going way: in body and soul, individually and corporately, domestic-
ally, politically and ethnically, in matters of bed and board, in the
private and public domain. Truly, a 'world turned upside down' (Acts
17.6). In helping to fill out the historical picture, social-scientific interpretation plays potentially an important role in bringing the church to
a more profound level of discernment about the nature of the reality
which God's Spirit is seeking constantly to transform and also where,
and in what manner, that same Spirit is leading God's people today.

---

[35]See, for example, Lash, *Emmaus*, esp. chs. 3 & 6; and Thiselton, *New Horizons*.
[36]*Cf.*, MacIntyre and Ricoeur, *Atheism*; also, Sutherland, *Atheism*.

CHAPTER 23

THE INFLUENCE OF JEWISH WORSHIP ON LUKE'S PRESENTATION OF THE EARLY CHURCH

Brad Blue

Summary

Archeological evidence indicates that the early Christians gathered in domestic residences until the monumental building program initiated by Constantine. Similarly, the Jewish communities often assembled in house-synagogues. In addition to the immediate availability of the house as a venue, the house provided the necessary culinary appurtenances which were important to the Jewish and Christian communities. In many respects the early house-church was a Christian synagogue. For the early church, reconciliation was manifest at the table and was founded on the very words of Jesus at table. Not coincidentally, Jesus' prayers while at the table proved to be mediatory and the means by which God's divine grace was experienced in the early Christian community. Together with instruction, the prayers and the communal meals constituted praise to God.

I. Introduction

The question, 'What did the early Christians do when they met?' is inseparable from the question, 'Where did the early Christians meet?' In fact, some of the early practices of the Christian communities were inextricably related to and determined by the venue. We will attempt to demonstrate, that the 'what' was, in part, determined by the 'where' and, reciprocally, the location was chosen so as to accommodate the practices to the early communities.

Early Christianity expanded throughout the Empire house by house. The literary and non-literary evidence speaks univocally that the domestic residence (adapted or otherwise) was the venue for early Christian gatherings.[1] This study, in part, examines the organization and practices of the early communities; subjects which cannot be fully understood without special reference to the house-church nature of early Christianity.

The assembly of Christians in the house church was not fortuitous; rather, four reasons suggest why the house was the chosen venue. First, the 'upper rooms' and domestic residences were immediately available. Second, the domestic structure was relatively inconspicuous. The house setting did not guarantee surety against persecution (*cf.,* Acts 8:3); however, during the inceptive years when fracas with the Jewish authorities (with Roman involvement) were not infrequent, when Christianity was viewed as surreptitious, the 'house' was categorically better than monumental architecture. Hostilities resulted in the ferreting out of those who aligned themselves with the gospel. Christianity was not given to public displays of flagrant violation; rather they used discretion in the face of possible threats, the more aggressive the threat, the deeper the retreat. The success of Christianity was, in this respect, a result of the 'ambivalent attitude of the Roman authorities to religious change, which was permitted in the private, but not the public, sphere'.[2]

Third, the Jews in Palestine and the Diaspora assembled in house-synagogues. Since most of the early believers were Jews and God-fearers, it is not difficult to envisage the Christian communities adopting Jewish patterns, particularly since many of the activities in the house-church resembled those of the house-synagogue.

---

[1]*Cf.,* Blue, 'Acts and the House Church', 119-222. This continued to be the norm until the early decades of the fourth century; thereafter, Constantine began erecting the first Christian Basilicas.
[2]Garnsey and Saller, *The Roman Empire,* 176-177, emphasis ours; *cf.,* 174.

Last, the 'house' provided the necessary appointments needed for Christian gathering. Most importantly, the post-sacrificial meal, *i.e.*, the Lord's Supper, required the culinary appurtenances afforded by the house.

The abundance of narrative material in Acts suggests that Luke is primarily concerned with the story of the expansion of the early church. Implicit within the texts are the attendant social realities: benefactors, venues, familial and collegial allegiances, etc. as well as the developing theology of the early Christians. Whatever else may be said, the attendant circumstances in the Palestinian and Diasporian communities shaped the stories in Acts and the emergent theology. Moreover, the structure and strategy of the emergent Christian community reflect the struggles within the new community in special reference to the broader communities, particularly the Jewish community. Therefore our task is to address the *realia* giving special attention to the organization, life, and theology of the early church.[3]

II. Jewish antecedents

When we look at the Jewish evidence from the NT period, we are struck by two significant facts. First, it was not uncommon for the Jewish community to assemble in a domestic residence (renovated or otherwise). Numerous inscriptions testify to benefactors who made venues available to the community.[4] Second, the reasons for the house-synagogue closely resemble the four mentioned above, including provisions for community meals. If the house (renovated or otherwise) was the preferred venue, the lack of material culture with 'synagogue' written all over it is perfectly reasonable.[5]

Synagogue communities and practices

'The synagogue concerned itself with matters of community identity, education and solidarity.'[6] The primary purpose of the synagogue was

---

[3]Herein, we affirm Marshall's comment that 'setting' and 'theology' form a hermeneutical circle; *cf.*, Introduction to this Volume.
[4]Brooten, *Women Leaders*.
[5]Meyers and Strange, *Archaeology*, 141; Kee, 'The Transformation of the Synagogue', 1-24.
[6]McKay, *Sabbath and Synagogue*, 154.

to serve as a place where people could meet for instruction.

The most helpful insight gained from a study of the few archaeological remains of the synagogue is the position of the Jewish
community in a given society: the synagogue functioned as a community centre. The synagogue complex clearly functioned as a place of
assembly; however, additional facilities suggest that other services
were important. Whether the synagogue was a converted private
residence (*e.g.,* Stobi, Delos, Dura and Priene), a converted public
building (*e.g.,* Sardis) or a synagogue constructed by the Jewish community (or a patron) (*e.g.,* Ostia, Khirbet Shema and 'Theodotus'–
Jerusalem) the facilities often included cooking and dining facilities, a
study hall and accommodations for guests or travellers. Perhaps the
most neglected aspect of these features is the presence of culinary
appurtenances. Since communal eating is such a strong feature in Acts,
the Jewish antecedent practices in the synagogue communities are all
the more interesting.

Dietary regulations in Jewish life were a means to maintain
identity in a pluralistic environment. Diodorus Siculus was the first
pagan author to mention the Jewish reluctance to engage in table-
fellowship with a Gentile. He comments that the Jews '...had made
their hatred of mankind into a tradition, and on this account had introduced utterly outlandish laws: not to break bread with any other race.'

Ritual laws of dietary purity were particularly important for the
Pharisees: 'One primary mark of Pharisaic commitment was the observance of the laws of ritual purity outside of the Temple.... Eating
one's secular, that is, unconsecrated food in a state of ritual purity, as
if one were a Temple priest in the cult, was one of the two significations
of party membership.... And the agricultural laws, just like the purity
rules, in the end affected table-fellowship'.[7]

The Pharisees' concern for ritual purity was translated into
everyday living: 'The setting for law observance was the field and the
kitchen, the bed and the street. The occasion for observance occurred
every time a person picked up a common nail....'[8] In this respect the
Pharisees can be called an 'Eating Club'.[9]

Evidently, this concern for dietary purity affected the selection of
venue for the gathering of the Jewish communities. Dietary purity

[7]Neusner, *Judaism,* 57. cf., *Rabbinic Traditions,* 3, 297; *From Politics to Piety,* 83ff. and
The Pharisees, 310ff. These traditions are pre-70 AD.
[8]Neusner, *From Politics to Piety,* 89.
[9]Neusner, 'Two Pictures', 525-557; cf., his 'The Use of Later Rabbinic Evidence',
223f.

would have been particularly important in the Diaspora where the synagogue would have been the community centre for a minority group faced with preserving its identity in a Gentile culture. This made the synagogue more important for a Diaspora Jew. Furthermore, because the synagogues often had cooking and dining facilities (or immediate access to them) the Jewish community could affirm its identity by observing the dietary regulations (what could and could not be eaten and what was the acceptable manner of preparation) and regulating who was (and was not) part of the community by their willingness to observe the accepted laws and customs.

At Ostia and Delos, there is clear indication that the Jewish community enjoyed meals together in the synagogue. In the case of the renovated domestic residences, the community would have had cooking and dining facilities on the premises; however, in the case of the synagogue building at Ostia, the construction of cooking facilities was included in the first building program.

It is not uncommon to find references in the papyri to dining rooms (commonly upstairs), a banqueting hall, or, generally, an auxiliary building in the precincts of the main (cultic) building.[10] Last, the mention of monies in connection with a dining facility and common meals in the synagogue community is well attested. Julius Gaius, according to Josephus, did not forbid the Jews from collecting money for common meals which were taken (we surmise) in the (former house) synagogue.[11] Likewise, the Jewish community at Apollinopolis Magna collected funds for common feasts which indicates that the community celebrated meals at a 'dining-club'.[12]

Similarly, Josephus records that at the provocation of certain Jews, including representatives from Delos, Julius Gaius was compelled to issue a statute regarding the legality of Jews desiring to follow their customs. According to Josephus he did not prohibit the Jews from collecting money for common meals.[13] The decree stated—'the essence of the Jewish cult, the major ritual necessitating public assembly and the public collection of money, was communal feasting'.[14]

The synagogue community at Sardis lobbied for the same community practices. Josephus affirms that the relations between the

---

[10]Nock, et al., 'The Guild of Zeus Hypsistos', 47f.
[11]The collection of monies was also for Jerusalem (*Ant.* 16.163; cf., Philo, *Leg.* 156f.).
[12]*CPJ* 139 ('Jewish dining-club at Apollinopolis Magna', 1st century BC=*OE* 368).
[13]Josephus, *Ant.* 14.214; cf., 14.215-216. Clearly, they are permitted to feast together (ἐστιᾶσθαι, 216).
[14]Cohen, 'Pagan and Christian Evidence', 165.

Jews and the *polis* were favourable and that the Jews were granted the privilege of following their ancient customs. Foremost, they enjoyed communal meals (*Jewish Antiquities* 14.359f.).

The synagogue complex and the sabbath

It is not inconceivable that the Jewish community in a given city would have spent most of the Sabbath in the precincts of the synagogue. According to tradition, the day was divided between eating and drinking and instruction.[15] The synagogue complex often included cooking and dining facilities to accommodate the evening meal on the day of preparation and the three meals on the Sabbath day.[16] With respect to the latter, following the morning service, the main meal at midday could have been enjoyed in the synagogue complex and instruction in the Torah could have been carried out in the main hall, a large forecourt, or an annexed room or building.

The fact that the Qiddush pronouncement (given at the beginning of each Sabbath or feast day) found its way into the synagogue service may be further demonstration that meals were often enjoyed in the synagogue complex. Normally, the head of the house would pronounce the Qiddush at home over the second cup; however, in the Amorean days it was also part of the synagogue service. Although this has traditionally been taken as the introduction of a synagogue service at the beginning of the Sabbath, it may well suggest that the Qiddush was sandwiched between the service on the day of preparation and the communal meal in the synagogue. Certainly, the Qiddush was not spoken in the synagogue and soon thereafter in the home. That would have been redundant. Rather, as Sukenik has suggested, the ceremony sanctifying the Sabbath and Festivals in the synagogue 'has its origin in the fact that very often some of the congregants had no home to go to after the services but remained to eat their evening meal'.[17]

The archaeological evidence for the first century synagogue is

---

[15]Lohse, *TDNT* VII:15f. Lohse (and others) refer to R. Joshua's statement in *b.Pes.* 68b., *cf.*, Bill. 1, 611-615.

[16]Three meals, instead of the customary two, were eaten on the Sabbath, the midday meal being the main meal of the day, *cf.*, Jeremias, *Eucharistic Words*, 44f., SB 1, 611-615; 2, 202-206; 4, 611-639.

[17]Sukenik, *Ancient Synagogues*, 49. Sukenik, however, did not have the archaeological evidence at his disposal, testifying to cooking/dining facilities in the synagogue complex.

fragmentary at best, or buried beneath subsequent accretion and renovation. Univocally, however, recent opinion argues for 'house synagogue'. That being so, it would be remiss not to mention the illustrious discoveries in Jerusalem and the trajectories for a study of Acts.

Some of the early Jewish-Christian benefactors may have been priests in Jerusalem. Acts 6:7 intimates that a significant (unspecified) number of priests responded in faith to the gospel. These two facts, taken together with the evidence that the Jewish communities gathered in domestic residences makes the recent evidence from the Palatial Mansion in Jerusalem illuminating.

The work of Nahman Avigad indicates that the priests lived on the Western Hill (the Upper City) in luxury villas, constructed in accordance with dominant fashions of the Hellenistic-Roman period.[18] The 'Palatial Mansion' included a reception hall (71.5 sq.m.) which could have accommodated 75 people. In addition, access to three other rooms was gained only by this room. The ornamental frescoes (Ionic columns bearing a schematic Doric frieze) in these rooms suggest a public character. Taken together, the hall and these rooms would have accommodated in excess of 100 people quite comfortably.[19]

One other appurtenance is noteworthy: the enormous water installations. These *mikvot*,[20] may find correlative importance if for no other reason than the proclivity for living water (later reiterated in the literary attestation of Mishnaic Judaism (so tractate *Mikwaoth*) which finds close resemblance to the early Christian practice of baptism in 'living' water (*cf.*, *Didache* 7).

III. Apostles, Christian benefactors and early gatherings

The early chapters of Acts indicate that thousands of people welcomed the salvific preaching of the Apostles (2:41; 4:4; 5:14). The numerous references to the gatherings of the Christians indicate that the believers in Jerusalem gathered in houses (2:46; 5:42; 12:12). In fact, residential properties were sold (4:34) in an effort to generate funds for other needs within the community without seemingly reducing the requisite number for assembly.

---

[18]Avigad, *Discovering Jerusalem*, 83; *cf.*, Mare, *Archaeology*, 174f.

[19]We are not suggesting that the early believers actually met in this residence nor does the material cultural evidence indicate Christian usage. Quite simply, we are proposing that this is archetypical of the residences envisaged in the Acts material.

[20]Avigad proposes the appellation: 'cult of immersion' (*Discovering Jerusalem*, 106).

The primary purpose of the specific mention of 120 people
assembled together (Acts 1) might well be an articulation of a new,
autonomous, self-governing community (*cf., M.San.* 1.6) in which
women were included in the count. At the same time, we are struck
with the immensity of the house (perhaps identified with or including
the 'upper room' mentioned in 1:13) and the degree of benefaction
operant in the communities. After all, it was exceptional to own a
domus; most residents of a large city lived in crowded *insulae*.[21]

Similarly, the accounts in Acts 13–28 indicate that the 'house'
served as the venue for the gathering of Christians. Believers in
Ephesus gathered in the house belonging to Priscilla and Aquila (1
Cor. 16:19; *cf.,* Acts 18:18, 26; 20:20; Rom. 16:3-5). The references to
houses and households are anything but incidental. Rather, the
conversion of a household/er was 'the natural or even the necessary
way of establishing the new cult in unfamiliar surroundings' and 'the
household remained the soundest basis for the meetings of
Christians'.[22] Clearly, believers in the Christian community were
known for their public benefaction and civic involvement.[23]

Leadership in the Christian communities

Acts also includes references to God-fearers who responded in faith to
Paul's preaching. Many of these God-fearers became benefactors in the
early communities. In fact, their homes became venues for Christian
gatherings (*e.g.*, Lydia, Acts 16:11f; Titius Justus, Acts 18:5f; Cornelius,
Acts 10).[24] The prosopographic information in Acts indicates that
these individuals were instrumental in the expansion and establishment of Christianity in the Diaspora. Familiar with the Hellenistic
world and monotheistic Judaism, these God-fearers were instrumental
in Luke's accounts. Recent evidence from Aphrodisias parallels the
important roles of the God-fearers in Diasporan communities.[25]

Whether these civic leaders and Christian benefactors were the

---

[21]In urban areas, the statistic was roughly 3%. For a fuller treatment see Blue, 'Acts
and the House Church', 152ff. and *Secure the Well-Being of the Family* (forthcoming).
[22]Judge, *Social Pattern*, 36.
[23]Winter, *Seek the Welfare of the City*. Among other studies in the *A1CS* see
particularly Gill, 'Acts and the Urban Élites', 105-118.
[24]Tradition suggests that Cornelius' house became the site of a church (*cf.,* St.
Jerome, Letter 108 to Eustochium). The centurion in Luke 7:5f. is not atypical.
[25]Reynolds and Tannenbaum, *Jews and God-fearers.*

leaders of the Christian communities is difficult to ascertain. In the case of Titius Justus, for example: did his conversion and the subsequent gathering of believers in his home infer that he would function as an 'elder' of the gathering?[26] Certainly, the conversion of Crispus aroused the attention of the Jews in Corinth (Acts 18:8f.). As ἀρχισυνάγωγος, he would have had an integral role in the synagogue community: his discretion would have been needed in selecting preachers (*e.g.*, Acts 13:15), as well as individuals to read from the Scriptures and offer prayers. Equally important, such an individual was chosen for past and/or potential benefaction. Although Acts is silent in reference to Crispus' role in the Christian community at Corinth, Paul was persuaded that the leadership in that city was adequate enough to allow the relocation of Priscilla and Aquila to Ephesus.

Lydia's position in the Christian community is equally uncertain. Luke's focus is on 'house' and 'household', *i.e.*, an individual who had control over an οἶκος[27] as well as benefactor to the Christian community. What role Lydia actually played in the gathering of believers is pure conjecture. Without doubt, however, we envisage a woman like Phoebe, who is described as a διάκονος in Cenchreae, a προστάτις of many including Paul (Rom. 16:1f.). Four related descriptions come to mind: Phoebe held the office of διάκονος,[28] she was a *patrona*—provided assistance to Paul, she provided the venue for Christian gathering and accommodation to travelling Christians, and, finally, she provided a degree of security from scrutiny during uncertain times during the expansion of the church.

The public activities of Christians

Acts differentiates between the activities which took place in the confines of a private, domestic residence (*i.e.*, house-church) and other activities which necessitated a different, that is a public, setting. Luke consistently pairs the public and private activities of the early church.

---

[26]No definitive catalogue of qualifications for this 'office' is forthcoming from the textual evidence. Kee intimates that 'elder' was an appellation for respected members who were capable of benefaction and decision making (*Good News*, 79). For the Jewish parallels in the synagogue, see Campbell, *Elders*.

[27]This was not uncommon. See further Horsley, 'The Purple Trade, and the Status of Lydia of Thyatira', 28f. and Hemer, 'The Cities of Revelation', 54.

[28]This was not uncommon for a woman (single or otherwise), *cf.*, Horsley, 'Sophia, "the second Phoebe"', 239-244.

On the one hand, the Temple precincts, synagogues, lecture halls, etc. served as platforms from which to preach the gospel. On the other, the converted hearers formed a community centered in the houses which were placed at the communities' disposal by affluent Christians.[29]

In his defence delivered to Agrippa II in the presence of Festus (Acts 26), Paul adamantly argued that his public activity was well-known, even to Agrippa 'for this was not done in a corner' (v. 26). Rather, there was a distinctly 'public' aspect of the life of the early church. Paul's defence in Acts 26 should, therefore, be seen as an apologetic against any claims that the Christianity was a reclusive, subversive religion. A. Malherbe has demonstrated that 'for at least seven hundred years…"to speak in a corner" was used pejoratively, especially by orators or philosophers of rhetorical bent, of people, particularly philosophers, who did not engage in public life'.[30] This statement by Paul, then, should be seen as a public apologetic which Luke uses to counter the charge of secrecy.

Luke presents Paul as the representative of Christianity in the Græco–Roman world and depicts the movement as legitimate in that milieu. But he is also careful to demonstrate the distinctive features of Christianity. Broadly speaking, there were two different spheres in which Paul and the early community operated: the public and the private, each requiring facilities to accommodate the different needs.[31]

Restrictive factors

Our starting point is the restrictive factors. In the terse description of the events of Pentecost, the vantage shifts from the activities in a room (ὑπερῷον, ἐπὶ τὸ αὐτό) to Peter's speech and the conversion of 3,000 people to a description of the attendant practices in the Christian community (v. 42). To be sure, Luke does not envisage some 3,000 people (or more, assuming that not all who heard believed) assembling *en masse* in the house when they heard the commotion. Rather, the scene changes: 'from inside to outside the house, from the speakers to the

---

[29]The scope of this discussion precludes a discussion of the overwhelming attestation for this dichotomy in the later tradition (especially the Apocryphal and Pseudopigraphical traditions) as well as the concern for 'locality' in the Synoptic Gospels. *cf.,* Blue, *Secure the Well-Being of the Family.*
[30]Malherbe, '"Not in a Corner"', 203.
[31]Walter, 'Preach the Word—Grippingly', 49; Evans, '"Preacher" and "Preaching"', 315-322.

hearers'.[32] Given the logistical problem of the large number and the change of perspective, the most natural location for Peter's address (2:14ff.) would have been the Temple precincts which, at that time of the day, were generally quite busy.[33] To find such a group in the Temple area would have been expected. Luke deliberately includes these references to the Temple precincts (the Beautiful Gate and Solomon's Portico) and specific times to indicate the strategic importance behind the activity. Both in 2:5ff. and 3:1ff. the times are quite significant. In 3:1ff. the specific hour is mentioned and in 2:1ff. Luke informs us that the events took place in the early morning. Both coincide with the times for prayer and sacrifice at the Temple.

In 3:1ff. Peter and John were going to Temple at the ninth hour of prayer[34] when they encountered a lame man. The subsequent healing of the man and the assembling crowds provides another opportunity for Peter to proclaim publicly the kerygma. According to Luke's portrayal, the public proclamation of the gospel message is the primary (if not the sole) reason behind the disciples' presence in the Temple precincts.

This is further supported by the cryptic summary in 5:12f., which, when understood in light of the previous events, is quite intelligible. Luke places little emphasis on the Jewish practices in the Temple area; reason for referring to the times and locations of the Temples is to illustrate that there was an audience and an acceptable place where the gospel could be proclaimed.

Summarily, the references to the Temple are specific and connote evangelistic efforts and the announcement of God's salvation in Christ. Nowhere is temple imagery used to refer to the church or the gathering of believers.[35] At what point the early Christian came to terms with the finality of Christ's sacrifice is difficult to determine; nevertheless, Luke

---

[32]Haenchen, The Acts, 168. cf., Marshall, Acts: Commentary, 70. Conzelmann's comment is most appropriate: 'The change in scene to a public place is not made clearly', Acts, 14.

[33]The Temple mount could have accommodated approximately 75,000 people. For a discussion of this area see Strange, 'Archæology and the Religion of Judaism in Palestine'.

[34]They did not participate in the customary prayers (although that may have been their intention). Contrary to the view of Haenchen, prayers are not said by the Christians with the Jewish congregation in the Temple (Acts, 192). Although Luke concludes his Gospel with a reference to the disciples in the Temple (24:52-53), there is a conscious shift subsequent to Pentecost. After Acts 2 the precincts became the prime locale in Jerusalem for a ready-made audience. (Esler, Community and Gospel, 131; cf., Peterson, Engaging, with God, 13ff.).

does not envisage the early Christian as engaged in the cultic activities in the Temple precincts.

Turning now to the synagogue activity recorded in Acts, we find no exception to this established pattern in reference to the Temple. Luke informs his readers that it was Paul's custom to seek out the local synagogue on the first Sabbath after his arrival in a new city (17:2). There he would deliver his instruction based on the OT text, concluding his message with the salvific message of the gospel.[36]

The vocabulary used to describe Paul's activity in the Diaspora synagogues is more diverse than earlier in Acts. Nonetheless, it is clear that the public message was intended to demonstrate that Jesus was the fulfilment of OT promises and that his death and resurrection were salvific. At the same time, Paul made every effort to ensure that the same city afforded a permanent meeting place for those who responded to the proclamation. As we demonstrated earlier, the conversion of a home owner (and his/her household) was extremely important for the founding of a Christian community.

In one instance we are explicitly told that Paul ensured that a house was available before he appeared in public in an effort to win converts. This was why Paul was accompanied by Priscilla and Aquila to Ephesus:[37] so that there would be a private house in which the believers could meet (cf., 1 Cor. 16:19). It is worth noting that despite this available house (church) we read nothing of Paul using it (or any other) for the presentation of the gospel. Rather, as was his custom, his initial platform was the synagogue. The subsequent rejection by the synagogue community at Ephesus necessitated securing another suitable place from which he could address the uninitiated. In the case of Ephesus, Paul used the Hall of Tyrannus as the publicly acceptable place in which to present the gospel message.[38] Of course the Hall would have been accessible to the Jews and Greeks (Gentiles); whereas the synagogue was only accessible to the Jew or the 'God-fearer'. The house of Aquila and Priscilla was indispensable for Paul and those who responded to the public proclamation. It (as well as perhaps others) became a place to gather (ἡ κατ' οἶκον αὐτῶν ἐκκλησία).

---

[35]Cf., Marshall, 'How Far Did the early Christians Worship God?', 224f. Temple imagery is used in the Epistles, as Marshall delineates. For example, the believers are described as the temple of the Holy Spirit (cf., 1 Cor. 3:16f.; 6:19).

[36]This can be seen most clearly in 13.16ff. (Pisidian Antioch).

[37]It is conceivable that Aquila and Priscilla's house was available to Paul in Corinth for the same purpose. Of this we cannot be sure, since Luke stresses the house belonging to Titius Justus (Acts 18).

This is precisely the scenario we find in Acts 18:24f. At Ephesus, Priscilla and Aquila heard Apollos speaking ἐν τῇ συναγωγῇ. Realizing that Apollos was already familiar with John's baptism, and spoke about Jesus accurately, the couple informs him of the 'the way of God more accurately'. The text indicates that they 'received him into their house' (προσελάβοντο αὐτόν),[39] i.e., the church meeting in their house (cf., 1 Cor. 16:19). In this context, Luke envisages that Priscilla and Aquila, once again, made their house available to the community. Here again, we see a Christian 'house' community and Christian believers attending public gatherings (synagogue). It is not Luke's purpose to show that Jewish-Christians and Jews were 'harmoniously gathered together';[40] rather, he delineates two distinct and separate spheres in which the Jewish-Christians operated: the public was for winning new converts (e.g., Apollos), the private for Christian gatherings (vv. 27f.; cf., 1 Cor. 16:19). In this instance Apollos became a part of that private house group (cf., vv. 27f.). Luke concludes the pericope by having Apollos return to the public sphere (i.e., the synagogue), where he refutes the Jews (v. 28).

In addition to Paul's public deliveries in the Hall of Tyrannus at Ephesus, he addressed the Greeks ἐν τῇ ἀγορᾷ κατὰ πᾶσαν ἡμέραν (17:18) and spoke concerning the relevance of the resurrection of Jesus within a framework which Epicureans, Stoics, and other residents of Athens would have comprehended. These and other public venues available to Paul should be seen as alternatives to the synagogue. In these places Paul's strategy was the same: evangelism.[41]

These observations lead us to support Klauck's commentary on Acts 5:42: the chiastic construction indicates private teaching in the

---

[38] According to Luke, his intention was to reach the unbeliever. In 19:10 Luke states that Paul's activity in the Hall lasted two years and the result was that all the residents in Asia heard the word of the Lord. To be sure, the Hall was used as a public stage and not a private meeting place for the Christians (cf., Pereira, *Ephesus*, 138f.). The believers met in homes (1 Cor. 16:19) and these homes did not facilitate the proclamation of the Gospel to the non-believer, as we shall substantiate below. Marshall is right when he writes that the synagogue was used for evangelism and that the Christians were already meeting as house groups (*Acts:*, 309f.). It seems only natural to conclude that the Hall functioned in the stead of the synagogue, serving the same purpose, i.e., evangelism.

[39] Although it is possible that the construction means that they received or invited Apollos into their house (cf., Acts 28:2), reception into the house church (for further instruction, which is precisely what took place) is more likely. Clearly, this is the intention behind Phm. 17.

[40] So Haenchen, *Acts*, 551f.

[41] Marshall, *Acts*, 310; cf., Haenchen, *Acts*, 560f.

'house church' was a distinct activity in relation to the public proclamation in the Temple precincts. The same distinction is found in the parallel construction in 20:20.[42]

Klauck's interpretation makes the cryptic summaries intelligible. In 2:46f., for example, constructions could be unravelled to mean that in the houses they broke bread (κλῶντές τε κατ᾽ οἶκον ἄρτον). The central feature of the private meetings was the common meal enjoyed together with intense gladness and joy. At the same time they were busy in the Temple area, proclaiming the gospel. The result of this activity was an increased number of followers:

καθ᾽ ἡμέραν
προσκαρτεροῦντες ὁμοθυμαδὸν ἐν τῷ ἱερῷ, κλῶντές τε κατ᾽ οἶκον ἄρτον,
    place (public)   place (private)
μετελάμβανον τροφῆς ἐν ἀγγαλλιάσει καὶ ἀφελότητι καρδίας,
    main clause: characteristics of private gatherings
αἰνοῦντες τὸν θεὸν   καὶ ἔχοντες χάριν πρὸς ὅλον τὸν λαόν.[43]
    private   public
   ὁ δὲ κύριος προσετίθει τοὺς σῳζομένους ἐπὶ τὸ αὐτό
   main clause: results of the public activity
          καθ᾽ ἡμέραν.

Paul distinguished between these two activities and places. We used as an example Paul's activity at Ephesus. Having been expelled from the synagogue he used the Hall of Tyrannus as the public place from which he proclaimed the gospel. As we mentioned earlier, there were also private houses in Ephesus which facilitated the Christian gatherings (cf., 1 Cor. 16:19; Acts 20:20).

If we have rightly understood the Lukan presentation of early Christianity, both in Palestine and the Graeco–Roman world, the gospel was first proclaimed in the publicly acceptable places. Subsequently, those who had responded were drawn into house gatherings. Luke never even suggests that during these private meetings of believers the gospel message was preached for the purpose of converting the hearers. On the contrary, for Luke, these private house meetings were for the benefit of the Christian community alone.[44]

---

[42]Klauck, Hausgemeinde und Hauskirche, 50; cf., Rordorf: 'Gottesdiensträume', 111-112.

[43]The recent discussion of this verse makes the dichotomy very clear, i.e., 'praising God [privately] and having goodwill towards all the people [public teaching]', see Andersen, 'The Meaning of ΕΧΟΝΤΕΣ ΧΑΡΙΝ ΠΡΟΣ in Acts 2:47', 604-610; cf., Cheetham, 'Acts ii.47', 214-215.

Formative factors

Luke reports that the early church did not neglect the poor and needy (Acts 2:43-47; 4:32-37). Benefactors voluntarily made arrangements to accommodate those in need, including selling property. This practice continued in subsequent generations and was done 'according to ancient custom' (cf., P.Oxy 1492-late third century AD).

Specifically, a synagogue practice was immediately adopted by the Christian community: the reference in Acts 6:1ff. intimates a *daily* distribution of food to widows (and perhaps others in need).[45] An inscription from Aphrodisias attests to a similar practice in Diasporan Jewish communities; there, benefactors maintained a community soup kitchen (πάτελλα). The *raison d'être* for the construction is given as: ...erected for the relief of suffering in the community...or, alternatively:...erected for the alleviation of grief in the community.[46] This

---

[44]Although the pattern mentioned above is, on the whole, a programmatic one, there are two notable exceptions. First, during his house arrest at Rome, Paul rents private accommodation for two years (Acts 28:16ff.). His intentions were not only the need of accommodation during his arrest but also to win converts, both Jew and Gentile (v. 28). The stress is on the public character of Paul's open door policy (vv. 30-31). Despite the emphasis on the public character of Paul's activity, it is conceivable that the second time, διδάσκων τὰ περὶ τοῦ κυρίου Ἰησοῦ Χριστοῦ, could be taken as private teaching. If so, two occasions are envisaged and, therefore, two distinct audiences. Thomas used his imprisonment in the same way. Although more restricted than Paul, he received outsiders (*e.g.*, Vazan the son of Misdaeus who was converted, *Acts of Thomas* 139f.). Second, Luke allows that a hospitable reception in a house could provide an acceptable venue for proclamation. In 10:1, Cornelius' house provided ample space and accessibility for Peter's address. This was feasible when the house was large and the crowd manageable. The fact that Peter was given a warm reception as an invited guest would have facilitated the proceedings. We find similar receptions and public addresses in large houses in the later tradition. In these instances, however, the reader is acutely aware that despite the house setting for the forum, the meeting is public. This is portrayed in contrast to the private nature of the house gatherings *subsequent* to the public meetings. In the private house gatherings only believers are present (see below). Whether Luke envisions such a contrast in the Cornelius episode is doubtful, since the entire audience responded in faith (hence, there was no need for a dismissal). With respect to the baptism of households, Luke, more often than not, refers to the entering of the house after the baptism, perhaps reflecting the tradition in which the house was for the private teaching of believers (*e.g.*, Acts 16:15, 33f.). Later, of course, it was not uncommon to have a baptismal font in a house (church) which may very well coincide with the later development which required the catechumen to be instructed before baptism (*e.g.*, Dura-Europos).

[45]Later, during a famine, collections from the believers in the Diaspora were sent to Judea to relieve the Christians from destitution (cf., Acts 11:27-30).

corresponds to the Hebrew *tamhui* (found both in the Mishnah and Tosephta and both Talmudim), a charitable institution organized in Jewish communities and required by Mishnaic law 'for the daily collection...and distribution of cooked food *gratis* to the poor and vagrant'.[47]

In Acts 2:42 Luke cryptically refers to practices which were characteristic of the gathered believers:

᾽Ησαν δὲ προσκαρτεροῦντες[48] τῇ διδαχῇ τῶν ἀποστόλων
καὶ				τῇ κοινωνίᾳ
				τῇ κλάσει τοῦ ἄρτου
καὶ				ταῖς προσευχαῖς.

Whether or not these are consecutive activities is difficult to determine, but the evidence points in this direction.[49] The διδαχὴ τῶν ἀποστόλων here is clearly a reference to instruction given by the apostles to those who had responded to the public proclamation. The teaching of the apostles needs little explanation, save to say that *false* teaching was a significant problem in the early church.

Instruction was intended for the benefit of the community and was basically the exposition of the Scriptures as well as the teachings of Jesus. Hence, there was a concern for Apostolic authority based on proximate experiences with Jesus (*cf.,* 1:21). The importance of instruction and of the 'office' of teaching is reiterated in the NT texts (*cf.,* 1 Cor. 12 and 14; 1 Tim. 5:17f.).

(a) Eating together

The second and third items are most interesting for our study at this juncture. In reference to κλάσις τοῦ ἄρτου, the Jewish rite of 'breaking the bread' or simply 'the breaking' was the coinage for the ritual for the opening of a meal. The ritual included the following elements: (1) the host (with bread in hands) would offer a prayer of thanksgiving to God; (2) those at the common table would respond

---

[46]Reynolds and Tannenbaum, *Jews and God-fearers*, 41.
[47]*Ibid.,* p. 27. For a description of the institution of *tamhui* in the first few centuries AD see also Schürer, *History*, II.437; Moore, *Judaism*, 2, 176-177
[48]The use of similar constructions to offset these two different spheres of activity is most striking. In 2:42 we read: ἦσαν δὲ προσκαρτεροῦντες τῇ διδαχῇ τῶν ἀποστόλων; and in v. 46 καθ᾽ ἡμέραν τε προσκαρτεροῦντες ὁμοθυμαδὸν ἐν τῷ ἱερῷ.
[49]Jeremias, *Eucharistic Words*, pp. 118f.; *cf.,* Marshall, *Last Supper*, 127.

with 'Amen'; (3) the host would then break and distribute the bread; (4) the host would begin to eat and would be followed by the guests. Thus the 'breaking (of bread)' is a metonym for the prayer of blessing and the distribution. With respect to the NT evidence, this meaning satisfies the contexts (cf., Luke 24:35; Acts 2:42, 46; 20:7, 11; 27:35).[50]

It is clear that 'the breaking' is always, at this early date, a constituent of a meal scene: by its definition it necessitates a meal scene here (even if the rite follows the meal). And while κοινωνία could be taken as 'table fellowship' while κλάσις τοῦ ἄρτου refers to the subsequent Eucharist, it is more likely that the latter is a cryptic reference to a meal which is highlighted by the blessing[51] and κοινωνία covers a broader range of activities, including the sharing of material properties.[52] Even if κοινωνία in 2:42 is not lexically broad enough to include the sharing of property, other passages are explicit about the practice (2:44f., 4:34-35; 6:1; cf., Rom. 15:26).

In 2:46f. again is a reference to breaking of bread. At first, it appears that Luke is being redundant; having just indicated that this was a characteristic feature of the early Christian gatherings in v. 42, he repeats (in summary form) that this was a regular feature. Upon closer examination, however, Luke's intentions become clear; he is on no account needlessly repeating himself. The quadruplex of activities in v. 42 comes immediately after the reference of the 3,000 new converts and is intended as a description of the activities characteristic of the private gatherings of the recent converts (in the houses). The summary in 2:43-47, on the other hand, is intended, like the other summaries in Acts, to serve as caesura between scenes, or rather as 'connective tissue by which memorabilia are turned into the beginnings of a continuous narrative'.[53] In v. 43f. is the first true 'summary' and it serves as a transition from the scenes of the Pentecost event and the subsequent confrontations with the Jewish authorities. As such, it is a summary of the public activities in the Temple precincts and the private activities in the house. After all, the material leading up to this summary requires that both be represented.

---

[50]The 'love feasts' in Jude 12 should be taken as a common meal including the Eucharist'.

[51]D. Crump has argued that if 'Breaking Bread' means the prayer over the meal, the summary account would read redundantly: 'they devoted themselves to the apostles' teaching and the fellowship, to "prayer" and to prayer"' (Jesus the Intercessor, 103, n. 103).

[52]See the contributions by D. Seccombe and B. Capper in this volume.

[53]Cadbury, 'The Summaries', 5, 395

According to 2:46 the breaking of bread was a daily practice. Later, in Acts 20:6f., Luke describes a gathering at Troas in an upper room on the third storey (τὸ ὑπερῷον; τρίστεγον) on the first day of the week. Luke describes a lengthy discourse (διαλέγομαι) given by the Apostle and a common meal (γευσάμενος) which, in the light of the previous texts, included the blessing/breaking.[54]

Above all, Luke's construction is consistent: he demonstrates that the church had been established and that its manifestation was these house gatherings:[55] Moreover, a central feature of the gathered Christians was the common meal.

(b) Table-fellowship between Jews and Gentiles

Without question, the community meal (i.e., Lord's supper) took on added significance when the number of Gentiles increased significantly and the evangelistic efforts reached the Diaspora. P. Esler argues:

> One issue in Luke–Acts towers above all others as significant for the emergence and subsequent identity of the type of community for whom Luke wrote: namely, table-fellowship between Jews and Gentiles. An almost universal failure to appreciate the centrality of this phenomenon, both to Luke's history of Christian beginnings and of the life of his own community, is one of the most outstanding deficiencies in Lucan scholarship.[56]

We have already intimated how important the Ritual Laws of Dietary Purity were for the Jewish communities (i.e., the synagogues included culinary appurtenances). Moreover, the non-Jewish writers were very direct about the Jewish insistence to remain 'pure/distinct' in reference to food and the protocols for consumption.

---

[54]Although Haenchen disputes this, his argument that only the Eucharist is intended here is based on the assumption that 'the congregation certainly did not wait until after midnight for their supper!' Contrariwise, the reference could very well be to a communal meal and the Eucharist, the former being in addition to the regular meal held much earlier, or, given that the context portrays a certain enthusiasm, the believers could have been more interested in Paul than the meal.
[55]Note for example the construction in 8.3: Σαῦλος δὲ ἐλυμαίνετο τὴν ἐκκλησίαν κατὰ τοὺς οἴκους εἰσπορευόμενος.
[56]Esler, Community and Gospel, p. 71. Meals and table-fellowship are prominent features, particularly in the Gospel of Luke (5:27-32; 7:36-50; 9:10-17; 10:38-42; 11:37-54; 14:1-24; 19:1-10; 22:4-38; 24:29-32, 41-43). cf., Smith, 'Table Fellowship', 613-638 and Corley, Private Women, Public Meals.

Luke suggests that the willingness of Jewish and Gentile believers to extend hospitality to one another and, in specific, to partake of a meal together was the litmus test in determining the validity of the gospel message. In this respect the house became the testing ground and within the confines of the domestic setting, the early believers were forced to define how the gospel message stood in relation to its Jewish heritage, society, and the world. Among other concerns, the Jewish-Christians re-examined the relevance and interpretation of the OT.

There are two incidents in Acts 10:1–11:18 which are relevant to our study: First, Luke indicates that when the entourage arrived in Joppa, Peter invited the men in (to the house) as his guests. This gesture would have been acceptable; despite the strict laws which governed table-fellowship between Jews and Gentiles these fundamental laws did not inhibit a devout Jew's entertainment of others since he was responsible for what was served and for the manner of its preparation. However, if we interpret Peter's hospitality in light of his vision and his subsequent willingness to be entertained by Cornelius, even this hospitality afforded by Peter in Joppa takes on new significance.

The second item of interest is Peter's willingness to be received by Cornelius in his home in Cæsarea (10:24ff.). These references to individuals being received as guests after long journeys (33 miles) might not seem particularly unexpected; however, this sort of behaviour on the part of a Jew was very rare, in fact it was treated with suspicion: a Jew in the home of a Gentile, eating at the same table! Addressing the people who had assembled in Cornelius' home Peter explains that such behaviour is considered unlawful. It was God, in fact, through the vision in Joppa, who had shown Peter that no man was unclean and, most importantly, God shows no partiality (10:34).

> The sheer length of this story and the way it is in effect told twice over...indicates the very great importance which Luke attached to it in the context of Acts as a whole. It deals with the decisive issue in the history of the church, namely the recognition that the gospel is for the Gentiles as well as the Jews, and it makes clear that this is no merely human decision, but that it was the result of God's clear guidance.[57]

The outpouring of the Spirit on the Gentiles prompts a further, equally important concern: Jewish-Gentile table-fellowship. Although

---

[57]Marshall, *Acts: Commentary*, 181.

his case is somewhat overstated, Esler is not far off the mark when he asserts that the central issue in Acts 10:1–11:18 '...is not that the gospel has been preached to the Gentiles, but the far more particular fact, of great ethnic and social significance, that Peter had lived and eaten with them'.[58] This, in fact, is the primary complaint voiced by the circumcision party in Jerusalem (11:3). These two events, the outpouring of the Spirit on the Gentiles and the table-fellowship in Cornelius' home must be seen together as Luke intended. Luke's way of confirming the validity of the former is demonstrated by Peter's willingness to eat with a Gentile.

For Luke, the obstacle of a Jew associating with the 'unclean' was overcome by the vision in Joppa. And, as Haenchen has aptly pointed out: 'only with reluctance, and constrained by divine miracles, visions, directives, did Peter take the step'.[59] After all, the inferences drawn from the Cornelius episode—that Gentiles can be admitted into the Christian community without undergoing circumcision (10:45; 11:18) and that table-fellowship between Jews and Gentiles was permissible —were avant-garde. After Cornelius and his household are baptized, they invite Peter to stay with them. Clearly, Luke intends to demonstrate that the authenticity of the reception is acknowledged by Peter's willingness to accept the invitation (cf., Acts 16:15).

Interpretively, 'Peter's vision, which ostensibly deals with the dissolution of the distinction between clean and unclean foods..., is interpreted as signifying the dissolution of the similar, but not identical, distinction between clean and unclean people'.[60]

For the Jewish Christians in Jerusalem, however, the issue was not so clear.[61] The inferences were so obvious to them; the ramifications were potentially damaging to the Jewish traditions. That God had poured out his Spirit on the Gentiles was amazing in its own right; but the subsequent inference that the Jewish believers would be required to accept (and even have table-fellowship) with the Gentile Christians without the latter having to undergo circumcision or to observe the law brought into question the legitimacy of the Torah.

The Cornelius incident, as much as Luke intends it to be paradigmatic, is only the beginning of the problem of defining appropriate

---

[58]Esler, *Community and Gospel,* 93.
[59]Haenchen, *Acts,* 463.
[60]Wilson, *Luke and the Law,* 68.
[61]Nor was Peter consistent in his willingness to associate with the Gentile believers, *cf.,* Gal. 2 which, in our opinion necessitated the Jerusalem gathering recorded in Acts 15.

social relations between Jewish and Gentile Christians. Failure to reconcile differences would nullify the possibility of fellowship and Christianity would be as segmented as first-century Judaism.

What, then, are we to make of the Apostolic Council in Acts 15? Why was it necessary for the Jerusalem church to consider the same concerns which had apparently been settled in Acts 10–11. The Jerusalem community could not have simply forgotten the events which Luke records in 10–11. The issues raised by the Cornelius incident were raised anew after the significant influx of Gentiles (13–14). Reports of Paul and Barnabas' success among the Gentiles had reached Jerusalem and instigated the believers who belonged to the party of the Pharisees to question the legitimacy of the mission. Their claim that circumcision was a necessary undertaking *sine qua non* for their salvation (15:1) and that even subsequent to the conversion of the Gentiles is dismissed and the law is displaced from the scheme of salvation. The fact that the question of the rescinding of the law is dealt with *after* the Gentiles had been admitted into the church[62] is a case in point *contra* the law as a vehicle of salvation.

In Acts 15 the issue of the Gentile obligation to the law is once again raised, as though it was never discussed in Chapter 11. Moreover, once again, it is Peter who defends the inclusion of the Gentiles and cites his summoning to preach to them as a defence of his position. Why in Acts 15 are certain levitical obligations required of the Gentile Christians when in Acts 11 Peter is willing to enjoy table-fellowship with Cornelius and his family without such contingencies?

First, we should establish that the Cornelius episode was exceptional only in respect to time and significance. As S.G. Wilson has demonstrated, the Cornelius episode has a '...paradigmatic significance. What applies to Cornelius applies to all Gentiles and the decisions made in his regard establish principles applied to them all'.[63] Luke clearly suggests that '...not only is Peter's experience referred to in 15:7-11 as in some sense normative, but also in that passage, as throughout 10-11, there is a constant shifting between Cornelius in particular and the Gentiles in general, such that the former is clearly representative of the latter (10:34, 45; 11:17-18)'.[64]

The real problem is the intervening events, in Acts 13–14, that is with regard to those Gentiles who were converted as a result of the

---

[62]Marshall, *Acts*, 181.
[63]Wilson, *Luke and the Law,72I*
[64]*Ibid.*, 72.

mission of Paul and Barnabas and the crisis in Galatia. Specifically, what would be the protocols for Jewish/Gentile commensality? Given the Jewish concern for dietary purity, the house venue for Christian gatherings and the common meal, and the inclusion of Gentiles, the texts concerning food and related matters are completely expected. While Acts 15 presents a number of difficulties for the interpreter, it is consonant with the other events in Acts and the Epistles to suggest that a chief matter of concern was table-fellowship.

The problem was augmented by the Gentile practice of eating food in the very precincts of a pagan temple, a practice which the Council concluded was unnecessarily offensive (15:29).[65] Above all, the verdict of the Council had in mind to unifying otherwise unreconcilable elements in the church. Circumcision is not requisite for faith or participation in the life of the community; however, certain sensitivities, particularly in reference to commensality should be observed.

(c) Prayer in Acts

D. Crump has skillfully articulated the significance of prayer in Luke–Acts. He concludes that 'all prayer gives opportunity for the expression of God's purposes'.[66] In reference to the early community, the summary account in 2:42 includes a reference to prayer which is devoid of specific content (cf., Acts 1:14; 6:4, 6; 9:11, 40; 10:2, 9, 30f.; 11:5; 12:5, 12; 14:23; 16:25; 20:36; 21:5; 22:17; 28:8).[67] Contextual inferences are possible in some cases. So, for example, the events which transpire on the Day of Pentecost are associated with prayer via Acts 1:14 (cf., 9:40; 12:5, 12; 14:23; 20:36). In other instances, the content is specifically related either verbally (1:24; 4:24-31; 7:59f.) or by implication through summary statements (8:15; 26:29; 27:29; 28:15).

Luke clearly correlates God's revelation and the prayers of the early believers. 'God's communication through prayer in Acts often takes the form of visions, angelic appearances or other supernatural phenomena (9:11; 10:2f, 9f, 30f; 11:5; 12:5ff, 12; 16:25f; 22:17f)'.[68]

Other references indicate that the church commissioned leaders with prayer (Acts 6:6; 13:13; 14:23) and prayed with, and for, one another (Acts 20:36; 21:5).

---

[65]Witherington III, 'Not so idle thoughts about *eidolothuton*', 237-254.
[66]Crump, *Jesus the Intercessor*, 123.
[67]See Crump, *op. cit.*, for an exhaustive analysis of Luke and Acts.

In reference to the prayers of Jesus, Crump makes these observations: (1) prayer is the means of communion between Jesus and the Father wherein God confirms the nature and direction of Jesus' ministry; (2) God communicates an element of encouragement, though not specifically requested; (3) the disciples receive new insight into who Jesus is as a result of Jesus' prayer.[69]

The first two are intended as paradigmatic for the disciples and the early community: 'Jesus' prayers serve as an avenue for the unpredictable, providential communion of God's will for his life. They were a means for his reception of revelation, visions, heavenly encouragement and the confirmation of actions performed in obedience to the Father, just as genuinely and spontaneously as for any later member of the church in Acts'.[70]

The third element is what differentiates Jesus from the disciples: 'Jesus' prayers are unique in that he alone is able to mediate the Father's revelation to others through them. No one else in Luke–Acts superintends the electing arm of God through their intercessions. Only Jesus prays so that others may come to see and hear who he truly is'.[71]

Two specific examples are particularly important for our discussion. First, the revelation given to the disciples during the meal at Emmaus—not coincidentally, Lukan material—Luke 24:13-35. As Crump intimates, the cardinal theme in this passage is 'recognition' (Luke 24:16, 31, 35) and is integral to Luke's seeing motif (cf., 24:24):[72] 'for these disciples to say that they were caused to recognize Jesus "in the breaking of bread" is tantamount to saying that he was made known to them *while he was at prayer'*.[73]

In reference to the practices of the early community, the Emmaus

---

[68]Crump acknowledges that God is not restricted to this paradigm. In Acts 11:15ff, the dispensation of the Spirit takes place at God's instigation, and his alone (*cf.*, 11:17): 'At times prayer serves to make God's will plain to the prayer, but his working need not be restricted by such acts of piety. God's plan is already in motion. Prayer does not change or affect that fact, it simply opens a window through which man may "see" God's activity and, perhaps, become a part of it', (*Jesus the Intercessor*, 126.; moreover, it should not go without notice that the laying on of apostolic hands yields similar results on one occasion, *cf.*, 8:14ff.).

[69]Crump, *Jesus the Intercessor*, 42-48 in reference to 9:28-36. Similar observations are made in reference to 9:18-27.

[70]*Ibid.*, 152.

[71]*Ibid.*, 153; Crump notes that when a specific request is made for intercession (Simon's request of Peter in 8:24), the request is denied by implication (8:22) since forgiveness is a result of repentance (*cf.*, Acts 2:38), *cf.*, 127.

[72]*Ibid.*, 102.

[73]*Ibid.*, 105-106.

story suggests that Jesus' messiahship and the necessity of his suffering are hidden (*cf.*, Luke 9:45; 18:34) until Jesus unveils the secret by interceding, praying. The solution to the 'blindness' is Jesus' prayers. Second, the prayer of Jesus affords the disciples with a clearer understanding of the Scriptures: 'It is not the opening of the Scriptures which opens their eyes; it is the opening of their eyes which causes them to perceive the meaning of the Scriptures...just as they have come to perceive Jesus'.[74]

Prayer is seen as integral to the practices of the early community, including commensality and the understanding of the Scriptures. Most importantly, Jesus is the mediator, in that only through his intercessory prayer does the community (here the disciples in Emmaus) come to terms with Jesus' messiahship and the meaning of the Scriptures.

In as much as ancient Judaism maintained that heavenly intercessors continued to do in heaven what they had done successfully on earth, it is not surprising that Acts 7:55-56 suggests that the intercession of Jesus is a continuing reality. That is 'Jesus continues to intercede for his disciples in heaven in order to testify to their faithfulness in times if trial, and to ensure their perseverance in discipleship at such moments. Both of these reasons appear in three gospel passages (Luke 12:8f; 22:31-32, 39-46), and both of them admirably fit the context of Stephen's vision. The Son of Man interceded for Stephen in acknowledgement of his faithful witness, but also to pray, as he did for Peter and the other ten, that his faith might not fail. Both heavenly recognition and earthly perseverance are secured for the church through their ascended advocate'.[75]

IV. Conclusion

McKay contends that the Jewish community did not worship in the synagogue. For her, worship includes the 'rites and rituals which pay homage, with adoration and awe, to a particular god or gods'.[76] Reading, studying and explaining sacred texts, according to her argument, do not constitute worship '*unless* given in a place in a planned session of worship'; otherwise, she regards these activities 'as educational, or

---

[74]*Ibid.*, 106-107.
[75]Crump, *Jesus the Intercessor*, 201-2. Hence, Jesus is 'standing' at the right hand, intimating ongoing heavenly intercession (*cf.*, Rom. 8:34; Heb. 7:25; 1 John 2:1).
[76]McKay, *Sabbath and Synagogue*, 3.

as serving the purpose of preserving and strengthening group identity, and not necessarily implying worship; the group's understanding
of the god as addressee of the worship'.[77]

While our study is not primarily concerned with the question of
'synagogues', it is abundantly clear that the Jewish antecedents to
Christian assembly—ἡ κατ᾽ οἶκον αὐτῶν ἐκκλησία—are felt
throughout. And, as we have intimated, the designation ἐκκλησία
was used in lieu of συναγωγή or προσευχή if for no other reason that
little else (particularly to an outsider) differentiated the practices of the
Jewish community of believers and the early Christian assembly. Yes,
the day of the week was changed,[78] but the venue was domestic in
nature and thereby provided the necessary culinary appurtances
necessary for communal meals, the Scriptures were the Hebrew texts
of the OT, the mechanisms for distribution were Jewish, and although
Acts does not make reference to the vexatious litigation in the early
Christian communities, the ἐκκλησία included provision for
arbitration which, in the Jewish community, fell under the auspices of
the synagogue.[79] The church, then, was a Christian synagogue.

This takes us back to McKay's assessment of the Jewish material
since she argues that the practices of the synagogue community do not
constitute worship. Must we infer that the early Christians did not
worship or is McKay's definition wanting? According to our study the
latter is the case provided that our understanding of worship
incorporates the activities of the early community including God's
communication with his people. In fact, the primary element of the
gathering was the flow of divine grace[80] which, according to Acts, was
mediated by Jesus. This includes the revelation of God's salvific
message particularly through the intercession of Christ. The resultant
activities were the response of the community; the meal, for example,
commemorates God's sacrificial love and unifies the community.

The prayers, including those of the heavenly intercessor, Jesus,
God's revelation to the believers (often as a result of the intercession of
Jesus), the meal and instruction from the Scriptures constituted their
praise to God.

---

[77]*Ibid.*, her emphasis.

[78]*Ibid.*, 176ff.

[79]For an excellent treatment of 1 Cor. 6.1-11, see Winter, *Seek the Welfare of the City*,
105-21.

[80]Well put by Marshall, 'How Far Did the early Christians Worship God?', 227.

CHAPTER 24

RECIPROCITY AND THE ETHIC OF ACTS

Brian Capper

Summary

Although Luke describes the community of goods of Acts 2–6 with remarkable enthusiasm, the later chapters of Acts do not suggest that he wished his readers to institute formal property-sharing arrangements. Rather, his model becomes almsgiving. The connection of community of goods with paradisal beginnings in Graeco–Roman literature suggests that Luke sought to underline that a new beginning was made for humanity through the birth of the Christian Church. His employment of proverbs of friendship, and the link in his Gospel between meal-fellowship and the inappropriateness of giving for a return after the model of Hellenistic friendship, suggest that he required the rich to transcend the conventions of reciprocity and eradicate poverty by entertaining the poor in their homes.

I. Introduction

I have argued elsewhere[1] that the community of goods depicted in
Acts (2:42-47; 4:32, 34-5:11, 6:1-6) has a demonstrable historical reference to events of formal property-sharing within a sector of the earliest
Jerusalem community. Although Luke's presentation is stylised with
Graeco–Roman philosophical commonplaces connected with community of goods, the communitarian patterns of Palestinian Jewish
sectarianism, evidenced particularly by our sources on Essenism,
appear to have materially influenced nascent Christianity.[2] The
terminology of the *Rule of the Community* from Qumran (1QS)
concerning the Essene יחד provides close linguistic parallels to difficult
Greek phrases which employ the equivalent ἐπὶ τὸ αὐτό at Acts 2:44
and 2:47.[3] Peter's challenge to Ananias and Sapphira's somehow
deceptive and culpably incomplete surrender of property at Acts 5:4
can be explained from the Essene procedure for provisional surrender
of property.[4]

Contributions to the study of Essene history by E. Bammel,[5] B.
Pixner[6] and R. Riesner[7] suggest that the early community in Jerusalem
developed in the immediate vicinity of a site on the southwest hill of
Jerusalem occupied three decades previously by the Essene community of Qumran itself. An Essene group which had broken ties with
the Qumran community probably continued on this site. Converts
from this community may have brought into the Jerusalem Church the
language and procedures of Essene property-sharing. The story of the

---

[1]'Community of Goods', 323-56.
[2]See further Bartchy, 'Community of Goods', who emphasises from a cultural-
anthropological perspective the historical value of these descriptions.
[3]The usage εἶναι ἐπὶ τὸ αὐτό at Acts 2:44 reflects the idiom להיות ליחד (1QS V:2);
the idiom להוסיף ליחד (1QS V:7) is reflected by the use of προστιθέναι ἐπὶ τὸ αὐτό
at Acts 2:47; *cf.,* Wilcox, *Semitisms of Acts,* 93-100. Barrett, *Acts I,* 167-168, cites
Wilcox on the proximity of ἐπὶ τὸ αὐτο at Acts 2:44 to the use of יחד in the *Rule of
the Community,* commenting 'It is...undoubtedly true that at the time of Christian
origins various forms of communal rather than private ownership were practised,
and it is quite reasonable to conclude that the christians followed a similar plan.'
On Acts 2:47 Barrett expresses a degree of caution (see 172-173).
[4]*Cf.,* esp. 1QS VI:20 and the linked rule regarding lies in matters of property, 24-25;
see Capper, 'Interpretation' and 'Ananias'.
[5]Bammel, 'Sadduzäer und Sadokiden'.
[6]See most recently Pixner, *Wege des Messias,* 402-407.
[7]Riesner, 'Essener und Urkirche'; 'Das Jerusalemer Essenerviertel'; 'Josephus'
"Gate of the Essenes"'; 'Das Jerusalemer Essenerquartier'; Betz and Riesner, *Jesus,*
141-156.

dispute between the 'Hellenists' and the 'Hebrews' over care for the Hellenists' widows (Acts 6:1-6) reveals that less socially integrated structures for mutual support were created as Christianity spread to the new context of diaspora-linked, Greek-speaking synagogues (6:9). These new social patterns became normative for the Christian communities which developed in the diaspora and beyond through the Hellenist mission.

Thus Acts may be shown to be 'good history'. But history always implies interpretation, and the purpose of this present piece is to go beyond the question of historical reference to ask what precisely Luke intended to convey to his readers through the inclusion of his account of earliest Christian community of property. What practical ethical model emerges from Acts for the handling of property? It is often noted that, in contrast with the tone of his Gospel, Luke includes apart from these descriptions of community of property very little further material of direct ethical import in Acts. He emphasises the almsgiving of Tabitha (9:36) and of the God-fearer Cornelius (10:2, 4, 31). He describes the support supplied by Christians in Antioch for the Church of Jerusalem in time of famine (11:27-30), and has Paul refer to what is apparently the arrival of his large-scale collection for the Church in Jerusalem as the bringing of 'alms for my nation' (24:17). Reference may also be made to Paul's speech to the Ephesian elders, which emphasises towards its close the topic of Paul's own lack of covetousness and virtue in working to supply both his own needs and the needs of others, concluding with the attribution to Jesus of the saying 'It is more blessed to give than to receive' (20:33-35).

C.F. Evans thinks that in Acts, 'Apart from references to community of goods, what conversion entailed in terms of moral life is not described'. He offers the explanation that Luke intended the ethical teaching of his first volume to be understood, noting that conversion involved listening to Jesus as the prophet like Moses (Acts 3:22-26), who has instructed God's people in the Gospel. This is surely, in general terms, correct.[8] Furthermore, in literary terms, to repeat Jesus' ethical material at length on the lips of Peter and Paul would hardly enhance Luke's second volume; the Saviour himself could be heard in the Gospel.

However, the problem of ethical concentration is not limited to a contrast between Luke's Gospel and Acts, but extends into the narrative of Acts itself. The reader of Acts 2–6 might be left with the

---

[8]Evans, *Luke*, 93-94; *cf.*, Bergquist, 'Good News to the Poor'.

impression that, for Luke, the thoroughgoing abrogation of private property and the social distinctions which it caused was the ideal and the goal of the widespread theme of possessions, the poor and the rich in his Gospel. The theme of community of property is emphatically introduced early in Acts by its repetition in the first two 'summaries' (cf., Acts 2:44-45 and 4:32, 34) and treated with obvious enthusiasm. Luke seems deliberately to have used similar wording in his version of the Gospel story of Jesus' challenge to the rich young man and the account of the sale and distribution of property in Acts 4:34-35. Whereas in Mark 10:21 Jesus commands the rich man merely to sell 'what' he has and 'give' to the poor, Luke would have the rich 'ruler' sell 'all' that he has and 'distribute' to the poor ((Luke 18:22, πάντα... πώλησον...διάδος).[9] Acts 4:34-35 uses the combination of selling and distribution (πωλοῦντες...διεδίδετο). Furthermore, the use of πάντα (or ἅπαντα)[10] at Acts 2:44 and 4:32 is reminiscent of the forceful demand, unique to the Lucan Jesus, that disciples renounce 'all' possessions (Luke 14:33).

In apparent fulfilment of such demands of the Saviour, Luke asserts boldly in Acts that the early believers 'had all things common' (2:44, cf. 4:32) and that 'as many as were possessors of houses or lands sold them, and brought (or used to sell and bring)[11] the proceeds of what was sold and laid it at the apostles' feet' (4:34-35). This statement implies participation in the property-sharing procedures by all who had substantial wealth and deserves attention in exegesis. Luke's remark that 'there were no needy (ἐνδεής) among them' (4:34) stresses fulfilment of the Mosaic law[12] in the earliest Christian community. Luke implies that the practice of the sale and surrender of property was the reason why 'great grace was upon them all' (4:33), since following this statement both the reminiscence on the absence of poverty in the community and the explanation that this was due to the practice of selling and surrendering property are introduced with γάρ (twice, 4:34). The exemplary and horrifying fate of Ananias and Sapphira in 5:1-11, who fail to share their goods with the church, is surely intended to have strong parenetic force.

However, after this powerfully expressed beginning, community of property as a theme receives no further mention after Acts 6:1-6. In what sense can it be Luke's intended ideal for the church of his day,

---

[9]Matthew 19:21 uses neither πᾶς nor διαδίδωμι.
[10]The manuscripts vary between πάντα and ἅπαντα in both verses.
[11]The imperfect ἔφερον may have iterative force.
[12]Deut 15:4, where the LXX also uses ἐνδεής.

and the appropriate realisation of Jesus' teaching on the dangers of wealth and the imperative demand to care for the poor? Community of property appears to be replaced by the theme of almsgiving which we have noted in 9:36, 10:2, 4, 31, 11:27-30, 20:35 and 24:17.[13] Moreover, Luke may even appear to imply in the individual stories which make up his account of earliest Christian community of property that he considered this a failed or impractical project. The sin of Ananias and Sapphira (5:1-11) can be read as a kind of fall of the first community from innocence (thereafter irretrievable), and the dispute over the supply of the Hellenist widows (6:1-6) might mean that Luke knew that as the community began to expand (6:1) a shared purse had to give way to organised poor-care. Possibly the solution to the problem of care of the Hellenist widows is meant to be taken as a kind of transition from community of property in Acts 2-5 to the almsgiving of the later church. How are we to give fair weight to Luke's obvious enthusiasm for the fragmentary record of Palestinian Jewish communitarian property-sharing which he had received? Can Luke really have yielded, as he wrote subsequent chapters, to the slightly cynical conviction that 'it was all too good to last'?

The tension between the ethical perspective of the account of communal sharing in Acts 2–6 and that of the later chapters of Acts has usually been implicitly solved by denying significant historical reality to the community of goods Luke described. The arguments in favour of the substantial historicity of the community of goods noted at the beginning aside, to deny the historical reference of these events does not solve, but rather heightens, the hermeneutical problem. If Luke, for example, was aware that only a few isolated events of substantial charitable giving had occurred in the earliest community, but embellished these to give the impression of substantial, community-wide communal sharing (the form-critical case of Dibelius),[14] why does he thereafter allow the theme to drop? What did he intend to achieve through the incorporation of language resonant of the widespread hellenistic theme of community of property?

---

[13]This contrast is emphasised by Johnson, *Literary Function*, who begins his analysis of Acts from chapters 9-28; cf. also his *Sharing Possessions*, 117-139.
[14]*Studies*, 8-10.

II. Literary resonances and the narrative tension of Acts

The theme of community of goods appears in a variety of contexts in
the Graeco–Roman period. The most important are the Golden Age (an
account of human beginnings), political theories of the proper
organisation for the state (beginning with Plato's *Republic*), the
association of community of goods with the ideal of friendship, and its
attribution to primitive peoples or location in fabled distant lands. The
interpreter of Acts must establish how this literary environment would
determine the ancient reader's approach to the attribution and apparent restriction of community of goods to the earliest Jerusalem church.

There are three clearly distinguishable theoretical accounts of
social and cultural history in early Greek thinking: the Golden Age, a
theory of decline and degeneration; a cyclical theory of eternal re-
currence; and theories of progress.[15] Those who believed that human
history began with the 'Golden Age' frequently asserted that the earliest human beings held all property in common.[16] The Golden Age
first appeared in Hesiod's *Works and Days* (106–201). Hesiod himself
seems to have combined a paradise myth, such as is common to virtually all ancient cultures, with an oriental scheme which divided world-
history into periods, named after various metals, which symbolise
their relative worth.[17] With Hesiod, the paradise myth became the
first, golden age of humankind, at once part of human history and yet
standing over against it as a condemnation of present moral decay.
Following subsequent, increasingly inferior races of silver and bronze,
and the age of heroes, the present 'iron' race was born. The Golden Age
appears extensively as an account of human beginnings in Graeco–
Roman literature,[18] where it attests the popular appeal of the image of
humanity's primeval common ownership of property:

> Before Jupiter's day no tillers subdued the land,
> Even to mark the field or divide it with bounds was unlawful.
> Humankind made gain for the common store, and earth

---

[15]Kerferd, *The Sophistic Movement*, 125. On the Golden Age theory of degeneration
and theories of progress, *cf.*, Guthrie, *History of Greek Philosophy*, I, 400; II, 182, 248.

[16]While the OT primeval history did not speculate a primitive human communism, Cain's murder of Abel, a key event in the destruction of primeval fellowship,
was under Greek influence attributed to avarice, *cf.*, Josephus, *Ant.* 1.2.1 §54.

[17]The scheme reached Hesiod in the same Iranian form which was later taken up
and modified in a different way by the author of Daniel.

[18]*Cf.*, Gatz, *Weltalter*. The Golden Age myth could easily be combined with the
story of Prometheus, see Uxkull-Gyllenband, *Kultur-Entstehungslehren*, 15-19.

> yielded all, of herself, more freely,
> When none begged her for gifts.   (Virgil, *Georgics* 1.125ff)

It is sometimes assumed that community of property was a component part of the Golden Age myth from its beginnings with Hesiod,[19] but the particular motif is absent from his work. The poet merely envisaged bounteous abundance.[20] Nevertheless Hesiod criticised, through his description of the present 'iron' race, the substitution of material values for human in his own society. The signal loss of the present age over against humanity's golden beginnings was the destruction of κοινωνία. This loss was characterised by unfaithfulness to the material obligations inherent in social relationships. Loved-one and companion were neglected for the pursuit of private wealth, which extended even to force of arms:

> The father will not agree with the children, nor the children with their father, nor the guest with the host, nor comrade with comrade; nor brother be dear to brother as aforetime. Human beings will dishonour their parents as they quickly grow old, and will carp at them, chiding them with bitter words, hard-hearted they, not knowing the fear of the gods. They will not repay their aged parents the cost of their nurture, for might shall be their right: and one will sack another's city. There will be no favour for the man who keeps his oath or for the good; but rather they will praise the evil-doer and violent dealing. (*Works and Days* 174–201)

One case of such broken fellowship was Hesiod's own dispute with his brother Perses over their inheritance, which forms the immediate context (11–41).

The poets of the Old Comedy (5th Century BC) made sport of the *automaton* motif, which emphasised the earth's spontaneous production of all the food humanity required,[21] but did not employ the Golden Age myth to express any ideal of community of property. Similarly, Orphic poetry before Plato spoke of the Golden Age,[22] but the *topos* of community of property does not appear in the fragments. When Aristophanes devoted a whole comedy to the sexist ridicule of

---

[19]Cf., Kurfess, 'Aetas aurea', *RAC* I, see 145.

[20]*Works and Days* 115.

[21]The development can be deduced from the numerous citations in Athenaeus *Deipn.* 6.267E–270A. Cf., Baldry, 'The idler's paradise'; Pöschl, 'Das Märchen vom Schlaraffenland'; Pöhlmann, *Geschichte*, I, 386-392.

[22]Cf., Gatz, *Weltalter*, 52-53.

communistic political theories as women's wisdom, the *Ecclesiazousae* (393 BC),[23] the figure of the Golden Age does not appear. Community of goods seems to have first found its way into the myth of the Golden Age with Plato's *Republic*, which appeared shortly after Aristophanes' satire. Plato proposed a state ruled by a class of 'Guardians', who practise community of both property and wives. The life without possessions is not prescribed for the wider community, but extends only to the Guardians, who are to live in a community amongst themselves without personal property. Plato's Republic was proposed in the context of hefty political struggle between oligarchy and democracy, and was not conceived as an unrealisable Utopia. His scheme of a possessionless ruling class was designed as a practical answer to the problems of government.[24] The Guardians are fitted to rule by their proposed common life, which removes any possibility of acting out of personal interest.

Plato drew an equation between the classes within his state and the successive races of Hesiod's myth:

> God in fashioning those who are fitted to hold rule mingled gold in their generation, but in the helpers silver, and iron and brass in the other craftsmen. (Republic 3 §415A, *cf.*, 5 §468E)

Plato's system for the state intends to recapture those aspects of the lost age of innocence necessary for its rulers. His connection of community of goods with the Golden Age reflects the growing suspicion of private property in Greek ethical thought. Plato's starting point is the righteousness of the first, golden men, which is now seen in the light of the growing suspicion that private property hopelessly taints moral integrity. After Plato the motif of community of property soon became a standard element of the legend. With this development, the term κοινωνία seems not only to denote the perfect human fellowship of the Golden Age, but to embrace as well the community of property as an expression of the primeval harmony.[25]

D. Mealand has emphasised that Acts 2:44 and 4:32 reflect two phrases used to describe the community of goods in Plato's *Republic*

---

[23]*Cf.*, *Ecclesiazousae* 590-594.
[24]*Cf.*, *Resp.* 6 §§499C-D; Wacht, 'Gütergemeinschaft', *RAC* XIII, 1-59, see 12-14.
[25]*Cf.*, Plutarch, *Cimon* 10.6f on the legendary generosity of Cimon, 'which restored the fabled communism (κοινωνία) of the age of Cronus', translation Bernadotte Perrin, Loeb edition. Athenaeus *Deipn.* 12.533A-C gives an account of Cimon's lavish social projects. Philo's use of κοινωνία at *Hyp.* 11.1 may denote not merely the Essene spirit of friendship, but its manifestation in formalised community of property.

which become standard elements in later descriptions of community of property.[26] 'All things common' (πάντα [or ἅπαντα] κοινά, Acts 2:44 and 4:32) and '(to consider) nothing one's own' (οὐδὲν [or μηδὲν] ἴδιον, cf. Acts 4:32) are both used to describe the community of goods of the Guardians of Plato's *Republic*,[27] and appear in Plato's other descriptions of the ideal state.[28] The significance of Plato's ideal state, however, for understanding the purpose of these descriptions in Acts is probably indirect. As the account of Acts 2–5 stands, there is no limitation of the community of goods to those ruling the community, but an implied universal participation. It might have apologetic weight to attribute a momentary greater realisation of community of goods to the earliest Christian community than Plato considered possible in his ideal state, but the absence of community of property from the later chapters of Acts suggests that Luke did not have in mind to claim that Christians were capable of exceeding the Platonic political ideal.

It is the wider effect of Plato's proposals that is significant for understanding Acts. Although communistic ideas were abroad prior to Plato's particular employment of them,[29] the impetus which he gave to their discussion led to the appearance, in a wide variety of literary contexts, of more idealised versions of community of goods than his own. Subsequent to the *Republic*, and in large measure conceptually dependent upon it, ideas of community of property are found in many idealised views of humanity. The earlier community of Pythagoras, the 'father of Philosophy' was portrayed as a communistic society under Platonic influence; later sources even extend Pythagorean communism to the whole population of the Greek colony in southern Italy (Magna Graecia).[30] The Cynic Diogenes devised a sceptical Republic in which the ordained currency would be dice.[31] The Stoic Zeno apparently wrote a Republic endorsing community of goods, although Stoicism did not endorse community of property as a practical possibility.[32] The marvellous communistic systems of tribal peoples,

[26]Mealand, 'Community of Goods and Utopian Allusions in Acts II-IV'.
[27]*Resp.* 3 §416D, 5 §464D, 8 §453B.
[28]*Crit.* §110D; *Tim.* 18B.
[29]Hence the satire of Aristophanes, *Ecclesiazousae* 590-594.
[30]*Cf.*, Porphyry, *Vit. Pyth.* 20; Iamblichus, *Vit. Pyth.*, esp. 16-17 §§70-74, Diog. Laert. 8.10. Further Burkert, *Weisheit und Wissenschaft* 92-94; Minar 'Pythagorean Communism' 36-40; Philip, *Pythagoras* 138-148; Hutter, *Politics* 48-51.
[31]*Cf.*, Athenaeus, *Deipn.* 4.159C.
[32]*Cf.*, Diog. Laert. 7.131. The Cynic Crates sees Utopianism as drunkard's talk, Diog. Laert. 6.85.

living beyond Greek and later Roman control, somehow preserved the
innocence of the lost Golden Age. Romances were penned of fabulous
distant lands where the primeval communistic behaviour of human
beings still persisted.[33]

Frequently the educated showed their culture by talk of the ideal
of community of goods and a certain disdain for private property, a
disdain which was calculated not to extend to any practical adjustment
of property relations in the real world.[34] Most Hellenistic instances of
enthusiasm for community of goods have in common that they do not
seek to invade everyday reality. They are dreams of a distant past,
distant lands, or a distant future.[35] For all their unreality, they convey
the commonly held ideal that, were it not for the complications which
human frailty brings to attempts of practical realisation, society ought
to avoid private ownership and hold its goods in common.[36]

The interpreter of Acts must acknowledge the tension between
the theoretical and the practical in this strand of ancient thought. The
ancient readers of Acts would anticipate that an account of community of goods might be in some sense withdrawn from everyday
reality. While Luke's account does not distance community of goods

---

[33]Cf., Euhemerus' (c. 300 BC) fable of Panchaia in the Indian Ocean, Diod. Sic. 5.41-
46, and Iambulus' 'Isle of the Sun', Diod. Sic. 2.55-60. Diodorus Siculus attributes
a communistic system to the Celtiberians of north central Spain, 5.34.3. Pseudo-
Scymnus, in a poem written about 110 BC, says the Scythians are 'very pious' and
'live in common, having their whole social life and property on a communal basis',
Orbis descriptio 850-859. Horace lauds the Scythians' simple life, 'whose unallotted
acres bring forth fruits and corn for all in common'; Scythian piety preserves the
κοινωνία of the Golden Age; children bereft of their natural mothers are readily
fostered by others, Carmina 3.24, c. 23 BC, cf., Pompeius Trogus, Hist. Phil. Epit. 2.2.
Strabo gave the Indians (15.1.13ff) a heavily idealised system of common
agriculture. Caesar pointed to the equality of possessions of the Germans, Bellum
Gallicum 6.22, cf. Seneca, De Providentia 4.14f. Tacitus says none of the German
tribe of the Chauci suffered poverty, Germania 35.
[34]Cf., esp. the discussion between the patron and the young scholar in Lucian, On
Salaried Posts in Great Houses, 19-21. The wealthy Seneca (e.g., Ep. 90) epitomises
this tendency.
[35]Kytzler commented on the marked contrast between the frequency of Utopian
presentations in antiquity and the virtual absence of attempts at practical
realisation, 'Utopisches Denken', esp. 68.
[36]Aristotle's critique of Plato reveals this tension. Aristotle believed that to attempt
to impose community of property politically would create disharmony because it
cut across the natural human drive for possessions, and that it would not result in
proper care for property. He developed the distinction that property should be
owned privately but should be made common in use, Pol. 2.1.2-2.2.6 (1261A-
1263B).

geographically, like the travel romances, beyond the edge of Graeco–Roman civilisation, it does set it back into the past, that is, at a chronological distance. The passing character of the Golden Age corresponds precisely with the narrative tension caused by the absence of community of goods from the later chapters of Acts. Readers familiar with the contemporary relegation of community of goods to the past Golden Age or to far-off places where its virtue persisted would have been cued to employ a reading strategy which would not demand that earliest Christian community of property would persist into the present experience of the Church.

Luke perhaps intended his reader to grasp that at the beginning of the history of the church there was momentarily realised again the idyllic state which all humanity enjoyed at the beginning of time. By restricting community of property to the earliest Christian community, Luke may mean to imply that foundation-events of unique import for world history were taking place. The fellowship of property which followed Pentecost may be, in effect, decoded as signifying that with the birth of the Church God worked a new creation for the whole human race.[37]

Luke's presentation of the coming of the Spirit upon the Church at Pentecost (Acts 2:1-41), the immediate context of the first description of community life (2:42-47), seems to confirm that Luke's present theme is 'new beginnings'. The preceding account of the gift of the Spirit at Pentecost seems clearly to allude to features of the developing Jewish legend concerning the giving of the Law at Sinai, the 'birthday-event' of the Jewish nation. The fully developed form of the legend seems to have indicated that not only Israel, but all the nations were present when God's voice promulgated commandments from the mountain. The divine voice was not only heard by all the nations but also seen, as a manifestation of flame spreading out above them.[38] A language miracle was associated with the event as all the nations heard, through the division of the voice into seventy 'tongues' the promulgation of the commandments in their own languages.[39] This was necessary since the defining feature of the earth's many nations was the variety of their languages. Only the nation of Israel consented

---

[37]Read as an account of new beginnings for the whole world, the account may have a universalist force parallel to Luke's extension early in his Gospel of the genealogy of Jesus back to Adam (Luke 3:23-38; Matt. 1:1-17 begins from Abraham, father of the Jewish nation).

[38]Philo, De Dec. 9, 11; cf., Targ. Yer. on Exodus 2:20.

[39]Midrash Tanhuma 26c; cf. B. Shab. 88b on Ps. 68:12.

to keep the commandments, however. By this consent Israel became God's chosen nation. The legend served to emphasise the divine origin of the Law of Moses and account for the Jews' unique role in the economy of God.

Certain features of the account in Acts of the birth of the Christian Church at Pentecost seem to be derived from this story. Luke tells of a manifestation which blended both flame and a great sound as the Holy Spirit came upon the church (2:2-3). Two features of the account of the Christian Pentecost, however, do not seem to derive from the developed Jewish legend of the giving of the Law at Sinai. First, in Acts human beings, the members of the nascent Church, are said to have spoken in foreign languages. In the developed Sinai legend it is the voice of God which is heard speaking in various languages. Second, the event in Acts is understood to have imparted the Holy Spirit to the believers; the embellished Sinai legend does not mention God's Spirit or any reception of him.

These two differences allow us to discern the seam between historical event and interpretive development in Luke's account. It is well attested that early Christianity understood the manifestation of glossolalia to be a sign of the Holy Spirit's reception. It appears that early events of glossolalia in the Jerusalem community were embellished, as their story was told, with the features of great sound and flame from the developed Sinai story. The stimulus for the connection of the two stories may have been the presence in both of the idea of strange language witnessed by an international audience (cf., Acts 2:5-13). The purpose of this development was twofold. The early Christian mission, in order to present a minority group within Judaism as the true heirs of the whole nation's religious heritage, usurped a Jewish symbolic vocabulary linked with foundation-events. It presented its own beginnings in the colours of the developed fable of the receipt of the Law. This legitimated the emerging church's claim to be the fulfilment of Jewish hopes. Moreover, the church thereby made the claim to fulfil Israel's role as 'light to the nations', as in the church by the glossolalic receipt of the Spirit the divisions between the nations are symbolically overcome. The consummate theological artistry of the development also served the church's more liberal stance on the Law of Moses by giving graphic representation to the conceptual pair, Law and Spirit; Christians may draw greater nourishment from recognising the symbolic vocabulary of the text than by reading it simply as an account of marvellous, strange events.[40]

Although Luke may not have been the theological innovator of the comparison drawn,[41] it can hardly have been lost on him.[42] In Jewish understanding the nation of Israel began properly with God's promises to Abraham, but the Sinai events were seen as a foundational event in the history of the nation, as it was redeemed from the bondage of servitude in Egypt, given its defining Law in the Mosaic covenant, and led onward into the land which God had promised to Abraham. The giving of the Law at Sinai was therefore a 'birthday-event' of the nation, and in the account of Pentecost the birth of the Christian Church is drawn as a parallel yet fulfilling and superseding event. In the following vignette of the Jerusalem community's life together (Acts 2:42-47), Luke seems to be making a parallel point about new beginnings through a symbolic vocabulary of Graeco-Roman provenance. Long before Luke wrote that the early Jerusalem disciples had 'all things common' (2:44; cf., 4:32), the poets of Greece had dreamed of a 'Golden Age', at the beginning of time, when the earth and its fruits were common to all. Luke's universalism is also expressed by first reversing the symbolism of the Sinai legend in the account of Pentecost, making God's Spirit available through repentance to all nations, and followed through by his reference to the community of goods in the subsequent depictions of the early Jerusalem community's life, which express the renewal of humanity through the symbolic vocabulary of the Golden Age myth.

Luke's intent is salvation-historical as well as ethical. As a salvation-historical reference, his account draws out the momentous significance of God's new act of the creation of the Church. God's Spirit of love, poured out on the community of his Messiah, brings a new ethical creation characterised by the κοινωνία which the first uncorrupted human beings shared. That a new phase of history has begun is symbolised by the momentary return of the paradisal state of the first human beings. Since the eschatological hope is hope for a return to paradise, Luke's description is also a glimpse of the eschatological future. The story of the Church's beginnings reveals its true essence as the vehicle of eschatological salvation through which all creation will be renewed. However, to restrict community of property to a past withdrawn from the present experience of the Church is also for Luke to postpone it to the eschatological future and not to demand its full realisation in the present community. We must

---

[40]On the whole comparison see most recently Wedderburn, 'Traditions'. For a different view see Marshall, 'Pentecost'.
[41]So Wedderburn, 'Traditions', 30, 52-53.
[42]Pace Wedderburn,'Traditions', 30, 35-36, 54.

turn to another literary resonance of community of property to understand precisely what kind of practical revision of property-relations Luke desired for the present, ongoing Christian community.

III. Friendship, reciprocity and meal-fellowship

As Acts continues, there is no hint that the almsgiving of Tabitha (9:36) and Cornelius (10:2, 4, 31) was anything less than an acceptable model for Christian behaviour. Luke did not intend the Christian communities of his day to formally institute property-sharing which disposed of the distinctions of ownership which secular law would acknowledge. What practical imitation of the community of goods of Acts 2-5 was possible in Luke's day? H.J. Cadbury observed that 'Possibly the community of goods is in part conceived... as providing a common meal...'[43] In these relatively brief descriptions, Luke notes three times the meal-fellowship of the early Jerusalem Christians. At 2:42 the community regularly attends to the 'breaking of bread', which seems to indicate the taking of full meals; at 2:46, the community daily breaks bread and takes food together 'from house to house'; the dispute of Acts 6:1-6 clearly shows that the poor were taken care of in the context of meal-fellowship (cf., διακονεῖν τραπέζαις, 6:2). The NT attests the Christian practice of domestic meal-fellowship (the Agape) in the ongoing church (Acts 20:7-11; 1 Cor. 11:17-34; Jude 12; 2 Peter 2:13 [some mss]). That Luke's interest is somewhat focused on the practice of meal-fellowship suggests that this may be the sphere in which he imagined that practical imitation of the community of goods of the early Jerusalem church could to some extent occur in the communities for which he wrote.

As I have emphasised in my earlier essay (see n. 1), impressions of community of goods within the Palestinian cultural context are distorted if the isolated Essene settlement of Qumran is taken as the typical social form of community of goods amongst the Essenes. As is particularly clear from the accounts of Philo, Essene community of property functioned principally through evening meal-fellowship, at which the wages of individual Essenes, earned separately in personal labour or crafts, were pooled in order to enable the purchase of the food for the meal and the other needs of the group.[44] As Philo emphasises in this context, community of goods was made possible

---

[43]Cadbury, *The Making of Luke–Acts*, 251.

through the *daily* process of the collection of wages and distribution of the necessaries of life to each member. While communal production may have occurred at Qumran, it did not occur in the Essene communities distributed through the towns and villages of Palestine. Similarly, while communal premises dominated the functioning of the community at Qumran, this appears to have been exceptional. There are significant indications in Philo's account which suggest that individual Essenes lived in their own houses, but used these where suitable for communal gatherings.[45] Community of goods as a Palestinian cultural phenomenon was essentially an economic structure created by the daily renewal of meal-fellowship between those who lived otherwise in their own houses. In addition, there were disposals of assets to the community on entry, but these probably did not extend to the disposal of the house in which a member actually lived, or of the land which the member personally worked or the workshop in which a craft was pursued. Disposal of assets probably only occurred where there was excess landed property which a member did not personally work. Philo emphasises that all Essenes (except the old and sick) worked;[46] retention of excess property irrelevant to the member's daily work may have been deemed unnecessary.

That Palestinian community of goods functioned principally through meal-fellowship has the consequence that, if one has to look for an 'end' to the practice of community of goods, one has principally

---

[44]Philo, *Hyp.* 11.4-10. At the beginning of paragraph 10 ἕκαστος refers to the wages of 'each member' rather than of 'each branch', a deduction of common production which the text does not support. Vermes and Goodman, *The Essenes* 29, translate: 'When each man receives his salary for these different trades...' The daily pooling of wages is also mentioned at *Quod. omn. prob.* 86.

[45]Note especially Philo, *Quod omn. prob.* 85, 'In the first place, there is no one who has a house so absolutely his own private property that it does not in some sense belong to all (οὐχὶ πάντων εἶναι κοινὴν συμβέβηκε)...', translation Yonge, *Philo Judaeus*, III, 525. Yonge pays closest attention among translators to the guarded nature of the phrasing. The continuation of this passage should perhaps be rendered '...since their homes are opened for the purpose of living together in meal-fellowships (κατὰ θιάσους), and to members of the sect arriving from elsewhere.' Philo's use of the term θίασος, which did not imply residential community but the gathering of members of a religious association for a meal (the term is typical of the Bacchic associations), implies that Essenes had individual homes which were open for the *use* of the fellowship; *cf.*, 81 on gathering on the sabbath in places called 'synagogues', which may imply separate dwellings, and *Hyp.* 11.6-10, where separated working lives are led from before dawn to nearly dusk, which may also imply separated dwellings, linked to workshops or personal pieces of farmland.

[46]*Quod omn. prob.* 79, 86; *Hyp.* 11.8-10.

to detect the point at which meal fellowship ceased to be a daily affair in Christianity. My suspicion is that meal-fellowship changed from being a daily process to a weekly affair as Greek-speaking believers in the Hellenist community started to organise themselves under the group led by Stephen (Acts 6:1-6). The Hellenists probably had less affinity with the Palestinian sectarian social pattern of communal sharing and modelled their worship on a weekly basis linked to the weekly pattern of the synagogues in which they worshipped (Acts 6:9). Christianity spread outside Palestine through their missionary enterprise, and weekly meal-fellowship became the norm. The parallel between 1 Corinthians 11:18 ('when you meet as a church') and Paul's resumption of his point at 11:20 ('When you come together, it is not the Lord's supper that you eat') shows that in Paul's communities every worship meeting of Christians entailed meal-fellowship. 1 Corinthians 16:2 shows that Paul's communities met on a weekly basis, on the first day of the week. What was gathered on these weekly occasions had to last through the week for the care of any in need through the offices of the community leaders.

The inherent danger as Christian meal-fellowship was transplanted from its original context of Palestinian communitarianism was that it would not be undertaken as a sharing which transcended social boundaries. The meal-fellowship of pagan religious associations did not share the social emphasis of Jewish meal-fellowship.[47] This problem is exemplified by Paul's severity (1 Cor. 11:17-34) with those who avoid ensuring that the needs of all who come to the Christian fellowship meal are met. At Corinth, the rich went ahead with their meal (προλαμβάνει, 11:21) without waiting for the president to make a distribution which gave each a share of what had been brought, whether they had contributed much, little, or nothing at all.[48] As has often been emphasised, Graeco–Roman ethical thinking did not share the characteristically oriental social emphasis on the need for the rich to care for the poor.[49] H.-J. Degenhardt and R.J. Karris have drawn attention to the importance of this cultural tendency for understanding Luke's emphasis on possessions, the poor and the rich in his

---

[47]*Cf.*, Uhlhorn, *Christian Charity*, 23-31. For example, Uhlhorn stressed that since the distributions made in the guilds gave greater shares to the officers than to ordinary members, their purpose was not charitable but the celebration of the giver (26).

[48]*Cf.*, Keating, *The Agape*, 47-48 and 178, on the distribution which Socrates undertakes in order to shame those who do not share at a meal in Xenophon, *Memorabilia* 3.14.

Gospel,[50] 'a tendency, which if left unchallenged, would lead to the abandonment of the poor'.[51] Actually, the key to understanding Luke's practical demands is gentile converts' potential neglect of the proper social function of meal-fellowship because of their cultural distance from Jewish ethical interest in the poor.

In his Gospel, Luke places remarkable emphasis on the meal-fellowship of Jesus, with many redactional touches which show its importance for him.[52] Luke's presentation of Jesus' meal-fellowship suggests that in the communities for which he wrote, as with Paul's Corinth, the proper function of meal-fellowship as a structure of social support was neglected. Characteristic is that Jesus eats with the rich and powerful, who overcome or are exhorted to overcome the social barrier between them and the poor and outcast in this context. Jesus dines with the tax-collector Levi and with 'sinners' despite the objections of the Pharisees (5:27-32). Jesus dines with a Pharisee who objects to the generous anointing of Jesus with ointment (7:36-50). Jesus dines with the wealthy chief tax collector Zacchaeus, who repents declaring the disposal of half of his goods to the poor and fourfold restitution to those whom he has defrauded (19:1-10).

The relevance of this material on meal-fellowship in Luke's Gospel to his presentation of the community of goods early in Acts is confirmed by a common reference to the Hellenistic motif of friendship. The opening of the second summary (Acts 4:32-35), in which

---

[49]This is the thesis of Bolkestein, *Wohltätigkeit*, *e.g.*, 'Dass sittliche Verpflichtungen der Reichen gegen den Armen fehlen, is um so bemerkenswerter, weil andere Gruppen, denen man zu helfen hat, ausdrücklich genannt werden...', 94; *cf.*, Degenhardt, *Lukas*, 180-181. Den Boer, *Private Morality*, 151-178, seeks to qualify Bolkestein's position. See further Winter, 'The Lord's Supper '.

[50]Degenhardt, *Lukas*, 221-223; Karris, 'Poor and Rich', 114-15.

[51]Karris, 'Poor and Rich', 115.

[52]Levi gives a 'great banquet' for Jesus, Luke 5:27-32, *cf.*, Matt. 9:9-13; Mark 2:13-17. The meal of 7:36-50 is unique to Luke. Of the Synoptics, only Luke has the meal of Luke 10:38-42. There is no Synoptic parallel to the meal-setting of Luke 11:37-54 or the eating references of 13:26 and 14:15; all of 14:1-24 occurs in the context of a meal. Luke apparently sets the parable of the lost sheep in the context of a meal (Luke 15:1-6, *cf.*, Matt. 18:12-14). Luke has the shepherd call his friends and neighbours together to rejoice as if for a meal (Luke 15:6), adding the parable of the lost coin, in which the woman does the same (Luke 15: 7-10, *cf.*, v. 9) and the parable of the prodigal, in the conclusion of which feasting is prominent (Luke 15:11-32, *cf.*, vv. 23-30). The rich man of 16:19-31 feasts sumptuously (v. 19). Zacchaeus repents in the context of a meal, 19:6-10. Luke emphasises the eating of the Passover meal at 22:16 (contrast Matt. and Mark). The road to Emmaus encounter concludes with a meal, 24:13-35. Only Luke has the meal of 24:41-43.

Luke's own hand in stylising his material on community of goods with Greek commonplaces is most evident, bears a remarkable similarity to a line of Aristotle's *Nicomachian Ethics* in which he lists proverbs of friendship. Luke writes that the early Jerusalem believers were of 'one heart and soul' and that 'all things were to them common' (4:32). Aristotle refers to the common Greek proverbs of friendship, 'the possessions of friends are common' (κοινὰ τὰ τῶν φίλων), and 'friends are one soul' (μία ψυχή).[53] The life of the earliest community in Jerusalem realised the vaunted Greek ideal of friendship.[54] Luke's Gospel uses φίλος more than any other NT book. The term has a close connection with meal-fellowship. Jesus is the friend of tax-collectors and sinners because he eats with them (7:34, *cf.*, Matt. 11:19). The term appears when the ranking of guests at meals is discussed (14:10, 12). The prodigal's brother desires to feast with his friends (15:29). When the shepherd rejoicing over the lost sheep (15:6) and the woman rejoicing over finding the lost coin (15:9) call their friends together to celebrate, meal-fellowship is probably envisaged. Luke is very aware of the reciprocal obligations which giving between friends established in the Graeco–Roman context. Friends can expect reciprocal duties of each other (11:6, provision of food; 16:9, the obligations under which the unjust manager places his friends by reducing their debts). When Herod Antipas and Pilate become friends (23:12), the term refers to political alliance which would be maintained by reciprocity.

When a social superior gave to an inferior who could not repay, the superior became the inferior's benefactor, entitled to a return of some other kind (service).[55] Luke shows his awareness of this by having elders of Capernaum plead the cause of the centurion who has built the town's synagogue, and then friends (social equals) speak for him when Jesus is at close quarters, Luke 7:3-6 (no parallel in Matt. 8:5-13).[56] Luke sets his face against the doing of good works by the rich in order to oblige a return of honour by changing the concept of tyranny at Mark 10:42 (Matt. 20:25), κατεξουσιάζουσιν, to that of benefactor, καὶ οἱ ἐξουσιάζοντες αὐτῶν εὐεργέται καλοῦνται, Luke 22:24.[57] As

---

[53] 9.8.2 §1116B. For instances of the very common maxim 'the possessions of friends are common', see Capper, 'Community of Goods', 325 n. 5.

[54] *Cf.*, Mitchell, 'The Social Function of Friendship'.

[55] On reciprocity *cf.*, Hands, *Charities*, 26-61; Veyne, *Bread*, 5-11; Eisenstadt and Roniger, *Patrons*, 52-64.

[56] *Cf.*, Moxnes, 'Patron-Client Relations', 241-268.

[57] On Luke's interest in benefactors *cf.*, Danker, *New Age*, 28-46 and 403 (on Acts 10:34-43).

well as showing distaste for the patron-client system, Luke rejects the self-interested flavour of the reciprocity linked with Hellenistic friendship by his additions to the Q saying of Matthew 5:42 on giving to those who beg.[58]

At Luke 14:1-14 Jesus is entertained by a ruler of the Pharisees. In the conclusion of the pericope extreme resistance is shown to meal-fellowship which is conducted by the rich with respect for the social boundaries between friends and non-friends:

> He said also to the man who had invited him, 'When you give a dinner or a banquet, do not invite your friends or your brothers or your kinsmen or rich neighbours, lest they also invite you in return, and you be repaid (14:13). But when you give a feast, invite the poor, the maimed, the lame, the blind, (14:14) and you will be blessed, because they cannot repay you. You will be repaid at the resurrection of the just' (14:12).

The casting of Jesus' reply in Luke's favourite Isaianic categories for the outcast strongly suggests that this section represents Lucan redaction.[59] Instead of the invitation of social equals (τοὺς φίλους, v. 12), in the expectation of reciprocal return, Luke expects the rich to extend their meal-fellowship to those who can offer no return.[60] In his Gospel Luke characterises the Pharisees as lovers of money, and hence as the rich, at Luke 16:14. They serve, therefore, as figures for behaviour inappropriate to the rich. In Luke's description of community of goods in Acts those overflowing with property are the 'owners of houses and lands' who eradicate poverty by their generosity (4:34). But this is no hands-off dispensing of charity to the poor; rather, it functions through meal-fellowship which takes place with rejoicing and genuinely overcomes social boundaries (2:42, 46).

As Graeco–Roman culture understood it, 'friendship' could not be created between superior and inferior. If meal-fellowship occurred between friends, that is social equals, it took place on the understanding that reciprocal invitations would be made. Horizontal social relationships would thus be cemented through a competition of reciprocal giving; what was given would be received again.[61] Luke, however, in

---

[58] Luke 6:30 adds: 'and if anyone takes away your goods, do not ask them again'; the addition of 6:34-35 speaks against lending which expects a return.

[59] Cf., Luke 4:18-19 (no synoptic parallel); 7:22 (=Matt. 11:4-5); 14:21 (contrast Matt. 22:9-10).

[60] On reciprocity and meal-fellowship in Luke–Acts, cf., Neyrey, 'Symbolic Universe', 271-304; Danker, 'Reciprocity', 49-58.

both his Gospel and Acts, has it that friendship could extend from the
rich to the poor through the vehicle of meal-fellowship.[62] The conclusion of Paul's speech to the Ephesian elders with the Jesus-saying 'It
is more blessed to give than to receive' (Acts 20:35) reads precisely as
a rebuttal of the reciprocity expected in Hellenistic friendship, and
makes explicit Luke's demand for open-ended property relations.[63]

For Luke, the rich were to abandon the self-interested connotations of meals between friends, and expend their resources in the
support of the poor through the vehicle of the Agape. We know that in
the period of Paul's letters the typical structure of the Christian
congregation of any city was as a group of connected house congregations which met in the houses of wealthier members who became
in effect 'patrons' of the groups which they hosted.[64] Luke may have
been emphasising the need to maintain the domestic meal-fellowship
possible through such social structures in the decades after Paul. He
may even have hoped for a return to the very early pattern of daily
meal-fellowship. However, the social integration implied by the
proper maintenance of any kind of regular meal-fellowship in his
community would have led to very substantial support for the poor. It
is inconceivable that a Christian community in which the under-
privileged were regularly entertained in the houses of the rich could let
them want for the essential human needs of food, clothing, and shelter
through the week.

---

[61]On the 'agonistic' nature of social intercourse in Mediterranean society cf.
Peristiany (ed.) *Honour and Shame*, 14.

[62]On the presence of both rich and poor in Luke's community *cf.*, Esler, *Community
and Gospel*, 183-187; Beavis, 'Expecting Nothing in Return'; Moxnes, 'Social
Context'.

[63]Some have thought the saying Μακάριόν ἐστιν μᾶλλον διδόναι ἢ λαμβάνειν
actually imitates in reverse the remark of Thucydides 2.97.4, λαμβάνειν μᾶλλον ἢ
διδόναι, which condemns the emphasis on reciprocity in the Thracian kingdom of
Sitalkes, where more disgrace was attached to not giving when asked than to
asking and being refused. *Cf.*, Plümacher, 'Eine Thukydidesreminiszenz'.

[64]For Rome, different house-groups are detectable at Rom. 16:3 (in the house of
Prisca and Aquila), 5 and 10-11 (Aristobulus and Narcissus). Meeks finds in the
three lists of names in Romans 16:14-15 three further household groups, *Christians*
75. At Corinth, groups met in the houses of Crispus (Acts 18:5-8), Gaius (Rom.
16:23) and Stephanas (1 Cor. 16:19). The participle προϊστάμενοι at 1
Thessalonians 5:12, which refers to the leaders of these house-groups at
Thessalonica, includes the nuance of patronage, cf. *TDNT* VI:700-701 and *BAGD*
707; προστάτις, used of Phoebe at Rom. 16:1-2, can mean 'patroness', *cf.*, *BAGD*,
718. Further Barrett, *Church*, 36.

CONCLUSION

CHAPTER 25

LUKE'S THEOLOGICAL ENTERPRISE: INTEGRATION AND INTENT

David Peterson

Summary

This essay seeks to integrate the theological themes that have been investigated throughout this volume. It affirms the central place of salvation in Luke's presentation and seeks to relate this to the idea of the plan of God. The way in which the message of salvation was proclaimed and advanced in the early church is also shown to be a dominant concern of Acts. The chapter further observes the extent to which the renewing work of God is a linking idea in Luke's work. Various theories about the purpose of Luke–Acts are reviewed in the light of this attempt at theological integration. The conclusion is reached that Acts is primarily a work for the encouragement of believers, offering them at the same time a confident basis from which to address their contemporaries.

I. Introduction

To some extent, each of the chapters in this book has advanced our understanding of the theological character and purpose of Acts. Luke addresses a wide range of issues in his work and it is important to assess the contribution that each one makes to the whole. But how do the various themes that have been identified relate together? Is there an overarching purpose to Acts or should we be content to identify a number of theological aims? This chapter seeks to integrate the insights of other contributors and to assess the relative importance of dominant themes in the total presentation of Acts. After some brief preliminaries, it reviews the conclusions of preceding chapters and proceeds to an assessment of Luke's purpose.

II. Some brief preliminaries

Luke's two volumes are different in style and genre and it is important to explore the consequences of that observation. At the same time, it is necessary to explain the links between the volumes at the level of story and theology. Acts is best interpreted as the intended sequel to the Gospel, whatever the process by which this two-volume work came to its present form.[1] It is valid to consider the emphases, style and purpose of Acts as a single document. In the final analysis, however, we are bound to consider the purpose of Luke and Acts together, even though their genres are different and various arrangements of the NT canon have traditionally kept them apart.

Investigations of the purpose of Luke–Acts have often begun with an examination of the prologues. But the difficulty in identifying Theophilus and the ambiguity surrounding certain terms in Luke 1:1-4 complicate any attempt to determine the character and concerns of the intended readers.[2] Was Luke–Acts addressed to an influential non-Christian, to counteract false views of Christianity and commend it to a wider public through him? Was there a special focus on defending Paul in the face of charges that had been laid against him? On the other hand, was Theophilus a representative of newly instructed Christians?

---

[1]Cf., Marshall, 'Former Treatise', 163-182; Maddox, *Purpose*, 3-6. *Contra* Parsons & Pervo, *Rethinking*.

[2] Brown, 'Prologues', 99-111, demonstrates that the prologues can be read in such a way as to support *any* of the main hypotheses which have been proposed about Luke's purpose. *Cf.*, Fitzmyer, *Luke I-IX*, 290-301.

Was Luke's intention to confirm and supplement their knowledge of the historical basis of Christianity or about some aspect of its teaching?

Although Luke 1:1-4 gives general indications of the author's theological intent, especially his desire to publish another account of 'the events that have been fulfilled among us',[3] the meaning and significance of this preface can only be determined by analysing the theological emphases and shape of Luke–Acts as a whole. 'We must allow Luke's work to provide the commentary for his stated purpose and then check our interpretation of the work against the author's statement in Luke 1:3-4.'[4]

III. Integrating the themes of Acts

The salvation of God

The centrality of salvation theology to both parts of Luke's work has often been noted. This is confirmed by several authors in the present volume. J. Green and B. Witherington highlight the special significance of this theme for readers in the Graeco–Roman world. But both insist on the primacy of OT Scripture as a background for understanding Luke's soteriology. At one level, Luke–Acts articulates a view of salvation that would have been broadly understood in the Graeco–Roman world, as well as in Judaism. At another, Luke's view challenges and even works to overturn contemporary alternatives.[5]

Salvation is essentially status reversal for Luke. The kingdom of God displaces other kingdoms, drawing Jews and Gentiles, even social outcasts, into a new community around Jesus. Salvation involves rescue from peril and judgement and is especially conceived of as release from bondage to Satan and sin. Ultimately, it means entering God's dominion and experiencing the blessing of eternal life in his

---

[3]Cf., Peterson, 'The Motif of Fulfilment', 87-104; Du Plessis, 'Once More', 259-71.
[4]Brown, 'Prologues', 100. Cf., Esler, Community and Gospel, 24-5.
[5]Witherington argues that we must speak of both continuity and discontinuity with what is found in Jewish and pagan sources. At its core, salvation in Luke–Acts has to do with God's gracious act of forgiving sins through Jesus, 'which causes the moral, mental, emotional, spiritual, and sometimes physical transformation of an individual'. Particularly when the terminology was used in a more exclusively spiritual or eternal sense, it would have caused some puzzlement to readers from a pagan background.

presence. But did Luke envisage certain people needing only enlightenment and the perfection of their existing attitude to God, rather than
salvation? C. Stenschke's thesis is that salvation in Luke–Acts is the
divine response to human failure in all its dimensions. It is closely
linked with the forgiveness of sins and a call for repentance. Luke
sketches the profound depths of human sinfulness and does not only
focus on the apparently superficial nature of separate sinful acts.

The gift of the Spirit is also central to the experience of this
salvation, marking out those who are members of the new community
and empowering them for ministry. J. Nolland notes that Luke envisages the kingdom of God having both a present (and developing), as
well as a climactic future dimension—both in connection with Jesus.
The day of salvation actually arrives in stages, each with their own
special quality and particular contribution. The Pentecostal outpouring of God's Spirit marks a decisive turning-point in Luke's
presentation of eschatological fulfilment. Green makes the further
observation that Luke's soteriology is theocentric before it is christocentric. God initiates salvation and is the primary actor in the salvific
activity of Jesus. In his suffering and exaltation, Jesus embodies 'the
fullness of salvation interpreted as status reversal', achieving
something unique for others and yet, in certain respects, providing a
model for disciples. Closely linked with the theme of soteriology is
Luke's christology.

The pulse of this, according to D. Buckwalter, is the presentation
of the exalted Jesus as co-equal with God. Jesus' heavenly reign images
that of God in the OT, in character and effect.[6] Given the number of
christological titles and emphases in Luke–Acts, the prominence of
this 'divine christology' was probably dictated by Luke's literary
motives and his knowledge of the christological grounding of his
intended readers. Luke's humiliation-exaltation christology shows
how God provided eschatological salvation for his people. In his
humiliation, Jesus willingly conformed his life to fulfil the Father's
plan. The vindication of Jesus' humiliation was God's exaltation of
him, yet in his exaltation he continues to serve the needs of his people.
In fact, Luke gears the christology of both volumes to redefine what
'benefaction' means. His presentation of 'a deity who waits on tables'

---

[6]Green also highlights the importance of Jesus' exaltation: 'as the enthroned one
(Messiah), as the Benefactor of the people (Lord), the exalted Jesus now reigns as
Saviour, pouring out the blessings of salvation including the Spirit, with whom he
was anointed at the outset of his ministry, to all'. *Cf.,* Hansen's argument that in
Acts 13 the benefits of salvation are shown to flow from the resurrection of Jesus.

acts as an encouragement to disciples to live a Christ-like life, simultaneously reflecting the pattern of the earthly Jesus and the exalted
Lord.

Although salvation is a major theme of Luke–Acts, J. Squires
proposes that it should be viewed in a wider theological context,
namely, the plan of God. The story of Jesus is to be understood within
the parameters of what God did through him to fulfil a cosmic and
universal plan, stretching from creation to new creation. Events within
the surface level narrative of both volumes are presented as taking
place specifically under the guidance of God. The divine plan
functions as 'the foundational theological motif for the complete
work', with the Hebrew Scriptures regularly being identified as the
interpretive framework. Luke writes in this way to encourage and
sustain his readers in their own witness to the fulfilment of God's
purposes. He draws on notions of divine providence for apologetic
reasons, to be considered more thoroughly in my section on Luke's
intention below.

D. Bock agrees that the plan of God is foundational to Luke's
theology: 'the events are recent and the era is new, but the plan is not'.
The message of the newly emerged Christian teaching spans the full
array of scriptural hope, at the centre of which is the Christ event.
Indeed, Scripture is used to support the community's claim to the
heritage of God revealed in Moses and the prophets.[7] Luke is not
simply interested in describing who Jesus is but in setting forth how he
functions within the divine plan. Jesus' vindication by God becomes
the occasion for a new appeal to Jews and Gentiles. Scripture is
particularly used to show how a suffering and exalted Messiah is
integral to the promised eschatological salvation. At the same time, the
community is shown how its current suffering is rooted in the way of
Jesus and the plan of God.

The call of God

The second section of this volume concentrates on the way the
message of salvation was proclaimed and advanced to Israel and then

---

[7]Like Squires, Bock argues that the claim that Christianity has a history and roots
spanning the generations was 'an ancient sociological necessity for obtaining
credibility'. Such a claim would have been impressive for Gentile readers, as well
as for Jews.

to the Gentiles. God's call to enjoy the benefits of eschatological salvation comes through the proclamation of the word about Jesus. From Luke's perspective, the twelve apostles played a critical role in this process. As Jesus' authorized witnesses to the Jewish people, they were foundational figures in the eschatological restoration of Israel.

A. Clark observes that the apostles are presented as having a first-hand knowledge of Jesus, both before and after his resurrection, so that they can 'affirm, guarantee and rightly interpret the facts about him'. Though rarely termed an apostle in Acts, Paul is also an authorized witness and expounder of the significance of the gospel events. As a leader in the mission to the Gentiles, he is portrayed in many ways as paralleling the ministry of Peter. Thus, the unity of the missions to Israel and to the Gentiles is highlighted.

P. Bolt notes that this apostolic work is set within the framework of two 'missions' of Christ. God sent him to Israel in the first place and will send him again at the time of the restoration of all things. Through the word of his Spirit-equipped witnesses, the exalted Lord Jesus continues to be sent to Israel (via the Twelve) and to the Gentiles (via Paul). The apostolic speeches, which regularly appear in a forensic setting, provide the reader with the illusion of hearing the testimony of Jesus' authorized witnesses first-hand. Although their distinctive role as witnesses is not transferable, the message which resulted from their commission has become public property because of Luke's work. 'By recording the witness, Acts maintains that witness. As Acts presents the word of witness, Jesus and his word of salvation continues to be sent to the nations.'[8]

B. Rosner confirms that the progress of the word, rather than simply 'missionary expansion', is a focus of Luke's narrative. The summaries that highlight this theme act as transitions from one period of growth to the next, revealing that expansion is impressive and far reaching. They also consistently stress divine causation. Although human characters overcome considerable barriers to preach the message, it is God who directs and enables them. Progress depends on the purpose, will and plan of God. The Spirit is also highlighted as the means by which God's saving purpose is advanced, so that, in Rosner's words, 'to trace the activity of the Spirit in Acts is to observe the progress of the gospel'.

---

[8]Bolt observes, however, that as Jews and Gentiles listen to the word, 'there is a natural movement towards evangelising the word (cf., 8:4; 11:20)'. Thus, the witness of the apostles continues to be shared by those who have received it themselves.

Acts 15 forms the centre of the book, structurally and theologically. The first half traces the movement of the gospel from a
Jewish to a universal context. Following the Jerusalem Council, the
progress of the gospel concerns primarily geographical boundaries
rather than ethnic or relational ones. Cycles of rejection and persecution throughout Acts warn us against seeing progress in triumph-
alist terms. Yet the open ending of the book suggests that progress will
continue and implicitly encourages readers to play their part in
spreading the word, even in the face of suffering.

B. Rapske develops the theme that, by God's enabling, Christian
witness prevails through resistance and hostility. The compelling
quality and divine origin of the Christian message is regularly
confirmed by the way the narrative is told. Opposition is shown to
come from inside and outside the church, fulfilling Jesus' prophetic
words about disciples experiencing trouble and persecution. Other
divine indications and apostolic catechesis confirm that persecution
will be a certainty for believers. Readers are encouraged by many
examples to rely upon the Spirit for boldness of speech and to
persevere in the face of opposition.

H. Bayer, W. Neudorfer and W. Hansen examine various
speeches in Acts, to show how they contribute to the literary structure
and development of thought. A close reciprocity between narrative
and discourse is regularly observed. The speeches demonstrate how
the message spread from Jerusalem to 'the end of the earth', adapting
to the respective circumstances along the way. Yet Luke gives the
impression that the message was proclaimed with an abiding core
shared by all the preachers he records.

Bayer insists that the eschatological foundation laid in the
Petrine speeches in Acts 1–3 sets the tone and framework for various
other themes developed and expounded in the unfolding narrative of
the book. Peter first appears as a preacher of repentance and final
salvation, calling Jews to return to the God of their fathers, in view of
what he had accomplished in Christ. Stephen's speech identifies him
as a Jew of the diaspora and displays a number of the theological
emphases of early Christian 'Hellenists'. Although Stephen manifests
a critical attitude towards temple and cultus, Neudorfer notes that 'the
law is only mentioned in passing and in an exclusively positive
manner'.[9] Most significantly, the speech links God's original revelation to Abraham with Jesus' present revelation of himself as the Righteous One and exalted Son of Man. Rejected by Israel, he has nevertheless been confirmed by God as a redeemer figure for his people.

Hansen notes the way Paul's mission speech to Jews in Acts 13 is characterized as the word of God. This is so because it is an exposition of scripture and proclaims the testimony of divinely authorized witnesses to the resurrection of Jesus. Paul's sermon expands major Lukan theological themes such as salvation history, promise and fulfilment, and the people of God, but its primary concern is with the resurrection and its implications.[10] Paul's incomplete address to pagan worshippers in Acts 14 needs to be read in the light of his speech to the Athenians in Acts 17. His command to forsake idolatry and turn to the living God is ultimately grounded on the proclamation of Jesus' resurrection, which indicates a turning point in God's dealings with the nations and gives proof of impending judgement. Paul's defence speeches before Jewish and Roman authorities (Acts 21–28) reveal him as essentially a witness to the resurrection, personally commissioned by the risen Lord. In these concluding chapters, Luke confirms that Paul's word must be accepted by both Jews and Gentiles as the word of the Lord.

The renewing work of God

The significance of the Spirit for Luke's view of salvation and the role of the Spirit in effecting the call to enjoy that salvation has already been noted. M. Turner begins the third section of this volume with a more extensive discussion of the pneumatology of Acts. This is based on Jewish conceptions of the 'Spirit of prophecy', now poured out on all who trust in Christ. Others in this section explore what Luke reveals about the character, activity and values of the new people of God.

Acts 2:38-39 paradigmatically associates the gift of the Spirit with conversional faith and baptism. Turner argues that the Spirit is not simply a prophetic empowerment for mission in Acts but is imparted to create and sustain the new community of believers. God's Spirit is firstly the means by which Israel is restored and renewed, in accordance with OT expectations. When Gentiles receive the Spirit and

---

[9]He allows, however, that the lack of explicit criticism of the law may be due to the fact that Stephen does not get to the second accusation mounted against him (cf., 6:13-14).

[10]Hansen rightly observes that, 'The sermon is an event which pulls the audience into the effective orbit of the resurrection event so that those who reject the message are judged 'unworthy of eternal life' (13:46) and those who believe it are 'destined for eternal life (13:48)'.

their hearts are cleansed by faith (15:9), it is clear that God has begun to fulfil the next stage in his saving plan. The blessing promised to Abraham's offspring can now be enjoyed by 'all the families of the earth' (3:25; cf., Gen. 22:18; 26:4), since God is taking from among the Gentiles 'a people for his name' (15:14). Through the Spirit, the exalted Lord Jesus fulfils the divine plan to renew Israel and uses his witnesses to bring his salvation to the ends of the earth (1:8; 13:47; cf., Isa. 49:6).

D. Seccombe develops this last theme, asserting that Luke wanted to show how the focus of God's saving plan had moved from a racially determined Jewish community to a non-racial, worldwide fellowship, composed of Jews, Samaritans and Gentiles. Thus, the notion of the people of God was transformed within early Christianity and 'world history turned in a radically new direction'. But the idea of a new people lagged behind the reality. Acts is structured to allow a proper understanding to emerge from the sequence of events it records. For example, Stephen's use of ἐκκλησία in Acts 7:37-8 makes it clear that, in calling themselves 'the church', Christians were claiming to be one with the congregation which gathered at Sinai. The rest of Acts shows how those from other races and cultures were drawn together with believing Jews into that fellowship, through faith in Christ and by receiving the Holy Spirit.

Seccombe suggests that the pattern of Paul's Jew-Gentile mission is commended by Luke as 'the way mission should be', because it expresses the sort of ecclesiology revealed in the first half of Acts. Paul's turning away from the Jews was never theologically motivated nor final, but forced upon him by Jewish rejection.[11] Indeed, many Jews and proselytes continued to respond positively to his preaching and join with converted Gentiles to form the church. Gentiles, however, could seek the Lord from within their own culture and not by becoming Jews, as the debate in Acts 15 makes clear. The covenant with Israel does not determine the full boundary of the eschatological people of God.[12]

Seccombe holds that Luke's respect for Judaism, together with his passionate concern to establish the validity of the new people of

---

[11]Even Acts 28 does not indicate 'the termination of any mission to the Jews in favour of a Gentile Christian church, to which is transferred all the covenant privileges of Israel'. Cf., Palmer, 'Mission', 62-73.
[12]The new people of God is neither 'a renewed Jewry expanded by an inflow of proselytes' nor a Gentile 'new Israel' from which Jews have departed but a fellowship of Jews, Samaritans and Gentiles, who share in the blessings of eschatological salvation through Christ.

God, particularly the legitimacy of Gentile Christianity, 'presupposes its novelty and fragility against a Judaism with strength and unquestioned antiquity'. This suggests that Acts may have been written before the outbreak of the Jewish War in AD 66. At that time, the interface between church and synagogue was still fluid and better opportunities remained for winning undecided God-fearers and Jews for Christ.

C. Blomberg confirms Seccombe's assertion that Luke is propounding a law-free view of the church. Step by step, Acts portrays Christianity's progressive departure from its nationalistic Jewish heritage. For example, in Acts 10 it becomes clear that the dietary laws are no longer applicable even for Jews. The Apostolic Decree in Acts 15 provides *ad hoc* advice to Gentiles about how to avoid giving offence to certain Jews. The Mosaic Law as a code of customs is given neither soteriological nor ecclesiological significance for Christians. Paul's flexibility with regard to the circumcision of Timothy and his observance of other Jewish customs is best understood in terms of his missionary strategy, (*cf.*, 1 Cor. 9:20). In the concluding chapters of Acts, Paul the prisoner proclaims that his religion is the true fulfilment of Jewish hopes. But that is no basis for claiming that he or Luke promoted a Torah-observant Christianity.

P. Towner argues that there is a change of Paul's missionary pattern in the portrayal of Acts. In the early period it was synagogue-based, seeking to replicate the model of the church in Syrian Antioch. Ministry to Gentiles was conducted more or less on the run, as Paul was forced to flee his Jewish opponents. In Corinth, however, a special word from the Lord encouraged him to stay for an extended period of time (18:9-11). He then carried out his ministry to Jews and Gentiles in a neutral setting, which was nevertheless in close proximity to the synagogue. Certain historical realities, together with a new or more developed definition of God's people, brought about this change of strategy. The same pattern emerges in the account of his stay in Ephesus, without any formal announcement of a turn to the Gentiles or specific word from the Lord. A considerable influence on both Jews and Gentiles resulted (19:10).[13]

With Seccombe, R. Wall notes the parallels between Paul's

---

[13]Towner argues that Paul's address to the Ephesian elders in Acts 20 reflects the convergence of developments in Corinth and Ephesus, both with respect to Paul's strategy and his view of the church. The letters of Paul that can be assigned to this period are also said to reveal in some way 'the growing realization of a new identification of God's people'.

teaching in Romans 9-11 and Luke's presentation of the partial hardening that has come upon Israel. Paul and Luke also affirm in different ways that divine election extends to Gentiles. One role of Acts within the NT canon is to supply a narrative setting that deepens our understanding of the redefinition of the people of God found 'at the epicenter of Paul's theological conception'. The extended citations from the prophecies of Joel in Acts 2 and Amos in Acts 15 play a major role in organizing the narrative and its theological subject matter. Both texts provide biblical justification for Luke's account of the movement of God's universal salvation from Jerusalem to Rome. The first half of Acts is viewed as a narrative commentary on Joel 3:1-5 (LXX) and the second half as a commentary on Amos 9:11-12 (LXX).[14]

My own contribution argues that a new theology of worship is being enunciated in Acts, with Jesus at its centre. The exalted Lord Jesus is presented as the new point of contact between heaven and earth, fulfilling the role of the temple in God's purpose for Israel and the nations. From another perspective, Christian life and ministry is viewed as the way to worship or serve God under the New Covenant. Ministry in the public sphere becomes the means of inviting people to call upon the name of Jesus and participate in the blessings of the new community. Ministry in the private sphere is an expression of the relationships engendered through faith in Christ and an exercise of the responsibilities entailed through membership of the church.

The community life depicted in the early part of Acts fulfils the OT hopes set forth in Luke 1–2 of an Israel free of oppressors, joyfully worshipping God without fear, serving him in holiness and righteousness, with poverty and hunger banished by the caring rich. Blue argues that many of the activities described resemble those of Jewish house-synagogues in Palestine and the Dispersion. Indeed, 'the structure and strategy of the emergent Christian community reflect the struggles within the new community in special reference to the broader communities, particularly the Jewish community'. As in Judaism, for example, there was a focus on communal meals, but without the concern to observe ritual laws and dietary purity. The community meal took on added significance when Gentiles were converted and eating together became '*the* litmus test in determining the validity of the gospel message'.

---

[14]In slightly different terms from Seccombe, Wall argues that Acts 'radically redraws the borders of a true Israel to include even those found in Rome'. It is doubtful, however, that Luke identifies the totality of the new people of God specifically as 'a true Israel'.

Although property-sharing is described with particular enthusiasm in Acts 2–6, this never becomes a formal requirement. Indeed, almsgiving becomes the model in later chapters. Noting the connection of this community of goods with the 'Golden Age' in Graeco–Roman literature, B. Capper suggests that Luke intended his readers to understand that a new beginning was made for humanity through the birth of the Christian Church.[15] Palestinian community of goods functioned principally through regular meal-fellowship. Luke's challenge to those he addressed was for such fellowship to extend 'beyond the conventions of reciprocity', transcending the barriers between rich and poor, so that 'some real imitation of earliest Christian community of goods could be made'.

IV. Luke's intention

Acts as an apology

Acts has sometimes been regarded as a precursor of the works of Justin Martyr and other apologists of the second and early third centuries A.D., but the apologetic aim of the book has been variously identified. For some, it is the defence of Christianity to a Roman audience, presenting it as a law-abiding movement, constituting no threat to imperial peace and order.[16] In particular it has been argued that Acts may have been offered as a kind of brief for use in connection with the trial of Paul. It is unlikely, however, that Luke wrote specifically to convince Roman officials about the innocence of Paul or of Christianity more generally. 'No Roman official would ever have filtered out so much of what to him would be theological and ecclesiastical rubbish in order to reach so tiny a grain of relevant apology.'[17]

Some scholars have therefore urged that the apologetic dimension to Luke's work was a means to another end. His ultimate purpose

---

[15]Seccombe also notes that Luke's presentation of the fellowship and generosity of the earliest Christian community would have signalled to Hellenistic readers that something remarkable was taking place in Jerusalem, 'for he uses evocative language suggesting the attainment of unattainable Greek ideals of true friendship'.

[16]E.g., Bruce, 'Apologetic', 379-393; 'Historical Record', 2598-2600. Bruce notes various life-settings when this particular apologetic may have been relevant.

[17]Barrett, *Luke*, 63. Cf., Maddox, *Purpose*, 91-9.

was to bring educated pagans to faith in Christ.[18] A strong argument in favour of this position is the fact that a Gospel precedes Acts and that many of the speeches in Acts are evangelistic. It must be said again, however, that much in Luke–Acts seems to be irrelevant to this purpose. Even a sympathetic outsider would have found it difficult to cope with the repetition and detail of Luke's narrative. The overall shape of Luke–Acts, its contents, and narrative style suggest that it was addressed to a Christian audience, rather than to outsiders.

Following this line, some have argued that Acts was intended to defend Paul's apostolic claims, especially in the matter of the Gentiles, against all attacks of the Judaisers.[19] Luke reports Paul's Jewish practices, omits every trace of Paul's renunciation of the Law, emphasises that Paul is on friendly terms with the primitive church and records parallel miracles, visions, sufferings and speeches of Peter and Paul. In shaping his narrative according to this apologetic purpose, Luke especially sought to establish Paul's good relationship with the primitive church and portray that church in the glory of its own traditions. Jerusalem became the centre of Luke's theological universe and the frame of Paul's ministry, leading him to emphasise the importance of Jerusalem and the temple for Jesus and his ministry. In so doing, he was able to draw important links between Jesus and Paul.[20]

There are valid and important observations in this approach, but with some distortion of the evidence. When everything is interpreted so as to establish the authority and authenticity of Paul's ministry, Paul, rather than Jesus, becomes the key character in Luke–Acts. The proposition that Luke was more concerned to stress continuity with Judaism than discontinuity is assessed by several contributors. More fundamental than a defence of Paul is the whole question of the way in which God's saving plan has been fulfilled, especially as that fulfilment bears on the identity and nature of the people of God.

---

[18]Cf., O'Neill, *Theology of Acts*, 172-185, and the contributions by Bruce mentioned in note 15.

[19]Cf., Mattill, 'Purpose of Acts', 108-122; Schneckenburger, *Zweck*, and 'Beiträge', 498-570; also Trocmé, *Le 'livre des Actes'*; Jervell, *Luke*.

[20]Mattill makes much of what he perceives as intentional parallels between Luke's Gospel and Acts. Cf., 'Jesus-Paul parallels', 15-46. In so doing, he also draws on the arguments of R. B. Rackham about Acts being composed in the early sixties, before the end of Paul's imprisonment, as a personal defence of Paul. Cf., Mattill, 'Date and Purpose', 335-350.

Acts as a work of edification

A growing number of scholars propose that the book of Acts is a work of edification for Christians, rather than an apology for outsiders or for dissident groups such as Judaisers. For example, with considerable scepticism about the historicity of Luke's account, E. Haenchen envisages it being written to edify the churches and 'thereby contribute its part in spreading the Word of God farther and farther, even to the ends of the earth'.[21] With greater confidence in the historical reliability of Acts, I.H. Marshall also argues that it was intended as 'an account of Christian beginnings in order to strengthen faith and give assurance that its foundation is firm'.[22]

(1) An eschatological corrective for a church in crisis. I will not dwell on the theory of H. Conzelmann, that Luke wrote to deal with problems created by the delay of Christ's return.[23] Conzelmann argued that Luke recast the prophecies of Jesus to locate the eschatological consummation in an indefinite future and represented the gift of the Holy Spirit as a substitute for that fulfilment, not as a part of it. Since the present life of the church has no eschatological quality, Luke's readers were urged to accommodate themselves to peaceful relationships with the Roman Empire, sustained by their knowledge of what God had done in Christ, and to live in the world without any expectancy of an imminent end.

Conzelmann's approach has been criticised in many ways.[24] Various articles in the present volume confirm that the period of the church is as much a time of fulfilment for Luke as the period of Jesus' ministry. Nolland, in particular, insists that Luke does not think in terms of sharply delineated periods of salvation-history: 'the same story keeps repeating, but in different keys and with a definite sense of escalation towards a climax represented by the Parousia'. The 'eschatological corrective' approach to Luke–Acts is quite inadequate.

(2) A reassurance for wavering believers. Noting that Luke offered his readers *kerygma*, rather than biography in his first volume, W.C. van Unnik proposed that 'Acts is the confirmation (βεβαίωσις) of what

[21]Haenchen, 'Source Material', 278.
[22]Marshall, *Acts: Commentary*, 21. *Cf.*, his 'Luke and his "Gospel"', 289-308.
[23]*Cf.*, Conzelmann, *Die Mitte der Zeit*.
[24]*Cf.*,Maddox, *Purpose*, 100-57, for a summary and critique of different approaches to Luke's eschatology.

God did in Christ in the first book'.[25] Luke's purpose in writing a sequel to his Gospel was not simply to recount the spread of Christianity from Jerusalem to Rome. His narrative is highly selective and is dominated by key words, phrases and themes such as witness, salvation, signs and wonders, the jealousy of the Jews, the persecution of Christians, exhortations, visions, and the constant refrain 'the word of God grew and multiplied' or something similar. These are indications of Luke's primary concern.

Van Unnik noted a number of parallels with Hebrews 2:3-4, the thrust of which he outlined in these terms:

> *There is a solid bridge between the saving activity of Jesus and people living at a distance who have had no personal contact with the incarnate Lord.* The solidity of this bridge consists in the *confirmation* of the salvation by the apostles, sanctioned by God through miraculous gifts. But it is possible to reject this eternal salvation in Christ through unbelief, disobedience and sin (*cf.*, ch. iii, iv). The exhortation of this letter is a call to firmness in the faith.[26]

Acts is said to have been similarly written for believers who were wavering in their faith, to reassure them that the gospel they received is the word of salvation for the whole world. To support his theory, van Unnik showed how the theme of salvation is central to the apostolic preaching in Acts, how the testimony of the apostles to that salvation is central to their role, and how God used signs and wonders to confirm their testimony in the face of much suffering and persecution. Despite the opposition from Jewish and pagan quarters, 'the word' continued to grow and multiply. This perspective on apostolic times is Luke's way of encouraging readers to hold fast to the gospel and the salvation it offers.

To some extent, Robert Maddox's significant work was a development of similar insights. Maddox set out to establish that Luke–Acts is a work aimed at 'reassuring the Christian community about the significance of the tradition and faith in which it stands'.[27] The preface in Luke 1:1-4 gives little immediate indication of the author's purpose, but two words stand out for Maddox as evident markers of Luke's intention. His subject matter is the things that have been 'fulfilled' (πεπληροφορημένων)[28] amongst God's people and

---

[25]van Unnik, 'Confirmation of the Gospel', 58. *Cf.*, Minear, 'Dear Theo.', 148-9.
[26]van Unnik, 'Confirmation of the Gospel', 48.
[27]Maddox, *Purpose*, 186.

Luke's aim is to allow the readers to perceive 'the reliability' (τὴν ἀσφάλειαν) of the message they have heard.

The story of Jesus, the apostles and the growing church is a story of 'fulfilment' in more than one sense. The full stream of God's saving action in history has flowed straight into the community life of those addressed. Luke writes to reassure them that 'their faith in Jesus is no aberration, but the authentic goal towards which God's ancient dealings with Israel were driving'.[29] With such a message of reassurance, Luke summons his fellow Christians 'to worship God with whole-hearted joy, to follow Jesus with unwavering loyalty, and to carry on with zeal, through the power of the Spirit, the charge to be his witnesses to the end of the earth'.[30]

Examining the total shape of Luke–Acts, Maddox notes how Luke emphasizes that 'the character of the Christian life in the church cannot be understood apart from its foundation in the incarnation, mission, death, resurrection and ascension of Jesus. Conversely, the story of Jesus cannot properly be appreciated without following it through to its outcome in the church.'[31] Maddox rightly points to the importance of the opening and closing sections of Luke–Acts for a consideration of the author's purpose. Luke 1–2 indicates how Jesus will fulfil the promises of Scripture and the hopes of Israel, while at the same time bringing 'a light for revelation to the Gentiles' (Luke 2:32). Acts 21–28 shows how that hope continued to be offered to Jews, even as the gospel was being received by Gentiles, from Jerusalem to Rome. But why should a concentration on Paul's imprisonment and trials be the concluding section of a work whose first half is in the form of a Gospel?

Luke's narrative method is normally to paint an individual portrait or scene, rather than to describe a general development. This is a warning against taking his concentration on Paul as 'necessarily implying a strictly personal interest in him'.[32] Paul is more important for what he represents than for his own sake. Maddox also insists that

---

[28]So NRSV, rightly improving on the bland rendering of RSV ('the things which have been *accomplished* among us'). Cf., Fitzmyer, *Luke I-IX*, 292-3.

[29]Maddox, *Purpose*, 187. Cf., Fitzmyer, *Luke I-IX*, 8-11; Peterson, 'The Motif of Fulfilment', 83-104.

[30]Maddox, *Purpose*, 187.

[31]Maddox, *Purpose*, 10. It is probably an overstatement to say that a major concern of Luke is 'to explore and explain the nature of the church'.

[32]Maddox, *Purpose*, 70. Luke would hardly have failed to report Paul's death if his interest was really in the person of Paul as such.

Luke chose to set Paul apart from the Twelve, rather than to assimilate him to them. The distinction is one of time and function, not of rank. 'The Apostles had to lay the true, historical foundation of faith in Jesus, but Paul and his contemporaries had the honour of carrying out a geographically far greater part of the Lord's commission in Acts 1:8.'[33] Paul is the bridge leading from the original, apostolic age down to Luke's own day and is 'chief representative and symbol of that great second generation of Christians, to whom Luke and his friends are indebted for their faith'.[34]

More precisely, Paul stands out as one who is persecuted and suffers for his faith in Christ. But nothing that happens to him can seriously weigh him down. Luke portrays Paul in his persecutions and long imprisonment in such a way as to warn and encourage his contemporary fellow-Christians that this is what the Christian life is like (cf., Acts 14:22). 'But through the Holy Spirit and the Word of God these afflictions are turned into mere annoyances, which a resolute Christian can easily endure.'[35]

These observations on the concluding chapters of Acts are an important contribution to the debate about Luke's purpose. I will return to such matters at the end of this chapter. Meanwhile, it is important to note theories that take account of some of Luke's other concerns.

(3) A defence of God's saving plan. L.T. Johnson revives the view that Luke–Acts is an apology,[36] but describes it as an apology directed to *believers* rather than to unbelievers. Luke followed the model of Jewish apologetic literature at that time, which had a dual function. It sought to defend Jews against misunderstanding and persecution by outsiders, while aiming to help Jews understand their own traditions within a pluralistic context, 'by bringing an outsider perspective to bear on them'.[37] Luke wrote to give his Christian readers 'full confidence' (τὴν ἀσφάλειαν, Luke 1:4) by the way he told his story 'in sequence' (καθεξῆς, Luke 1:3).[38]

---

[33]Maddox, *Purpose*, 75.

[34]Maddox, *Purpose*, 77.

[35]Maddox, *Purpose*, 82. In my view, however, opposition and persecution in Acts are more than 'mere annoyances, which the resolute Christian can easily endure'. They are part of the very process by which God furthers his purpose in the world.

[36]Johnson, *Acts*, 7. Although Johnson is reasonably confident about Luke's accuracy as a historian, he insists that, 'recognizing the *ways* in which Luke literarily shapes his narrative, in fact, is an important step toward recognizing the *kind* of history he was attempting to write'.

In the broadest sense, his apology is a theodicy, defending God's activity in the world. Ostensibly it addresses a wider audience in the clothing of Greek literature, but its main interest is 'to construct a continuation of the biblical story for Gentile believers in order to help them come to grips with a profound puzzle generated by their own recent experience'.[39] This conclusion fits well with many of the insights found elsewhere in this volume. On the one hand, Luke develops a biblical theology for readers with some biblical knowledge and insight. On the other hand, he uses language and concepts that would have been understood in particular ways against a Graeco–Roman background. In so doing, he shows how Christianity fulfils biblical hopes in a way that is relevant for Jews and Gentiles together.

Luke–Acts celebrates the success of the Gentile mission, with Theophilus and those he represents being among its fruit. The success of that mission, however, has created a serious problem of confidence in the very God who accomplished it. Gentiles have only been converted, it seems, because the Jews have rejected the gospel. Are the Jews correct and Jesus is not Messiah? It follows that Gentile believers are not authentically God's people. Or has God not been faithful to his promises and abandoned the Jews as his people?

Luke shows by the sequence of events that he presents how God first brought salvation to Israel. His skilful development of the plot has persuasive force. Acts 1–8 first highlights the eschatological 'restoration of Israel', illustrating the fulfilment of hopes and promises enunciated in the opening chapters of the Gospel. Acts 9–28 then goes on to describe the Gentile mission, 'not as a replacement of Israel but as its legitimate continuation'.[40] Since God has shown himself faithful to the Jews, the word that has reached the Gentiles can be trusted. Johnson argues that a number of frequently noticed tendencies in Acts

---

[37]Johnson, *Luke*, 9. Such literature could provide security or reassurance to Jewish readers 'by demonstrating within a pluralistic context the antiquity and inherent value of their traditions'. *Cf., idem.*, 'Luke–Acts', 404-20.

[38]It appears from Luke's use of καθεξῆς in Luke. 8:1; Acts 3:24; 11:4; 18:23, and his delight in telling how events happened 'in order' (*e.g.*, Acts 9:26-7; 15:12-14), that he thought this narrative method to have 'a distinctively convincing quality' (Johnson, *Luke*, 4).

[39]Johnson, *Acts*, 7. Johnson notes the literary devices by which Luke achieves his end: narrative summaries, speeches, journey narratives and parallelism in the accounts of what happened to Peter and Paul. *Cf.*, Snook, 'Luke's Theodicy', 304-11.

[40]Johnson, *Acts*, 9. Johnson rightly argues that 'the crisis concerning God's fidelity to his people is resolved in the narrative of Acts 1–7' (14).

make particular sense within this overall framework.[41]

Luke's most comprehensive way of structuring his entire two-volume work is by means of 'literary prophecy'. In a variety of ways, he stresses the fulfilment of OT expectations, as well as the fulfilment of prophecies uttered by characters within his own narrative. This serves to strengthen his presentation of the missionaries as 'prophetic figures moved by the Spirit' and his work as a continuation of biblical history.[42] It also helps Luke's readers to perceive how 'the matters that have been brought to fulfilment among us' are events directed by God.

C.H. Talbert and J.T. Squires have both argued in a somewhat similar way, demonstrating parallels between Luke's use of the prophecy-fulfilment motif and the emphasis in Hellenistic histories that history fulfils divine oracles.[43] It is likely that Luke highlighted the OT roots of Christianity and the fulfilment of Scripture in the events that he records for more than strictly theological or hortatory reasons. His approach would have given Greek-speaking Christians the chance to appeal to an argument from antiquity, allowing them to feel 'not the least bit inferior to pagans with their cultural and religious claims allegedly rooted in antiquity'.[44] In a social context where such matters were considered important, Luke–Acts offered Christians a confident basis from which to address their contemporaries.

Squires notes the need to consider two special features of Luke's work: '(1) the Jewishness of Christianity throughout the whole of Luke–Acts, especially concerning the role of Hebrew scripture; (2) the Hellenization of Christianity, especially (but not exclusively) in the appropriate sections of Acts.'[45] He concludes that Luke–Acts is a kind of cultural 'translation', an attempt to explain and defend Christianity to Hellenized Christians. Various techniques familiar to educated

---

[41]Johnson, *Acts*, 9-12.

[42]Johnson, *Acts*, 12. Johnson argues that Luke's literary use of prophecy extends to the portrayal of his characters and to the overall structuring of his two-volume work (12-14). *Cf.*, more fully, Johnson, *Luke*, 15–21, and Peterson, 'The Motif of Fulfilment', 83-104.

[43]*Cf.*, Talbert, 'Promise and Fulfillment', 91-103; as well as his *Reading Luke*, 234-240; Squires, *Plan of God*.

[44]Talbert, *Reading Luke*, 240. At one level, therefore, the prophecy-fulfilment motif is 'a legitimation device' in the Lukan narrative, just as it was in Mediterranean antiquity generally.

[45]Squires, *Plan of God*, 190. Luke's readers (typified by Theophilus) would have been personally aware 'both of the Jewish origins and heritage of Christianity and of the generally "hellenized" context within which the Gospel spread and within which they now live' (191).

readers from contemporary histories are embedded into the story of Luke–Acts to show how the gospel related to their thought-world. Luke's appeal is to 'insiders', using categories provided by 'outsiders'.

Although the primary audience for which Luke wrote is the Christian community, his apologetic method offered Christians a 'missionary tool', to assist them in evangelism.[46] This attempt to outline the continuity between Christians and Israel and between the events of Jesus' career and OT prophecies was an important aspect of Luke's response to criticisms of Christianity that may have been made by Jews and pagans. Moreover, his presentation of Jesus and the early church facing objections and offering plausible explanations in their times would enable the readers to do the same, should the need arise in their own time.

Johnson, Talbert and Squires agree that Luke–Acts is primarily a work for the encouragement of Christians, simultaneously providing them with resources for dealing with outsiders. In particular, Johnson has shown that a central concern is to demonstrate God's faithfulness in fulfilling his promises to Israel. Luke offered a valuable reassurance for Gentile converts about their own position as well as an encouragement to continue evangelising unbelieving Israel. With this I wholeheartedly agree.

In my judgement, however, these scholars have not given adequate place to the motifs of suffering and of the progress of the word through opposition and conflict, highlighted in several contributions to this volume and noted by Maddox. Their reconstruction of the life-situation of the original recipients is helpful as far as it goes, but each one envisages the readers' struggle in somewhat rarefied and cerebral terms, focusing on theological uncertainties and debates with intelligent outsiders. What follows is an attempt to supplement the conclusions of Johnson, Talbert and Squires with a *pastoral* aim that is also suggested by Luke's narrative.

(4) A reassurance about the triumph of the word through suffering. The degree to which opposition and division are represented as the context for gospel growth in the apostolic period implies that Luke was concerned to encourage those who were under similar threat in his own time. Luke's pastoral aim was achieved by the way he structured his narrative, juxtaposing various accounts of suffering with assurances about the triumph of 'the word'. 'Persecution, hard-

---

[46]Cf., Squires, *Plan of God*, 192-4.

ships, troubles, martyrdom, and disputes between Christians and non-Christians (sometimes even between Christians and Christians) provide the theological and literary framework for Acts.'[47]

Opposition from unbelievers normally follows gospel ministry in Luke's narrative, where the focus is on God's use of such situations to further his purposes.[48] Within this framework, Acts also records the resolution of significant difficulties in the nascent Christian communities[49] and deliverance from other disasters that could have impeded the work of the gospel.[50] Suffering regularly provides the opportunity for more ministry[51] and is intimately connected with the growth of 'the word'.

This last point is extremely significant. Many commentators have observed the use of narrative summaries as a literary device in Acts. Three key summaries are used throughout the book to indicate the way 'the word of God continued to spread' (ηὔξανεν, 6:7), how 'the word of God continued to advance and gain adherents' (ηὔξανεν καὶ ἐπληθύνετο, 12:24) and how 'the word of the Lord grew mightily and prevailed' (ηὔξανεν καὶ ἴσχυεν, 19:20). This unusual application of the language of growth signifies the advance of the gospel and the movement it creates.[52] Churches continued to be founded and nurtured by the power of the message about Jesus.

In addition to these key texts, there are many references to the way the word of the Lord was proclaimed and received (e.g., 8:4, 14, 25; 10:44; 11:1, 19; 13:5, 7, 44, 48; 14:3, 25; 15:35-6; 16:6, 32; 17:11, 13; 18:5, 11), so that it 'spread' (διεφέρετο, 13:49) through previously unreached regions (cf., 19:10). The word is the real 'hero' of Luke's narrative![53] Other references speak more specifically about the growth of churches

---

[47]House, 'Suffering', 320, notes at least five basic functions of suffering in Acts and relates it to: (1) the expanding gospel, (2) the defence of Christianity, (3) the defence of Paul, (4) the foundations of Christianity, (5) Luke's portrayal of Paul.

[48]Acts 4:1-22; 5:17-40; 6:8-14; 7:54–8:3; 12:1-23; 13:6-11, 44-5, 50-1; 14:2-6, 19-20; 16:16-39; 17:5-9, 13-14; 18:12-17; 19:13-16, 23-41; 20:3; 21:27-40; 22:22-9; 23:12-35; 25:1-7; 28:24-9.

[49]Acts 5:1-11; 6:1-6; 8:18-24; 9:1-30; 11:27-30; 15:1-34, 36-41; 21:20-6.

[50]Acts 11:27-30; 27:1-44; 28:1-6.

[51]Acts 4:23-37; 5:12-16, 41-2; 6:7-8; 6: 15–7:53; 8:4-40; 9:31–11:26; 12:24–13:5; 13:12-43, 46-9; 13:52–14:1; 14:7-18, 21-8; 15:35; 16:1-15; 17:1-4, 10-12; 17:15–18:11; 18:18 - 19:12; 19:17-22; 20:1-2; 20:4–21:19; 22:1-21; 22:30–23:11; 24:1-27; 25:8–26:32; 28:7-23, 30-31.

[52]'Luke sees the word so bound up with the community life and witness that he can say 'The word of God grew' when the church adds new members', (Kodell, 'Word', 518).

resulting from gospel ministry (*cf.*, 9:31; 16:5). Acts concludes with the picture of Paul under house arrest in Rome, 'proclaiming the kingdom of God and teaching about the Lord Jesus Christ with all boldness and without hindrance' (28:31).

Luke's placement of the three critical statements about the word of God growing and multiplying (6:7; 12:24; 19:20) is far from casual or ornamental. Each climaxes a section of the narrative recording the resolution of some conflict or the cessation of opposition and persecution. The gospel is shown to prosper in spite of, and even because of, suffering. By implication, 'nothing can stop the gospel but its spread still causes grief and loss'.[54] In fact, four major sections of Acts are demarcated by these texts:[55]

1:1–6:7 Development of the church in Jerusalem under the leadership of the Twelve. The transitional summary in 6:7 indicates that 'growth' of the word followed the satisfactory resolution of conflict in the church with the appointment of the Seven (*cf.*, 6:1-6).

6:8–12:24 Unplanned expansion to Judea, Samaria and Gentile areas, with a widening of ministry to include the Seven and others scattered because of the persecution in Jerusalem. The transitional summary in 12:24 indicates that growth of the word followed the release of Peter from prison and the death of Herod, the persecutor of the church (*cf.*, 12:1-23).[56]

12:25–19:20 Planned and organised geographical expansion into Asia Minor and Europe, under the leadership of Paul, emanating from Antioch in Syria. The transitional summary in 19:20 indicates that growth of the word was specifically related to the overcoming of demonic opposition in Ephesus (*cf.*, 19:11-19).[57]

---

[53]'The word of God' is actually mentioned twelve times in Acts, 'the word of the Lord' ten times, 'the word' ten times, 'the word of his grace' twice, 'the word of the gospel' and 'the word of this salvation' once each.
[54]House, 'Suffering', 323.
[55]*Cf.*, Grumm, 'Another Look at Acts', 335-6. The growth and progress of the word is what Grumm calls 'the *cantus firmus* of the message of Acts' (336). He observes a 'natural' growth of the word as well as a growth stemming directly from opposition and persecution.
[56]A further subdivision could be indicated by 9:31, where the church throughout Judea, Galilee and Samaria enjoys peace, encouragement and growth, as a result of Saul's conversion and the persecution for which he was responsible (*cf.*, 9:1-30).

19:21–28:31 The word of the Lord continues to grow and prevail, even though Paul is persecuted and arrested. The focus is on Paul's testimony to the gospel when he is on trial, climaxing with the statement about the free course of the word when he is under arrest in Rome (28:30-1). At the same time, various travel companions are mentioned, suggesting that the progress of the word will continue through such as these.

In each major division of the book there are speeches by key characters that clearly advance the action. Far from being merely 'narrative filler',[58] they are different expressions of 'the word' that is the focus of Luke's story and the basis of Christian life and witness. The speeches represent the apostolic witness to Jesus, with an interpretation of gospel events in the light of Scripture.[59] As such, they continually challenge the reader with the apostolic claims about Jesus. They may also be challenging or anticipating false interpretations of the gospel in the churches addressed by Luke through his patron Theophilus. Luke is not simply assuring the readers of the continuing power and effectiveness of the word but reminding them of the authentic content which God uses to change lives and advance his saving purpose for the world. At the same time, he shows the reader the essential unity of early Christianity in the claims of these speeches.[60]

Acts 21–28 portrays Paul as the missionary prisoner, fulfilling in a particular way the call to suffer for Christ given to him in 9:16. As he endures suffering, he learns to use it to serve the gospel. Seen in this way, Acts gives the reader a theology of suffering that is particularly exemplified by the life and work of the apostle. The dominance of Paul's suffering in the narrative precludes the view that Luke simply attempted to defend Paul against the attack of Jewish Christians. It also calls into question the adequacy of theories about Acts serving in some way as a document in Paul's defence before Caesar. 'Rather than

---

[57]A further subdivision could be indicated by 16:5, where the South Galatian churches are said to have been strengthened in the faith and 'grew daily in numbers'. This is related in the context to Paul's revisiting of those churches with Silas and Timothy, delivering the decisions reached by the Council in Jerusalem (*cf.*, 15:36–16:4).

[58]This unfortunate phrase is used by Johnson, *Acts*, 7.

[59]'Luke tells the story of the early church's bearing witness to God's will and work in Jesus Christ in such a way that the witness itself is offered in the speeches' (Soards, *Speeches*, 194).

[60]Through repetition, 'the unified witness is emphasized and articulated in a manner greater then the capacity of any single speech' (Soards, *Speeches*, 199).

serving a polemical purpose, Paul's suffering defends him as a Christian and as a worthy servant of Jesus'.[61]

Rapske has also noted how Paul, 'far from inspiring the shame and revulsion of associates in ministry, co-religionists and interested pagans, is surrounded by helpers. Christian co-workers stand by the prisoner-missionary rather than taking the easier and safer route of slipping away from him.'[62] Furthermore, Luke is at considerable pains to show how the prisoner-missionary Paul has divine approval. Such observations support the view that Acts was written to strengthen the early Church's witness in the face of opposition and persecution.

Just as one of the chief bases of Christianity is the suffering of Christ, so a main characteristic of the early church is its own suffering. The prominence of Jesus' suffering in the Gospel and the extension of that suffering to his representatives in Acts provides a profound link between the two volumes of Luke's work. Readers are encouraged to follow the example of the earliest believers, and Paul in particular, by holding fast to the same gospel and continuing to be active in its dissemination, even in the face of persecution from without and conflict from within the churches.[63]

---

[61]House, 'Suffering', 328.
[62]Rapske, *Paul in Roman Custody*, 434-35.
[63]*Cf.*, Maddox, *Purpose*, 82.

Bibliography

Adna, J. *Jesu Kritik am Tempel. Eine Untersuchung zum Verlauf nd Sinn der sogenannt-en Tempelreinigung Jesu, Mk 11,15-17 und Parallelen.* Tübingen/Stavanger: Unpublished PhD dissertation, 1993.

Agnew, F.H. 'The Origin of the New Testament Apostle-Concept: A Review of Research', *JBL* 105 (1986) 75-96.

Aker, B. 'New Directions in Lucan Theology: Reflections on Luke 3:21-22 and Some Implications' in P. Elbert (ed.), *Faces of Renewal*. Peabody, MA: Hendrickson, 1988, 108-127.

Alexander, L.C.A. 'Acts and Ancient Intellectual Biography' in A.D. Clarke and B.W. Winter (eds.), *The Book of Acts in Its Ancient Literary Setting*, A1CS, vol. 1. Grand Rapids/Carlisle: Eerdmans/Paternoster, 1993, 31–63.

Alexander, L.C.A. *The Preface of Luke–Acts*. Cambridge: CUP, 1993.

Allison, D.C. 'Was There A "Lukan Community"?', *Irish Biblical Studies* 10 (1988) 62-70.

Andersen, T.D. 'The Meaning of ΕΧΟΝΤΕΣ ΧΑΡΙΝ ΠΡΟΣ in Acts 2.47', *NTS* 34 (1988) 604-610.

Arrington, F.L. *The Acts of the Apostles*. Peabody, MA: Hendrickson, 1988.

Attridge, H.W. 'The Philosophical Critique of Religion under the Early Empire', *ANRW* II. 16.1, (1978) 63-4.

Aune, D.E. *Prophecy in Early Christianity and the Ancient Mediterranean World.* Grand Rapids: Eerdmans, 1983.

Aune, D.E. 'The Significance of the Delay of the Parousia for Early Christianity' in G.F. Hawthorne (ed.), *Current Issues in Biblical and Patristic Interpretation.* Grand Rapids: Eerdmans, 1975, 87-109.

Aune, D.E. *The New Testament in its Literary Environment*. Philadelphia: Westminster Press, 1987.

Avigad, N. *Discovering Jerusalem: Recent Archæological Excavations in the Upper City.* Oxford: Basil Blackwell, 1984.

Bachmann, M. *Jerusalem und der Tempel. Die geographisch-theologischen Elemente in der lukanischen Sicht des jüdischen Kultzentrums*, BWANT 109. Stuttgart,

Berlin, Cologne and Mainz: Kohlhammer, 1980.

Balch, D.L. 'The Areopagus Speech: An Appeal to the Stoic Historican Posidonius against Later Stoics and the Epicureans' in D.L. Balch, E. Ferguson and W. Meeks (eds.), *Greeks, Romans and Christians: Essays in Honor of Abraham J. Malherbe*. Minneapolis: Fortress, 1990, 52-79.

Baldry, H.C. 'The idler's paradise in attic comedy', *Greece and Rome* 65 (1953) 49–60.

Bammel, E. 'Sadduzäer und Sadokiden', *ETL* 55 (1979) 107-15.

Banks, R. *Paul's Idea of Community*. Grand Rapids: Eerdmans, 1980.

Barnard, L.W. 'Saint Stephen and Early Alexandrian Christianity', *NTS* 7 (1960/1) 31-45.

Barrett, C.K. 'Shaliah and Apostle' in E. Bammel *et al* (eds.), *Donum Gentilicium. New Testament Studies in Honour of David Daube*. Oxford: Clarendon, 1978, 88-102.

Barrett, C.K. 'Stephen and the Son of man', in W. Eltester and F.H. Kettler (eds.), *Apophoreta*. Berlin: Topelmann, 1964, 32-38.

Barrett, C.K. 'The Acts of the Apostles' in *New Testament Essays*. London: SPCK, 1972, 70-85.

Barrett, C.K. 'Theologia crucis —in Acts?' in C. Andresen and G. Klein (eds.), *Theologia crucis —signum crucis: Festschrift für Erich Dinkler zum 70. Geburtstag*. Tübingen: J.C.B. Mohr (Paul Siebeck), 1979, 73-84.

Barrett, C.K. *A Critical and Exegetical Commentary on the Acts of the Apostles I: Preliminary Introduction and Commentary on Acts I-XIV*. Edinburgh: T. & T. Clark, 1994.

Barrett, C.K. *Church, Ministry and Sacraments in the New Testament*. Carlisle: Paternoster, 1985.

Barrett, C.K. 'Imitatio Christi in Acts' in J.B. Green and M. Turner (eds.), *Jesus of Nazareth, Lord and Christ. Essays on the Historical Jesus and New Testament Christology*. Grand Rapids/Carlisle: Eerdmans/Paternoster, 1994, 251-62.

Barrett, C.K. 'Submerged Christology in Acts' in C. Breytenbach *et al.* (eds.), *Anfänge der Christologie*. Göttingen: Vandenhoeck & Ruprecht, 1991, 237-44.

Barrett, C.K. *The Holy Spirit and the Gospel Tradition*, 2nd edn. London: SPCK, 1966.

Barrett, C.K. *The Signs of An Apostle*. London: Epworth, 1971.

Barrett, C.K. 'Apollos and the Twelve Disciples of Ephesus' in W.C. Weinrich (ed.), *The New Testament Age: Essays in Honor of Bo Reicke*, vol.1. Macon, GA: Mercer, 1984, 29-39.

Barrett, C.K. *Luke the Historian in Recent Study*. London: Epworth, 1961.

Bartchy, S.S. 'Community of Goods in Acts: Idealization or Social Reality?' in B.A. Pearson (ed.), *The Future of Early Christianity: Essays in Honour of Helmut Koester*. Minneapolis: Fortress, 1991, 309-18.

Bartchy, S.S. 'Table Fellowship' in J.B. Green and S. McKnight (eds.), *Dictionary of Jesus and the Gospels*. Downers Grove, IL/Leicester: IVP, 1992, 796-800.

Barton, S.C. 'Early Christianity and the Sociology of the Sect' in F. Watson (ed.), *The Open Text: New Directions for Biblical Studies?* London: SCM, 1993, 140-62.

Barton, S.C. *The Spirituality of the Gospels*. London: SPCK, 1992.

Bauer, W., W.F. Arndt, F.W. Gingrich and F. Danker, *A Greek-English Lexicon of the New Testament and Other Early Christian Literature*. Chicago: University of Chicago Press, 1979.

Baumbach, G. *Das Verständnis des Bösen in den synoptischen Evangelien*, Theologische Arbeiten 19. Berlin: Evangelische Verlagsanstalt, 1963.

Bayer, H.F.*Jesus' Predictions of Vindication and Resurrection*. WUNT 2,20.Tübingen: J.C.B. Mohr (Paul Siebeck), 1986.

Bayer, H.F. 'Christ-Centered Eschatology in Acts 3:17-26' in J.B. Green and M. Turner (eds.), *Jesus of Nazareth, Lord and Christ. Essays on the Historical Jesus and New Testament Christology*. Grand Rapids/Carlisle: Eerdmans/Paternoster, 1994, 236-250.

Beavis, M.A. '"Expecting Nothing in Return": Luke's Picture of the Marginalised', *Interpretation* 48 (1994) 357-368.

Beckwith, R.T. 'The Jewish Background of Christian Worship', in C. Jones, G. Wainwright, and E. Yarnold (eds.), *The Study of Liturgy*. London: SPCK, 1978, 39-51.

Beckwith, R.T. *Daily and Weekly Worship: From Jewish to Christian*. 2nd ed., Bramcote: Grove, 1989.

Berger, K. *Formgeschichte des Neuen Testaments*. Heidelberg: Quelle & Meyer, 1984,

Berger, P.L. and T. Luckmann, *The Social Construction of Reality: A Treatise in the Sociology of Knowledge*. New York and London: Doubleday, 1966.

Bergquist, J.A. '"Good News to the Poor"—Why does This Lukan Motif Appear to Run Dry in the Book of Acts?', *Bangalore Theological Forum* 18 (1986) 1-16.

Betori, G. 'Luke 24:47: Jerusalem and the Beginning of the Preaching to the Pagans in the Acts of the Apostles' in G. O'Collins and G. Marconi (eds.), *Luke and Acts*, ET. New York and Mahwah, NJ: Paulist, 1991, 103–120.

Betz, O. and R. Riesner, *Jesus, Qumran and the Vatican*. London: SCM, 1993.

Blomberg, C.L. 'Marriage, Divorce, Remarriage and Celibacy: An Exegesis of Matthew 19:3-12', *Trinity Journal* 11 (1990) 161-96.

Blomberg, C.L. 'The Law in Luke–Acts', *JSNT* 22 (1984) 53-80.

Blomberg, C.L. *1 Corinthians*. Grand Rapids: Zondervan, 1994.

Blue, B.B. 'Acts and the House Church' in D.W.J. Gill and C. Gempf (eds.), *The Book of Acts in Its Graeco-Roman Setting* , A1CS , vol.2. Grand Rapids/Carlisle: Eerdmans/Paternoster, 1994, 119-222.

Blue, B.B. *Secure the Well-Being of the Family: Christians as Householders and Servants. First-Century Christians in the Graeco-Roman World*. Grand Rapids/Carlisle: Eerdmans/Paternoster, forthcoming.

Bock, D.L. *Luke 1:1–24:53*, BECNT, 2 vols. Grand Rapids: Baker, 1996.

Bock, D.L. 'Use of the Old Testament in the New' in D.S. Dockery, K.A. Mathews and R.B. Sloan (eds.), *Foundations for Biblical Interpretation*. Nashville: Broadman & Holman, 1994, 97-114.

Bock, D.L. *Proclamation from Prophecy and Pattern: Lucan Old Testament Christology*, JSNTSS 12. Sheffield: JSOT Press, 1987.

Bock, D.L. 'The Use of the Old Testament in Luke–Acts: Christology and Mission' in D.J. Lull (ed.), *Society of Biblical Literature 1990 Seminar Papers* 126, 29. Chico, CA: Scholars Press, 1990, 494-511.

Bockmuehl, M.N.A. *Revelation and Mystery* , WUNT 2, 36. Tübingen: J.C.B. Mohr (Paul Siebeck), 1990.

Bolkestein, H. *Wohltätigkeit und Armenpflege im vorchristlichen Altertum*. Utrecht: Oosthoek, 1939.

Booth, W.C. *The Rhetoric of Fiction*, 2nd edn. Harmondsworth: Penguin, 1983.

Borg, M.J. *Conflict, Holiness & Politics in the Teachings of Jesus*. Lewiston: Mellen, 1984.

Borgen, P. 'Jesus Christ, the Reception of the Spirit, and a Cross-National

Community' in J.B. Green and M. Turner (eds.), *Jesus of Nazareth: Lord and Christ. Essays on the Historical Jesus and New Testament Christology.* Grand Rapids/Carlisle: Eerdmans/Paternoster, 1994, 220-35.

Bovon, F. 'Studies in Luke–Acts: Retrospect and Prospect', *HTR* 85 (1992) 175-96.

Bovon, F. *Luc le théologien: Vingt-cinq ans de recherches (1950-1975).* Neuchatel/Paris: Delachaux et Niestlé, 1978; translated and updated as *Luke the Theologian: Thirty-three Years of Research (1950-1983).* Allison Park: Pickwick, 1987.

Bovon, F. 'Das Heil in den Schriften des Lukas' in *Lukas im neuer Sicht: Gesammelte Aufsätze,* BThSt 8. Neukirchen-Vluyn: Neukirchener, 1985, 61-74.

Boyarin, D. *Intertextuality and the Reading of Midrash .* Bloomington: Indiana University Press, 1990.

Braund, D.C. *Augustus to Nero: A Sourcebook on Roman History. 31 BC–AD 68.* London: Crook Helm, 1985.

Brawley, R.L. *Centering on God: Method and Message in Luke–Acts.* Louisville: Westminster and John Knox, 1990.

Brawley, R.L. *Luke–Acts and the Jews: Conflict, Apology, and Conciliation,* SBLMS 33. Atlanta: Scholars Press, 1987.

Brett, M.G. *Biblical Criticism in Crisis?* Cambridge: CUP, 1991.

Brooten, B.J. *Women Leaders in the Ancient Synagogue. Inscriptional Evidence and Background Issues,* Brown Judaic Studies, 36. Chico, CA: Scholars Presss, 1982.

Brown, R.E. *The Birth of the Messiah: A Commentary on the Infancy Narratives in the Gospels of Matthew and Luke,* rev. edn., London/New York: G. Chapman/Doubleday, 1993.

Brown, S. *Apostasy and Perseverance in the Theology of Luke,* AnBib, 36. Rome: Pontifical Biblical Institute, 1969.

Brown, S. 'The Role of the Prologues in Determining the Purpose of Luke–Acts' in C.H. Talbert (ed.), *Perspectives on Luke–Acts.* Danville, VA: Association of Baptist Professors of Religion, 1978, 99-111.

Brox, N. *Zeuge und Märtyrer,* Munich: 1961.

Bruce, F.F. 'Paul's Apologetic and the Purpose of Acts', *BJRL* 69 (1987) 379-393.

Bruce, F.F. 'The Acts of the Apostles: Historical Record or Theological Reconstruction?', *ANRW* II 25.3 (1984) 2570-2603.

Bruce, F.F. 'The Church of Jerusalem in the Acts of the Apostles', *BJRL* 67 (1985) 641-61.

Bruce, F.F. *The Acts of the Apostles: The Greek Text with Introduction and Commentary,* 3rd edn., Grand Rapids/Leicester: Eerdmans/Apollos, 1990.

Bruce, F.F. *The Book of Acts,* rev. edn., Grand Rapids: Eerdmans, 1988.

Bryan, C. 'A Further Look at Acts 16:1-3', *JBL* 107 (1988) 292-94.

Buckwalter, H.D. *The Character and Purpose of Luke's Christology.* University of Aberdeen: Unpublished PhD Dissertation, 1991. Published as *The Character and Purpose of Luke's Christology,* SNTSMS 89. Cambridge: CUP, 1996.

Burchard, C. 'Paulus in der Apostelgeschichte', *TLZ* 100 (1975) 881-95.

Burchard, C. *Der dreizehnte Zeuge. Traditions–und kompositionsgeschichtliche Untersuchungen zu Lukas' Darstellung der Frühzeit des Paulus.* Göttingen: Vandenhoeck & Ruprecht, 1970.

Burkert, W. *Weisheit und Wissenschaft. Studien zu Pythagoras, Philolaos und Platon.* Nürnberg: xx, 1962.

Buss, M.F.-J. *Die Missionspredigt des Apostels Paulus im Pisidischen Antiochie.*

Stuttgart: Katholisches Bibelwerk, 1980.

Busse, U. *Die Wunder des Propheten Jesu: Die Rezeption, Komposition und Interpretation der Wundertradition im Evangelium des Lukas,* FB 24. Stuttgart:
Katholisches Bibelwerk, 1977.

Cadbury, H.J. 'The Summaries in Acts' in F.J. Foakes Jackson and K. Lake (eds.),
The Beginnings of Christianity. Part 1: The Acts of the Apostles, vol. 5. London:
Macmillan, 1933, 392-402.

Cadbury, H.J. *The Book of Acts in History.* New York: Harper, 1955.

Cadbury, H.J. *The Making of Luke–Acts.* London: SPCK, 1958.

Caird, G.B. *The Language and Imagery of the Bible,* Duckworth Studies in Theology.
London: Duckworth, 1980.

Callan, T. 'The Background of the Apostolic Decree (Acts 15:20, 29; 21:25)', *CBQ* 55
(1993) 284-97.

Calvin, J. *The Acts of the Apostles 1-13,* ET. Grand Rapids: Eerdmans, 1979.

Campbell, R.A. *The Elders: Seniority within Earliest Christianity.* Edinburgh: T. & T.
Clark, 1994.

Capper, B.J. 'In der Hand des Ananias. Erwägungen zu 1QS VI,20 und der urchristlichen Gütergemeinschaft', *RQ* 12 (1986) 223-236.

Capper, B.J. 'The Palestinian Cultural Context of Earliest Christian Community of
Goods', in R. Bauckham (ed.), *The Book of Acts in Its Palestinian Setting,* A1CS
Vol. 4. Grand Rapids/Carlisle: Eerdmans/Paternoster, 1995, 324-356.

Capper, B.J. 'The Interpretation of Acts 5.4', *JSNT* 19 (1983) 117-131.

Carroll, J.T. 'Luke's Portrait of the Pharisees', *CBQ* 50 (1988) 604-21.

Carroll, J.T. and J.B. Green, *The Death of Jesus in Early Christianity.* Peabody, MA:
Hendrickson, 1995.

Carroll, J.T. *Response to the End of History: Eschatology and Situation in Luke–Acts,*
SBLDS 92. Atlanta: Scholars Press, 1988.

Carroll, J.T. 'Jesus as Healer in Luke–Acts' in E.H. Lovering, *Society of Biblical Literature 1994 Seminar Papers.* Atlanta: Scholars Press, 1994, 269-85.

Casey, R.P. 'μάρτυς' in F. J. Foakes Jackson and K. Lake (eds.), *The Beginnings of
Christianity. Part 1: The Acts of the Apostles,* vol. 5. London: Macmillan, 1933,
30–37.

Cassidy R.J. and P.J. Scharper (eds.), *Political Issues in Luke–Acts.* Maryknoll, NY:
Orbis, 1983.

Cassidy, R.J. *Society and Politics in the Acts of the Apostles.* Maryknoll, NY: Orbis,
1987.

Catchpole, D.R. 'Paul, James and the Apostolic Decree', *NTS* 23 (1977) 428-44.

Cerfaux, L. 'Témoins du Christ d'après le Livre des Actes', *Recueil Lucien Cerfaux*
(Gembloux, 1954–62) 157–174.

Chance, J.B. *Jerusalem, the Temple and the New Age in Luke–Acts.* Macon, GA: Mercer
University Press, 1978.

Cheetham, F.P. 'Acts ii.47: ἔχοντες χάριν πρὸς ὅλον τὸν λαόν; *ET* 74 (1963) 214-
215.

Cheung, A.T.M. 'A Narrative Analysis of Acts 14:27-15:34: Literary Shaping in
Luke's Account of the Jerusalem Council', *WTJ* 55 (1993) 137-54.

Chevallier, M.A. 'Luc et l'Esprit Saint. A la mémoire du P. Augustin George (1915-
77)', *Revue des Sciences Religieuses* 56 (1982) 1-16.

Clark, A.C. 'Apostleship: Evidence from the New Testament and Early Christian
Literature', *VE* XIX (1989) 49-82.

Clark, D.L. *Rhetoric in Greco-Roman Education.* New York: Columbia University Press, 1957.

Clarke, W. L. 'The Use of the Septuagint in Acts' in F.J. Foakes Jackson and K. Lake (eds.), *The Beginnings of Christianity. Part 1: The Acts of the Apostles*, vol. 2. London: Macmillan, 1922, 66-105.

Cohen, S.J.D. 'Pagan and Christian Evidence on the Ancient Synagogue' in L.I. Levine (ed.), *The Synagogue in Late Antiquity.* Philadelphia: ASOR, 1987, 159-181.

Cohen, S.J.D. 'Was Timothy Jewish (Acts 16:1-3)? Patristic Exegesis, Rabbinic Law, and Matrilineal Descent', *JBL* 105 (1986) 251-68.

Conzelmann, H. 'The Address of Paul on the Areopagus' in L.E. Keck and J. L. Martyn (eds.), *Studies in Luke–Acts: Essays in Honor of Paul Schubert.* Nashville: Abingdon Press, 1966, 217-30.

Conzelmann, H. *Acts of the Apostles*, Hermeneia, ET. Philadelphia: Fortress, 1987.

Conzelmann, H. *An Outline of the Theology of the New Testament*, ET. London: SCM, 1969.

Conzelmann, H. *Die Mitte der Zeit: Studien zur Theologie des Lukas.* Tübingen: J.C.B. Mohr (Paul Siebeck), 1954; ET: *The Theology of St. Luke*, London and New York: Faber & Faber and Harper & Row, 1960.

Conzelmann, H. Reviews of the two editions of J. C.O'Neill, *The Theology of Acts*, in *TLZ* 87 (1962) 253-55 and *TLZ* 96 (1971) 584f.

Cook, M.J. 'The Mission to the Jews in Acts: Unraveling Luke's "Myth of the Myriads"', in J.B.Tyson (ed.), *Luke–Acts and the Jewish People: Eight Critical Perspectives*.Minneapolis: Augsburg, 1988, 102-123.

Corley, K.E. *Private Women, Public Meals: Social Conflict in the Synoptic Tradition.* Peabody, MA: Hendrickson, 1993.

Cosgrove, C.H. 'The Divine ΔEI in Luke–Acts: Investigations into the Lukan Understanding of God's Providence', *NovT* 26 (1984) 168-90.

Crump, D.M. 'Jesus, The Victorious Scribal-Intercessor in Luke's Gospel', *NTS* 38 (1992) 51-65.

Crump, D.M. *Jesus the Intercessor. Prayer and Christology in Luke–Acts*, WUNT 2.49. Tübingen: J.C.B. Mohr (Paul Siebeck), 1992.

Cullmann, O. 'Dissensions Within The Early Church', *USQR* 22 (1967) 83-92.

Dahl, N.A. '"A People for His Name" (Acts XV.14)', *NTS* 4 (1957-58) 319-27.

Dahl, N.A. *Studies in Paul.* Minneapolis: Augsburg, 1977..

Danker, F.W. 'Graeco-Roman Cultural Accommodation in the Christology of Luke–Acts' in K.H. Richards (ed.), *Society of Biblical Literature 1983 Seminar Papers.* Chico, CA: Scholars Press, 1983, 391-414.

Danker, F.W. 'Imaged through Beneficence' in D.D. Sylva (ed.), *Reimaging the Death of Jesus*, BBB 73. Frankfurt: Anton Hain, 1990, 57-67,184-86.

Danker, F.W. 'Reciprocity in the Ancient World and in Acts 15:23-29' in R. J. Cassidy and P. J. Scharper (eds.), *Political Issues in Luke–Acts.* Maryknoll, NY: Orbis, 1983, 49-58.

Danker, F.W. *Benefactor: Epigraphic Study of a Graeco-Roman and New Testament Semantic Field.* St. Louis: Clayton, 1982.

Danker, F.W. *Jesus and the New Age: A Commentary on St. Luke's Gospel*, 2nd edn. Philadelphia: Fortress, 1988.

Darr, J.A. *On Character Building: The Reader and the Rhetoric of Characterization in Luke–Acts.* Louisville: Westminster and John Knox, 1992.

Degenhardt, H.-J. *Lukas: Evangelist der Armen*. Stuttgart: Katholisches Bibelwerk, 1965.

Delebecque, E. *Les Actes des Apôtres*. Paris: Belles Lettres, 1982.

Den Boer, W. *Private Morality in Greece and Rome*. Leiden: E.J. Brill, 1979.

DeSilva, D.A. 'Paul's Sermon in Antioch of Pisidia', *BSac* 151 (1994) 32-49.

Dibelius, M. *Studies in the Acts of the Apostles*. London: SCM, 1956.

Dickinson, R.Jr. 'The Theology of the Jerusalem Conference: Acts 15:1-35', *ResQ* 32 (1990) 65-83.

Dietrich, W. *Das Petrusbild der lukanischen Schriften*. Stuttgart: Kohlhammer, 1972.

Dillon, R.J. 'The Prophecy of Christ and His Witnesses according to the Discourses of Acts', *NTS* 32 (1986) 544-56.

Dillon, R.J. 'Easter Revelation and Mission Program in Luke 24:46–48' in D. Durken (ed.), *Sin, Salvation and the Spirit*. Collegeville, MN: Liturgical Press, 1979, 240–270.

Dillon, R.J. 'Previewing Luke's Project from his Prologue (Luke 1:1-4)', *CBQ* 43 (1981) 205-27.

Dillon, R.J. *From Eye-Witnesses to Ministers of the Word: Tradition and Composition in Luke 24*, AnBib 82. Rome: Pontifical Biblical Institute, 1978.

Doble, P. *The Paradox of Salvation. Luke's Theology of the Cross*, SNTSMS 87. CUP, 1996.

Dockery, D. 'Acts 6–12: The Christian Mission Beyond Jerusalem', *RevExp* 87/3 (1990) 423–438.

Dollar, H.E. *A Biblical-Missiological Exploration of the Cross-Cultural Dimensions in Luke–Acts*. San Francisco: Mellen Research University Press, 1993.

Dömer, M. *Das Heil Gottes: Studien zur Theologie des lukanischen Doppelwerkes*, BBB 51. Köln and Bonn: Peter Hanstein, 1978.

Downing, F.G. 'Freedom from the Law in Luke–Acts', *JSNT* 26 (1986) 49-52.

Downing, F.G. 'Law and Custom: Luke–Acts and Late Hellenism' in B. Lindars (ed.), *Law and Religion: Essays on the Place of the Law in Israel and Early Christianity*. Cambridge: Clarke, 1988, 148-58.

Dschulnigg, P. 'Die Rede des Stephanus im Rahmen des Berichtes über sein Martyrium (Apg. 6,8-8,3)', *Jud* 44 (1988) 195-213.

Du Plessis, I. 'Once More: The Purpose of Luke's Prologue (Lk. 1.1-4)', *NovT* 16 (1974), 259-71.

du Plooy, G.P.V. *The Narrative Act in Luke–Acts from the Perspective of God's Design*. University of Stellenbosch: Unpublished Th.D. Dissertation, 1986.

Dubois, J.D. *De Jean-Baptiste á Jesus: essai sur la conception lucanienne de l'Esprit á partir des premiers chapitres de l'évangile*. University of Strasbourg: Unpublished PhD Dissertation, 1977.

Dunn, J.D.G. 'Baptism in the Spirit: A Response to Pentecostal Scholarship on Luke–Acts', *Journal of Pentecostal Theology* 3 (1993) 3-27.

Dunn, J.D.G. *Baptism in the Holy Spirit: A Re-examination of the New Testament Teaching on the Gift of the Spirit in Relation to Pentecostalism Today*. London: SCM, 1970.

Dunn, J.D.G. *Jesus and the Spirit*. London: SCM, 1975.

Dunn, J.D.G. *Romans 9-16*. Dallas: Word Press, 1988.

Dunn, J.D.G. *The Partings of the Ways Between Christianity and Judaism and their Significance for the Character of Christianity*. London and Philadelphia: SCM and Trinity Press International, 1991.

Dunn, J.D.G. *Unity and Diversity in the New Testament*, 2nd. edn. London: SCM, 1990.

Dupont, D.J. 'Un peuple d'entre les nationes (Actes 15,14)', *NTS* 31 (1985) 321-35.

Dupont, D.J. 'ΛΑΟΣ ΕΞ᾽ΕΘΝΩΝ (Actes 15,14)' in *Études sur les Actes des Apôtres*, Lectio Divina 45. Paris: Editions du Cerf, 1967, 361-65.

Dupont, D.J. *Le Discours de Milet: Testament Pastoral de Saint Paul*, Lectio Divina 32. Paris: Les Éditions du Cerf, 1962.

Dupont, D.J. 'ΤΑ ΟΣΙΑ ΔΑΥΙΔ ΤΑ ΠΙΣΤΑ(Ac XIII 34=Is LV 3)', *Revue Biblique* 68 (1961) 91-114.

Dupont, D.J. *The Salvation of the Gentiles: Studies in the Acts of the Apostles*, ET. New York: Paulist Press, 1979.

Dupont, D.J. 'Ascension du Christ et don de l'Esprit d'apres Actes 2.33' in B. Lindars and S.S. Smalley (eds.), *Christ and Spirit in the New Testament*. Cambridge: CUP, 1973, 219-28.

Dyrness, W. *Themes in Old Testament Theology*. Exeter: Paternoster, 1979.

Eichrodt, W. *Theology of the Old Testament*, 2 vols, ET. Philadelphia: Westminster, 1967.

Eisenstadt, S.N. and L. Roniger, *Patrons, Clients and Friends*. Cambridge: CUP, 1984.

Elliott, J.H. 'Household and Meals vs. Temple Purity: Replication Patterns in Luke–Acts', *BTB* 21 (1991) 102-8.

Elliott, J.H. *What Is Social-Scientific Criticism?* Minneapolis: Fortress, 1993.

Ellis, E.E. 'Midrashic Features in the Speeches of Acts' in A. Descamps and A. de Halleux (eds.), *Melanges Bibliques en hommage au R. P. Beda Rigaux*. Gembloux: J. Duculot, 1970, 303-312.

Ellis, E.E. '"The End of the Earth" (Acts 1:8)', *Bulletin for Biblical Research* 1 (1991) 123-32.

Ellis, E.E. *The Gospel of Luke*, 2nd edn. Grand Rapids: Eerdmans, 1981.

Enuwosa, J. ῾Η φύση τοῦ θανατοῦ τοῦ ᾽Ιησοῦ στή Σωτηριολογία τοῦ Λουκᾶ.' *DBM* 22 (13, 1993) 49-65.

Esler, P.F. *Community and Gospel in Luke–Acts. The Social and Political Motivations of Lucan Theology*, SNTSMS 57. Cambridge: CUP, 1987.

Evans, C.A. '"Preacher" and "Preaching": Some Lexical Observations', *JETS* 24 (1981) 315-322.

Evans, C.A. 'Prophecy and Polemic: Jews in Luke's Scriptural Apologetic' in C.A. Evans and J.A. Sanders (eds.), *Luke and Scripture: The Function of Sacred Tradition in Luke–Acts*. Minneapolis: Fortress, 1993.

Evans, C.A. and J.A. Sanders, *Luke and Scripture*. Minneapolis: Fortress, 1993.

Evans, C.F. ' "Speeches" in Acts' in A. Descamps and A. de Halleux (eds.), *Melanges Bibliques en hommage au R. P. Beda Rigaux*. Gembloux: J. Duculot, 1970, 287-302.

Evans, C.F. *Saint Luke*. London and Philadelphia: SCM and TPI, 1990.

Falk, D.K. 'Jewish Prayer Literature', in R. Bauckham (ed.), *The Book of Acts in Its Palestinian Setting*, A1CS Vol. 4. Grand Rapid/Carlisle: Eerdmans/Paternoster, 1995, 268-276.

Faw, C.E. *Acts*. Scottdale and Kitchener: Herald, 1993.

Feldman, L.H. *Jew and Gentile in the Ancient World: Attitudes and Interactions from Alexander to Justinian*. Princeton: Princeton University Press, 1993.

Fenton, J. 'The Order of the Miracles Performed by Peter and Paul in Acts', *ExpT* 77 (1965-6) 381-3.

Filson, F.V. *Three Crucial Decades: Studies in the Book of Acts*. London: Epworth, 1963.

Fishbane, M. *The Garments of Torah*. Bloomington: Indiana University Press, 1989.

Fitzmyer, J.A. 'Jesus in the Early Church through the Eyes of Luke–Acts', *ScrB* 17 (1987) 26-35.

Fitzmyer, J.A. 'The Use of the Old Testament in Luke–Acts', in E.H. Lovering (ed.), *Society of Biblical Literature 1992 Seminar Papers*. Chico, CA: Scholars Press,1992, 524-38.

Fitzmyer, J.A. *Romans*. Garden City, NY: Doubleday, 1994.

Fitzmyer, J.A. *The Gospel According to Luke: Introduction, Translation and Notes I-IX*. Garden City, NY: Doubleday, 1981.

Fitzmyer, J.A. *The Gospel according to Luke Introduction, Translation and Notes X-XX-IV*. Garden City, NY: Doubleday, 1985.

Fitzmyer, J.A. 'Crucifixion in Ancient Palestine, Qumran Literature, and the New Testament' in *To Advance the Gospel*. New York: Crossroad, 1981, 125-46.

Fitzmyer,J.A. *Luke the Theologian: Aspects of His Teaching*. New York: Paulist,1989.

Flanagan, N. 'The What and How of Salvation in Luke–Acts' in D. Durken (ed.), *Sin, Salvation, and the Spirit* Collegeville, MN: Liturgical Press, 1979, 203-13.

Flender, H. *Heil und Geschichte in der Theologie des Lukas*, BeT 41. München: Chr. Kaiser Verlag, 1965; ET: *St Luke: Theologian of Redemptive History*. London: SPCK, 1967.

Foakes Jackson, F.J. *Peter: Prince of Apostles. A Study in the History and Tradition of Christianity*. London and New York: George H. Doran, 1927.

Foakes Jackson, F.J. *The Acts of the Apostles*, MNTC. London: Hodder & Stoughton, 1931.

Forbes, C. 'Comparison, Self-Praise and Irony: Paul's Boasting and the Conventions of Hellenistic Rhetoric', *NTS* 32 (1986) 1-30.

Ford, J.M. *My Enemy Is My Guest: Jesus and Violence in Luke*. Maryknoll, NY: Orbis, 1984.

Foulkes, F. *The Acts of God: A Study of the Basis of Typology in the Old Testament*. London: Tyndale Press, 1958.

France, R.T. 'The Worship of Jesus: A Neglected Factor in Christological Debate?', in H.H. Rowdon (ed.), *Christ the Lord: Studies in Christology Presented to Donald Guthrie*. Leicester: IVP, 1982, 17-36.

Franklin, E. *Christ the Lord: A Study in the Purpose and Theology of Luke–Acts*. London: SPCK, 1975.

Franklin,E. *Luke: Interpreter of Paul, Critic of Matthew*, JSNTSMS 92. Sheffield: JSOT Press, 1994.

Franklin, E. 'The Ascension and the Eschatology of Luke–Acts', *Scottish Journal of Theology* 23 (1970) 191-200.

Frei, H.W. *The Eclipse of Biblical Narrative*. New Haven: Yale University Press, 1974.

Frein, B.C. 'Narrative Predictions, Old Testament Prophecies and Luke's Sense of Fulfilment', *NTS* 40 (1994) 22-37.

Fuller, R.H. 'Luke and the Theologia Crucis' in D. Durken (ed.), *Sin, Salvation, and the Spirit*. Collegeville, MN: Liturgical Press, 1979, 214-20.

Fusco, V. 'Problems of Structure in Luke's Eschatological Discourse (Luke 21:7-36)' in G. O'Collins and G. Marconi (eds.) , *Luke and Acts* , ET. New York and Mahwah, NJ: Paulist, 1991, 72-92.

Gager, J.G. 'Jews, Gentiles and Synagogues in the Book of Acts',*HTR* 79 (1986) 91-99.

Garnsey, P. and R.P. Saller, *The Roman Empire: Economy, Society and Culture*. London: Duckworth, 1987.

Garrett, S.R. 'Sociology (Early Christian)', *Anchor Bible Dictionary*, 6,89-99.

Garrett, S.R. *The Demise of the Devil: Magic and the Demonic in Luke's Writings*. Minneapolis: Fortress, 1989.

Garrett, S.R. 'The Meaning of Jesus' Death in Luke', *WW* 12 (1992) 11-16.

Gärtner, B. *The Areopagus Speech and Natural Revelation*, ASNU 21. Lund and Copenhagen: C.W.K. Gleerup and Ejnar Munksgaard, 1955.

Gasque, W.W. *A History of the Criticism of the Acts of the Apostles*. Tübingen and Grand Rapids: J.C.B. Mohr (Paul Siebeck) and Eerdmans, 1975.

Gatz, B. *Weltalter, goldene Zeit und sinnverwandte Vorstellungen*. Hildesheim: Georg Olms, 1967.

Gaventa, B.R. *From Darkness to Light: Aspects of Conversion in the New Testament*. Philadelphia: Fortress, 1986.

Gaventa, B.R. 'Towards a Theology of Acts. Reading and Rereading', *Interpretation* 42 (1988), 146-57.

Gaventa, B.R. 'The Eschatology of Luke–Acts Revisited', *Encounter* 43, 1 (1982) 27-42.

Geertz, C. *The Interpretation of Cultures*. New York: Basic Books, 1973.

Geldenhuys, N. *Commentary on the Gospel of Luke*. Grand Rapids: Eerdmans, 1951.

Gempf, C.H. 'Public Speaking and Published Accounts' in A.D. Clarke and B.W. Winter, *The Book of Acts in Its Ancient Literary Setting*, A1CS, vol 1. Grand Rapids and Carlisle: Eerdmans and Paternoster, 1993, 259-303.

Gempf, C.H. 'Paul at Athens' in G.F. Hawthorne and R.P. Martin (eds.), *Dictionary of Paul and His Letters*. Downers Grove, IL and Leicester: IVP, 1993, 51-54.

Gempf, C.H. *Historical and Literary Appropriateness in the Mission Speeches in Acts*. University of Aberdeen: Unpublished PhD Dissertation, 1988.

George, A. 'Le parallèle entre Jean-Baptiste et Jésus en Lc 1-2' in *Études sur l'oeuvre de Luc*, SB. Paris: Gabalda, 1978, 43-65.

George, A. 'L'Emploi chex Luc du vocabulaire de salut', *NTS* 23 (1977) 308-20.

George, A. 'L'Esprit Saint dans l'Oeuvre de Luc', *Revue Biblique* 85 (1978) 500-42.

George, A. 'Le sens de la mort de Jesus pour Luc', *Revue Biblique* 80 (1973) 186-217.

George, A. 'Le vocabulaire de salut' in *Études sur L'Oeuvre de Luc.*, SB. Paris: Gabalda, 1978, 307-20.

Gerhardsson, B. 'Die Boten Gottes und die Apostel Christi', *SEÅ* 27 (1962) 89-132.

Gerhardsson, B. *The Gospel Tradition*, ConBNT 15. Lund: Gleerup, 1986.

Giblin, C.H. *The Destruction of Jerusalem according to Luke's Gospel*, AnBib 107. Rome: Biblical Institute, 1985.

Giles, K. 'Apostles Before and After Paul', *Churchman* 99 (1985) 241-56.

Giles, K. 'Is Luke an Exponent of "Early Protestantism"? Church Order in the Lukan Writings'*EQ* 55 (1983) 3-20.

Giles, K. 'Present-Future Eschatology in the Book of Acts', *RTR* Part I, 40, 3 (1981) 65-71; Part II, 41, 1 (1982) 11-18.

Giles, K. 'Salvation in Lukan Theology',*RTR* 42 (1983) 10-16, 45-49.

Gill, D.W.J. 'Acts and the Urban Elites' in D.W.J. Gill and C. Gempf (eds.),*The Book of Acts in Its Graeco-Roman Setting* , A1CS, vol 2. Grand Rapids/Carlisle: Eerdmans/Paternoster, 1994, 105-118.

Gill, D.W.J. and B.W. Winter, 'Acts and Roman Religion' in D.W.J. Gill and C.
   Gempf (eds.),*The Book of Acts in Its Graeco-Roman Setting,* AICS, vol 2. Grand
   Rapids/Carlisle: Eerdmans/Paternoster, 1994, 79-103.
Gill, D.W.J. 'Behind the Classical Facade: Local Religions of the Roman Empire' in
   A.D. Clarke and B.W. Winter (eds.), *One God, One Lord. Christianity in a
   World of Religious Pluralism.* Grand Rapids: Baker, 1992, 85-100.
Glöckner, R. *Die Verkündigung des Heils beim Evangelisten Lukas,* WSTR 9. Mainz:
   Matthias-Grünewald, 1975.
Goodwin, W.W. *A Greek Grammar.* London: Macmillan, 1894.
Goppelt, L. *Typos: The Typological Interpretation of the Old Testament in the New,* ET.
   Grand Rapids: Eerdmans, 1982.
Gowler, D.B. *Host, Guest, Enemy and Friend: Portraits of the Pharisees in Luke and
   Acts.* New York: P. Lang, 1991.
Green, E.M.B. *The Meaning of Salvation.* London: Hodder and Stoughton, 1965.
Green, J.B. 'Jesus on the Mount of Olives (Luke 22.39-46): Tradition and Theology',
   JSNT 26 (1986) 29-48.
Green, J.B. 'The Death of Jesus, God's Servant' in D.D. Sylva (ed.), *Reimaging the
   Death of Jesus,* BBB 73. Frankfurt: Anton Hain, 1990, 18-28, 170-73.
Green, J.B. 'The Demise of the Temple as Culture Center in Luke–Acts: An Explo-
   ration of the Rending of The Temple Veil (Luke 23.4-49)', *Revue Biblique*
   (1994) 495-515.
Green, J.B. 'The Problem of a Beginning: Israel's Scriptures in Luke 1-2', *Bulletin
   for Biblical Research* 4(1994) 61-85.
Green, J.B. *The Death of Jesus: Tradition and Interpretation in the Passion Narrative,*
   WUNT 2.33. Tübingen: J.C.B. Mohr (Paul Siebeck), 1988.
Green, J.B. '"The Message of Salvation" in Luke–Acts', *Ex Auditu* 5 (1989) 21-34.
Green, J.B. *The Theology of the Gospel of Luke,* New Testament Theology. Cam-
   bridge: CUP, 1995.
Green, J.B. 'Good News to Whom? Jesus and the "Poor" in the Gospel of Luke' in
   J.B. Green and M. Turner (eds.), *Jesus of Nazareth, Lord and Christ. Essays on
   the Historical Jesus and New Testament Christology.* Grand Rapids and Car-
   lisle: Eerdmans and Paternoster, 1994, 59-74.
Green, J.B. 'Jesus and a Daughter of Abraham (Luke 13:10-17): Test Case for a Lu-
   kan Perspective on the Miracles of Jesus', *CBQ* 51 (1989) 643-54.
Green, J.B. '"Proclaiming Repentance and Forgiveness of Sins to All Nations": A
   Biblical Perspective on the Church's Mission' in A.G. Padgett (ed.), *The
   World Is My Parish: The Mission of the Church in Methodist Perspective,* SHM
   10. Lewiston, NY: Edwin Mellen, 1992, 13-43.
Grumm, M.H. 'Another Look at Acts', *ExpT* 96 (1985) 335-6.
Gunkel, H. *Die Wirkungen des heiligen Geistes nach der popularen Anschauung der ap-
   ostolischen Zeit und nach der Lehre Apostels Paulus.* Göttingen: Vandenhoeck
   & Ruprecht, 1888.
Gunkel, H. *The Influence of the Holy Spirit.* ET. Philadelphia: Fortress, 1979.
Guthrie, D. *New Testament Theology.* Downers Grove: IVP, 1981.
Guthrie, W.K.C. *History of Greek Philosophy.* Cambridge: CUP, 1962.
Haacker, K. 'Das Bekenntnis des Paulus zur Hoffnung Israels nach der Apostelge-
   schichte des Lukas', *NTS* 31 (1985) 437-51.
Haacker, K. 'Verwendung und Vermeidung des Apostelbegriffs im lukanischen
   Werk', *NovT* 30 (1988) 9-38.

Haenchen, E. 'The Book of Acts as Source Material for the History of Earliest Christianity' in L. E. Keck and J. L. Martyn (eds.), *Studies in Luke–Acts*. Nashville and London: Abingdon and SPCK, 1966, 1968, 258-278.

Haenchen, E. *Die Apostelgeschichte*, KEK 3. Göttingen: Vandenhoeck & Ruprecht, 1977; ET: *The Acts of the Apostles:A Commentary*. Philadelphia and Oxford: Fortress and Basil Blackwell, 1971.

Hahn, F. 'Der Apostolat im Urchristentums. Seine Eigenart und seine Voraussetzungen', *KD* 20 (1974) 54-77.

Hahn, F. *Mission in the New Testament*. Naperville and London: Allenson and SCM, 1965.

Hall, R.G. *Revealed Histories: Techniques for Ancient Jewish and Christian Historiography*, JSPSup 6. Sheffield: JSOT Press, 1991.

Hamm, D. 'Acts 3:12-26: Peter's Speech and the Healing of the Man Born Lame', *PRS* 11, 3 (1984) 199-217, 205.

Hamm, D. 'Sight to the Blind: Vision as Metaphor in Luke', *Bib* 67 (1986) 457-77.

Hands, A.R. *Charities and Social Aid in Greece and Rome*. London: Thames and Hudson, 1968.

Hansen, G.W. 'Galatia' in D.W.J. Gill and C. Gempf (eds.), *The Book of Acts in Its Graeco-Roman Setting*, AICS vol 2. Grand Rapids/Carlisle: Eerdmans/Paternoster, 1994, 377-395.

Hanson, R.P.C. *The Acts in the Revised Standard Version*. Oxford: OUP, 1967.

Hastings, A. *Prophet and Witness in Jerusalem: A Study of the Teaching of Saint Luke*. London: Longmans, Green and Co. 1958.

Haya-Prats, G. *El Espiritu en los Hechos de los Apostolos*. Rome: Gregorian University, 1967; French Translation: *L'Esprit Force de l'église*. Paris: Editions du Cerf, 1975.

Hays, R. B. *Echoes of Scripture in the Letters of Paul*. New Haven: Yale University Press, 1989.

Hedrick, C.W. 'Paul's Conversion/Call: A Comparative Analysis of the Three Reports in Acts', *JBL* 100 (1981) 415-432.

Hegermann, H. 'Mensch IV. Neues Testament', *TRE* 22 (1992) 481-93.

Hemer, C.J. 'Paul at Athens: A Topographical Note', *NTS* 20 (1974) 341-50.

Hemer, C.J. 'The Speeches of Acts II. The Areopagus Address', *TynB* 40.2 (1989) 239-259.

Hemer, C.J. 'The Cities of Revelation', *New Docs 1978* (1983), Item 17.

Hemer, C.J. *The Book of Acts in the Setting of Hellenistic History*. Tübingen: J.C.B. Mohr (Paul Siebeck)1989.

Hengel, M. 'Die Ursprünge der christlichen Mission', *NTS* 18 (1971-72) 15-38.

Hengel, M. 'Jesus als messianischer Lehrer der Weisheit und die Anfänge der Christologie' in E. Jacob (ed.), *Sagesse et Religion*. Paris: France, 1979, 147-88.

Hengel, M. *Between Jesus and Paul*. London: SCM, 1983.

Hengel, M. 'Die Synagogeninschrift von Stobi', *ZNW* 57 (1966) 145-83.

Hengel, M. *Zur urchristlichen Geschichtsschreibung*, Stuttgart: Calver Verlag, 1979; ET: *Acts and the History of Earliest Christianity*. London: SCM, 1979.

Hengel, M. 'Zwischen Jesus und Paulus. Die "Hellenisten", die "Sieben" und Stephanus (Apg 6,1-15; 7,54-8,3), *ZThK* 72 (1975) 151-161.

Hill, C.C. *Hellenists and Hebrews*. Minneapolis: Fortress, 1992.

Hill, D. 'The Spirit and the Church's Witness. Observations on Acts 1:6–8', *IBS* 6 (1984), 16–26.

Hitchcock, F. 'Is the Fourth Gospel a Drama?', *Theology* 7 (1923) 307-317.

Holmberg, B. *Sociology and the New Testament*. Minneapolis: Fortress, 1990.

Holtz, T. *Untersuchungen über die alttestamentliche Zitate bei Lukas*, TU 104. Berlin: Akademie Verlag, 1968.

Holtz, T. 'Zum Selbstverständnis des Apostels Paulus', *ThLZ* 91 (1966) 321-30.

Horsley, G.H.R. 'Sophia, "the second Phoibe"', *New Docs 1979* (1987), Item 122.

Horsley, G.H.R. 'The Purple Trade, and the Status of Lydia of Thyatira', *New Docs 1977* (1982), Item 3.

Horsley, R.A. *Sociology and the Jesus Movement*, 2nd edn. NY: Continuum, 1994.

House, P.R. 'Suffering and the Purpose of Acts', *JETS* 33, (1990), 317-330.

Hui, A.W.D. *The Concept of the Holy Spirit in Ephesians and its Relation to the Pneumatologies of Luke and Paul*. University of Aberdeen: Unpublished Ph.D Dissertation, 1992.

Hultgren, A.J. 'Paul's Pre-Christian Persecutions of the Church: Their Purpose, Locale and Nature', *JBL* 95 (1976) 97-111.

Hurst, L.D. 'Ethics of Jesus' in J.B. Green and S. McKnight (eds.), *Dictionary of Jesus and the Gospels*. Downers Grove, IL and Leicester: IVP, 1992, 210-222.

Hurtado, L.W. *One God, One Lord: Early Christian Devotion and Ancient Jewish Monotheism*. London: SCM Press, 1988.

Hutter, H. *Politics as Friendship*. Waterloo, Ontario: Wilfred Laurier University Press, 1978.

Isaacs, M.E. *The Concept of Spirit*. London: Heythrop Monographs, 1976.

Jacob, E. *Theology of the Old Testament*, ET. London: Hodder & Stoughton, 1958.

Jannaris, A.N. *An Historical Greek Grammar Chiefly of the Attic Dialect*. Hildesheim: G. Olms Verlag, 1897.

Jeremias, J. *The Eucharistic Words of Jesus*. London: SCM, 1966.

Jervell, J. 'Paulus in der Apostelgeschichte und die Geschichte des Urchristentums', *NTS* 32 (1986) 378- 92.

Jervell, J. 'Retrospect and Prospect in Luke–Acts Interpretation' in E. H. Lovering, Jr. (ed.), *Society of Biblical Literature 1991 Seminar Papers*. Chico, CA: Scholars Press, 1991, 383-404.

Jervell, J. 'The Church of Jews and Godfearers' in J.B.Tyson (ed.), *Luke–Acts and the Jewish People: Eight Critical Perspectives*, Minneapolis: Augsburg, 1988, 11-20, 138-140.

Jervell, J. *Luke and the People of God: A New Look at Luke–Acts*. Minneapolis: Augsburg, 1972.

Jervell, J. *The Theology of the Acts of the Apostles*, New Testament Theology. Cambridge: CUP, 1996.

Jervell, J. *The Unknown Paul: Essays on Luke–Acts and the Early Christian Church*. Minneapolis: Augsburg, 1984.

Jervell, J. 'The Future of the Past: Luke's Vision of Salvation History and its bearing on his Writing of History' in B. Witherington, III (ed.), *History, Literature and Society in the Book of Acts*. Cambridge: CUP, 1996.

Johnson, D.E. 'Jesus against the Idols: The Use of Isaianic Servant Songs in the Missiology of Acts', *WTJ* 52 (1990) 343-53.

Johnson, L.T. 'Luke–Acts, Book of', *Anchor Bible Dictionary*, 4, 404-20.

Johnson, L.T. 'On Finding the Lukan Community: A Cautious Cautionary Essay' in P.J. Achtemeier (ed.), *Society of Biblical Literature 1979 Seminar Papers*, vol.1. Missoula, MT: Scholars Press, 1979, 87-100.

Johnson, L.T. *Sharing Possessions. Mandate and Symbol of Faith*. Philadelphia: Fortress, 1981.

Johnson, L.T. *The Acts of the Apostles*. Collegeville, MN: Liturgical Press, 1992.

Johnson, L.T. *The Gospel of Luke*. Collegeville, MN: Liturgical Press, 1991.

Johnson, L.T. *The Literary Function of Possessions in Luke–Acts*, SBLDS 39. Atlanta: Scholars Press, 1977.

Johnstone, W. 'Guilt and Atonement: The Theme of 1 and 2 Chronicles', *JSOT* 42 (1986) 113-38.

Jones, D.L. 'The Title Author of Life (Leader) in the Acts of the Apostles', in E.H. Lovering, Jr. (ed.), *Society of Biblical Literature 1994 Seminar Papers*. Atlanta: Scholars Press, 1994, 627-36.

Judge, E.A. 'The Social Identity of the First Christians: A Question of Method in Religious History', *Journal of Religious History* 11 (1980) 201-217.

Judge, E.A. *The Social Pattern of Christian Groups in the First Century: Some Prolegomena to the Study of the New Testament Ideas of Social Obligation*. London: Tyndale, 1960.

Juel, D. *Messianic Exegesis: Christological Interpretation of the Old Testament in Early Christianity*. Philadelphia: Fortress, 1988.

Juel, D. *Luke–Acts*. London: SCM Press, 1984.

Kähler, M. 'Die Reden des Petrus in der Apostelgeschichte, Sprachlich untersucht', *Theologische Studien und Kritiken* 3 (1873) 492-536.

Kaiser, W.C. *Toward an Old Testament Theology*. Grand Rapids: Zondervan, 1978.

Kaiser,W.C. 'The Davidic Promise and the Inclusion of the Gentiles (Amos 9:9-15 and Acts 15:13-18): A Test passage for Theological Systems', *JETS* 20 (1977) 97-111.

Karris, R.J. 'Poor and Rich: the Lukan Sitz im Leben' in C. H. Talbert (ed.), *Perspectives on Luke–Acts*. Danville, VA: Association of Baptist Professors of Religion, 1978, 112-25.

Karris, R.J. *What Are They Saying About Luke and Acts?* New York: Paulist, 1979.

Kaye, B.N. 'Acts' portrait of Silas', *NovT* 31 (1979) 13-26.

Keating, J.F. *The Agape in the New Testament*. London: Methuen, 1901.

Kee, H.C. 'The Transformation of the Synagogue after 70 CE: its Import for Early Christianity', *NTS* 36.1 (1990) 1-24.

Kee, H.C. *Good News to the Ends of the Earth: The Theology of Acts*. London and Philadelphia: SCM and Trinity Press International, 1990.

Kee, H.C. *Knowing the Truth. A Sociological Approach to New Testament Interpretation*. Minneapolis: Fortress, 1989.

Kerferd, G.B. *The Sophistic Movement*. Cambridge: CUP, 1981.

Kilgallen, J.J. 'The Function of Stephen's Speech (Acts 7,2-53)', *Bib* 70 (1989) 173-93.

Kilgallen, J.J. 'Acts 13, 38-39: Culmination of Paul's Speech in Pisidia', *Bib* 69 (1988) 480-506.

Kilgallen, J.J. *The Stephen Speech*. Rome: Pontifical Biblical Institute, 1976.

Kim, H.S. *Die Geisttaufe des lukanischen Doppelwerks*. Berlin: Lang, 1993.

Kim, S. *The Origin of Paul's Gospel*, WUNT 2, 4. Tübingen: J.C.B. Mohr (Paul Siebeck), 1981.

Kimball, C.A. *Jesus' Exposition of the Old Testament in Luke's Gospel*, JSNTMS 94. Sheffield Academic Press, 1994.

Kirk, J.A. 'Apostleship Since Rengstorf: Towards a Synthesis', *NTS* 21 (1975) 249-64.

Klauck, H.-J. (ed.), *Monotheismus und Christologie: Zur Gottesfrage im hellenistischen Judentum und in Urchristentum*. Freiburg: Herder, 1992.

Klauck, H.-J. *Hausgemeinde und Hauskirche im frühen Christentum*, SBS 103. Stuttgart: Katholisches Bibelwerk, 1981.

Klauser, T. *et al.* (eds.) *Reallexikon für Antike und Christentum*. Stuttgart: Hiersemann Verlags,1950ff.

Klein, G. *Die zwölf Apostel: Ursprung und Gehalt einer Idee*, FRLANT 77. Göttingen: Vandenhoeck & Ruprecht, 1961.

Klein, W.W., R.L.Hubbard, Jr. and C.L. Blomberg (eds.), *Introduction to Biblical Interpretation*. Dallas: Word Press, 1993.

Kliesch, K. *Apostelgeschichte*. Stuttgart: Katholisches Bibelwerk, 1986.

Klinghardt, M. *Gesetz und Volk Gottes*, WUNT 2.32. Tübingen: J.C.B. Mohr (Paul Siebeck), 1988.

Kodell, J. '"The Word of God grew": The Ecclesial Tendency of Λόγος in Acts 1,7; 12,24; 19,20', *Biblica* 55 (1974) 505-19.

Kodell, J. 'Luke's Theology of the Death of Jesus' in D. Durken (ed.), *Sin, Salvation, and the Spirit*. Collegeville, MN: Liturgical Press, 1979, 221-30.

Koet, B.J. *Five Studies of Interpretation of Scripture in Luke–Acts*, Studiorum Novi Testamenti Auxilia XIV. Leuven: Leuven University Press, 1989.

Korn, M. *Die Geschichte Jesu in veränderter Zeit: Studien zur bleibenden Bedeutung Jesu im lukanischen Doppelwerk*, WUNT 2, 51. Tübingen: J.C.B. Mohr (Paul Siebeck), 1993.

Kraabel, A.T. 'The Disappearance of the God-Fearers', *Numen* 28 (1981) 113-26.

Kremer, J. 'Weltweites Zeugnis für Christus in der Kraft des Geistes. Zur lukanischen Sicht der Mission' in K. Kertelge (ed.), *Mission im Neuen Testament*. Freiburg: Herder, 1982, 145–163.

Kränkl, E. *Jesus der Knecht Gottes. Die heilsgeschichtliche Stellung Jesu in den Reden der Apostelgeschichte*. BU 8. Regensburg: Pustet, 1972.

Krodel, G.A. 'The Functions of the Spirit in the Old Testament, the Synoptic Tradition and the Book of Acts' in P.D. Opsahl (ed.), *The Holy Spirit in the Life of the Church*. Minneapolis: Augsburg, 1978.

Krodel, G.A. *Acts*. Minneapolis: Augsburg, 1986.

Külling, H. *Geoffenbartes Geheimnis: Eine Auslegung von Apostelgeschichte 17. 6-34*, ATANT 79. Zürich: TVZ, 1993.

Kümmel, W.G. *Einleitung in das Neue Testament*. Heidelberg: Quelle & Meyer, 1973.

Kümmel, W.G. *Man in the New Testament*, ET. London: Epworth, 1963.

Kurz, W.S. *Reading Luke–Acts: Dynamics of Biblical Narrative*. Louisville: Westminster and John Knox, 1993.

Kytzler, B. 'Utopisches Denken und Handeln in der klassischen Antike' in R. Villgradter and F. Krey (eds.), *Das Utopische Roman*. Darmstadt: Wissenschaftliche Buchgesellschaft, 1973, 45-68.

Ladd, G.E. 'The Christology of Acts', *Found* 11 (1968) 27-41.

Lake, K. and H.J. Cadbury, *The Acts of the Apostles*, Vol 4 of *The Beginnings of Christianity, Part I: The Acts of the Apostles*, F. J. Foakes Jackson and K. Lake (eds.), London: Macmillan, 1933.

Lampe, G.W.H. 'The Lucan Portrait of Christ', *NTS* 2 (1955-56) 160-75.

Lampe, G.W.H. *God as Spirit*. Oxford: Clarendon, 1977.

Lampe, G.W.H. *The Seal of the Spirit*, 2nd edn. London: SPCK, 1967.

Lampe, G.W.H. 'The Holy Spirit in the Writings of Saint Luke' in D.E. Nineham (ed.), *Studies in the Gospels: Essays in Memory of R.H. Lightfoot*. Oxford: Blackwell, 1955, 159-200.

Larsson, E. 'Temple-Criticism and the Jewish Heritage: Some Reflections on Acts 6-7', *NTS* 39 (1993) 379-395.

Lash, N. *Theology on the Way to Emmaus*. London: SCM Press, 1986.

Leaney, A.R.C. *The Gospel according to St. Luke*, 2nd ed. London: Black, 1966.

Leisegang, H. *Der Heilige Geist: Das Wesen und Werden der mystisch-intuitiven Erkenntnis in der Philosophie und Religion der Griechen*. Berlin: Teubner, 1919.

Leisegang, H. *Pneuma Hagion: Der Ursprung des Geistesbegriffs der synoptischen Evangelien aus der griechischen Mystik*. Leipzig: Hinrichs, 1922.

Lentz, J. *Luke's Portrait of Paul*, SNTSMS 77. Cambridge: CUP, 1993.

Liebeschuetz, J.H.W.G. *Antioch: City and Imperial Administration in the Later Roman Empire*. Oxford: Oxford University Press, 1977.

Lofthouse, W.F. 'The Holy Spirit in the Acts and the Fourth Gospel', *ExpT* 52 (1940-41) 334-36.

Lohfink, G. *Die Sammlung Israels: Eine Untersuchung zur lukanischen Ekklesiologie*, SANT 39. Munich: Kösel-Verlag, 1975.

Lohfink, G. *Jesus and Community*. London: SPCK, 1985.

Lohmeyer, M. *Der Apostelbegriff im Neuen Testament*, SBB 29. Stuttgart: Katholisches Bibelwerk, 1995.

Long, B.O. 'Prophetic Call Traditions and Reports of Vision', *ZAW* 84 (1972) 494-500.

Longenecker, R.N. 'The Acts of the Apostles' in F.E. Gaebelein (ed.), *The Expositor's Bible Commentary*, vol. 9. Grand Rapids: Zondervan, 1981.

Löning, K. 'Gottesbild der Apostelgeschichte' in H.-J. Klauck (ed.), *Monotheismus und Christologie*: Freiburg: Herder, 1992, 88-117.

Loumanen, P. (ed.) *Luke–Acts*. Scandinavian Perspectives, Publications of the Finnish Exegetical Society 54. Göttingen: Vandenhoeck und Ruprecht, 1991.

Louth, A. *Discerning the Mystery*. Oxford: Clarendon, 1983.

Lövestam, E. *Son and Saviour. A Study of Acts 13.2-37. With an Appendix: "Son of God" in the Synoptic Gospels*, ET. Lund & Copenhagen: Gleerup & Munksgaard, 1961.

Lüdemann, G. *Das frühe Christentum nach den Traditionen der Apostelgeschichte*. Göttingen: Vandenhoeck & Ruprecht, 1987; ET. *Early Christianity according to the Traditions in Acts. A Commentary*. London: SCM, 1989.

Lull, D.J. 'The Servant-Benefactor in Luke 22:24-30'. *NovT* 28 (1986) 289-305.

MacIntyre, A. and P. Ricoeur, *The Religious Significance of Atheism*. New York: Columbia University Press, 1969.

MacRae, G.W. '"Whom heaven must receive until the time": Reflections on the Christology of Acts', *Int* 27 (1973) 151-65.

Maddox, R. *The Purpose of Luke–Acts*. Göttingen & Edinburgh: Vandenhoeck & Ruprecht and T. & T. Clark, 1982.

Maddox, R. *Witnesses to the End of the Earth. The Pattern of Mission in the Book of Acts*. Enfield, NSW: UTC Publications, 1980.

Mainville, O. *L'Esprit dans l'Oeuvre de Luc*. Montreal: Fides, 1991.

Malherbe, A.J. 'Not in a Corner: Early Christian Apologetic in Acts 26:26', *The Second Century* 5 (1986) 193-210.

Malherbe, A.J. *Paul and the Popular Philosophers*. Minneapolis: Fortress, 1989.

Malherbe, A.J. *Social Aspects of Early Christianity*, 2nd edn. Philadelphia: Fortress, 1983.

Mangatt, G. `The Gospel of Salvation', *Biblebhashyam* 2 (1976) 60-80.

Mare, W.H. 'Acts 7: Jewish or Samaritan in Character?', *WThJ* 34 (1972) 1-21.

Mare, W.H. *The Archæology of the Jerusalem Area*. Grand Rapids: Baker, 1987.

Marguerat, D. '"Et quand nous sommes entrés dans Rome": L'énigme de la fin du livre des Actes (28,16-31)', *RHPR* 73 (1993) 1-21.

Marguerat, D. 'The End of Acts (28.16-31) and the Rhetoric of Silence' in S. E. Porter and T. H. Olbricht (eds.), *Rhetoric and the New Testament: Essays from the 1992 Heidelberg Conference*, JSNTSS 90. Sheffield: JSOT Press, 1993, 74-89.

Marshall, I.H. 'Acts and the "Former Treatise"' in B.W. Winter and A.D. Clarke (eds.),*The Book of Acts in Its Ancient Literary Setting*, AICS, vol 1. Grand Rapids and Carlisle: Eerdmans and Paternoster, 1993, 163-82.

Marshall, I.H. 'How Far Did the Early Christians Worship God?', *Churchman* 99 (1985) 216-29.

Marshall, I.H. 'The Significance of Pentecost', *SJT* 30 (1977) 347-369.

Marshall, I.H. *Last Supper and Lord's Supper*, Didsbury Lectures 1980. Exeter: Paternoster, 1980.

Marshall, I.H. *Luke: Historian and Theologian*, 3rd edn. Exeter: Paternoster, 1988.

Marshall, I.H. *The Acts of the Apostles*. Sheffield: JSOT Press, 1992.

Marshall, I.H. *The Acts of the Apostles: An Introduction and Commentary*. Leicester and Grand Rapids: IVP and Eerdmans, 1980.

Marshall, I.H. *The Gospel of Luke. A Commentary on the Greek Text*, 3rd edn. Exeter and Grand Rapids: Paternoster and Eerdmans, 1983.

Marshall, I.H. 'The Interpretation of the Magnificat: Luke 1:46-55' in C. Bussmann and W. Radl (eds.), *Der Treue Gottes Trauen*. Freiburg: Herder, 1991, 181-96.

Marshall, I.H. 'The Resurrection in the Acts of the Apostles' in W.W. Gasque and R.P. Martin (eds.), *Apostolic History and the Gospel: Biblical and Historical Essays Presented to F.F. Bruce on his 60th Birthday*. Grand Rapids: Eerdmans, 1970, 92-107.

Marshall, I.H. 'Luke and his "Gospel"', in P. Stuhlmacher (ed.), *Das Evangelium und die Evangelien*, WUNT 2, 28. Tübingen: J.C.B. Mohr (Paul Siebeck), 1983, 289-308.

Marshall, I.H. *Die Ursprünge der neutestamentlichen Christologie*. German translation; Gießen-Basel: Brunnen, 1985.

Martin, L.H. 'Gods or Ambassadors of God? Barnabas and Paul in Lystra', *NTS* 41 (1995) 152-156.

Martin, R.P. 'Salvation and Discipleship in Luke's Gospel', *Interpretation* 30 (1976) 366-80. `

Martin, R.P. 'Some Reflections on New Testament Hymns', in H.H. Rowdon (ed.), *Christ the Lord: Studies in Christology Presented to Donald Guthrie*. Leicester: IVP, 1982, 37-49.

Matera,F.J. 'Responsibility for the Death of Jesus according to the Acts of the Apostles', *JSNT* 39 (1990) 77-93.

Mather, P.B. 'Paul in Acts as "Servant" and "Witness"', *BR* 30 (1985) 23-44.

Matson, D.L. *Household Conversion Narratives in Acts. Pattern and Interpretation*, JSNTSS 123. Sheffield Academic Press, 1996.

Mattill, A.J. Jr. 'The Purpose of Acts: Schneckenburger Reconsidered' in W.W. Gasque and R.P. Martin (eds.), *Apostolic History and the Gospel*.

Grand Rapids: Eerdmans, 1970, 108-22.

Mattill, Jr. A.J. 'The Date and Purpose of Luke–Acts: Rackham Reconsidered', *CBQ* 40 (1978) 335-350.

Mattill, Jr. A.J. 'The Jesus-Paul parallels and the purpose of Luke–Acts: H.H. Evans reconsidered', *NovT* 17 (1975) 15-46.

McBride, D. *Emmaus: The Gracious Visit of God according to Luke*. Dublin: Dominican, 1991.

McKay, H.A. *Sabbath and Synagogue. The Question of Sabbath Worship in Ancient Judaism*. Leiden: E.J. Brill, 1994.

McKelvey, R.J. *The New Temple: The Church in the New Testament*. London: Oxford University, 1969.

McKnight, S. *A Light among the Gentiles*. Minneapolis: Fortress, 1991.

Mealand, D.L. 'Community of Goods and Utopian Allusions in Acts 2-4', *JTS* 28 (1977) 96-99.

Meeks, W.A. 'A Hermeneutics of Social Embodiment', *Harvard Theological Review* 79 (1986) 176-186.

Meeks, W.A. *The First Urban Christians*. New Haven: Yale University Press, 1983.

Menzies, R.P. *The Development of Early Christian Pneumatology with Special Reference to Luke–Acts*, JSNTSup 54 Sheffield: JSOT, 1991.

Menzies, R.P. 'Luke and the Spirit: a Reply to James Dunn', *Journal of Pentecostal Theology* 4 (1994) 115-38

Menzies, R.P. 'Spirit and Power in Luke–Acts: A Response to Max Turner', *JSNT* 49 (1993) 11-20.

Metzger B.M. *et al,A Textual Commentary on the Greek New Testament*. New York: UBS, 1971; 2nd ed. Stuttgart: German Bible Society, 1994.

Metzger, B.M. 'Seventy or Seventy-Two Disciples?', *NTS* 5 (1958-9) 299-306.

Meyer, B.F. *The Aims of Jesus.*London: SCM, 1979.

Meyers, E. and J. Strange, *Archaeology, the Rabbis, and Early Christianity*. Nashville: Abingdon, 1981.

Michel, O. 'Die Rettung Israels und die Rolle Roms nach den Reden im "Bellum Iudaicum". Analysen und Perspektiven', *ANRW* II.21.2.945-976.

Minar, E.L. 'Pythagorean Communism', *Transactions and Proceedings of the American Philological Association* 75 (1944) 34-46.

Minear, P.S. 'Dear Theo. The Kerygmatic Intention and Claim of the Book of Acts', *Interpretation* 27 (1973), 148-49.

Mitchell, A.C. 'The Social Function of Friendship in Acts 2:44-47 and 4:32-37', *JBL* 111 (1992) 255-272.

Moessner, D.P. *Lord of the Banquet: The Literary and Theological Significance of the Lukan Travel Narrative*. Minneapolis: Fortress, 1989.

Moessner, D.P. 'Paul in Acts: Preacher of Eschatological Repentance to Israel', *NTS* 34 (1988) 96-104.

Moessner, D.P. '"The Christ must suffer": New Light on the Jesus-Peter, Stephen, Paul Parallels in Luke–Acts', *NovT* 28 (1986) 220-256.

Moessner, D.P. 'The Script of the Scriptures in the Acts of the Apostles' in B. Witherington, III (ed.), *History, Literature and Society in the Book of Acts*. Cambridge: CUP, 1996.

Moessner, D.P. 'Paul and the Pattern of the Prophet Like Moses in Acts' in K.H. Richards (ed.), *Society of Bibilical Literature 1983 Seminar Papers*, 22. Chico, CA: Scholars Press, 1983, 203-12.

Montague, G.T. 'Pentecostal Fire: Spirit-Baptism in Luke–Acts' in K. McDonnel and G.T. Montague (eds.), *Christian Initiation and Baptism in the Holy Spirit*. Collegeville, MN: Liturgical Press, 1991, 22-41.

Moore, G.F. *Judaism in the First Centuries of the Christian Era: The Age of the Tannaim*, 3 vols. Cambridge, MA: Harvard University Press, 1927-1930.

Morgan, R. with J. Barton, *Biblical Interpretation*. Oxford: Oxford University Press, 1988.

Morgenthaler, R. , *Die Lukanische Geschichtsschreibung als Zeugnis: Gestalt und Gehalt der Kunst des Lukas* Teil II. Zürich: Zwingli-Verlag, 1949.

Morris, L. *The Gospel according to St. Luke*, 2nd edn. Grand Rapids: Eerdmans, 1989.

Moule, C.F.D. 'The Christology of Acts' in L.E. Keck and J.L. Martyn (eds.), *Studies in Luke–Acts*. Philadelphia: Fortress, 1980, 159-85.

Moule, C.F.D. *An Idiom Book of New Testament Greek* , 2nd edn. Cambridge: CUP, 1959.

Moule, C.F.D. *Worship in the New Testament*. London: Lutterworth, 1961; rep. Bramcote: Grove, 1977.

Mowery, R.L. 'God the Father in Luke–Acts' in E. Richard, (ed.), *New Views on Luke and Acts*. Minnesota: Michael Glazier, 1990, 124-32.

Moxnes, H. 'Patron-Client Relations and the New Community in Luke–Acts', in J. H. Neyrey (ed.), *The Social World of Luke–Acts*. Peabody, MA: Hendrickson, 1991, 241-268.

Moxnes, H. 'Social Relations and Economic Interaction in Luke's Gospel' in P. Luomanen (ed.), *Luke–Acts. Scandinavian Perspectives*. Göttingen: Vandenhoeck & Ruprecht, 1991, 58-75.

Moxnes, H. 'The Social Context of Luke's Community', *Interpretation* 48 (1994) 379-389.

Munck, J. *Paul and the Salvation of Mankind*. London: SCM, 1959.

Munck, J. *The Acts of the Apostles*, rev. edn. New York: Doubleday, 1967.

Murphy, L.E. *The Concept of the Twelve in Luke–Acts as a Key to the Lukan Perspective on the Restoration of Israel*. Southern Baptist Theological Seminary: Unpublished Ph.D Dissertation, 1988.

Murphy-O'Connor, J. 'Lots of God-Fearers? *Theosebeis* in the Aphrodisias Inscription', *Revue Biblique* 99 (1992) 418-24.

Murphy-O'Connor, J. *St. Paul's Corinth: Texts and Archaeology*, Good News Studies, 6. Wilmington, DE: Michael Glazier, 1983.

Mussner, F. *Die Apostelgeschichte*. Würzburg: Echter, 1984.

Neirynck, F. 'The Miracle Stories in the Acts of the Apostles: An Introduction' in J.Kremer (ed.), *Les Actes des Apôtres. Traditions, rédaction, théologie*, BETL 48. Leuven: Leuven University Press, 1979, 169-213.

Nellessen, E. *Zeugnis für Jesus und das Wort. Exegetische Untersuchungen zum lukanischen Zeugnisbegriff*. Köln: Peter Hanstein Verlag, 1976.

Nelson, P.K. *Leadership and Discipleship: A Study of Luke 22:24-30*, SBLDS 138. Atlanta: Scholars Press, 1994.

Neudorfer, H.-W. *Der Stephanuskreis in der Forschungsgeschichte seit F.C. Baur*. Gießen: Brunnen, 1983.

Neudorfer, H.-W. *Die Apostelgeschichte des Lukas* 1. Stuttgart, 1986.

Neudorfer, H.-W. 'Lukas', GBL 2. Wuppertal: Brockhaus, 1988, 900.

Neudorfer, H.-W. 'Urchristentum', ELThG 3. Wuppertal: Brockhaus, 1994.

Neusner, J. 'The Use of Later Rabbinic Evidence for the Study of First-Century Pharisaism' in W.S. Green (ed.), *Approaches to Ancient Judaism: Theory and Practice,* Brown Judaic Studies 1. Missoula, MT: Scholars Press, 1978.

Neusner, J. 'Two Pictures of the Pharisees: Philosophical Circle or Eating Club', *AThR* 64 (1982) 525-557.

Neusner, J. *From Politics to Piety: The Emergence of Pharisaic Judaism.* Englewood Cliffs, NJ: Prentice Hall, 1973.

Neusner, J. *Judaism in the Beginning of Christianity.* London/Philadelphia: SPCK/ Fortress, 1984.

Neusner, J. *The Pharisees: Rabbinic Perspectives. Studies in Ancient Judaism.* Leiden/ Hoboken, NJ: E.J. Brill/KTAV, 1973, 1985.

Neusner, J. *The Rabbinic Traditions about the Pharisees before 70,* 3 vols. Leiden: E.J. Brill, 1971.

Newman, C.C. , 'Acts' in L. Ryken and T. Longman (eds.), *A Complete Literary Guide to the Bible.* Grand Rapids: Zondervan, 1993, 436-44.

Neyrey, J.H. 'Acts 17, Epicureans and Theodicy: A Study of Stereotypes' in D. L. Balch, E. Ferguson and W. Meeks (eds.), *Greeks, Romans and Christians: Essays in Honor of Abraham J. Malherbe.* Minneapolis: Fortress, 1990, 118-134.

Neyrey, J.H. *The Passion according to Luke: A Redaction Study of Luke's Soteriology.* New York: Paulist, 1985.

Neyrey, J.H. *The Social World of Luke-Acts: Models for Interpretation.* Peabody, MA: Hendrickson, 1991.

Neyrey, J.H. 'The Symbolic Universes of Luke–Acts: "They Turn the World Upside Down"', in *The Social World of Luke–Acts: Models for Interpretation.* Peabody, MA: Hendrickson, 1991.

Nielsen, H.K. ‚*Heilung und Verkündigung: Das Verständnis der Heilung und ihres Verhältnisses zur Verkündigung bei Jesus und in der ältesten Kirche,* ATDan 22. Leiden and New York: E.J. Brill, 1987.

Nock, A.D., C. Roberts and T.C. Skeat , 'The Guild of Zeus Hypsistos', *HThR* 24 (1936) 39-89.

Nolland, J. 'A Fresh Look at Acts 15:10', *NTS* 27 (1980) 105-115.

Nolland, J. *Luke 1 - 9:20.* Dallas: Word Press, 1989.

Nolland, J. *Luke 9:21-18:34.* Dallas: Word Press, 1993.

Nolland, J. *Luke 18:35 - 24:53.* Dallas: Word Press, 1993.

Nolland, J. *Luke's Readers: A Study of Luke 4.22-8; Acts 13.46; 18.6; 28.28 and Luke 21.5-36.* University of Cambridge: Unpublished PhD Dissertation, 1977.

O'Brien, P.T. 'The Church as a Heavenly and Eschatological Entity' in D. A. Carson (ed.), *The Church in the Bible and the World.* Exeter and Grand Rapids: Paternoster and Baker, 1987, 88–119.

O'Collins, G.G. 'Salvation', in *ABD* 5:907-14.

O'Neill, J.C. *The Theology of Acts in its Historical Setting,* 2nd edn. London: SPCK, 1970 (1st edn., 1961).

O'Reilly, L. *Word and Sign in the Acts of the Apostles.* Rome: Pontifical Biblical Institute, 1987.

O'Toole, R.F. 'Christ's Resurrection in Acts 13:13-52', *Bib* 60 (1979) 361-372.

O'Toole, R.F. 'Parallels Between Jesus and His Followers: A Further Study', *BZ* 27 (1983) 195-212.

O'Toole, R.F. 'Paul at Athens and Luke's Notion of Worship', *RB* 89 (1982) 185-197.

O'Toole, R.F. 'Reflections on Luke's Treatment of Jews in Luke–Acts', *Bib* 74 (1993) 529-55.

O'Toole, R.F. 'The Kingdom of God in Luke–Acts, in W. Willis (ed.), *The Kingdom of God in Twentieth-Century Interpretation*. Peabody, MA: Hendrickson, 1987.

O'Toole, R.F. *Acts 26: The Christological Climax of Paul's Defense (Acts 22:1-26:32)*, AB 78. Rome: Pontifical Biblical Institute, 1978.

O'Toole, R.F. *The Unity of Luke's Theology: An Analysis of Luke- Acts*, GNS 9. Wilmington, DE: Michael Glazier, 1984.

O'Toole, R.F. 'Activity of the Risen Christ in Luke–Acts', *Biblica* 62 (1981) 471-98.

Ogilvie, R.M.*The Romans and their Gods in the Age of Augustus*. London: Chatto & Windus, 1969.

Overman, J.A. 'The God-Fearers: Some Neglected Features', *JSNT* 32 (1988)17-26.

Palmer, D.W. 'Acts and the Ancient Historical Monograph', in A.D. Clarke and B.W. Winter (eds.), *The Book of Acts in Its Ancient Literary Setting*, A1CS, vol 1. Grand Rapids/Carlisle: Eerdmans/Paternoster, 1993, 1-29.

Palmer, D.W. 'Mission to Jews and Gentiles in the Last Episode of Acts', *RTR* 52 (1993) 62-73.

Parsons, M.C. and R. I. Pervo, *Rethinking the Unity of Luke and Acts*. Philadelphia: Fortress, 1993.

Parsons, M.C. *The Departure of Jesus in Luke–Acts: The Ascension Narratives in Context*, JSNTSS 21. Sheffield: JSOT Press, 1987.

Pelling, C.B.R. 'Synkrisis in Plutarch's Lives' in F.E. Brenk and I. Gallo (eds.), *Miscellanea Plutarchia, Giornale Filologico Ferrarese* 8 (1986) 83-96.

Penny, J.M. *The Missionary Emphasis of Lukan Pneumatology*, JPTS 12, Sheffield Academic Press, 1997.

Pereira, F. *Ephesus: Climax of Universalism in Luke–Acts. A Redactional Study of Paul's Ephesian Ministry (Acts 18:23-20:1)*, Jesuit Theological Forum 10.1. Anand, India: Gujarat Sahitya Prakash, 1983.

Peristiany, J.G. (ed.), *Honour and Shame: The Values of Mediterranean Society*. London: Weidenfeld and Nicolson, 1965.

Perkins, P. '"I Have Seen the Lord" (John 20:18): Women Witnesses to the Resurrection', *Interpretation* 46/1 (1992), 31–41.

Perkins, P. *Peter: Apostle for the Whole Church*. Columbia: University of South Carolina Press, 1994.

Perlewitz, L.A. *A Christology of the Book of Acts: Modes of Presence*. St Louis: Unpublished Dissertation, 1977.

Perry, G.R. *"No Other Name": Luke's Recentralization of the Cult of Israel*. Columbia Theological Seminary: Unpublished Masters Dissertation, 1995.

Pervo, R.I. *Luke's Story of Paul*. Minneapolis: Fortress, 1990.

Pesch, R. *Die Apostelgeschichte*, 2 vols, EKKNT 5. Zürich and Neurkirchen-Vluyn: Benziger and Neukirchener, 1986.

Peterson, D. 'The Motif of Fulfillment and the Purpose of Luke–Acts' in B.W. Winter and A.D. Clarke (eds.), *The Book of Acts in Its Ancient Literary Setting* , A1CS, vol 1. Grand Rapids/Carlisle: Eerdmans/Paternoster, 1993, 83-104.

Peterson, D. *Engaging with God. A Biblical Theology of Worship*. Grand Rapids/ Leicester: Eerdmans/Apollos, 1992.

Pfitzner, V.C. 'Continuity and Discontinuity: The Lucan View of History in Acts' in H. P. Hamann (ed.), *Theologia Crucis. Studies in Honour of Hermann Sasse*. Adelaide, SA: Lutheran Publishing House, 1975.

Pfitzner, V.C. '"Pneumatic" Apostleship? Apostle and Spirit in the Acts of the Apostles' in W. Haubeck and M.Bachmann (eds.), *Wort in der Zeit. Neutestamentliche Studien: Festgabe für Karl Heinrich Rengstorf.* Leiden: E.J. Brill, 1980, 211-35.

Philip, J.A. *Pythagoras and Early Pythagoreanism,* Toronto: University of Toronto Press, 1966.

Pilch, J.J. 'Sickness and Health in Luke–Acts' in J.H. Neyrey (ed.), *The Social World of Luke–Acts.* Peabody, MA: Hendrickson, 1991, 181-209.

Pilgrim, W.E. *The Death of Christ in Lukan Soteriology.* Princeton Theological Seminary: Unpublished Th.D. Dissertation, 1971.

Pillai, C.A.J. *Apostolic Interpretation of History: A Commentary on Acts 13:16-41.* Hicksville, NY: Exposition, 1980.

Pitt-Rivers, J. *The Fate of Shechem or, The Politics of Sex.* Cambridge: CUP, 1977.

Pixner, B. *Wege des Messias und Stätten der Urkirche.* Gießen and Basel: Brunnen, 1991.

Plümacher, E. 'Eine Thukydidesreminiszenz in der Apostelgeschichte (Act., 20,33-35—Thuk. II 97, 3f.)', *ZNW* 83 (1992) 270-275.

Plummer, A. *The Gospel according to St. Luke,* 3rd edn. Edinburgh: T. & T. Clark, 1900.

Polhill, J. *Acts.* Nashville: Broadman Press, 1992.

Porter, S.E. 'Excursus: The "We" Passages' in D.W. J. Gill and C. Gempf (eds.), *The Book of Acts in Its Graeco-Roman Setting,* A1CS, vol 2. Grand Rapids/Carlisle: Eerdmans/Paternoster, 1994, 545–574.

Pöschl, J. 'Das Märchen vom Schlaraffenland', *Beiträge zur Geschichte der Deutschen Sprache und Literatur* 5 (1878) 391–393.

Powell, M.A. 'The Religious Leaders in Luke: A Literary-Critical Study', *JBL* 109 (1990) 93-110.

Powell, M.A. *What Are They Saying About Acts?* New York: Paulist Press, 1991.

Powell, M.A. 'Salvation in Luke–Acts', *WW* 12 (1992) 5-10.

Praeder, S.M. 'Jesus-Paul, Peter-Paul and Jesus-Peter Parallels in Luke–Acts: A History of Reader Research' in *Society of Biblical Literature 1984 Seminar Papers,* 23. Chico, CA: Scholars Press, 1984, 23-39.

Pred, A. *Making Histories and Constructing Human Geographies: The Local Transformation of Practice, Power Relations, and Consciousness.* Boulder: Westview, 1990.

Preuschen, E. *Die Apostelgeschichte,* HNT 4.1. Tübingen: J.C.B. Mohr (Paul Siebeck), 1912.

Price, R.M. 'Confirmation and Charisma', *Saint Luke's Journal of Theology* 33 (1990) 173-182.

Price, S.R.F. *Rituals and Power: The Roman Imperial Cult in Asia Minor.* Cambridge: CUP, 1984.

Prince, G. *Narrative as Theme: Studies in French Fiction.* Lincoln and London: University of Nebraska, 1992.

Quesnel, M. *Baptisés dans L'Esprit.* Paris: Cerf, 1985.

Rackham, R.B. *The Acts of the Apostles.* London: Methuen, 1901.

Radl, W. *Das Lukas-Evangelium,* ErFor 261. Darmstadt: Wissenschaftliche, 1988.

Räisänen, H. 'The Redemption of Israel: A Salvation-Historical Problem in Luke–Acts' in P. Luomanen (ed.), *Luke–Acts. Scandinavian Perspectives.* Göttingen:

Vandenhoeck & Ruprecht, 1991, 94-114.

Räisänen, H. 'Freiheit vom Gesetz im Urchristentum', *ST* 46 (1992) 55-67.

Rapske, B. *The Book of Acts and Paul in Roman Custody*, A1CS, vol. 3. Grand Rapids/ Carlisle: : Eerdmans/Paternoster, 1994.

Rasco, E. *La teologia de Lucas: origen, desarrollo, orientaciones*. Rome: Gregorian University, 1976.

Recker, R.R. 'The Lordship of Christ and Mission in the Book of Acts', *RefRev* 37/3 (1984) 178.

Refoulé, F. 'Le discours de Pierre à l'assemblée de Jérusalem', *Revue Biblique* 100 (1993) 239-51.

Rehm, B. (ed.), *Homilien*, Die PseudoKlementinen, vol 1, GCS 42. Berlin: Akademie, 1953.

Rehm, B. (ed.), *Rekognitionen in Rufins Übersetzung*, Die PseudoKlementinen, vol 2, GCS 51. Berlin: Akademie, 1965.

Reicke, B. 'Some Reflections on Worship in the New Testament', in A.J.B. Higgins (ed.), *New Testament Essays: Studies in Memory of T.W. Manson*. Manchester: Manchester University, 1959, 194-209.

Reicke, B. 'The Risen Lord and His Church: The Theology of Acts', *Interpretation* 13 (1959) 157-69.

Rengstorf, K.H. , 'The Election of Matthias Acts 1:15ff.', in W. Klasson and G. F. Snyder (eds.), *Current Issues in New Testament Interpretation: Essays in Honor of Otto A. Piper*. London: SCM, 1962, 178–192.

Rese, M. *Alttestamentliche Motive in der Christologie des Lukas*. Gütersloh: Gütersloher, 1969.

Rese, M. 'Die Funktion der alttestamentlichen Zitate und Anspielungen in den Reden der Apostelgeschichte' in J. Kremer (ed.), *Les Actes des Apôtres: traditions, rédaction, théologie*. Leuven: Leuven University Press, 1979, 61-79.

Rétif, A. 'Témoigne et prédication missionaire dans les Actes des Apôtres', *NRT* 73 (1951) 152–165.

Reynolds, J. and R. Tannenbaum, *Jews and God-fearers at Aphrodisias: Greek Inscriptions with Commentary*, CambPS Suppl. 12. Cambridge: Cambridge Philological Society, 1987.

Richard, E. *Acts 6.1-8.4: The Author's Method of Composition*, SBLDS 42. Missoula: Scholars Press, 1978.

Richard, E. 'Acts 7: An Investigation of the Samaritan Evidence', *CBQ* 39 (1977) 190-208.

Richard, E. 'The Creative Use of Amos by the Author of Acts', *NovT* 24 (1982) 37-53.

Richard, E. 'The Polemical character of the Joseph Episode in Acts 7', *JBL* 98 (1979) 255-267.

Richardson, P. *Israel in the Apostolic Church*, SNTSMS 10. Cambridge: CUP, 1969.

Riches, J. 'The Synoptic Evangelists and Their Communities' in J. Becker (ed.), *Christian Beginnings. Word and Community from Jesus to Post-Apostolic Times*. Louisville: Westminster and John Knox, 1993, 213-241.

Ridderbos, H.N. *The Speeches of Peter in the Acts of the Apostles*. London: Tyndale Press, 1962.

Riesner, R. 'Das Jerusalemer Essenerquartier und die Urgemeinde', forthcoming in *ANRW*, II, 26. 2.

Riesner, R. 'Das Jerusalemer Essenerviertel. Antwort auf einige Einwände' in Z.J.

Kapera (ed.), *Intertestamental Essays in honour of Józef Tadeusz Milik*. Kraków: Enigma Press, 1992, 179-186.

Riesner, R. 'Essener und Urkirche in Jerusalem', *Bibel und Kirche* 40 (1985) 64-76.

Riesner, R. 'James's Speech (Acts 15:13-21), Simeon's Hymn (Luke 2:29-32) and Luke's Sources' in J.B. Green and M. Turner (eds.), *Jesus of Nazareth,Lord and Christ*. Grand Rapids/Carlisle: Eerdmans/Paternoster, 1994, 263-78.

Riesner, R. 'Josephus' "Gate of the Essenes" in Modern Discussion', *ZDPV* 105 (1989) 105-109.

Riesner, R. *Die Frühzeit des Apostels Paulus: Studien zur Chronologie, Missionsstrategie und Theologie*, WUNT, 71. Tübingen: J.C.B. Mohr (Paul Siebeck), 1994.

Robinson, Jr.,W.C. 'On Preaching the Word of God (Luke 8:4-21)' in L.E. Keck and J.L. Martyn (eds.), *Studies in Luke–Acts*. Philadelphia: Fortress, 1966, 131-138.

Rolland, P. 'L'organisation du Livre des Actes et de l'ensemble de l'oeuvre de Luc', *Bib* 65 (1984) 81-86.

Roloff, J. *Apostolat-Verkündigung-Kirche*. Gütersloh: Gütersloher, 1965.

Roloff, J. *Die Apostelgeschichte*. Göttingen and Berlin: Vandenhoeck & Ruprecht and Evangelische Verlagsanstalt, 1981, 1988.

Rordorf, W.D. 'Was wissen wir über die christlichen Gottesdiensträume der vorkonstantinischen Zeit?', *ZNW* 55 (1964) 110-128.

Rosenblatt, M-E. *Paul the Accused: His Portrait in the Acts of the Apostles*, ZS. Collegeville, MN: Liturgical Press, 1995.

Rosner, B. 'Acts and Biblical History' in B.W. Winter and A.D. Clarke (eds.), *The Book of Acts in its Ancient LiterarySetting*, A1CS, vol. 1. Grand Rapids/Carlisle: Eerdmans/Paternoster, 1993, 65-82.

Runia, D.T. *Philo in Early Christian Literature: A Survey*. Assen: Van Gorcum, 1993.

Russell, W. 'The Anointing with the Holy Spirit in Luke–Acts', *Trinity Journal* 7 (1986) 47-63.

Ryken, L. *Words of Life: A Literary Introduction to the New Testament*. Grand Rapids; Baker, 1987.

Salmon, M. 'Insider or Outsider? Luke's Relationship with Judaism' in J.B. Tyson (ed.), *Luke–Acts and the Jewish People: Eight Critical Perspectives*. Minneapolis: Augsburg, 1988, 76-82.

Salo, K. *Luke's Treatment of the Law. A Redaction-Critical Investigation*, Annales Academiae Scientiarum Fennicae, Dissertationes Humanorum Litterarum 57. Helsinki: Suomalainen Tiedeakatemia, 1991.

Sanders, J.T. 'Chapter 10: The Pharisees in Luke–Acts' in D.E. Groh and R. Jewett (eds.), *The Living Text: Essays in Honor of Ernest W. Saunders*. London and New York: University Press of America, 1985, 141-88.

Sanders, J.T. 'The Jewish People in Luke–Acts' in J.B. Tyson (ed.), *Luke–Acts and the Jewish People: Eight Critical Perspectives*. Minneapolis: Augsburg, 1988, 51-75.

Sanders, J.T. 'Who Is a Jew and Who Is a Gentile in the Book of Acts?', *NTS* 37 (1991) 434-55.

Sanders, J.T. *The Jews in Luke–Acts*. London and Philadelphia: SCM and Fortress, 1987.

Sanders, J.T. 'The Salvation of the Jews in Luke–Acts' in C. H. Talbert (ed.), *Luke–Acts: New Perspectives from the SBL Seminar*. New York: Crossroads, 1984.

Sandmel, S. *Philo's Place in Judaism: A Study of Conceptions of Abraham in Jewish Literature*. New York: KTAV Publishing House, 1971.

Satterthwaite, P. E. 'Acts against the Background of Classical Rhetoric, in B.W. Winter and A.D. Clarke (eds.), *The Book of Acts in its Ancient Literary Setting* A1CS, vol 1. Grand Rapids/Carlisle: Eerdmans/Paternoster, 1993, 337-79.

Scharlemann, M.H. 'Stephen's Speech: A Lucan Creation?', *ConJ* 4 (1978) 52-57.

Schille, G. *Die Apostelgeschichte des Lukas.* Berlin: Evangelische Verlagsanstalt, 1983.

Schille, G. *Die urchristliche Kollegialmission,* AThANT 48. Zürich: Zwingli, 1967.

Schlatter, A. *Das Evangelium des Lukas aus seinen Quellen erklärt,* 3rd edn. Stuttgart: Calwer, 1975.

Schlatter, A. *Die Geschichte der ersten Christenheit,* 4th edn. Gütersloh: Bertelsmann, 1927.

Schmithals, W. *The Office of Apostle in the Early Church.* ET; London: SPCK, 1971.

Schmithals, W. *Die Apostelgeschichte des Lukas.* Zürich: Theologischer Verlag, 1982.

Schnackenburg, R. 'Apostles Before and After Paul's Time' in W.W. Gasque and R.P. Martin (eds.), *Apostolic History and the Gospel.* Grand Rapids and Exeter: Eerdmans and Paternoster, 1970, 287-303.

Schneckenburger, M. *Ueber den Zweck der Apostelgeschichte.* Bern: xx, 1841.

Schneckenburger, M. 'Beiträge zur Eklärung und Kritik der Apostelgeschichte...', *Theologische Studien und Kritiken* 28 (1855)498-570.

Schneider, G. *Die Apostelgeschichte,* 2 vols. Freiburg, Basel and Wien: Herder, 1980, 1982.

Schneider, G. 'Die zwölf Apostel als "Zeugen": Wesen, Ursprung und Funktion einer lukanischen Konzeption', in *Lukas, Theologe der Heilsgeschichte: Aufsätze zum lukanischen Doppelwerk,* BBB 59. Bonn: P. Hanstein, 1985, 61-85.

Schneider, G. 'Die Petrusrede vor Kornelius; das Verhältnis von Tradition und Komposition in Apg 10,34-43' in *Lukas, Theologe der Heilsgeschichte: Aufsätze zum lukanischen Doppelwerk,* BBB 59. Bonn: P. Hanstein, 1985, 253-279.

Schnelle, U. 'Neutestamentliche Anthropologie: Ein Forschungsbericht', *ANRW* II.26.3 (forthcoming)

Schnelle, U. *Neutestamentliche Anthropologie: Jesus - Paulus - Johannes,* Biblisch-Theologische Studien 18. Neukirchen-Vluyn: Neukirchener, 1991.

Schoedel, W.R. *Ignatius of Antioch.* Philadelphia: Fortress Press, 1985.

Schubert, P. 'The Final Cycle of Speeches in the Book of Acts', *JBL* 87 (1968) 1-16.

Schürer, E. *History of the Jewish People in the Age of Jesus Christ,* Vols. I-III, rev. edn. Edinburgh: T. & T. Clark, 1973-87.

Schürmann, H. *Das Lukasevangelium, Erster Teil: Kommentar zu Kap. 1.1-9-50,* HTKNT III.1, 4th edn. Freiburg, Basel and Wien: Herder, 1990.

Schütz, F. *Der leidende Christus: Die angefochtene Gemeinde und das Christuskerygma der lukanischen Schriften,* BWANT 89. Stuttgart: W. Kohlhammer, 1969.

Schwartz, D.R. 'The End of the ΓH (Acts 1:8): Beginning or End of the Christian Vision?', *JBL* 105 (1986): 669-76.

Schwartz, D.R. 'The End of the Line: Paul in the Canonical Book of Acts', in W.S. Babcock (ed.), *Paul and the Legacies of Paul.* Dallas: Southern Methodist University Press, 1990, 1-23.

Schwarz, D.R. 'The Futility of Preaching Moses (Acts 15:21)', *Bib* 67 (1986) 276-81.

Schweizer, E. *Church Order in the New Testament,* SBT 32. ET; London: SCM, 1961.

Schweizer, E. *Luke: A Challenge to Present Theology.* London and Atlanta: SPCK and John Knox, 1980, 1982.

Scott, J.J. Jr. 'Stephen's Defense and the World Mission of the People of God', *JETS* 21 (1978) 131-141.

Scott, J.J. Jr. 'Stephen's Speech: A Possible Model for Luke's Historical Method', *JETS* 17 (1974) 91-97.

Scott, J.M. 'Luke's Geographical Horizon' in D.W.J. Gill and C. Gempf, *The Book of Acts in Its Graeco-Roman Setting*, A1CS, vol. 2. Grand Rapids and Carlisle: Eerdmans and Paternoster, 1994, 483-544.

Scroggs, R. 'The Earliest Christian Communities as Sectarian Movement' in J. Neusner (ed.), *Christianity, Judaism and Other Greco-Roman Cults*, Part Two. Leiden: E.J. Brill, 1975, 1-23.

Scroggs, R. 'The Sociological Interpretation of the New Testament: The Present State of Research', *NTS* 26 (1980) 164-179.

Seccombe, D.P. 'Luke and Isaiah', *NTS* 27 (1981) 252-59.

Seccombe, D.P. *Possessions and the Poor in Luke–Acts*. Linz: SNTU, 1982.

Seeligmann, I. 'Voraussetzungen der Midrashexegese', *SVT* 1 (1953) 150-81.

Seifrid, M.A. 'Jesus and the Law in Acts', *JSNT* 30 (1987) 39-57.

Seifrid, M.A. 'Messiah and Mission in Acts: A Brief Response to J. B. Tyson', *JSNT* 36 (1989) 47-50.

Selwyn, E.G. *The First Epistle of St. Peter*. London: Macmillan, 1946.

Shelton, J.B. *Mighty in Word and Deed: The Role of the Holy Spirit in Luke–Acts*. Peabody, MA: Hendrickson, 1991.

Shelton, J.B. '"Filled with the Holy Spirit" and "Full of the Holy Spirit": Lucan Redactional Phrases' in P. Elbert (ed.), *Faces of Renewal*. Peabody, MA: Hendrickson, 1988, 81-107.

Shepherd, W. *The Narrative Function of the Holy Spirit as Character in Luke–Acts*. Atlanta: Scholars Press, 1994.

Siegert, F. 'Mass Communication and Prose Rhythm in Luke–Acts' in S. E. Porter and T. H. Olbricht (eds.), *Rhetoric and the New Testament*. Sheffield: JSOT Press, 1993, 42-58.

Siegert, F. 'Gottesfürchtige und Sympathisanten', *JSJ* 4 (1973) 109-64.

Simpson, J.W. Jr. 'Letters to the Thessalonians' in G.F. Hawthorne, R. P. Martin and D. G. Reid (eds.), *Dictionary of Paul and His Letters*. Downers Grove, IL: IVP, 1993, 932-39.

Simon, M. 'Saint Stephen and the Jerusalem Temple', *JEH* 2 (1951) 133-137.

Simon, M. *St. Stephen and the Hellenists in the Primitive Church*. London: Longmans, 1958.

Simon, M. 'The Apostolic Decree and Its Setting in the Ancient Church', *BJRL* 52 (1970) 437-60.

Sloan, R. '"Signs and Wonders": A Rhetorical Clue to the Pentecost Discourse', *EvQ* 63 (1990) 225-40.

Smend, R. & U. Luz, *Gesetz*. Stuttgart: Kohlhammer, 1981.

Smith, D.E. 'Table Fellowship as a Literary Motif in the Gospel of Luke', *JBL* 106 (1987) 613-638.

Smith, T.V. *Petrine Controversies in Early Christianity*, WUNT 2,15. Tübingen: J.C.B. Mohr (Paul Siebeck), 1985.

Smyth, H.W. and G.M. Messing, *Greek Grammar*, rev. edn. Cambridge, MA: Harvard University Press, 1956.

Snook, L.E. 'Interpreting Luke's Theodicy for Fearful Christians', *WordWorld* 3 (1983) 304-11.

Soards, M.L. *The Speeches in Acts: Their Content, Context and Concerns*. Louisville: Westminster and John Knox, 1994.

Soards, M.L. 'The Speeches in Acts in Relation to Other Pertinent Ancient Literature', *Ephemerides Theologicae Lovanienses* 70 (1994) 65-90.

Soja, E.W. *Postmodern Geographies: The Reassertion of Space in Critical Social Theory*. London: Verso, 1989.

Spencer, F.S. 'Acts and Modern Literary Approaches' in B.W. Winter and A.D. Clarke (eds.), *The Book of Acts in Its Ancient Literary Setting* , A1CS, vol 1. Grand Rapids / Carlisle: Eerdmans / Paternoster, 1993, 381-414.

Spencer, F.S. *The Portrait of Philip in Acts. A Study of Roles and Relations*. Sheffield: JSOT Press, 1992.

Squires, J.T. *The Plan of God in Luke–Acts*, SNTSMS 76. Cambridge: CUP, 1993.

Stählin, G. *Die Apostelgeschichte*. Göttingen: Vandenhoeck & Ruprecht, 1970.

Stählin, G. 'Τὸ πνεῦμα 'Ιησοῦ' (Apostelgeschichte 16.7)' in B. Lindars and S.S. Smalley (eds.), *Christ and Spirit in the New Testament*. Cambridge: CUP, 1973, 229-52.

Stalder, K. 'Der Heilige Geist in der lukanischen Ekklesiologie', *Una Sancta* 30 (1975) 287-293.

Stanton, G.N. 'Literary Criticism, Ancient and Modern' in *A Gospel for a New People*. Edinburgh: T. & T. Clark, 1992, 54-84.

Steck, O.H. *Israel und das gewaltsame Geschick der Propheten*. Neukirchen-Vluyn: Neukirchener, 1967.

Steichele, H. *Vergleich der Apostelgeschichte mit der antiken Geschichtsschreibung*. München: Unpublished Dissertation, 1972.

Stein, R.H. *Luke*. Nashville: Broadman, 1992.

Stemberger, G. 'Die Stephanusrede (Apg 7) und die jüdische Tradition', in A. Fuchs (ed.), *Jesus in der Verkündigung der Kirche*. Linz, 1976, 154-174.

Sterling, G.R. *Historiography and Self-Definition: Josephus, Luke–Acts and Apologetic Historiography*. Leiden: E.J. Brill, 1992.

Stibbe, M.W.G. *John's Gospel*, NT Readings. London and New York: Routledge, 1994.

Stowers, S.K. 'The Social Sciences and the Study of Early Christianity' in W.S. Green (ed.), *Approaches to Ancient Judaism*, Vol. V. Atlanta: Scholars Press, 1985, 149-181.

Strack, H.L. and P. Billerbeck, *Kommentar zum Neuen Testament*. München: C.H. Beck, 1924.

Strange, J.F. 'Archæology and the Religion of Judaism in Palestine', *ANRW* II.19.1 (1979) 646-685.

Strauss, M.L. *The Davidic Messiah in Luke–Acts: the Promise and its Fulfillment in Luke's Christology*, JSNTMS 110. Sheffield Academic Press, 1995.

Stronstad, R. *The Charismatic Theology of St Luke*. Peabody, MA: Hendrickson, 1984.

Stuhlmacher, P. *Biblische Theologie des Neuen Testaments I: Grundlegung, Von Jesus zu Paulus*. Göttingen: Vandenhoeck & Ruprecht, 1992.

Sukenik, E.L. *Ancient Synagogues in Palestine and Greece*. London: Oxford University Press, 1934.

Sutherland, S.R. *Atheism and the Rejection of God*. Oxford: Başil Blackwell, 1977.

Syreeni, K. 'Matthew, Luke, and the Law: A Study in Hermeneutical Exegesis' in T. Veijola (ed.), *The Law in the Bible and in Its Environment*. Helsinki and Göttingen: Finnish Exegetical Society and Vandenhoeck & Ruprecht,1990,126-55.

Taeger, J.-W. *Der Mensch und sein Heil: Studien zum Bild des Menschen und zur Sicht der Bekehrung bei Lukas*, SNT 14. Gütersloh: G. Mohn, 1982.

Tajra, H.W. *The Trial of St. Paul*, WUNT 2,35. Tübingen: J. C. B. Mohr (Paul Siebeck), 1989).

Talbert, C.H. 'An Anti-Gnostic Tendency in Lucan Christology', *NTS* 14 (1967-68) 259-71.

Talbert, C.H. 'Promise and Fulfillment in Lukan Theology, in C. H. Talbert (ed.), *Luke–Acts: New Perspectives from the Society of Biblical Literature Seminar*. New York: Crossroads, 1984, 91-103.

Talbert, C.H. 'Shifting Sands: The Recent Study of the Gospel of Luke' in J.L. Mays (ed.), *Interpreting the Gospels*. Philadelphia: Fortress, 1981, 197-213.

Talbert, C.H. *Reading Luke: A Literary and Theological Commentary on the Third Gospel*. New York: Crossroads, 1989.

Talbert, C.H. (ed.), *Perspectives on Luke–Acts*. Edinburgh: T. & T. Clark, 1978.

Talbert, C.H. *Acts*. Atlanta: John Knox, 1984.

Talbert, C.H. *Literary Patterns, Theological Themes and the Genre of Luke–Acts*, SBLMS 20. Missoula, MT: Scholars Press, 1974.

Talbert, C.H. *Luke and the Gnostics: An Examination of the Lucan Purpose*. Nashville: Abingdon, 1966.

Tannehill, R.C. *The Narrative Unity of Luke–Acts: A Literary Interpretation*, 2 vols. Philadelphia: Fortress, 1986, 1990.

Tannehill, R.C. 'Israel in Luke–Acts: A Tragic Story', *JBL* 104 (1985) 69-85.

Tannehill, R.C. 'Rejection by Jews and Turning to Gentiles: The Pattern of Paul's Mission in Acts' in J.B.Tyson (ed.), *Luke–Acts and the Jewish People: Eight Critical Perspectives*. Minneapolis: Augsburg, 1988, 83-101.

Tannehill, R.C. 'The Functions of Peter's Mission Speeches in the Narrative of Acts', *NTS* 37, 3 (1991) 400-414.

Taylor, N. *Paul, Antioch and Jerusalem: A Study in Relationships and Authority in Earliest Christianity*, JSNTSS 66. Sheffield Academic Press, 1992.

Thüsing, W. *Erhöhungsvorstellung und Parusieerwartung in der Ältesten nachösterlichen Christologie*, SBS 42. Stuttgart: Katholisches Bibelwerk, 1969.

Thiselton, A.C. *New Horizons in Hermeneutics*. London: Marshall Pickering, 1992.

Thornton, C.-J. *Der Zeuge des Zeugen*, WUNT 56.Tübingen: J.R.Mohr (Paul Siebeck), 1991.

Thrall, M.E. *A Critical and Exegetical Commentary on the Second Epistle to the Corinthians,Vol.I*. Edinburgh: T. & T. Clark, 1994.

Throckmorton, B.H. 'Σῴζειν, σωτηρία in Luke–Acts', *Stiudia Evangelica* 6 (1973) 515-26.

Tiede, D.L. *Luke*. Minneapolis: Augsburg, 1988.

Tiede, D.L. 'Contending with God: The Death of Jesus and the Trial of Jesus in Luke–Acts' in B.A. Pearson et al. (eds.),*The Future of Early Christianity: Essays in Honor of Helmut Koester*. Minneapolis: Fortress, 1991, 301-8.

Tiede, D.L. 'The Exaltation of Jesus and the Restoration of Israel in Acts 1', *Harvard Theological Review* 79 1986, 278-86.

Tiede, D.L. *Prophecy and History in Luke–Acts*. Philadelphia: Fortress, 1980.

Trites, A.A. *The New Testament Concept of Witness*, SNTSMS. Cambridge: CUP, 1977.

Trocmé, E. *Le 'livre des Actes' et l'histoire*. Paris: Presses Universitaires de France, 1957.

Turner , M. and J.B. Green(eds.), *Jesus of Nazareth, Lord and Christ*. Grand Rapids and Carlisle: Eerdmans and Paternoster, 1994.

Turner, C.H. 'Chronology of the New Testament', *Hastings' Dictionary of the Bible*, 1, 421-23.

Turner, M.M.B. 'Prayer in the Gospels and Acts' in D.A. Carson (ed.), *Teach Us to Pray: Prayer in the Bible and the World*. Grand Rapids: Baker, 1992, 52-83.

Turner, M.M.B. 'Spiritual Gifts: Then and Now', *Vox Evangelica* 15 (1985) 7-64.

Turner, M.M.B. 'The Sabbath, Sunday, and the Law in Luke–Acts' in D.A. Carson (ed.), *From Sabbath to Lord's Day*. Grand Rapids: Eerdmans, 1982, 99-158.

Turner, M.M.B. 'The Spirit and the Power of Jesus' Miracles in the Lucan Perception', *NovT* 33 (1991) 124-52.

Turner, M.M.B. 'The Spirit of Christ and "Divine" Christology' in J.B. Green and M. Turner (eds.), *Jesus of Nazareth Lord and Christ*. Grand Rapids and Carlisle: Eerdmans and Paternoster, 1994, 413-36.

Turner, M.M.B. *Power From On High: The Spirit in Israel's Restoration and Witness in Luke–Acts*, JPT Monograph series: 9. Sheffield: Sheffield Academic Press, 1996.

Turner, M.M.B. '"Empowerment for Mission"? The Pneumatology of Luke–Acts: An Appreciation and Critique of James B. Shelton's *Mighty in Word and Deed*', *Vox Evangelica* 24 (1994) 103-22.

Turner, M.M.B. 'Holy Spirit' in J.B. Green and S. McKnight (eds.), *Dictionary of Jesus and the Gospels*. Downers Grove, IL/Leicester: IVP, 1992, 341-51.

Turner, M.M.B. 'Jesus and the Spirit in Lucan Perspective', *TynB*. 32 (1981) 3-42.

Turner, M.M.B. 'The Significance of Receiving the Spirit in Luke–Acts: A Survey of Modern Scholarship', *Trinity Journal* 2 (1981) 131-58.

Turner, M.M.B. 'The Spirit of Christ and Christology' in H.H. Rowdon (ed.), *Christ the Lord: Studies in Christology Presented to Donald Guthrie*. Downers Grove, IL and Leicester: IVP and Apollos, 1982, 168-90.

Turner, M.M.B. 'The Spirit of Prophecy and the Ethical/Religious Life of the Christian Community' in M. Wilson (ed.), *Spirit and Renewal: Essays in Honor of J. Rodman Williams*. Sheffield Academic Press, 1994, 166-90.

Turner, M.M.B. 'The Spirit of Prophecy and the Power of Authoritative Preaching in Luke–Acts: A Question of Origins', *NTS* 38 (1992) 66-88.

Tyson, J.B. 'The Emerging Church and the Problem of Authority in Acts', *Interpretation* 42/2 (1988), 132-45.

Tyson, J.B. (ed.), *Luke–Acts and the Jewish People: Eight Critical Perspectives*. Minneapolis: Augsburg, 1988.

Tyson, J.B. *Images of Judaism in Luke–Acts*. Columbia: University of South Carolina, 1992.

Uhlhorn, G. *Christian Charity in the Ancient Church*. Edinburgh, T. & T. Clark, 1883.

Uxkull-Gyllenband, W.G. *Griechische Kultur-Entstehungslehren*. Berlin: Leonard Simion, 1924.

van Aarde, A.G. '"The Most High God Does Live in Houses, but Not Houses Built by Men...": The Relativity of the Metaphor "Temple" in Luke–Acts', *Neot* 25 (1991) 51-64.

van de Sandt, H. 'An Explanation of Acts 15.6-21 in the Light of Deuteronomy 4:29-35 (LXX)', *JSNT* 46 (1992) 73-97.

van Pelt, J.R. 'Witness, in J. Hastings (ed.), *Dictionary of Christ and the Gospels*, 2 vols. Edinburgh: T. & T. Clark, 1908, II.830-32.

van Unnik, W.C. 'Der Ausdruck ἕως ἐσχάτου τῆς γῆ (Apostelgeschichte 1:8) und sein alttestamentliche Hintergrund', in van Unnik, W.C. and A.S. van der Woude (eds.), *Studia Biblica et Semitica: Theodoro Christiano Vriezen,*Wageningen: H. Veenman, 1966, 335-49; reprinted in *Sparsa Collecta: The Collected Essays of W.C. van Unnik*, vol 1. Leiden: E.J. Brill, 1973, 386-401.

van Unnik, W.C. 'The Christian's Freedom of Speech in the New Testament', *BJRL* 44 (1961) 466-88.

van Unnik, W.C. 'The "Book of Acts" the Confirmation of the Gospel', *NovT* 4 (1960), 26-59; reprinted in *Sparsa Collecta: The Collected Essays of U.C. van Unnik*, vol 1. Leiden: E.J. Brill, 1973, 340-373.

Vanhoye, A. 'Les Juifs selon les Actes des Apôtres et les Épîtres du Nouveau Testament', *Bib* 72 (1991) 70-89.

Veltman, F. 'The Defense Speeches of Paul in Acts' in C.H. Talbert (ed.), *Perspectives on Luke–Acts*. Danville, VA: Association of Baptist Professors of Religion, 1978, 243-256.

Verbeke, G. *L'Evolution de la doctrine du pneuma du Stoicisme a S. Augustin*. Paris: Brower, 1945.

Vermes, G. *The Dead Sea Scrolls in English*. Harmondsworth: Penguin, 1962.

Vermes, G. and M.D. Goodman, *The Essenes according to the Classical Sources*. Sheffield: JSOT Press, 1989.

Veyne, P. *Bread and Circuses*. Harmondsworth: Penguin, 1990.

Vielhauer, S.P. 'On the "Paulinism" of Acts' in L.E. Keck and J.A. Martin (eds.),*Studies in Luke Acts: Essays in Honor of Paul Schubert*. Nashville/Philadelphia: Abingdon/Fortress, 1966, 1980, 33-50.

Vielhauer, S.P. 'Zum "Paulinismus" der Apostelgeschichte', *EvTh* 10 (1950-51) 1-1/ in *Aufsätze zum Neuen Testament*. München: Chr. Kaiser, 1965, 9-27.

von Baer, H. *Der Heilige Geist in den Lukasschriften*. Stuttgart: Kohlhammer, 1926.

von Pöhlmann, R. *Geschichte der sozialen Fragen und des Sozialismus in der antiken Welt*, 2nd edn. München: Beck, 1912.

von Rad, G. *Old Testament Theology*, 2 vols, ET. New York: Harper and Row, 1962.

Voss, G. 'Zum Herrn und Messias gemacht hat Gott diesen Jesus' (Ap 2,36). Zur Christologie der lukanischen Schriften', *BibLeb* 8 (1967) 236-48.

Voss, G. *Die Christologie der lukanischen Schriften in Grundzügen*, SNT 2. Bruges-Paris: Brouwer, 1965.

Vriezen, T.C. *An Outline of Old Testament Theology*, ET. Oxford: Blackwell, 1970.

Walker, P.W.L. *The Holy City: New Testament Perspectives on Jerusalem*. Grand Rapids: Eerdmans, forthcoming.

Walker, W.O. Jr. 'The Timothy-Titus Problem Reconsidered', *ET* 92 (1981) 231-34.

Wall, C.M. 'Acts 2:22 - 15:12 as Narrative Commentary on Joel 3:1-5 (LXX)'. Seattle Pacific University: Unpublished MA Thesis, 1992.

Wall, R.W. 'The Acts of the Apostles in Canonical Context', *BTB* 18 (1988) 16-24.

Wall, R.W. and E.E. Lemcio, *The New Testament as Canon: A Reader in Canonical Criticism*, JSNTSS 76. Sheffield: JSOT Press, 1992.

Walter, V.L. 'Preach the Word—Grippingly', *TrinJ* 2 (1981) 49-61.

Watts, R.E. *The Influence of the Isaianic New Exodus on the Gospel of Mark*,. University of Cambridge: PhD Dissertation, 1990, forthcoming SNTSMS.

Weatherley, J.A. 'The Jews in Luke–Acts', *TynB* 40 (1989) 107-17.

Weatherly, J.A. *Jewish Responsibility for the Death of Jesus in Luke–Acts*, JSNTS 106. Sheffield Academic Press, 1994.

Webb, R.L. 'The Activity of John the Baptist's Expected Figure at the Threshing Floor (Matthew 3:12=Luke 3:17)', *JSNT* 43 (1991) 103-111.

Wedderburn, A.J.M. 'The "Apostolic Decree": Tradition and Redaction', *NovT* 35 (1993) 362-89.

Wedderburn, A.J.M. 'Traditions and Redaction in Acts 2:1-13', *JSNT* 55 (1994) 27-54.

Wehnert, J. *Die Wir-Passagen der Apostelgeschichte: Ein lukanisches Stilmittel aus jüdischer Tradition*, GTA 40. Göttingen: Vandenhoeck & Ruprecht, 1989.

Weinert, F.D. 'Luke, Stephen and the Temple in Luke–Acts', *BTB* 17 (1987) 88-90.

Weiser, A. 'Das "Apostelkonzil" (Apg 15, 1-35): Ereignis, Überlieferung, lukanische Deutung', *BZ* 28 (1984) 145-67.

Weiser, A. 'Zur Gesetzes- und Tempelkritik der "Hellenisten"' in K. Kertelge (ed.), *Das Gesetz im Neuen Testament*. QD 108. Freiburg: Herder, 1986, 146-68.

Weiser, A. *Die Apostelgeschichte 1-12*. Gütersloh and WÄrzburg: Mohn and Echter, 1981, 1985.

Wendt, H.H. *Die Apostelgeschichte*. Göttingen: xx, 1913.

Wenham, D. 'Acts and the Pauline Corpus' in B.W. Winter and A.D. Clarke (eds.), *The Book of Acts in Its Ancient Literary Setting*, A1CS, vol 1. Grand Rapids/Carlisle: Eerdmans/Paternoster, 1993, 215-58.

Wiefel, W. *Das Evangelium nach Lukas*, THKNT 3. Berlin: Evangelische, 1988.

Wikenhauser, A. *Die Apostelgeschichte*. Regensburg: Pustet, 1961.

Wilckens, U. *Die Missionsreden der Apostelgeschichte*, 3rd edn. Neukirchen-Vluyn: Neukirchener Verlag, 1974.

Wilcox, M. 'The "God-Fearers" in Acts–A Reconsideration', *JSNT* 13 (1981) 102-22.

Wilcox, M. *The Semitisms of Acts*. Oxford: Clarendon Press, 1965.

Wilcox, M. 'A Foreword to the Study of the Speeches in Acts', *SJLA* 12, 1 (1975) 206-25.

Wilcox, M. '"Upon the Tree"—Deuteronomy 21:22-23 in the New Testament', *JBL* 96 (1977) 85-99.

Williams, C.S.C. *The Acts of the Apostles*, BNTC 5. London: A. & C. Black, 1964.

Williams, D.J. *Acts*. San Francisco and Peabody, MA: Harper & Row and Hendrickson, 1985, 1990.

Willimon, W.H. *Acts*. Atlanta: Knox, 1988.

Wills, L.M. 'The Depiction of the Jews in Acts', *JBL* 110 (1991) 631-54.

Wilson, S.G. *Luke and the Law*. SNTSMS 50. Cambridge: CUP, 1983.

Wilson, S.G. *Luke and the Pastoral Epistles*. London: SPCK, 1979.

Wilson, S.G. *The Gentiles and the Gentile Mission in Luke–Acts*, MSSNTS 23. Cambridge: CUP, 1973.

Winter, B.W. 'In Public and in Private: Early Christians and Religious Pluralism' in A.D. Clarke and B.W. Winter (eds.), *One God, One Lord: Christianity in a World of Religious Pluralism*, 2nd edn. Grand Rapids: Baker, 1992, 125-148.

Winter, B.W. 'The Lord's Supper at Corinth: An Alternative Reconstruction', *RTR* 27.3 (1978) 73-78.

Winter, B.W. 'Official Proceedings and the Forensic Speeches in Acts 24-26' in B.W. Winter and A.D. Clarke (eds.), *The Book of Acts in Its Ancient Literary Setting*, A1CS, vol. 1. Grand Rapids/Carlisle: Eerdmans/Paternoster, 1993, 305-336.

Winter, B.W. *Seek the Welfare of the City: Citizens as Benefactors and Citizens*. Grand Rapids: Eerdmans, 1994.

Witherington, III, B. 'Lord', in R.P. Martin and P.H. Davids (eds.), *Dictionary of the*

New Testament (provisional title),Vol. III. Leicester: IVP, forthcoming.

Witherington, III, B. (ed.), *History, Literature and Society in the Book of Acts.* Cambridge: CUP, 1995.

Witherington, III, B. *Conflict and Community in Corinth: A Socio-Rhetorical Commentary on 1 and 2 Corinthians.* Grand Rapids: Eerdmans, 1994.

Witherington, III, B. 'Not so idle thoughts about εἰδολόθυτον',*TynB* 44 (1993) 237-254.

Witherup, R.D. 'Cornelius Over and Over and Over Again: Functional Redundancy in the Acts of the Apostles', *JSNT* 49 (1993) 45-66.

Woodhouse, J.W. 'Evangelism and Social Responsibility' in B. G. Webb (ed.) *Christians in Society* , Explorations 3. Homebush West, NSW: ANZEA, 1988, 3–26.

Wren, M. 'Sonship in Luke: The Advantage of a Literary Approach', *SJT* 37 (1984) 301-11.

Wright, N.T. 'How Can the Bible Be Authoritiative?', *Vox Evangelica* 21 (1991) 7-32.

Wright, N.T. *The New Testament and the People of God,* vol 1. London and Minneapolis: SPCK and Fortress, 1992.

Wuthnow, R. *Communities of Discourse: Ideology and Social Structure in the Reformation, the Enlightenment, and European Socialism.* Cambridge, MA and London: Harvard University Press, 1989.

Xeres, S. 'Il nome χριστιανοί come espressione dell'autocoscienza di un popolo nuovo' in M. Sordi (ed.), *Autocoscienza e rappresentazione dei popoli nell'antichità* , Contributi dell'Istituto di storia antica 49. Milano: Vita E. Pensiero, 1992, 211-225.

Yonge, C.D. *The Works of Philo Judaeus.* London: Bohn, 1855.

York, J.O. *The Last Shall Be First: The Rhetoric of Reversal in Luke.* Sheffield Academic Press, 1991.

Young, F.M. *The Use of Sacrificial Ideas in Greek Christian Writers from the New Testament to John Chrysostom.* Cambridge, MA: Philadelphia Patristic Foundation, 1979.

Zehnle, R. 'The Salvific Character of Jesus' Death in Lucan Soteriology', *TS* 30 (1969) 420-44.

Zerwick, M. and M. Grosveor, *Grammatical Analysis of the Greek New Testament,* Vol. 1. Rome: Pontifical Biblical Institute, 1974.

Zerwick, M. *Biblical Greek.* Rome: Pontifical Biblical Institute, 1963.

Ziesler, J.A. 'The Name of Jesus in the Acts of the Apostles', *JSNT* 4 (1979) 28-32.

Zmijewski, J. *Die Apostelgeschichte.* Regensburg: F. Pustet, 1994.

Zmijewski, J. *Die Eschatologiereden des Lukas-Evangelium: Eine traditions- und redaktionsgeschichtliche Untersuchung zu Lk 21,5-36 und Lk 17,20-37,* BBB 40. Bonn: P. Hanstein, 1972.

Zmijewski, J. 'Die Stephanusrede (Apg 7,2-53)—Literarisches und Theologisches', in *Das Neue Testament. Quelle christlicher Theologie und Glaubenspraxis.* Stuttgart: Katholisches Bibelwerk, 1986, 85-128.

Zweck, D. 'The Exordium of the Areopagus Speech, Acts 17.22,23', *NTS* 35 (1989) 94-103.

Index of Authors

A
Agnew, F.H. 170, 178
Aker, B. 339
Alexander, L.C.A. 20, 192, 213
Allison, D.C. 464
Andersen, T.D. 486
Arrington, F.L. 402, 415
Attridge, H.W. 310
Aune, D.E. 267, 425
Avigad, N. 479

B
Bachmann, M. 399
Balch, D.L. 309-10
Baldry, H.C. 505
Bammel, E. 500
Banks, R. 424
Barnard, L.W. 292
Barrett, C.K. 13, 96, 100, 108, 117, 132,
    134, 141, 170, 177, 183, 186,
    199, 206, 213, 216, 222, 304-5,
    328, 339, 378, 401, 406, 422,
    500, 518, 532
Bartchy, S.S. 91, 121, 500
Barth, K. 4
Barton, J. 461
Barton, S.C. 463, 469
Baumbach, G. 134
Baumgärtel, F. 113
Bayer, H.F. 259-60, 265-7, 269,

272-3
Beavis, M.A. 518
Beckwith, R.T. 395
Behm, J. 393
Berger, K. 186
Berger, P.L. 102
Bergquist, J,A. 501
Bertram, G. 138-39
Betori, G. 202, 401
Betz, O. 500
Beyer, H.W. 384
Bietenhard, H. 114, 119, 381
Bihler, J. 277
Blomberg, C.L. 398-400, 403, 408-9
Blue, B.B. 392, 474, 480, 482
Böcher, O. 420
Bock, D.L. 22, 43, 45-8, 54, 108, 111-
    13, 118, 123, 269, 302-4, 413
Bockmuehl, M.N.A. 425
Bolkestein, H. 515
Booth, W.C. 96
Borg, M.J. 343
Borgen, P. 92
Bovon, F. 12, 87, 328, 337, 399
Boyarin, D. 442
Braund, D.C. 88
Brawley, R.L. 78, 102, 189, 218-9,
    223-4, 399
Brett, M.G. 462
Brooten, B.J. 431, 475

Brown, C. 147
Brown, R.E. 73, 132-3, 186
Brown, S. 73, 522-23
Brox, N. 192-93
Bruce, F.F. 45, 52, 150, 183, 206, 237-8,
    240-1, 243, 248-9, 252, 254, 302-
    3, 306-7, 311, 314, 316, 359, 383-
    4, 386, 388, 401, 403, 412, 414,
    422, 431, 532-3
Bryan, C. 411
Büchsel, F. 135, 137-8
Buckwalter, D. 333
Buckwalter, H.D. 108-9
Bultmann, R. 4
Burchard, C. 170, 178, 192
Burkert, W. 507
Burkett, W. 148-50
Buss, M.F.-J. 406
Busse, U. 94

C
Cadbury, H.I. 15
Cadbury, H.J. 15, 20, 172, 219, 222,
    229, 237, 239, 246, 248-9, 412,
    512
Caird, G.B. 69
Callan, T. 410
Campbell, R.A. 177, 422, 424, 481
Capper, B.J. 391, 500, 512, 516
Carroll, J.T. 67, 100-1, 150, 152,
    266-7, 399
Casey, R.P. 192-3
Cassidy, R.J. 93
Catchpole, D.R. 408
Cerfaux, L. 192-93
Chance, J.B. 75, 174, 176, 374, 399
Cheetham, F.P. 486
Cheung, A.T.M. 410
Chevallier, M.A. 329, 339, 348
Clark, A.C. 170, 184
Clark, D.L. 185
Clarke, W.K.L. 43
Cohen, S.J.D. 411, 477
Cole, R.A. 378, 394
Conzelmann, H. 8, 12-13, 28, 64-5, 72-
    3, 109-10, 112, 122-3, 126-7,
    133, 139, 144, 155, 166, 183,
    190, 207, 209, 216, 224, 229,
    233, 237, 239, 246, 260, 311,

    312, 315, 318, 344, 431, 467,
    483, 534
Conzelmann. H. 8
Cook, M.J. 350
Corley, K.E. 490
Cosgrove, C.H. 23, 90, 188, 237, 246
Crump, D.M. 108, 378, 394, 489, 494-6
Cullmann, O. 244

D
Dahl, N.A. 408, 426, 452
Danker, F.W. 87, 108, 110-11, 120,
    409, 516-17
Darr, J.A. 232, 399, 403, 414
Degenhardt, H.-J. 514-15
Delebecque, E. 415
Den Boer, W. 515
deSilva, D.A. 301, 306
Dibelius, M. 259, 301, 311, 313-14,
    317-18, 503
Dickinson, R., Jr. 409
Dietrich, W. 198
Dillon, R.J. 100, 177-8, 193, 195-7,
    211, 413
Dittenberger, W. 158
Dockery, D. 211
Dodds, E.R. 147
Dollar, H.E. 216, 219-21, 226-8
Dömer, M. 87
Downing, F.G. 398
Driver, S.R. 155-6
Dschulnigg, P. 281, 285
Du Plessis, I.I. 523
du Plooy, G.P.V. 90
Dubois, J.D. 328
Dunn, J.D.G. 22, 188, 263, 332, 335,
    337-8, 340, 344, 456
Dupont, J. 179, 303, 345, 408, 426, 434
Dyrness, W. 113-14

E
Ebel, G. 387
Eichrodt, W. 113-14
Eisenstadt, S.N. 516
Elliott, J.H. 405, 462
Ellis, E.E. 85, 111, 218, 299, 401
Enuwosa, J. 99
Esler, P.F. 20, 95, 367, 398, 467-9, 471,
    490, 492, 518, 523

Evans, C.A. 49, 442, 482
Evans, C.F. 196, 198, 324, 501

F
Fabry, H.-J. 91
Falk, D. 375, 394-5
Faw, C.E. 403, 415
Feldman, L.H. 89
Fenton, J. 187
Filson, F.F. 222
Fishbane, M. 442
Fitzmyer, J.A. 45, 99, 101, 120, 123,
    165-6, 176, 179, 181, 188, 298,
    366, 385, 401, 453, 455, 522, 536
Flanagan, N. 87
Flender, H. 8, 426
Foakes-Jackson, F.J. 183, 261-2, 266
Foerster W. 287
Foerster, W. 131, 147, 155-6, 159, 392
Fohrer, G. 147
Fontenrose, J. 146
Forbes, C. 185
Ford, J.M. 93
Foulkes, F. 47
Fox, R.L. 147
France, R.T. 386
Frankemölle, H. 426
Franklin, E. 8, 73, 111, 174, 344,
    376-8, 381
Frei, H.W. 461
Frein, B.C. 246
Fuller, R.H. 98
Fusco, V. 66

G
Gager, J.G. 430
Garnsey, P. 474
Garrett, S.R. 94, 99, 460
Gärtner, B. 133, 309, 311-12, 314
Gasque, W.W. 212-13, 419, 461
Gatz, B. 504, 505
Gaventa, B.R. 12-13, 104, 226, 266,
    296, 324
Geertz, C. 465
Geldenhuys, N. 120
Gempf, C.H. 133, 296
Gempf, C.L. 8
George, A. 87, 91, 93, 96, 117, 186, 329
Gerhardsson, B. 108, 170

Giblin, C.H. 375, 378
Giles, K. 87, 170-71, 190, 260
Gill, D.W.J. 121, 147, 382-3, 480
Glöckner, R. 87, 99
Goodman, M.D. 513
Goppelt, L. 47
Goulder, M.D. 229
Gowler, D.B. 399
Green, E.M.B. 87
Green, J.B. 45, 47, 85-7, 89-90, 94, 96,
    99, 100-1, 103, 110, 221
Grosvernor, M. 249
Grumm, M.H. 542
Grundmann, W. 246, 390
Gunkel, H. 331-2, 339, 342
Guthrie, D. 108
Guthrie, W.K.C. 504

H
Haacker, K. 170, 184, 413
Haenchen, E. 51, 64, 79, 183, 207, 209,
    237, 240, 248, 276, 305, 311,
    314, 318, 322, 357, 367, 381,
    388-9, 408, 483, 485, 490,
    492, 534
Hahn, F. 170, 183-4, 226
Hall, R.G. 102
Hamm, D. 103, 258-9
Hands, A.R. 516
Hansen, G.W. 308
Hanson, R.P.C. 123, 248, 251
Hauck, F. 390, 391
Haya-Prats, G. 331-2, 334, 338-9,
    341-2
Hays, R.B. 43, 442
Hedrick, C.W. 322
Hegermann, M. 126
Hemer, C.J. 20, 133, 229, 311, 481
Hengel, M. 117, 216, 278, 290, 293,
    386, 418, 420-3
Hill, C.C. 162
Hill, D. 193, 211
Hitchcock, F. 227
Holmberg, B. 462
Holtz, T. 43, 421
Horsley, G.H.R. 481
House, P.R. 541, 542, 544
Hubbard, R.L. 400
Hui, A.W.D. 347

Hultgren, A.J. 238
Hurst, L.D. 343
Hurtado, L.W. 386
Hutter, H. 507

I
Isaacs, M.E. 328

J
Jacob, E. 114
Jeremias, J. 389, 392, 478, 488
Jervell, J. 11-12, 60, 79, 155, 173-4,
        178, 180-1, 183, 190, 226, 244,
        300, 318-22, 324, 347, 350-1,
        365, 369, 398, 405-7, 426,
        442, 533
Johnson, L.T. 21, 35, 38, 53, 89, 157,
        162, 174-5, 185-6, 189, 230, 307,
        403, 407, 450-51, 463-4, 503,
        537-40, 543
Johnstone, W. 227
Jones, A.H.M. 158
Jones, D.L. 150
Judge, E.A. 461, 463, 480
Juel, D. 96

K
Kähler, M. 265
Kaiser, W.C. 113, 351
Karris, R.J. 20, 399, 514-15
Kaye, B.N. 228
Keating, J.F. 514
Kee, H.C. 11, 20-22, 29, 32, 166, 211,
        224, 230, 330, 465-6, 475, 481
Kerferd, G.B. 504
Keydell, R. 149
Kilgallen, J.J. 280, 303-5, 357, 403, 406
Kim, H.S. 338, 345, 348
Kim, S. 420, 421, 423
Kimball, C.A. 46
Kirk, J.A. 170
Klauck, H.-J. 486
Klein, G. 170, 183, 184
Klein, W.W. 400
Kliesch, K. 402, 406, 415
Klinghardt, M. 398, 406-7, 409-10
Kodell, J. 99, 180, 223, 541
Koet, B.J. 56, 398
Korn, M. 100

Kraabal, A.T. 430
Kränkl, E. 109, 116
Kremer, J. 197, 335
Krodel, G.A. 116, 183, 406, 411, 415
Külling, H. 133
Kümmel, W.G. 126, 276, 278
Kurz, W.S. 232, 413
Kytzler, B. 508

L
Ladd, G.E. 122-23
Lake, K. 237, 239, 246, 248-9, 412
Lampe, G.W.H. 109, 116, 118, 123,
        329, 331, 337, 380
Larsson, B. 75, 403
Lash, N. 472
Leaney, A.R.C. 111
Légasse, S. 277
Leisegang, H. 328
Lemcio, E.E. 439-40
Lentz, J. 441
Liebeschuetz, J.H.W.G. 422
Link, H.-G. 246
Lofthouse, W.F. 116
Lohfink, G. 343, 427, 434
Lohmeyer, M. 170
Lohse, E. 478
Long, B.O. 425
Longenecker, R.N. 238-9, 248, 251,
        254, 305, 315, 322, 400
Louth, A. 461
Lövestam, E. 204
Luckmann, T. 102
Lüdemann 7
Lüdemann, G. 7, 184, 186
Lull, D.J. 120
Luz, U. 400, 410

M
MacIntyre, A. 472
MacMullen, R. 146-47, 149
MacRae, G.W. 116, 118, 333
Maddox, R. 20, 80, 170, 183-4, 190,
        194, 198, 211, 213, 220, 398,
        522, 532-7, 540, 544
Mainville, O. 328-9, 331, 333, 338,
        339, 341, 344
Malherbe, A.J. 310, 318, 461, 482
Mangatt, G. 87

Mare, W.H. 293, 479
Marguerat, D. 216, 222, 231, 415
Marshall, I.H. 12, 16, 20, 21, 43, 45,
    51, 87, 96, 110, 115, 120-1, 127-
    8, 138, 178, 183, 188, 198, 211,
    216, 219, 238, 241, 248, 251-2,
    267, 286, 301, 305, 316, 343-4,
    386-9, 392, 403, 411-12, 414,
    423, 466, 483-5, 488, 491, 493,
    497, 511, 522, 534
Martin, L.H. 307
Martin, R.P. 87, 386
Matera, F.J. 363
Mather, P.B. 189
Mattill, A.J., Jr. 186, 533
McBride, D. 190
McKay, H.A. 476, 496-97
McKelvey, R.J. 377, 394
McKnight, S. 163
Mealand, D.L. 506-7
Meeks, W.A. 424, 428, 462, 466, 518
Mellor, R. 146
Menzies, R.P. 22, 117, 328, 331-2, 335,
    337-9, 341, 343-5
Metzger, B.M. 181, 248, 385
Meyer, B. 388
Meyer, B.F. 343
Meyers, E. 475
Michel, O. 282-83
Minar, E.L. 507
Minear, P.S. 535
Mitchell, A.C. 516
Mitford, T.B. 148
Moessner, D.P. 56, 108, 111, 159, 186,
    263-64, 324
Montague, G.T. 338
Moore, G.F. 488
Morgan, R. 461
Morgenthaler, R. 172, 213
Morris, L. 117
Moule, C.F.D. 116, 154, 249, 389, 391,
    393, 446
Moxnes, H. 464-5, 516, 518
Müller, P.-G. 97
Munck, J. 254, 421
Murphy, L.E. 173
Murphy-O'Connor, J. 407, 424
Mussner, F. 402, 413

N
Neirynck, F. 186
Nellessen, E. 192
Nelson, P.K. 174, 177
Neudorfer, H.-W. 277-8, 290, 292
Neusner, J. 476
Newman, C.C. 216, 229
Neyrey, J.H. 20, 87, 312-13, 470-1, 517
Nielsung, H.K. 70
Nock, A.D. 477
Nolland, J. 60, 65, 70-2, 74, 77, 80,
    120, 171, 181-2, 190, 369, 407

O
O'Brien, P.T. 211
O'Collins, G.G. 89
O'Neill, J.C. 3, 8, 10, 11, 13, 348, 357,
    533
O'Reilly, L. 339
O'Toole, R.F. 21, 87, 104, 123, 171,
    186, 189, 300, 302, 306, 320-1,
    323-4, 333, 384, 399, 414
Overman, J.A. 430

P
Palmer, D.W. 21, 529
Parsons, M.C. 15, 43, 126, 128, 144,
    217, 522
Pelling, C.B.R. 186
Pereira, F. 427, 428-29, 431, 434, 485
Peristiany, J.G. 518
Perkins, P. 196, 262
Perry, G.R. 382
Pervo, R.I. 15, 43, 126, 128, 144, 411,
    522
Pesch, R. 84, 117, 129-31, 285, 294,
    402, 420, 425, 430, 432
Peterson, D.G. 23-24, 36, 47, 179, 224,
    373-74, 376, 384, 393, 483, 523,
    536, 539
Pfitzner, V.C. 170, 185, 187, 189,
    198-9, 212
Philip, J.A. 507
Pilch, J.J. 150
Pilgrim, W.E. 87, 96, 100
Pillai, C.A.J. 301, 305-6
Pitt-Rivers, J. 466
Pixner, B. 500
Plümacher, E. 518

Plummer, A. 120
Polhill, J.B. 61, 84, 413
Porter, S.E. 213
Pöschl, J. 505
Powell, M.A. 87, 399, 460
Praeder, S.M. 186-7
Pred, A. 85
Price, R.M. 337
Price, S.R.F. 88
Prince, G. 86

Q
Quesnel, M. 337-8

R
Rackham, R.B. 359
Radl, W. 87
Räisänen, H. 347, 398
Ramm, B. 4
Rapske, B. 129, 154, 192, 213, 245-6,
    250, 253, 544
Rasco, E. 12
Recker, R.R. 198, 211
Refoulé, F. 407
Reicke, B. 116, 388
Rengstorf, K.H. 170, 194, 198
Rese, M. 46, 269
Rétif, A. 192
Reynolds, J. 481, 488
Richard, E. 52, 286, 289, 293
Richardson, P. 399
Riches, J. 464
Ricoeur, P. 472
Ridderbos, H.N. 258-61
Riesner, R. 277, 407, 418, 421, 433,
    435, 500
Robinson, W.C., Jr. 298
Rolland, P. 400
Roloff, J. 108, 170, 183, 433
Roniger, L. 516
Rordorf, W.D. 486
Rosenblatt, M.-E. 94, 188, 297, 299
Rosner, B. 216
Rosner, B.S. 23, 37, 224, 227, 263
Russell, W. 339
Ryken, L. 225

S
Saller, R.P. 474

Salmon, M. 399
Salo, K. 75, 398, 406-7
Sanders, J.A. 442
Sanders, J.T. 58, 80, 161-62, 242,
    350-5, 354, 365, 405, 432
Sandmel, S. 292
Satterthwaite, P.E. 21
Sawyer, J.F.A. 89, 156
Schille, G. 184, 399
Schlatter, A. 127, 263
Schmithals, W. 170, 184, 402, 405
Schnackenburg, R. 170
Schneckenburger, M. 533
Schneider, G. 130-31, 183, 189, 206,
    246, 259, 270-1, 286, 402, 407,
    420, 422, 425, 435
Schneider, J. 147
Schnelle, U. 126, 127
Schreiber, J. 101
Schubert, P. 300, 320
Schürer, E. 431, 488
Schürmann, H. 5, 132
Schütz, F. 100, 110
Schwartz, D.R. 177, 218, 401, 408
Schweizer, E. 21, 119, 122, 331-2,
    335, 388
Scott, J.J.Jr. 276, 279, 286, 290
Scott, J.M. 216, 218
Scroggs, R. 462-63, 466
Seccombe, D.P. 85, 189, 346, 355,
    389-1
Seeligmann, I. 442
Seifrid, M.A. 398, 405
Selwyn, E.G. 270
Shelton, J.B. 22, 331, 339, 341
Shepherd, W. 329, 338, 342, 346
Siegert, F. 230, 430
Simon, M. 378, 408
Simpson, J.W., Jr. 422
Sloan, R. 178
Smend, R. 400, 410
Smith, D.E. 490
Smith, T.V. 261-2
Smyth, H.W. 79, 209
Snook, L.E. 538
Soards, M.L. 24, 26, 47-8, 97-8, 259,
    261, 266-8, 270-1, 296, 317, 543
Soja, E.W. 85
Spencer, F.S. 210, 216, 229, 264

Sperry Chafer, L. 4
Squires, J.T. 20, 22-6, 30, 32, 38-9, 90, 163, 239, 539-40
Stählin, G. 116, 332-3, 408
Stalder, K. 344
Stanton, G.N. 185
Steck, O.H. 263-64
Stein, R.H. 117, 120
Stemberger, G. 294
Stenschke, C. 16
Sterling, G.E. 21, 23, 38, 42
Stibbe, M.W.G. 227
Storch, R. 277
Stowers, S.K. 462, 469
Strange, J.F. 475, 483
Strathmann, H. 192, 196, 211-12, 388
Strauss, M.L. 46, 108, 337
Stronstad, R. 22, 331, 338-39, 341
Stuhlmacher, P. 126, 277-8, 288, 291, 293
Sukenik, E.L. 478-9
Sutherland, S.R. 472
Syreeni, K. 398

T
Taeger, J.-W. 126-27, 143-44
Tajra, H.W. 319, 414
Talbert, C.H. 22, 65, 109, 112, 185, 211, 229, 259, 339, 400, 539-40
Tannehill, R.C. 93, 96-7, 184-5, 218-9, 223, 231-2, 259, 299, 311, 364, 399, 409, 411, 415, 418, 420, 423, 425, 426-9, 431-4, 447, 449
Tannenbaum, R. 481, 488
Taylor, N. 422, 423
Thiselton, A.C. 472
Thornton, C.-J. 213
Thrall, M.E. 435
Throckmorton, B.H. 87, 95
Thüsing, W. 119
Tiede, D.L. 99, 120, 345
Tiedtke, E. 246
Torgovnick, M. 231
Trites, A.A. 172, 177, 189, 192-4, 213
Trocmé, E. 533
Turner, C.H. 222
Turner, M.M.B. 96, 108, 116, 174, 179, 186, 328, 330-8, 341, 344-7, 380, 394, 398

Tyson, J.B. 162, 198, 399

U
Uhlhorn, G. 514
Uxkull-Gyllenband, W.G. 504

V
van Aarde, A.G. 405
van de Sandt, H. 407
van Pelt, J.R. 192
van Unnik, W.C. 85, 218, 250, 534-5
Vanhoye, A. 399
Veltman, F. 318
Verbeke, G. 328
Vermaseren, M.J. 148
Vermes, G. 513
Veyne, P. 516
Vidman, L. 148
Vielhauer, S.P. 260, 304-5, 317, 441
von Baer, H. 8, 328-32, 339
Von Pöhlmann, R. 505
von Rad, G. 113, 114
Voss, G. 112
Vriezen, T.C. 114

W
Walker, P.W.L. 399
Walker, W.O., Jr. 411
Wall, C.M. 449
Wall, R.W. 439, 440
Walter, V.L. 482
Watts, R.E. 347
Weatherly, J.A. 140, 399
Webb, R.L. 343
Wedderburn, A.J.M. 345, 409, 511
Wehnert, J. 213
Weinert, F.D. 375, 399
Weiser, A. 117, 398, 406-7, 410, 418, 422, 430, 434
Weiss, K. 220
Wendt, H.H. 207
Wenham, D. 453
Wiefel, W. 76
Wikenhauser, A. 411
Wilckens, U. 259-60, 265
Wilcox, M. 91, 101, 265, 430, 500
Williams, C.S.C. 247
Williams, D.J. 249, 403-4, 415
Willimon, W.H. 399

Wills, L.M. 399
Wilson, S.G. 108, 219, 226, 398, 409,
        492-93
Winter, B.W. 121, 194, 308, 310, 312,
        316, 318, 382-3, 480, 497, 515
Witherington III, B. 146, 148-9, 158,
        494
Witherup, R.D. 173, 404
Woodhouse, J.W. 193
Wren, M. 112
Wright, N.T. 232, 344, 453
Wuthnow, R. 106

X
Xeres, S. 422

Y
Yonge, C.D. 513
York, J.O. 343, 346

Z
Zehnle, R. 87
Zerwick, M. 249, 406
Ziesler, J.A. 381
Zmijewski, J. 76, 271
Zweck, D. 315

Subject Index

A

Abraham 37, 49, 51, 195, 284, 357,
365, 372, 377-8, 387, 527, 529
Acts
> date of 367
> ending of 229–33
> historicity of 460
> narration in 232
> plan of 225–9
> preface 523, 535
> speeches 212, 527

acts of God 26, 31
Aelius Theon 185
Areopagus 308, 310, 312, 314, 317
Aeschylus 317
Agabus 30, 32, 341
Agape 512, 518
Agrippa 34, 102, 208-9, 320-1, 323
Alexander the Great 382
alienation from God 144
almsgiving 501, 503, 532
Amorean 478
Ananias 115, 186, 322, 341, 346, 386,
389, 414, 446-8, 500, 503
angel 23, 25, 30, 33, 35, 39, 113, 356
Anna 374
anthropology 126-9, 140
anti-gnostic 109
Antioch 30, 218, 227, 308, 361-2,
405, 407, 421-3, 427, 435
anti-semitism 161, 369
Aphrodisias 487
Apollinopolis Magna 477
Apollo 317

Apollos 338, 340, 429, 432, 485
apologists 80, 262, 532
> function 38

apology 389, 532, 534, 537-8
apostles 170, 204, 212, 340, 346, 351,
356, 359, 365, 371
> preaching of 21, 24, 26
> testimony of 535
> teaching of 143, 175

Apostolic 407, 410, 493
> Decree 408-10, 412
> appeal to Caesar 414

Aquila 429, 480, 484-5
Aratus 309
Aristotle 516
ascension 154
> account of 20, 23, 84, 112,
> advocate 496
> benediction 217
> end of epoch 330, 332
> eschatological event 73
> event 351, 373, 375, 381, 394
> foundation for Christian 536
> fulfilment 50
> historic fact 189
> of Jesus 55, 72, 74, 171, 175,
> 95, 97-8, 198, 214, 217
> parousia 67
> preaching of 216
> session 53
> site of 175

Athens 102, 383
atonement 98-100, 111
Augustus 158

B
Babel 352
baptism 91, 119, 290, 339, 353, 410,
    487
    Crispus 424
    Cornelius 346, 492
    Ethiopian 360
    Gentiles 176, 361
    John 74, 178, 198, 249, 485
    Holy Spirit 49
    households 487
    of Jesus 303, 328, 396
    repentance 95, 133, 153, 157,
    338, 342, 401, 528
    Paul 447
    Philipian jailor 104, 154, 253
    name of Jesus 104-5, 323
    water 241, 337, 479
Bar-Jesus 33, 448
Barnabas 31, 37, 175, 182-4, 186,
224, 297, 306, 308, 340, 362, 365, 388,
420, 422-3, 444, 493
Baucis 308
bear witness 38
benefaction 87-8, 106, 120, 123,
480-1
benefactor 97, 106, 110, 120-1, 123,
469, 475, 479, 480-1, 487, 516
biblical theology 538
biography 534
Bithynia 115
blood-guiltiness 420
boldness 201
boundary difficulties 72
breaking of bread 389, 392-3
burnt offering 375
C
Caesar 543
Caesar Augustus 218
Caesarea 21, 29, 31, 34
canonical
    approach 455
    context 438
Cenchrea 411-2
charismatic
    empowering 341
    intensifications 342
    praise 334, 346
    preaching 334
    revelation 347

teaching 334, 342, 346
wisdom 334, 342
chiasm 425
christology 46, 50, 52, 108–23, 344,
441
    absentee 154
    categories 70
    climax of Peter's speech 96
    exaltation 154
    focus of OT 415
    functional 272
    interpretation of OT 414
    subordinationist 13
    titular 272
church 210, 347, 353, 358-9, 473,
475, 481-8, 490-1, 493-7, 527, 529,
530-4, 536, 541, 543-4
    growth of 180
    Jerusalem 493
    synagogue 530
Cicero 148
circumcision 357, 365, 368, 372,
407-8, 410
Claudius Lysias 209, 319
cleanse Zion 343
Clement of Alexandria 185
commission 57, 180, 182, 188-9
common meal 392, 477, 486, 489-90,
494, 531
common ownership 391
community 346-7
    mission 52, 55
    of believers 528
    of goods 500, 532
comparison 185, 186
Confirmationist 337
conflict 540, 542
conversion 116, 127, 141, 204, 340,
467, 469
    faith 528
    initiation 333, 337, 339, 347
Corinth 18, 117, 418, 424-9, 432,
434-5
Cornelius 58, 102, 203-4, 227, 341,
346, 361, 404, 448, 480, 491-3
corrupt generation 132, 134-5, 140
covenant 363, 365, 529
    and promise 49
    realisation 50
creation 45

credal statements 386
Crispus 78, 424, 430-2
crucifixion 20, 110, 132, 377
culture 365-6, 372
Cynics/Cynicism 507
Cyrenaica 218
D
Damaris 312
Damascus 297, 323
David 50, 143, 366
Davidic
    covenant 49
    figure 336
    hope 52
    house 52
    Messiah 336, 345
    promise 50-1, 54
    rule 344
    seed 204
Day of Judgment 160-1
death 133, 207
deity 142
delay 64, 66
Delos 476-7
Demetrius 433
demons 119, 122
denominations 359
destruction of Jerusalem 367, 370
dialectical process 419
Diaspora 268, 275, 277-9, 284-6, 289-90, 292-4, 352, 359, 474, 477, 480, 484, 487, 490
Didache 392
dietary laws 404
    purity 476-7, 490, 494, 531
    regulations 476
Dio Chrysostom 309
Diodorus Siculus 38, 476
Dionysius 149, 311
discipleship 112
discrimination 362, 366
Dispersion 531
divine 37
    accreditation for Jesus 53
    action 28
    agents 22, 25, 28, 30, 32-3, 35, 37
    causation 222
    design 45
    guidance 24, 34, 39

oracles 539
pattern=typology 47
plan 37-38, 45, 50, 188, 529
promise 42
providence 38
retribution 129
vindication 129
will 130
donum superadditum 333, 339, 342
Doric frieze 479
doxology 347
dreams 334
Dura 476
E
early Catholicism 461
ecclesiology 52, 529
Egypt 118
election 364, 371
Eleusinian mysteries 148
Eleusis 148
Eleven, the 170-1, 182
Elymas 34
Emmaus 287, 495, 496
empowering
    for mission 338-9
    for the messianic task 336
    for witness 330, 339
ends of the earth 80, 344, 347
enlightenment 127
enthronement 111
Ephesian elders 435, 341
Ephesus 32-4, 383, 387, 417-9, 421, 424, 427-30, 432-6, 480, 484, 485-6
Epicurean 310, 312-3, 485
epochs 329
eschatology 102, 110, 206, 534
    age 166
    context 121, 136
    discourse 65
    early apostolic 267
    event 136, 174, 265-7, 274
    expectation 176
    framework 260, 266
    foundation 527
    fulfilment 73, 524
    hope 511
    Imperial 148
    influx of Gentiles 346
    Isaianic vision 85
    Israel 336, 451

judgement 66, 447, 452
outpouring of spirit 73
people of God 366, 529
prophet 51, 90, 260, 381
Petrine 259, 274, 266
realised 148, 247
repentance 264
restoration 445, 526, 538
rule 69
salvation 72, 164, 150, 176,
   377, 394, 511, 524, 529
salvation-history 8, 12, 63ff.
sonship 332, 336, 340
Spirit 73, 335
spirit of prophecy 343
work of God 85, 102
Zion 197
Essenes 500, 513
eternal life 194, 206, 523
ethical life of the community 335
Ethiopia 218
Ethiopian 29, 104, 223, 226, 360
Eucharist 489
evangelism 182, 485, 540
event and text 48
exaltation 110
exalted Messiah 332
exhortations 535
Exodus/wilderness testing 336
exorcisms 179, 186
eyewitnesses 192
F
failure of Jewish people 76
faith 130, 134, 206, 214, 338
faithful remnant 376
famine 362
fear of the Lord 331
Felix 208, 209, 319
fellowship 350, 355, 359, 362, 366,
372
Festus 34, 209, 323
first missionary journey 194, 204
fore ordination 271
foreknowledge 271
forensic 305
forgiveness 74, 118, 122, 127, 140,
201, 405
forgiveness of sins 132, 132–4, 140,
160, 197, 204-6, 212, 268, 524
form-criticism 503

friendship 356, 372, 504, 515, 518
fulfilment
   of prophecy 22-5, 27, 30, 32,
      35-7, 39, 130
G
Gallio 209, 320, 431, 433
Gamaliel 402
general resurrection 208, 210
generation 135–140
genre 128, 213
Gentiles 46, 60, 78, 130, 133-4, 142,
189, 195, 203, 206, 208, 212, 214, 306,
320, 346, 353, 360, 372, 404-5, 407,
411, 426, 526, 529, 530-1, 536, 538
   Christians 398, 405, 408,
      415-6
   good news to 76
   inclusion of 52, 57, 219
   involvement 52
   mission 30, 32, 48, 69, 71, 77,
      80, 177, 220, 227, 298-9, 306,
      318-20, 363-5, 402, 428, 440,
      444, 446, 450, 453-4, 456
Gideon 113
glorification 111, 113-15
glossolalia 510
God 130-1, 133-4, 138, 141, 162,
   223-5
God of the Fathers 272
God's
   guidance 22, 34
   impartiality 31
   plan of 19-21, 23, 34-5, 37,
      39, 44, 46, 55, 131, 189, 521,
      525
   providence 31
   right hand 344
   word 202
God-fearers 59-60, 162, 368, 383,
399, 422-24, 430, 432, 474, 480-1,
488, 530
Golden Age 504-5, 509
gospel 45, 118, 122, 209, 540
   movement of 527
   progress of 526
   ministry 542
Graeco–Roman 105-6, 108, 110, 112,
119, 121, 374, 384, 486, 538
   people 106
   rhetor 318

world 12, 83, 87, 92, 105, 523
guarantors 178
guidance of God 22, 334
H
haircut 411
hardening 369, 370, 372
healings 68, 151, 179, 186
health 150
hearing and responding 79
heavenly voice 25
Hebrew Scriptures 22, 25, 525
Hellenistic
  histories 38
  Judaism 8,
  world 86
Hellenists 226, 275, 277-80, 289-90, 403, 501
  early Christian 527
Hellenisation 539
heritage 50-1
hermeneutical axioms 43-4
Hermes 307-8, 382
Herod 120
historical criticism 472
historicity 459
holiness 355
Holy and Righteous one 272
Holy Spirit 112, 122, 131, 175, 202, 204, 224, 359, 361, 366, 372, 510
Homer 307
honour and shame 470
hope
  of the Spirit 49
  for redemption 196
  of Israel 208, 210
hospitality 471
house 375, 474
house-church 424, 473-5, 481
household 392, 394-5, 471, 480-1, 484, 487, 492
house-synagogues 473-4, 531
human failure 130, 132, 140, 143
Hygieia 148
hymn fragments 386
I
Iconium 308
identifying Christ as God 273
idols 45, 207
Ignatius 392
ignorance 131, 143, 353

imitation of Christ 109
immanence 113-4, 116
immortality 146
incense 375
indictment 58
intimation 76
irreversible judgement 268
Isis 147-49
Israel 46, 59, 174, 190, 195, 214, 352
  challenge and warning to 58
  hardness of heart 202, 209
  hopes 197, 208
  pattern of rejection 61
  promise 50
  renewal 211
  restoration 327, 343, 345-6
  transformation/salvation 345
Jacob 113
James 5, 52, 172, 366, 407, 412, 441
jealousy 356, 363, 370
Jeremiah's call 421
Jerusalem 115, 117, 131, 133, 137, 141-2, 175, 176, 180, 399-400, 402, 404-5
Jerusalem Council 176, 204, 206, 261, 365, 400, 423, 449, 527, 543
Jerusalem Synod 441
Jesus 126, 130-1, 133, 135-7, 139, 143, 265
  ascension 536
  death 54, 202, 536
  incarnation 536
  mission 536
  prophecies of 534
  resurrection of 524, 526, 536
  suffering/exaltation 524
  the righteous one 203
  vindication of 525
  innocent sufferer 54
  as Son 54
  companions 171
  Righteous One 205, 210, 213
Jew-Gentile 173
  relations 42, 423
  unity 421
Jewish
  Christians 398, 404, 411, 416
  hope 46

mission 80, 441
ritual 413
unbelief 76
War 530
Jews 357-8, 362, 366-7, 538
Christian relationship 350
jealousy of 535
of the Dispersion 9
and Greeks 432, 434, 436
John 116, 136, 172, 180, 483
John Mark 340
John the Baptist 32, 45, 49-50, 60,
72, 75, 181, 186, 220, 223, 265, 271,
330, 335, 343, 345-6, 352, 432
Jonah 135-36
Joppa 404
Josephus 155, 227
Judaisers 408, 533-4
Judaism 48, 142, 225, 375, 379,
387-8, 389, 395, 523, 529-31, 533
Judas 55, 351
Judge 123, 207
judgement 67, 75, 126, 130, 132, 137,
206, 447, 523, 528
judgement day 207
Julius Gaius 477
justification 205, 406
Justin Martyr 532
K
kerygma, 534
Khirbet Shema 476
Kingdom of God 65, 68-9, 111, 198,
209-10, 343, 523-4
kingship 111
L
land of Israel 218, 350, 357
last days 49-50, 130
law 138, 143, 365, 366, 397, 509
law of Moses 134
laying on of hands 359
leaders 174
leaders of the church 175
leadership 354-7, 363, 366, 371
leadership authority 174
legitimation 329
legitimizing 173, 176-7
Levites 388
light 56, 58
light to the Gentiles 56
light to the nations 344

literary
analysis 258
approach 216
context 258
patterns 229
liturgical sequence 389
Lord 120, 123, 130-1
Lord's Supper 389, 392-3, 475
Lordship 110, 120, 122
Lot 137
Lukan
anthropology 128, 144
beliefs 48
Luke 140
christology 524
claim of heritage 42, 49
Luke's Gospel 219–21
literary intention 419
Luke–Acts 43, 57
addressed to 533
social context 539
christology in 524
OT Scripture in 523
purpose of 521-2, 536
readers of 522
salvation in 521, 523-4
style and genre 522
theme of 525
purpose of 522
theological emphasis 523
Lycaonian 382
Lydda 404
Lydia 480
lying to the Spirit 341
Lysias 319
Lystra 307, 315, 382-3
M
Macedonia 33, 115
Mantic prophetism 328
Matthias 55, 171, 177, 198
meal-fellowship 512, 517, 532
Media 218
mediator 110
messengers 183
Messiah 131, 133, 141, 143, 180, 189,
346, 538
suffering and exalted 525
executive power 344
messianic 111
empowering 329

jubilee 337
Servant 272
Meter 148
midrashic technique 43
miracles 3, 19, 22, 26-9, 31, 33-5, 37,
130, 179-80, 186-7, 335, 355-6, 492,
533
Mishnah 488
missiology
    modern debate 192, 210–14
mission 56, 109, 115, 117, 123, 180,
182, 194–214, 341, 347
    in Acts 528
    of the church 210
    practice 417-9, 423-4, 426-9,
    432-4, 436
    to the Gentiles 182
    to Jews and Gentiles 181
Mithras 147, 148
Mosaic
    law 502
    Prophet 345
    prophetic-Servant
    christologies 337
Moses 51, 111, 113-4, 118, 138,
    357-8, 402-3
    and the prophets 525
most high God 129
Mt. Olympus 147
mysticism 328
N
name 113-5, 118, 122, 134, 200-1,
204, 208
name of the Lord 130
narrative
    travel 111
national rejection of Jesus 59
natural revelation 130
Nazareth 122
Nazirite vow 411-2
near expectation 266-7
new community 524, 531
New Covenant 49, 51, 373, 376, 380,
384, 388, 394, 531
New Exodus 337
Noah 137
Noahic commands 409
O
Old Covenant 380
OT citations 111

expectations 539
prophecies 540
opposition 426, 432, 540, 542, 544
    from the Jews 421
    to God 136
oppressors 346
Orphic 149, 505
Ostia 476-7
Ovid 308
P
pagan 147, 149, 433, 444, 535
    religion 147
paganism 385
pagans 368, 539-40, 544
Palestine 531
Paphos 383
Papias 262
paradox 426
paraklesis 331
parallels 184, 185-7
Parousia 63, 64-7, 69-70, 75-6, 81,
109, 260, 266-7
Parthia 218
particularism 229
patronage 470, 476
patron-client relations 470
pattern of prophetic call 264
Paul 5, 50, 59, 117, 118-9, 127, 142,
181-4, 186-89, 192, 195, 199, 203,
208, 210-11, 340-1, 357, 360, 363,
365-6, 406-7, 493, 514-5, 536-7
    apostle to the Gentiles 209
    apostolic claims 533
    as witness of 526
    defence of 522
    imprisonment 537
    status of 189
    trial of 532
    and Barnabas 56
    and Cornelius 57
    preacher of repentance 264
    in Damascus 340
    under house arrest 542
Paul's
    defence 42
    imprisonment 536
    mission 228
    witness 117
Pauline mission practice 424
    soteriology 305

Pentecost 23, 26, 30, 85, 98, 101-2, 112, 116, 122, 142, 329, 333, 345, 352, 401, 489, 509

people of God 353-5, 357-8, 372, 531, 533

persecution 55, 100, 203, 229, 357, 360, 370, 394, 527, 540, 542, 544

Peter 3, 5, 53, 108, 115-6, 118, 130-1, 135, 138, 140-1, 143, 172, 179-80, 186-8, 198-9, 200, 203, 258, 261-2, 264, 266, 268-9, 361, 401-2, 404, 407, 441, 446, 448, 483, 491, 526-7, 533, 542

Pharisees 358, 361, 365, 399, 413, 515

Philemon 308

Philip 28-9, 37, 104, 226, 264, 340, 359, 404

Philippian jailer 105, 450

Philo 292, 512

Pilate and Herod 59

Pisidian Antioch 187, 265, 297, 423

Plato 504, 506

Plutarch 185

pneumatology 528

Polytheism 382

poor 502, 515

poverty and wealth 468

prayer 122, 402

preaching 187, 189, 347

precincts 486

predestination 353

pre-existence 108

Priene 476

principle of duality 213

Priscilla 429, 480, 484-5

prisoner 413

proclamation 122, 129-30, 136, 143

prologues 522

promise 50, 64, 335
    and fulfillment 47-8, 71-3
    of Scripture 53
    of the Father 345
    of the Spirit 58

promised Son 55

prophecy 48, 347

prophet 71, 119, 136, 200, 202, 270

prophetic
    Isaianic Servant-Herald 336
    preacher of repentance 262

    prediction 46
    speeches of repentance 263

propitiation 268

proselytes 352, 360-1, 364-5, 529

punishment 139

purge/cleanse Zion 346

purging of Israel 346

purification rites 379, 389

purpose 350, 363, 371

Pythagoras 507

Q

Qiddush 478

Qumran 156, 387, 391, 395, 500, 512

R

race 361-2

racial community 350

reader 210-11, 213

reciprocity 516, 518

redaction criticism 12

rejection of Jesus 132, 139, 141-3

religious/ethical effects 336

remnant 352-3, 355, 369

repent 201

repentance 118, 122, 127, 131-3, 136-7, 140-2, 197, 207, 214, 265, 268, 524

repentance
    centrality of 264

rescue 152

restoration 141, 346, 351, 355, 371, 526
    of all things 195
    of things prophesied 268
    of Israel 197, 198

resurrection 84, 95, 97, 101, 109, 143, 172, 177, 180, 187, 190, 201, 381, 383-4, 413
    bodily 50, 53
    meaning of 54
    of Jesus 20, 24, 37, 42, 50, 55, 57, 193, 195, 199-200, 205-8
    of woman 29
    witness to 528

revelation 375

revelatory
    discernment 334
    visions 334
    words 334

rhetorical approach 216

ritual laws 531

Roman

cult 383
Empire 20, 37, 218, 227, 382, 534
imperial authority 468
imperial cult 121
law 431
officials 209
Rome 117-8, 208-9, 218, 366, 368, 414-5
S
Sabbath 478, 484
sacramentalist 337
sacrifice 375
Sadducees 312, 356, 358
salvation 72, 111, 118-9, 126-34, 140-1, 143, 146, 194, 204, 207, 209, 214, 268, 338, 343-4, 347, 365, 375, 377, 381-2, 387, 394, 448, 454, 529, 531, 535
status reversal 523
salvation history 70, 72, 109-10, 184, 187, 423
Samaritans 226, 341, 359, 372, 529
Sanhedrin 116, 201-2, 206, 208-10, 312, 356
Sapphira 115, 389
Sardis 478
Satan 134, 344, 523
Saul 203, 404
Scripture 143, 173, 179-80, 187, 189
and event 45-6, 51
as interpreter 47
faithful to 38
fulfilment of 32, 37, 39, 58, 539
guided by 55
Luke's use of 42ff
promises of 46, 53, 536
prophetic 62
realisation of 44
sect 356, 358, 365, 368, 371
typology 468-9
sectarianism 462
seed 51
seed of Abraham 51
Sergius Paulus 297
servant 56-7, 109, 122, 188, 195, 204, 206, 272
citation 54
of Yahweh 110

passage 421
Seven, the 542
Seventy, the 180-2
sifted Israel 343
signs and wonders 122, 143, 178, 184, 355, 443, 535
Silas 103, 105, 340
Simeon 157, 374
Simon
the magician 359
the tanner 404
sins 126-7, 131-2, 134, 140-2
slaves 121
sociology 459-62, 463, 466-7, 470-1
Socrates 310
Son 379
of David 270
of God 112
of Man 66, 75, 135, 286, 378-9, 496, 527
sonship 331
soteriology 339, 343-4, 523, 530
Spain 218
speeches 186-7, 199, 204, 207, 212, 367, 533-43
farewell speech 433, 435
repentance 264
similarities–Peter/Paul 261
Stephen's 276, 299, 527
Temple 266-67, 272
Spirit 35-37, 39, 44, 115, 141, 143, 187, 198, 200, 212, 379
activity of 19, 32, 526
as witness 381
baptise with 73
christocentric functions 332
coming of 69, 380
distribution of 50
empowered by 387
filled with 324
fulfilment 27, 35ff
gift of 333, 338, 377, 380, 524, 534
guidance of 22ff., 74
impact of 472
indwelling 380
inspired by 38
of Jesus 33, 332
of prophecy 327, 334
of the Lord 332

on Gentiles 492
out-pouring of 29, 73, 260,
373, 376, 395
power of 536
promised 272, 380
role of 23-4, 31, 73, 528
sent by 184
spiritual
life of the church 341
wisdom 346
renewal of individual 331
Stephen 5, 24, 26, 28, 37, 71, 80, 116,
117, 162, 186, 192, 202, 208, 226, 261,
264, 277, 340, 356-7, 360, 377-9, 386,
403-4, 444-5, 496, 514, 529
Stobi 476
Stoics/Stoicism 310-13, 485, 507
suffering 55, 527, 533, 535, 540, 543
Suffering Servant 200
summaries 221–3, 331, 345
supernatural powers 115, 119
synagogue 358, 363, 368-9, 377, 383,
392, 394-5, 420, 423-4, 427, 430-2,
475-7, 481-2, 484-7, 490, 496-7, 530
Synoptic Gospels 126
Syrian Antioch 411, 530
T
table fellowship 174, 223, 361-2,
372, 389, 391-3, 467-8, 471
Talmudim 488
Temple 476, 483-4, 486, 489
temple 61, 142, 356, 358, 360, 399,
402, 468, 471, 494, 533
role of 531
the law 527
theodicy 538
Theodotus 476
theophany 345
Theophilus 60, 469, 522, 538-9, 543
Timothy 340, 410
circumcision of 530
Titius Justus 424, 427, 430, 432, 484
Torah 399-400, 404-5, 409-11, 414,
431, 478, 492
Tosephta 488
transcendence 113-4
trial before Caesar 210
Troas 392, 490

Twelve, the 170-1, 175, 181-2, 190,
197, 202, 211, 338, 340, 344, 346, 526,
537, 542
typology 70
Tyrannus 428, 484, 486
U
unity 182, 359, 372
unity of message 259
universal restoration 141
universalism 419, 429, 430
universality 334
of the message 268
Utopia 506
V
vindication of Jesus 524
visions 492, 494, 495, 533, 535
W
'we' passages 213
wicked generation 132, 141
wisdom 117, 122, 341, 347
witness 116, 170, 172, 188, 192–214,
327, 330-2, 334, 340, 347, 535
of the Holy Spirit 179
corporate and collective 262
witnesses 38, 173, 177, 180, 190
to the Jewish people 526
works and faith 131
worship 357, 531
wrath 130
Z
Zechariah 85, 92-4, 132
Zeno 309
Zeus 307-8, 382

Index of Biblical References

Genesis
6:3 335
7:1 137
9:1 223
9:7 223
12:1-2 200
12:3 365
15:14 529
16:10 113
16:13 113
17:9-14 365
21:18 113
21:33 114
22:12 113
22:14 113
22:16-18 113
22:18 346, 402, 529
25:9 285
26:4 402, 529
28:3 223
31:13 113
32:30-31 113
33:19 285
35:11 223
47:27 223
48:4 223
50:13 286

Exodus
1:7 223
2:6 113
2:14 287
3:2 251
3:4 251
3:7 251
3:15 114
4:12 117

16:10 114
16:7 114
19:3 345
19:5 99, 426
20:24 114
22:28 414
23:12 409
23:20-21 113
23:22 426
24:15-17 114
29:38-43 375
33:11 113
33:18-23 114
33:19 114
33:20-23 113
34:14 114
40:34-35 114

Leviticus
9:23-24 114
16:19 409
17:9 410
17:13-15 409
17:14 410
17-18 366
18:29 410
20:2 409
23:29 58, 60
26:9 223

Numbers
6 412
6:1-21 411
12:8 113
14:10 114
14:14 113
15:30 409

Deuteronomy
4:19 61
5:24 114
6:4 315
7:6 436
12:5-11 382
14:2 426
14:23 114
16:11 409
16:14 409
17:3 61
18:13 302
18:15 51, 195, 200, 210, 287, 291, 402
18:19 58, 60, 114
19:15 172, 213
21:22-23 100, 202, 204, 288
28:58 114
31:12 409
32:5 93, 138, 447
33:3 99

Joshua
1:9 425
24:32 286

Judges
2:1-3 113
6:16 113
6:18 113
6:22 113
6:24 113
13:22 113

1 Samuel
10:19 88

595

1 Maccabees
3:9 218
3:18-22 89
4:11 89
4:30 88
9:46 89

2 Samuel
7:5 289
7:8-16 50
7:10-14 303
7:11 289
7:12 302
7:13 114

1 Kings
6:11-13 61
8:11 114
8:27 61, 378
8:28-30 382
9:3 114
9:6-7 382
17:17-24 165

2 Kings
21:3-5 61
21:7 114
23:4-5 61

1 Chronicles
6:8 61
29:16 114

2 Chronicles
11:14 388
33:3 61
33:5 61

Nehemiah
1:9 114
9:30 202

Job
1:21 114

Psalms
2 200, 204
2:1-2 55, 58-9, 201
2:7 50, 54, 201, 205,
298, 302-3, 336

2:8 201
8:1-9 114
16 199
16:10 50, 53-4, 187,
205, 298, 302-4
16:8-11b 50
32:1 304
63:2 114
68:18 345
69:25 23
69:26 55
75:1 114
77:8 138
78 281
78:5-7 138
106 281
109:8 55
110:1-2 50, 53, 200,
201-2
118:10 114
118:22 201
118:26 114
124:8 114
132:11 50, 199

2 Maccabees
1:11 89
1:25 89
2:17-18 89
7:1-42 89
8:27-29 89

Proverbs
18:10 114

Isaiah
2:1-4 176, 379
4:4 343
6 322
6:1-4 114
6:9-10 36, 58, 80, 209,
323, 415
8:9 218
9:2 208
11:1-4 335, 343
11:1-9 336
12:2 155
13:10 208
18:7 114
25:9 157

26 200
26:18 157
30:26 208
30:27 114
32:15 336, 345
34:16 115
35:5 189
40 196
40:3-5 157
41:10 421, 425
41:13 425
41:41 196
42:16 189, 208
42:1-7 336-7
42:6 208, 220
42:7 189
43:5 425
43:11 119
43:14 196
43:21 99, 434
44:3 335
44:24-28 196
45:15 88
45:17 155, 157
45:20 156
45:21-23 88, 156
48:20 218
49:2 425
49:5-6 345, 376
49:6 32, 56-7, 156,
184, 197, 201, 206-8,
218, 306, 344, 423, 529
49:24-25 336
50:10-11 208
51:4 208
52:7 203
52:9-10 196
52:10 197, 201, 204
52:13 200
53:7-8 31, 54, 56
53:11 208, 273, 286
54 196
55:11 119
55:3 50, 54, 205, 298,
302-4
55:4 200
56:4 360
57:15 61
57:19 92, 226
58:6 151

58:8 208
58:10 208
59:9 208
60 379
60:1-3 208
60:19-20 208
61:1-2 151, 157, 189,
201, 220, 336
62:11 218
63:10-14 115, 202
63:16 114
66 196
66:1-2 59, 61, 202,
289, 379
66:2 202
66:4-6 202
66:10 202
66:18 114

Jeremiah
1:5-8 189, 421
1:7 189, 421
1:8 421, 425
1:10 323
1:12 119
1:18-19 421
3:12-16 223, 263
3:17-18 379
4:14 89
7:1-34 61
7:3-25
7:12 114
7:18 61
8:2 61
12:15 32
14:6 263
19:13 61
23:3 223
29:9 114
31:31-34 49, 89, 380,
387
44:26 114
46:27 156, 263

Ezekiel
1:25-28 114
2:1 189
3:23 114
18:30 263
20 281

20:19 281
20:35 113
20:41-42 281
33:4 420
36:22-32 49 335, 380
37:14 380
39:25 114
39:7 114
39:29 380
43:8 114
45:4 388

Daniel
7:13 202
9:6 114
10:11 323

Hosea
12:3-5 113

Joel
2:17 388
2:28-32 24, 49, 58,
158, 200, 332-4, 380
2:32 85, 105, 108, 118,
160, 200, 334, 352, 381
3:1-5 441, 443, 531
3:5 445, 457

Amos
2:7 114
4:13 114
5:25-27 59, 61, 385
9:11 243
9:11-12 32, 204, 407,
441, 449, 531
9:11-15 52, 55, 57
9:12 445, 451
9:14 407

Micah
3:9-11 61
4:1-5 176, 379

Habakkuk
1:2-4 206
1:3 205
1:4 205, 406
1:5 32, 58, 194, 205,
206, 210, 305, 406

1:6-7 205
1:12-13 206
2:14 114
2:3 206
2:4 206, 406
2:6 206

Zephaniah
1:5 61
3:9 352

Haggai
2:7 114

Zechariah
1:3 263
2:5 114
7:8-10 263
7:11-14 202
8:7 156
14:9 114

Malachi
2:2 114
3:7 263

Matthew
5:42 517
8:11 219
10:2 170
10:14 420
10:18b 118
10:23 265
11:19 516
19:28 174
20:25 516
23:15 361
28:18-20 197

Mark
3:14 170, 180
6:7-13 182
6:11 420
6:30 170
7:24-30 219
9:1 76
10:21 502
10:25-45 265
10:42 516
10:45 98, 120, 287

11:17 219
13:9b 118
13:10 219
14:9 219
14:24 98

Luke
1:1 44
1:1-4 4, 165, 279, 464,
522-3
1:2 188, 190, 192
1:3 240, 537
1:4 537
1:5-22 374
1:5–2:52 85
1:11-20 33
1:14-17 45
1:23 388
1:26-38 33
1:32-33 336, 344
1:35 331, 336
1:46-55 89
1:47 85, 90, 157, 165
1:54-55 49
1:68-79 49, 92, 287,
336, 344
1:69-70 85, 90, 159
1:71 85, 165
1:74 387
1:75 387
1:77 90, 132-3, 387,
406
1:78-79 103, 133
1:79 323
2:1 157, 220, 218
2:1-20 87
2:9 115
2:11 85, 90, 97, 157
2:25-26 196, 336
2:25-38 374
2:26 115
2:27-32 375
2:29-32 156, 163
2:29-35 336
2:30 85, 157
2:30-32 181
2:32 56-7, 77, 159,
166, 220, 418, 536
2:34 184, 352
2:36-38 375

2:38 196, 287, 336
2:40 154
2:40-52 336, 374
3:1 218, 220
3:1-6 90, 157
3:1-20 104
3:2-17 224
3:3 72, 74, 95, 133,
406
3:4-6 157
3:6 157, 163, 181
3:7-9 90, 130
3:9 130
3:10-14 104
3:14 220
3:15-17 49-50, 72, 75,
130, 343
3:18 72
3:21-22 336
3:21–4:30 90
3:22 54, 331
4:1 336
4:1-13 98, 336
4:2 321
4:5 219
4:13 73
4:14 336
4:16-30 77, 220, 336
4:17 447
4:18 22, 323, 406
4:18ff. 68, 94, 72, 120,
122, 151, 157, 299,
336, 339, 362
4:24-27 71, 76-7
4:43 68
5:1 224
5:2 298
5:8 130
5:10 180
5:12-16 90, 178
5:17-26 178
5:20 323
5:27-32 515
5:27-39 220
6:1-11 403
6:9 150, 165
6:12-16 198
6:13 180
6:20 69
6:40 178

7:1-10 405
7:2-10 361
7:3-6 516
7:11-17 90
7:16 90
7:18-23 120
7:20 72
7:21-22 122, 157
7:27 45
7:28 45, 68, 72
7:31-35 72, 136
7:34 220, 516
7:36-50 90, 515
7:49-56 178
7:50 150
8:1 171
8:4-15 223
8:8 298
8:10 369
8:11 224
8:26-39 90
8:36 165
8:40-56 90
8:48 150, 165
8:50 165
9:1 180
9:1-6 182
9:2 139, 265
9:5 420
9:6 139, 180
9:11 70
9:13 182
9:21 72
9:23 100
9:24 152
9:24a 165
9:24b 161
9:27 65, 76
9:28 76
9:35 51
9:36 178
9:41 137, 139, 447
9:45 496
9:48 74
9:51-56 220
10:1-20 181-2
10:4 74, 182
10:5 265
10:9 68, 180
10:10-11 420

10:21 342
10:25 300
10:25-37 220
11:2 69
11:4 94
11:13 96
11:15 73
11:18 73
11:20 68
11:20-22 336
11:29 137, 139, 447
11:37-41 403
11:47-51 71
11:51-52 75
12:4 76
12:8f 496
12:11-12 36, 44, 115, 117
12:31-32 69, 74
12:35-40 67, 121
12:42-46 67
12:45 67
12:49 66
12:54-56 66
13:10-17 90, 94
13:18 69
13:20 69
13:22 160
13:28-29 69
13:33-34 71, 130
13:35 66, 115
14:1-14 517
14:10 516
14:12 516, 517
14:22 100
14:33 502
15:6 516
15:8 73
15:9 73, 516
15:11-32 406
15:29 516
16:9 516
16:14 517
16:16 45, 72
16:19-31 161
17:11-19 90, 220
17:19 150, 165
17:20 267
17:25 136
17:26 137

17:27ff 137
18:9-14 375, 406
18:16-17 69
18:18 300
18:22 502
18:26-27 160
18:30 300
18:34 496
18:42 150, 165
19:1-10 90, 160, 164, 515
19:5-7 220
19:9 70, 72, 157
19:10 85, 144, 160
19:11-27 66, 69, 344
19:13 67
19:16-25 67
19:41-44 130
19:45-46 375
19:46 219, 375, 402
19:47-48 375
19:50-53 66
20:9-19 354
20:19-20 60
20:35-36 161
20:41-44 53
21:5-28 403
21:12-13 117
21:12b 118
21:13-19 99
21:14-15 115-7, 122, 248, 334, 342
21:16 74
21:18 74
21:21 250
21:22 75
21:24 76
21:25-26 219
21:27 76, 161
21:28 65, 196
21:29-36 267
21:30 69
21:32 66
21:37-38 375
22:14-30 171, 344
22:19-20 98, 99
22:24 122, 516
22:24-27 120, 122
22:28-30 171-4, 351
22:31 73

22:31-2 172, 188, 496
22:32b 198
22:35-36 73, 182
22:36 74
22:39-46 98, 496
22:53 99
22:54 324
22:69 53
23:4 54
23:12 516
23:14-15 54
23:22 54
23:32-43 152
23:34f. 165, 377, 386
23:37 165
23:39 100, 165
23:42-43 99, 344
23:44-49 99, 190, 386
24:1-12 172, 196
24:13-43 196-7, 495
24:16 495
24:20f. 196-7, 370
24:22-24 196
24:24 495
24:26f. 179, 196
24:30f. 392, 495
24:33-49 74, 172, 196 392, 489, 495
24:41-43 174, 287
24:43-47 44, 53, 54, 179, 197
24:44-48 189, 401
24:45-49 159, 180
24:46 196
24:46-47 197
24:47 56, 57, 58, 118, 133, 304, 344, 381, 401, 414, 415
24:47-49 339, 340, 344
24:48 177, 192, 197
24:49 49, 58, 84, 96, 112, 175, 195, 197, 329-30, 344-5
24:50-53 23, 74, 112, 217, 375, 385

John
2:20 120
12:20 385

13:1-16 120
17:20 232
20:29 232
20:30 222
21:25 222

Acts
1:1 21, 44, 91, 171, 214
1:1-11 197, 217, 233, 400
1:1-26 23
1:2-4 171, 198, 206, 334
1:3 70, 196-7, 224, 231
1:3-8 344
1:4-5 44, 96, 112, 174-5, 195, 197, 199, 334-5,
1:5 335, 345
1:6 197, 231, 401, 450
1:6-8 62, 351, 370
1:8 23, 36, 38, 49, 57, 92, 177, 180, 184, 189, 192-3, 195, 197, 199, 201, 204, 211, 216-9, 221-2, 224, 226, 230-1, 236, 245, 329-30, 334, 339, 340, 344-5, 347, 400-1, 415, 421, 444, 529, 537
1:8b 280
1:9-11 112
1:10 23
1:11 74, 94, 195, 199
1:12-13 27
1:12-26 198, 330
1:13 172, 198, 480
1:14 91, 177, 391, 394, 494
1:14-15 199
1:15 91, 329, 351, 353
1:16 23, 143, 172, 299, 334
1:17 329
1:20 23, 55
1:21 171, 177, 488
1:21-22 91, 198, 211

1:22 84, 192-3, 262, 266, 271
1:24 91, 394, 494
1:24-26 198
1:25f. 171, 194, 199
1:32-35 329
1:42-43 329
1:67-79 329
2 91-4, 96, 112, 198, 299
2:1 27, 91, 199, 342
2:1-4 24, 265
2:1–8:3 27
2:1-13 345
2:1-41 509
2:1-13 345
2:1-39 377
2:2-3 510
2:2-4 199
2:3ff. 27, 92, 142, 218, 224, 329, 334, 401
2:5-13 199, 510
2:5f. 483
2:7 199
2:9-11 92, 218
2:10ff. 96, 143, 339, 352
2:13-36 187
2:14ff. 24, 27, 171, 173, 199, 258-9, 261, 266, 335, 352, 380, 483
2:15-16 199
2:15-21 333
2:16 27, 172
2:16-18 26, 380
2:16-21 158, 267
2:16-39 49
2:17 22, 24, 92, 102, 226, 323, 334
2:17-18 330, 335
2:17-21 195, 200, 401, 441, 443
2:19 178, 443
2:20 130, 161
2:21 85, 92, 94, 105, 108, 118-9, 153, 160, 200, 266, 268, 332, 352, 380-1, 445, 451, 457

2:22 22, 26, 33, 98, 178, 200-1, 271, 272, 352, 443
2:22-24 26, 143
2:22-36 24
2:23 54, 97, 139, 199, 271
2:23-24 130
2:24 26, 54, 199, 302
2:24-32 172, 199, 205
2:25-28 25, 401
2:25-34 299, 329
2:27ff. 94, 143, 187, 266, 271
2:29-31 270
2:30f. 25, 50, 143, 199, 271
2:31b 53
2:32 26, 54, 177, 190, 192-3, 200, 266, 271, 302
2:32-36 50, 112, 199, 380
2:33 96, 115-6, 122, 187, 195, 200, 271, 272, 330, 332-5, 344, 385
2:33-36 200-1, 330, 332, 344-5, 380
2:33-38 158
2:34 25, 401
2:34-39 53, 200
2:35 180
2:36 26, 91, 96, 131, 135, 143, 266, 270-1, 288, 352, 385, 446, 450
2:37 102, 171, 173, 199, 261
2:37-42 91, 104, 200, 380
2:38 91, 95, 104-5, 118, 122, 133, 140-1, 187, 200, 224, 262-3, 268, 272, 304, 323, 381, 385, 401, 406, 448
2:38-39 199, 212, 258, 330, 332-3, 335, 338, 342-3, 528
2:38-41 140, 259, 352. 376, 391

2:39 50, 92, 226, 268, 272, 348, 353, 360, 451
2:39-40 142
2:40 85, 93, 132, 135, 137-40, 152, 199, 258, 262, 268, 443, 447
2:40-47 342
2:41 104, 338, 443, 479
2:42 175, 179, 180, 213, 225, 261, 389, 390-2, 394, 482, 488-9, 494, 512, 517
2:42-47 331, 340, 342, 345, 355, 387, 389, 402, 500, 509, 511
2:43 27, 178-9, 186, 355, 443
2:43-47 487, 489
2:44 104, 352, 448, 500, 502, 506-7, 511
2:44-47 91, 179, 389-90, 502
2:44ff. 179, 180, 362, 375, 390-2, 394, 402, 479, 489-90, 512, 517
2:46-47 225, 375
2:46f. 28, 85, 200, 225, 352, 394, 448, 450, 486, 489, 500
3:1 172, 375, 394, 402
3:1-4:12 92
3:1-8 307
3:1-10 27, 172, 178, 186
3:1f. 483
3:3f. 172, 261
3:6 91, 119, 122, 270-1, 381, 447
3:5 174
3:7 131
3:8f. 175, 447
3:11 172, 402
3:11-26 375, 390
3:12 98, 182, 261, 272
3:12-26 258, 259, 380, 381
3:13 26-7, 200, 270-2, 287
3:13-15 97

3:13a 272
3:13b-15 200
3:13b-18 272
3:14 141, 206, 270, 272, 286
3:14-15 272
3:15 26, 94, 122, 177, 192-3, 201, 208, 266, 270-1, 273, 353, 385
3:16 27, 91, 97-8, 104-5, 118, 122, 271-3, 381, 447
3:17 163, 200
3:17-26 93, 376
3:18 97, 180, 200, 267, 271
3:18-23 51, 345
3:19 67, 95, 104, 141, 201, 262-3, 268, 371
3:19-21 94, 268, 272, 330
3:19-26 198, 346
3:20 67, 141, 180, 200, 271
3:20-21 195
3:21 25-6, 67, 112, 141, 200, 271, 447
3:22 26, 54, 172, 195, 267, 270, 287, 302, 402, 444
3:22-23 51, 58, 200, 201-2, 210, 348, 353
3:22-26 501
3:23 451
3:24 25, 51, 200
3:24-26 51, 59
3:25 51, 182, 200, 226, 354, 360, 402, 529
3:26 51, 54, 141, 172, 226, 268, 270-2, 354, 402, 420
3:43 355
4:1 102, 225
4:1-20 246
4:2 175, 177, 179-80, 182, 201, 375
4:3 246, 377
4:4 28, 479
4:5 354
4:7 261

4:7-18 118
4:8 122, 172, 182, 248, 334, 354
4:8-12 380
4:8-22 116
4:9 150, 165, 268
4:9-10 448
4:9-12 268
4:10 91, 98, 122, 177, 180, 182, 201, 266, 270, 271, 315, 381, 451
4:10-12 381, 447
4:11 25, 201, 288, 402
4:11-12 97
4:12 26, 91, 119, 150, 157, 159, 201, 268, 271, 354, 381, 385, 406, 448
4:13 171-2, 175, 248
4:14ff. 175, 178, 180, 237, 330
4:17-18 447
4:17-20 208
4:18-21 330, 344
4:19 172, 237, 261, 266
4:20f. 175, 237
4:23 340
4:23-31 201, 204, 245, 251
4:24 26, 261, 271, 391
4:24-26 55
4:24-30 62, 394
4:24-31 494
4:25 299, 334
4:25-26 25, 58, 59, 402
4:26 175, 201, 354, 448
4:27 201, 270, 271, 273
4:27-28 97, 201, 55
4:29-30 98, 201, 224, 248
4:30 27, 33, 91, 119, 122, 178-9, 270, 273, 443, 447
4:31 27, 224, 248, 251, 329-30, 334, 340, 394
4:31-32 130

4:32 261, 500, 502,
506-7, 511, 516
4:32-35 346, 387, 515
4:32-37 225, 331, 342,
389, 487
4:32–5:11 91, 94
4:32-35:16 355
4:32-37 389, 391
4:33 28, 177, 179, 193,
331, 340, 355, 362, 502
4:33-35 130
4:34 479, 502, 517
4:34-35 391, 489, 502
4:34–5:11 500
4:35 175
4:37 175, 391
4:38-39 130
5:1-10 331
5:1-11 172, 179, 187,
389, 502, 503
5:1-11 201
5:2 175, 261
5:3 27, 187, 334, 341,
346
5:4 115, 266, 391, 500
5:5 179, 443
5:9 115, 130, 341, 346
5:10 27, 172, 448
5:11 179, 355
5:12 27, 98, 175, 178,
182, 184, 186, 375,
391, 443-4, 451
5:12-13 225
5:12-16 92, 179, 389
5:12f. 483
5:13ff.
28, 172, 179, 186, 355,
479
5:17 225, 246, 358
5:18 251
5:18-23 246
5:19 28, 33, 237, 246
5:20 179-80, 182, 201,
251
5:21 28, 390
5:25 175, 180, 182,
251
5:25-26 377
5:26 175, 251
5:27-40 116, 246, 251

5:28 91, 119, 175, 179,
208
5:29 26, 28, 173, 237,
261, 266
5:30 26, 54, 100, 133,
202, 271, 288, 324
5:30-31 97, 165
5:31 53, 95, 103-4,
122, 133, 141, 158-9,
180, 201-2, 208, 226,
262-3, 268, 270-1, 272,
298, 304, 323, 356, 406
5:31–32 193
5:32 24, 177, 179, 192,
195, 202, 224, 266,
329, 330, 334
5:33–40 202
5:34-39 403
5:34-40 208, 236
5:38 237
5:38-39 28, 98
5:39 201, 237
5:40 91, 119, 175, 188,
208
5:40-41 26
5:41 91, 119
5:41-42 202
5:42 179-80, 188, 238,
251, 375, 385, 479, 486
6:1 238, 251, 293, 489,
503
6:1a 28
6:1-2 391
6:1-3 224
6:1-6 500, 502, 503,
512, 514
6:1-7 202
6:1-11 226
6:1f. 487
6:2 171, 175, 179, 224,
261, 298, 340, 512
6:3 27, 176, 285, 334,
341, 342
6:4 179, 494
6:5 27, 251, 291, 334,
342
6:6 171, 175, 394, 494
6:7 28, 180, 221, 223-
4, 298, 356, 400, 479,
541-2

6:8 251, 340, 443-4
6:8-8:3 226
6:9 246, 292, 501, 514
6:9-14 246
6:10 27, 116, 122, 238,
248, 285, 291, 334, 340
6:11 377, 403
6:13 61, 202, 291, 403
6:13-14 377, 403
6:14 287-8, 291, 403
6:15 248, 291
6:27-32 103
6:30-31 406
6:49-53 202-3
6:55-56 202
7:1 403
7:1-53 378
7:2 280, 283, 285, 289
7:2-8 26
7:2-50 26
7:2-53 263, 403
7:4ff. 284-5, 288-9
7:7ff. 279, 284-5, 388
7:9-16 26
7:10ff. 279, 284, 285
7:13f. 279, 284
7:17 284, 451
7:17-18 223
7:20 284
7:20-38 26
7:21ff. 284, 285, 323
7:24 288
7:24-25 26
7:25 93, 152, 153, 165,
224, 284
7:26 288
7:29f. 283-5, 289, 291
7:30-38 25
7:33ff. 25, 194, 279,
283, 285, 287, 291,
451, 444
7:35-39 287, 378
7:36 26, 279, 285,
443-4
7:37 54, 202, 210, 270,
302, 444
7:37-38 358
7:38ff. 279, 284-5,
287, 291
7:42 388, 450

7:42-43 59
7:43f. 283, 289, 385
7:45-46 299
7:47f. 289, 314, 323
7:48-50 379
7:49 289
7:49-50 59, 61
7:51 24, 71, 225, 291,
334, 369
7:51-53 61, 195, 284
7:51-8:3 221
7:52 71, 206, 270, 279
7:52-53 283, 378
7:53ff.
24, 27, 102, 115, 251,
283-4, 286, 291, 357
7:55-56 53, 76, 334,
378, 496
7:56 192, 281, 283,
286, 291
7:58 203, 238
7:59 284, 286, 291,
293, 445
7:59-60 202, 386
7:59f. 494
7:60 59
8:1 28, 180, 182, 203,
226, 281, 359, 404
8:1-3 203, 238, 245
8:1b-3 203
8:2 176
8:3 28, 208, 238, 246,
474
8:4 28, 180, 182, 213-
4, 238, 281, 340, 359,
541
8:4-12:25 28
8:4-24 220
8:4-25 226
8:4-40 29
8:4-40 203
8:4-5 444
8:4-8 238
8:5-40 340
8:5-8 28
8:6 443-4
8:7 29, 92
8:10 29, 31
8:12 70, 104-5, 119,
224, 359, 444

8:12-14 238
8:12-17 338
8:13 29, 31, 443, 444
8:14 172, 175, 176,
224, 261, 541
8:14-17 180
8:14-23 444
8:15 494
8:15-17 29, 176
8:16 91, 105, 119, 338
8:16-17 225
8:17 347
8:17-18 329
8:18-24 98
8:20 272
8:22 141, 262
8:25 31, 176, 180, 541
8:26 30, 360
8:26-39 360
8:26-40 226, 238
8:27 385
8:29 29, 329, 334
8:32-33 54, 56
8:32-35 31
8:34 54
8:36 104, 241, 368
8:36-38 338
8:39 29
8:39-40 225
8:40 31
8:51 172
9:1 221, 238, 246, 387
9:1–2 203, 208
9:1-31 29
9:2 246
9:3-6 30
9:3-19 238
9:4-6 31
9:5 201, 386
9:6 26, 31, 203
9:8 323
9:10-16 30
9:10-17 386
9:10-18 334
9:11 494
9:13-22 446
9:14 91, 105, 119, 238,
386, 446
9:15 29, 119, 188, 246,
360, 419, 446, 447

9:15-16 117
9:15–16 195, 203
9:16 26, 31, 91, 100,
119, 446
9:17 29, 95, 194, 195,
225, 248, 329, 334, 340
9:17-19 116
9:18 104
9:19-30 203
9:20 239, 288, 297,
340, 446
9:20-22 29
9:20-23 246
9:21 91, 105, 119, 238,
246, 446
9:22 248, 288, 297,
385
9:23 248
9:26-28 176
9:27 176, 248
9:27-28 119
9:27-29 29, 182
9:28 172, 249, 297
9:29 246, 446
9:30 203, 446
9:31 31, 203, 221, 239,
329, 331, 334, 341,
400, 450, 542
9:32 261
9:32-11:18 29, 227
9:32-35 187
9:34 122
9:35 180
9:36 501, 503
9:36-42 29
9:36-43 92, 187
9:40 494
9:42 180
9:48 105
9:54 172
10 203, 530
10:1-11:18 29, 92,
404, 491, 492
10:1-48 173
10:2 240, 405, 494,
501, 503, 512
10:2f. 494
10:3 22, 33, 405
10:3-6 30
10:3-7 240

10:4 240, 501, 503, 512
10:9 494
10:9-16 404
10:9-48 379
10:9f. 494
10:10 187
10:10-16 30, 240
10:10-20 334
10:13-16 31
10:14 241
10:15 31, 106
10:15-18 158
10:17-19 187
10:19 240, 329, 334
10:19-20 29
10:20 194, 241, 361, 362
10:22 240, 405
10:23 241
10:24f. 491
10:25 240
10:27 241
10:28 29, 31, 240, 268, 404
10:29 180
10:30-32 240
10:30-33 30
10:30f. 494
10:31 240, 501, 503, 512
10:33 31
10:34 266, 268, 269, 362, 491, 493
10:34-35 404
10:34-36 31, 106
10:34-43 258, 259
10:36 26, 42, 195, 203, 204, 268, 269, 379, 385
10:36-39 192, 337
10:36-43 404
10:37-38 204
10:37-43 31
10:38 24, 90, 94, 98, 120, 122, 201, 270, 271, 272, 323
10:39 100, 178, 192, 193, 204, 266, 268, 288
10:40 26, 54, 271, 272
10:40-41 193

10:40-42 204
10:41 174, 177, 188, 190, 192, 196, 198, 266
10:42 67, 182, 262, 270, 271
10:42-43 42, 45
10:43 92, 95, 119, 122, 134, 193, 204, 268, 304, 323, 406, 447
10:43-44 95
10:44 24, 30, 102, 241, 329, 335, 404, 541
10:44-45 329
10:44-46 241
10:44-48 204, 353, 380
10:45 29, 95, 162, 225, 241, 261, 268, 272, 335, 492, 493
10:46 30, 334
10:47 241, 258, 329, 335
10:47-48 104
10:48 91, 119, 176, 361
11:1 29, 176, 224, 240, 261, 298, 541
11:1-18 203, 204, 280
11:2 361, 362
11:3 240, 361, 492
11:4 240
11:4-10 240
11:5 494
11:5-17 173
11:8 241
11:9 31, 271
11:12 29, 106, 225, 240, 241, 261, 329, 334, 361, 362
11:13 240
11:13-14 30
11:14 153, 204, 268, 448
11:15 30, 241, 280, 335, 448
11:15-16 225
11:15-17 50, 95, 380
11:15-18 58, 92, 329
11:16 271, 335, 346

11:17 30, 31, 104, 241, 272, 362, 368, 448
11:17-18 493
11:18 29, 31, 104, 141, 176, 204, 227, 241, 268, 404, 492
11:19 31, 182, 221, 242, 281, 359, 541
11:19-12:25 30
11:19-14:28 227
11:19-20 278, 340
11:19-21 203, 213, 214, 361
11:19-26 422
11:19-30 405
11:20 242, 514
11:21 31, 242, 514
11:21-26 423
11:22 176
11:23 31, 362
11:24 30, 225, 242, 341, 342
11:25 203
11:25-26 390
11:26 422
11:27-30 362, 501, 503
11:28 30, 219, 334, 341
11:29 135
11:30 135, 176
11:31 136
11:32 136
11:50 136
11:52 136
12:1-3 225, 246
12:1-4 225, 246
12:1-23 29
12:2 172
12:3-17 187
12:4-10 246
12:5 31, 225, 245, 252, 394, 494
12:5f. 494
12:6 225
12:7 187
12:7-11 30, 225
12:9 252
12:11 225, 253, 451

12:12 252, 391, 394,
479, 494
12:12-17 225, 245
12:15 187, 252
12:17 253
12:23 30, 225
12:24 31, 180, 221,
222, 223, 224, 298,
400, 541, 542
12:25 31
13 528
13:1 182
13:1-2 56, 225
13:1-3 30, 31
13:1-4 183, 184
13:1–4 211
13:2 194, 247, 329,
334, 388, 389, 406, 425
13:2-3 388
13:3 394
13:3b 303
13:4 32, 194, 195, 329,
334
13:5 224, 297, 423,
541
13:6-12 246, 383
13:6-41 296
13:7 224, 297, 541
13:8-12 187
13:9 32, 187, 249, 334
13:10 187
13:11 34, 448
13:12 247, 297
13:13 494
13:13-41 50
13:14 423
13:15 297, 481
13:16 103, 301
13:16-22 301
13:16-25 205
13:16-41 98, 187, 259,
263, 380, 383, 405
13:16b-41 281
13:16-48 204
13:17 21, 22, 451
13:17-22 26
13:21 301
13:22 26, 54, 195, 301,
302
13:22-24 53

13:22a 301
13:23 158, 205, 270,
297, 301, 302, 306
13:24 451
13:25 195, 541
13:26 194, 195, 205,
207, 297, 299, 301, 306
13:27 97
13:27-29 204, 301
13:27-31 205
13:28 301
13:29 100, 298, 299
13:30 26, 178, 301,
306
13:30-31 53, 205, 302
13:30-33 301
13:31 182, 187, 188,
192, 193, 199
13:31-32 299
13:32 205, 212, 299,
302
13:32-33 54, 302, 303
13:32a 302
13:33 54, 204, 205,
271, 299, 302, 303, 306
13:33-35 25
13:33-37 205
13:33a 303
13:33b 303
13:34 205, 302, 305
13:34-38 205
13:34a 303, 304
13:34b 303
13:35 53, 187, 304
13:35-37 205, 303,
305
13:36 26
13:36-37 304
13:37 306
13:38 95, 103, 173,
187, 205, 299, 301,
304, 305, 323
13:38-39 103, 122,
161, 212, 304, 305, 406
13:39 104, 205, 304,
305, 405
13:40 369
13:40-46 264
13:41 25, 32, 58, 103,
194, 206, 210, 406

13:41-47 59
13:43 32, 173, 242,
247
13:44 224, 297, 541
13:44-45 102
13:44-49 100, 189
13:44ff 420
13:45 246, 247, 249,
423
13:45-47 429
13:46 32, 76, 78, 162,
206, 221, 224, 231,
249, 298, 300, 306,
364, 420, 421, 449
13:46-47 157, 296,
419
13:46-48 206
13:47 25, 32, 55, 56,
57, 84, 184, 208, 217,
218, 220, 224, 298,
299, 306, 345, 347,
420, 423, 529
13:47-48 94
13:48 32, 206, 224,
242, 247, 254, 298,
300, 306, 353, 364, 541
13:49 298, 541
13:50 32, 246, 247
13:51 420
13:52 249, 331, 334,
341, 342
14 528
14:1 78, 91, 242, 246,
247, 364, 423
14:1-7 184
14:1-18 100
14:2 247, 423
14:3 22, 98, 184, 186,
189, 193, 249, 443,
444, 541
14:4 170, 181, 182,
183, 184, 247, 444
14:5 246, 247
14:7 249
14:8-10 92, 186
14:8-18 382
14:8-20 228
14:9 104, 165, 307
14:11 92
14:11-12 307

14:12 308
14:14 170, 182, 183,
184, 307, 308
14:14-15 98
14:15 26, 207, 308,
314, 315
14:15-16 103
14:15-17 296, 405
14:16 103, 315
14:17 207, 315
14:19 152, 247, 423
14:21 242, 247
14:21-28 424
14:22 26, 70, 188, 224,
247, 249, 537
14:23 394, 494
14:26 194, 247
14:27 22, 34, 224, 242,
308, 405
15 493, 527, 529
7 173
15:1 204, 242, 407,
448, 493
15:1-16:4 411
15:1-35 182, 379
15:1ff 423
15:2 175, 177, 242
15:2-4 407
15:2-5 365
15:2-29 407
15:4 22, 34, 177
15:5 176, 204, 242,
356, 358, 365, 407
15:6 177, 261
15:6-8 203, 204
15:6-11 204, 212, 407
15:7 104, 162, 422
15:7-11 104, 173, 253,
261, 493
15:7-8 92
15:7-9 243
15:8 95, 193, 225, 262,
272, 330, 335
15:9 95, 106, 346, 362,
366, 529
15:10 243, 365, 407
15:11 70, 160, 204,
206, 243, 268, 365,
406, 422, 448

15:12 33, 186, 224,
243, 443, 444
15:13 449
15:13-18 407
15:13-21 177
15:14 32, 118, 353,
407, 445, 450, 451
15:14-18 52, 57, 346
15:15 449
15:15-18 55
15:16 32, 204, 299,
351, 445, 450
15:16-17 25, 162, 441,
449
15:17 32, 115, 118,
163, 204, 445, 446,
450, 451
15:19 243, 407, 408
15:19-29 408
15:20 221, 409
15:21 366
15:22 176, 177, 243
15:23 177, 243, 408
15:24 243, 408
15:25 243
15:26 119
15:28 32, 243, 329,
334, 341, 407, 408
15:28b 409
15:29 221, 409, 494
15:30 243
15:35 182, 189
15:35-36 541
15:36-21:16 228
15:36-41 33
15:38 194
15:41 188
16:1-3 244
16:3 410
16:3-4 411
16:4 177, 243, 410,
411
16:4-5 424
16:5 221, 243, 400,
542
16:6 33, 329, 541
16:6-10 195, 425
16:6-7 332, 334
16:6-9 33

16:7 33, 115, 116, 122,
329
16:9 33, 187, 423
16:9-10 334
16:10 33
16:11 480
16:15 104, 338, 424,
450, 492
16:16 152
16:16-34 450
16:17 34, 450
16:18 119, 122, 334
16:19-22 246
16:23-37 246
16:25 187, 494
16:25-34 187
16:25f. 494
16:26 253
16:30 129
16:30-31 104, 153
16:30-34 104, 253
16:31 105, 134, 353
16:32 224, 541
16:33 338
16:40 424
17 528
17:2 423, 484
17:2-3 25
17:2-4 383
17:3 103, 288
17:5 246
17:6 219
17:10 423
17:11 541
17:13 224, 246, 541
17:15 382
17:16 309, 316, 383
17:16-33 375
17:17 310, 423
17:18 207, 310, 311,
313, 315, 382, 383, 485
17:18-21 42
17:19 310
17:19-20 383
17:19-21 311
17:21 310
17:22 428
17:22-23 315, 383
17:22-28 309
17:22-31 297, 382

17:23 313, 316
17:24 314, 316
17:24-25 312, 384
17:24-29 316, 384
17:24b 316
17:25 316, 384
17:25-26 316
17:25a 316
17:26 312, 316
17:26-27 384
17:27 316
17:28 25, 309, 316
17:28-29 384
17:29 309, 316
17:29-30 309
17:29a 316
17:29b 316
17:30 104, 141, 142, 315, 316, 317, 353
17:30-31 45, 46, 312, 317, 384
17:30a 103
17:30b 103
17:31 26, 67, 97, 130, 161, 207, 270, 309, 317
17:32 311, 317
17:32-33 102, 380
17:33 312
18:1-17 424
18:2 218
18:2-6 100
18:3 435, 450
18:4 424, 429
18:4-7 429
18:5 480, 541
18:5-6 33, 221, 231, 449
18:6 76, 78, 162, 264, 420, 421, 424, 428, 429, 434
18:6-7 428
18:7 78, 228, 253, 424, 427, 429, 430
18:8 78, 105, 338, 418, 428, 430, 431, 481
18:9 253
18:9-10 33, 117, 122, 334, 421, 425
18:9-11 195, 530

18:10 408, 426, 427, 434
18:11 189, 224, 390, 427, 541
18:12 218, 246
18:12-16 253
18:12-17 117, 209, 246, 383, 425, 429, 431, 433, 435
18:13 387, 432
18:14-15 320
18:18 412, 480
18:18–19:10 427
18:18–19:22 428
18:18b 411
18:19 427, 429
18:22 411
18:23 188, 424
18:24-26 429
18:24-28 338
18:24f. 485
18:25 334
18:26 249, 480
18:27–19:1 429
18:27f. 485
18:28 249, 485
19:1 429, 432
19:1-6 249, 338
19:1-7 75
19:3 339
19:4 75, 338
19:5 91, 105, 119, 338, 339
19:6 32, 334, 339
19:8 70, 224, 249, 250, 427, 429
19:8-10 103
19:8-9 231, 429
19:9 387, 428, 429, 432
19:9-10 390
19:9-20 250
19:10 418, 428, 430, 431, 434, 530, 541
19:11 34, 186
19:11-12 164
19:13 91, 119
19:17 119
19:17-20 433

19:20 180, 221, 223, 298, 400, 541, 542
19:21 32, 34, 36, 188, 209, 254, 329, 334, 452
19:21-22 433
19:23 387
19:23-27 383
19:23-38 246
19:23-41 250, 429
19:25-27 433
19:26 250
19:28 428
19:34 428
19:40 242
20:3 246, 435
20:6f. 490
20:7 392, 489
20:7-11 389, 512
20:7-12 92, 390
20:9-12 187
20:11 393, 489
20:17-35 429, 433, 435
20:18-35 297
20:19 387, 435
20:20 188, 207, 480, 486
20:20-21 390
20:21 104, 142, 207, 434
20:22 32, 195, 334
20:22-23 329, 425
20:23 24, 32, 208, 246, 334, 341
20:24 207, 434
20:25 70, 207
20:25-35 348
20:26 420
20:26-27a 434
20:27 189, 207, 434
20:28 32, 60, 98, 99, 207, 341, 358, 434
20:28-32 390
20:30 208
20:31 207, 427
20:32 99, 208, 323, 434, 450
20:32–36 207
20:33-35 501
20:34 435

20:35 207, 503, 518
20:36 494
21:4 208, 246, 334, 341
21:5 494
21:8 340
21:10 246
21:10–14 208
21:11 32, 334, 341
21:13 91, 119
21:14 34, 246
21:15-16 34
21:17-25 34
21:17-28:33 228
21:17-32 228
21:19 177, 244
21:20 80
21:20-26 375
21:21 244, 411, 412
21:22 319
21:23-24 412
21:23-24a 412
21:24 412
21:25 221, 244, 412
21:26 34, 412
21:26-30 379
21:27 245
21:27-30 377
21:27-32 34
21:27-36 413
21:28 231, 245, 319, 413
21:30 245, 246
21:31-36 35
21:32 136
21:33-28:31 246
21:34 245
21:36 245
21:37-38 319
22:1 35
22:1-21 208, 254, 297
22:2-4 238
22:3 228, 319, 415
22:4 238, 387
22:4–5 208
22:4-16 322
22:5 238
22:6 25, 323
22:6-16 34
22:6-21 238

22:7 323
22:7-11 25
22:8 201
22:8-9 25
22:9 25
22:10 386, 409
22:11 25, 323
22:12 322
22:12-16 322
22:13 323
22:14 25, 188, 206, 270, 286, 322
22:14-15 26, 192
22:15 25, 35, 36, 188, 190, 193, 434
22:16 91, 95, 105, 119, 380, 386, 447
22:17 187, 494
22:17-18 334
22:17-21 117, 203, 375, 386
22:17f. 494
22:18 193, 324
22:19 238, 246
22:20 192
22:21 188, 194, 195, 228, 322, 334, 425, 436
22:21-22 413
22:22 102, 245
22:22-23 322
22:23 245
22:25-27 120
22:25-29 319
22:28 451
22:30 208
22:30–23:11 254
23:1 414
23:1-5 414
23:1-6 297
23:1–10 208
23:3 415
23:5a 415
23:5b 415
23:6 231, 319, 321, 413, 436
23:6-10 312
23:6-7 312
23:7 242
23:8 415
23:9-10 35

23:10 242, 246
23:11 34, 35, 36, 117, 118, 188, 193, 195, 209, 245, 254, 334, 452
23:12 35
23:16-24 93
23:24 117
23:26 117
23:26-27 415
23:26-30 319
23:27 451
23:28 208
23:29 209, 320
23:33 117
23:33–24:2 246
24:5 242, 356, 358
24:10 36
24:10-21 297
24:11 385
24:11-18 228
24:14 319, 356, 358, 387, 414
24:14-15 322
24:14–16 208
24:15 231
24:17 501, 503
24:21 208, 231, 321, 413
24:22 387
24:22-27 209
24:23 245
24:25 130, 208
25:1-26 32, 246
25:2-11 297
25:8 36, 228, 320, 414
25:10 288
25:11 451
25:12 451
25:13-14 117
25:13–21 209
25:13-26:32 246
25:16 36
25:19 208
25:21 451
25:23 323
25:24 117
25:25 451
25:26 117, 323
26 322
26:1 36

26:1-23 208
26:2 36, 117
26:2-3 320
26:2-29 297
26:5 320, 356
26:6 321, 322, 413
26:6-8 208, 231
26:7 117, 322
26:9 119, 201
26:9-11 208
26:10 238
26:11 238
26:12-18 34, 238, 322
26:13 25, 117, 323
26:13-18 25
26:14 201, 239, 323
26:14-18 25
26:15 323
26:15-18 42, 62, 386
26:15-23 203
26:16 25, 36, 189, 192, 323
26:16-18 26, 189, 323
26:16-23 188
26:17 189, 228, 421, 430, 436
26:17-18 103, 134, 194, 195
26:18 95, 99, 304, 323, 406
26:18b 408
26:19 117, 239, 324
26:20 58, 104, 133, 141, 142, 189
26:20-21 379
26:21 324
26:22 22, 24, 189, 193, 322
26:22-23 42, 44, 208, 229, 414
26:23 24, 26, 36, 57, 58, 117, 122, 189, 201, 207, 231, 323, 324, 413
26:24 36, 102
26:24-31 209
26:26 482
26:26-27 117
26:27 103
26:29 494
26:30 117

26:30-31 320
26:31-32 209
26:32 34, 321, 451
27:18-19 35
27:20 35, 152, 165
27:21-26 228
27:23 187, 387
27:23-24 33, 35
27:24 34, 452
27:29 494
27:31 93, 165
27:33 34
27:34 150, 153, 165
27:35 392, 489
27:35-36 228
27:42-44 35
28:1-6 209
28:4 79
28:7 187
28:8 494
28:9 186
28:10 228
28:14 36, 218, 452
28:14-31 440
28:15 36, 494
28:16 36, 452
28:16-30 250
28:17 231, 415
28:17-18 320
28:17-22 36
28:17-28 297
28:17-29 100
28:17-31 415
28:19 451
28:20 78, 231, 321, 413, 415
28:22 79, 356
28:23 36, 70, 209, 210, 224, 415, 436
28:23-24 324
28:23-28 36, 221, 454
28:24 162, 367
28:24-28 250
28:25 24, 36, 334
28:25-27 36, 59, 71, 324, 369
28:25-28 76, 78, 264, 430
28:26 79
28:26-27 58, 209

28:26ff 420
28:27 79
28:28 78, 79, 80, 157, 209, 224, 231, 369, 421, 430, 449
28:30 229
28:30-31 36, 62, 118, 210, 221, 230, 231, 390
28:31 36, 70, 210, 224, 250, 324, 400, 415

Romans
1:1-15 440
1:3-4 54, 386
1:14-16 455
1:16 59
1:24-32 61
2:11 362
2:25-26 293
3:2 456
3:24 287
3:25-26 293
4:10-12 293
4:5 304
4:5-7 304
6:7 305, 406
9 420
6-29 453
9:11 454
9:12 454
9:14-23 454
9:1-5 454
9:24 455
9:24-29 454
9:25-26 455
9:26 455
9:27-29 455
9:30 456
9:30 - 10:21 453
9:32 456
9:6-13 454
9:6-7 454
9:7 454
9-11 445, 452, 453, 454
10:4 456
10:5-13 456
10:8 456
10:9 456
10:9-10 386

10:9-13 385
10:12-14 457
10:13 457
11:12 371
11:13 421
11:14 370
11:15 370, 371
11:16 370
11:23 370
11:25 370
11:25-31 370
11:25-32 454, 455
11:28 354
14:1–15:13 411
15:26 489
15:29 455
16:1 481
16:3-5 480

1 Corinthians
1:2 434
1:9 390
2:1-5 117
5:21 293
8:5-6 386
9:19-21 420
9:20 411, 530
10:16-17 393
10:32 434
11:17-34 393, 512, 514
11:18 514
12 488
14 488
15:3 278
15:9 434
15:29 149
16:2 514
16:5 433
16:19 480, 484, 485, 486
16:22 386

2 Corinthians
1:1 434
8:23 183
13:1-2 433
13:14 390

Galatians
1:5 421
1:8 415
1:9 415
1:13 434
2 423
2:2 425
2:11-14 415
3:11 305
3:13 100
3:16 51
4:6 115

Ephesians
1:21 119
2:11 293
2:13 353
2:17 42, 353

Philippians
1:5 390
1:19 115
2:5-11 386
2:6-11 108
2:9-11 119
2:25 183
3:2 415

Colossians
1:15-20 386
1:28 385
2:6-7 385
2:11 293
3:11 293
4:14 464

1 Thessalonians
1:9-10 384, 385
2:14 434

1 Timothy
2:15 153
5:17f. 488

2 Timothy
4:11 464

Hebrews
1:3-4 108
1:5 54

2:3-4 535
3:1 385
4:14 385
10:11 388

1 Peter
1:1 359
2:7 268
2:10 268
2:24 100
3:18 271
3:21 268
4:5 270

2 Peter
2:13 512

1 John
1:3 390

Jude
12 512

Revelation
7 323
8 224
21:14 351